Isolation and Engagement

Isolation and Engagement

PRESIDENTIAL
DECISION MAKING ON CHINA
from KENNEDY *to* NIXON

WILLIAM WALTMAN NEWMANN

UNIVERSITY OF MICHIGAN PRESS
ANN ARBOR

For questions or permissions, please contact um.press.perms@umich.edu

Published in the United States of America by the
University of Michigan Press
Manufactured in the United States of America
Printed on acid-free paper
First published July 2022

A CIP catalog record for this book is available from the British Library.

Library of Congress Cataloging-in-Publication Data

Names: Newmann, William W., author. | Michigan Publishing (University of
  Michigan), publisher.
Title: Isolation and engagement : Presidential decision making on China from
  Kennedy to Nixon / William Waltman Newmann.
Other titles: John Kennedy, Lyndon Johnson, Richard Nixon, and Presidential
  decision making on China
Description: Ann Arbor, Michigan : University of Michigan Press,
  2022. | Includes bibliographical references and index.
Identifiers: LCCN 2022003928 (print) | LCCN 2022003929 (ebook) | ISBN
  9780472133086 (hardcover ; alk. paper) | ISBN 9780472220281 (ebook)
Subjects: LCSH: Kennedy, John F. (John Fitzgerald), 1917–1963. | Johnson,
  Lyndon B. (Lyndon Baines), 1908–1973. | Nixon, Richard M. (Richard
  Milhous), 1913–1994. | United States—Foreign relations—China—20th
  century. | China—Foreign relations—United States—20th century.
Classification: LCC E183.8.C5 N43 2022 (print) | LCC E183.8.C5
  (ebook) | DDC 327.7305109/04—dc23/eng/20220222
LC record available at https://lccn.loc.gov/2022003928
LC ebook record available at https://lccn.loc.gov/2022003929

For Judy and Jeri

Someday you may well be sitting here where I am now as President of the United States. And when you are, you'll be looking at that door over there and knowing that practically everybody who walks through it wants something out of you. You'll learn what a lonely job this is, and you'll discover the need for somebody like Harry Hopkins who asks for nothing except to serve you.

—FDR to Wendell Wilkie, January 1941

∿ Contents

Digital materials related to this title can be found on the Fulcrum platform via the following citable URL: https://doi.org/10.3998/mpub.11684577

⌁ Acknowledgments

This one took a long time.

It's been over a decade since I thought "it might be interesting if I looked at decision making this way . . ." The book may have been inevitable: on the day I was born the Kennedy administration held a National Security Council meeting to discuss US policy toward China.

Once I traveled to my first presidential library and began looking through documents, I was hooked. Reading through primary sources and seeing the day-to-day debates, as described by the participants in their own handwriting or miserable typing, is the ultimate in historian geekiness. I plead guilty. I can give a tour of all the best diners near every presidential library from Simi Valley (Reagan) to Boston (Kennedy) geographically and Abilene (Eisenhower) to Little Rock (Clinton) chronologically.

I am grateful to the staffs at the Dwight D. Eisenhower Presidential Library in Abilene, Kansas; the John F. Kennedy Presidential Library in Boston, Massachusetts; the Lyndon B. Johnson Presidential Library in Austin, Texas; the Richard M. Nixon Presidential Library in Yorba Linda, California; the Gerald R. Ford Presidential Library in Ann Arbor, Michigan; and the Jimmy Carter Presidential Library in Atlanta, Georgia. Every trip was a wonderful research experience and a pure pleasure.

I owe a great debt to the University of Michigan Press. Elizabeth Demers believed in the book very early on (a great relief to me when I was sure it was too big to ever be published). Kevin Rennells and John Raymond helped make sure I was saying what I thought I was saying. Shana Milkie prepared the index and caught a really big mistake I made!

Portions of this book have appeared in earlier form. Thanks go to the journals *Presidential Studies Quarterly* (44, no. 4: 640–72) and *Congress and the Presidency* (42, no. 2: 119–46) for permission to use revised portions of material from my articles.

Of course, I am also thankful for my colleagues in the Department of Political Science at Virginia Commonwealth University who helped me think about foreign policy and presidential power, and also taught big sections of Introduction to International Relations or took on service responsibilities so I could focus on the book. Thanks go to Chris Saladino, John Aughenbaugh, and Herb Hirsch; the latter was just as excited as I was when I showed him LBJ's Daily Diary with the first meeting of the Tuesday Lunch Group penciled in. Thanks also to VCU's Humanities Research Center for financial support. The biggest thanks go to students in my US Foreign Policy class over the years, who brought fresh perspectives to their research papers on foreign policy decision making every year since 1994. They made sure it always remained fun.

Unending gratitude goes to Paul Hammond. Without him, I'd be doing something else for a living. Also, I owe a significant debt to Bert Rockman, who was willing to share his expertise and guidance when I was just beginning to think seriously about these issues.

Of course, the biggest thanks go to Judy and Jeri. They believed I could write this book even when I wasn't so sure. That's really true about everything in my life. Without them, I'm not even here.

～ List of Figures and Tables

Figures

Tables

∾ Note on Chinese Transliteration and Sources

This research uses Pinyin transliteration for Chinese names except in cases when quoting archival material that used the older Wade-Giles transliteration. Quotations from earlier eras may use Peking instead of Beijing or Formosa instead of Taiwan.

Most of this research is based on archival material from presidential libraries. To make citing this material less complicated and lengthy, the following acronyms/abbreviations are used in the endnotes.

DDEL	Dwight David Eisenhower Presidential Library
FRUS	*Foreign Relations of the United States*
GRFL	Gerald R. Ford Presidential Library
HAK	Henry A. Kissinger
JFKL	John F. Kennedy Presidential Library
LBJL	Lyndon B. Johnson Presidential Library
NIE	National Intelligence Estimate
NSDM	National Security Decision Memorandum
NSC	National Security Council
NSC H-Files	National Security Council Institutional ("H") Files
NSC H-Files Misc	NSC Institutional ("H") Files, Miscellaneous Institutional Files of the Nixon Administration
NSF	National Security Files
NSSM	National Security Study Memorandum
RMNL	Richard M. Nixon Presidential Library
SNIE	Special National Intelligence Estimate

～ Abbreviations

ADST   Association for Diplomatic Studies and Training Foreign Affairs

ANSA   assistant to the president for national security affairs or national security adviser

CJCS   Chairman of the Joint Chiefs of Staff

CWG   China Working Group

DCI   Director of Central Intelligence

DoD   Department of Defense

EAIG   East Asian Interdepartmental Group

EOP   Executive Office of the Presidency

ExComm   Executive Committee of the National Security Council

FAS   Federation of American Scientists

FE/IRG   Far Eastern Interdepartmental Regional Group

IG   Interdepartmental Group

IRG   Interdepartmental Regional Group

JCS   Joint Chiefs of Staff

NARA   National Archives and Records Administration

NSAM   National Security Action Memorandum

OCB   Operations Coordination Board

PB   Planning Board

PLA   People's Liberation Army (China)

PRC   People's Republic of China

RG   Review Group

ROC   Republic of China

SANSA   special assistant to the president for national security affairs

SIG   Senior Interagency Group

SIG/IRG	Senior Interagency Group/Interdepartmental Regional Group
SRG	Senior Review Group
TLG	Tuesday Lunch Group
UN	United Nations
UNGA	United Nations General Assembly
UNSC	United Nations Security Council
USAID	United States Agency for International Development
USC	Undersecretaries Committee
USIA	United States Information Agency
VSSG	Vietnam Special Studies Group
WSAG	Washington Special Actions Group

ONE

∿ Introduction

On September 18, 2019, Donald Trump appointed Robert O'Brien as his *fourth* national security advisor. A few days later Mark Pottinger was chosen as Trump's *seventh* deputy national security advisor. Such turnover at the top of the National Security Council (NSC) staff is unprecedented.[1] Trump's first national security advisor, Michael Flynn, was fired after roughly a month following accusations that he lied to the FBI and to Vice President Mike Pence about his conversations with the Russian ambassador to the US. Flynn twice pleaded guilty to lying to the FBI, but was ultimately pardoned by Trump in November of 2020. The second and third men who occupied the office, General H. R. McMaster and Ambassador John Bolton, left after their attempts to manage the president's decision making process and the direction of policy had failed. Trump is famously known as impulsive, making decisions based on instinct rather than thorough analysis, setting and changing long-standing policies with a flurry of tweets, and relishing his freedom to be unpredictable. Building a national security process that could manage Trump's haphazard style or integrate it into a formal interagency process might have been an impossible task. Observers often argued that Trump initially surrounded himself with an "axis of adults"—Rex Tillerson at State, General James Mattis at Defense, Chief of Staff General John Kelly, and McMaster and Bolton at the NSC staff—who would channel him toward a stable process and temper his shoot-from-the-hip nature. One by one, the "adults" lost their battles to manage the president; by 2019 all of them had resigned or been fired.[2] No NSC system, no chief of staff or national security advisor, was able to tame the president. He made decisions in his own style and anyone who attempted to change that style soon found themselves out of a job and updating their resumes.

Trump might be considered an outlier, a president with no governmental or military experience in his background, a businessman unaccustomed to decision making in an environment where the clash of competing interests is the fundamental reality. The story, however, is a familiar one: attempts to change the president's decision style seem never to succeed. Barack Obama's first national security advisor, General James Jones, lasted less than two years. He had no strong relationship with Obama before he was chosen and Obama never allowed him to play the role of honest broker or enforced his authority as the manager of the NSC process. Most analyses see it as a result of poor fit between the two men (Obama's collegial instincts vs. Jones' military-style faith in hierarchy and formal processes) and a result of Obama's preferences; he wanted a set of loyal presidential assistants—Thomas Donilon, Denis McDonough, Mark Lippert, and Ben Rhodes—to have free-flowing access to the Oval Office and refused to allow any notions of structure or process to get in the way.[3] In particular, Donilon, the initial deputy national security advisor, was the official who knew what Obama wanted. Instead of trying to build a hierarchy to manage the president, he fed Obama's preferences for a more collegial system with Obama at the center. By mid-2010, insiders saw Donilon as the "shadow National Security Advisor."[4] Jones tried to rein in the president while Donilon nurtured the president's style. In October 2010, Jones resigned and Donilon became national security advisor.

Two successive presidents refused to be boxed in or restricted by their staffers; neither Obama nor Trump adapted to what their staffers argued was a need for greater reliance on structured interagency processes. On the other side of the spectrum was Dwight Eisenhower, a man wedded to formal interagency processes, who eventually chafed at the amount of time and energy his own system required of him and the lack of imaginative policies produced by its priority on consensus at the expense of creativity. By 1959, Eisenhower was seriously contemplating the creation of a "First Secretary of the Government," who "would be the President's principal assistant in the field of international relations and head of a new 'super department,'" tentatively named the Department of Government.[5] He had tasked his President's Advisory Committee on Government Organization with developing a reorganization plan. Ultimately it recommended against a department of government, instead placing the first secretary in the Executive Office of the Presidency. The first secretary, however, would "rank above members of the Cabinet" and "be designated by statute as fourth in the succession to the Presidency."[6] Vice President Richard Nixon described it as the "most revolutionary change" to the structure of gov-

ernment "in 150 years."[7] In essence, Eisenhower was contemplating centralizing decision making in the White House in an effort to free himself
from his own formality. Delegation of the day-to-day decision process to
the first secretary would allow Eisenhower to decide where he wanted to
devote his time and energy. Ultimately, he never implemented the plan.
Eisenhower could not change his own nature; he believed in the need for
formal hierarchy, and even a recognition of its weaknesses did not persuade
him to abandon the style he had become accustomed to over decades of
service in the military and government.[8]

These brief tales of Trump, Obama, and Eisenhower's deliberations
over changing their foreign policy decision making structures touch on
all the key themes of the study of foreign and national security policy
making—the centralization of the process; the necessity of coordination,
formal systems, and informal avenues for open and honest advice; attempts
to ensure that multiple organizational and individual perspectives are
included in the process; the conservation of time and effort at the upper
levels of decision making; and, perhaps most importantly, the personalized
nature of the office of the presidency. It is an office built around the needs
of a single individual.

A first look at these issues, based on the premise that decision making
within any administration changes over time, led to my development of an
evolution model.[9] The model explained the centralization of the national
security decision making process on nuclear strategy and arms control
within the Jimmy Carter, Ronald Reagan, and George H. W. Bush administrations, arguing that over time an administration's decision making
structure narrows the range of participation, adds more informal and ad
hoc processes, and bypasses the standard interagency system with greater
frequency. The centralization is a response to the institutional pressures
buffeting the president. Presidents end up with three structures: a formal
structure (the full National Security Council system); an informal structure (a smaller group of key advisors who hold staff-free meetings, with
and without the president, to iron out a consensus on policy); and a confidence structure (the president and the one or two advisors he trusts the
most). How a president uses each depends on the idiosyncratic aspects of
the president's style—his personal preferences for making decisions.

The earlier study concluded that all three structures were necessary
for an administration to manage its decision process well. The glue that
holds the policy process together, however, is the informal structure. It is
there that the administration works out the necessary consensus that can
break interagency gridlock, smooth out organizational rivalry, and con-

vince senior officials that while the president wants diverse opinions and full-throated debate, he also needs that debate to end when he makes up his mind.[10]

This book takes the next step by adapting the evolution model into an evolution-balance model, and by testing that model with case studies on China policy. The new model argues that administrations never stop their assessment of the process even after the three structures form in the first six months to a year and a half of an administration's tenure. The process of making decisions about how to decide—a search for ways to make the system work better for the president—never ends. Presidents have their own management styles that they cannot or will not change, and the purpose of continued refinements of process is to compensate for the weaknesses of that style, the inability of officials or executive departments, or both, to adapt to that style, or the need to protect specific areas of policy innovation and implementation. These adaptations in an administration's decision making process represent attempts to balance out competing tensions within the administration, tensions based in the idiosyncratic needs of individual presidents, and institutional factors, such as the complexities of interagency relationships, and the political pressures of domestic and international politics.

Two Scholarly Debates

The need for refinement of the original evolution model became obvious after further research. The model itself needed to address more directly two key areas of study that are hallmarks of modern presidential scholarship: (1) what matters more, *idiosyncratic factors*—the influence of the personality and character of the individual president, or *institutional factors*—the legal, administrative, and political context in which the presidency operates; and (2) how do presidents deal with the competing pressures to maintain formal interagency-based structures vs. the temptation to use more informal and centralized structures.

The first debate can be summed up simply: Do individual presidents matter, or are presidential character, experience, and political skill irrelevant? Presidents and their advisors are absolutely certain that their individual contributions to American foreign policy are significant, unique, and often heroic. An administration's legacy in foreign affairs is the product of the president's vision or at least the result of an opportunity seized by a shrewd and decisive leader. In this sense, it is more than literary convention when scholars personify a policy, naming it the "Truman Doctrine" or "Johnson's War" or the "Reagan Doctrine." The more personality-centered model, often called some variation on persuasion or bargaining and derived from the seminal work of Richard Neustadt, sees the ways in which individual presidents choose to wield their power as the crucial characteristic of the executive branch. Presidents use their powers of persuasion to bargain with organizations and individuals in an effort to direct policy in a desired direction.[11] They directly manage decision making. The management strategies different presidents use are idiosyncratically defined. For convenience, this model is called the idiosyncratic model.

In contrast, an institutional model downplays the importance of the president's decision making impact, contending that as the presidency has become more institutionalized—more constrained by legislation, regulatory rules, administrative complexity, routinized structures, and the constant pressures of a domestic and international political context that handed the US president a greater and greater load of responsibility—the importance of the actual individual behind the desk has been nearly nullified.[12] This body of scholarship often argues that characteristics of individual presidents are irrelevant; political and legal forces create a context for presidential policy making and all presidents will react to those forces in a similar manner, using rational choice calculations. Presidents face rivalry and organizational interests, and all react to increase their control, regardless of their character or management preferences.

This debate over whether individual presidents matter is critical to the evolution of presidential studies. While scholars may be pleased with their ability to develop parsimonious and more rigorous models of the presidency, veteran policy makers might argue that scholars are missing the essence of decision: people make decisions, and different people make different decisions even in similar situations.

The evolution-balance model suggests that it is the interaction of institutional political forces (Congress, public opinion, and domestic and international political trends) and idiosyncratic aspects (presidential political skill, management style, and character) that define the nature of decision making. In short, both matter. The evolution-balance model, however, also argues that the president matters more. His management style is the one constant in the administration.

The second debate—on centralization and the need for formal interagency processes—begins with an observation and then the obvious question. Presidents have increasingly moved policy making into the White House, centralizing the process, adding more informal and ad-hoc procedures, ignoring their own executive departments, and essentially performing end runs around their own hand-picked political appointees and executive department expertise. In the context of the evolution and evolution-balance models, this centralization shows the development of the confidence structure—the president's growing reliance on a few trusted advisors. This second field of study is in many ways a subset of the first. Scholars who focus on institutional variables contend that the institutional context wraps presidents in chains and their only rational choice once locked in that embrace is to search for the obvious wiggle room: centralization of the process in the White House through an often informal reliance on staff, a cadre of "Assistants to the President" outside of statutory, congressional, and public oversight. Scholars have often called it an unofficial fourth branch of government, a "presidential branch," that replicates the full functions of the executive branch on a smaller scale and under the direct and unchallenged control of the president.[13] The counterargument zeroes in, once again, on the management style of each president, contending that centralization is not a knee-jerk reaction to the pressures of the Oval Office. Presidential biographies and administrative histories often highlight the unique characteristics of each president's management style, his preferred method of decision making. Some are hands-on (Carter), while others prefer to delegate (Reagan); some feel comfortable with elaborate structures (Eisenhower), while others want it more free form and swift (John F. Kennedy); some are experts who pride themselves on that mastery of policy (George H. W. Bush), while others know they have much to learn and rely heavily on the advice of specific officials (Clinton, George W. Bush). In this sense, centralization of the process is overstated. Different presidents centralize to different extents and in very idiosyncratic ways and some work toward decentralization of the process. The level of formality and informality varies based on the individual.

The evolution-balance model hypothesizes that the trend toward centralization and more informality is not completely linear; presidents and their advisors are aware of the pitfalls of centralization or an overreliance on informality that might undermine the standard interagency process. A key goal of the administration's ongoing assessment of the decision making process is to maintain a balance between formality, informality, and the centralization that is the hallmark of the confidence structure.

An Evolution-Balance Model

This research begins where the initial study of the evolution model left off. The revised model accepts the notion that national security and foreign policy decision making evolves over time, but it refines the idea in several ways. The original evolution model hypothesized that administrations begin their time in office using a formal interagency process and then develop informal and confidence structures during the first six months to a year of their terms. The case studies chosen—Carter, Reagan, and George H. W. Bush—confirmed that hypothesis. That evolution described in the original model, however, is too linear to capture the complexity of all presidential administrations' decision styles. For example, two questions were left unanswered by the original evolution model. First, what if an administration begins with an informal process on day one? Second, what happens after the initial evolution of the three structures? The evolution-balance model is designed to answer both of these questions.

The evolution-balance model has four elements. Each element needs to be seen as a function of time. As in the case of the original evolution model, the ideas are based on the notion that administrative decision making is dynamic, not static. Administrations enter office with an initial standard structure based on the president's preferences. Over time, that process is deliberately changed in an effort to make it work better. Chapter 2 gives a full description of the model. Figure 2.2 provides an illustration.

The first element, *presidential management style*, is the key independent variable. Following the election, a victorious president and his advisors explicitly design a process for decision making. This initial structure represents a theory about what a new president thinks he needs and wants based on his management preferences and the administrative challenges he expects to face. As the original evolution model suggests, presidents will typically (but as we will see not always) create formal, informal, and confidence structures over the first six months to a year in office. Importantly, the balance between the three structures is also determined by the president's decision making style. In short, presidential management style is nearly a constant, determining the original administrative design and functioning as the key factor in any structural adaptations.

Second, once in office, administrations engage in a *continuous assessment of the decision process in an effort to identify weaknesses*. The initial standard process is really a theory about how the administration believes it can operate. Once the theory is put into practice amid international and domestic political pressures, and the realities of making decisions within the institutional framework of the US government, its flaws may be revealed. Essentially, the new administration learns on the job. This is typically one of the key functions of senior officials and the National Security Council staff. Advisors to the president or the president himself initiate a dialogue about the shortcomings of the process and methods for fixing those shortcomings—new committees, new channels for the policy process up and down the hierarchical levels of the bureaucracy, or special interagency structures designed for specific issues. That debate about changes to process, or the decision about making decisions, may extend for months before it leads to any actual proposal. This reassessment and search for a better process may extend throughout the entire tenure of the administration. Perhaps the most important assessment is that of personnel. The president has chosen departmental officials and staff based, again, on a theory of how each individual will work within the system and how each will fulfill the president's administrative and personal needs. As an administration makes more and more decisions, a president will learn how well he chose his original advisors.

The third element is *proposals for change to compensate and find better balance*. The president or his senior advisors, or both, design modifications to decision making that compensate for the shortcomings of the president's style. The ultimate goal is to establish a better balance between the formal, informal, and confidence structures. Though they would not necessarily use this terminology, the president and his senior advisors are actively thinking about that balance. If a president's preferred style leans too far toward formal interagency systems that slow the process or rob it of creativity and flexibility, his advisors may lobby him on the need to add informal structures; if a president's style leans too far toward informality, bypassing the formal process to such a degree that key individuals and even departments feel as though they have been excluded from policy making, his advisors may recommend adding more formality. If the president feels that the formal system and even the informal structures are not giving him advice he can trust or counsel that is politically attuned to his needs, he may seek the private and absolutely frank advice he can get from one or two advisors/aides who have never let him down—his confidence structure.

Finally, whether meaningful modifications in the process are actually implemented is ultimately a *presidential choice to accept or reject changes*. The presidency is an institution designed to serve the needs of whoever occupies the Oval Office. It is a tall order to ask the preeminent politician in the nation, who also happens to be the most powerful person in the world, to do things differently now that he has reached the pinnacle of success. He may be unable to adapt after decades of making decisions in one manner or he may, understandably given his seat at the top of the governmental hierarchy, ask everyone else to simply deal with it. Ultimately, presidents choose one of three options: a president may reject the new ideas;

he may accept the proposal and find that it is helpful; or he may approve the changes on paper and fail to implement them faithfully, using the new mechanisms or committees temporarily, then letting them fall into disuse.

The independent variables are the president's management style and the international, domestic, and administrative pressures placed on the administration. Intervening variables come from three sources: the formal, informal, and confidence structures that develop early in the administration; what the president and his advisors believe they have learned through repeated decisions and their assessment of the process; and their proposals for how to remedy the problem. The dependent variable is the decision making structure (whether it is changed or unchanged). In a nutshell, a president enters office with a simple premise: this is the way I like to do things. Over time, he and his advisors may feel that style is not working well. They design plans to repair the system, and the president ultimately decides whether he can or will change the way he does his business.

These events occur over time and may go through repeated cycles of assessment, identification of weaknesses, proposed adaptations, debate, and acceptance or rejection by the president. Capturing the dynamics of this evolution of the process means viewing it as a linear sequence of decision making events occurring over time.

Case Studies and Methodology

The evolution-balance model is developed here using case studies and a methodology that highlights why the president and senior officials might feel the need for change, why and when change does or does not occur, and what types of changes are made. The purpose of using multiple case studies is to inductively tease out patterns in the answers to those questions across administrations. The case studies in this book focus on two levels. First, the overall foreign policy decision making process of each administration is examined to illustrate the debates about potential adaptations to the process, the reasons when and why the process was modified or not modified, and the types of changes made, if any. Second, each administration's decision making on China is used as the narrower lens for examining the evolution of the process. The issue-area focus provides for a comparison of the general to the specific—are the patterns in the evolution of the overall process similar to those for a specific issue. The comparison can reveal how shifts in the overall process impact decision making on a single issue. Case study methodology also needs to isolate independent and dependent variables as well as identify whether these variables are idiosyncratic (specific to the men and women in the administration) or institutional (based in the political context or structural nature of governmental decision making).

From the idiosyncratic perspective, individual presidents and advisors are the key independent variables. What is the impact of their character, ambition, interpersonal styles, and cognitive needs? Of course, the key variable is the president himself. The case studies in this book cover the presidencies of Kennedy, Johnson, and Nixon. The three men could hardly be more different. Kennedy was brash and untested, the youngest elected president taking over from the oldest man ever to occupy the White House, confidently taking the torch passed to him by the previous generation. Johnson was a pro's pro, a master of politics who thought his chance to be president had passed him by. To him, the government and even the nation were simply uncooperative bulls who were no match for his own unlimited energy and stubborn nature; he would grab it by the horns and wrestle it to the ground. Nixon, whose brilliance was surpassed only by his viciousness, saw clearly how the use of power shaped history, but was often paralyzed by face-to-face conflict within his own administration.

Importantly, presidents are not the only idiosyncratic actors. Major players in the process, such as the secretary of state or national security advisor, are singularly important enough to influence the process independently of their department and even the president. Secretary of State Dean Rusk ran the State Department for both Kennedy and Johnson. His relationship with Kennedy was awkward and formal, but his southern roots endeared him to Johnson. Kennedy's national security advisor, McGeorge Bundy, served as Kennedy's alter ego, honest broker of the process, and confidential advisor. He continued in that job for Johnson but eventually gave way to Walt Rostow, who played an even more central role than Bundy as manager and confidant. Henry Kissinger dominated Nixon's foreign policy process as national security advisor, adding the secretary of state position as well for Nixon's final year in office.

This era from 1961 to 1974 also saw the rise of the national security advisor and the NSC staff and a growing rivalry between these White House-based advisors and the secretary of state and State Department. How Bundy, Rostow, and Kissinger navigated this minefield and how the president conceived of their advisory responsibilities is crucial. It is an institutional variable that serves as both an independent and dependent variable for this study in the sense that its impact on the process has changed over time. It is a dependent variable for the Kennedy case study as Kennedy's dissatisfaction with the State Department and Rusk's advice led him to move more authority into Bundy's NSC staff. It becomes an independent variable in the Johnson and Nixon case studies. The NSC staff's new prominence was institutionalized by that point and would shape the way these incoming administrations thought about their choices for foreign policy decision making.

International and domestic political events and trends are independent variables that represent dynamic institutional pressures. The China case studies exist within a changing political landscape. At the macro level, US containment policy reversed course from intervention in Vietnam to withdrawal from the war and a new détente with both the Soviet Union and China. Kennedy and Johnson entered the Vietnam War as firm believers in the dangers of falling dominoes, even as the Sino-Soviet split widened. The notion that greater engagement with the Soviet Union and China should be an aim of the US was a key feature of the debate in the Kennedy administration, especially following the Cuban Missile Crisis. Two weeks at the brink of war brought a sudden clarity about how to avoid future crises. The Johnson administration moved tentatively toward détente even as the US ramped up involvement in Southeast Asia. Only the Soviet invasion of Czechoslovakia in August 1968 prevented Johnson from beginning strategic arms negotiations with the USSR. Détente became the core of US foreign policy during the Nixon years, a belief that management of the rivalry served US interests better than continued confrontation, intervention, and the possibility of escalation that might heat up the Cold War.

Policy toward China tracks in a single direction, from isolation to engagement. Though the Nixon administration gets the credit it deserves for making the historic diplomatic breakthroughs, the debate over whether to reach out to China began in the Kennedy administration and continued under Johnson. If change in decision making is the subject of study, a policy where innovation occurs and the outcome of debates had real consequences is the most fruitful case study. Most of the key elements of that debate—balancing Soviet and Chinese relations, the level of US involvement in Vietnam, managing relations with Taiwan—provide a consistent contextual framework for the entire era.

Domestic public opinion as an independent variable matters in two ways. First, an America ready to "bear any burden" to fight the Cold War suffered from a "Vietnam Syndrome" by the late 1960s—an aversion to the use of force, or perhaps it had learned a brutal, but important lesson about when and how to intervene in regional conflicts. The US public wholeheartedly supported détente as an antidote to intervention until the late 1970s. Engagement with China fit into the trend away from political-military containment. Second, for the occupant of the Oval Office, fending off charges of being soft on Communism, and the domestic political fallout of such accusations, may have been the overriding determinant of China policy. Kennedy and Johnson understood that vulnerabilities on their approach to China would be used by Republicans to quash Democratic domestic initiatives. The domestic imperative placed limits on their ability to innovate, limits that Nixon, who could never be seen as soft on Communism, did not have. In this sense, domestic political partisanship was an absolutely crucial variable.

Another reason for choosing these presidencies is purely methodological. Designing solid case study methodology requires thinking about what variables can vary and what should stay the same. Given that the aim of any study such as this is a better understanding of the foreign policy process, examining case studies from before the national security advisor and NSC staff became the president's personal machinery is perhaps an apples to oranges comparison—interesting, but not as useful for developing scholarly and practical recommendations for future presidents and officials who operate in a world where the national security advisor and NSC staff remain prominent. That is why the research here begins with the Kennedy era. The case study period ends with the Nixon administration for a different methodological reason. At the time of this writing, the archival records available in presidential libraries and the *Foreign Relations of the United States* series that give the declassified record of US foreign relations are only readily available through the Ford administration. Though the *Foreign Relations of the United States* volume covering the Carter administration's relations with China was published in 2013, almost all of the NSC Institutional "H" Files are still classified as of 2020. The Reagan administration documents on China are years away from being released. The China volumes for 1981–83 and 1984–88 are listed as "Under Declassification Review."[14] Research that compares presidential administrations necessitates that the quality of information is comparable. Results can be skewed if scholars have archival documents for one administration and only journalistic accounts, biographies, and memoirs for another. A planned Ford case study has been cut to bring this work to a manageable size.

This study uses a process tracing and structured-focused comparison methodology. For each president there are two chapters: one that traces the overall evolution of decision making, and one that examines the evolution of decision making on China through the use of episodic case studies (chapters 3 and 4 on Kennedy; chapters 5 and 6 on Johnson; chapters 7 and 8 on Nixon). Through process tracing, these episodes (for example, a China decision in year one, a China decision in year two, and a China decision in year three) can be compared to see how their characteristics may have changed over time. The chapter conclusions include some big-picture analysis of each administration and the episodic case studies.

The concluding chapter of the book explicitly uses the structured-focused comparison questions to make five types of comparisons: overall decision making and China decision making within a single administration; overall decision making across the Kennedy, Johnson, and Nixon administrations; China decision making within each administration; China decision making across administrations; and, finally, the difference between overall and China decision making across each administration. In short, the test of this model and the aim of the case studies is to see if the Kennedy, Johnson, and Nixon administrations made attempts to improve their decision making styles by creating a better balance among their formal, informal, and confidence structures. If so, what explains why they did or did not actually make the proposed changes?

Chapter 2 illustrates the two scholarly debates introduced above (idiosyncratic vs. institutional models; centralization/decentralization and formality/informality). This scholarly context is followed by a summary of the original evolution model, a full presentation of the evolution-balance model, and a deeper look at the process tracing case study methodology.

Chapters 3 through 8 are paired chapters on each presidency: the first focuses on overall decision making, and the second narrows the examination to China-related decisions.

Chapter 3 illustrates the Kennedy informal style and the generally unsuccessful attempts by national security advisor McGeorge Bundy to add more formal interagency processes. Consciously rejecting the formal NSC-based architecture of Eisenhower, Kennedy built an informal system that operated like the spokes of a wheel with Kennedy at the center and multiple channels leading to and from the presidential hub. Though Kennedy hoped to absorb much of the strategic and diplomatic weight of the secretary of state, he also wished to place the State Department at the heart of the foreign policy process. His disappointment with Secretary of State Rusk and the State Department's lack of creativity led to greater informality, more White House-based decision making, the use of special assistants, and the emergence of a more central role for Bundy and the NSC staff (Kennedy's confidence structure). It was Bundy who recognized the weaknesses of the informal style—unpredictability, a disconnect between departments and the White House, and an uncertainty within the departments when decisions were even made. He hoped to compensate by creating an NSC Standing Group, a weekly meeting of principals that could regularize the schedule of decisions and make sure everyone was on the same page. Twice Kennedy agreed to establish such a committee, and twice he grew tired of its formality and allowed it to fade away. The tale of the overall evolution conforms the evolution-balance model. Chapter 4 examines two case studies of Kennedy policy on China: the 1961 United Nations decision on a new US strategy for keeping the US-allied Republic of China in and the Communist People's Republic of China out of the United Nations (UN); and the 1962 Return to the Mainland decision on how to make it clear to the Republic of China that the US would not support its attempts to use force to overthrow the People's Republic of China. In both cases, the State Department took the lead, but the 1961 decision conforms more closely with the original evolution model. The 1962 decision confirms the evolution-balance model; a formal interagency Offshore Islands Working Group was created to complement the informal processes.

Chapter 5 examines Johnson's style and the ultimate success Rostow had in convincing Johnson to add formality to his informal Tuesday Lunch Group as well as rebuild an NSC-based formal interagency system. Johnson's spokes-of-the-wheel style differed from Kennedy's in Johnson's heavier hands-on approach and his faith in and reliance on Rusk more than any other cabinet-level official (confidence structure). As with Kennedy, Bundy suggested that greater formality be built into the process, but Johnson continued to lean on the Tuesday Lunch Group, a scheduled principals-only, no-note-taking weekly luncheon. When Rostow replaced Bundy in 1966, he was able to make the case that the lack of a formal process placed too much of the burden on Johnson, allowed too many issues to be crowded out of consideration by Vietnam-related decisions, and prevented Johnson from receiving the diverse and inclusive advice he needed. The result was the 1966 creation of the Senior Interagency Group/Interdepartmental Regional Group (SIG/IRG) system, a formal set of interagency committees run by the Department of State with assistant secretaries of state chairing the regional and functionally based IRGs. At roughly the same time, the Tuesday Lunch Group was transformed into a more formally staffed committee, essentially the NSC in all but name. The Johnson administration shows the clearest illustration of the evolution-balance model and the way an overreliance on informality is compensated for by new committees or modifications to existing committees that add formality. Chapter 6 focuses on two decisions: the 1965–66 Long Range Study of China Policy, and Johnson's July 1966 speech on China as well as the resulting debate on US strategy at the UN in the fall of 1966. Both cases confirm the evolution-balance model. The initiation of a formal long-range bottom-up interagency review of China policy reflects the same desire for more formal processes. The results of the study itself were considered in the new interagency Far Eastern IRG; an interagency China Working Group within the Far Eastern IRG was formed to examine the Long Range Study report. Johnson's 1966 speech and the need to reevaluate US policy at the UN led to proposals for formal committees and a new assistant-secretary-level committee that reported to Rusk through the SIG/IRG system.

Chapter 7 examines Nixon's hopes to improve upon the Eisenhower NSC by plugging it directly into the White House, thereby making it an arm of the presidency, rather than, in Nixon's eyes, a nearly independent machine that determined policy for the president. Nixon gave Kissinger the role of managing a formal system based on a surprisingly large number of detailed interagency studies. Within six months, Nixon concluded that the NSC was too decentralized and even encouraged interpersonal conflict of the type that Nixon had hoped to avoid. He established interagency committees chaired by Kissinger in 1969 and 1970 that accepted the weight of the interagency process. The new system bypassed the NSC and the senior cabinet officials in favor of deputy- and undersecretary-level committees controlled by Kissinger and connected to Nixon through Kissinger. The changes, in effect, merged the formal and confidence structures. The infamous battle between Kissinger and Secretary of State William Rogers was part of the reason for the reorganization. That rivalry prevented the development of an informal structure that might have resolved the differences between principals and departments. Nixon sought a way to remove himself from the cabinet-level battles, and delegating management to Kissinger was the method. Nixon's confidence in and reliance on Kissinger was so great that in September 1973, Nixon replaced Rogers, making Kissinger secretary of state and national security advisor. Perhaps Nixon had dusted off Eisenhower's plans for a first secretary of the government. These changes confirm the evolution-balance model. This case is unique in that it was Nixon himself who identified the flaws in his own initial administrative design. Chapter 8 looks at three case studies of decision making on China: National Security Study Memorandum (NSSM) 14 of 1969; Chinese representation at the UN during 1970 and 1971; and the drawdown of US troop levels on Taiwan during 1973–74. The 1969 case does not confirm the evolution-balance model; decision making began with a large formal interagency study, NSSM 14, and did not deviate from the initial formal design. The Chinese representation case is best explained by the original evolution model; the formal interagency process was used through NSSM 107, but the final decision on whether to revise US policy at the UN in 1971 was made in small group meetings including only Nixon, Rogers, and Kissinger. The 1973–74 case partially confirms the evolution-balance model. Though another interagency study, NSSM 171, formed the backbone of the process, an early informal dialogue between Kissinger and Secretary of Defense Elliot Richardson guided the outcome. The heavy reliance on the formal interagency process is surprising given that the standard picture of Nixon decision making suggests a centralized system that nearly excludes the interagency process. A larger lesson can be learned here. Nixon and Kissinger used a formal interagency process to fine-tune and analyze their options, but bypassed these same structures when implementing policy during the Paris Peace Talks, Middle East negotiations, the Strategic Arms Talks with the USSR, or the actual diplomacy that led to the opening to China.

Chapter 9 considers the usefulness of the evolution-balance model by comparing all three presidencies and the China case studies. Each administration considered changes to their decision making processes as the model predicts, and each change does represent a search for balance in the process. In all cases, the president only accepted modifications to the process if they were suggested or supported by the key official in the confidence structure, did not interfere with the confidence structure, or better yet, enhanced its effectiveness. Case studies of China also show the utility of the model. Seven case studies of China decision making are included here. Four confirm or partially confirm the hypotheses of the evolution-balance model (Kennedy's 1962 Return to the Mainland case, both Johnson case studies, and Nixon's 1973–74 Taiwan troop decision); two confirm the original evolution model (Kennedy's 1961 and Nixon's 1971 Chinese representation decisions); and one exhibits no change (Nixon's NSSM 14).

The mixed results reflect an interesting feature: the longer an administration has been in office, the greater the explanatory power of the model becomes. Time matters. Administrations learn what works and what does not work over time. As time goes on, the pressure to make modifications increases, and real change to a decision making process becomes more likely.

Chapter 9 also examines the key determinant of China policy in each administration. Importantly, the case studies suggest that domestic politics was the determining factor. Though both Kennedy and Johnson felt that US isolation of China was foolish and counterproductive, they continued the policy, fearing the domestic political repercussions if they appeared to be soft on China. Nixon, an anti-Communist second to none, could move toward engagement with fewer consequences; his right flank was protected.

The evolution-balance model has predictive value that relates to its policy implications. The debate about the proper presidential role in American life will never end. Without question, however, the presidency is a place of decision. The US electoral process fails to recognize that fact. We spend precious little time wondering how presidential candidates have organized their administrative tasks during their careers. That approach to making decisions might be the key variable for the job, but Americans generally ignore the question. The evolution-balance model contends that not only is the president's initial management style crucial, but it is likely to be challenged in ways that will have significant implications for both process and policy. Two suggestions flow from this notion. First, the decision making style of candidates needs to be a greater focus of the vetting process by the parties, the press, and the public. Two, we should all assume that incoming presidents will modify their decision making processes, perhaps several times during an administration. Typically, change is greeted with a headline reading essentially "Administration in Disarray." That knee-jerk judgment may be exactly wrong. A better headline might be "Administration Learns."

TWO

∼ The Evolution-Balance Model

The detailed case studies in this volume are designed for theory-building. The process is inductive, and the most important (and most enjoyable) aspect of this research is the time spent in presidential archives neck deep in boxes and folders. If the question is this—how did presidents use their advisors and structure their administrations for making foreign policy decisions?—the answer rests in the documentary record of those decisions, a record that includes a significant number of memos on decisions about decision making. New models, however, are the descendants of earlier models. Scholarship is a ladder of discovery. Each new theory, model, or hypothesis can only be reached by standing on previous rungs of the ladder—the theories, models, and hypotheses that came before.

This chapter develops the evolution-balance model by first illustrating two debates on decision making and then identifying ways to reconcile these competing models. The first scholarly debate is an argument about the role of the president, and pits an idiosyncratic model against an institutional model. The idiosyncratic model is supported by scholars and practitioners who feel that presidents are unique actors; their administrations are intimately personal creations, and their management styles define the shape of decision making. The institutional model argues the opposite. An individual president's character, political skill, and management styles are essentially irrelevant; all presidents respond to the political pressures of international events, domestic political trends, and the constitutional, legal, and administrative relationships among the three branches of government and within the executive branch in similar ways, through a series of rational calculations intended to protect or enhance presidential power and prerogatives. The evolution-balance model views these models as complementary perspectives rather than irreconcilable rivals. The interaction of institutional pressures and idiosyncratic style shapes decision making. In short, presidents are buffeted by institutional forces that constrain, compel, or empower. They often react in similar ways, but they also often react in different ways. A president's character explains why this is so. In the context of decision making, a president's management style is the one constant amid all the policy making battles, the one independent variable that is most unlikely to change.

The second debate flows from the first. Scholars note that presidents typically centralize decision making in the White House, adding more informality, or ultimately relying on only a handful of trusted aides, what is labeled here as a confidence structure, or they do both. Most research on the evolution of the National Security Council staff is essentially an examination of that centralization. Sometimes, however, there are attempts by an administration to do just the opposite—add decentralized and formal interagency processes. This formalization is particularly true after centralization or poor oversight lead to scandals (e.g., Iran-Contra) or dysfunction. The evolution of decision making is not always a straight linear trend toward centralization and informality.

These debates leave scholars with a dilemma: how to reconcile idiosyncratic and institutional models, and how to explain why a general tendency toward centralization and informality in administrative decision making sometimes makes a U-turn by decentralizing its system and adding formal structures.

The evolution model was the first step toward explaining this dynamism.[1] It started with a simple premise: decision making changes over time. That change has an identifiable pattern: after six months to a year and half in office, administrations begin to make fewer decisions through their formal interagency system; they alter the process by narrowing participation in decisions to fewer officials and agencies, adding more informality, and bypassing or streamlining the formal interagency process more frequently. An administration eventually uses three structures to make decisions: the standard formal interagency structure; an informal structure including only a handful of presidentially chosen senior officials; and a confidence structure composed of the president and his one or two most trusted advisors. Fitting all three together in a way that serves the competing needs of the president, his advisors and executive departments, and the political context is the trick to a stable process. Presidents who fail to achieve a coherent mix among the structures have serious decision making difficulties.

Though useful in its focus on change over time, the evolution model does not fully capture the shifts in the process. It remains too linear and too unidirectional, suggesting that the evolution of decision making flows in one direction, toward centralization and informality. The evolution-balance model refines the idea, hypothesizing that administrations are seeking a better balance between the formal, informal, and confidence structures of the administration, and that such efforts may lead different administrations in different directions—increasing or decreasing reliance on formal, informal, or confidence structures.

This chapter considers the two scholarly debates, summarizes the evolution model, then gives a full explanation of the evolution-balance model.

Does the Individual President Matter?

This section describes the idiosyncratic and institutional models with the goal of reconciling the competing images of the role of the president. As a contextual benchmark, it is useful to begin by pointing out what the models do explain well. The institutional model works best when explaining why all presidents behave the same way in similar political contexts, and the idiosyncratic model is most useful in explaining why specific presidents behave differently in similar political contexts. That leaves obvious dilemmas: when and why do individual presidents respond as if they had no unique characteristics, as simple rational choice machines, regardless of their party, their biography, or their agenda (institutions matter; centralization and informality are the result), and when and why do individual presidents respond as unique actors fighting to remain true to their instincts even when pressured to conform to institutional pressures (presidents matter; decision style goes where the president wants it to go).

The Idiosyncratic Model: The Individual President Matters

There is a large literature on the ways in which individual presidents or other executives matter.[2] Most of those that concern the US presidency are based in the study of character or cognitive psychology.[3] Obviously, presidential biographies concentrate on a single person, while comparative studies, generally with several chronologically arranged chapters on specific presidents, also highlight personality and character.[4] The role of the individual within organizational decision making is the focus here. In the idiosyncratic model the individual president is the independent variable—his character, political skill, perception of the world, personal ambitions, and relationship with his advisors. The structures and processes of decision making are the dependent variable. These are often called "first image" studies.[5] Interest in the "personal biography approach" has been growing in recent years after almost being eclipsed by institutionalism.[6] The study of policy entrepreneurs—individuals who seek to use decision making opportunities as avenues to push their pet projects—has also become an important area of research.[7] Scholarly studies, memoirs, oral histories, and declassified documents make the case for the importance of the individual president in the policy process. In this view, the presidency is a personal institution, designed to work for the individual who occupies the Oval Office, and any attempt to understand the presidency must begin by understanding that individual.[8] The office of the presidency is newly remade after Inauguration Day, like a reverse chameleon transforming to match the individual who occupies the Oval Office. This will be true in terms of three key aspects: the way the president uses his senior advisors and their departments, the way the president uses his own staff, and the president's relationships with the advisors he trusts the most.

In the scholarly literature, Neustadt's persuasion model is the starting point for the modern study of how presidents navigate the labyrinth of policy making.[9] The premise of this model is that individual presidents bring a set of skills to the White House that they use to persuade their way through the internal deliberations of the executive branch and the external arena of executive-legislative relations; that power of persuasion is an art, not a science, the result of almost otherworldly skills of manipulation, bargaining, salesmanship, and political will, bestowed by heaven (or hell) to a single gifted individual. Though the statutory tools of each president are relatively the same, each president's political talents make the difference between success and failure, between a one-term oft-maligned butt of jokes and a candidate for a second Mt. Rushmore. Institutions are not irrelevant, but they are not deterministic of presidential decision structures; they create a set of legal rules, standard procedures, and political realities. What determines the nature of any presidency, however, are the strengths, weaknesses, and skill sets of individual presidents—how presidents navigate through these constraints and compelling forces.

This basic idea helped produce a surge of scholarship in the 1960s and 1970s, promoting what is often called the governmental politics model. The model was a sharp contrast to the rational actor model of decision making, where all decisions are made through cost-benefit calculations of carefully constructed options by a unified government functioning almost as one supremely rational and strategic mind. In the rational actor model, the president's individuality is not relevant. Think of sweeping historical studies or biographies that contain sentences beginning with phrases such as "Washington decided . . . ," as if a city itself produces policy or decisions spring forth from buildings through alchemy. The governmental politics school challenged the rational actor model in two fundamental ways. First, the new school argued that the unitary or unified vision of government was inaccurate. Government is made up of organizations and individuals, and there may be nothing unified about it. A second point drew the logical conclusion of the first—decisions are not made by cost-benefit analysis, but by political infighting among those organizations and individuals.[10] Two models initially flowed from this reconceptualization. The organizational process model focuses on departmental and agency competition. The government is composed of competing organizations, rivals who fight over budgetary allocations, or the division of labor; each has its own interests, culture, and standard operating procedures based on a view of the world that it inculcates to all employees.[11] The bureaucratic politics model narrowed the focus further to individual officials. In this view, the government is composed of ambitious men and women with their own goals, perceptions of the world, and pet projects they hope to see implemented. Rivalries are personal and ugly, and every decision is an opportunity for someone to win a battle and take charge of a specific policy.[12] In both the organizational process and bureaucratic politics models, decisions are the result of bargaining and compromise between organizations, individuals, factions, or coalitions that fight it out until a consensus is reached. No one is entirely happy with the outcome—a solution that was likely no one's first choice. Everyone gets a little something, however, and they live to fight again another day. Importantly, in both these models, the president's key job is to bring order to potential chaos, though he is often described as just another player in the bargaining game, with no special role.

A third model, the presidential management model, brought the idea back toward Neustadt's original target: leadership.[13] It argued that the president is not just another player in the game of bargaining and compromise. He has managerial resources and skills that allow him to bring order to what may seem chaotic, and perhaps most importantly, he has a strong motivation for making sure that the policy process is designed to produce decisions that can serve the overall national interest as well as his political goals. He has been elected, and the responsibility for US national security is on his shoulders; a president's place in history will partly depend on his legacy in that area. To ensure a process that serves him, the president uses specific management strategies to manipulate the size of decision making groups, the level and pace of debate, centralization and delegation within the group, horizontal and vertical participation in decisions, the relationships among the individuals and organizations, and his own expenditure of time and effort. At a more basic level, he hires advisors for their specific skills, expertise, and temperament and fires people who no longer satisfy those initial advisory needs; he sets deadlines for decisions, ends debates, or allows them to continue. Most importantly, he controls access to the Oval Office; some officials can see the president on a regular basis and some cannot. Access itself can be used as the ultimate reward (you have it) or punishment (you don't) for senior officials in the government. In this model, the bottom line is simple: the president has a preferred method of making decisions, and that is the way decisions will be made. Decision making structures are designed to fit the needs of the individual president.

Based on these ideas, scholars developed a typology of presidential management that hypothesized three distinct styles in the early postwar presidencies: competitive, formalistic, and collegial.[14] In the competitive style, a president pits his advisors against one another in the belief that competition breeds excellence. He forces them to become rivals and uses that battle to make a place at the table next to him as the ultimate prize. It is a hands-on approach that asks the president to be principal policy maker and chief of staff. Franklin Delano Roosevelt is seen as the primary example of the competitive; Trump may have favored a variant of it as well. The formalistic style is a more traditional notion of hierarchy and order. Advisors have roles and responsibilities, and a formal chain of command through which options are assessed flows from cabinet departments upward to the president. Staff work is crucial, and all opinions are fully vetted before a recommendation is made to the president. Saving the time and effort of the president is one of the motivations for constructing such a system. It leaves him making the big decisions without having to manage the day-to-day operations of his administration. Truman, Eisenhower, Johnson, and Nixon are typically seen as more formalistic presidents. The collegial style again places the burden of management back onto the president. Here, decision making is made in a more informal grouping where all advisors are equals and expertise does not grant anyone special authority on a subject. Great minds gather and wrestle with a problem as they search for the best possible solution. The president is a participant in the group, either listening and learning or actively engaging with it. Teamwork is the key value; the president wants a consensus opinion and wants to see that it is reached through vigorous, but not acrimonious, debate. Kennedy is seen as the quintessential example of collegiality.

Former governmental officials strongly support the argument that the individual president matters, that his character, his political skills, and his ambitions are the defining features of an administration. Secretary of State Dean Rusk, who served both Kennedy and Johnson, stated it most eloquently: "The real organization of government at higher echelons is not what you find in textbooks or organization charts. It is how confidence flows down from the president."[15] McGeorge Bundy, national security advisor for Kennedy and Johnson (until 1966), wrote of national security decision making in a 1961 memo to Kennedy: "This is really your private business. . . . The essence of it is that the organization should reflect your style and methods, not President Eisenhower's."[16] Walt Rostow, a veteran of the Kennedy State Department and the successor to Bundy as Johnson's national security advisor, stated, with conviction, that when it came to organizing for national security, "there is only one truly important thing to be said on the subject: the work should be organized in ways congenial to the incumbent president."[17] Henry Kissinger, Nixon's national security advisor and secretary of state, argued that "presidents listen to advisors whose views they think they need, not to those who insist on a hearing because of the organizational chart."[18] H. R. Haldeman, Nixon's White House chief of staff, argued the same sentiment:

"Each presidency is almost completely unique because it is under our constitution, an office held by one man, and that's all there is to the office of the President, that one man. . . . You have to structure each President's staff to fit that President's method of working. You cannot institutionalize on any permanent basis the Office of the President. You must build a new Office of the President for each president, and it must evolve as that president evolves in office.[19]

The president matters; all other considerations are secondary.

The Institutional Model: The President Does Not Matter

Most of the literature that fits into the framework of the institutional model touches upon the advisory process only indirectly. The independent variables in this model are the pressures of statutory provisions (legal and regulatory), congressional action, interest groups, the bureaucracy, domestic political and electoral trends and events, as well as international commitments and political developments. The dependent variable in these studies is the way presidents behave while in office. The general conclusion of these studies is that all presidents react in similar ways to the institutional forces arrayed around the presidency. It is an "impersonal" approach "that treats presidents as generic types rooted in an institutional system,"[20] one that endeavors to eliminate "personal factors" from the analysis.[21] Presidential management of the process is not an idiosyncratic phenomenon, but the rational choice response of presidents to their institutional context. That rational response is typically to centralize decision making in the White House.

A key assumption of the institutional perspective is similar to the presidential management model: presidents want control of the policy process. However, in the institutional model, presidents desire this control because it is rational for them to do so, and the way they seek to gain that mastery has no relation to the characteristics of the individual president.

The framers of the constitution were successful in designing a political and administrative architecture where, in Madison's words of Federalist 51, "ambition must be made to counteract ambition." No branch of government should dominate, and the institutional structure has been carefully constructed to place limits on each branch of government. This is an "invitation to struggle" that protects each branch of the federal government (as well as individuals and states) from the other branches of the federal government.[22] Institutions limit or channel presidential action by "imposing elements of order" in the relationships inside and outside the executive branch.[23] The rational choice aspects of the model suggest that presidential actions are calculated responses to those institutional forces.[24] Changes in presidential decision making are a function of presidents rightfully defending their statutory turf against encroachment by other institutions.

In particular, three types of forces seem most relevant: constraining, compelling, and empowering. For example, by professionalizing the bureaucracy into a nonpolitical civil service, Congress was attempting to place the career personnel of the executive branch outside presidential influence, constraining his ability to direct them. A president can respond by choosing political appointees for the upper levels of executive departments who have absolute loyalty to the president and his ideology. A second arena of battle is over agency design. Congress may tinker with executive department structures to insulate or isolate an agency from politics, professionalizing a department by making it more civil service-heavy.[25]

Compelling and empowering forces are also factors in agency design. Presidents and their allies in Congress can create new agencies or bureaus that institutionalize certain missions and perspectives, thereby favoring them over competing missions and perspectives; this strategy can empower a president by giving him the administrative tools to pursue an agenda.[26]

The creation of the Arms Control and Disarmament Agency (ACDA) during the Kennedy administration and the State Department Bureau of Human Rights and Humanitarian Affairs during the Carter administration are examples. Compelling a president to deemphasize a policy area or to grant more congressional oversight on a policy is the same dynamic in reverse. The downgrading of ACDA from a semi-independent agency under the State Department to a one-man bureau within State in 1999, by a Republican Congress skeptical of arms control, shows the ability to undermine a perspective.[27] Following the September 11 attacks, the George W. Bush administration had hoped to ensure presidential dominion over homeland security issues when it created the Office of Homeland Security, a unit in the Executive Office of the President, as the hub for decision making in the area. The establishment of the Department of Homeland Security over the initial objections of the administration is an example of Congress designing in institutional oversight and gaining power to compete with the executive branch for authority over the issue.[28]

The creation of the National Security Council itself is an excellent example of a congressional attempt to force the president to make national security decisions in a forum that by statute must include officials whom the Senate has approved and who must report to Congress (the secretaries of State and Defense). In this way, Congress wedged its foot in the door of the most secret deliberations a president makes. The presidential response was to make an end run around the NSC by giving more and more prominence to presidential staff. The evolution of the national security advisor and NSC staff from neutral administrators to the president's main advisor and his personal foreign policy staff during the 1960s and 1970s (addressed in chapters 3, 5, and 7) is the rational way for the president to regain control of the agenda in the face of what he sees as congressional meddling.[29]

Presidential empowerment is at the root of the debates over the "imperial presidency" and the "unitary executive." If the president is the dominant actor in government, it is because he cannot be constrained or compelled in certain areas. The executive is already empowered by statutory authority or by "plenary" or "inherent" prerogatives over foreign affairs that are exclusively presidential, regardless of whether they are enumerated in the Constitution.[30] Rationally, presidents seek an understanding of the institution of the presidency that enhances their control over policy. Arthur Schlesinger's notion of the imperial presidency argued that during the era of the modern presidency (FDR through the early 1970s), there had been a steady usurpation of congressional power by the presidency;[31]

crises accelerated the trend, enabling the president to absorb even greater entitlement as a necessary response to the need for swift decisions, unity of command, and national solidarity in the face of threats.[32] A recent reformulation of the imperial presidency thesis argues that the rise of the dominant presidency is as much a function of an "invisible Congress" as it is of presidential aggrandizement; presidents are "contingently imperial," rationally expanding the presidency when other institutions fail to balance against the executive.[33]

The "unitary executive" idea is much broader, suggesting that Congress has no legitimate constitutional oversight role in executive branch policy implementation. Presidential power to implement the law, especially during wartime, is nearly absolute; checks and balances from the legislative or judicial branch that might interfere with the president's ability to protect the nation are essentially voided.[34] Here the president is empowered to interpret the rules in a way that favors his institutional jurisdiction. Not only does the president have a rational desire to control the policy process, but he has the mechanisms for doing so. The president has a multitude of unilateral tools: executive orders, presidential memoranda, presidential proclamations, national security directives, and signing statements.[35] The "administrative presidency" version of this model focuses on the more practical side—the president's administrative toolkit that can be used to manipulate federal government actions.[36] These ideas are not peripheral to presidential management of the executive branch. They suggest that a president's institutional authority is expansive enough that he can shrug off most challenges from Congress and structure his policy process to maximize his hands-on command of the executive branch, regardless of congressional interpretation of legislation or the law. Trump defenders took this argument to the extreme during the impeachment, essentially making the case that Congress has no right to question or limit presidential actions. Trump himself stated that Article 2 of the Constitution gives him the "right to do whatever I want as president."[37]

If the president does not matter, then the key variables on decision making will be congressional pressure (the partisan mix, the liberal or conservative balance, and the congressional approval/disapproval of specific policies), public opinion, and the president's rational need to own the policy process. All presidents will react in the same manner to the political forces around them: they will attempt to maximize their control and expand their freedom to do as they please and make decisions as they please, typically through centralization of power in the White House.

When Does the President Matter, if He Matters, and How Would We Know?

In a thoughtful analysis of the debate between the institutional and idio-syncratic models, Bert Rockman speculates that "people matter more when other things matter less."[38] Testing that premise requires assuming that the president does matter, but how much he matters may depend on institutional forces. Rather than an either/or approach, it calls for assuming that both institutional and idiosyncratic factors are independent variables, and the interaction between those variables is the real answer to the question of what determines the shape of the decision making process. Put in more general terms, agency and structure are both important.[39]

Centralization, Formality, and Informality

Most studies of presidential decision making assume that presidents cen-tralize the process and add more informality to its structures. The trend is almost always described as linear. Even studies that suggest it is not necessarily linear still lean heavily on the hypothesis that there is nearly a straight line between inauguration and centralization and informality.[40] Of the three presidents studied in this volume, however, two added or con-sidered adding formal decentralizing structures to their decision making processes (Kennedy and Johnson). Here, the discussion of centralization and formality/informality is placed into the context of the debate on idio-syncratic and institutional models, allowing for direct linkage between the concepts.

Centralization

The study of centralized presidential decision making begins with a sim-ple observation. Since FDR, presidents have moved more power into the White House, often draining authority and relevance from the statutory departments and agencies of the executive branch. The institutional model explains this pattern best: pressures on each president are the same; all presidents reacted similarly, with increasing centralization of the process. The idiosyncratic model obviously has less explanatory utility here—its challenge is to explain why a set of uniquely different individuals all made the same choices. Analytical parsimony makes the institutional model the clear preference. Here the independent variables are institutional pressures from Congress, the formal departmental organization of the executive branch, public opinion, and political trends; the dependent variable is a centralization of the decision group into the White House, or a presidential reliance on one or two individuals for most advice, what is labeled the confidence structure in the evolution and evolution-balance model. Scholars of public administration and foreign policy decision making have often remarked that there are only two methods of coordination: centralization of the process, or developing a common purpose within the organization.[41] Given how difficult it is to build consensus within an administration through an interagency process that will generate unanimous support behind anything reflecting a "common purpose," the only rational choice seems to be centralization.

The Executive Office of the Presidency (EOP), the institution that supports the president within the executive branch, was created in 1939. Before its establishment, presidents had roughly 130 staff members supporting them. The number swelled to over 600 almost immediately after the EOP was up and running and has hovered since the Ford administration at 1,500 to 1,900.[42] More important than the overall size are the functions of that staff. Units within the EOP replicate the expertise of the statutory executive branch agencies. As a sort of "presidential branch" that mirrors the executive branch, successive presidents use a personally designed bureaucracy to manage their agendas.[43] A quick sampling of EOP analogs include the White House Counsel's Office (Department of Justice), the Office of the US Trade Representative (Department of Commerce), and the National Economic Council staff (Departments of Treasury and Labor).

The evolution of the NSC staff into the president's own foreign and national security machinery is that same style of EOP-based centralization in its most extensive form. The NSC was established by the National Security Act of 1947 to be a cabinet-level interagency body that advised the president. A professional staff that served the president was not on the radar at the time. The growth of a professional presidential staff, not affiliated with specific departments and not part of the NSC itself, occurred during the Kennedy administration. That centralization of foreign policy advice within the NSC staff has been a subject of intense debate and the rivalry between the national security advisor and other officials is a central theme of numerous studies, including this book (and a question on my PhD comprehensive exam in 1990).[44] Since Kennedy, there has been a consistent trajectory over time toward a larger and larger staff. While Kennedy had under 20 professional staff members, the Obama administration reportedly grew a mix of professional and administrative staff that reached nearly 400.[45] Congress acted to constrain subsequent growth in Section 1085 of the National Defense Authorization Act (Public Law 114–328) of December 13, 2016, limiting the professional staff to 200.[46] The NSC staff performs analytical functions that are assigned by statute to the Department of State, Department of Defense, Office of the Director of National Intelligence, Central Intelligence Agency, and Department of Homeland Security, among others.

Scholars who use the perspective of the institutional model disagree about the roots of centralization, but they generally identify the centralization trend as a rational choice reaction to presidential needs for numerous reasons. First, institutional pressures in the form of more and more responsibility placed at the front door of the White House lead the president to react rationally by building up his capability to respond to those pressures.[47] Second, the failure of the interagency process to reach consensus or produce usable advice for the president is a staple of the governmental politics model, whether in its organizational process or bureaucratic politics form. Though scholars often worry about the problem of a senior decision making group forming an early consensus or feeling pressure to conform (groupthink), a bigger problem may be "polythink," where a lack of consensus, perhaps caused by organizations or individuals pushing their parochial interests, leads to conflict, gridlock, and leaks.[48] This inability of the president to get the departments and agencies to work together through the standard interagency process leads the president to move the process into the White House. Third, even with the ability to appoint several thousand officials at the top layer of the governmental pyramid, a president faces the great challenge of moving the government in a desired direction. The president might use centralization as a means to bypass executive departments and agencies that are seen as less than committed to his agenda. Fourth, presidents use the administrative tools that serve them best. Presidents often adapt some of the adhockery that has helped them resolve critical time-urgent issues, essentially a use of crisis decision making for routine policy making.[49] As the NSC staff proves itself to be flexible and adaptable to crises, presidents see it as a reliable stand-in for the routine interagency process in areas that are important to them. Fifth, White House-based assistants may be more attuned to the political needs of the president than departmental or agency-based officials. National security is still about politics; domestic political feasibility is always a factor. The poliheuristic model explains it well: decision making is a two-step process, a first stage where politically unacceptable options are rejected and a second stage where decision makers choose among the remaining, feasible options.[50] Sixth, all of these factors suggest that the time and effort required for a president to run the government might be like a snowball rolling down a hill for four or eight straight years. To conserve time and energy, a president may act on an "economy principle" and find ways to do things faster even if this requires bypassing his own interagency processes or ignoring departments and agencies that are too slow.[51] Ironically, the solution of centralization may represent an unenviable choice to overburden the White House while analyzing policy options and making decisions, instead of overburdening the White House supervising other people analyzing policy options and making decisions.

All of the above suggests that presidents are simply rational actors responding to institutional forces, not idiosyncratic actors. Centralization of the advisory process in the White House or a reliance on a few individuals (confidence structure) is the rational reaction of all individuals who are elected president. Decentralization is generally ignored in these studies; it is a central aspect, however, of research on formality and informality.

Formality/Informality

The level of formal versus informal processes within an administration is the second key element in understanding the evolution and changes within that process. Formal structures are those based on standard committees, hierarchical relationships between committees and individuals, and regularized channels of paperwork and reports. These may be rooted on statute or presidential directive. Decisions made through ad hoc structures or meetings not officially established in statute or directive, even if interagency in nature, are defined as informal.

From the institutional perspective, formality and decentralization are built into decision making by tradition and statute in two ways. First, the US government is designed by law as a cabinet-style architecture of departments and agencies with codified line officers tasked with set roles and responsibilities. Major reorganizations, such as the National Security Act of 1947, the Goldwater-Nichols Act of 1986, the Homeland Security Act of 2002, and the Intelligence Reform and Terrorism Prevention Act of 2004, are negotiated by the executive and legislative branches and can only be changed by further legislation. In this sense, presidents are handed a formal system when they enter office. Even at the highest level of decision making, presidents are by law instructed to use the NSC, a formal interagency committee, for advice. Second, the same organizational rivalry and bureaucratic feuding that create pressure for centralization also lead to informality. These internal institutional pressures motivate the president to tinker with the formal statutory design that comes with the job. He may begin to create alternate structures or shortcuts in hopes of minimizing these organizational and bureaucratic battles. The new modifications may be designed to create consensus within a small group of senior officials or to break bureaucratic gridlock through bypassing the formal interagency process.[52]

Scholars of the idiosyncratic perspective address formality and informality in the context of the presidential management model. Former governmental officials agree, arguing that the level of formality or informality in an administration is based on the needs of the individual president. Some presidents prefer formal structures (formalistic), while others prefer informality (competitive and collegial). For example, a president with little experience in foreign affairs, an uncertain sense of his ability to manage the executive branch, and a dislike of political conflict might choose a formal process where the interagency process runs itself, producing a choice the president can then ratify. In contrast, a president with a complex view of the world, a high level of confidence in his administrative skills, and a natural comfort with political conflict might lean toward an informal process where his direct participation is the key factor in the process. Underneath these models, however, is an assumption about all presidents' decision making goals: they all seek wide-ranging debate, thorough analysis, and a diversity of perspectives. The difference rests in how they expect to produce that outcome, through either fierce competition, the inclusivity of the formal interagency process, or teamwork among equals.[53]

If centralization is not a linear phenomenon and if the level of formality and informality differs between presidents and often changes even within one presidency, models of decision making need to account for this variation.

The Evolution Model

The evolution model is the stepping-stone to the evolution-balance model (see fig. 2.1). It flows out of one critical idea: decision making in any administration changes over time. The way decisions are made in the first month of an administration's tenure in office will differ from the way they are made a year later and the way they are made two years later. From a methodological standpoint, an administration's processes cannot truly be understood by describing a specific decision made at a specific point in time; a more comprehensive understanding can be gained by taking snapshots of

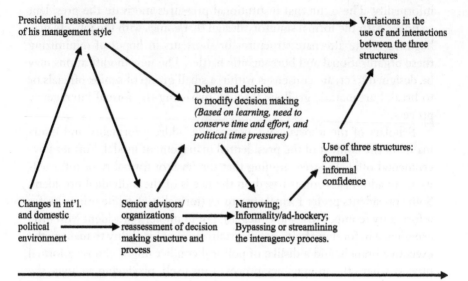

Fig. 2.1. The Evolution Model

the process made at different times during an administration's tenure. The model was developed inductively through a study of Carter, Reagan, and George H. W. Bush decisions on nuclear strategy and arms control.[54]

Importantly, the evolution model contended that these changes over time have a distinct pattern for all presidencies: a narrowing of participation, the addition of informal and ad hoc processes, and more frequent bypassing of the full interagency system.

Three principles of decision making explain this pattern.[55] The economy principle highlights the ever-expanding demands on the time and effort of the president and senior officials. During the transition, presidents and their advisors try to create a system that will maximize their use of executive branch expertise while also conserving their effort and making the best use of their time.[56] They realize very quickly that the time and effort required to maintain that original system expands exponentially. The solution to conservation of time and effort is the use of more informal and streamlined processes. The principle of political time focuses on the international and domestic political demands on an administration and how they influence decision making. There are anticipated pressures, such as the budget cycle or other legislative requirements, as well as the intense pressure of the electoral cycle, which emphasizes the need for policy accomplishments on a timetable. Power is like political capital placed in a bank after an election; it immediately begins to decrease whether used or not, and therefore presidents must use that power according to a pressurized time frame.[57] Unanticipated pressures such as crises may have a deep impact on organization as well if decision makers feel that crises have reshaped their views of current political issues or decision making itself. Both anticipated and unanticipated pressures move an administration to consider ways its processes could be more responsive to its political environment. The learning principle suggests that the original structure designed before Inauguration Day is a theory of how decision making should work. Only after making decisions over a period of months can a president and his senior advisors learn if the theory had any value. Perhaps most importantly, presidents and their senior advisors learn about each other.[58] Do they fit the president's pre-inauguration perceptions of their strengths and weaknesses, assets and liabilities, and placement within the decision making system?

Ultimately, the administration develops three different structures: formal, informal, and confidence. The *formal structure* is the initial NSC-based interagency process, typically codified in the first two presidential directives of the administration. The *informal structure* is a smaller group of senior officials who work with the president on a daily basis to smooth over the rough spots and to move the government in the desired direction. The group may have an actual committee name, but it generally operates without staffing—no one but principals attend. There may be no agenda and no minutes. The group usually meets in two forms—with and without the president. The assumption of all the principals is that their ability to insulate themselves from organizational rivalries, staffers fighting for their parochial interests, and the cacophony of pundits, the press, and ideologues within the administration is the key to formulating decisions based on a strategic assessment of the threats and opportunities facing the US. The adults need to get in a room away from all the screaming children so they can think clearly. The *confidence structure* is the smallest unit—the president and one or two of his close advisors alone. These are the people the president trusts the most, who serve as his alter egos, and the last people the president asks for advice before he finally makes a decision. These relationships provide critical psychological support for the president.

Much of the above discussion leans in the direction of the institutional model. Institutional pressures push the president to change the system, and each president reacts in roughly the same manner: narrowing, informality and adhocracy, and streamlining or bypassing the interagency process, adjustments that led to the use of three structures. At first glance, individual presidents do not matter. The case studies, however, made it clear that an administration's use of the three structures and success in developing a stable process was defined by the president's specific and unique decision making preferences. Institutional variables may lead to change, but successful adaptation depends on idiosyncratic variables.

Ultimately, the research concluded that all three are necessary for a smoothly functioning process. If the formal process dominates, administrative rivalry and gridlock may be the result (Reagan). If the confidence structure eclipses the others, ideas are not vetted well enough and policy can spin in unexpected and unwanted directions (Carter). The informal process seems to be the sweet spot. If it is used as a mechanism to tame rivalry, build or maintain teamwork, break gridlock, and serve as the bridge between the formal process and confidence structures, then decision making can proceed smoothly (George H. W. Bush).

The Evolution-Balance Model

The evolution-balance model moves beyond the evolution model in two ways. First, the original evolution model focused on how three administrations that began with formal processes developed their informal and confidence structures. The choice of case studies rendered the model too linear; decision making changes flowed in one direction. The evolution-balance model is intended to explain change in administrations that begin with either formal or informal processes. Second, and most importantly, the evolution-balance model focuses the lens of analysis more deeply on the impact of the president and his management style—as an independent variable that defines an administration's initial processes, as a strength or weakness of that process, and as the determining factor in whether corrective medicine is applied to policy making pathologies or whether they are left as is to plague future efforts at effective decision making.

The evolution-balance model has four elements: presidential style; continuous assessment in an effort to identify weaknesses; proposals for change that compensate for the shortcomings of the president's style by finding a better balance between the formal, informal, and confidence structures; and presidential choice to accept or reject changes. Importantly, the model views decision making as a sequence of events occurring in a linear fashion beginning when a president enters office. Figure 2.2 illustrates the model. In the figure and in the discussion below each element is identified as taking place at T_1 to T_4, indicating that each occurs in that

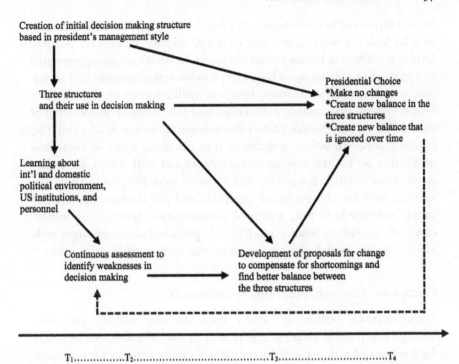

Fig. 2.2. The Evolution-Balance Model

linear sequence. That sequence may repeat itself again during the tenure of an administration. Following T_4, assessment begins again (a return to T_2 is indicated in figure 2.2 as a dashed line). If no changes were made, the president's advisors may continue to press for something new. If changes were made, those advisors assess the impact of the new adaptations or whether they are actually being used at all.

Presidential Management Style (T1)

At the inception of an administration, presidents and their senior advisors design a decision making process that they believe will best serve the president, a process based on the president's preferred management style. The best definition of presidential management is still Alexander George's trio of variables.[59] First, an incoming president has a cognitive style: he knows, for example, whether he is an intuitive or analytical decision maker, the level of information he requires before he makes decisions, if he prefers written reports or oral briefings as the best method to receive information, or if he feels the need to seek out or quash alternative opinions. Second, he may not admit it, but he carries a sense of his decision making strengths and weaknesses. He knows if he prefers hands-on management or a surrogate manager; whether he works better in small informal settings or more formal systems that provide well-staffed, and fully vetted, consideration of issues; if he errs on the side of deciding too quickly or too slowly; and if he requires consensus before choosing or if he can make decisions regardless of whether he has the support of his cabinet and staff. Third, he understands his orientation toward conflict. Does he enjoy the give and take and sparring with his advisors or are organizational and bureaucratic rivalries simply unbearable to him, a sign of administrative dysfunction? Importantly, the evolution-balance model treats presidential management style as idiosyncratic models do; it is a constant that does not change over time.[60]

Continuous Assessment to Identify Weaknesses (T2)

Administrations continually assess their decision making processes. Though every administration begins with its carefully designed structure for foreign and national security policy, it is simply a theory for how decision making might or should work—the president's beliefs about what he thinks he needs drawn on an organizational chart. Once codified through a presidential directive or directives, the system is up and running; that theory meets reality the day of the inauguration and every day thereafter. The president and his senior advisors learn if their theory was correct as they make decision after decision within an international and domestic political context and the institutional context of US governmental structures.

Continuous assessment of the system is an explicit and recognized job of the White House staff.[61] Since the Kennedy administration, the assistant to the president for national security affairs or national security advisor (hereafter ANSA) and the NSC staff have led these reevaluations both formally and informally. As assistants to the president whose primary responsibility is coordination, the ANSA and NSC staff are the canaries in the coal mine of the interagency process; they are likely to see problems before anyone else and will be the most concerned with how the overall process operates. Presidential archives contain memo after memo from NSC staffers examining the deficiencies, inefficiencies, and illogic of their daily routine and offering administrative remedies. That dialogue continues throughout the administration. The main goal of reassessment is to identify weaknesses in structure and process. The top-down question is simple: Does the system serve the president well? The bottom-up question is more complex: Does the system serve the needs of the interagency concept—analysis that considers all options and uses the full range of resources within the executive branch? The political question is perhaps most daunting: Does the system allow the president to respond promptly and effectively to the demands placed upon him by the international and domestic political environment?

A more fundamental area of assessment is personnel. Presidential selection of departmental advisors (cabinet and subcabinet officers) and presidential assistants (NSC and White House staff) is also a theory about which individuals will work best in what roles, how each person will serve the president, and how the group will work together. In the latter case, the relationships may be built into the system as the key elements of the formal, informal, and confidence structures. Presidents and their senior advisors learn whether these personnel choices—again, theories on how it should all operate—were strong or weak ones. The personalities of the key advisors are crucial factors in that determination.

Proposals for Change to Compensate and Find Better Balance (T3)

An awkward conclusion of an administration's assessment may be that the president's management style is the single biggest cause of weaknesses in the decision making process. These weaknesses are best described as a poor balance between the formal, informal, and confidence structures. Changes to the process are suggested as ways of compensating for the imbalances caused by the president's decision making preferences. A president who relies on the formal may be asked to shift more weight to informal (using the informal to break gridlock in the formal). A president who relies too much on the informal structure may be advised to use a formal interagency process in order to backstop the informal processes or to relieve the informal process of a workload that is overwhelming it. A president who leans too heavily on the confidence structure may be advised to use the formal and informal structures more to gain alternate perspectives. At the opposite end of the spectrum, a president may decide that only his confidence structure has real value and ignore the formal and informal processes. In many cases, someone has to walk into the Oval Office and say: "Sir, you are the thing that needs fixing." Presidents are surrounded by "assistants to the president" and "special assistants to the president" and an army of staff whose mission is to serve the president; few will dare to say "no," and even fewer will dare to tell the president that his basic decision making style is faulty.[62] It seems intuitive then that a president's response to this advice might be to show that official the door. The record, however, does not reflect a history of senior advisors being fired for suggesting changes (until the Trump administration). Presidents seem to want to get it right; they take the assessment process seriously enough to value even critical advice. When it comes to making improvements in decision making, presidents do not seek a palace court filled with "yes men."

Presidential Choice (T4)

Ultimately, the president will decide whether any proposed changes are actually implemented. The key question is this: Is a president willing or able to do his job differently? Presidents rely on familiar strategies and a style that has brought them to the highest office on earth. In that sense, they are old dogs. Can they learn new tricks? The president can go in three directions: accept the proposed reorganization; reject the reorganization; or accept the recommendations, but implement them only half-heartedly or for a short period of time before falling back on old habits. If changes are made, it is because someone has convinced the president that the modifications will benefit him; if the proposed changes are rejected or only partly implemented, it is because a president either cannot or will not adapt. Again, the president's management style is the crucial variable. All proposals for change will live or die based on his preferences. Presidents make decisions the way they want.

The illustration in figure 2.2 shows the dynamics of the evolution-balance model over time. The president's management style (idiosyncratic) and the international, domestic, and administrative pressures (institutional) the administration faces every day are the independent variables. These pressures strain the administration's ability to make decisions in an efficient and timely manner. The formal, informal, and confidence structures that develop early in the administration, what the president or his advisors, or both, believe they have learned through repeated decisions and their assessment of the process, and their proposals for how to remedy the problem, are the intervening variables. The changes or lack of change in the administration's decision making structure is the dependent variable.

One important aspect should be highlighted. At T_4, after a president makes a choice, the process returns to T_2—continuous assessment of decision making—regardless of what the president decides about previous proposals (indicated in fig. 2.2 with a dashed line). The president and his senior advisors continue to monitor the process to identify weaknesses in an unchanged process, new problems in a new process, or weak implementation of new processes.

Developing and testing the evolution-balance model requires research that is inductive and casts a wide net for independent variables, essentially examining all the influences on an administration—external and internal—and then identifying what type of impact they may have had on decision making. The dependent variables for this research are proposed changes and accepted changes in decision making, both structures and processes. In all the case studies, special attention needs to be paid to influences on the process that come from idiosyncratic variables and institutional variables. Idiosyncratic independent variables are defined here as personality traits of the key individuals in the decision making unit, relationships among them, and the policy preferences of individuals. Independent variables that come from institutional pressures are defined as any congressional, public, legal, or political/electoral forces that constrain, compel, or empower the president; legislative or public pressures that reduce presidential independence and flexibility; and organizational rivalries within the executive branch that create obstacles to presidential control of an issue. In short, defining variables as idiosyncratic or institutional is a function of answering a question: Are the actors or players in the process behaving in a way expected by their institutional interests, or is there something unique, unexpected, or personal about their behavior at that particular time in the process?

Case Studies and Methodology

This study uses a qualitative process tracing and structured-focused comparison methodology. The narrative of an administration's decision is the key data source. Process tracing is designed to tease out patterns of change over a given time period by examining a defined set of variables or characteristics at different points in time. For example, what were the characteristics of decision making in the first weeks of an administration's tenure? What did they look like one year later and two years later? In this study, that means literally tracing the changes in the process over time. Accomplishing this type of analysis requires the use of a structured-focused comparison methodology that allows the characteristics of decision making to be compared over time and across multiple case studies (different administrations and a specific issue area).[63] The changes over time in the overall pattern of decision making in the Kennedy, Johnson, and Nixon administrations are evaluated in chapters 3, 5, and 7. The China case studies of each administration, chapters 4, 6, and 8, are divided into what are essentially episodes, focusing on specific China policy decisions made at different points in an administration's term in office.

Best practice process tracing uses a single set of questions to draw out the characteristics of decision making. The questions are applied to overall Kennedy, Johnson, and Nixon decision making and each China case study; the answers to the questions reveal the key aspects of the administration's processes and if they have evolved—over time, do the characteristics vary? The questions themselves are based on past studies of the presidency that emphasize the multiple influences on the process, the dynamic nature of the process, and the mix of formal, informal, and ad hoc arrangements.[64] The set of questions is not explicitly asked in each chapter. That would make the study unreadable. Instead, the key questions are placed into larger categories for comparison that enable the chronological narrative of each case study to answer those questions. Each chapter uses the same format to organize its narrative.

While a process tracing methodology is used to understand the relationships between the independent and dependent variables, causation is, of course, the most difficult hurdle for any methodology to clear.[65] Judging causation in process tracing requires examining a set of variables over time and making sure that all connections between them support the causal chain; every ingredient must be necessary to bake the cake. The study of decision making therefore requires historical case studies.[66] The case studies in this book satisfy that necessity by telling the story of each administration's decision making as a detailed narrative. In particular, the research in this study focuses on passing the "hoop test"—targeting a variable that absolutely must be present to accept the hypothesis.[67] In specific terms this means searching for memos and records of conversations that document evidence of each element of the evolution-balance model: an identifiable presidential management style; assessments of the process and identification of weaknesses; proposals for change that explicitly reference the balance between formal, informal, and the level of reliance on the most trusted advisors (confidence structure); and a presidential choice about them. Instead of a set of formal hypotheses, the test of the evolution-balance model is whether the documentary record provides evidence for each of these elements.

The concluding chapter will not explicitly compare the answers to each of the structured-focused comparisons below. It will compare them through the use of the overall categories through which each question is derived. Five comparisons are made: overall decision making across the

Kennedy, Johnson, and Nixon administrations; overall decision making and China decision making within a single administration; China decision making within each administration; China decision making across administrations; and, finally, the difference between overall and specific decision making across administrations.

The case studies for the overall evolution of each administration use the following format that embeds the structured-focused comparison questions into a set of categories that form the narrative for the chapters on each presidency.

Structured-Focused Comparison Questions

1. Initial Decision Making Process: What is the standard decision making process established when the administration enters office?
   - *How is the initial decision making structure decided upon, and what are the reasons for designing a structure in that particular way?*
   - *What are the committees and roles and responsibilities designed into the initial process (both statutory and administration-designed structures)?*
   - *What is the standard paper flow of administration interagency studies and directives?*
   - *What is the mix of formal and informal elements at the outset of the administration?*

2. Role of the President: How does the president fit into the process, and what is his preferred management style?
   - *What is the president's orientation toward conflict; does he join any intra-administration battles or shy away from them?*
   - *Does he want options from which he can choose, or does he want specific recommendations?*
   - *Does he want consensus from his advisors, or does he seek a full vetting of the complexity and dilemmas for any issue?*

3. Organizational Dynamics: Are there organizational and bureaucratic conflicts within the administration and how are they resolved (if they are resolved)?
   - *What are the key individual and organizational rivalries within the administration?*
   - *What is the coalition structure of the individuals and organizations in the process?*
   - *Who has the responsibility to manage or resolve these conflicts?*

4. Development and Use of Three Structures: Why and how did the administration create its informal and confidence structures?
   - *What are the informal decision groups that exist outside the standard process?*
   - *What is the role of the president in the informal process?*
   - *Are there individuals (prime movers) who have the first-among-equals role in the policy process in terms of management and in terms of specific policy issues?*
   - *Are there individuals who have more access to the president than others? Are there advisors whom the president trusts and relies on more than others?*
   - *What is the horizontal range of participation in the process for organizations and individuals?*
   - *Is a standard interagency model used, or is any agency or individual excluded?*
   - *What is the vertical range participation in the process from the working level to the senior levels?*

5. Balancing and Compensating: Do the president or other senior advisors identify weaknesses in the system and propose significant changes to remedy those weaknesses?
   - *What are the reasons for consideration of these changes, and why did they consider these changes at this particular time in the administration's tenure?*
   - *Who initiated these changes?*
   - *How will these changes reshape the operation of the three structures?*
   - *What is the relationship between the proposed changes and the president's management style?*
   - *Are these changes related to balancing and compensating for the president's management style?*
   - *Are these changes related to issues of centralization or decentralization of the decision process?*
   - *Why did the administration decide to implement the changes, or why did it decide not to implement the changes?*

Case studies on China decision making are developed using an abbreviated case study structure of political context, narrative, and analysis. Again, this modification is made to keep the case studies readable. The political context section asks the questions that follow; the analysis section considers the structured-focused comparison categories.

Political Context: How does the political context shape institutional pressures on the administration's decision making for China?

- *What were the president's views of China and Taiwan and Cold War politics in Asia upon entering office?*
- *What is the nature of the perceived threat level concerning the issue area, and has that perception changed? If that perception of threat is changing, why?*
- *How do the foreign policies of China and Taiwan impact US decision making?*
- *Is there congressional pressure on the administration regarding the issue area and, if so, what is its nature and level of change?*
- *Is there significant public opinion regarding the issue area and, if so, what is its nature and level of change?*

The concluding chapter of this book compares the evolution of overall decision making and China decision making across each administration. It draws lessons from the case studies about decision making, the Kennedy, Johnson, and Nixon presidencies, and policy making toward China. It also identifies where the evolution-balance model works well and where it falls short, and suggests areas for further study. Tables that detail the specific answers to the structured-focused comparison categories for each presidency and each China case study (figs. 9.1 to 9.3) are included there.

The key sources for this research are the archival record in the Kennedy, Johnson, and Nixon presidential libraries as well as the State Department's *Foreign Relations of the United States* series. The research methodology is traditional in that sense, but best suited for this study. Trends in political science research have opened up new possibilities in the form of quantitative methods and experimental methods. The qualitative method of process tracing is best suited for this research since the objective is to find out exactly what these specific officials did in a given situation. Experimental methods can add to this type of research by testing the models explained here to see if different randomly selected decision groups experience the same phenomenon (changing the style of decision making) when faced with similar challenges in experimentally designed simulations. Studies have used experiments to assess important phenomena: the impact of new options after deliberation has begun; the relationship between experience and confidence in available evidence, the range of opinion, and the possibility of new information; the influence of complexity on decision making;

and even the relationship between signaling, perceptions of hostility, and rapprochement.[68] Experiments hold a useful place in testing some of the ideas developed here. The concluding chapter suggests avenues for experimental research.

THREE

∿ John F. Kennedy

"A Livelier Sense of Duty"

"The sole and undivided responsibility of one man will
naturally beget a livelier sense of duty and a more exact regard
to reputation."
—Alexander Hamilton, *Federalist* 76[1]

In a November 16, 1962 memo to President Kennedy, Special Assistant to
the President for National Security Affairs McGeorge Bundy summed up
nearly two years of the administration's foreign policy decision making in
this way:

> It will remain true that our operating style will be somewhat differ-
> ent from General Eisenhower's. Your own instinct is to work closely
> with the men who are most directly concerned with a particular
> problem, and to seek advice from a wider and more varied circle
> than General Eisenhower used. For this reason, your tendency is
> to use frequent small meetings with those who have an immediate
> concern with a problem. . . . This is simply the way you do your job,
> and I see no chance that you will want to take the opposite course
> of reviewing the agreed papers laboriously ground forward by a
> third-level bureaucracy and presented to you through the medium
> of weekly meetings of 30 to 40 people.[2]

Kennedy's decision making is the quintessential example of an informal
process attuned to the president's own style. He wanted control; he was
a hands-on manager who felt that layers of staff work would only delay
policy making and dilute sharp analysis. His White House aide Arthur

Schlesinger Jr. concluded that he was "impatient with systems" and wanted an open Oval Office where it would be "relatively easy to get to him."[3] Above all else, Kennedy craved freedom to act as president, and movement in a foreign policy unencumbered by bureaucratic foot-dragging, inertia, and lack of imagination. George Ball, undersecretary of state for Kennedy, felt that Kennedy's "main concern was action and day-to-day results." He quoted Kennedy as often saying "politely, but impatiently 'let's not worry about five years from now, what do we do tomorrow.'"[4] Kennedy himself reflected on his frustration with a State Department that he felt was too wedded to the past, too content with the status quo.

> The President can't administer a department, but at least he can be a stimulant. . . . There is a great tendency in government to have papers stay on desks too long. . . . One of the functions of the President is to try to have it move with more speed. Otherwise you can wait while the world collapses.[5]

Kennedy was not a man who liked to wait.

The notion of the president as a "stimulant" may be the key to understanding the Kennedy decision process. If the Eisenhower era was staid and buttoned-down, Kennedy's presidency jump-started an era of action. If Eisenhower's foreign policy bureaucracy was too formal, slowed to a crawl by the weight of its own paper trail and paralyzed by its own requirements for consensus, Kennedy's administration inaugurated a level of activity not seen since FDR. If Eisenhower represented the fading of World War II–era senior leadership too set in its ways to imagine anything other than incremental change, Kennedy's junior officers pushed the government toward creativity in any way possible. Along with soaring inspirational rhetoric, Kennedy's inaugural speech implied a great deal about his approach to foreign policy and its management: "Let the word go forth from this time and place, to friend and foe alike, that the torch has been passed to a new generation of American."[6] Kennedy was not about to let executive branch agencies slow or water down the agenda of this new generation; great achievements demanded action, and that meant action now, not in two weeks after the proper committees had met or in six months after the interagency study was done. If he had to run everything from the Oval Office, if he had to go around his own departments or under people's heads to get the information he needed, so be it.

Kennedy's initial standard decision making process had three main features: an informal design based in small groups debating with the president in a collegial manner; downgrading the formal National Security Council in favor of these small groups; hopes to use the State Department as the center of decision making; and a reliance on Bundy and the NSC staff as his own personal foreign policy bureaucracy.

The role of the president flowed from Kennedy's management style. He wanted to be at the heart of the process. A spokes-of-the-wheel system was designed where all avenues of communication led to the president, and all key decisions were in his hands. Kennedy was his own secretary of state in matters of interest to him and in areas where he thought his selected secretary, Dean Rusk, failed to deliver the types of policies he sought. The administration's organizational dynamics were surprisingly stable given the growth in prominence of Bundy and the NSC staff, a shift in administrative power resulting from Kennedy's conclusion that State and Rusk were either unwilling or unable to accomplish the task Kennedy had assigned them. Rusk and Bundy never became serious rivals because of their loyalty to Kennedy and the absolute priority of retaining a collegial environment.

The development and use of the three structures occurred quickly under Kennedy. His administration began with informal structures dominating the decision process—small groups that included all the key officials from departments with responsibilities on the issue backstopped through the use of Bundy and the NSC staff as Kennedy's own machinery for foreign affairs. The informality expanded during the first year as the Bundy/NSC staff deepened its role and White House-based special assistants were added to the mix. At the center of Kennedy's confidence structure was Bundy. If Kennedy was his own secretary of state, Bundy served as his chief of staff for foreign affairs and ultimate sounding board/reality check.

As part of its continuous assessment of the decision making process, the administration began considering changes not long after the Bay of Pigs debacle of April 1961. Though most of his advisors saw the need to balance out Kennedy's informal style with more formal interagency procedures, Kennedy emerged from the Cuban failure convinced of the opposite; he needed to place more faith in people he actually trusted—his confidence structure—rather than in those the organizational chart told him he should trust. In spite of Kennedy's reluctance, three new formal groups were created to balance out the informal system with formal structures: an assistant-secretary level NSC Planning Group (1961) and two NSC Standing Groups, the first in 1962 and the second in 1963. The Standing Groups were serious attempts to add a formal senior-level interagency group below the NSC level, something Bundy saw as an absolute necessity. In both cases, Kennedy agreed to create a formal group that could meet as a subcommittee of the NSC and, in both cases, Kennedy then ignored it. The Standing Groups were simply too formal; he would not allow them to replace the informal meetings and he never allowed their operations to connect to the informal processes. Interestingly, the ExComm (the executive committee of the NSC), famous for its role in the Cuban Missile Crisis, was also an innovation in decision making. Its creation, however, was directly related to a crisis and therefore beyond the scope of this study. It is described briefly in the context of how it continued meeting after the crisis and how it related to the creation of the Standing Groups. The only changes that did gain some permanence were Kennedy's increased use of special assistants as his own personal checks on the advisory process, an additional source of informal rather than formal advice. In the wake of any problems, Kennedy fell back on his initial preferences. From a theoretical perspective, institutional pressures pushed Kennedy toward adding more formality, but his own idiosyncratic instincts won the day. The overall development of Kennedy's foreign policy decision making confirms the evolution-balance model. The administration attempted to balance against too much informality, but Kennedy ultimately chose to reject those balancing structures.

Table 9.1 summarizes the evolution of the overall Kennedy administration decision making process as well as the China decisions using the structured-focused comparison questions. Figure 3.1 provides an illustration of the changes described in this chapter; it is a Kennedy-specific diagram based on figure 2.2 that traces the administration's decision making in the context of the evolution-balance model.

Initial Decision Making Process

Kennedy's informal process has become the archetype for collegial presidential management.[7] Often, the response to the Cuban Missile Crisis and the use of the Executive Committee of the NSC, or "ExComm," is considered Kennedy's finest hour and the quintessential example of his style. The modern study of foreign policy decision making often begins with Graham Allison's classic 1969 article and 1971 book on the rational actor, organizational process, and bureaucratic politics paradigms, which used the missile crisis as its case study.[8] Decision making during the crisis presents a heroic portrait of a president throwing great minds into a room, instructing them all to treat each other as equals, and urging them to find a solution to avert World War III. Kennedy is portrayed as sober and analytical, rationally assessing the wisdom of every participant, like a wise judge evaluating the

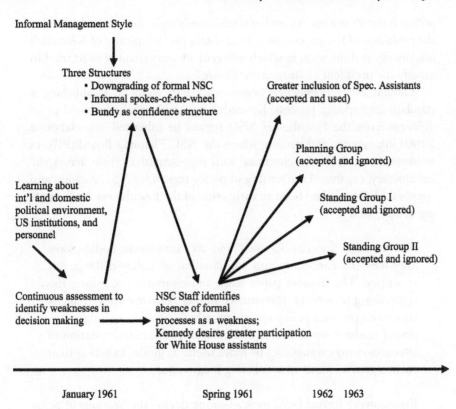

Informal Management Style

Three Structures
• Downgrading of formal NSC
• Informal spokes-of-the-wheel
• Bundy as confidence structure

Greater inclusion of Spec. Assistants
(accepted and used)

Learning about
int'l and domestic
political environment,
US institutions, and
personnel

Planning Group
(accepted and ignored)

Standing Group I
(accepted and ignored)

Standing Group II
(accepted and ignored)

Continuous assessment to
identify weaknesses in
decision making

NSC Staff identifies
absence of formal
processes as a weakness;
Kennedy desires greater participation
for White House assistants

January 1961   Spring 1961   1962   1963

NSC – National Security Council

Fig. 3.1. The Evolution of Kennedy Administration Decision Making

arguments of beseeching plaintiffs. Occasionally he is seen taking the helm of the meeting, steering his advisors in the right direction, but his inclination is for letting the ExComm go where the current takes it. In the end, Kennedy rejected the advice of the ExComm, which had recommended an air strike to destroy the soon-to-be-deployed Soviet medium and intermediate range ballistic missiles. Instead, he opted for a naval blockade that forced the Soviets into the position of firing the first shot against an opponent that had overwhelming nuclear superiority at the time. The Soviets backed down; a period of détente began; and a legend was born that mythologized the administration and its collegial model rooted in informal decision making.

The missile crisis, however, was a crisis decision, something very different from the day-to-day decision making that characterizes foreign policy. It serves as a microcosm of the Kennedy style, but a broader look at the evolution of the process over time shows the complexity of Kennedy's informality and the ways in which different advisors adapted to or tried to modify the president's management choices.

Though every presidency begins with a decision on establishing a standard interagency process, Kennedy's was deliberately designed to be different from the Eisenhower NSC system he inherited—an elaborate formal interagency architecture where the NSC Planning Board (PB), an assistant-secretary-level committee with representatives from across the bureaucracy, organized the writing of policy papers for NSC revision and approval.[9] Kennedy had been an early critic of the Eisenhower NSC, writing in 1957 that

> the National Security Council and its companion bodies have improved the continuity and coordination of policy-making, but at a price. The massive paper work and clearance procedure, the compulsion to achieve agreements among departments and agencies, often produce policy statements which are only a mongrelization of clashing views. Sparks of dissent and a clear confrontation of alternatives may sometimes be more useful as guides to action than an amalgam on paper of conflicting judgments.[10]

Eisenhower's formal NSC took a beating during the hearings of Senator Henry Jackson's Subcommittee on National Policy Machinery of the Senate Committee on Government Operations. The subcommittee began its work in 1959 and still hammered away at Eisenhower even after Kennedy was elected. Jackson's main criticisms can be read as indictments of the Eisenhower process: the disconnect between the work of the NSC and the key national security questions facing the nation; the lack of budgetary considerations in NSC deliberations; the emphasis on consensus decisions in the NSC Planning Board's policy papers, that watered down analysis to the lowest common denominator; the ever-growing size of NSC meetings; and the formality of it all, which rendered it slow, rigid, and always behind the rapid movement of world events.[11]

Kennedy and his incoming advisors seemed to agree with much of the criticism. The president himself stated it outright as he announced the appointment of McGeorge Bundy as his special assistant to the president for national security affairs (SANSA) on January 1, 1961: "I have been much impressed with the constructive criticism contained in the recent staff report by Senator Jackson's Subcommittee on National Policy

Machinery. The Subcommittee's study provides a useful starting point for the work that Mr. Bundy will undertake in helping me to strengthen and simplify the operations of the National Security Council."[12]

A president-elect receives more advice than he wants, but all incoming administrations seek out those who have experience in the White House or scholarly expertise on the presidency. In Kennedy's case, much of the private counsel during the transition echoed the public sentiments of the Jackson subcommittee. In December 1960, the subcommittee staff gave the incoming administration its recommendation: get rid of Eisenhower's Operations Coordination Board (OCB)—a subcabinet-level interagency committee that oversaw implementation of NSC decisions—and much of the formal interagency paperwork and routine meetings of Eisenhower's NSC system. They referred to it as "deinstitutionalizing and humanizing the NSC process" in an effort to make the NSC an "intimate forum."[13] Richard Neustadt, a veteran of the Truman White House who had just published *Presidential Power*, a book destined to be a classic of presidential studies, sent a memo to the campaign on October 30, 1960. He detailed staffing choices that Kennedy would need to make in the first few weeks after the election (assuming he was the winner):

> The interim staff that I suggest below is closer to Roosevelt's pattern than to Eisenhower's: You would be your own "chief of staff." Your chief assistants would have to work collegially, in constant touch with one another and with you. . . . There is room here for a *primus inter pares* to emerge, but no room for a staff *director* or arbiter, short of you. Neither is there room for sheer, unguided struggle . . . commit yourself not to each detail of Rooseveltian practice . . . but to the *spirit* of his presidential operation; whereby *you* would oversee, coordinate, and interfere with virtually everything your staff was doing. A collegial staff has to be managed; competition has to be audited. (italics in original)

He emphasized maintaining Kennedy's flexibility in the early stages, arguing that "you will want to take a careful look at NSC machinery and avoid a premature commitment to procedure." Interestingly, Neustadt felt that in the case of the SANSA—the role Bundy would transform into the president's most important advisor on foreign affairs—"this post should be avoided by all means until you have sized up your new secretaries of state and defense."[14]

In a memo to the transition organization from November 1960, Clark

Clifford, another White House aide to Truman, pointed out how Truman was, and Kennedy would be, different from Eisenhower: "A vigorous President in the Democratic tradition of the Presidency will probably find it best to act as his own chief of staff, and to have no highly visible majordomo standing between him and his staff (and incidentally, between him and the public)." In making recommendations for Kennedy, he focused on Kennedy's style, suggesting that something similar to the Truman White House, with the president at the center of the process, would be "best suited to Kennedy's style and personality . . . a White House chief of staff was not desirable for an activist hands-on man like John F. Kennedy."[15] Those who knew Kennedy best reminded him that he was not Eisenhower, could not be Eisenhower, and should not want to be Eisenhower. His administration needed to reflect his personality.

Importantly, the incoming secretaries of state and defense, Dean Rusk and Robert McNamara, also agreed that the Eisenhower system was too formal and elaborate. In Bundy's words, the two men "had argued strongly" for "a streamlined organization." Rusk wanted State Department leadership rather than NSC "staff committees without the power of decision."[16] He also saw Eisenhower's NSC as "muscle-bound with too much machinery, too many meetings, too much wasted time."[17]

Kennedy began the planning process for dismantling many of the central features of Eisenhower's NSC very quickly. Much of the work on a new system during the transition was done by Robert Johnson, a holdover from Truman and Eisenhower's NSC staffs; Walt Rostow, the newly appointed deputy SANSA; James Lay, the NSC executive secretary (a holdover from Eisenhower); and NSC staffer Robert Komer.[18] Their work was reflected in a January 24, 1961 memo to the president from Bundy that stands as the opening of the Bundy-Kennedy dialogue on the nature of the NSC system, a dialogue that continued throughout the Kennedy presidency. Bundy explicitly understood that this was the beginning of a discussion and that part of his job was to keep Kennedy thinking about the process and what he wanted out of it. In the memo, he states that his reason for sending it was to "stir your reactions." The premise for that dialogue was fundamental: decision making must be geared to presidential style. According to Bundy, "Everyone who has written or talked about the NSC agrees that it should be what the president wants it to be; this is right." He was clearly aware, however, that what the president might want can change over time. He wrote to Kennedy that "the Council can readily be shaped and reshaped to your taste as we learn from experience."[19]

The initial decision making process as established in the first six months of the administration contained three key elements: de-emphasizing the role of the NSC system; leadership by the State Department; and the use of the NSC staff as the president's personal foreign policy staff under the leadership of the SANSA.

De-emphasizing the Role of the NSC

As the preinaugural memos suggest, Kennedy desired a process that would stand in direct contrast to Eisenhower's: informal, flexible, and swift, where Eisenhower's was deemed formal, rigid, and sluggish. The notion that incoming presidents hope to differentiate themselves from the predecessor and learn from their mistakes holds true for Kennedy. The quote at the beginning of the chapter illustrates the administration's open acknowledgment that Kennedy would do things differently than Eisenhower. Bundy, noting the dominance of the NSC in the Eisenhower process, wrote in a January 31 memo that when it comes to decision making,

> formal meetings of the Council are only part of its business; you will be meeting with all of its members in other ways, and not all decisions or actions will go through this one agency. . . . This is really your private business. . . . The essence of it is that the organization should reflect your style and methods, not President Eisenhower's. The jobs it can do for you are two: one is to help in presenting issues of policy, and the other is to keep in close touch with operations that you personally want to keep on top of. Both of these things were done in theory by a large, formal, paper-producing staff for President Eisenhower. I'm sure you don't want that.[20]

A move away from formality required de-emphasizing the NSC. The January 31 memo from Bundy detailed how Kennedy needed to make that idea clear to NSC members in the very first NSC meeting. Everyone needed to know that the NSC was not a venue for decisions, period: Kennedy would make decisions. Bundy said: "The Council is *advisory*: it does *not* decide. . . . *You* will decide—sometimes at the meeting, and sometimes in private after hearing the discussion" (italics in original). Theodore Sorensen, counsel to the president and a Kennedy loyalist since his Senate days, suggested that Kennedy did put this idea into practice, making "minor decisions in full NSC meetings or pretended to make major ones actually settled earlier."[21] Bundy saw the NSC as a way to make sure all senior advisors to the president would know "what is cooking" and what the president wants.[22] Commensurate with this, NSC meetings were shifted from weekly to biweekly meetings.[23] The size was a key problem; with too many people present, the NSC would lose its usefulness. Bundy's January 24 memo, however, only proposed a cut from slightly over 20 to around 16. That list included the statutory members at that time (the president, vice president, secretaries of state and defense, and director of the Office of Civil Defense and Mobilization); statutory advisors (director of Central Intelligence and the chairman of the Joint Chiefs); cabinet-level invitees (secretary of the treasury and director of the Bureau of the Budget); the executive secretary of the NSC; and potentially six White House or NSC staff members. The first meeting of the NSC on February 1, 1961 included 17 people, though the roster of attendees differed slightly from Bundy's list; it added officials of cabinet departments rather than NSC staffers.[24]

Minutes of Kennedy's first NSC meeting made it clear that the NSC would not function as the top of an interagency pyramid: "Policy recommendations would be brought to the NSC without being obscured by inter-agency processing but with adequate previous consultation and the presentation of counterproposals."[25] Making that a reality required dismantling much of Eisenhower's NSC machinery. The OCB was abolished officially on February 18, 1961 by Executive Order 10920.[26] Though these changes received much scrutiny at the time, a more important modification to the process was the quiet elimination of the PB and its extensive paperwork, also in February 1961.[27] The PB's prodigious production of policy papers was seen by many as the main culprit that had rendered the NSC an unimaginative, consensus-driven behemoth.

In place of the OCB and PB, the Kennedy administration established a process centered on departmental leadership rather than NSC interagency committee leadership. The State Department received most of the responsibility.

The NSC itself rarely played a central role in Kennedy decision making. Though the NSC schedule was shifted to biweekly meetings and regularly scheduled for every other Thursday morning by October 1961, actual meetings did not hold to that intended ideal (see table 3.1 for data on meeting frequency). The Kennedy administration held 45 NSC meetings, the first on February 1, 1961 and the last on October 2, 1963. In 34 months, the administration averaged roughly one NSC meeting every three weeks, but only one a month in 1962 and 1963. The frequency of meetings by year shows a steady decline in use, from 21 in 1961 to 12 each in 1962 and 1963. Meetings typically came in spurts and were related to specific issues

TABLE 3.1. Committee Meetings of the Kennedy Administration

Date (by Quarter)	National Security Council	Standing Group I	Standing Group II
January–March 1961	3	0	0
April–June 1961	9	0	0
July–September 1961	4	0	0
October–December 1961	5	0	0
January–March 1962	3	10	0
April–June 1961	2	3	0
July–September 1962	4	2	0
October–December 1962	3	0	0
January–March 1963	2	0	0
April–June 1963	5	0	8
July–September 1963	3	0	5
October–November 1963	2	0	1

Source: Clinton administration, National Security Council Archives, https://clintonwhitehouse4.archives.gov/media/pdf/Kennedy_Admin.pdf

that had reached a critical point; they functioned partly as crisis management and partly as a check to make sure everyone was on the same page. For example, the NSC's most active period came when the NSC held six meetings between April 27 and May 9, 1961. The main issue was the crisis in Laos, though other subjects were discussed. Another active period saw three NSC meetings between July 13 and 20, 1961 over Berlin. Unsurprisingly, three NSC meetings were held between October 20 and 22, 1962 on the Cuban Missile Crisis (though the ExComm dominated decision making on Cuba). Laos was also the subject of three meetings between April 10 and 22, 1963.[28] This data seems to confirm the impressions of Sorensen that the NSC would be more active during crises, but only to get every official "on the record" or to "silence outside critics who equated machinery with efficiency."[29] In 1963, one NSC staffer summed it by saying that the NSC was "little more than a name."[30]

Leadership of the State Department

Kennedy hoped that Secretary of State Dean Rusk and the State Department could lead the process and produce innovative solutions for international problems; to him, a strong secretary of state should be the backbone of foreign policy. The downgrading of the NSC could leave a void in decision making and cripple the administration's interagency process unless the State Department picked up the slack. This was precisely how Kennedy saw the enhanced role of the secretary of state and his department. Kennedy wanted to place himself at the heart of it all, but State would be his primary tool for controlling foreign policy. He was formally handing interagency leadership to Rusk and State, a full replacement of the NSC-based system under Eisenhower. Importantly, PB coordination and long-term planning functions were also reassigned as State Department responsibilities.[31] Bundy emphasized to the Jackson subcommittee the "clear authority and responsibility of the Secretary of State, not only in his own Department, and not only in such large-scale related areas as foreign aid and information policy, but also as an agent of coordination in all our major policies toward other nations."[32] In a September 4, 1961 letter to the Jackson subcommittee, Bundy explained that the elimination of the OCB was done in part to return that authority over implementation of foreign affairs to the secretary of state.[33] Rusk told senior-level officials in the State Department soon after the inauguration that the president had made it clear that there was "an active expectation on his part that this Department will in fact take charge of foreign policy."[34] Sorensen argued that while Kennedy wanted to be his own secretary of state, reality made this "incapable of practical application." In reality, "Kennedy looked to Rusk for the bulk of this work, and made it clear that the latter—not McNamara, Bundy, or any one of the many he consulted on foreign affairs—was his principal advisor and agent in foreign affairs."[35]

To achieve this, routine matters were assigned to the appropriate regional assistant secretary of state, who would take on coordination responsibilities. Often a special interagency group or "task force" was created to deal with a more critical area; those described as "unusually urgent, difficult and complex" were assigned to a "single full-time office under the Secretary of State." This might be the assistant secretary for the region or an official specifically designated to handle the issue. Its chair served under the direction of the president and secretary of state. These groups often met on a weekly basis while the topic was still relevant. Some issues, such as those focusing on defense or economic policy, were managed by the relevant agency. Task forces were established for particularly critical issues, such as counterinsurgency, the nuclear test-ban negotiations, foreign aid, and critical regional topics (Cuba, Vietnam, Berlin, Iran, Laos, the Congo, and the Ryukyus). Though all these ultimately reported to the NSC, coordination responsibility was assigned to a specific department or agency, rather than an NSC-based coordinating committee, as was the case under Eisenhower's OCB and PB.[36]

The President's Own Foreign Policy Staff

Kennedy's greatest decision making legacies are the transformation of the NSC staff and the emergence of a powerful national security advisor, officially the special assistant to the president for national security affairs at that time. Today, scholars and even the general public think of the NSC staff as the president's personal foreign policy bureaucracy. It is almost taken for granted that the NSC staff will operate as the hub of decision making in foreign affairs under the direction of a prominent national security advisor, who also serves as the president's top advisor on foreign and national security policy. The smaller, flexible, and agile NSC staff developed by Kennedy and Bundy was the first to reach that status.

Though overall cuts were made in the staff, downsizing from around 71 to roughly 50, the number of professional staff (experts in international relations, economics, intelligence, or military affairs, some on loan from other cabinet departments and agencies) was actually increased, eventually becoming as high as 17. In addition, the staff was reorganized along functional or regional lines, with members having portfolios for their specific area. It took on the job of evaluating departmental papers and reports to the president, conducting its own analysis, and eventually reviewing outgoing State Department traffic.[37] In short, the NSC staff began to work in an oversight and management role in foreign affairs. Kennedy brought this approach to both the foreign and domestic sides of his administration. Numerous staff members had access to the Oval Office, and the number of "Assistants to the President" expanded. The president made it explicitly clear that, on foreign policy issues, he wanted "direct communication and command with" Bundy and Rostow, as well as with White House staffers such as Special Assistants Arthur Schlesinger and Ralph Dungan, Special Counsel Theodore Sorensen, Deputy Special Counsel Myer Feldman, Special Assistant Counsel Richard Goodwin, and Kennedy's military aide, General Chester Clifton.[38]

Importantly, this use of the NSC staff as the president's private foreign policy brain trust was not due to any gradual but inexorable expansion of the staff or related to the aftermath of a crisis. It was a deliberate decision at the outset of the administration. The general conception of the NSC staff up to this point was that it worked for the NSC. Bundy explicitly refers to the NSC staff in his January 31, 1961 memo to Kennedy as "*your* Staff" (italics in original).[39] A memo to Kennedy of June 22, 1961 makes this statement even more powerfully. The memo is from a White House official but has no specific authorship; it is absolutely clear about the role of the NSC staff: "The President's staff is to serve as an extension of himself—as his eyes and ears and his source of nondepartmental comment. The President's staff is his own instrument."[40] Schlesinger eloquently described it as a "supple instrument to meet the new President's distinctive needs."[41]

Bundy was the first of the celebrated national security advisors, the early prototype for the position of first among equals, process manager, and presidential alter ego. He had unlimited access to the president and was considered as influential as any cabinet officer (as was Sorensen); one journalist referred to him as a "one man National Security Council."[42] A basic part of the SANSA role, then as now, was managing the paper flow. The elimination of the PB meant that departmental reports were coming directly to the White House, in effect directly to the president. Bundy's task was to manage that paper flow to make sure the president received what he needed and was not bothered by issues that could be resolved below the presidential level.[43] Kennedy described Bundy's management mission succinctly: "All matters of international security go through McGeorge Bundy."[44] In both the assessment of analytical reports and in advising the president, Bundy saw the challenge as trying to get "to the bored bones of the problem as cleanly and clearly as you could and state the alternatives as sharply as possible." Bundy's new centrality became so widely reported that Kennedy even joked with the press about it, responding to a question about Bundy's huge responsibilities with the quip: "I will continue to have some residual functions."[45]

Scholars have noted that one of the most important roles of a national security advisor is honest brokerage—making absolutely sure that the president gets all the advice he needs from everyone who has expertise and that all options are fully vetted; no ideas or analyses can be excluded because of organizational parochialism or rivalry or because some official favors a rival idea. To perform this well, the national security advisor cannot choose sides in the interagency debate; he must make sure that the debate is an open and inclusive one that serves the president's needs.[46] Sorensen noted Bundy's honest brokerage: "McGeorge Bundy made certain that no responsible office or point of view was omitted from meetings on foreign policy."[47] In the Kennedy administration that meant keeping both Rusk and McNamara in the loop. Bundy, however, also saw himself as an advocate of polices he believed supported administration priorities. He was not always a neutral broker. Walt Rostow, deputy SANSA until November 1961 (when he became chairman of the State Department Policy Planning

Council), pointed out Bundy's dual contributions, writing that Bundy was a "source of advice, as well as a manager of advice."[48]

The new role of the national security advisor and his staff did have a key formal component. Presidential directives in the form of the National Security Action Memoranda (NSAMs) were written by Bundy and distributed to the departments as the formal decision of the president. The power to shape the president's formal communications to the bureaucracy should not be underestimated. Early NSAMs were either written by Bundy following NSC meetings or were dictated by Kennedy to his secretary. They functioned as records of policy actions or tasking documents for the departments, identifying questions that the president wanted answered. Draft NSAMs were reviewed by the departments to make sure that everyone shared a common understanding.[49] Bundy's authorship of these memos, however, gave him substantial clout.

Role of the President

If Eisenhower's presidency and his decision making style are seen as a reflection of the corporate culture of postwar America, where everyone finds their role and accepts their responsibility as a cog in a large machine, the Kennedy administration was more akin to a small business, where every aspect is geared to the whims and needs of the founder. Where Eisenhower served as chairman of the board of the USA, ruling over layers of bureaucracy, delegating power to specialists, and searching for consensus, Kennedy's style allowed everything to flow into his office, giving him authority and responsibility over all the key issues. His desire for an informal process, free of all the bureaucratic superstructure that Eisenhower built, was at its core a desire for flexibility. Scholarly work traces this informality to Kennedy's love of the pulling and hauling of politics and his need to be immersed in it, his competitive nature, or his general skepticism toward experts, particularly those in the military.[50] Schlesinger described it this way: "Kennedy, who had been critical of the Eisenhower effort to institutionalize the Presidency, was determined to restore the personal character of the office and recover presidential control over the sprawling feudalism of government."[51] Sorensen saw it as establishing the "primacy of the White House within the Executive Branch."[52] It was a style more similar to Roosevelt than to Truman or Eisenhower.

From a broader perspective, Kennedy wanted to be his own secretary of state—the US spokesman and representative to the world. In terms of process, Kennedy was his own chief of staff for foreign affairs in a system described as a "spokes-of-the-wheel" approach. At the hub was Kennedy. Direct access to the president was open to numerous advisors. Bundy was given an office in the West Wing and might see the president several times during an average day, while numerous White House staffers had easy access to the president. Reportedly, Kennedy had a "two-door policy." The main entrance to the Oval Office was manned by Special Assistant to the President Kenneth O'Donnell, a Kennedy loyalist from Massachusetts, who guarded formal access. A second door was designated for presidential assistants and often left open just a bit, as a deliberate message to staff—come in if you need to. One of the hallmarks of informal processes is a reliance on people, rather than regularized procedures, and Kennedy had greater faith in people than in organizations.[53]

Kennedy thrived on information. He rejected summarized reports or one-page versions of larger papers; he preferred full reports to read and digest before he made decisions. He also sought reports from multiple channels and often would reach down to the second or third layers of the bureaucracies of the State and Defense Departments. A system designed to funnel everything toward the president meant that Kennedy operated as a "desk officer at the highest level," in the words of one White House assistant.[54]

Such a task, when added to all the other responsibilities of a president, seems outside the capability of a single person. How long can a president act as his own chief of staff? The answer is: not long at all. That partially explains why Kennedy and other presidents have enlarged the size of the White House and NSC staffs. They use these all-purpose assistants as the management tools that allow them to run *their* presidency. Bundy and the NSC staff allowed Kennedy to manage foreign policy without all the formal interagency committees that Eisenhower had used. Where Eisenhower used the NSC process as a filter, Kennedy tossed aside the filters in favor of managing information and advice within his own staff. The creation of his own foreign policy bureaucracy was Kennedy's innovative method of placing himself at the center of everything without being overwhelmed by day-to-day requirements.

Related to this is Kennedy's clear desire to make the administration's decisions his decisions, rather than a compromise between agencies that the president accepts. He had a suspicion that the cabinet departments would try to manage him, rather than allow themselves to be managed by him. This wariness is one of the reasons he sought such diverse sources of counsel, seeking advice from within the cabinet departments, the White

House, and even outside government.[55] He put it this way: "I can't afford to confine myself to one set of advisors. If I did that, I would be on their leading strings."[56] Kennedy made it clear that the quality of ideas mattered, not their source. From Cabinet officers to presidential staff, everyone was encouraged to add their opinions and analysis, and all of them would be treated equally by the president. He craved diversity and debate. The last thing he wanted was insulation from the challenges of governing or the crush of the policy process.[57] This notion of diverse ideas stretched all the way to the core of the administration. Kennedy's treasury secretary, and regular member of the NSC, was C. Douglas Dillon, a Republican. Bundy himself was a Republican. These are core characteristics of the collegial style—all opinions are treated equally, no matter their origin; the decision group functions as a team of excellent minds working on solving a problem. Bundy explained it clearly: "Members should be free to comment on problems outside their 'agency' interests. It's not good to have only State speak to 'politics' and only Defense speak to 'military matters.' You want free and general advice from these men (or you don't want them there)."[58]

Organizational Dynamics

A central role for the secretary of state and State Department is hard to square with Kennedy's desire to be his own secretary of state. Given that reality, what did Kennedy want from the actual secretary of state? He wanted innovation, boldness, decisiveness, and responsiveness from State; it was the secretary's job to make that happen. Like most presidents, Kennedy arrived in the Oval Office with a bit of suspicion toward the State Department and its ability to subordinate its bureaucratic goals to those of the new president. He chose most of the senior staff at the State Department rather than allowing Rusk to choose them, something he did not insist on when staffing McNamara's Pentagon. In spite of his hope to make the State Department into a fountain of energy and innovation, Kennedy was underwhelmed by State. That ultimately was one of the reasons that Bundy and the NSC staff gained influence in decision making.[59] Kennedy was often exasperated: "Damn it," he once complained. "Bundy and I get more done in one day in the White House than they do in six months in the State Department. . . . They never have any ideas over there, never come up with anything new." He concluded that the "State Department is a bowl of jelly."[60] Whether this was a problem of bureaucratic inertia or one of leadership—Rusk's comfort with the status quo—remains a subject of debate.[61] Neither Rusk nor State were ever excluded from the process, but management and creative leadership came from the NSC staff or the White House (Kennedy included). In frustration, Kennedy even made significant changes at the top of the State Department in late November 1961; dubbed the "Thanksgiving Day Massacre," it shifted key officials in the top level of the department in hopes of fashioning a team that could reinvigorate State with new ideas and energy.[62] The shuffling of personnel seemed to fail. In late 1962, Bundy was still lamenting the shortcomings of the State Department's coordination role: "The State Department has not proved to be as effective an agency of executive management as we had hoped, and above all, it has not shown the capacity for interdepartmental coordination which we hoped to force upon it."[63] State's lackluster performance reinforced Kennedy's belief in maintaining a tight hold on the reins of foreign policy.[64]

It seems counterintuitive that rivalry did not shatter administrative harmony as the clout of Bundy and the NSC staff grew. The legendary feuds that are the bread and butter of scholarship on national security decision making did not occur during the Kennedy administration. There is no battle in the administration that resembles the William Rogers vs. Henry Kissinger, Cyrus Vance vs. Zbigniew Brzezinski, George Shultz vs. Caspar Weinberger, or Colin Powell vs. Donald Rumsfeld/Dick Cheney conflicts. The emergence of Bundy and the NSC staff did not lead to a counteroffensive by State to regain control of foreign policy. Three elements of the administration's organizational dynamics explain this relative harmony: Kennedy's collegial style that prioritized open debate and access for all the senior advisors; Bundy's and Rusk's absolute loyalty to Kennedy and his preferences; and Rusk's conception of the role of secretary of state.

The first aspect of the administration's organizational dynamics that muted rivalry was the nature of the president's style. Collegial management has at its core inclusion, open communication, and a sense of teamwork in which all participants in the decision are equals, with access to each other and the president. Eliminating all conflict is a fairy tale, but the collegial style channels the ambitions of agencies and individuals to serve the president rather than frustrate him. As studies of the collegial process point out, this dynamic creates a large burden for the president.[65] Kennedy's elevation of Bundy and the NSC staff, however, was partly with this problem in mind; it was Bundy's job to make certain senior cabinet officers had access to the president. De-emphasizing the formal interagency NSC, while at the same time moving power back to the formal statutory advisors at the State and Defense Departments and the CIA, would serve no purpose if the new NSC staff had the same impact—disconnecting the president from the advice of the departments and agencies. Bundy put it plainly: the "President's staff must not attempt to replace the President's chief constitutional and statutory advisors." The president's "own plain sense of the matter is that the White House must be the center of both final authority and initiatives, but that the great roles of the State and Defense Secretaries must never be undermined."[66] To this end, Kennedy met with his principals (Vice President Lyndon Johnson, Bundy, Rusk, McNamara, and Director of Central Intelligence Allen Dulles [January to November 1961] then John McCone) three to four times every week. Bundy made sure Kennedy met one-on-one with his senior cabinet officials whenever he wanted, and Rusk and McNamara regularly met on Saturday mornings to coordinate their policies and to work out any departmental differences.[67] Bundy always saw himself and the NSC staff as extensions of the presidency, not as a new institution or a rival bureaucracy. Of the NSC staff, he said: "Their role is to help the President, not supersede or supplement any of the high officials who hold line responsibilities in the executive departments and agencies. Their task is that of all staff officers: to extend the range and enlarge the direct effectiveness of the man they serve" (underlining in original).[68]

Second, both Bundy and Rusk were absolutely loyal to Kennedy and therefore fully committed to the collegial process. Understanding that the president wanted to use the State Department as the centerpiece, Bundy deferred to Rusk in foreign affairs. Reportedly, their relationship actually grew closer as time went on. Bundy and Rusk both claimed that Bundy never sent any important foreign affairs-related messages without clearing them with Rusk, even as the NSC staff began reviewing outgoing State Department telegrams regarding policies of interest to the president. For his part, Rusk had been an assistant secretary of state in the Truman administration and remembered the bitter feud between Secretary of State Dean Acheson and Secretary of Defense Louis Johnson. He worked to prevent that type of feud from happening again.[69] In his memoirs, Rusk is clear: "I looked upon McGeorge Bundy and his successor, Walt Rostow, as allies rather than competitors. . . . We worked so closely that I regarded the National Security staff at the White House almost as another wing of the State Department." He felt that the NSC staff helped him serve the president better:

> I could not spend my day scurrying back and forth to the White House, carrying papers and memoranda. We sent those papers to Bundy, who organized them, highlighted and underlined key points, and identified critical questions and decisions for the president's

attention. He also insured that the president reacted on time and checked with the various departments to see that presidential decisions were executed.[70]

His relationship with Kennedy was never subject to any committee schedules or procedures: "I had instant access to John Kennedy twenty-four hours a day. . . . Intermediaries never came between us. White House operators and staffers always put through my calls. The layering of the later Nixon White House just didn't exist under Kennedy or Johnson; it was inconceivable to us."[71] Most officials took it for granted that Bundy would become secretary of state in Kennedy's second term, and Rusk suggested moving Bundy to deputy secretary as preparation for such a transition.[72] In this sense, the rivalry never occurred because the key advisors to the president would not allow it.

This observation raises the third element of the administration's organizational dynamics: Rusk's conception of his role and Kennedy's disappointment with that concept. Ironically, Rusk's inability or unwillingness to become what Kennedy hoped he would be may have helped the decision making process run more smoothly. If Rusk and State had been able and willing to become energetic movers of innovation, they might have gone to war with Bundy and the NSC staff over control of foreign policy. Instead, a vacuum developed when State did not fulfill the mission Kennedy envisioned for it. This may have been partly a result of State's legendary bureaucratic inertia, but Rusk's view of his job is crucial. He once described the presidency as "an office of almost unbearable responsibility."[73] His goal as secretary of state was to make it easier for the president to carry out that responsibility by sharing the load, not by adding more burdens. Rusk was absolutely loyal to Kennedy. He believed that his duty was not to advocate for policies, certainly not on behalf of the State Department, or to fight forcefully for innovation, but instead to implement Kennedy's ideas faithfully and follow his lead scrupulously; his assessment of his role is described as being "at the President's side, as a judge."[74] Rusk explained that when it comes to the secretary of state and the president: "A president is entitled to his secretary of state's support for the decisions he makes. . . . There should be no blue sky between them on foreign policy issues. . . . If the secretary of state disagrees with a presidential decision, he has only two choices of action: support the decision or resign."[75] For example, Rusk opposed the Bay of Pigs invasion and expressed this to Kennedy privately. Since the president approved the policy, Rusk never mentioned his opposition in meetings that included the other advisors. Following its failure, Rusk never pointed out that he had been against it.[76] Rusk's reticence in meetings became legendary. He preferred to give his advice to the president one-on-one.[77]

Rusk, however, may have had another reason for withholding his views until he could advise the president in person. Holding that advice until he had an audience of one might also be seen as a strategy that guarantees there will always be an audience of one. In this sense, Rusk never fought back against Bundy because he saw Bundy's elevated role as something the president desired, and if Kennedy wanted it that way, Rusk had to learn to live with it or resign. Rusk apparently only complained about Robert Kennedy's encroachment on his turf. When he raised the subject with the president, Kennedy reassured him: the attorney general "can have his say . . . However, if he ever gets in your way, let me know, and I'll take care of it."[78]

Development and Use of the Three Structures

The Kennedy administration challenges the most fundamental aspects of the original evolution model. That model suggests that administrations create a formal structure at their start and then evolve informal and confidence structures over time. Kennedy, however, came into office critical of Eisenhower's formal system and determined to use informal arrangements from day one. There was no yearlong learning period when the administration discovered that its formal system needed informal adjuncts in order to function smoothly. Instead, the opposite seems to be true: the members of the administration decided that the informality had gone too far and more formality was required. The confidence structure was centered on Kennedy's White House staff; Bundy was Kennedy's first-among-equals advisor; Sorensen became a part of the foreign policy confidence structure after the Bay of Pigs, but he never approached the importance of Bundy in that area. Bundy led the managing and monitoring of the system, ultimately deciding that it needed to be modified through the addition of more formal structures.

Informal Structure

Though Kennedy's initial collegial decision making was informal, as described above, the core of this informal advisory process lay in the small informal meetings, typically three to four per week, between Kennedy and the cabinet-level principals.[79] These informal sessions replaced the NSC, granting the president the ability to hear the opinions of his closest advisors in a more leak-proof, free-ranging venue where teamwork could be built. Even the NSC itself had an informal element to it. Typically, before or after NSC meetings, Kennedy met with Rusk and McNamara, where in Rusk's words "the real decision would be taken."[80] Most importantly, this informal structure placed Kennedy at the center of a series of channels of communication and multiple sources of information and advice, enabling him to maintain control of the pace and content of decisions. These sessions allowed him to be his own chief of staff for foreign affairs, realizing the spokes-of-the-wheel approach. In a sense, the informal system was a throwback to the days of FDR and Truman where everything flowed to the Oval Office, the president spoke with the key advisors, and then made up his mind. As Sorensen describes it, the smaller the venue, the more comfortable Kennedy felt; he wanted to consult with only those individuals "whose official views he requires or whose unofficial judgment he values, and to reserve crucial decisions for a still smaller session or for solitary contemplation in his own office."[81]

One additional aspect of Kennedy's informal process has been detailed above but should be reiterated here. Kennedy surrounded himself with special assistants whose advice he sought on issues of domestic and national security affairs. These were the officials "whose unofficial judgment he values." A White House memo from June 22, 1961, explicitly reminded the senior staff that Kennedy demanded "direct communication and command with" at least eight White House-based staff on foreign affairs. Three of them were national security specialists—Bundy, Rostow, and Military Aide Clifton. The rest were simply loyal staffers whose advice Kennedy had learned to trust during his Senate years and presidential campaign, and who had titles such as special assistant or special counsel to the president: Sorensen, Schlesinger, Dungan, Theodore Feldman, and Goodwin.[82] This preference fits a collegial style where general intelligence is as important as specific expertise.

Confidence Structure

Though Kennedy wanted diverse opinions, multiple sources of information, and a way to prevent the interagency process from limiting his options, he did not treat all advisors the same. Bundy clearly became the first among equals in foreign affairs. This relationship was based initially on the two men's natural affinity and on their shared conception of decision making as an appendage of the president. Kennedy also relied on Bundy to guarantee that he had heard all relevant opinions and that the secretaries of state and defense would always have access to the Oval Office.[83] This was a matter of trust. As Kennedy began to sense that the State Department and Rusk could not lead as he had hoped, Bundy soaked up unused authority, enhancing his role and his importance to Kennedy. Sorensen may have been Bundy's equal in the president's eyes, but his priorities in domestic affairs made him more of a monitor of foreign policy, a set of extra eyes and ears for Kennedy. After the Cuban Missile Crisis, Kennedy had considered moving Bundy to State and Sorensen to the SANSA post. He decided against it for political reasons; White House staffer Kenneth O'Donnell argued that Sorensen's conscientious objector status during World War II would have been a lightning rod for Republican attacks in the 1964 election. Any major changes needed to wait until after the next election.[84] Of course, Attorney General Robert Kennedy had a unique position in the Kennedy confidence structure; however, it only manifested itself in foreign affairs on rare occasions, such as the Cuban Missile Crisis.[85]

Balancing and Compensating

The evolution-balance model suggests that administrations will begin to modify their decision making to compensate for weaknesses in the system preferred by the president. In the case of the Kennedy administration, a debate on modifications in the standard processes began in the spring of 1961. Four changes were made. Following the Bay of Pigs, Kennedy actually strengthened his informal structure by increasing the participation of special assistants in foreign policy making. The other three adaptations—establishment of the Planning Group (1961) and two Standing Groups (1962, 1963)—were explicit attempts by Bundy to build more formal interagency processes into the system, based on a growing belief in the NSC staff and cabinet departments that informality was creating problems. Importantly, Kennedy and his advisors were moving in opposite directions. A fifth, the ExComm, was created specifically to deal with the Cuban Missile Crisis; its assignment was to deal with a crisis, a very different type of decision making than what is being examined in this study, but its existence was a learning experience that contributed to the proposals for the second Standing Group. Though Bundy had tried to compensate for the weaknesses of the informal process, an attempt to create a better balance between informal and formal decision machinery, in the end Kennedy simply ignored the new interagency groups; he favored the free-wheeling informality of his spokes of the wheel. As Bundy wrote to him in November 1962: "This is simply the way you do your job."[86]

After the Bay of Pigs

The story of the Bay of Pigs is well known and need not be recounted here. What matters in the context of this study are what lessons different members of the administration believed they had learned from its first significant, and very public, mistake. In April 1961, Kennedy gave the green light to a plan conceived during the Eisenhower administration for the US to help Cuban exiles overthrow Fidel Castro. The plan failed miserably and became an embarrassment for the new administration. For Kennedy, the outcome reinforced his instincts toward collegiality and informality. He had trusted the CIA, deferring to the experts on the issue. In that sense, Kennedy had made a formalistic decision—the CIA had the role and responsibility for covert action, and therefore its judgment was considered better than anyone else's. Even though Kennedy had already dismantled Eisenhower's NSC system and implemented his informal spokes-of-the-wheel system, he deferred to the CIA leadership on this decision because of its formal area of responsibility. Following the defeat of US-backed rebels at the Bay of Pigs, Kennedy explicitly questioned that reliance on the standard division of labor. His remedy was clear: more presidential control over the process and more generalist staff oversight of departmental activities, in other words, a strengthening of the informal structure.

Attorney General Robert Kennedy and the President's Special Military Representative General Maxwell Taylor led a Cuba Study Group, an after-action study of the decision and what went wrong that was commissioned by Kennedy on April 22, 1961, less than a week after the failed invasion.[87] Their recommendations fit along the lines of the president's instincts and the assessment of others in the administration: advisors need to be generalists when they are analyzing policies, not advocates representing their agencies; too much reliance on the specialists is a mistake; more informal processes need to be added to important decisions, particularly the use of advisors who were not involved directly in developing or implementing the policy; and, perhaps most importantly, there had to be a greater role for Kennedy loyalists in overseeing the work of the departments.[88] The latter point led to observable changes in decision making—more White House assistants were included in national security decisions and given access to intelligence data. Schlesinger, one of those White House assistants, wrote that the Bay of Pigs "made us all more aggressive in defending the interests of the president and therefore in invading on his behalf what the foreign affairs bureaucracy too often regarded as its private domain." These were Kennedy's generalist advisors; their advice was seen as untainted by organizational interests and closely aligned with presidential interests. They were also people he trusted implicitly, having been members of his Senate and campaign staff. Schlesinger puts it succinctly: "We were the President's men, and the government knew it, in part welcoming it, in part resenting it."[89]

This beefed-up use for special assistants was made explicit. A White House memo of June 22, 1961 emphasized the inclusion of the White House and NSC staff in foreign policy, describing it as a mission of oversight, to make sure that policies are "adequately controlled and coordinated" and to make sure that if something is potentially heading for disaster, the staff can "spot it early and stimulate remedial action."[90] Related to the enhanced role of the staff was the movement of Bundy's office from the Old Executive Office Building across the street from the White House to the West Wing itself, where he would be within view of the Oval Office. Logistically this made it easier for the president to consult with Bundy as needed, but it also had a symbolic impact. Since access is power, Bundy's new address sent a message about his status; Bundy will be at the president's right hand at all times. In addition, Robert Kennedy and Special Counsel Sorensen were now made important members of the national security decision making team. Robert Kennedy's advice to the president during the Cuban Missile Crisis is now the stuff of legend. Sorensen also served as an additional alter ego for the president.[91]

The Planning Group

The Planning Group was the first structural change to the administration's decision making. It was an attempt to add formality. In May and June of 1961, in the wake of the Kennedy-Taylor study and prompting by Bundy, voices within the NSC staff, as well as other parts of the executive branch, began a discussion of the weakness of the decision making process. The shortcomings were related to its informality, an informality that prevented the NSC and the NSC staff from regularizing their procedures and providing thorough analytical support for the president. The debate centered around three themes: more regularized interagency meetings, better use of the NSC staff, and a routine schedule for the NSC. A memo from Undersecretary of the Treasury Henry Fowler to Treasury Secretary Dillon made its way to Bundy in early May. It argued that the NSC system did not fully vet policies through the departments and agencies before the president made decisions. Departments did not get enough time to express their views and analyze the positions of other departments, and the NSC staff did not have the opportunity to examine those views. In this way, the president was not part of the administration debate. He suggested re-creating the senior staff of the NSC that had existed during the Truman administration as "built-in assurance that the Chief Executive will not have to depend primarily upon ad-hoc measures in the awesome task of finally determining national security policy."[92]

It is unclear how much influence the Fowler memo had, but the Planning Group was established sometime in the summer of 1961. It had representation at the assistant-secretary level from the Departments of State, Defense, the CIA, and the NSC staff. The mandate remained vague, however; it was unclear to the group how its deliberations were related to policy making initiatives or ongoing decisions at other levels, and even members did not seem clear about how the group was designed to function. NSC staffer Komer described one meeting of the Planning Group on the Chinese nuclear program as "the usual disorderly affair." Though it met on a set schedule, its work was not staffed out, and records of the group's activities are sparse.[93] It remained an essentially irrelevant exercise in the sense that it had little connection to decision making at the upper levels. It could be seen, however, as a useful mechanism for assistant-secretary-level officials to communicate, share ideas, and trade information within an environment where it was often unclear how close senior decision makers were to making decisions on many issues.

The First Standing Group

One of Bundy's most trusted assistants, Robert Komer, summed up the flaws of the NSC staff as he saw them in a May 1961 memo to Deputy SANSA Rostow. He felt that Bundy and Rostow were not "making much use of your staff. Essentially, you are running a two man, self-contained operation . . . you just can't afford to handle all these problems on the fly or from the hip." He suggested more on-paper staff work and more delegation of work to the NSC staff "to handle and follow through under your general eye." He emphasized strongly that the "main problem is for you and Mac to decide what *you* want us to do, *and to tell us!*" (italics and exclamation point in the original).[94]

NSC executive secretary Bromley Smith echoed this idea in mid-June. Smith had been an Eisenhower NSC staffer, elevated to the NSC management post at the beginning of the Kennedy administration. Smith suggested that deputies of NSC members (undersecretary-level representatives of the NSC principals), who had been meeting informally at a

Thursday luncheon, should play a larger part in the interagency process. The group he dubbed "The National Security Council Deputies" would be "responsible for facilitating the making and carrying out of presidential decisions in the international field." It would be chaired by Bundy and "function" as a "steering group for the Council." Its key charges would be to propose policies that needed presidential attention, monitor implementation, and recommend new ad-hoc task forces as necessary. This group would also meet monthly with the regulars from the Rostow-led NSC staff meetings. Smith also supported formal meetings of the NSC with a set agenda scheduled for every two weeks.[95]

Bundy had already been lobbying the president to change his seat-of-the-pants style of planning, suggesting more routinized operations and "planning of assignments that have long term meaning." Bundy felt that the "National Security Council, for example, really cannot work for you unless you authorize work schedules that do not get upset from day to day. Calling these meetings in five days is foolish—and putting them off for six weeks at a time is just as bad." Bundy also thought Kennedy should restrict access to the Oval Office by ending the "two-door policy"; staffers who walk in through the back door unannounced disrupted Kennedy's time and schedule. In an October 1961 memo to the president, Bundy continued to make his case. He noted that the absence of a regular schedule for the NSC and the habit of having "short notice" meetings of the NSC "has produced incomplete staff work and given unreasonable difficulty to members of the Council and their staff." Kennedy finally approved biweekly meetings of the NSC on October 13, 1961, a few days after receiving this memo.[96]

At roughly the same moment, Kennedy and Bundy recognized what they saw as a deep flaw in their standard decision process. That initial system, with the State Department at the heart of the interagency process and the NSC staff supporting the presidential hub, foundered on Rusk's and the State Department's inability or unwillingness to perform the task adequately. If State could not coordinate, Kennedy had three possible choices for management adjustments: add greater structure to the NSC, centralize the process in the NSC staff even more, or simply muddle through with the informal coordination that dissatisfied so many at the working levels. Kennedy chose the first option but ultimately fell back on the second and third.

The NSC Standing Group, created at the end of 1961, but only operational by February 1962, was the ultimate result of all this debate. Based on Smith's "National Security Council Deputies" committee, it re-created a group with some of the functions of Truman's senior staff or Eisenhower's Planning Board; it added some of the implementation oversight responsibilities of Eisenhower's OCB as well.[97] The main purpose of the group was as Smith had envisioned; it backstopped and organized the work of the NSC on a weekly basis. Chaired by the undersecretary of state for political affairs, it included the deputy secretary of defense, deputy director of central intelligence, SANSA Bundy, the executive secretary of the NSC, and other invitees based on the issue. It was scheduled to meet every Friday at 2:30 in the White House Situation Room and met for the first time on January 5, 1962. As a committee working underneath the NSC, the Standing Group required membership that mirrored the composition of the NSC. The Standing Group, however, also gave greater power to the NSC staff by having it serve in the same supporting role for the new interagency committee.[98] The addition of the Standing Group was a way to add more staff work and coordination to the NSC process without adding more responsibility to the National Security Council itself. The NSC could therefore remain a more informal place for the president to receive the uncensored opinion of his advisors and build the collegial teamwork he desired for his principals. In this sense, the Standing Group gave everyone what they wanted.

The implementation of these new procedures, however, was halfhearted. Neither biweekly NSC meetings nor weekly Standing Group meetings survived for very long. The NSC met twice in November and December of 1961, as hoped, but then met once every month from January to April 1962 and not at all in May 1962. Its schedule through the rest of 1962 followed specific topics: a June meeting on the United Nations; two back-to-back meetings (July 9 and 10) on the Soviet Union and nuclear missile deployment issues; a September meeting on nuclear testing; and three meetings in October during the Cuban Missile Crisis.[99] The Standing Group met nearly weekly through March 1962 (missing one week in February and one in March), then not at all in April, twice in May, and once in July and August before it stopped meeting (see table 3.1).[100] After only eight months, the Standing Group simply faded away; the desire for informality throughout the administration rendered it superfluous. Executive Secretary Smith felt that "its usefulness varied, but lack of driving support from the State Department representative resulted in a rather desultory life."[101] In short, State still held the formal coordination role and it chaired the Standing Group. If State did not elevate it to a central place in the process, the Standing Group would become irrelevant. Bundy did not have the authority to manage it and Kennedy did not have the interest.

The ExComm

During the rest of 1962, the heavy work flowed deeper and deeper into the White House and NSC staff. The interagency process, however, was modified temporarily, innovating in the area of crisis decision making. The missile crisis is famous for the creation of the Executive Committee of the NSC (ExComm), a special ad-hoc committee of principals and wise men from outside of the government who advised the president for the crucial days when the US and Soviet Union seemed to be edging toward World War III.[102] The success of ExComm left its mark on overall decision making as much as the failure of the Bay of Pigs did. Given that the ExComm was a crisis decision making committee, it is somewhat beyond the scope of this research; however, it did last long after the 13 days of the Cuban Missile Crisis. It served as a rival to the NSC and a learning experience for the administration. It was an ad hoc committee, in theory connected to the NSC, that met in the immediate aftermath of the discovery of Soviet missiles in Cuba. It consisted of NSC members and advisors, as well as the attorney general, the secretary of the treasury, Bundy, Sorensen, and retired ambassador Llewellyn Thompson; 21 other officials met with the core membership on an as-needed basis at different times. The heroic model of decision making in a crisis represented by the ExComm is not easily translatable to noncrisis situations. If the crisis is considered to be October 16 through 28, the ExComm met 11 times during the crisis and 31 times after the immediate crisis ended (a total of 42 times between October 1962 and March 1963). During this same period, the NSC itself met only twice, and the first Standing Group had already stopped meeting by October 1962. It did not need the ExComm to drown out its activities (see table 3.1). Nearly all of the ExComm meetings, even after the missile crisis had ended, focused on Cuba. Its last meeting was on March 29, 1963 and the subject again was Cuba.[103] This meant that from the end of 1962 through early 1963, the only regularly scheduled even slightly formal committee operating in the administration was the crisis decision making body centered almost exclusively on a single issue.

The Second Standing Group

In November 1962, roughly three months after the last Standing Group meeting, Bundy wrote to Kennedy again worrying about some of the unresolved problems with the NSC process. He felt that while the president and all the principals agreed on doing away with the Eisenhower system, they did not truly establish anything to replace it. In short, there needed to be some formal architecture for decision making and neither Rusk nor his chief undersecretaries (Chester Bowles and then George Ball) had taken on the responsibility for coordination. That left State Department counselor George McGhee or Deputy Undersecretary of State for Political Affairs U. Alexis Johnson in the coordinator role, but neither had the bureaucratic heft to tease out an interagency consensus given their subcabinet positions. While musing that perhaps the ExComm could work as a venue for noncrisis interagency coordination, Bundy again made it clear where he thought the job must be located: "Under a strong President even more than under a relatively inactive one, there can be no final coordination except from the White House."[104]

Bundy tried one last time to repair the NSC machinery. This time, importantly, the interagency group was firmly under his authority. The creation of the second Standing Group represented a conscious decision to move interagency planning out of the State Department and under the auspices of the NSC staff. On April 2, 1963, Bundy suggested the formation of a "Plans and Operations Committee" of the NSC. The new group was seen as an antidote to the current informal system's shortcomings in the areas of "interdepartmental planning and coordination on major national security issues." Bundy noted that the ExComm had done the job for Cuba as a "good instrument for major interdepartmental decisions," but had not worked at all for "lesser matters of coordination" or "forward planning." Conversations between Bundy, Rusk, Robert Kennedy, and new Undersecretary of State for Political Affairs Averill Harriman produced a proposal for a committee chaired by Bundy and composed of a mix of principal-level and deputy-level officials, but not the statutory members of the NSC. The committee would meet weekly and, befitting Kennedy's devotion to the generalist idea, members "should attend as individuals, not as representatives of agencies." For this reason, if someone could not be at a meeting, no replacement would be sent. The new committee would also have limited staff infrastructure attached to it. That would be Bundy's responsibility. The purpose of the committee would be to look at a medium-term focus, such as Cuba over the next year or China over the next two years.[105]

The name was quickly changed to Standing Group of the NSC. Bundy informed the president on April 12 that it would begin meeting the next week, "and we intend to have absolutely no publicity about it in order to avoid useless chatter about seizing initiative from the State department or restoring the OCB or otherwise reorganizing ourselves in the spring of our discontent."[106] A draft NSAM (that was never signed as official policy and entered into the numbered series) specified its role as "responsible for consideration of such issues relating to the national security as do not immediately require the attention of the president; in this sense it will supplement the work of the Executive Committee of the National Security Council and of the National Security Council itself." Membership included Bundy (chair), the undersecretary of state for political affairs, deputy secretary of defense, undersecretary of the treasury, the attorney general, chairman of the Joint Chiefs, director of central intelligence, director of the United States Information Agency, the administrator of the Agency for International Development, and the special counsel to the president.[107] Interestingly, this membership list includes only one cabinet-level official: Attorney General Robert Kennedy. Though this new committee was intended to serve as a semiformal group, it had some built-in aspects of the president's confidence structure: Bundy chaired, the president's brother sat in on it, and so did Sorensen. The original idea for the group suggested limited staff participation, but the actual meetings were supported by intensive staff work—intelligence reports, briefing papers, documentation. In this sense, it was similar in nature to Eisenhower's Planning Board. Meetings were held on Tuesdays at 10:30 a.m.[108]

The second Standing Group met the same fate as the first. Its first meeting on April 16, 1963 was followed by weekly meetings through May 28. Thereafter the frequency tailed off: once in June; twice in July; and one each in August, September, and October (see table 3.1). Two things of note about its demise are important. First, the administration had successfully used a weekly formal interagency committee for a full seven weeks, the most routinization of the decision process it had ever sustained. Second, the Standing Group never did function in the way it was intended to when it came to long-term planning and coordination. Nine of the 14 meetings focused on Cuba.[109] Given that the ExComm stopped meeting in March and the Standing Group began meeting in April, the Standing Group, in part, simply replaced the ExComm as the venue for dealing with Cuba. It did not become the venue for general interagency foreign policy planning or backstopping the NSC.

The pattern in the Kennedy administration is quite clear. Every attempt to add more formal and routine procedures or committee processes to supplement or energize the NSC seemed to fade over time. Like a new toy that is played with every day for a month but then left on a shelf to gather dust, the Standing Group fell into disuse. The best management intentions cannot compete with the inattention of the president.

Conclusion

The analysis of Kennedy's overall foreign policy process confirms the evolution-balance model (see table 9.1). Bundy repeatedly tried to add formality that would compensate for the president's informal habits; he felt the demands of policy making and the needs of the departments required it. Every attempt to add more formal and routine procedures or committees, however, seemed to fade over time. The best of intentions for managing the process could not compete with the preferences of the president; Kennedy was simply not terribly interested in anything that restricted his involvement or narrowed the range of debate. The Standing Groups capture the dynamic well. The president agreed to Bundy's repeated pleas for more formal committees to supplement the freewheeling nature of the spokes-of-the-wheel system, but he quickly lost interest in them. In the context of the institutional vs. idiosyncratic models, institutional forces led to pressure for more formality, but Kennedy's idiosyncratic desire for informality prevailed. It is simply not possible to make the president do anything in the decision realm that he does not want to do.

Two aspects of this conclusion are relevant to the evolution-balance model. First, most administrations seem to begin with formal processes that emphasize decentralization. They move to compensate with more informality and some centralization. Kennedy started his time in office at the opposite end of the spectrum—informality—and felt deep pressures for more formality. This confirms the evolution-balance model, that all administrations try to achieve a balance, no matter where their starting point is. Second, Kennedy did centralize his administration's decision making to a certain degree—the increasing significance of the NSC staff. The administration began with a built-in contradiction: desire for a State Department–managed system and a greater NSC staff role in foreign policy. That contradiction was never resolved. Consider the two Standing Groups. The first was chaired by State, but the second was chaired by Bundy. In a nutshell that fact illustrates Kennedy's disappointment in State and his preferred remedy. In the context of the institutional and idiosyncratic models, a clear dynamic emerged. Variables explained by the idiosyncratic model won the day. The experience of making decisions in the White House only reinforced Kennedy's instincts for informality and reliance on his confidence structure, no matter how often Bundy and the NSC staff tried to bring more formality to the process.

FOUR

∿ Kennedy and China

It really doesn't make any sense—the idea that Taiwan represents China.
—President Kennedy[1]

Every presidency inherits both the processes and policies of the previous administration. As Kennedy sought to distance himself from the foreign policy decision making style of Eisenhower, he also had to consider whether to reshape specific policies. US policy on China had remained remarkably consistent since the Korean War. After serious deliberation, the Kennedy administration maintained that continuity, reconfirming the Truman-Eisenhower policies.

This chapter examines two decision episodes. First, in 1961 the Kennedy administration accepted the Truman-Eisenhower goal of preserving the United Nation's recognition of the Republic of China (ROC) as the legitimate government of China, while preventing the People's Republic of China (PRC) from displacing the ROC or earning a seat of its own in the UN; it did, however, change the strategy for achieving those ends. Second, in 1962 the administration chose to deny ROC president Chiang Kai-shek assistance for his plans to retake mainland China from the PRC. This chapter deviates slightly from the Johnson and Nixon chapters in that it begins with the context for Kennedy's decisions—policy as it existed under Truman and Eisenhower. Other than that additional section, each case study follows the structure outlined in chapter 2: political context, narrative, and analysis. The chapter conclusion compares the two decisions.

The 1961 decision on how to keep the PRC out of the UN provides an excellent example of Kennedy's informal system. Though there was interagency participation from all the key departments, it was not based on the NSC or any regularized set of committees in any set hierarchical relationship. Throughout 1961, the State Department maintained its leadership; however, at key moments Kennedy relied on Bundy and his White House assistants for advice. The use of special assistants here was not a function of Kennedy's frustration with State's lack of creativity, nor was the expanded power of Bundy and the NSC staff a crucial factor. In fact, State was far more ready for innovative ideas on China than Kennedy, who defended the status quo. The increased role of Bundy, Sorensen, and Schlesinger was a post–Bay of Pigs development, a worry that delegation of the Chinese representation issue to the State Department, even if outside any standard Eisenhower-like process, was too formal. The 1961 Chinese representation case confirms the original evolution model, but not the evolution-balance model. Though the State Department always led the policy making on the subject, Kennedy narrowed participation from time to time as he grew more involved in the decision, a decision made through an informal process based in his initial spokes-of-the-wheel concept. No new structures and no significant attempts to balance the process took place; the only adjustments were refinements to the informal structure. The 1962 Return to the Mainland case, regarding aid to the ROC, does confirm the evolution-balance model. Kennedy again used the informal spokes-of-the-wheel style; however, he was encouraged to add more formal structures. In June 1962 the administration discussed Taiwan's request for military assistance at two full interagency meetings, one of which was the formal NSC. As a result of the first meeting, a formal interagency Offshore Islands Working Group was created to serve as a venue for routine decisions on the issue, but it never was given the opportunity to be anything other than an adjunct to the informal process, here dominated by both State and the NSC staff.

Kennedy's China decisions are compared to the overall evolution of the decision making process using the structured-focused comparison questions in table 9.1. Figure 4.1 diagrams the evolution of Kennedy China decision making using figure 2.2—the full evolution-balance model—as a guide.

China Policy before Kennedy

When Kennedy entered office, he became the custodian of policies toward China still defined by events that occurred between 1949 and 1951. The end of World War II brought a withdrawal of Japanese forces from China, but also renewed hostilities between Mao Zedong's Communists and Chiang Kai-shek's Nationalists (the Kuomintang or Guomindang). During the 1946–49 civil war the US expended a great amount of diplomatic effort

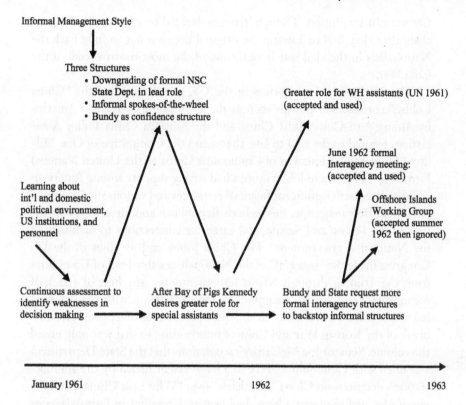

Fig. 4.1. The Evolution of Kennedy Administration Decision Making on China

trying to broker a peace based on a power sharing agreement; the effort failed.[2] Truman, however, made an explicit decision not to intervene to save the Nationalists, believing that such an effort would be futile and held the potential to entangle the US in a war in China that might last years. Since the Communist victory and the declaration of a new People's Republic of China in Beijing on October 1, 1949, the US faced a dilemma—to recognize the reality of Communist control over mainland China or to support the Nationalists, now an exiled government in Taipei occupying the island of Taiwan (often called Formosa at the time) and seeking US assistance to launch a counteroffensive against the Communists. That choice was made easier by China's alliance with the USSR and commitment to worldwide

Communist revolution. Though Truman decided to support the Nationalists after they fled to Taiwan, the original decision not to fully back the Nationalists in the civil war became one of the most controversial of the Cold War.

The Nationalists' supporters in the US, generally called the "China Lobby," consisted of groups such as the Committee to Defend America by Aiding Anti-Communist China and the America China Policy Association, formed in the mid to late 1940s, and the Committee of One Million (Against the Admission of Communist China to the United Nations) formed in 1953. These lobby groups had strong support among American conservatives with significant financial resources and various media centers including *Time* magazine, ties to both Republican and Democratic members of the House and Senate, and extensive connections to members of the Nationalist government.[3] The China lobby and its allies in the US Congress made the "betrayal" of the Nationalists a third rail of US politics from the Truman through Nixon administrations. Any hint of a lack of commitment to Chiang or support for rapprochement with Mao's China led to immediate condemnation and often accusations of treason. The outbreak of the Korean War and Chinese intervention in that war only raised the volume. Senator Joe McCarthy's accusations that the State Department was filled with Communists were to a large extent fueled by the administration's decisions on China. The debate over "Who Lost China?" and the era of McCarthyism cast a long shadow over US policy in East Asia, contributing greatly to President Johnson's decision to intervene in Vietnam rather than face the question of "Who Lost Vietnam?"

The Korean War renewed the US commitment to the Nationalists. The Truman administration reinstituted military aid to the ROC and deployed the US 7th Fleet to physically protect the island.[4] The defense of Taiwan became an integral part of a new US policy in Asia that included intervention in Korea, massive US purchases from and investments in the Japanese defense industry, the beginning of Japanese rearmament, and the US-Japanese Security Treaty of 1952.[5] US policy on Taiwan from the Korean War to the end of the 1950s had a clear trajectory from this point on. Both Truman and Eisenhower were willing to defend the Nationalists as part of an expanded containment strategy and as a way to shore up the credibility of US commitments to fight Communist aggression in Asia and worldwide. In a nine-month period, Mao's forces had taken mainland China and North Korea had made a bid for possession of the entire Korean Peninsula. The US could no longer give an inch. When the Eisenhower administration signed the US-ROC Mutual Defense Treaty with the government in Taipei on December 2, 1954, however, it agreed to defend Taiwan and the Pescadores (Penghus) from China, but not Quemoy, Matsu, or the Tachen Islands, territory under ROC control but geographically closer to the mainland, typically labeled the Offshore Islands. Additionally, Eisenhower asked Congress for formal authority to defend Taiwan. The Formosa Resolution, passed in late January 1955, gave the president explicit congressional authorization to use force to defend Taiwan and the Pescadores without further legislative approval if he deemed it necessary; the resolution, again, left the Offshore Islands outside the explicit US commitment.[6] It was a clear deterrent threat to China and a reassurance message to Taiwan. These policies held firmly through the 1954–55 crisis and in 1958, when China once again attacked Quemoy and Matsu.

The question of whether the US would recognize or even communicate with the new Communist-led regime after October 1949 again seems obvious in hindsight. US policy had three elements. First, the US continued to recognize the ROC as the legitimate government of the mainland. Communist control in Beijing was judged to be temporary, but US obligations to defend Taiwan under the Mutual Defense Treaty did not include helping Taiwan retake the mainland.[7] Second, the US worked to keep the Nationalist-led government of the ROC in the United Nations, accepted as the legitimate government of all of China and in possession of the permanent UN Security Council (UNSC) seat and the coveted veto. To that end, Truman and Eisenhower lobbied US allies to postpone the UN's decision on whether the ROC government in Taipei or PRC government in Beijing was the legitimate representative of China, a policy that would in effect maintain the ROC's ownership of the UN seat. These lobbying efforts were aimed at yearly votes on postponement at the UN General Assembly (UNGA). In opposition, the Soviet Union worked to build a coalition of nations at the UN that could vote the PRC in and the ROC out. Third, even while denying recognition, refusing to consider a PRC seat in the UN, and supporting Taiwan, both the Truman and Eisenhower administrations were open to dialogue with the PRC under specific conditions: the PRC needed to accept certain international norms and not threaten its neighbors, particularly the ROC, if any serious discussions were to be held. The Eisenhower administration, taking note of growing tensions between the PRC and the USSR, considered the possibility of a strategy to drive a "wedge" between Moscow and Beijing.[8] Although the Sino-Soviet split began in the 1950s, accelerating after 1958, it was not until the Kennedy and Johnson administrations that the split was seen to have real strategic significance, and only under Nixon did the US truly act on this knowledge.[9] Talks between the US and mainland China began in Geneva in August 1955 before moving to Warsaw in 1958. Since the two nations did not recognize each other, they were represented by their ambassadors to nations in Eastern Europe. The talks did not address fundamental issues except in a polemical fashion on the Chinese side and the laying down of conditions on the US side, but draft language was developed on topics such as civilian repatriation, a rejection of the use of force, and potential visits by journalists.[10]

Kennedy inherited all three policies when he entered office: a commitment to defend Taiwan, but not assist Chiang in assaults on the mainland; the postponement strategy at the UN; and the Warsaw-based talks.

Chinese Representation at the United Nations

The 1961 case study on Chinese representation at the UN fits aspects of the original evolution model, but does not fit the evolution-balance model. The administration maintained its spokes-of-the-wheel informal process throughout the decision, relying on Bundy and White House special assistants, but never considering major changes in decision making to shore up perceived weaknesses. Though the administration debated moving to a two-China strategy in 1961, Kennedy ultimately rejected the notion, overruling the sentiment of the State Department; ironically, Kennedy, who complained about the lack of imagination at State, quashed State's attempt to modernize China policy, instead reaffirming the status quo. In this case, Kennedy's priorities were clearly defined by domestic political considerations, specifically the savage backlash he expected to face if he chose to recognize the PRC, a revolutionary Communist state, the prime opponent of the US in the Korean War, and the perceived nemesis in the expanding Vietnam conflict. Perhaps this logic explains why the final decision was made outside even the informal senior advisory group and instead with Kennedy surrounded by his political, rather than foreign policy, staff.

Political Context

The political context consists of three elements. First, Kennedy was a committed cold warrior and had been one since he entered politics; he was unlikely to make any major changes to US policy toward China and Taiwan. His expansion of the US military commitment to South Vietnam is a better indicator of his ideas. Second, internationally, even as the Sino-Soviet split deepened, the Soviet bloc's commitment to forcing the ROC out and the

PRC in to the UN had not wavered. Newly independent nations added to the UN also leaned toward the PRC, and even US allies were questioning the wisdom of a US policy that continued to pretend that the PRC did not control mainland China. In short, the postponement strategy was perceived to be on its deathbed. Third, on the domestic front, Kennedy faced Republican criticism that he was neither experienced enough to lead the US in foreign policy, nor committed enough to anti-Communism. He felt the pressure of the China lobby intensely.

Kennedy and China before the Presidency

Kennedy could be judged a hard-liner on China, not a likely candidate to seriously consider accepting China into the UN without significant changes in Chinese foreign and domestic policy. As a member of the House of Representatives, Kennedy had been a sharp critic of Truman when that administration faced the charge of "losing" China in the late 1940s and early 1950s.[11] Kennedy attacked Truman policy with McCarthy-level viciousness in a speech on January 30, 1949, saying that "it is of the utmost importance that we search out and spotlight those who bear the responsibility for our present predicament. . . . This is the tragic story of China whose freedom we once sought to preserve. What our young men had saved, our diplomats and our president have frittered away."[12] By the late 1950s and during the 1960 campaign, Kennedy had come to regret that criticism of Truman, though he still saw the defense of Taiwan as a necessity.[13] Often he was allied with the right wing of the Republican Party, arguing that Eisenhower was too soft on China and too equivocal on Taiwan, Quemoy, and Matsu, voting with Senators Joseph McCarthy and Barry Goldwater to cut US economic aid to nations that traded with the PRC, a policy opposed by the more moderate Eisenhower.[14] In a *Foreign Affairs* article of 1957, perhaps a first toe in the water for presidential ambitions, Kennedy defined his thinking on China with some nuance; the US could change its approach when China changed its behavior: "There have been—and still are—compelling reasons for the non-recognition of China; but we must be very careful not to straightjacket our policy as a result of ignorance and fail to detect a change in the objective situation when it comes."[15]

Kennedy based his China policy during the 1960 campaign on that essential notion of a willingness to respond to improvements in Chinese behavior. In a June 14 speech, he criticized Eisenhower while suggesting flexibility, based on China's level of hostility to its Asian neighbors and the West. The speech proposed a strategy of bringing China into the nuclear test-ban talks as a path to greater communication and possibly to convincing China to forego the development of nuclear weapons:

> We must reassess a China policy which has failed dismally to move toward its principal objective of weakening communist rule on the mainland—a policy which has failed to prevent a steady growth of Communist strength—and a policy which offers no real solution to the problems of a militant China. . . . And, although we should not now recognize Red China or agree to its admission to the United Nations without a genuine change in her belligerent attitude toward her Asian neighbors and the world . . . we must nevertheless work to improve at least our communications with mainland China. Perhaps a way could be found to bring the Chinese into the nuclear test ban talks at Geneva—so that the Soviets could not continue their atomic tests on the mainland of China without inspection—and also because Chinese possession of atomic weapons could drastically alter the balance of power. If that contact proves fruitful, further cultural and economic contact could be tried. For only in this way can we inform ourselves of communist activities, attempt to restore our historic friendship with the Chinese people, and make sure that we are not plunged into war by a Chinese miscalculation of our determination to defend all of free Asia.[16]

The Democratic platform of 1960, published a month later, generally a reflection of the nominee's beliefs, reaffirmed this idea:

> We deeply regret that the policies and actions of the Government of Communist China have interrupted the generations of friendship between the Chinese and American peoples. We reaffirm our pledge of determined opposition to the present admission of Communist China to the United Nations. Although normal diplomatic relations between our Governments are impossible under present conditions, we shall welcome any evidence that the Chinese Communist Government is genuinely prepared to create a new relationship based on respect for international obligations, including the release of American prisoners.[17]

International Context

As the Kennedy administration entered office there was a clear recognition that US policy on the "Chirep" issue faced huge challenges. The international situation made the postponement strategy increasingly anachronistic. The dilemma for the US was the growing closeness of the vote year after year. The 1951 vote was 42 in favor of postponement, 7 against, and 11 abstaining. By 1960 the vote was 42 in favor, 34 against, and 22 abstaining.[18] The 22 abstentions represented a group of nations poised to swing away from US policy, defeating the postponement resolution, and switching UN recognition from Taipei to Beijing. As decolonization proceeded in Africa and Asia, the number of developing nations in the UN General Assembly increased. Their sympathies generally leaned to the left or toward other formerly colonized states. The PRC had set itself up as a model for these newly independent developing states. In 1950, UN membership stood at 60 nations. In 1961 membership had swelled to 104 nations, almost all of them developing states, likely to side with the PRC rather than with the ROC. Taipei's insistence on pretending that the Communists had not won the civil war further alienated the developing world as well as most major US allies.[19]

Though the Sino-Soviet alliance had begun to shatter, the Soviet bloc maintained its support for the PRC's addition to the UN in place of the ROC, voting against the postponement resolution every year.[20] The United Nations was one of several places where the hard bipolarity of the Cold War raged on as if the Sino-Soviet split had not occurred.

In some ways the US had its hands tied behind its back by PRC and ROC foreign policies. For both the PRC and ROC, there could only be one China at the UN. Neither friend nor foe gave the US any wiggle room for change in policies. The ROC under Chiang Kai-shek's leadership was a core US ally, strategically and legally—the two nations were bound together by the Mutual Defense Pact of 1954. Its foreign policy was absolutely clear.[21] First, there was only one China—unified and indivisible—and only one legitimate Chinese government, the one that lived in Taipei. The Communist rulers in Beijing were illegitimate, temporary usurpers of the mainland. A second idea followed: the Nationalists would someday return to China and regain their lost territory. To that end, Taiwan had launched raids against the mainland throughout the 1950s, trained in unconventional operations with the US, and tried to build a resistance within China that might link up with Nationalist forces to undermine the Beijing regime from the inside and the outside. Dozens of operations were conducted in and against the mainland through the 1950s and 1960s.[22] A third element of ROC policy was an absolute commitment to retention of the UN seat. Chiang spelled it out in an April 1, 1961 letter: "I personally and my government cannot possibly accept the so called 'two Chinas' or any other arrangement which would affect the character of China's right of representation in the United Nations."[23] In the early 1960s, no issue had more symbolic relevance to the ROC's status in Asia and the international system than its hold on the UN seat.

Chiang had domestic political concerns of his own. He ruled Taiwan through a one-party dictatorship, and challenges to his leadership were not tolerated. Basic democratic freedoms—freedom of speech, press, and assembly, as well as the formation of opposition parties—were restricted or banned. The notion that two Chinas might be acceptable was treason. Chiang understood that the longer it took to regain the mainland, the more tenuous his hold on power could become. He suspected that if his policies at home and abroad became too inflammatory for the US, it might move against him.[24] The Kennedy administration is bookended by cases where the US helped remove anti-Communist Asian leaders who had been solid allies of the US: South Korea's Syngman Rhee in April 1960 and South Vietnam's Ngo Dinh Diem in November 1963.

The PRC's foreign policy had evolved during the 1950s but was relatively stable during the Kennedy years.[25] First, the PRC had made it clear from Mao Zedong's first proclamation of the People's Republic of China on October 1, 1949: it considered itself the legitimate government of China; there could be only one China; Taiwan was an indivisible part of it; and Chiang's government in Taipei was secessionist and traitorous. Second, the PRC had ambitions to return China to its natural place as the preeminent power in Asia and ultimately sought to become a major global power. It was not satisfied with its status as a junior partner to the USSR, and hoped to one day become the equal of Japan or the US.[26] Territorial unity was the most basic aspect of this notion (maintaining control over Tibet and recovering Taiwan), a nationalism that was one of the cures for the humiliation of colonialism.[27] Third, China aspired to be a revolutionary force in the world just as it was at home. It would become the champion of the developing nations, fighting against the remnants of colonialism and the stunting effects of imperialism on Asia, Africa, the Middle East, and Latin America, by supporting wars of national liberation throughout the world. Its colonial experience gave it a special understanding of and solidarity with the developing world.[28]

The notion of spreading revolution is deeply related to a fourth aspect of China's foreign policy—the importance of ideology and the Sino-Soviet split. Mao vehemently rejected Soviet premier Nikita Khrushchev's post-1956 reform era, his "DeStalinization," and the nascent Soviet détente with the US. He viewed himself as the true Communist. Since 1957, Mao had been pushing a more radical line as a counterweight to

Soviet pragmatism. The mid-1950s' more moderate tones, embodied by Foreign Minister Zhou Enlai's Five Principles of Peaceful Coexistence, had been replaced by an effort to speed up and intensify the revolution at home and abroad. The massive collectivization campaign of the Great Leap Forward (1958–63), which ultimately led to the death of an estimated 20 million Chinese, was in part a reflection of Mao's yearning to prove that he was the most revolutionary Communist leader of them all. The great break in PRC-USSR relations came in 1958, with the withdrawal of Soviet technical advisors to China and Khrushchev's tepid support for China during the 1958 Offshore Islands Crisis over Quemoy and Matsu.[29] By the time Kennedy came to office, Mao was in no mood to be conciliatory. Obviously, his efforts to assist Communist movements in Laos, Indonesia, and Vietnam would have a tremendous impact on US perceptions of China.

Fifth, when it came to the issue of the United Nations and PRC membership, China's line remained consistent through the 1950s and into the 1960s: the UN seat belonged to the government of Beijing; it would never accept any form of representation that did not expel the ROC from the UN. It went even further, stating unequivocally that it refused to recognize any nation that also recognized the ROC or belong to any international organization that also allowed ROC membership. China saw the US as the reason for its exclusion from the UN and the continued ROC possession of the China seat at both the UNSC and UNGA.[30]

At the time of Kennedy's inauguration, China gave the new administration a sampling of its views in the January 27, 1961 issue of *Peking Review*, calling the US the "main force of aggression and war of our time" and "the main enemy of the peoples of the whole world." This was not simply rhetoric for public show. The secret internal Communist Party publication *Bulletin of Activities* from April 25, 1961 called the Kennedy administration "more reactionary, treacherous, elusive, and deceitful" than the Eisenhower administration.[31]

Domestic Context

Every member of the administration understood domestic political realities very clearly. The shadow of the "Who Lost China?" debate hovered over the administration. Democratic vulnerability on national security issues, in particular the McCarthy-era charges that the party was too soft on Communism, placed limits on what Kennedy could do on China policy. On the last day of his presidency, Eisenhower gave Kennedy a warning about what might await him if he moved too quickly on China. During their January 19, 1961 meeting between the outgoing and incoming president, Eisenhower stated it explicitly: he would support Kennedy's foreign policy—there could be only one president at a time. If Kennedy chose to recognize China, however, Eisenhower would challenge him, strongly, publicly, and with the intent of mobilizing public opposition. Clark Clifford, in attendance at the meeting, stated that "Kennedy did not comment, but I had no doubt that Eisenhower's warning had its desired effect."[32]

Public and congressional opinion were also clear. A September 1961 Gallup poll found that PRC admission to the UN was opposed by a 65–18% margin; the percentage of the public that saw the PRC, not the USSR, as the greatest threat to the US grew in the early 1960s. A survey of print media attitudes in 1961 found that major newspapers and magazines opposed PRC entry into the UN 55–13.[33] The Committee of One Million had deepened its ties to members of Congress and found its cause reinvigorated by the 1954–55 and 1958 Quemoy and Matsu crises. Congress had reciprocated with resolutions or legislation opposing China's admission to the UN several times during the 1950s. For example, a resolution condemning any attempt to recognize the PRC as the legitimate representative of China at the UN passed the House with bipartisan support in August 1959 by a margin of 368–2. The Committee of One Million lobbied both parties vigorously during the 1960 election and gained strength through its alliance with the Republican Party in opposition to Kennedy. The Committee placed an advertisement in the *Washington Post* on February 20, 1961, signed by 54 Senators and 285 Representatives, arguing against PRC admission into the UN. The Senate had already passed a Sense of the Senate resolution against admission (January 1961), and the House had considered 14 similar resolutions during that single year.[34] The expectation that a liberal Democrat might upend the consensus of conservative Democrats and Republicans awaited the administration. There were suspicions surrounding the administration's intentions, and every one of the senior decision makers held that in the forefront of their minds as they considered China policy during their first year in office.

This context was a shadow over every administration decision on China and Taiwan. In his nomination hearings, Kennedy's choice for secretary of state, Dean Rusk, stated it succinctly: "I see no prospect at the present time that normal relations could be established with the authorities in Peiping because they seem to feel that the abandonment of the government and people on Formosa would be a prerequisite to any such normal relations."[35] Notice the care Rusk took in crafting the answer. The PRC leaders were referred to as the "authorities" rather than "government"; "government" would confer some legitimacy. That word was reserved for the leaders in Taipei.

Narrative of Decision

Decision making in 1961 took place within four arenas: the State Department between bureaus; the NSC staff; the full interagency process; and small senior-level meetings during the summer and fall that included the president. The debate and decision were marked by inclusion of every individual and organization that had responsibility for the issue. For everyone the central challenge was the same: The postponement strategy looked like it would fail soon; what could the US do to keep its preferred China in the UN?

From January to May, bureaus within the State Department debated two options. The Far Eastern and International Organization Bureaus first suggested a variant of the two-China solution—the PRC could apply to the UN as a new nation.[36] The US needed to somehow convince the ROC not to veto PRC admission to the UN. The Legal Bureau opposed this version of two Chinas, arguing that it would ultimately devolve into a question of whether the PRC was the "successor state" to the ROC. If so, then the PRC deserved the UNSC seat and the ROC was in effect demoted to a UNGA seat without the power of the veto. It countered with a proposal that might consider both the ROC and PRC as successor states. Each would become members of the UNGA with equal status there. The proposal also handed the issue of the permanent UNSC seat with its veto to the UNSC itself.[37] The latter idea had the effect of allowing the ROC to keep the permanent seat; it could veto any resolution asking it to give up its seat to the PRC.

To the working level in the State Department and the NSC staff, the two-China solution in some form was seen as inevitable; the US would not be able to keep the PRC out of the UN forever. It needed to focus on strategies to keep the ROC in. Importantly, US Ambassador to the UN Adlai Stevenson and State Department ambassador at large Averill Harriman agreed with this assessment.[38]

Secretary of State Rusk was an old State Department Asia hand. He had served in the US Army in the military intelligence field for the War Department in the China-Burma-India Theater. From 1947 to 1949, Rusk served as the director of the State Department Office of Special Political Affairs, essentially the United Nations desk at State. In 1949 and 1950, he held several positions: deputy undersecretary of state, assistant secretary

for United Nations affairs (the post was renamed International Organization Affairs in 1954), then was named the very first assistant secretary
of state for Far Eastern affairs in March 1950 (a post created in 1949).[39]
He had been a strong advocate for Taiwan.[40] He also played a key role in
developing the Truman postponement policy in 1951. Rusk claimed that
he did not enter office with any "Rusk Plan" for China, though he "did lean
toward a two-Chinas approach." To him, China's entrance into the UN was
inevitable, regardless of US actions.[41]

In an April memo, State Department counselor George McGhee tried
to move the debate back to first principles. US objectives were to keep the
PRC out and the ROC in. If keeping the PRC out was not possible, then
the US should strive to keep the PRC off the Security Council.[42] This was
still the line drawn in the sand for the US. In any case, officials throughout
the bureaucracy believed that the PRC would never accept two Chinas;
it would never agree to join the UN unless the ROC was simultaneously
stripped of membership.[43]

Talk of two Chinas had two advantages: it looked like the US was making a gesture toward compromise and peace, and its rejection by the PRC
would be seen as a sign of Beijing's intransigence. As Rusk said in a March
1961 meeting with UK ambassador Sir Harold Caccia:

> It is fundamental to the United States that Formosa retain a seat
> in the United Nations. If this is unacceptable to Peiping then they
> are at fault. We don't believe we should have to pay the ticket for
> Peiping's admission at Formosa's expenses. If Peiping won't accept
> admission under these conditions, then that is their choice and we
> would not be responsible.[44]

In a meeting with Prime Minister Keith Holyoake of New Zealand, also
in March, Kennedy spoke frankly about his worries, citing three dilemmas
for US policy: fear that PRC membership would erode US public support
for the UN; widening of political divisions in the US if the PRC were to
gain membership; and "damage which would be done to United States
prestige if we were to suffer a defeat on this issue."[45] In a meeting with
British prime minister Harold Macmillan on April 5, Kennedy summed up
the diplomatic challenge at the UN and of the US approach to the PRC:
"We needed to find a formula for keeping them from wanting to get in."[46]

Though the State Department had the lead, the NSC staff had been
considering China policy since January in its regularly scheduled Tuesday staff meetings. Bundy and Rostow were both included in the meet-

ing with Macmillan. NSC staffer Robert Komer seemed to be the NSC official most involved in keeping Bundy up to speed. He had been sending memos to Bundy in the hopes that a long-term study of China might be undertaken.[47] Komer shared the administration consensus. US policy at the UN had reached its shelf life; it was an area "where we're likely to get clobbered."[48] He continued to whisper in Bundy's ear. In a May memo he stated bluntly that when it came to UN representation and the defense of Quemoy and Matsu, "most Free World countries will no longer support us on these issues."[49]

A crucial May 5, 1961 meeting between Rusk and Kennedy solidified administration thinking. Rusk briefed Kennedy on the discussions within the State Department and the possibility of shifting to a two-China policy. As mentioned above, Rusk felt it may have been time to move in that direction, and he firmly believed that the postponement tactic was drawing its last breath. He admitted to Kennedy that at the time he and others in the State Department had developed the postponement policy, it was a short-term remedy, useful, he thought, for maybe four or five years. The fact that it had survived for so long was an unexpected bonus. Kennedy quickly rejected the two-China idea, primarily on domestic political grounds. His small margin of victory in 1960 combined with the strength of the China lobby among Republicans made a change in China policy a political land mine for the administration, and a clear candidate for the agenda of a second term. Rusk described the president as calculating that the "the potential benefits of a more realistic China policy didn't warrant risking a severe political confrontation." In keeping with Rusk's belief that there should be no "blue sky" between the president and the secretary of state, Rusk accepted Kennedy's decision. The two-China option seemed dead, no matter how many officials in the State Department supported it. The president also told Rusk, in a polite admonishing of the State Department, that "I don't want to read in the *Washington Post* or the *New York Times* that the State Department is thinking about a change in our China policy."[50] Again, Rusk was faithful to his president. He never told members of the senior level of the State Department that he met with Kennedy to discuss China. Rusk explained it this way:

> I went back to the department, and when Adlai Stevenson, Chester Bowles, and others would drop by to talk about China and especially their hopes for a two-Chinas policy at the UN, I stonewalled them and played the "village idiot." I didn't tell them about my talk with the president because I would have read about *that* in the *Washing-*

ton Post or the *New York Times*. Nor did I initiate any new studies on China policy; in the leaky Kennedy administration even that would have gotten to the press. (italics in original)[51]

Rusk's task at that point was to develop a strategy that could prevent China from attaining a seat at the UN and to discourage the State Department from making any more noise about a two-China policy.

At first glance it seems like the decision was done; the president had spoken; all discussion of two Chinas were over. The president and Rusk, however, did not enforce their decision; no directives were issued, and the two-China solution was continually brought back to the president as an option. In the larger tale, the meeting became essentially irrelevant. Both the president and Rusk continued to allow the State Department, in particular, to brainstorm on a two-China policy.

It was not until three weeks later that the rest of the administration was given a hint, and only a hint, that Kennedy had made up his mind. On May 24 the president, Rusk, Stevenson, Assistant Secretary of State for International Organization Harlan Cleveland, and Deputy Under Secretary for Political Affairs U. Alexis Johnson met at the White House. It is notable that even though the NSC staff and White House Staff had begun taking a larger role in decision making, the records of this meeting suggest that it was exclusively attended by the president and members of the State Department. The discussion centered on a State Department memo for Kennedy, likely the product of negotiations between the Far Eastern, International Organization, and Legal Affairs Bureaus, which called for the US to take the lead in presenting a two-China formula at the UN. Stevenson explained to Kennedy that "the purpose of the exercise is to keep the Chinese Communists out of the UN" in a manner that keeps the ROC in, but appears to be a good faith effort by the US to resolve the matter. The issue, however, was not one where the US should risk "a major loss, on a question which we had staked the whole of our prestige and leadership." As expected, given Rusk's reluctance to state his views unless meeting privately with Kennedy, the memorandum of conversation for this meeting contains no mention of Rusk's opinions. Kennedy scuttled the idea of the US taking the lead on proposing two Chinas, but recognized that unless the US moved quickly the ROC could be voted out of the UN. He suggested a larger diplomatic effort to reach out to congressional leaders, US allies, and Eisenhower.[52]

No decisions were made at the meeting, but a Rusk memo of May 26 formally drew up a range of options. It began with the premise that the postponement policy might last one more year, and if the UNGA had to choose between Chinese governments, it would select Beijing. Rusk suggested a UNGA resolution that could lead to two Chinas in the UN by reconfirming the ROC as a UN member, but allowing the entry of the PRC as if it already had membership. This would likely pass the UNGA and be rejected by the PRC, making them the obstructionist party. The ROC had already stated that it would not publicly do or say anything that implied it accepted two Chinas and that it wanted to hold on to its UNSC seat. The memo implied that the ROC would accept two Chinas, but this was not explicitly stated. Rusk asked for and received permission to staff out the policy and to begin laying the groundwork for its implementation with Chiang's government, other Western allies (Australia, Norway, Canada, and Japan), and members of Congress.[53]

By mid-June, State had begun testing the waters for the two-China proposal. Cleveland, the assistant secretary for international organization affairs, had already contacted Norway, Canada, and the UK; none of them was very interested in taking the lead on the new approach. This led to a bit of policy reformulation at State and the preparation of a new memo for the president. Kennedy was scheduled to meet with Prime Minister Ikeda Hayato of Japan in late June, and some felt that Japan might carry the diplomatic load for the US if the president personally asked Ikeda. The administration had also been readying its pitch to members of Congress. The dilemma, however, still remained: the purpose of the policy (to keep the PRC out of the UN and make it appear to be the result of Beijing's intransigence) was the exact opposite of what it appeared to be (a formula for bringing the PRC into the UN). Keeping that quiet once Congress was involved loomed as an almost impossible task. As Komer of the NSC staff put it:

> It will be very hard to explain to the Congress and the public why we must shift our policy, without telling them we really hope by this "shift" to keep the CPR [PRC] out. Then we run the risk that various Congressmen might start playing this theme in public, which would be fatal. If it gets widely noised about that the US expected this new technique to keep the CPR out of the UN, we will lose crucial votes from the less-developed countries.[54]

Even worse was the possibility that members of Congress took the proposal at face value, believing that the administration really welcomed the addition of the PRC to the UN. That might create a rerun of the "Who Lost China?" accusation that dogged Truman.

On June 26, Kennedy met with Stevenson and Rusk. Stevenson was instructed to tell the Senate in upcoming testimony that US policy was to keep the PRC out but that its postponement tactic was sure to collapse in the near future. Kennedy also asked for more information on the "successor states" concept that would allow the PRC to enter the UN without changing the status of the ROC. By early July, Stevenson reported back to the president that he had been sounding out several influential Republicans and media figures with ties to the ROC government, such as former US ambassador to the UN Henry Cabot Lodge, *Time* magazine's Hedley W. Donovan, and the former president of Scripps-Howard newspapers, Roy W. Howard, who had strong connections to Chiang.[55] The administration was using a two-pronged strategy for the ROC—lobbying it through government-to-government channels and through the ties between Taiwanese and American elites.

The administration's diplomacy here was complicated by the position of the ROC government. It explicitly rejected even the appearance of accepting a two-China policy, even if the purpose was to corner the PRC into rejecting the idea. Correspondence between Kennedy and Chiang had been ongoing since the beginning of the administration. The dynamic had a pattern. First, Chiang insisted on a hard rejection of PRC admission to the UN and expressed doubt about the US commitment to defense of the ROC, both militarily and at the UN. Kennedy then responded with reassurance on both counts, and an added reminder that Chiang's unyielding adherence to the postponement tactic would be self-defeating. A June letter explained that in suggesting the "successor states" idea, the US hoped to prevent a credentials vote in the UN—a simple up or down vote on which government was the legitimate representative of China, a vote the ROC would lose. The letter stated it bluntly: the administration predicted that the ROC strategy of asking the US to continue the postponement was doomed; the ROC was certain to be expelled from the UN.[56] At the time, the State Department's assessment was that a 1961 postponement vote would fall short by 12 votes in the UNGA; it estimated a vote of 31 nations for the postponement, 43 against, and 25 abstentions.[57]

On June 27, 1961, at the regularly scheduled weekly Planning Group between State, Defense, and the CIA, Counselor to the State Department George McGhee was given the role as "the focal point of interdepartmental consideration of the problem of our over-all policy toward Communist China."[58] The meeting was not initially scheduled as a meeting on China, but the lingering conversation about how to shape the interagency debate on China in the longer term was resolved by the Planning Group in favor of State Department leadership, in full concurrence with the initial design of the administration's decision process. The Planning Group had been considering China policy throughout 1961, but similar to its fate on other issues, it is unclear what relationship its activities had to the State Department and NSC staff work. For example, a March 1961 Planning Group meeting did specifically focus on China, but the outcome of the discussion was not recorded, and subsequent minutes and memoranda of other committees do not mention the Planning Group.[59]

Memoranda concerning China and the interagency debates were being closely followed by the NSC and White House staff.[60] In terms of decision making, this is important. Though the meetings with the president on this issue clearly showed the dominance of the State Department, Komer of the NSC staff was up to speed on every aspect of the policy and consistently provided Bundy with his analysis. This fact suggests that behind the scenes Kennedy consulted Bundy and others in the White House staff (Schlesinger in particular) on every aspect of the ongoing deliberations. For example, a July 7 memorandum from Bundy to Kennedy summarizes Bundy's conversations with Ray Cline, the CIA station chief in Taipei. The memo also reviews the situation as of early July. It highlights Cline's view that State's diplomacy toward the ROC had backfired. State's emphasis on the coming failure of the postponement and continued lobbying on behalf of two Chinas had made the ROC government "deeply uneasy about the U.S." Cline told Bundy that if the US and the ROC could not resolve this issue and several other contentious problems, he expected "a grievous split." Bundy lamented what he saw as the irony of the administration coming full circle to the "Who Lost China?" domestic uproar: "What makes all this so sad is that in fact we have no intention of deserting Chiang and every reason to support real progress in Formosa. Yet we seem headed for the same impasse Marshall and Acheson got into—and with equally bad political results at home and abroad."[61]

As if emphasizing Bundy's warnings, the China lobby, led by the Committee of One Million, began flexing its muscles. The fact that the administration was considering a two-China formula leaked in July. Whether the leak came from within the administration, from the administration's discussions with the media, from Congress, or from the ROC government is unclear. The power of the ROC and the China lobby was reflected in the efforts of the Republican Party, including former vice president Richard Nixon, and decisive Senate action. On July 25, the Senate gave the administration a shot across the bow, voting 76–0 on a resolution rejecting the PRC's admission to the UN and supporting the ROC as the legitimate representative of China. The House approved a similar resolution 395–0 on August 31.[62]

In the last few days of July and first few of August, US policy shifted toward a strategy that might keep the PRC out, the ROC in, and the administration safe from accusations of being soft on China or an unreliable ally for the ROC. A two-hour meeting on July 28 made significant progress. The meeting included the president and the key figures in the State Department and NSC staff, excluding all other departments and agencies: Kennedy, Rusk, Under Secretary for Economic Affairs George Ball, Assistant Secretary for Far Eastern Affairs Walter McConaughy, Cleveland, US ambassador to the ROC Everett Drumright, Bundy, Rostow, Komer, and acting director for Chinese affairs at the NSC Robert Rinden. After some convincing arguments by the State Department representatives, Kennedy showed a preference for a strategy that would change the status of the China issue to an "important question" for the UNGA. Article 18 of the UN Charter specified that a two-thirds vote was required on "important questions." The parliamentary maneuver would raise the bar for challenges to the status of the ROC and the consideration of PRC admission from a simple majority to a two-thirds supermajority. Making representation an "important question" might add years to the life of US policy. It would also avoid even the appearance of support for two Chinas. The State Department, however, had a slight internal dilemma on its hands; Stevenson and many in the US delegation to the UN continued to support the successor state idea. Kennedy suggested pairing the "important question" with the Swedish proposal for a commission to study the entire China representation problem. He was reminded by State Department attendees that the ROC was, in Cleveland's words, "allergic to the Swedish proposal."[63]

Withholding his opinion from the group meeting of July 28, Rusk gave the president his view in a private memorandum on July 31. He indicated his support for the "important question" tactic and an additional resolution creating a study committee to examine general criteria for UN membership in the UNGA, the Economic and Social Council, and the UNSC. Though the study committee would be tasked to report back to the UN in one year, its mandate was be so broad in scope that it would be nearly impossible for it to reach a consensus. The gambit was similar to the one used by the Truman administration in 1950 and 1951. Rusk even included language for a draft UNGA resolution.[64]

An additional complication related to a package proposal for the admission of Mongolia and Mauritania to the UN. The ROC was mulling a veto of that application; it argued that, historically, Mongolia was part of China.

This would have been a disaster for US policy and the future of the ROC at the UN. The US believed that if the ROC vetoed Mongolia's application, the Soviet Union would veto the application of Mauritania in return, and the ROC would be blamed for its exclusion. African states, an estimated 10–15 votes, might then punish the ROC by voting to seat the PRC when the next postponement resolution was proposed. The US spent considerable diplomatic effort successfully convincing the ROC not to jeopardize its membership at the UN over the Mongolia issue.[65]

Through August and September, the US firmed up its two-pronged tactic of making the representation an "important question" and establishing a UNGA commission. The record shows several meetings to discuss the Mongolia-Mauritania problem, a potential Kennedy speech on the issue, and the "important question"/commission tactic. An August 5 meeting between Kennedy, Stevenson, Cleveland of the State Department, and Arthur Schlesinger of the White House staff was typical of the conversations. The meeting, held at Kennedy's Hyannis Port, Massachusetts residence, illustrated the informality of the administration. Neither Rusk nor Bundy was there, but an assistant secretary of state and a White House staffer were. According to Schlesinger, the meeting covered several subjects, beginning with Berlin. When the topic of PRC admission to the UN came up, Kennedy called to the First Lady: "Jackie, we need the Bloody Marys now." Kennedy stated that he felt US policy toward the PRC was "irrational," in Schlesinger's words. He believed, however, that none of the options for admitting the PRC into the UN was worth the domestic backlash they would produce. Though Stevenson made it clear on August 5 and in other meetings that he was prepared to introduce the important question/commission resolutions, he continued to lobby for a fallback position that included the successor state formula and therefore an acceptance of two Chinas.[66] At this point the US began to work on its allies to lock up diplomatic support for the new strategy.

On September 5, Kennedy met with Rusk, Stevenson, Cleveland, Bundy, Sorensen, and Schlesinger. The addition of Sorensen and Schlesinger, White House staffers with license to freelance, is notable. This meeting was essentially the final meeting before Stevenson was to receive his instructions for the upcoming UNGA session. Kennedy added his "generalist" alter egos to the meeting as a last-minute political reality check. The meeting centered on a Rusk memo to the president that asked for explicit confirmation of Stevenson's instructions. Kennedy gave Stevenson the green light to use the possibility of a two China idea in 1962 as an enticement for allies. They may disapprove of the important question/commission idea, but they might vote for it if they believed the US was preparing for a more permanent resolution of the problem down the road.[67] Kennedy then summed up Stevenson's mission:

> You have the hardest thing in the world to sell. It really doesn't make any sense—the idea that Taiwan represents China. But if we lost this fight, if Red China comes into the UN during our first year in town, your first year and mine, they'll run us both out. We have to lick them this year. We'll take our chances next year. It will be an election year; but we can delay the admission of Red China till after the election. So far as this year is concerned, you must do everything you can to keep them out. . . . At least for a year.[68]

This meeting was the administration's official decision on its strategy at the UN for 1961.

Stevenson's formal instructions of September 13, 1961 outlined the new policy in detail. These were his last official marching orders for the UNGA's 16th session, which began on September 19, 1961. In a memo from Rusk, Stevenson was given a great deal of latitude to accomplish his tasks. The instructions explicitly stated in writing that Stevenson could tell allies that "the United States does not exclude the possibility that a study committee would recommend to the 1962 session a successor state solution if that becomes necessary." Stevenson was allowed to bring up this successor state issue if he believed it was "essential" to moving the important question/commission idea through the 1961 UNGA. If the entire proposal seemed doomed and the UNGA appeared ready to take a simple up or down vote on which nation was the legitimate China, Stevenson was told to "seek instructions as to whether we should adopt the successor state approach."[69]

This should have been the end of the decision making process. From that point on the administration moved toward implementing the policy—Stevenson focusing on diplomacy at the UN, and Kennedy, Rusk, Bundy, and others in the State Department, White House, and the CIA lobbying to gain international, domestic, and ROC support. Stevenson, however, used his implementation authority as an excuse to continue his lobbying effort to include a successor state option—essentially a two-China initiative—in the 1961 UNGA session. Though many within the State Department supported the successor state idea, Bundy led efforts to restrain Stevenson's freelancing, emphasizing at an October 9 White House staff meeting that "the President, regardless of any personal views he may have, probably cannot afford to be officially associated with a two China idea."[70] Stevenson was not alone in his dissatisfaction with the policy. Komer felt that the imminent failure of the postponement strategy meant that they should fall back on the successor state notion and faith that the PRC would reject it; he acknowledged, though, that this meant an on the record acceptance of two Chinas.[71]

In spite of Stevenson's unhappiness and the grumbling from the working level of the administration, Stevenson carried out his instructions. Resolution 1668(XVI), Representation of China in the United Nations, was introduced into the UNGA on December 1, 1961. The resolution called for making the issue of Chinese representation an "important question," but it did not contain language calling for a commission. At some point during the diplomatic dance between the US and its allies, the necessity for a commission as an extra enticement for nations to support the important question idea faded away. The resolution was, however, cosponsored by the US, Australia, Colombia, Italy, and Japan. The inclusion of the US illustrates the difficulty the US expected. The other cosponsors seemed to have needed US cover before they acted. The resolution passed on December 15, 1961, 61–34 with 7 abstentions.[72] A Soviet-sponsored resolution, calling for the removal of the ROC from the UN and replacing it with the PRC, failed with 36 votes for, 48 against, and 20 abstentions.[73] The administration had averted a crisis. The use of the "important question" resolution succeeded until 1971; the PRC remained out and the ROC remained in for another decade, until Nixon's rapprochement with China changed the strategic calculus of the UN representation dilemma.

Analysis

Kennedy's decision making for the Chinese representation issue is a quintessential example of Kennedy's overall style—informal, inclusive, and reliant on meetings of small groups of advisors. Kennedy made the ultimate choice here, relying on Rusk and the State Department as the foundation for ideas and advice. Participation did narrow at key points and included more White House assistants loyal to Kennedy who could warn him of the political consequences of new policies, in this instance the Republican assault on anything that hinted at the acceptance of two Chinas. No one made suggestions to change the decision making process to shore up perceived weaknesses. In that sense, this case study fits the original evolution model better than the evolution-balance model. Though the original evolution model described how formal systems become more informal, bypass interagency processes, and narrow participation, Kennedy began with an informal system. He always maintained that informality, but he did narrow participation at times. Consideration of balancing the informal system with more formal elements began after about six months; these did not, however, take any form until February 1962 when the first Standing Group was established. The idea of adding formality had not yet ripened.

What is most interesting here from a policy perspective is the consensus within the administration that what they were trying to defend was foolish and would eventually fail. For domestic political reasons, however, the administration committed itself to strengthening the policy and hiding the fact that it believed a two Chinas approach was more realistic. Once Kennedy ruled out a two-China proposal, both Rusk and Bundy stepped into line and looked for an alternative solution to the postponement that did not include two Chinas. In spite of this, the rest of the State Department and NSC staff continued to staff out two-China options and key officials did not stop lobbying for it. Kennedy's informal process revealed one of its weaknesses—a difficulty in communicating and enforcing decisions.

Return to the Mainland: The Crisis That Almost Was

The 1962 decision on military aid to Taiwan does fit the predictions of the evolution-balance model. The administration initially tackled the issue using Kennedy's informal spokes-of-the-wheel style. ROC president Chiang Kai-shek's intensified lobbying for US military assistance and approval for a full-scale ROC invasion of the mainland raised the potential for a serious military confrontation with China. In response, the administration added more formal decision structures: a cabinet-level meeting, explicitly not labeled as an NSC meeting on June 20; consideration of the public roll-out of the policy at an actual NSC meeting on June 27; and the formation of a new interagency Offshore Islands Working Group. This move to set up a permanent committee was likely based on the judgment that Chiang's requests for US assistance would be an ongoing problem. The new interagency group was established, and then, as in the case of the Standing Groups, ignored, as policy making remained dominated by informal groups. Kennedy, again, made all the final decisions. In choosing to limit US assistance to Chiang, the administration considered both international and domestic factors. First, there was a consensus that intervention against the mainland by the ROC would never dislodge the Beijing government. Chiang's adventurism could only fail miserably and force the US into an unacceptable choice of allowing the ROC to embarrass itself, tilting the balance of power across the Taiwan Strait even further toward the mainland, or rescuing Taiwan through more direct US intervention. To Kennedy and his advisors, this dilemma was the Bay of Pigs all over again, but on a much larger scale, both in terms of its impact on the international reputation of the US and Kennedy's political standing at home.

Political Context

This case study begins in January 1962, only two months after the United Nations vote had taken place. For that reason, the international and domestic political contexts are discussed in one section. Internationally, both China and Taiwan had walked away from the 1961 UN vote with a sense that the diplomacy across the Taiwan Strait had changed. The defeat in 1961 was particularly bitter for Beijing. The two-thirds vote necessary to consider the PRC's admission to the UN raised the bar so high that the PRC's leadership became explicitly hostile to the UN, calling it an alliance of "imperialist" and "revisionist" forces controlled by the US and the USSR. It even considered establishing alternative international organizations based on a large alliance of African, Asian, and Latin American states that might form a counterweight to the "Western-dominated" UN.[74] The ROC felt vindication and perhaps more confidence in the US-ROC alliance and in its belief that Mao's policies were undermining the Communist hold on China. The Great Leap Forward (1958–63) continued producing famine and economic catastrophe, taking an immense toll on the mainland. Chiang and his advisors saw the crisis in China as an opportunity. In their view, the failure of the Great Leap Forward weakened Mao Zedong, making the PRC ripe for counterrevolution. Such a counterrevolution could be successful if led by an ROC invasion of the mainland. Though Chiang had no illusions that his military was a match for the People's Liberation Army (PLA), he believed the food crisis might lead to rebellion by the Chinese people. US intelligence was tracking the crisis as well; by mid-1962, it estimated that 5,000 refugees were fleeing to Hong Kong daily. It was the sense of crisis on the mainland that convinced the ROC leadership that they must move quickly or lose the window of opportunity to overthrow the government in Beijing. In addition, there were still debates about whether the Communist hold on the mainland was permanent. From the perspective of the ROC, the longer they waited for action, the more deeply entrenched the Communists became.[75] The domestic political context had not changed from 1961–62; the China lobby was still powerful and Kennedy was still wary of giving his political opponents any reason to doubt his commitment to the containment of Communism or support for Taiwan.

Narrative of Decision

During the first three months of 1962, Chiang led an often-intense lobbying effort to gain US approval for some type of military action against the mainland. The US had given tentative approval for a limited ROC incursion consisting of an "airdrop" of "six 20-man teams" into southern regions of the PRC. The initial recommendation to support Chiang in July 1961 may have been by the "Special Group"—an interagency committee with a mandate to review all counterinsurgency policies of the US government; Kennedy then approved the idea.[76] It became clear to the administration early in 1962 that the ROC saw this training as the preparatory phase for a military campaign against the mainland later that same year. On January 24, Chiang met with the CIA's Ray Cline and asked about Kennedy's views of military action against the PRC. Cline detailed the meeting in a January 26 memo, which Komer of the NSC staff summarized for Bundy in another memo dated January 29. According to Cline, Chiang hoped to initiate a discussion "on the circumstances under which GRC [Government of the Republic of China] intervention on the mainland might be feasible and necessary or desirable." Komer examined the full range of possibilities, from "limited probes" to larger-scale ROC attempts to ignite a revolution overthrowing the Communists. His assessment concluded that the US had little to gain from any ROC military operations. Larger attacks might bring the Soviet military in to defend the mainland, defeating ROC forces and repairing the Sino-Soviet split at the same time. Smaller operations would achieve little unless they incited revolts against Beijing, which if serious enough might again lead to a Soviet military response. In either case, the administration would feel pressure, domestically and internationally, to fight alongside ROC forces. Komer based some of his analysis on a July 1961 paper entitled "Unrest and Uprisings in Mainland China" written by China specialist Edward Rice of the State Department's Policy Planning Council. Rice felt that any ROC attacks against the mainland would only work "if there were a major revolution in Red China." The possibility was seen as "unlikely." The bottom line for Komer was that "no matter how weak the ChiComs are, the Soviets won't let us succeed." Avoiding a war with the Soviets over China was the top priority. He recommended to Bundy that the US keep Chiang on a "tight leash."[77] In February, both deputy assistant secretary of defense for international security affairs William Bundy and US ambassador to Taiwan Everett Drumright sent similar messages to their departments: Chiang was preparing for a counterattack on the mainland; he expected logistical support, but not direct US intervention.[78]

The interagency aspects of US decision making at this point are unclear, but there was participation by the Department of State, Department of Defense, the CIA, and NSC staff. There was also consensus on caution. Through March and April of 1962, Chiang received a less than enthusiastic reaction from the administration. On instructions from Harriman, Drumright met with Chiang on March 6 and explained US policy. Though the US was skeptical about military action against the mainland, it wanted the ROC to continue its dialogue with the US. Drumright's telegram to Harriman explained that "above all" he had emphasized the "need . . . for joint agreement respecting use of force against mainland." In his assessment, "it was utterly clear that Chiang is bent on taking some kind of action this year against mainland and that it will take skillful, adept responses on our part to channel his actions in directions we deem appropriate to situation."[79] On March 8, Roger Hilsman, director of the State Department Bureau of Intelligence and Research, met with Chiang Ching-kuo, Chiang Kai-shek's son and heir apparent to the presidency, who repeated the ROC line: the year 1962 was the optimal time to strike, and although US assistance was preferable, the ROC would achieve victory even if acting alone. Hilsman's response to Chiang Ching-kuo reinforced the US position that it did not view the Beijing regime as ready to topple and that "premature action" could "heal" the Sino-Soviet rift.[80]

Kennedy entered the process at this point, sending Harriman to Taipei to discuss the issues with Chiang. It is unclear how Kennedy decided the matter. There are no records of specific interagency meetings, but Kennedy and Harriman did speak directly. In the first week of March, the administration also used a back channel from Bundy to Cline to Chiang Ching-kuo to lay the groundwork for Harriman's meeting. Bundy told Cline to emphasize that US views on any military action by the ROC were still based on the December 1954 "exchange of notes" between Eisenhower's secretary of state, John Foster Dulles, and ROC foreign minister George Yeh: "the use of force will be a matter of joint agreement." He also told Cline to stress that while in Taipei, Harriman "will be empowered to speak in the most direct and authoritative way for the President himself."[81] Kennedy's written instructions to Harriman of March 9 reiterated these points. Taking note of Chiang's sensitivities, that he might be insulted by an admonition coming from an assistant secretary of state, Kennedy told Harriman to make it clear that Kennedy and Harriman had spoken directly and Harriman had been given the president's "full authority."[82]

The administration continued to send its message to Taipei through multiple channels. On March 12, two days before Harriman was scheduled to meet with Chiang in Taipei, Bundy had spoken with Yeh, now ROC ambassador to the US, and mentioned what became an important theme in the US response to Chiang's plans. Assessments by the US intelligence community were not optimistic about efforts to dislodge the Beijing government, and the US was especially wary of stepping into another situation like the aborted attempt to overthrow Castro during the Bay of Pigs fiasco. Bundy stated it explicitly to Yeh, saying that the US "would always be alert to any real opportunity," but he "referred to the Cuban episode, indicating that both our governments must be careful not to mistake hopes for realities." By the time of the Harriman meeting on March 14, Chiang had already been bombarded with the US position. The meeting evolved into another of Chiang's ongoing attempts to lobby the US for support. Chiang explained that "people on mainland are ripe for revolt." He would only need US assistance to transport troops to the mainland; no large contingent of US forces was necessary. Harriman and Chiang disagreed about the possibility of Soviet intervention. Chiang thought the rift was a personal one between Mao and the current Soviet leaders, and that Moscow was no longer willing to intervene to help Beijing. Harriman saw the Sino-Soviet split as "fundamental"; however, he believed that the Soviets would still protect the mainland if US forces were part of any intervention. The summary of Harriman's meeting was sent from the US Embassy in Taipei to the president and Rusk. Harriman sent a separate telegram to Kennedy explaining that he received the sense during the meeting that Chiang did not believe he needed US permission before launching military action. This differed from the US interpretation in the 1954 agreement and added potential complications.[83] Hypothetically, Chiang could intervene unilaterally and nearly force the administration to support him. If the intervention met with success, the US might feel compelled to seize the opportunity presented to it. If the mission began to fail, the US would be accused of abandoning an ally unless it came to the rescue.

The key meeting on the issue was held March 31 at the White House. Attending were representatives of State, the CIA, and NSC staff, but not the Department of Defense: the president, Rusk, Bundy, Cline (in from Taipei), General Marshall "Pat" Carter of the CIA, Michael Forrestal (an Asian expert from the NSC staff), and Hilsman. In spite of the broad, but not comprehensive, interagency attendance, it was not an NSC meeting and had no formal connection to any other decision processes. The only real interagency backstopping for the White House session was a meeting earlier in the day between Cline and Harriman, arranged by Harriman's deputy Edward Rice at Cline's request. Several decisions came out of the White House meeting, including a seven-point guidance that defined US policy on the issue for the rest of the administration. During the meeting, Cline first detailed some of the ROC's proposals. Rusk quickly interceded, arguing that the notion of ROC forces accomplishing anything significant was "nonsense, and the idea that we could keep it covert was nonsense." The Bay of Pigs debacle shadowed the debate in the room. Hilsman even referred to the ROC plans as "an even grander Bay of Pigs." He argued, however, that immediate rejection of the idea might lead the ROC to "start a public campaign to arouse the China Lobby." Kennedy suggested training ROC pilots to fly C-123 transport planes within the United States as a preparatory move. The planes must stay in the US, however, as a precaution and as another way of telling Taipei that the US was not making a commitment to military intervention. Cline felt that this would be enough to reassure Chiang. The group seemed to focus on October as a date for reassessment of the potential for military action. Interestingly, though Cline of the CIA was still the main US messenger to Chiang at that time, he was instructed at the meeting to tell Chiang that, once appointed, a new US ambassador to the ROC would assume the role that had been played by the CIA as the direct conduit between the US and Taipei.[84] This latter decision fits in with the administration's initial hope to elevate the State Department's leadership.

Following the meeting, Cline was given a formal statement of the seven-point US policy. The statement was drafted in the White House, and early versions of it contained the handwriting of both Kennedy and Bundy. An additional memo to Cline from Bundy explicitly informed him that Rusk and Harriman had approved the document. Though decisions were being made informally, the administration was careful to make sure that all the relevant players were involved and that those who implemented policy knew that it had full interagency support. The statement was deliberately left unsigned by Kennedy as a way of insulating him from evidence that he had approved covert action against the mainland. Cline was instructed not to give the document to ROC officials, but to use it as a reference for his diplomacy. The seven points in the instructions covered both operational and diplomatic aspects. The administration did not believe that the conditions on the mainland were dire enough to make intervention "feasible," but that the US supported "probing operations and specifically the joint training, equipping, and supervising of the formation of probing teams of the type previously authorized." The operations and preparations for further action were designed to test the mainland forces and be ready if those tests discovered serious weaknesses. The document gave Cline permission to work with the "planning and preparation for larger scale clandestine operations on a contingent basis involving up to a maximum of 200 men in a single airdrop," but it also insisted that the US had not yet agreed that the ROC should proceed with larger operations and that any US role, even in the planning process, would be publicly denied.[85]

Cline received Chiang's response and relayed it to Washington in an April 14 memo. Chiang had decided to postpone action from June to October 1962. He set a date for an airdrop of troops into China for October 1. Bundy quickly met with the president to develop a response to Chiang's timetable and explicit plans for military action. Bundy then responded to Cline on April 17, telling him to reemphasize that the US had not made any commitments to support military action. It had only agreed to "studying the feasibility" of such action. Bundy did not want Cline to beat around the bush on this: "The USG position must be that it stands on what is outlined in the president's seven-point statement. We cannot safely get ourselves in the position of negotiating on this." It was not a discussion. The US had set its policy, and Chiang could not lobby his way to changing it until the intelligence assessment of the situation suggested that new and significant vulnerabilities had emerged.[86] During this part of the decision, the channel of Kennedy to Bundy to Cline to Chiang left the State Department as an informed observer.

Chiang was not giving up. Cline returned to the US to report on how Chiang had responded to the US decisions of late March. Interestingly, a May 17 meeting on the issue was attended by the president, Bundy, CIA director John McCone, and Cline. No State or Defense Department personnel were present. Cline gave Chiang's assessment of the mainland political situation: the "system of public security controls was beginning to crumble," and "it is essential for it to plan and prepare for both clandestine and military actions to support anti-Communist resistance forces on the Mainland." Chiang acknowledged that the US would not be a part of any operations, but sought "strategic" and "joint agreement" with the US on the next step in an allied strategy against the PRC. Chiang had told Cline that October 1 was the longest he could delay action. The absence of any State Department representatives from the meeting may be explained by what Cline described as Chiang's sense that State was hostile to him.[87]

A few days later, on May 22, an interagency meeting led by State, including officials from State, Defense, the CIA, and the White House, met to consider an arms request from the ROC. Deputy Undersecretary of State

U.A. Johnson had requested the meeting; it was held in his office. The group drafted a response, which was considered at a White House meeting with Kennedy on May 29. Attending were Johnson and Harriman, new ambassador to the ROC Admiral Alan Kirk, Assistant Secretary for International Security Affairs Paul Nitze from Defense, Carter and Desmond FitzGerald (director of the Far Eastern Division of the Directorate of Plans) from the CIA, Bundy, and Forrestal from the NSC staff. The meeting was based, in part, on an analysis by Hilsman from State's Intelligence and Research Bureau that had been written for Rusk; Rusk had written on his copy "President should see." Everyone at the meeting remained skeptical that a large-scale uprising could be instigated by ROC commandos. Kirk felt that the request for greater military assistance was Chiang's way of "dragging us into GRC plans for an invasion of the mainland." Kennedy worried that a lack of US support for ROC military options would be seen as a lack of commitment to the ROC itself. He thought that the administration's best avenue to discourage ROC action should be to emphasize that US intelligence had concluded that "a landing on the mainland was doomed." If ROC intelligence suggested otherwise, the US needed to see that information.[88]

Soon after these meetings, the situation across the Taiwan Strait pushed the US toward another major decision. In mid-1962, an estimated half million PRC troops redeployed to the coastal regions on the mainland opposite Taiwan and Quemoy. Hilsman described it as a major mobilization from Manchuria, north China, and central China, large enough and public enough to take control of civilian rail infrastructure for a few days.[89] Regardless of Chiang's seriousness, this redeployment indicated that China believed the ROC was dedicated to action sometime in the summer or fall of 1962. Though this was not discussed at the time (at least in any documentation of the period), the PRC must have known that such a large-scale movement of troops would be noticed by the ROC and US intelligence. That was likely the purpose—sending a message across the Taiwan Strait and across the Pacific that if you are planning something, we are ready.

The administration held several meetings in mid-June to deal with what some thought was the beginning of an urgent crisis. On June 18 the president met with DCI John McCone and Deputy DCI for Plans Richard Helms. McCone had met with Chiang on June 5 in Taipei (detailing the meeting in a memo to Bundy for transmission to Kennedy, to Hilsman at State, and to the Office of the Secretary of Defense). In person, he summarized that conversation again. Chiang made it clear that he saw 1962 as his best chance to retake the mainland, and was awaiting a green light from the US. Kennedy asked McCone his impressions of what Chiang might do if the US refused to support any ROC military operations against the mainland. The consensus in the room was that Chiang might launch attacks anyway.[90]

The next morning's President's Intelligence Checklist, a CIA-written roundup of key global events that had occurred since the day before, upped the intensity of the moment through its analysis of Chinese troop activities: "our confidence in the assessment that this movement is primarily defensive is dwindling." Bundy's copy of the brief added his handwritten notation: "Meeting today on this. More info tonight."[91] That evening Kennedy met with McCone and E. Henry Knoche of the CIA, Bundy, Forrestal, and the President's military representative, General Maxwell Taylor of the NSC staff. McCone gave Kennedy a copy of the memo he had sent to Chiang asking him for more information on his plans. Most importantly, the group decided that the president should have a full interagency meeting on the issue; it was scheduled for June 20.[92]

Up to this point in the decision process, there had been no significant meetings that included the president and full interagency participation. Meetings had typically been of two types: either the president, the CIA, and NSC staff; or the president, State, the CIA, and NSC staff. Importantly, the seriousness of the crisis led to greater interagency participation, rather than a narrowing or centralization of the process. The President's Intelligence Checklist of the morning of June 20 heightened the sense of impending crisis, noting that civilians were being evacuated from the coastal areas of China where PLA troops were deploying.[93] The June 20 evening meeting (6:00 p.m. to 7:30 p.m.) was attended by the full range of interagency representation: the president; Vice President Johnson; Undersecretary George Ball, U.A. Johnson, Harriman, Hilsman, and Ambassador Kirk from State; Defense secretary Robert McNamara, Joint Chiefs chair General Lyman Lemnitzer, and Commander in Chief of Pacific Command Admiral Harry Felt from Defense; McCone of the CIA; and Taylor, Bundy, and Forrestal of the NSC staff. Rusk was traveling in Europe at the time. In spite of the broad and cabinet-level attendance, this was not labeled an NSC meeting. Hilsman's summary of the meeting describes a serious and frank discussion. McCone briefed the group on a Special National Intelligence Estimate (SNIE 13-5-62, "Chinese Communist Short-Range Military Intentions," of June 20), which viewed the PLA actions as very significant, either a move to pressure Quemoy or preparation for an attack on Taiwan. It described the troop deployments as "the largest such movement since the Korean War." McNamara thought the possibility that the PRC could invade Taiwan or even Quemoy with its unimpressive logistical capabilities and nonexistent sealift was, in Hilsman's words, "pretty silly." McCone stated the intelligence community consensus: this was not a preparation for a Pearl Harbor–style surprise attack.

The meeting led to a series of administration actions. First, the CIA and the Pacific Command stepped up their intelligence activities to gain a greater understanding of the PLA buildup. Second, the State Department was assigned the task of communicating the US position to the important players. State's mission was to finally convince the ROC that the US absolutely would not support any bid to retake the mainland that might lead to requests for larger-scale US military operations; the US, however, would continue to defend Taiwan from China. State also had the trickier job of sending the same message to the PRC and the Soviets. Under the direction of Harriman, the Far Eastern Bureau worked on the proper diplomatic language. Ironically, the US was in the predicament of restraining an ally, while deterring and reassuring its rivals.

From a decision making perspective, the most important outcome of this meeting was the creation of a new interagency group to study the situation: the Offshore Islands Working Group. It existed during this crisis only, from June 21 to July 17, and its meetings were not on any set schedule. Participants included the full range of agencies; the individuals who actually attended seemed to vary by meeting, but the key players were Harriman and Hilsman from State, Nitze from Defense, Cline from the CIA, and Forrestal from the NSC staff. Actual attendance at the meetings was reportedly not very good. The Working Group's story is similar to that of the Planning Group (1961) or Standing Groups (1962 and 1963). It was added as a formal committee to give some interagency backbone to the informal process. Though created with a serious purpose, it was ultimately not taken very seriously.[94]

Over the next few days, the administration moved into high gear. On June 21, Eisenhower was briefed on the situation at his home in Gettysburg, PA. He agreed that the US should deter China from attacking the Offshore Islands, but when asked what his administration's position had been on ROC forces returning to the mainland, he rather unhelpfully "replied that the policy of his Administration was to avoid the question."[95] In a memo to Kennedy, also on June 21, Ball laid out a strategy for dealing with the Soviets and sending a clear message to PRC leaders. Kennedy gave Ball permission for Harriman to contact the Soviet ambassador to the US, Anatoly Dobrynin. On June 22, at Harriman's house, Harriman conveyed the basic parameters of US policy to the Soviet ambassador: deterrence of PRC action against the Offshore Islands and Taiwan, and US opposition to ROC actions against the mainland. Harriman was frank about that deterrent:

> Mr. Khrushchev should understand our treaty with the GRC and I referred to the dangerous situation arising from any aggressive action on the part of the ChiComs. With an air of surprise, he commented "you wouldn't help defend the off-shore islands?" I replied, "why not?" "But these islands are Chinese territory," he asserted. I said we believed in peaceful settlement of differences but we could not stand by if the ChiComs took aggressive action.

On the same day, Harriman gave the UK ambassador to the US the same message and explicitly asked the UK to send that message to Beijing.[96]

Most importantly, on June 23, US ambassador to Poland John Moors Cabot met with Chinese ambassador Wang Bingnan in an unscheduled meeting of the Warsaw channel, now in its seventh year of on-again-off-again ambassadorial communications.[97] In response to Wang's complaints about ROC actions, Cabot sent the critical message straight to Beijing.

> I said that I was authorized to state that US Government had no intention of supporting any GRC attack on Mainland under existing circumstances. I pointed out GRC committed not to attack without our consent. I then noted ChiCom military build-up opposite Taiwan and said if this defensive, it was unobjectionable. However, I invited his side's attention to our formal treaty with GRC and to 1955 resolution re defense of Taiwan and Pescadores. I said that any effort to take off-shore islands would require major military operation which could not be easily limited and in such event there was serious danger US forces would become involved.[98]

Having sent messages to China through intermediaries (the USSR and UK) and through the Warsaw talks (as direct a contact as current US-PRC relations allowed), the issue might seem to have been settled.

Kennedy, however, had one more task to perform, and it concerned public opinion in the US and the impact of this crisis on overall US-PRC relations as well as China representation. On June 26, an NSC meeting considered a range of topics related to the upcoming UN General Assembly session. This meeting was the first time that representation was addressed at a formal NSC meeting. Stevenson felt that Chiang's talk of retaking the mainland was the type of rhetoric that would complicate US efforts to keep the ROC in the UN. He suggested a proposed public statement in which Kennedy declared officially that the US "had no intention of supporting Chiang's attack on the Mainland." No further discussion of Stevenson's ideas exists on the record.[99]

The next day, at a June 27, 1962 press conference, Kennedy finessed his way through the complexity of the situation. He noted the PRC buildup of troops and stated clearly that the US was strongly against the use of force in the area. It would, however, continue to uphold the Formosa resolution of 1955—the US would defend Taiwan and the Pescadores. Kennedy also added that the US would defend Quemoy and Matsu if attacks on the Offshore Islands were part of a larger attack on Taiwan and the Pescadores. This framing left the administration wiggle room not to use force to defend attacks on the Offshore Islands only. In this way, Kennedy followed the politically safest route—remaining faithful to Eisenhower's policy. He even quoted Secretary of State John Foster Dulles to make his point. What Kennedy left out was perhaps more important than what he included. He did not say what the administration had decided—that the US would not and could not support any ROC actions against the mainland. That would surely bring the China lobby out in full force. In response to a question asking about US policy if the ROC tried to "return to the mainland," Kennedy again said that his policies were not a shift from the past. A second question speculated on whether the 1954 understanding that the ROC would not take any military action against the mainland without US consent was still in effect. Kennedy reiterated that "no such action as you mention would take place without the agreement of the United States and I have indicated that our interest in this area is defensive, and we would like to have a renunciation of the use of force."[100]

Chiang interpreted the lack of public statements on his requests for assistance as permission to continue lobbying the US for support and approval for initiating small probing operations onto the mainland, missions that were easily crushed by the PLA.[101] The US was akin to a parent who said "no ice cream, no ice cream, no ice cream, okay, try some different flavors and tell me which you like best, but that doesn't mean we're getting ice cream."

Analysis

In contrast to the UN representation case, the 1962 decision on Taiwan's hopes to return to the mainland fits the evolution-balance model: consideration of the problem at a cabinet-level interagency meeting on June 20, a brief discussion of it at an NSC meeting on June 27, and the establish-ment of the Offshore Islands Working Group. Like the Standing Groups, the latter was created to add a more formal interagency structure to the process, but then was generally ignored. In terms of policy, the interna-tional and domestic political pressures had to be fine-tuned by the admin-istration, a search for the sweet spot between showing a commitment to Taiwan and an unwillingness to be drawn into a war in China. That mes-sage had to be sent to all major players in the area: Taiwan, China, and the USSR, while leaving enough ambiguity for the US public and the China lobby to believe that the US might support ROC actions against the mainland. The bottom line for the administration here was its belief that support for ROC action would be another Bay of Pigs disaster, a replay of the administration's greatest international and domestic failure.[102] The administration had been burned once by grand ideas of small forces insti-gating a large revolution that overthrows a supposedly tottering regime; a war across the Taiwan Strait promised to be an ever-larger fire. Though not explicitly mentioned in meetings, all participants must have known that a ROC-led debacle in October 1962, whether the US supported or did not support an intervention, might spell doom for Democrats in the 1962 midterms. Table 9.1 summarizes the structured-focused comparison questions for this case study.

Conclusion

The conclusions from this chapter will ultimately be used to compare presidencies in the last chapter of this book. First, the original evolution model does a better job of illustrating the patterns in the Chinese repre-sentation case; the evolution-balance model does a better job of explaining the Return to the Mainland case. The most logical reason for this differ-ence is timing; ideas for adding more formality only became serious in 1962. The 1961 representation issue was decided before Bundy had been able to convince Kennedy that more formal structures might be needed. By the time the administration was considering Chiang's planned inva-sion of the mainland, the Standing Group was in the works; Kennedy was already more amenable to adding some level of formality to the process, formality seen in the 1962 Taiwan decision. It is noteworthy that Chinese representation itself was discussed at an NSC meeting in 1962, but not in 1961 when it was of far more critical importance. Second, as in the case of the overall process, Kennedy's spokes-of-the-wheel system still defined the administration's style. The consistency of Kennedy's preferences explains the low level of adaptation. The fact that Kennedy himself did not and possibly could not change his views on decision making lends weight to the idea that presidential management style is the one constant in a volatile domestic, international, and administrative setting. The question of whether institutional factors or the idiosyncratic character of the individual president exert the most influence over decision making is answered here decidedly in favor of the latter.

Third, the actual substance of Kennedy's China policy illustrates the impact of institutional forces. Kennedy may have insisted on making decisions his way, but the decisions he made on China were shaped by the international and domestic political pressures on the administration. In spite of being advised by the State Department that he should consider a two-China solution and his own conclusion that the US nonrecognition policy toward the PRC was irrational, Kennedy refused to buck the China lobby and its friends in Congress. In 1962, Kennedy also played the cautious game as Chiang lobbied for US support of his intervention plans. Kennedy would try to keep the ROC from taking provocative action, but in deference to Chiang's allies in the China lobby, Kennedy never said "No" to Chiang explicitly.

Kennedy's assassination meant that any decision making changes or strategic innovations that might have evolved over a second term would never arrive. His death left Lyndon Johnson with an informal system designed for Kennedy's needs and a China policy solidly supporting the status quo inherited from Eisenhower.

FIVE

～ Lyndon B. Johnson
"Energy in the Executive"

"Energy in the Executive is a leading character in the definition
of good government."
—Alexander Hamilton, *Federalist* 70[1]

Lyndon Johnson was a force of nature, in possession of an elemental political power to persuade, seduce, intimidate, or coerce individuals and institutions until he gained mastery over them. Once in control, he found the
right angle of leverage to make a deal and achieve his goals, often convincing his opponents that they were reaching their goals at the same moment.
White House staffer Joseph Califano put it this way:

> The Lyndon Johnson I worked with was brave and brutal, compas-
> sionate and cruel, incredibly intelligent and infuriatingly insensitive,
> with a shrewd and uncanny instinct for the jugular of his adversar-
> ies. He could be altruistic and petty, caring and cruel, generous and
> petulant, blatantly honest and calculatingly devious—all within the
> same few minutes.[2]

Johnson's second secretary of defense, Clark Clifford, an old hand of Democratic politics going back to the Truman administration, described Johnson as "the most complex man I ever met . . . on occasion, he reminded
me of a powerful, old-fashioned locomotive roaring unstoppably down the
track."[3] Bill Moyers, a White House staffer who had a father-son relationship with Johnson, noted the ferocity and generosity of the Johnson art
of management by calling him "thirteen of the most interesting and difficult men I ever met."[4] Johnson had clear preferences in his decision mak-

117

ing style, using cabinet officers and their departments often in a formal way and his staff of White House loyalists in a more ad-hoc manner that demanded absolute loyalty and obedience. On the use of that staff, Johnson remarked, "I was determined to make them more dependent on me than I was on them."[5] Whether delegation or dominance, Johnson's administrative strategies were designed to give him ownership of decision making. That drive took its toll on every member of the administration. George Reedy, who began working for Johnson as a Senate staffer in 1951, then as a White House assistant until 1966 and then again in 1968, explained his reasons for finally writing a memoir about Johnson in 1982: "For nearly two decades, he was the physically dominant force in my life. What I discovered after leaving him was that geographical, social, and political separation did not put an end to his presence. Even dead, he remained a force. What is happening here is an effort to get some things off my chest. In a very real sense, this is an exercise in exorcism."[6] No staffers or advisors could defend themselves against Johnson's overwhelming overwhelmingness.

The fundamental reality of life in the administration was Johnson's need to manipulate all the people around him and to push them in every manner imaginable until he got what he wanted. It was called the "Johnson Treatment," and everyone who came in contact with Johnson during his political run knew exactly what that treatment felt like, with one exception: Secretary of State Dean Rusk. In his memoirs, Rusk explained Johnson and their relationship: "Johnson was the most dynamic man I ever knew, simply overpowering at times. And he knew where his opponent's vulnerable points were, when to appeal seductively, and when to apply pressure. Fortunately, LBJ never used the 'treatment' on me; he never had to!"[7] Rusk's status as first among equals was at the core of the Johnson foreign policy process.

Johnson's initial decision making structure had four key elements. First, Johnson came to office in the most tragic way, as a vice president replacing an assassinated president. During that transition, Johnson decided to retain Kennedy's advisors and in many ways Kennedy's system: centered on the president, State Department-led, backstopped by an important but deferent national security advisor—McGeorge Bundy until late 1966, and then Walt Rostow—leading a professional NSC staff. Second, Johnson's system is often described as formalistic, a clear departure from Kennedy's more freewheeling approach. Johnson's style, however, was based on informal elements much closer to Kennedy than to Eisenhower in in its structure, in particular in Johnson's reliance, like Kennedy, on face-to-face consultations with his key advisors. If Johnson was more formal than Kennedy, that formalism was rooted in Johnson's decision to rely on his cabinet-level advisors for their specific areas of expertise, rather than build a larger collegial mix of generalists and experts at cabinet and subcabinet levels. Also like Kennedy, Johnson downplayed the NSC, instead using cabinet-level meetings to reach his goal: producing consensus. Third, Johnson delegated key foreign policy issues to Rusk and the State Department. Johnson and Rusk shared a southern background, an often poor one at that. In an administration populated by Kennedy's men—sons of the wealthy Northeastern aristocracy—Johnson and Rusk, initially outsiders, became extremely close. Fourth, the White House staff and NSC staff functioned as Johnson's loyal extra eyes and ears on foreign policy, similar to the Kennedy administration.

The role of the president was one of deep involvement; when LBJ turned his attention to foreign policy he grabbed it with both hands and wrestled with it twenty-four hours a day. Decision making still resembled the spokes of a wheel, placing Johnson at the center of everything. Ultimately, he wanted absolute control of the process, more like a whip pushing a bill through Congress than a president deciding foreign policy. Johnson's energy and brilliance allowed him to function as his own chief of staff, more hands-on than any president since FDR. The organizational dynamics in the administration were stable. No major rivalries occurred. The senior members of the administration continued to operate as a team, just as they had during the Kennedy administration. Rusk and the State Department were never seriously challenged by Bundy and the NSC staff.

The informal structure was based in the Tuesday Lunch Group (TLG)—a weekly meeting of initially only Johnson, Rusk, Secretary of Defense Robert McNamara, and Bundy. It is typically seen as an informal version of the NSC, composed of principals, but no staff. Though Johnson was the ultimate decision maker, the TLG was the place where policy consensus was created at the senior level. The TLG was created very early on in the administration (in February 1964, about ten weeks after Johnson was sworn in). This quick evolution of an informal structure and its centrality to the interagency process may reflect the unique nature of the administration—late 1963 to early 1964 was the beginning of the administration's third year in office. Only the president was new. Johnson's confidence structure initially had two levels, Rusk as the official he trusted explicitly more than any other, and several staffers, most prominently Bill Moyers, who gave him the loyalist view of foreign policy.

The balancing and compensating came in 1966 and 1967 with two reforms. Each confirms the evolution-balance model. As the model predicts, both changes added formal structures to an administration dominated by informality. The origins of each were rooted in a consensus among Johnson's advisors that too much informality was causing major problems. First, the administration created a formal interagency process through the Senior Interagency Group/Interdepartmental Regional Group (SIG/IRG) system, a semi-resurrection of the Eisenhower NSC architecture. The SIG/IRG had three main goals: to redesign the foreign policy system in an explicitly hierarchical manner; to institutionalize the formal participation of all the relevant agencies; and to place routine matters under the State Department and its regional assistant secretaries. The SIG/IRG system, however, never became the backbone of a formal interagency process. It was generally ignored by Johnson, not connected to the NSC itself, and underused by Rusk. As in the case of Kennedy, Johnson could not change his own style to conform to a bottom-up process. Second, the TLG became a potent semiformal structure when Rostow became assistant to the president for national security affairs (ANSA) in April 1966. Rostow quickly became a crucial element of Johnson's confidence structure. Through that influence, he was able to persuade Johnson to add formality to the TLG. Its agendas became more detailed; extensive readout was the norm; and it evolved into a committee that in effect was a working NSC, minus full staff presence.

The evolution-balance model predicts that the president or his chief advisors will identify the weaknesses in the system the president prefers and then try to compensate for them. Both the SIG/IRG and Rostow's TLG were exactly those types of balancing innovations. Table 9.2 illustrates the evolution of Johnson's overall process and China decisions through the lens of the structured-focused comparison questions. Figure 5.1 is a Johnson-specific diagram of the overall process based on figure 2.2.

Initial Decision Making Process

Scholars often argue that it is impossible to think about Johnson's foreign policy without focusing on Vietnam. The war consumed every aspect of the foreign and domestic agenda, every advisor, and Johnson himself.[8] While the standard tale of the Kennedy administration is one of heroism and heartbreak, the Johnson administration was of Shakespearean dimensions, beginning and ending in tragedy, where the best of intentions led to futile war, an ever-escalating spiral of deceit, and the political and personal destruction of a president. A study of policies on China overlaps with the Vietnam War for obvious reasons. A look at Johnson's standard process,

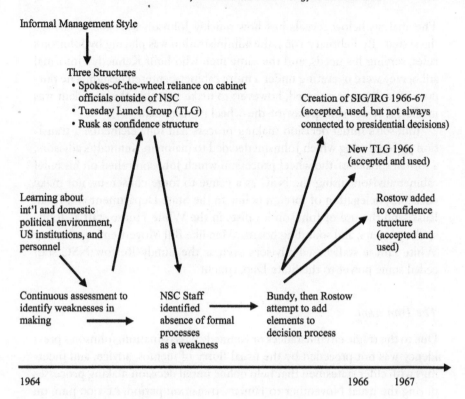

Informal Management Style

Three Structures
- Spokes-of-the-wheel reliance on cabinet officials outside of NSC
- Tuesday Lunch Group (TLG)
- Rusk as confidence structure

Creation of SIG/IRG 1966-67
(accepted, used, but not always connected to presidential decisions)

New TLG 1966
(accepted and used)

Learning about int'l and domestic political environment, US institutions, and personnel

Rostow added to confidence structure (accepted and used)

Continuous assessment to identify weaknesses in making

NSC Staff identified absence of formal processes as a weakness

Bundy, then Rostow attempt to add elements to decision process

1964   1966   1967

NSC – National Security Council
SIG/IRG – Senior Interagency Group/Interdepartmental Regional Group

Fig. 5.1. The Evolution of Johnson Administration Decision Making

however, must be careful not to equate Vietnam decision making with Johnson's decision making overall. The war was not the entirety of the administration's responsibilities in foreign policy.

Initially, Johnson administration decision making procedures were those inherited from Kennedy. However, morbid as it may be, the first year of Johnson's administration provides a case study to assess the importance of a president. An entire administration suddenly had a new leader. While all processes and personnel remained the same, the occupant of the Oval Office had changed. Did it make a difference? If so, then idiosyncratic models are accurate: the man makes the administration. If not, institutional models have a stronger case: Kennedy and Johnson as leaders are footnotes; once an internal decision making system is established within a given political environment, it defines the process no matter who leads.

The analysis below reveals just how quickly Johnson was able to change the system. By February 1964, the administration was playing by Johnson's rules, serving his needs, and the same men who built Kennedy's informal adhocracy were operating under a more cabinet-centered design. The purpose of it all never wavered, however: to make sure that the president was in charge. It was still spokes-of-the-wheel management.

Johnson's initial decision making process had four elements: a transition period during which Johnson decided to maintain Kennedy's advisors; a formal spokes-of-the wheel process in which Johnson relied on his chief cabinet advisors, using the NSC as a venue to forge consensus, not make decisions; delegation of foreign policy to the State Department and Dean Rusk; and the use of Johnson loyalists in the White House staff as Johnson's eyes, ears, and sounding boards. Men like Bill Moyers emerged as key White House staff-based advisors even as the Bundy/Rostow NSC staff ceded some power to the State Department.

The Transition

Due to the tragic circumstances of Kennedy's assassination, Johnson's presidency was not preceded by the usual flurry of memos, advice, and meetings with elder statesmen that help define initial decision making processes during the usual November to January transition period. At 1:00 p.m. on November 22, 1963, the death of President Kennedy was officially pronounced; less than two hours later Johnson was sworn in. He immediately decided to keep Kennedy's advisors until after the 1964 election, signifying continuity and maintaining stability; to that end he met with the entire cabinet, asking them to stay on.[9] Politically, Johnson would fulfill Kennedy's term as the understudy, not making waves of his own until after he was elected president in his own right. Rusk had been on his way to Japan with several other cabinet members. Just west of Hawaii they heard the news of the assassination and headed back to the US. Rusk met with Johnson the next day, November 23, and offered to submit his resignation, effective as soon as Johnson could identify his own hand-picked replacement. Johnson would have none of it and told Rusk to stay.[10] On the same day Bundy also sent in a draft resignation letter, undated, for Johnson to use in case he wanted to make a change at the NSC staff.[11]

Though he maintained the Kennedy team, Johnson and his advisors understood that the new president would ultimately use them and the existing decision making structures differently. Johnson met with Clark Clifford for five hours on November 27 to discuss management of the White

House. Later that day, Johnson gave his first major address to a joint session of Congress. His intentions were to introduce himself as the new president of the nation, to reassure a shaken public, and to stress the strength of US institutions at a time of crisis. The speech was written by Theodore Sorensen, one of Kennedy's closest confidants, along with Johnson's newly elevated staffers, all of them trying to translate the Kennedy style to a Johnson style.[12] Johnson added his own White House staffers, his own loyalists, bit by bit through 1964. In effect, the Johnson White House had a two-tiered staff system of Kennedy men and Johnson men until the Kennedy men left.[13] All understood that there would be a period of transition and that the new president would eventually develop his own decision making style. They also understood that the task was daunting. The administration had to deal with all the current domestic and foreign policy issues and crises that were already on the table before Kennedy's assassination, prepare for the challenge of adapting the administration for the new president, and gear up for the presidential election of 1964. To that end, in mid-December Bundy asked Rostow, then chair of the State Department's Policy Planning Council, "for ideas on how the policy planning process might be tied to the evolving style of the new President."[14] It is unclear if "policy planning process" refers to the entire advisory process or just aspects tied to Rostow's team. In any case, Bundy recognized that Johnson was different from Kennedy and everyone within the administration had to be prepared to make adjustments. For Johnson, the ultimate dilemma was serving in Kennedy's shadow, even as he assumed command. He was well aware that he would forever be compared to Kennedy and hoped to lay a foundation for the nation to accept the new leadership and new style. In preparation for an interview with Roscoe Drummond, a syndicated columnist whose writing appeared under the byline "State of the Nation" in dozens of newspapers, NSC executive secretary Bromley Smith submitted to Johnson a memo of talking points on January 31, 1964. Smith suggested that Johnson emphasize that "each President works differently. . . . President Kennedy did his work in one way. I will be doing mine in my way." Smith felt Johnson should emphasize that "each President has a shakedown period. The most effective system is rapidly developing. It will take final form shortly and as needs become apparent with the passage of time."[15]

Informality, Formality and Consensus

While Kennedy's management is seen as the epitome of collegiality, Johnson is viewed as a formalistic manager by most scholars.[16] This seems to contradict the notion that both presidents used a spokes-of-the-wheel style and that Johnson's advisors urged him to add more formal elements. The Kennedy and Johnson systems were similar in two ways. Both men placed themselves at the center of the process, determined to make their own choices, and both refused to use the NSC as a true decision making body. Kennedy's NSC was for information purposes only if it was used at all. Johnson's NSC was a vehicle for building and enforcing consensus, often not even for advice; fear of leaks meant that the relatively large size of the NSC and attendance by those below the cabinet level made it a poor setting for serious deliberation of issues. His style has been characterized as formalistic because it established a hierarchy in place of Kennedy's more free-wheeling collegial process. Johnson sought advice from the cabinet-level advisors of the key bureaucracies (State, Defense, the CIA, the Joint Chiefs of Staff, and NSC staff), rather than reaching down to lower levels of the administration. In that sense, it was a formalistic style in that it sought full interagency participation, but only at the highest levels of the bureaucracies. Actual decisions were made in the informal Tuesday Lunch Group, which had its first meeting on February 4, 1964. The TLG rather than the formal NSC was the main venue for decision making. That swift evolution to a TLG process is detailed below in the section on informal structure.

This deemphasis on the NSC was explained by Bundy in 1965: "The NSC as a formal council has had even less to do under President Johnson than it did under President Kennedy."[17] In preparation for the first NSC meeting of December 5, 1963, Bundy provided Johnson with talking points:

> Not all the work of National Security can be done in meetings of this Council, and I expect to go on with special meetings for special purposes, but I do plan to use this Council from time to time as a forum in which these matters can be examined. I welcome candid and open expressions of views and differences of opinion, and they also welcome the opportunity which these meetings give for making my own positions clear.[18]

Johnson used the NSC for the latter purpose (giving his opinions) more than the former purpose (candid and open expression of views). At that first meeting Johnson reiterated Bundy's talking points: the NSC would not be the center of decision making.[19] The downgrading of Eisenhower's vision of the NSC had survived its first institutional test; a second president reaffirmed its reduced importance at his very first NSC meeting.

Johnson's reasons for de-emphasizing the NSC included the typical complaints about the NSC and one unique circumstance. First, Johnson felt the NSC was too formal, not the venue where actual candid viewpoints could be shared, in spite of what he may have suggested at the first meeting. That formality meant that attendance at the meetings would grow; more officials would argue for invitations and all of them would want to bring their key staffers. This tendency was evident to Johnson at the first meeting. He had wanted to have an NSC meeting on the day after Kennedy's death, but several of his cabinet officials, Rusk included, had not yet returned to Washington. Hoping to have a full meeting at his very first NSC, Johnson delayed the meeting for two weeks. Forty people attended the meeting.[20] All the senior decision makers—Johnson, Rusk, McNamara, and Bundy— felt the size of the NSC precluded real open debate and discussion. Rusk's reticence, described in the previous chapter, may have been an extreme case, but all the senior officials shared his concern to a certain degree. The inclusion of subcabinet-level officials and staff meant that NSC meetings could never be a place where the president and his top advisors could really brainstorm, or think out loud, or disagree with each other.[21] After the first three NSC meetings, Johnson asked Bundy to reduce the attendance at the next meeting, scheduled for March 5, 1964. Bundy and White House special assistant Jack Valenti developed lists of people who might be invited to an NSC meeting depending on the subject matter; Johnson reviewed the list for each meeting and decided who should be invited.[22] Meetings generally were attended by anywhere from 12 to over 30 attendees.[23] To say that Johnson disliked leaks is a vast understatement; he was obsessed with them. A large NSC might stifle frank dialogue, but even worse, a large NSC with staff and backbenchers was prone to leaks. Johnson described it best in his own words: "The National Security Council meetings were like sieves. I couldn't control them. You knew after the National Security Council meeting that each of those guys would run home to tell his wife and neighbors what they said to the President."[24]

A second feature of Johnson's NSC was atypical (but not as atypical as many imagine). The US government had no vice president between November of 1963 and January 1965. Until the ratification of the 25th Amendment on February 10, 1967, the US had no procedure for replacing a vice president.[25] Hubert Humphrey did not become Johnson's vice president until January 20, 1965. To prevent a possible succession crisis in case Johnson could no longer serve as president, a serious concern for a man who had suffered his first heart attack in 1955, the administration invited Speaker of the House of Representatives John McCormick to all

NSC meetings. In the absence of a vice president, McCormick, a Democrat from Massachusetts, was first in line of succession to the presidency. McCormick was not happy about the situation and tried to sit against the wall with the staff during the first meeting. Johnson forced him to sit in the traditional vice president spot, next to the president. The two carried out this same dance each meeting, McCormick trying to hide in plain sight and being forced reluctantly to move center stage each meeting.[26] McCormick's presence was not simply a quirk; it was a serious issue for the administration. A member of the legislative branch had a seat at the table of a key decision making body of the executive branch. If Johnson worried about the separation of powers or the tendency for Congress to leak, the NSC would certainly be handicapped in its ability to address serious national security issues. Bundy realized the problem quickly and also knew that any adjustments made to deal with the situation set precedents for the administration. In a March 1964 meeting with the White House staff, he explained that certain topics would be off limits for discussion at NSC meetings, perhaps indefinitely: "This being the case, it seems the NSC can play no crucial role until after the election at least, and by then the pattern will have been set to live without it, assuming the president is reelected."[27]

Bundy summed up Johnson's view: "Scheduled NSC meetings drove him crazy. He liked the NSC as an instrument for placing the great seal on a decision he'd already made, or making it perfectly clear that he was in the process of making a great decision. I never saw him make a decision in that [body] and I'm not sure any president does."[28] In fact, there was no set schedule for NSC meetings until the spring of 1966.[29] A look at the frequency of NSC meetings under Johnson shows a similar pattern to Kennedy, with early interest in using the NSC fading over time (see table 5.1). After holding five meetings from December 1963 to March 1964, Johnson increased the number of meetings to 18 from April to September, an average of three per month. One analysis of this increase suggests that this was a response to Eisenhower's criticism of Johnson's sporadic use of the NSC. More meetings may have been to inoculate the administration from these charges during the 1964 election campaign.[30] During the latter part of 1964, immediately before and after the election, from October to December, the administration held one NSC meeting. From January 1965 to June 1966, NSC meetings were held on average once per month. Seventeen of the 18 meetings during this period concerned Vietnam and seven of them were held from January 1965 to March 1965, a crucial period when the US began bombing North Vietnam in a systematic way through Operation Rolling Thunder and US troops began their first major deployment

TABLE 5.1. Committee Meetings of the Johnson Administration

Date (by Quarter)	National Security Council (NSC)	Tuesday Lunch Group (TLG)	Senior Interagency Group (SIG)
December 1963	1	0	N/A
January–March 1964	4	5	N/A
April–June 1964	10	12	N/A
July–September 1964	8	9	N/A
October–December 1964	1	1	N/A
January–March 1965	7*	4	N/A
April–June 1965	3*	5 or 11***	N/A
July–September 1965	2*	8	N/A
October–December 1965	0	0	N/A
January–March 1966	2*	5	4
April–June 1966	4*	3	7
July–September 1966	2	9	3
October–December 1966	2	3	0
January–March 1967	2	11	2
April–June 1967	3	17/18	0
July–September 1967	4	11	5
October–December 1967	4	11	6
January–March 1968	5	16	5
April–June 1968	4	16	6
July–September 1968	3	10	3
October–December 1968	3**	15****	5

Sources: NSC Meetings: Clinton administration, National Security Council Archives, https://clinton-whitehouse4.archives.gov/media/pdf/Johnson_Admin.pdf. TLG Meetings: President Lyndon B. Johnson's Daily Diary Collection, LBJL, http://www.lbjlibrary.net/collections/daily-diary.html; National Security Files, Files of Walt W. Rostow, Box 1, LBJL; and David Humphrey, "Tuesday Lunch at the Johnson White House," *Diplomatic History* 8, no. 1 (Winter 1984): 82–88. SIG Meetings: NSF, Agency File, State, Department of State Senior Interdepartmental Group, Box 56, LBJL; and Folder title list, National Security Files, Agency Files, Folder title list, LBJL, https://www.discoverlbj.org/item/ftl-nsf-agency

* All NSC meetings during these quarters focused on Vietnam except for one (June 9, 1966; the topic was "India, Nuclear Weapons").

** None in December 1968.

*** Lower number indicated meetings with just the four core TLG members; higher number includes Tuesday "off the record" meetings that also included 6–9 additional advisors.

**** Includes January 1969 (two meetings).

to Vietnam.[31] Meetings from 1966 through 1968 will be discussed below in the section on balancing and compensating. All told, 93 people attended various meetings of the NSC, a rotating roster that did not lend itself to building a collegial body of decision makers. Early on Johnson deliberately or inadvertently sent a message about the insignificance of NSC meetings. He arrived late for meetings, missing more than half the meeting in many cases, a clear indication that he did not see them as a crucial aspect of the decision making process.[32] Meetings held after the creation of the SIG/IRG system and Rostow's replacement of Bundy as ANSA took on a different character.

Johnson used his formal decision making structures as a method for building and enforcing consensus. The NSC became a place for Johnson to broker that consensus and manipulate his advisors into approving the decisions he had already made outside the NSC.[33] White House staffer Richard Goodwin describes meetings on foreign and domestic policy this way: "The purpose of the meeting was not deliberation, but to enforce unanimity. And all the participants knew it, knew also that Johnson would let them know what 'decision' they were supposed to decide."[34] Johnson's need for control meant that he did not want conflict or bureaucratic rivalry; dissent against the prevailing views and Johnson's wishes was a risky choice for any advisor. He did want alternative opinions, but there might be a price to pay for those who pushed those alternative opinions too far. In particular, Johnson wanted debate to end once he made the decision. After he had made up his mind, further discussion was seen as disloyalty.[35] Scholars often use the Johnson administration, particularly its Vietnam decisions, as examples of the danger of "groupthink," where Johnson's desire for consensus was so strong that other senior officials felt enormous pressure to agree with him.[36] Though Johnson did want consensus, he did ask Rusk and Bundy to make sure he received alternative opinions. Famously, he used Undersecretary of State for Political Affairs George Ball as a "devil's advocate" during critical decisions on Vietnam in 1965, specifically giving Ball the task of challenging the consensus that had emerged on escalating the US presence in the war.[37]

Much of what has been described above indicates that Johnson was as informal a decision maker as Kennedy and that these informal elements are defining aspects of Johnson's administration. Where Johnson is described as formalistic is in his relationship with his key advisors. Johnson believed in a chain of command and a decision making hierarchy. He relied on his formally defined cabinet advisors in foreign policy and saw each as the expert and chief advisor in their issue areas. From this perspective, some scholars see Johnson's style to be nearly as formalistic as Eisenhower's.[38] An NSC staff assessment of the process written by Harold Saunders, however, emphasized the informality, placing Johnson closer to Kennedy than Eisenhower, the two extremes of informality and formality, respectively:

> President Johnson is between the two extremes I've described but much closer to Kennedy than to Eisenhower. There is, of course, the obvious historical fact the President Johnson developed his system from what he inherited from President Kennedy. But there is the far more important fact that President Johnson, like President Kennedy

in this way, determined to keep his own hand on the foreign policy helm.[39]

In this sense, Johnson did not want to bypass the bureaucracies by relying on the NSC staff; he wanted to manipulate the bureaucracies by managing the cabinet officers directly. Johnson used his NSC staff and White House staff extensively (as described below), but, ultimately, he enforced a hierarchy when it came to dealing with the departments and agencies. He focused on the top and sought counsel from the senior people. This was not a collegial or flat decision making structure. As Bundy describes it, "The President felt it very important to emphasize his cabinet officers against his staff officers. I think he genuinely had two or three reasons for that. One is a real one. He really feels that way. He thinks the cabinet officers are more important than the staff officers."[40] Rusk's assessment of the decision process reinforces this idea: "He believed in the chain of command, delegated extensively, and operated through cabinet officers themselves."[41] The style pleased Rusk. Kennedy often reached down to the lower levels of the State Department, but Johnson never bypassed Rusk.[42] In particular, Johnson had immense respect for Rusk and McNamara. The Johnson-Rusk relationship was a special one and is detailed in the next section. Johnson and McNamara were never as close, but Johnson described McNamara "as the ablest man I ever met," stating flatly "that man with the Sta-Comb in his hair is the best of the lot."[43] Johnson did use staff as his eyes and ears in much the same way Kennedy had. The difference was that Johnson did not view the staffers as equals to the cabinet officers: they were his people; their job was to prepare Johnson for dialogue with his cabinet officers, so that when they entered the room Johnson had as much expertise in their issue areas as they did. Even in his interactions with the NSC staff, however, Johnson held fast to a hierarchy, dealing with only the top people, his ANSA and perhaps one or two others, not with individual staff members with regional and functional expertise.[44] This use of staff is detailed below.

Delegation to the State Department

As was the case with Kennedy before him, Johnson wanted State to lead. Johnson's choice of Rusk as his first among equals (detailed in the confidence structure section) allowed the State Department more leeway and arguably more power. This was an across-the-board attempt to reinforce the State Department's authority in foreign policy under the new president. In effect, this reduced the influence of the NSC staff, reversing a trend that had occurred under Kennedy.[45] NSC staffers sat in on Kennedy and Rusk's meetings with foreign officials and therefore had the task of writing the memoranda of conversation for the visit, a position that gives great wiggle room to the drafter to interpret or emphasize as he desires. Johnson ended the practice, pushing the NSC staffers out of the room, and leaving the State Department in charge of documentation.[46] Benjamin Read, the State Department executive secretary, felt that under Johnson there was much less "detailed monitoring" of State Department activity than under Kennedy: "We used to clear things with Mac Bundy and his people which I wouldn't dream of clearing today. . . . And in that sense there's a greater degree of independence and has been under President Johnson from the beginning."[47]

Several of the first National Security Action Memoranda of the administration, the presidential directive series that officially codified presidential decisions, explicitly delegated responsibility to the State Department. NSAM 280 of February 14, 1964 established a coordinating committee for Vietnam. The NSAM states: "After consultation with the Secretary of State, I have designated Mr. William Sullivan of the Department of State to serve as Chairman of this committee, under the direct supervision of the Secretary of State."[48] Sullivan was Rusk's special assistant on South Vietnam at the time. NSAM 281 of February 11, 1964, initially drafted on January 7, 1964, gave the job of drafting national policy papers to the State Department.[49] These papers were long-term planning documents and did not necessarily have any real bearing on the day-to-day operations of foreign policy. The creation of the NSAM, however, showed a desire to enhance the role of the State Department or at least a determination to appear to do so.

The Use of Staff

Johnson's relationships with his more domestic-policy-focused staff are the stuff of legend; his use and abuse of his own White House staff as they replaced the Kennedy men led to resignations and a fascinating set of memoirs brimming with both bitterness and admiration.[50] Two aspects of Johnson's relationship with his staff are particularly relevant: the institutionalization of the upgraded NSC staff and the slow, but certain, inclusion of the White House staff in foreign affairs. Johnson inherited the nimble foreign policy shop in the White House under Bundy that Kennedy had established. Given his intention to rely on his cabinet officers and transfer authority to the State Department, the NSC staff should have been significantly downgraded. Bundy, however, felt that very little had changed during the transition; the NSC staff was only marginally affected. It still operated as it had under Kennedy.[51] For example, Bundy continued to manage paper flow on foreign policy headed for the president. Early in the transition, when State reduced the number of memos and papers headed for the president through the NSC staff, in essence cutting both the NSC staff and Johnson out of the loop on many topics, Bundy quickly reversed the practice by reminding State of his implicit and explicit prerogative. He explained the new institutional muscle of the NSC staff: "We stopped that really I think out of our own bureaucratic strength, and they didn't want to make an issue of this. I just said, 'I'd have to tell the President that he's not getting telegrams that his predecessor got,' and that stopped that."[52] Johnson, like Kennedy, saw the value of the NSC staff as a presidential instrument, something that belonged to him, not the NSC.[53] For that reason, the NSC staff remained a presidential foreign policy group, and Bundy was treated with the deference and advisory impact of a cabinet member.

In general, Johnson used his staff the same way all presidents do, as an extra president-focused source of advice, as eyes and ears of the president seeking information, as a method of oversight to make sure that the bureaucracies are actually faithful to presidential decisions, and to judge the political feasibility of policy. In 1964, Johnson's double staff of Kennedy and Johnson loyalists made its transition to Johnson loyalists alone. Men such as Sorensen, Schlesinger, Pierre Salinger, and Kenneth O'Donnell were replaced by Walter Jenkins, George Reedy, Jack Valenti, and Bill Moyers. The two groups actually differed little in their essential nature. They were all liberal Democrats who moved from various fields into the world of campaigns and Senate staffs. Salinger, Reedy, and Moyers had a journalism background. O'Donnell and Jenkins were career staffers. Schlesinger, Sorensen, and Valenti took detours from other professions—historian, lawyer, and advertising work, respectively—to join the staffs or campaigns of politicians who rallied them to a cause. Even with a preference for the advice of cabinet officers, Johnson still saw himself as the one and only decision maker. In the spokes-of-the-wheel metaphor, this presidential staff served as the grease that allowed the spokes to rotate around the president. Through 1964 and 1965, Bill Moyers, a special assistant to the president (and press secretary from 1965 to 1967), participated more and more in the foreign policy realm. Moyers was interested in foreign affairs and Johnson used him as a source of informal advice on its political aspects. That influence was magnified as he took on more prominent speech-writing tasks. Johnson directed that Moyers should be in the loop for all important foreign policy traffic—memos, reports, and incoming cables from overseas.[54] A memo from September 1965 identifies the officials who would receive the President's Daily Brief, the CIA's morning intelligence briefing. The list included the usual cabinet and chief subcabinet officers, and Moyers.[55] When Bundy decided to leave his post as ANSA in early 1966, Moyers was seriously considered as his replacement.[56] Though passed over for the position, likely because he was too important to Johnson as an all-purpose staffer, he still retained his informal but central impact in foreign policy. For example, in September 1966, CIA director Richard Helms was reporting to Moyers on the president's suspicion that members of the CIA were leaking information to the press.[57]

The Role of the President

Johnson's approach to administration or management was to focus on relationships, not systems or institutions.[58] That fits the style of a former member of the House and Senate. In that sense, Johnson sought command through a hands-on process, in which he controlled all the rewards and punishments; he dominated both decision making and the other decision makers. Incorporating Johnson into the already functioning foreign policy machinery would be the major operation for all Johnson's advisors and holdover staff. To a certain extent, Kennedy and Johnson wanted the same thing—a spokes-of-the-wheel, presidential-centered process. Johnson differed in the level of absolute authority he wanted and the level of micromanaging he was willing to perform. Kennedy wanted to be his own secretary of state, but Johnson was his own chief of staff.[59] Johnson's philosophy was simple: "You know, one of the things that you learn in politics is that most of the people you have working for you are incompetent and as a result you've got to do all of this yourself."[60]

In the policy area, as in the case of civil rights on the domestic side, when Johnson was energized on a subject, he mastered it, and forced his will on the rest of the executive branch (and Congress if necessary). In Johnson's spokes-of-the-wheel system, above all else, Johnson would be making the decisions.[61] Early critics of Johnson argued that he was so inexperienced in foreign policy that his senior advisors, Rusk, McNamara, and Bundy, actually made the decisions. Bundy called that "baloney."[62] When asked if it was true that Johnson had little foreign policy knowledge when he became president, Bundy said that "it is and it isn't." Johnson's leadership position in the Senate (Democratic whip in 1951, minority leader in 1953, majority leader from 1955 to 1961) and years in the vice presidency made him an eyewitness or participant in every foreign policy decision from 1951 to 1963.[63] Both Rusk and Rostow extol Johnson's capacity for learning quickly and his continuously expanding expertise in foreign affairs. In an oral history interview, Rostow even quotes Eisenhower acknowledging that he would not have been able to achieve his foreign policy goals if it had not been for the support of Johnson in the Senate. Eisenhower called Johnson "my strong right arm when I was President."[64] If Johnson had gaps in his knowledge, he worked tirelessly to fill in the holes. He was a "voracious reader," ending each day by reading reports, briefings, and intelligence, everything he could get his hands on. His "night reading," as he called it, would begin at roughly 10:30 p.m. and continue until 1:00 or 2:00 a.m.[65] The amount of reading might be 80–100 memos a night.[66] On foreign policy, Johnson received a constant flow of information from his cabinet departments and agencies, but he also supplemented that channel with memos from Bundy and lower level NSC staffers, such as Robert Komer, a specialist on strategic issues and South Asia, and Alfred Jenkins, a specialist on China.[67] On any subject where he had a strong interest, his information needs could be summed up by one word: more.

Interest and access to information are necessary, but what set Johnson apart may have been his level of energy. He was president every single second of the day. NSC staffer Komer contrasted Kennedy and Johnson this way: "Kennedy almost deliberately turned off the hearing aid when he left the Oval Office. LBJ—completely different. He lived the Presidency seven days a week, 24 hours a day. . . . He really loved it."[68] During the Dominican intervention of 1965, the Six-Day War of 1967, the Soviet invasion of Czechoslovakia in 1968, and throughout the Vietnam War, Johnson grabbed hold of foreign policy and held tight; he micromanaged. Undersecretary of State George Ball even called him the "Dominican desk officer" during the 1965 crisis.[69] Rusk expressed the same sense on Vietnam:

> You see, as far as Viet Nam is concerned. President Johnson was his own desk officer. He was actually the Commander-in-Chief. This was a great preoccupation with him so that every detail of the Viet Nam matter was a matter of information to the President, and the decisions on Viet Nam were taken by the President.[70]

Memoirs and scholarship on Johnson all give the same impression of his indisputable energy; men half his age could not keep up with him.[71] He slept roughly four hours per night; Rusk wrote that this constant energy level and need for action may have stemmed from the experience of his heart attack in 1955: "He was a driven man, a president in a hurry, partly because he never knew from one day to the next if he would still be alive the following day."[72] Johnson was legendary for having discussions with staffers that continued while he used the bathroom or while he took a shower. He generally had a White House staffer in his bedroom with him, going over various items until he finally fell asleep.[73]

Bundy noted that on many other noncrisis topics Johnson decided on his own internal timetable and sometimes did not decide at all. He lamented Johnson's "greatest executive weakness . . . He excessively delayed things that were not critical because when he got into a problem at all, he was obsessive about getting into it all the way, keeping all the threads in his own hand." Bundy lamented "the number of things that the President would neither decide nor let anyone else decide." In general, Bundy felt that in the administration Johnson "decided what was ready for decision. His notion of what was ready for decisions would be almost anybody else's view of over-ready for decision."[74] In this sense, Johnson's hands-on management could obstruct rather than facilitate in cases when the need for action was not immediate.

On an interpersonal level, Johnson was legendary for the famous "Johnson treatment," where manipulation was accomplished through a mix of fawning persuasion, single-minded, inexhaustible lobbying, and intimidation, both psychological and physical.[75] The treatment was used on cabinet officers as well as on members of Congress, but staffers bore the worst of it. The goal was to maximize Johnson's leverage over the aspects of policy he wanted in his hands. That meant control of both policy and people. He wanted absolute loyalty and often used brutal means of rewards and punishment to guarantee that loyalty. The words staffers used to describe how Johnson enforced that loyalty included "devour," "possess," and "dominate."[76]

To use the spokes-of-the-wheel metaphor, the administration rotated around Johnson and he decided the speed of that rotation. Johnson truly was his own chief of staff. While White House staffers Walter Jenkins (with Johnson since the 1950s, but gone by October 1964), then Marvin Watson, from 1965 to 1968, served as the unofficial chiefs of staff, Johnson was the true center of management. He used access or denial of access to the president as the ultimate reward and punishment.[77] One White House staffer explained that there really was no management in the administration at all and, in effect, its operation should have collapsed, but it did not: "The reason that the chaos of the White House did not often have serious consequences is that basically Lyndon Johnson ran everything."[78]

Organizational Dynamics

The typical rivalry that might form in any administration would be between the secretary of state and either the ANSA-led NSC staff or the Department of Defense. As in the case of the Kennedy administration, organizational rivalry within the Johnson administration was largely absent. This relative bureaucratic harmony derived from four sources: the sense of teamwork that all the senior advisors had already developed before Johnson entered the Oval Office and the continuation of that president-centered collegiality at the senior levels; the dominance of Johnson himself; the access that Johnson gave all the senior advisors; and Johnson's very clear and very well-known choice of Rusk as first among equals. As mentioned above, analyses of the administration often focus not on organizational rivalry, but on the problem of too little debate and argument, the dilemma of groupthink.[79]

First, by the time Johnson assumed the presidency, issues of rivalry and the roles of each department had been ironed out. All the key players saw their priority as serving the president, and each saw teamwork as the method for serving the president well. This amity could have changed when Johnson took office. Ambitious officials and departments that felt they were undervalued might have seen an opportunity to change the nature of the organizational relationships. Johnson, however, benefited from nearly three years of collegial decision making in the Kennedy administration. Secretary of Defense McNamara describes it this way:

> My basic feeling about the relationship between Defense and State is that Defense is a servant of State . . . and that the Secretary of Defense was subordinate to the Secretary of State. And I always made very clear to Dean Rusk that I believed that . . . but also because I admired him immensely.[80]

Rusk echoed this idea, saying that he and McNamara prioritized making sure that their departments worked well together, encouraging communication between the departments at the senior and lower levels. Rusk also claimed that his relationship with McNamara was such that the two men ironed out their differences on their own, "almost never" bringing a disagreement to Johnson for the president to settle. Though Kennedy had elevated the ANSA and NSC staff, these White House-based advisors never usurped the role of the State and Defense Departments. When asked if the NSC staff had ever tried to "block out the views of the Department to the President in any way?" Rusk answered unequivocally: "No, I'm sure that didn't happen." Rusk continued to see the NSC staff as a necessary arm of the presidency, not a rival to State Department prerogatives. He felt the NSC staff "function is indispensable to a President partly because there's such a mass of business that it is important to have, right at the President's elbow, some staff who can help manage the flow of papers."[81] As long as Bundy and the NSC staff were seen as extensions of the president and not independent actors in their own right, they were not seen as rivals to the departments.

A second reason for the lack of rivalry emerges from the first. Johnson's will was so powerful and his dominion in important issue areas so pervasive that organizations focused on pleasing the president, not competing with each other. Another way of characterizing it is to say that competition between departments and agencies, when it existed, consisted of efforts to keep on Johnson's good side and away from his bad side, an exercise in following his orders, performing tasks that he delegated to the department, and embracing whatever he assigned to you or your department. In this sense, the only relevant tensions might have been those between Johnson and anyone who would not bend to his will.

The third reason that organizational rivalry did not become a major factor in the administration reflects the rapid emergence of Johnson's informal and confidence structures. Kennedy's assassination meant that Johnson became president in the administration's thirty-third month. Johnson did not have or need a great deal of time to assess the decision making style and consider how he wanted to proceed. He had been involved in most of the major administration decisions and he knew all the players in the lineup. The evolution of his informal and confidence structures was rapid and helped tamp down organizational rivalry. As detailed below, the creation of the Tuesday Lunch Group, instituted in February 1964, meant that all senior decision makers, Rusk, McNamara, Bundy, and eventually director of Central Intelligence John McCone and Chair of the Joint Chiefs General Earle Wheeler, had direct access to Johnson on a regular basis. That informal process became the glue that kept the group unified.

The fourth reason that organizational rivalry never became a great factor in the administration was Johnson's clear and well-communicated preference for Rusk over his other advisors. That confidence structure, detailed below, mitigated organizational rivalry. It was clear very early on that no official could rival Rusk in the eyes of Johnson and, through Rusk, the State Department had primacy. McNamara's Pentagon may have gained greater prominence when Vietnam made Johnson a wartime president; Bundy may have been an essential tool in helping manage foreign policy for a hands-on executive; Moyers's close relationship with Johnson may have given him a place at the table, literally at the Tuesday Lunch meetings. Ultimately, however, Johnson dominated the decision process and Rusk was the most trusted voice in the administration. No organizational or bureaucratic politics could challenge that.

An additional source of potential rivalry within the administration was the possibility that the administration might have fractured along the lines of Kennedy holdovers vs. Johnson's newly minted staff. Johnson kept Kennedy's people in both cabinet and subcabinet positions and within the White House staff. The White House staffers, such as Sorensen and Schlesinger, soon left, and the departmental officials transferred their loyalty to Johnson. Underneath the smooth transition, however, was some simmering resentment that went in both directions. Kennedy admirers deplored Johnson's crudeness and his non-establishment roots, while Johnson was obsessed with the notion that people saw Robert Kennedy, Johnson's own attorney general, as the real heir to John Kennedy; Johnson was just a placeholder, destined to be a footnote in between Kennedy presidencies.[82] Johnson was paranoid enough about Robert Kennedy that White House assistant and unofficial chief of staff Marvin Watson was ordered to keep a watch out for Kennedy loyalists.[83] Rusk also saw Robert Kennedy as a potential rival, wary of what Rusk described as his "dabblings in foreign policy." He never shook the feeling that Kennedy believed that his brother had chosen the wrong man for secretary of state. Rusk states that the problem of Robert Kennedy's habit of trying to expand his authority into foreign policy increased under Johnson, the opposite of what might be expected.[84] As in the case of other Kennedy men, however, Robert Kennedy left the administration in 1964, announcing his candidacy for a US Senate seat from New York on August 25 and handing in his resignation on September 3. That moved the increasingly vicious rivalry between Johnson and Kennedy to an external electoral, rather than internal administrative, issue.[85]

Development and Use of the Three Structures

The development of Johnson's informal and confidence structures came swiftly, within the first three months of Johnson's tenure in the White House. The evolution model suggested that these changes might take six months to over a year. In Johnson's case, the learning curve had been truncated. By November of 1963 the administration had been making foreign policy decisions for two years; by this time each member had a very good idea of what they wanted and what they did not want. Johnson's informal structure, the Tuesday Lunch Group, first met on February 4, 1964, roughly ten weeks after Johnson's swearing in. His confidence structure had already been formed while he was vice president. Of Kennedy's cabinet officers, Johnson trusted Rusk.

Informal Structure

It may have seemed inconsequential at first, but an entry in Johnson's Daily Diary of February 4, 1964 reading "Lunch with Secy. McNamara, Mr. Bundy, Secy. Rusk" could be seen as the beginning of the real Johnson administration decision making process.[86] What became Johnson's Tuesday Lunch Group can be described in many ways. Both Rusk and NSC staffer Komer called it a "war cabinet"; the earliest journalistic account of the TLG focused almost exclusively on its role in making Vietnam decisions.[87] The TLG, however, was much more than a management tool for running the war. It was Johnson's method for controlling foreign policy and steering the process in the desired direction. Johnson's preference for dealing with his senior cabinet advisors alone, without staff, was perhaps the most important factor in the creation of the TLG. Johnson wanted a place where he and a select few could brainstorm out loud without leaks, gossip, and push back from lower levels, the press, or Congress. Critically, he wanted a place to receive unvarnished advice before he made decisions. Johnson also desired a place to cement consensus; he knew what he wanted and sought advice on how to implement and reinforce it within the executive branch and how to persuade Congress and the American people of its wisdom. Eliminating dissenting voices from the discussion allowed Johnson to move more quickly toward action, rather than get bogged down in debate that would ultimately be irrelevant when Johnson had already made up his mind.[88] Bundy characterized the formation and utility of the TLG in this way:

> It just plain evolved out of a sense of its convenience and the fact that he liked it. It was a comfortable institution and everything else that we'd tried on for size wasn't. . . . The Tuesday lunch had virtues from his point of view. It was an agreeable social occasion. . . . Tuesday lunch didn't commit him to having anything in the presence of anybody that he wasn't comfortable with. It turned out to be a very useful way of sort of cleaning things that he couldn't clean otherwise. It turned out to be the only instrument of staffed com-

munication, oral communication, between him and the Secretary of State that there was, really.[89]

The latter point relates to the Johnson-Rusk relationship and Rusk's reluctance to give his advice to the president in any setting other than a private meeting. The TLG satisfied Rusk's definition of private; he would share his thoughts within the TLG. In this sense, anyone participating in the TLG, and the departments/agencies they represented, received perhaps the only clear glimpse available of the Rusk-Johnson friendship and the ideas they shared.

To Rusk, the TLG was invaluable in the frankness it brought to the principals' discussions and the swiftness with which they could create consensus.

> President Johnson discovered that, at least, that group knew how to keep their mouths shut, whereas in a large meeting of the Cabinet or a large meeting of the National Security Council the chances for leaks to the outside were always present. He knew that he could talk in the most intimate way, the most provisional or tentative way, at that Tuesday Luncheon without having things leak out to the press. . . . We'd have a full discussion, and it was in a relaxed fashion. We could debate with each other, we could expose different points of view, we could look at all the alternatives, we could talk about the attitude of other personalities and individuals such as Senators or leading Congressmen. It was a most valuable institution and made a great difference to the ease of working relationships among those who were carrying the top responsibility.[90]

McNamara echoed these ideas, feeling that the TLG provided

> extremely useful opportunities for the President to exchange views with his key national security advisors . . . to probe intensively the views of each of the participants and for each of them to express their views with a candor that is very difficult for a senior official if his views are being expressed in front of the usual thirty or forty listeners in major national policy discussions.[91]

Bromley Smith, executive secretary of the NSC, also saw the benefits of the TLG for Johnson and the senior advisors, even though he was rarely a participant: "Tuesday luncheon was one of the most valuable pieces of machinery that I've encountered."[92]

The TLG was an extension of Johnson's preferences for making decisions. After becoming Democratic leader in the Senate in 1953, Johnson transformed the Democratic Policy Committee into a similar type of grouping, a legislative branch ancestor to the TLG, where the senior leadership of the Democratic Party could meet informally, without staff, to work on strategy. The committee did not leak, and for Johnson its entire purpose was to build party unanimity by allowing its leaders to create a consensus and then present it to the other members of the Senate as a done deal. That committee also met on Tuesdays for lunch.[93]

Attendance at the TLG varied over time. Clearly, Johnson hoped to keep it small, and the vast majority of meetings fit the classic description: a Tuesday luncheon in the White House family dining room between Johnson, Rusk, McNamara, and Bundy, on a weekly basis, depending on the president's schedule. As time went on, other administration officials joined the meetings, either on a semiregular basis (Chairman of the Joint Chiefs General Earle Wheeler; Directors of Central Intelligence John McCone and Richard Helms; and Special Assistants to the President/Press Secretaries Bill Moyers and George Christian) or on an as-needed basis (Undersecretary of State George Ball, Nicholas deB. Katzenbach as attorney general and undersecretary of state; Special Assistant to the President General Maxwell Taylor; White House Assistant Joseph Califano; Vice President Hubert Humphrey; NSC staffer Komer; NSC Executive Secretary Bromley Smith; Deputy Secretary of Defense Cyrus Vance [sitting in for McNamara or accompanying him]; Assistant Secretary of Defense for International Security Affairs John McNaughton; and members of the Joint Chiefs of Staff). With Walt Rostow's replacement of McGeorge Bundy as national security advisor in April 1966, Rostow became one of the inner core attendees and White House special assistant Tom Johnson became a regular note taker at meetings.[94] The clear goal was to keep the meeting small—the four core members with one or two additional people if needed.

The meetings were somewhat irregular and their pattern tells an interesting tale (see table 5.1). Of the first four meetings in February and March 1964, two were held on Tuesday and two were scheduled for Friday. From March 17 to October 17, 1964 a total of 23 meetings were held. Eleven (48%) of these meetings followed an NSC meeting.[95] Johnson wanted the smaller group to discuss the outcome of the meeting and channel the aftermath in the proper direction. The decision strategy here was similar to the Eisenhower style. Following NSC meetings, Eisenhower selected those whose advice had been most useful and asked them to join him in the Oval Office to fine-tune the policy options.[96] Beyond October, no additional meetings were held for the rest of 1964 as Johnson focused on the 1964 election contest. All told, 27 meetings of the TLG were held in 1964. Rusk, McNamara, and Bundy occasionally met alone earlier in the day to prepare for a TLG session with Johnson.[97] The TLG met less frequently in 1965. The exact number is somewhat unclear. Depending on how meetings are judged, the number is either 17 or 23. The smaller number includes meetings of the core group alone or with one other member. The larger number includes meetings on Tuesdays that included the core group and six to nine additional officials (White House staff, State and Defense Department officials, and Johnson friend and future Supreme Court justice Abe Fortas). Given the size of the meetings, they would not be considered TLG meetings except for two factors. First, the meetings occurred on Tuesdays. Second, the president's Daily Diary entry for the meeting explicitly states "Off the Record," an unusual designation. These larger meetings in May and June 1965 could be viewed as the TLG process getting out of hand; the president hoped to keep them small, but the departments and agencies fought for a place at the table and won the argument. In that sense, the TLG had malfunctioned or ended as its original purpose was undermined by the bureaucracy. The record indicates that Johnson was unhappy with the situation and in June asked Bundy to "get the Tuesday lunches going again."[98] Meetings of just the original TLG members were held from June to September (10 meetings in 16 weeks), but no meetings of either type (the core group or expanded meetings) were held from October to December 1965. Only four were held in the first six months of 1966. Rostow's move into the ANSA position as of April 1, 1966, gave new life to the TLG. It met on average every two weeks from May to December 1966, the bulk over the summer of 1966 (nine from July to September). The 1967–68 TLG was a completely different animal, so different that its characteristics and functions are discussed below as part of the evolution of the administration's decision making and the rebalancing of the process.[99]

From 1964 to 1966 the TLG served, in effect, in the role initially intended for the NSC when it was created in 1947. It was the place where the president could hear the views of his senior advisors, grill them on those views, and map out administration national security and foreign policy.[100] Rusk makes that aspect clear: "During the Johnson years Tuesday luncheons were, in fact, meetings of the National Security Council. . . . We didn't call these luncheons NSC meetings because if we had, twenty-five or thirty staff people would have lined the walls."[101]

Critics of the TLG claimed that it had no agenda and no connection to the departments and agencies. Decisions were made at the meetings and the rest of the executive branch was left in the dark. William Bundy, assistant secretary of State for East Asian and Pacific Affairs, and someone who was not an attendee of the TLG, called it "a procedural abomination—rambling, lacking in a formal agenda or clear conclusions, infinitely wearing to the participants, and confusing to those at the second level who then had to take supporting actions . . . the process was a nightmare."[102] Smith, a supporter of the TLG, understood their frustration: "The staffs of those attending didn't like it. They didn't know what was on the agenda. They did not get full report of everything that took place."[103] The basic dilemma was two-fold: the informal TLG was not designed to connect to any formal system, but even if such a linkage was desired, no formal system existed.

Those who attended or helped staff the TLG claimed it always had an agenda and each member of the group was tasked with informing the departments and agencies of the decisions made at meetings. The initial TLG did not produce a paper trail itself; the written record was left up to each of the principals.[104] The documentary record shows significant staff work between the NSC staff and the Departments of Defense and State beginning in 1966, when Rostow took over the ANSA position. Agendas were prepared; records of decisions were kept; background papers from the departments were distributed. Under Bundy, the documentary record is almost negligible, but participants say that the staffing did occur. Though most scholars and even some nonattendees of the TLG contend that Vietnam dominated the agenda, the record shows that, even if the TLG served as a war cabinet at times, other topics were addressed, particularly if they required immediate attention (for example, NATO troop levels, Indonesia, Rhodesia, F-4 sales to Iran).[105] The memo traffic between Rostow and the departments refers to issues that might be addressed at the TLG because they are "nearly ripe for Tuesday luncheon handling" or others that should remain at the "working level . . . action at lunch will be premature."[106]

Confidence Structure

For administrative and personal reasons, Secretary of State Rusk was the key advisor in the formulation of Johnson's foreign policy from the start. Describing his transition to the presidency, Johnson stated:

> Among the top officials I inherited from President Kennedy were some extraordinary men who served me with fidelity, brilliance, and distinction. That list begins with Dean Rusk . . . he stood by me and shared the President's load of responsibility and abuse. He never

complained. But he was no "yes man." He could be determined and he was always the most determined when he was telling me I shouldn't do something that I felt needed to be done.[107]

First, as detailed above, Johnson's desire to rely on his cabinet guaranteed that Rusk always had Johnson's ear. Johnson himself summed it up this way, comparing his style to Kennedy's: "They say he called the fifth desk officer (in the State Department) about things. I call Rusk."[108] Second, and even more important, perhaps, was Johnson's sense that he and Rusk were the odd men out, poor southerners in an administration filled with wealthy northeasterners established by an even wealthier northeasterner. Rusk even joked that they "would argue which one of us was born in a smaller house."[109] The Johnson-Rusk bond provides an excellent confirmation of the thesis that presidents listen to those advisors they trust the most. It was Rusk himself who issued the now famous quote: "The real organization of government at higher echelons is not what you find in textbooks or organization charts. It is how confidence flows down from the President."[110] Rusk would know. Johnson's move into the Oval Office transformed Rusk's connection with the presidency. Kennedy had given Rusk the respect due a secretary of state, but never felt a strong personal affinity. In contrast, Johnson felt Rusk was an "outcast" from the Kennedy inner circle, just as he had been.[111] That relationship began while Johnson was vice president. Rusk briefed Johnson informally and assigned a Foreign Service officer from the State Department to brief him regularly.[112] In this sense, Rusk gave Johnson the respect he felt he did not get from Kennedy and the rest of Kennedy's advisors. Rusk described his relationship with Johnson as one "reinforced by personal friendship." He felt that it had been deepened by the difficulties of the Vietnam War: "He and I occupied the same foxhole together for so long, and when you are in a foxhole with somebody, you get to know him rather well."[113] Bundy describes it eloquently:

> With Rusk there was a real sense that, "This is my kind of man, and I can get along with him, and I understand him and he understands me, and we are both aware that the country is full of Yankees." He had that feeling about Dean Rusk, very strongly. And he never had any reason to change his mind. He was a man that he relied on, he trusted, he could be sure there would never be a side-bar play.[114]

That confidence empowered Rusk, and Johnson actively supported that increased power. For example, he communicated to the State Department through Rusk, never communicating with even the assistant secretaries without Rusk being in the loop. When assistant secretaries tried end runs around Rusk, Johnson informed Rusk.[115] In short, Johnson and Rusk were as close as Truman and Acheson or Eisenhower and Dulles.

Balancing and Compensating

As the evolution-balance model suggests, the experience of decision making within the Johnson administration led key advisors to try to convince Johnson to add more formality to his informal structure. Two major modifications of the process were instituted in 1966 and 1967. Both were intended to add more formality. In each case, Johnson was lobbied over a period of months by advisors who felt that the system was no longer working effectively. Taken together they seem like a complete bottom-up reorganization. The first change was initiated by Bundy's continued sense that the State Department could not or would not lead, and the TLG was not sufficiently connected to the departments to provide adequate policy guidance. The Senior Interdepartmental Group–Interdepartmental Regional Group (SIG-IRG) system, established in March 1966 by NSAM 341, was a formal State Department–led interagency process, closer to the Eisenhower NSC than to the spokes-of-the-wheel Kennedy/Johnson style. Though it seems counterintuitive to hand responsibility for decision making to the very department whose lack of leadership has created problems, the hope may have been that an explicitly formal hierarchy might force State to take hold of the reins of policy firmly and decisively. The SIG/IRG was the first formal decision making system in the Kennedy-Johnson era, the first since the dismantling of Eisenhower's Planning Board and Operations Coordination Board. The results of the changes were mixed. The SIG never fulfilled its promise as the manager of the foreign policy process, but the IRGs, designed to be formal interagency committees with jurisdiction for specific areas of the world, often played that exact role, depending on how serious a regional assistant secretary of state was about his leadership of the IRG. The second change followed the elevation of Rostow to the position of ANSA. Rostow convinced Johnson to allow him to transform the TLG from an ad hoc grouping into an analogue for the NSC that met nearly weekly and was backed up by intense staff work from departments, agencies, and the NSC staff. The new TLG was able to bridge the gap between the bureaucracies' hope for a more formal process and the president's need for control. The new TLG served Johnson's preferences for dealing with cabinet officers only in small, hopefully leak-proof meetings as well as the need to subject policy to more formal staffing that connected the TLG to the cabinet departments and the NSC staff. In a sense, Bundy and Rostow finally achieved what Bundy had been trying to accomplish since 1962, plugging the president's informal system for making decisions into the departments that would actually have the task of implementation.

The SIG/IRG System

Though NSAM 341, *The Direction, Coordination and Supervision of Inter-departmental Activities Overseas*, which created the SIG/IRG system, was issued on March 2, 1966, its roots can be traced back to 1961. Among the recommendations of the after action report that had assessed the Bay of Pigs decision making process was the creation of a "Strategic Resources Group" that might report directly to the president on large-scale strategic analysis. General Maxwell Taylor, cochair of the Bay of Pigs review group and Kennedy's White House-based military representative, referred to it as "a sort of Cold War operations center," composed of senior civilian and military leadership.[116] Kennedy rejected the idea, but did accept a scaled down advisory body that would concentrate only on counterinsurgency— the Special Group (Counter-insurgency), chaired by Taylor until he became US ambassador to South Vietnam in 1964.[117] Taylor never gave up on the Strategic Resources Group and continued to believe that the president needed some centralized advisory body that could manage foreign policy operations on a global scale. Upon his return from South Vietnam in July 1965, Taylor became a special consultant to the NSC and was charged by Bundy with the job of assessing overall US counterinsurgency policy. His report, issued in January 1966, is typically seen as the impetus for the SIG/IRG design, but Taylor's ideas eventually merged with ideas coming from Bundy and the State Department.

After the failure of the second Standing Group under Kennedy, Bundy dropped the plan for creating a formal interagency committee. He would try again under Johnson, but not until the transition period had ended. Bundy drafted a memo on the eve of the 1964 election, November 2, that stated bluntly his worries about the lack of organization within the administration. He recommended that Johnson take some time before the inauguration

> to have very frank and private talks with the men you trust most, about the general business of organizing the Presidency for your administration. This is the job which we have not attacked in the

last 11 months, and getting it right is absolutely indispensable if the Johnson Administration of 1965 is to escape the frustrations that overtook Truman in 1949 and Roosevelt in 1937.[118]

Johnson gave Bundy the green light to consider organizational modifications within weeks of his landslide election. In mid-December Johnson asked Rusk for a memo describing State Department operations; Rusk gave Johnson a full accounting on December 31, 1964.[119] Johnson also asked Bundy for a confidential assessment of State's role in decision making and an overall analysis of how State could provide more effective leadership in foreign affairs. Bundy wasted no time in lobbying Johnson for some type of change to his seat-of-the-pants style. Bundy submitted his memo the day after Johnson's January 20 inauguration.

The memo summed up what Bundy had learned from four years managing the foreign policy decision making of two presidents. Though Bundy applauded the State Department, he also made it clear that he saw its problems as critical. He stated that the "Department of State probably has more talented men incompletely used than any other department of government." He admitted that he had been holding his tongue: "I have probably watched the Department as closely as anyone outside it for the last four years, and I have been so careful to avoid comment to others that the temptation in reporting to you is irresistible." He identified the main dilemma. Neither Rusk nor the number-two man in the department, Undersecretary of State George Ball, were managers. If Johnson planned to keep Rusk, which Bundy assumed he did, then changes might be hard to make. Rusk himself was an impediment to effective management:

> He is not a manager. He has never been a good judge of men. His instincts are cautious and negative, and he has only a limited ability to draw the best out of those who work with him. His very discretion seems like secretiveness in his dealings with subordinates; it is a constant complaint in the bureaus that even quite high officials cannot find out what the Secretary himself thinks and wants. . . . the Secretary has little sense of effective operation. He does not move matters toward decision with promptness. He does not stimulate aggressive staff work. He does not coordinate conflicting forces within his own department.

He believed, however, that the State Department could lead if some changes were made. His suggestions in the memo were preliminary, but included a renewed presidential effort to place State at the center of managing foreign policy.[120] Bundy was sparse on details; he may have not wanted to step on Rusk's toes, which he clearly understood were more important to Johnson than his own.

Johnson seems to have shared Bundy's disappointment with State's coordination efforts. For example, interagency direction for Vietnam had been placed under the State Department by NSAM 280 of February 14, 1964, but then shifted to NSC staff direction by NSAM 310 of July 8, 1964.[121] In only a few months, Johnson and Bundy pulled management of Vietnam policy out of State's hands.

State also used the transition to a new president as an opportunity to reassess its functions. In December 1964, Rusk had suggested some modifications—adding an additional undersecretary, changing the lines of authority from assistant to undersecretary, and tinkering with the geographical boundaries of the regional bureaus. A more detailed plan for changing State Department operations, contained in an internal State Department memo, from July or August 1965, mirrors the eventual SIG/IRG system precisely.[122] Authorship is unidentified, but the memo was seen by much of the senior leadership of the department. It was no less than a complete restructuring of the interagency process that would make the State Department responsible for the coordination of all administration foreign policy.

The memo noted that the Johnson administration used the NSC and State Department bureaucracy even less than the Kennedy administration. If, as the senior leadership of the State Department believed, "primary responsibility for the proper handling of foreign affairs must rest with the bureaus and the regional Assistant Secretaries," State had to develop a method for "strengthening bureau leadership." The solution would be to make the regional assistant secretaries the primary administrative managers within their given regions by creating "*interdepartmental regional policy committees in each of the bureaus under the chairmanship of the respective regional Assistant Secretary*" (italics in original). Importantly, each assistant secretary would have the power to approve attendance at meetings. The memo suggested that "the regional committees would have jurisdiction over any and all aspects of US policy toward the countries covered by the bureaus" except perhaps counterinsurgency and covert operations. In addition, it proposed a way for State to resume senior-level leadership of the interagency process. A new "*State Coordinating Committee*" chaired by the deputy undersecretary of state for political affairs would "*deal with the most important problems requiring highest level inter-agency consideration*" (italics in original). The new committee would have membership at the highest sub-cabinet level.

In late July, at roughly the same time that this memo floated around the upper levels of the State Department, Taylor left his appointment as US ambassador to South Vietnam, taking on a new position as a special consultant to the president. Returning at the same time was Taylor's deputy, U. Alexis Johnson. Johnson had served as deputy undersecretary of state for political affairs from April 1961 to July 1964, when he was assigned to Saigon. He resumed the State post in September 1965. Given that Rusk and Ball, the top two men at the State Department, were often inattentive to administration, Johnson, Ball's deputy, had often assumed the management challenge.

Taylor and U.A. Johnson became the prime movers in the creation of the SIG/IRG system. On September 1, 1965, Taylor was asked by the president to evaluate the work of the Special Group (CI, for counterinsurgency) and the interagency process that directed US counterinsurgency efforts in Vietnam.[123] Taylor's review had a wide bureaucratic profile. Four working groups reported to him; each had representatives from the State and Defense Departments as well as the Joint Chiefs of Staff (JCS), the CIA, and the United States Information Agency (USIA). Taylor and U.A. Johnson continued their strong partnership once they arrived back in Washington, using their joint experience in Saigon as a template for their analysis. Their recommendations were based, in part, on the country team concept that operated within an embassy; the ambassador led an interagency effort that focused on coordinating the activities of the US government toward a nation. U.A. Johnson described the "primacy of the Ambassador" as one of the key aspects of success, a primacy that overall US foreign policy lacked when the president's attention was elsewhere. Taylor and his working groups expanded their mandate into an overall appraisal of Johnson foreign policy decision making, feeling that the problem of interagency coordination in Vietnam was a microcosm of the larger problem of overall interagency coordination.[124]

The timing of Johnson's request for the counterinsurgency review and the Taylor group's determination to assess the full scope of the administration's system may have been related to the July 1965 increase in US troop levels in Vietnam, in hindsight a clear turning point in the war.[125] At the July 27 NSC meeting, the administration decided to announce publicly that it would increase troop levels from 75,000 to 125,000 and double the monthly draft allotment from 17,000 to 35,000. It did not make public a further plan to raise troop levels to at least 350,000 during 1966.[126] The lack of interagency staff work leading up to the decision and the absence of interagency follow through afterwards made a strong impression on many officials throughout the bureaucracy. It also seemed to leave a mark on Johnson; within a month of the NSC meeting, he asked Taylor to examine the interagency process for counterinsurgency, the primary military tactic that ultimately was used by the additional troops.[127]

U.A. Johnson drafted a memo for Rusk dated November 5, 1965 based on the July/August memo.[128] It recommended setting up regional inter-agency groups chaired by the assistant secretaries of state for each regional bureau and reconstituting the Special Group (CI) as a high-level inter-agency group chaired by a senior State Department official. He did not explicitly state in the memo that he and Taylor had been working on the ideas in tandem, but the November proposal and Taylor's eventual report were likely the products of close cooperation.[129] It is unclear, however, if Rusk ever saw the memo.[130]

Taylor's final report was given to Johnson on January 19, 1966.[131] The report is a study in how to widen the scope of an issue without seeming to widen the scope of an issue. It does not explicitly state its intention of redesigning the entire structure of foreign policy decision making in the administration, but Taylor wrote that he intended to "limit my com-ments in this letter to what I believe to be the basic problem—the need to improve the executive direction, coordination and supervision of interde-partmental activities overseas." In short, he "limited" his report to every aspect of foreign policy.

The report suggested a structure to empower the secretary of state to act as the agent of interagency coordination on behalf of the president and to establish a method to make decisions on issues that did not need presidential attention. It recommended a set of hierarchical committees to formalize the interagency process. The primary interagency bodies for making decisions on foreign policy topics that did not need presidential-level attention would be "Regional Coordination Groups" led by State's regional assistant secretaries. The Regional Coordination Groups would report to a senior level "Overseas Operations Group." He wrote: "It is my view that the Special Group (Counter-insurgency) with a broader direc-tive and a new name . . . could be converted into an agency for supporting the secretary of state in discharging his broadened responsibilities for the direction, coordination and supervision of overseas affairs (less exempted military matters)."

In the report's covering memo to Johnson, Taylor assured the president that he had discussed these ideas and reached agreement on them with

Rusk, McNamara, JCS chair General Earle Wheeler, Bundy, and Director of the Bureau of the Budget Charles Schultze; only DCI Admiral William Raborn had reservations regarding how intelligence matters might be handled. Taylor also included a draft NSAM laying out the new system. In his memoirs, Taylor described his ideas as logical conclusions drawn from his original mandate. His own Special Group (CI) had a higher level of interagency representation than anything other than the NSC. Under Taylor's chairmanship were the attorney general, the deputy undersecretary of state, the deputy secretary of defense, the chairman of the Joint Chiefs of Staff, the director of central intelligence, the ANSA, the director of the USIA, and the administrator of the Agency for International Development (USAID).[132] If such a high-level group existed to review counterinsurgency policy, how did it make sense not to have a committee at that level to review overall foreign policy? Taylor had successfully repackaged his proposal for the senior level Strategic Resources Group that he had first proposed in 1961. As he described it, "in an odd way, the quest for a way to deal with subversive insurgency led to the adoption of a whole new organization for dealing with foreign affairs in general."[133]

Interdepartmental debate on the merits of the ideas began immediately after the report was submitted. On January 21, Rusk wrote to Johnson, approving Taylor's proposal. The letter was short and short on details, befitting Rusk's preference for giving Johnson his opinion face to face rather than on paper. Johnson then met with Taylor on January 24. A meeting between Rusk, Ball, Taylor, and Bundy on February 1 led to a new Taylor/Bundy-authored NSAM. This draft was further refined by meetings throughout February between Taylor and officials from all the relevant agencies and departments.[134] By March 1, a final draft had been ironed out. Importantly, U.A. Johnson was the lead negotiator for State, giving Taylor a strong ally from the very department that would be the key to the new system. The departments of defense, treasury, agriculture, and commerce, the JCS, the CIA, USAID, USIA, and the Budget Bureau all approved the draft (with some reservations from Agriculture and Treasury about State's dominion over international economic issues). Rusk reassured them that their departments would have full participation when topics related to their agencies were considered.[135]

NSAM 341, *The Direction, Coordination and Supervision of Interdepartmental Activities Overseas*, was signed on March 2, 1966.[136] It represented Johnson's acknowledgement that his decision making had serious weaknesses and needed restructuring. The NSAM, at least on paper, established a formal interagency structure, closer to the Eisenhower system than to the Kennedy or Johnson system that immediately preceded it; importantly, again, it signifies the first formal decision making structures in the Kennedy-Johnson era. It had three key elements. First, it explicitly made the secretary of state the key official responsible for US foreign policy, excluding military policy, stating, "I have assigned to the Secretary of State authority and responsibility to the full extent permitted by law for the overall direction, coordination and supervision of interdepartmental activities of the United States Government overseas." Second, it created a Senior Interagency Group (SIG), chaired by the undersecretary of state. Membership included the "Deputy Secretary of Defense, the Administrator of the Agency for International Development, the Director of the Central Intelligence Agency, the Chairman of the Joint Chiefs of Staff, the Director of the United States Information Agency, and the Special Assistant to the President for National Security Affairs. Representatives of other departments and agencies with responsibility for specific matters to be considered will attend on invitation by the Chairman." The list of SIG responsibilities essentially amounted to overall coordination of "interdepartmental activities," issues referred to it by the assistant secretaries of state, and the responsibilities of the Special Group (CI). In short, the SIG was intended to be the committee that managed the day-to-day operations of foreign policy, resolving interagency disagreements, handling things that could not be settled at the assistant secretary level, and identifying problems that needed to be bumped up to the presidential level. Third, NSAM 341 created the Interdepartmental Regional Groups (IRGs), one group for each of the geographic bureaus of the State Department and chaired by the regional assistant secretaries of state. IRGs included members from the Department of Defense, the JCS, the CIA, USAID, USIA, and the White House or NSC staff. The primary responsibilities of the IRGs were "assisting the Assistant Secretaries of State" to "assure the adequacy of United States policy for the countries in their region and of the plans, programs, resources and performance for implementing that policy." If an IRG thought an issue needed to be moved up the hierarchy into the SIG, it would recommend that the SIG address the issue. NSAM 341 also gave the SIG and all the IRGs their own staff.

Publicly and within internal memos, the administration explicitly acknowledged that the new system was an attempt to decrease informality and an effort to "formalize relationships and clarify responsibilities." It would not, however, reduce Johnson's central role in the process. In a press briefing, Taylor and U.A. Johnson stated it directly: "The President has taken a portion of his own Presidential responsibility and given it to the Secretary of State as his agent." The SIG would be the "focal point" for interagency decision making, and to that end, the chairs of the SIG and each IRG had real power that derived from the president's elevation of the secretary of state. The committees were described as "more than normal committees." The chairs did not simply "preside." They also had the right to "decide," possessing the "authority and responsibility to decide all matters coming before his committee, subject to the right of any member to appeal his decision to a higher authority." While the IRGs dealt with day-to-day operations, the SIG would tackle the "major problems," issues referred to it by the IRGs or brought to the SIG by any member or nonmember who felt the topics needed addressing. In this way a formal structure was created, one that included a method for breaking interagency gridlock (the chairs) and an appeals avenue for departments unhappy with any decision. The paper flow in and out of the Oval Office would also be reduced by the new system, with the SIG in charge of "major problems" and the IRGs handling their own geographic areas. Issues that could not be resolved in the SIG might be brought to the secretary of state or president.[137]

In the context of the evolution-balance model, acceptance of the SIG/IRG idea represents the bureaucracies' success in finally convincing Johnson that he needed some more formal decision structures; the informal spokes-of-the-wheel system rooted in Johnson's own inextinguishable energy was not enough.

Still, this does not answer the question of why Johnson accepted this proposal when he did, in the winter of 1966. Part of the reason is the State Department's movement in this direction during 1965. Part of it was the respect the president had for Taylor and those who supported the idea (senior levels of the State Department and NSC staff, including Bundy). Bundy's departure in February 1966, in the works since at least January 1965, may also account for the timing. He submitted his resignation officially on February 28, 1966, five weeks after the report had been submitted to Johnson.[138] His coming departure may have been the final argument for creating a more formal structure; absent Bundy, Johnson needed to start from square one. Bundy was gone on February 28; NSAM 341 was signed on March 2; the first SIG meeting was held on March 8; and Rostow began his tenure as ANSA on April 1.

As the evolution-balance model hypothesizes and the Kennedy case study suggests, you can lead a president to a better foreign policy decision making process, but you cannot make him use it. Like Kennedy's Standing Groups, the SIG/IRG system did not play the central role it was designed to play. For roughly the first year and a half of its existence, the SIG's prominence in decision making declined; it met less frequently as time went on, again a new toy that was played with less and less over time (see table 5.1). It was reenergized in mid-1967 as a useful forum for dealing with topics that did not require cabinet-level or presidential-level attention. In that sense, it regained some importance, perhaps picking up the slack on lesser issues that might have been lost as the senior officials were pulled deeper and deeper into Vietnam priorities. It did not serve, however, as the formal foundation for the administration's decision making. The IRGs functioned more as intended, depending on how seriously an individual regional assistant secretary of state considered his IRG chairmanship.

The new system had three interrelated problems. First, surprisingly, State did not initially use the SIG as a way to preside over the foreign policy process. Neither Rusk nor Ball, executive chairman of the SIG, took the SIG very seriously.[139] Given the usual scramble for power that is the reality of governmental decision making, it is unusual for any department not to jump at the chance to take charge. It becomes doubly unusual given the fanfare accompanying the NSAM: an official White House announcement on March 4, a White House briefing for the press from Taylor and U.A. Johnson, a message from Rusk to the State Department reprinted in the March 28 issue of the *State Department Bulletin*, a speech by Taylor to the American Foreign Service Association on March 31, an article by U.A. Johnson in the *Foreign Service Journal* in April, and a report by Senator Henry Jackson's Subcommittee on National Security and International Operations.[140] The administration wanted the public and members of Congress to know about the new system, hoping it would quell any doubts about Johnson's foreign policy. Johnson and Rusk, however, valued the informal process, their relationship with each other, and other cabinet members. The SIG would essentially get the leftovers. Vietnam decision making was specifically excluded from the SIG.[141] This division of labor may have sent the signal that the SIG was not central to the administration's decision making. Another indication of its less than critical nature was the fact that it was not chaired by the secretary of state; if Rusk chose not to use the SIG as a management tool, it was not an important committee.[142]

The second dilemma for the SIG was that its relationship to the NSC and the TLG was undefined in NSAM 341. Though there is reference to SIG disagreements being appealed "to the next higher authority," that authority is not named.[143] While the hierarchical linkage between the SIG and the IRGs was clearly hashed out at the first SIG meeting, the connection between the NSC and SIG was left unaddressed. Again, the view was looking downward, not upward. One official likened the SIG to an old rope trick: "It has no top and leads nowhere. You climb the rope with your problem and both of you disappear."[144]

The third reason the SIG did not fulfill its promise was simple. Though Johnson wanted to increase the power of the State Department in foreign affairs, it would not come at the expense of Johnson's power. In essence, Johnson needed to be at the center of a process that served his specific needs. The SIG was designed to handle second-tier issues that the president had no time to deal with. The State Department could expand its role in decision making only so far. Anything that might get in the way of Johnson or the Johnson-Rusk relationship was simply not an option.

State and particularly Ball's disinterest in the SIG became obvious after only a few meetings. The first meeting of the SIG took place on March 8.[145] In attendance at the first meeting were Ball (as chair), Deputy Secretary of Defense Cyrus Vance, Director of USAID David Bell, Director of Central Intelligence Admiral William Raborn, Director of USIA Leonard Marks, General Andrew Goodpaster representing the JCS, Deputy Undersecretary of State for Political Affairs U.A. Johnson, SIG staff director Harry Schwartz, as well as additional staff. Robert Komer, interim ANSA at the time between Bundy's resignation and Rostow's appointment, was not invited to the meeting, even though NSAM 341 includes the ANSA as a member. Knowing that this was the surest way to get a message to the president, Komer wrote a note to White House staffer Bill Moyers, pointing out that he had not been invited to the meeting, and that no one had even told the NSC staff that the meeting was taking place.[146] At the second meeting, the SIG declared an ambitious mandate. It would "seize the initiative on whatever matters its members find of interest and help to guide the other apparatus of government by its agreements and decisions." During the third meeting the SIG decided which already-existing interagency groups would be absorbed by the SIG or various IRGs. The SIG met every week in March, and the flow of paperwork and agenda items thickened.

After this bold start—outlining what committees the SIG would swallow, even bypassing bureaucratic rivals—the SIG began to fade. It met twice in April, three times in June, and twice in July. In a sign of inattentiveness to its own directive, it was not until July 26, 1966, the thirteenth meeting of the SIG, that the group finally tasked each IRG with specific assignments.[147] Its last meeting in 1966 was in September (see table 5.1). The SIG was essentially no longer a functioning interagency committee by late fall of 1966, even as some IRGs did continue to meet. This fact was not lost on either Taylor or Rostow. Taylor suggested a review of SIG/

IRG operations for September or November delivery to the president, but he never received approval to launch it.[148] Taylor described the SIG/IRG process by 1967 as "in impressive display of inactivity."[149]

The SIG did hold a one meeting per month in January and February 1967, but then stopped meeting altogether. After a five-month hiatus, the SIG was resurrected in mid-July 1967, meeting roughly every two to three weeks from July 1967 to the end of 1968. State's official history refers to post-July1967 as the SIGs "Second Incarnation."[150] Personnel changes and Rostow's growing frustrations led to the renewal of the SIG. Ball had been replaced by Nicholas deB. Katzenbach in October 1966. Though Katzenbach initially also had reservations about expending efforts to make the SIG operate as advertised, Rostow was able to convince Katzenbach that the SIG could be a useful tool for interagency management.[151] In March 1967, Rostow wrote in a memo to Johnson that "I am convinced that this town cannot work effectively unless the State Department really acts from day to day in the spirit of NSAM 341; and making the SIG work is a critical element in that process."[152] In June 1967 Rostow even drafted a memo for Johnson to send to the State Department that issued a clear threat. Rostow wanted the president to tell State: "The simple fact is that for 15 months now NSAM 341 has not been implemented." Either the State Department accepts this management role, or "I shall have to organize this kind of leadership and coordination out of the White House."[153] Though Rostow was ready to crack the whip, Johnson was not. The memo was never sent. Even without the extra incentive, however, Rostow had made an impression on Katzenbach and the SIG had a second life, though its place in Johnson's decision making was never truly formalized or clarified.

The IRGs, however, in some cases did work exactly as intended: functioning as subordinate committees to the NSC; ironing out interagency policies that could be decided below the presidential level; and staffing out issues that needed to be made at the presidential level (preparing reports, developing policy options, and highlighting interagency agreement and disagreement). The difference between an active IRG and an inactive IRG rested with the regional assistant secretary of state who chaired the IRG. If the regional assistant secretary took advantage of the opportunity to manage foreign policy for his region, scheduling regular meetings, taking hold of issues that could be decided at the working level, and pushing others to the SIG for decision, the IRG became the main decision venue for a formal process. If the assistant secretary did not, policy making for the area remained informal and somewhat haphazard.[154]

The New Tuesday Lunch Group

Walt Rostow replaced Bundy officially on April 1, 1966. His ability to convince Johnson to make adjustments to his decision making process was based in the faith Johnson had in Rostow; though secondary to Rusk, Rostow had earned a place in Johnson's confidence structure. He tamed the TLG to a certain degree, adding formality to it in a way that did not interfere with Johnson's hands-on, small group style. Johnson liked the TLG because it eliminated staff from the room, allowing the principals to interact free of bureaucratic gossip and, most importantly, free of leaks. Rostow did not bring staff into the room; instead, he formalized the agendas and used staff to prepare Johnson, McNamara, and Rusk for what occurred during the TLG meetings. He also increased the frequency of meetings to make the TLG essentially a stand-in for a weekly NSC meeting. In addition, he made some modifications to the NSC itself; these changed the role of the NSC, but did not enhance its value within the administration. Rostow did what the evolution-balance model would suggest: he saw the weaknesses in the Johnson style—its overreliance on informality and lack of connection to the bureaucracies—and found a remedy that fit with Johnson's decision making preferences.

Bundy was the last of the Kennedy men Johnson replaced. After the obligatory resignation letter of November 1963, he became a core advisor to Johnson. Bundy seriously began considering leaving as early as January 1965.[155] Johnson saw his value and urged him to stay, keeping him in the White House until February 28, 1966. Most analyses of Bundy's departure attribute it to a falling out between Johnson and Bundy over Vietnam strategy; Bundy came to see the escalation of the war as a mistake. He lost the trust of the president and could no longer support the policy.[156] Even before Bundy left, the jockeying for selecting his replacement had begun. In February 1965, Bundy recommended White House special assistant Moyers as the best man for the job. McNamara also saw Moyers as the top choice.[157] By late 1965, Bundy had changed his mind, suggesting NSC staffer Komer as his replacement in November, and also offering him as an excellent interim replacement in February 1966 as Bundy's departure date grew closer and Johnson had yet to pick a replacement. Jack Valenti, a White House assistant and confidant to Johnson, also recommended Komer as an interim solution.[158] Johnson, however, seems to have favored Rostow. Komer did become the interim ANSA, but Rostow received the permanent position. The decision was pure Johnson—in his control and designed to avoid leaks—in that it was unclear until the last minute whom

Johnson was going to pick or if he had even made a decision. Francis Bator, the deputy ANSA, actually sent a memo to Moyers suggesting comments Moyers might make at the March 31 NSC staff meeting; he assumed that no official would be named to replace Bundy soon and Moyers would be acting as the interim ANSA for quite a while.[159] Later that day, however, Johnson announced Rostow's appointment at his weekly press conference.

Clark Clifford, then a consultant to the White House, favored eliminating the post altogether. Johnson seemed to agree in part, stating that he did not want "another Bundy in the basement."[160] Rostow's role would be different from Bundy's. At his March 31 press conference, Johnson stated that Rostow would specialize in long-range planning and Latin American development, but would not be working on foreign affairs exclusively. In his mind, all his special assistants could slide from issue to issue as needed. Rostow's advantage was that he was more of a thinker in Johnson's eyes, there to help him with strategic planning, rather than a day-to-day manager of the policy process like Bundy. At the press conference, Johnson described his special assistants as flexible, all-around assistants: "Most of the men play any position here." Rostow, he said, would be "at the service of the President, and if he needs to play first base or second base or third base, I hope that he can do it." Johnson saw Rostow's brainpower as his key asset, an asset that now belonged to him.[161] Rostow was known as an idea man, one of the reasons he was moved from deputy ANSA to the chairman of State's Policy Planning Council, the Department's in-house think tank, in November 1961.[162] The broader mandate was indicated by Rostow's official title: he served as a special assistant to the president, rather than special assistant to the president for national security affairs.

First, Rostow made some changes to the nature of Johnson's NSC itself. In May 1966, Johnson indicated that he wanted NSC meetings every two weeks. At that point the NSC meeting schedule was irregular and infrequent. From February 1965, when the NSC met six times during the intense period that followed the North Vietnamese attack on Pleiku and the beginning of Rolling Thunder bombing campaign, to May 1966, the administration had held eight NSC meetings, an average of slightly more than once every two months. It is unclear why Johnson asked for the change. Perhaps it was the creation of the SIG and the accompanying talk of the need for organization, or the way Vietnam decisions crowded out other issues, or the expectation that the lack of NSC meetings would be a 1968 campaign issue (Eisenhower had already publicly criticized the administration over its nonuse of the NSC, and the two leading candidates for the 1968 Republican nomination, Richard Nixon and Nelson

Rockefeller, were both veterans of the Eisenhower administration; Rockefeller had been the chair of Eisenhower's President's Advisory Committee on Government Organization). Rostow agreed to schedule meetings more frequently, but he also understood what Johnson wanted. In a May 25, 1965 memo from Rostow and Bromley Smith, the two assistants mentioned "conditions" under which they felt the NSC could function well for Johnson: "We must not pretend the NSC meetings are the occasion when you will actually be making your major foreign policy decisions. . . . On the other hand, we must avoid creating a paper mill that would produce unimportant or uninteresting briefings for you."[163] Initially, the NSC met the new schedule with three meetings in June and two in July. After these meetings, however, the administration held one NSC meeting per month from August 1966 to February 1967 (none in November) and then did not meet at all in March and April 1967.

It was not until May 1967 that a biweekly schedule became semiroutine. From May 3, 1967 to November 25, 1968 (the last Johnson NSC meeting), the NSC met twice per month in 11 of 19 months. Again, the pattern of formal committees being used until the president loses interest is partially confirmed. In this case, however, Johnson began to meet the schedule at least half the time. The meetings focused on long-range issues. Johnson had hoped Rostow would add his expertise in strategic planning, and this became the main function of the NSC process. Rostow had been chair of the State Department's Policy Planning Council, and may have been attempting to turn the NSC into a policy planning council for the entire administration.[164]

Rostow's real impact was felt in the transformation of the TLG. The TLG added increased formality and became what the NSC was intended to be when it was first proposed: a venue for the top decision makers to informally and openly debate policy that was cemented into the administration by formal staffing of issues and a clear readout of decisions made at the meetings. During its first year of use, 1964, the TLG met 27 times, roughly biweekly. In 1965, as described above, estimates of TLG meeting frequency vary from 17 to 23 times. Even in the larger estimate, the TLG met only biweekly. In 1966, the TLG met 20 times, less than biweekly. Rostow's transformation of the TLG is most easily seen in the increased frequency of meetings; it met weekly during both 1967 and 1968: 50 meetings in 1967 and 57 meetings in 1968 (including two in January 1969) (see table 5.1).[165]

More importantly, the 1967–68 TLG was managed and staffed by Rostow in a more formal manner, as close to a fully staffed cabinet-level committee as Johnson might allow. Detailed records of the proceedings were kept, overruling Johnson's 1964 order to end record-keeping of TLG meetings.[166] Agenda setting for the TLG became an important responsibility for Rostow, a task he shared with Benjamin Read, executive secretary of the State Department. Rostow and Read finalized the agenda the day before a TLG meeting. Read explained how the State Department and its regional bureaus were plugged into the TLG process through the contact between Read and Rostow. To a certain degree, these contacts were made under Bundy as well.

> Usually a day before a Tuesday lunch, I will be in touch by phone with the President's Special Assistant and we'll swap ideas of what might go on the agenda and start the list and add to it in that manner. . . . It's a constant interchange and we supplement this process by a procedure in State in which the Secretariat officers contact each of the bureaus, maybe two days in advance or a day or so in advance at least, to get their ideas of what is of sufficient importance and timeliness to put on the luncheon platter. So it's not as unstructured as some of the recent newspaper accounts of the incoming crowd would have you believe. The staff work is done over here, in some cases for the President as well as for the Secretary. . . . But there's a great deal of staffing which precedes it.[167]

Rostow also talked to Rusk and McNamara about what items they thought should be included.[168] Analyses by various departments and the NSC staff accompanied the agendas. Often, he kept issues out of the TLG until they were "ripe for Tuesday Lunch handling," meaning that the issue was not be brought to the TLG before Defense and State had reached agreement. In this way, the NSC staff became the coordination body for a senior-level committee that formally developed a consensus on advice to the president, effectively the purpose of the NSC.[169] Often the TLG has been described as essentially a war cabinet for Vietnam.[170] The documents and staff records of the TLG in 1967–68, however, show the TLG looking at a full range of foreign policy issues: Indian sensitivity to arms transfers to Pakistan; Iranian interest in aircraft sales from the USSR; NATO; Indonesia; Rhodesia; German offset payments to the US for the stationing of troops; Anti-Ballistic Missile programs; the PL-480 aid program; and, most importantly for this study, trade with China and Chinese representation at the UN.[171]

Importantly, the results of the meetings were communicated to the departments and agencies, plugging the TLG into the interagency process in a way that corrected many earlier criticisms of the TLG as a body that made decisions but did not disseminate them to the rest of the administration. As Read explained: "After the lunch Walt Rostow has been scrupulous in calling me to run down the list of items, item by item, to relay any action instructions which may flow from the discussion at the meal." Not surprisingly, Read also mentioned that the results of the meeting were not always clear: "I get a double-shot at it because I talk independently to the Secretary and get his account as well. On occasions these accounts have not meshed, and you would think that they had attended separate lunches. But they're usually quite similar."[172]

Attendance at the meetings was kept small. The core group of Johnson, Rusk, McNamara, and Rostow was often joined by JCS chair Wheeler, DCI Helms, Komer, Press Secretary George Christian, and from July 1967 on White House staffer Tom Johnson as the official note taker. Others attending the meetings on an irregular basis included Katzenbach, commander of US forces in Vietnam General William Westmoreland, other members of the JCS, Vice President Hubert Humphrey, White House staffer Harry McPherson, Deputy Secretary of Defense Cyrus Vance, General Taylor, Secretary of the Treasury Henry Fowler, Johnson confidant Abe Fortas, and Clark Clifford (first as a special consultant to the administration, then as secretary of defense and a regular member of the TLG after March 1, 1968).[173] During 1967–68, the TLG was only paired with the NSC— meeting on the same day—on four out of 107 TLG meetings.

Several conclusions can be drawn about the 1967–68 TLG. First, it seems to have done what the SIG could not—serve as the top committee on the interagency ladder. Johnson rejected use of the full NSC because of its size and propensity for leaks. The TLG had been his informal substitute, but until Rostow's tenure, it was not plugged into the departments and agencies well enough. Rostow's management of the TLG—the staffing and agenda setting—allowed the TLG to become the real center of interagency decision making in a more formal way than ever before. Second, connection to the interagency process and the SIG/IRG was still semiformal, reliant on Rostow, the NSC staff, and its participation on those committees. This is related to a third point: Rostow managed the TLG in a way that maximized interagency participation; it was not a committee that replaced the interagency process, but relied heavily on the relationship between Rostow, Rusk, and McNamara. As noted above, Rostow was careful to make sure that the TLG did not get ahead of the State or Defense Departments. Fourth, Rostow's management efforts did not lead to a rivalry between Rostow and Rusk. Rostow seems to have conceived of his job as managing foreign policy for Rusk and the president, not just for the president. Rostow knew that anything that might come between Johnson and Rusk would be rejected. Perhaps equally important was the fact that when Rostow had been a member of the State Department from 1962 to 1966, Rusk had been his boss. That relationship remained one of a superior to a subordinate.[174]

None of this could have had any impact on decision making unless Johnson himself had been convinced that the transformation of the TLG was necessary. He allowed Rostow to manage it in a much more hands-on way than he had allowed Bundy, an indication of his confidence in Rostow. This new power was calculated and deliberate on both men's behalf. Rostow was given real ability as ANSA to establish and enforce a new chain of command. He explained that "the rule was laid down at State and in the White House that nothing was to come to the President on foreign policy except through my shop."[175] As the channel for communication to the president, Rostow was clearly delegated the task of managing the process. It is unclear if the very positive reviews of the TLG given to it by those who attended are commentary on the Bundy-era or Rostow-era TLG, but the difference between them is important. Given that Bundy had been trying to add more formality to decisions under both Kennedy and Johnson, Rostow's success must be a function of Johnson changing his mind or Rostow's relationship with Johnson, or both.

Conclusion

The evolution of Johnson's foreign policy decision making confirms the evolution-balance model. The administration began to discuss making modifications to the process in 1965, following roughly a year and a half of an informal system that was sustained through the brute force of Johnson's will and the continuity of the Kennedy cabinet. Johnson approved the elements of the new system in 1966 and 1967. The SIG/IRG and the new TLG were both attempts to add what was missing: a formal interagency process. Two points about these changes highlight the importance of the relationships between the president and his advisors. First, the SIG/IRG should be seen as a delegation of some authority to Rusk, based on Johnson's faith in him (the confidence structure). Johnson's personality suggests that he would rather cut off his own arm than give anyone more power to manage or control his own administration. The new SIG/IRG system, however, was Johnson's recognition that he simply could not be his own chief of staff for every foreign policy issue his administration faced; the less critical decisions had to be delegated to someone. Rusk was the obvious choice. Only Johnson's certainty that Rusk would never make a move that contradicted Johnson's own preferences allowed him to say yes to the innovations. Rusk's inability or disinterest in the SIG/IRG, however, made it unsuccessful. In any case, the SIG/IRG was never going to become the central arena for important issues. Johnson was never going to let go of any decisions that he himself wanted to make. The SIG/IRG could deal with issues that were outside presidential attention, but little else. This observation leads to the second point. For topics where Johnson had an interest, any increased formality had to be layered onto the informal structure he preferred, into the TLG. Rostow did not set out to completely tame Johnson's instinct, as a full blown SIG/IRG or NSC-based Eisenhower-style system might have. He built a formal structure around the TLG, institutionalizing it into the executive branch in ways that did not prevent Johnson from using the TLG as an inner sanctum for himself and his cabinet officers, but did allow the TLG to provide guidance for the departments and agencies. It could only work for Johnson because at its core was Johnson's confidence in both Rusk and Rostow. Figure 9.1 summarizes the Johnson administration's overall decision making.

SIX

❧ Johnson and China

> You know, there are some young men in this government who
> think we're going to change our China policy, and I can tell you
> they're dead wrong.[1]
> —Dean Rusk

Continuity rather than change was the hallmark of US foreign policy from the late 1940s to the mid-1960s. Though Eisenhower criticized Truman's tactics in Korea, he accepted the foundation of Truman's containment strategy. Similarly, Kennedy's attacks on Republican foreign policy during the 1960 campaign were over means, not ends. Inheriting the Kennedy presidency meant that Johnson was even less likely to rock the boat in foreign affairs or on China.

This chapter contains two case studies: the Long Term China Study of 1965–66, and Johnson's speech of July 1966 that guided the fall 1966 decisions on Chinese representation at the UN. A brief look at the December 13, 1963 speech by Assistant Secretary of State for Far Eastern Affairs Roger Hilsman precedes the case studies to highlight the policies bubbling up from the working levels of the bureaucracy and the uncertain nature of policy making during the transition period.

Both cases confirm the evolution-balance model. In the case of the Long Range Study, the administration desired a comprehensive evaluation of China policy to set a baseline for Johnson's initial complete term as president. In the absence of a standard interagency process, it established an ad hoc task force with full departmental/agency participation to do the job, a formal structure. Though the study began before the SIG/IRG system had been created, it was ultimately plugged into that system through the Far Eastern IRG (FE/IRG) and a new subcommittee of the FE/IRG, the interagency China Working Group (CWG) (both formal structures).

Similarly, the July 1966 speech and decision on Chinese representation later that fall included several suggestions for the addition of formal processes to improve the administration's organization. Two new committees were proposed. An assistant-secretary-level committee to examine the administration's response to congressional hearings on Asia was added, though a new high-level group was rejected. Following Johnson's speech, responsibility for thinking about the next steps on China was delegated to the China Working Group of the FE/IRG. In each of the case studies, as in the evolution of the overall decision process, advisors felt that the informal system was incapable of fully analyzing the key policy issues. The confidence structure was also unable to produce the type of bottom-up analysis that was necessary. The role of the confidence structure here was Rusk's, Bundy's, and Rostow's support for the inclusion of greater interagency formality, the key to getting Johnson's assent to potentially meaningful modifications to the process.

A comparison of the evolution of the Johnson China decisions and the evolution of the overall process is provided in table 9.2. Figure 6.1 serves as an illustration of the changes in Johnson's China decisions based on the framework of figure 2.2.

The case studies suggest several conclusions about the administration's decision making and its overall thinking on China. First, China policy was like all other policies, usually determined through an informal process heavily reliant on Johnson, Rusk, and their relationship. Second, both case studies in this chapter illustrate the continuity of the international and domestic political dynamics. The debate centered on the dangerous growth in Chinese power, the necessity of using military force to block the advance of China and its North Vietnamese proxy in Southeast Asia, and consideration of whether engagement might be an alternative strategy for reducing that Chinese threat. Third, lower-level China and Asia area officials had formed a consensus on the need to engage China, but saw Rusk as the key obstacle to any change in administration policy on China. Fourth, domestic politics was a key factor in Johnson's calculations on China. He and Rusk allowed the bureaucracies to consider the implications of new ideas on China, but consistently rejected them. Ultimately, Johnson and Rusk were unwilling to commit to any real change in policy or serious steps toward an engagement strategy while the Vietnam War continued.[2] Partly, this was a decision based on geopolitics: How could the US move toward engagement with China while fighting a war in Vietnam to stop the spread of China-supported wars of national liberation? The domestic politics of the situation seemed to be even more important: No Democrat

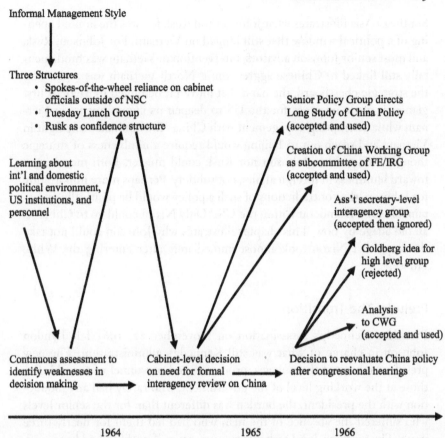

Informal Management Style

Three Structures
- Spokes-of-the-wheel reliance on cabinet officials outside of NSC
- Tuesday Lunch Group
- Rusk as confidence structure

Learning about int'l and domestic political environment, US institutions, and personnel

Senior Policy Group directs Long Study of China Policy (accepted and used)

Creation of China Working Group as subcommittee of FE/IRG (accepted and used)

Ass't secretary-level interagency group (accepted then ignored)

Goldberg idea for high level group (rejected)

Analysis to CWG (accepted and used)

Continuous assessment to identify weaknesses in decision making

Cabinet-level decision on need for formal interagency review on China

Decision to reevaluate China policy after congressional hearings

1964   1965   1966

NSC – National Security Council
FE/IRG – Far Eastern Interdepartmental Regional Group
CWG – China Working Group

Fig. 6.1. The Evolution of Johnson Administration Decision Making on China

could support engagement without being accused by Republicans and the China lobby of surrendering to Communist aggression, a political attack that might jeopardize the entire Johnson legislative agenda, Democratic control of Congress, and Johnson's prospects for reelection. Fifth, by 1966, the public and congressional view on China had evolved significantly, but not enough to convince Johnson that an all-out push for an engagement strategy was possible. Johnson and Rusk felt the administration had political cover for a trial balloon along the same lines as the Hilsman speech. Johnson's July 12, 1966 nationally televised speech implying a willingness to reevaluate the isolation policy pending China's end to aggression in

Southeast Asia illustrates what Johnson and Rusk felt was the limited opening of a political window that still hinged on Vietnam. For Johnson, Rusk, and most senior Johnson advisors, intervention in Vietnam was fundamentally still linked to Chinese aggression; if North Vietnam was a pawn on the strategic chessboard, the hand that moved it belonged to Mao. At first glance, it made no sense for the US to deepen its commitments in Vietnam while attempting engagement with China. To simultaneously fight in Vietnam and reach out to Beijing would require a nimbleness of strategic thought that neither Johnson nor Rusk could muster. Both men leaned toward bluntness in foreign affairs, not subtlety. Perhaps more importantly for Johnson, the contradictions of such a policy would be politically unsustainable for a Democrat within the US. "Only Nixon could go to China" is an old adage by now. This chapter illustrates why Johnson could not take the steps that Nixon took almost immediately after entering the White House.

Prelude: The Transition

President Kennedy's assassination on November 22, 1963 left Lyndon Johnson in charge of what was still Kennedy's administration. The new president inherited the policies, processes, and personnel of the old. For those at the working level of the government, who rarely had any interaction with the president, the burden was different than for the senior levels who suffered the absence of the man who had led them for nearly three years. The working-level task was to carry on as if nothing had happened. Routine decisions had to be completed; policy had to be implemented. Assistant Secretary of State for Far Eastern Affairs Roger Hilsman had been scheduled to give a speech on China at the Commonwealth Club in San Francisco on December 13, 1963. In spite of the tragedy of November, Hilsman was instructed to keep the date; the show of continuity was important for the nation.

This brief look at the transition serves two purposes. First, it establishes the baseline thinking of those at the working level at the start of the Johnson administration—they still hoped to move past the isolation policy. Second, it illustrates the state of decision making on China during the transition. Greater study of this case is warranted in future research. In a tragic way, it is an experimental design: What happens if the president is removed in the middle of the policy process? The answer seems to be that some officials in an administration will try to take advantage of the absence of a formal interagency framework and a leadership in transition to advance the policies they favor. In short, when the parents are away for the weekend, the kids will throw a party.

Since the early days of the Kennedy administration, the working levels of the NSC staff and the State Department had called for a fundamental reevaluation of US policy toward Communist China. NSC staffer Robert Komer had lobbied Bundy, calling isolation "unproductive." A big-picture review of China policy was also the subject of frequent discussion during NSC staff planning lunches. At the State Department, Undersecretary of State Chester Bowles and James Thomson, then his assistant for Far Eastern Affairs, argued for a fundamental reexamination of the policy, while Edward Rice of the Policy Planning Council wrote a 700-page paper on alternative options. The Assistant Secretary of State for Far Eastern Affairs, Walter McConaughy, an Eisenhower holdover, saw no reason to change the policy, but he was removed during Kennedy's November 1961 "Thanksgiving Day Massacre," a shakeup in the State Department. His replacement, Averill Harriman, eager for innovation on China, hired Rice as his deputy for economic affairs. At the same time, Bowles was replaced by George Ball, who shared the skepticism of the working levels.[3] A draft of a presidential speech calling for recognition of two Chinas was developed in the fall of 1961 by Bowles, Thomson, and Thomas Hughes of the Intelligence and Research Bureau. It is unclear if the draft ever found its way to the White House.[4]

A subtle but important shift in the structure of State's Far Eastern Bureau occurred in 1962 when a new Mainland China Affairs desk was created as a distinct institutional office. Previously, all China-related issues fell under the purview of the Republic of China Affairs desk; its name indicated its priorities.[5] If organization reflects priorities, then the change reflects the sense of the China watchers at State that US policy was inadequate, specifically in its persistent belief in the fiction that Communist control over the mainland was temporary.[6]

The year 1962 was marked by consensus at the State Department that the Sino-Soviet split was real and of strategic significance; a State Department task force, led by Ball, even considered the possibility of grain trade to China. Rusk, however, counseled that these types of discussions were not yet for public consumption.[7] By 1963, the potential for a Chinese atomic bomb test began to take center stage in the administration. Other issues related to China were placed on the back burner.[8] When Harriman moved up to the post of undersecretary for political affairs in March 1963, he told Roger Hilsman, his replacement as assistant secretary for Far Eastern affairs: "You must immediately begin to think about laying the groundwork

for what the president might do about China policy in his second administration."[9] Harriman was pushing Hilsman to prepare for changes, but was
also warning him that this was a second-term task due to domestic political
constraints.[10]

Kennedy made the case for détente between the West and the Soviet
bloc in a commencement speech at American University on June 10, 1963,
stating that Americans should "reexamine our attitude toward the cold
war" and that it was possible to seek a "relaxation of tension without relax-
ing our guard."[11] While Kennedy did not specifically mention China in
June, he did state at a press conference on November 14, 1963, "When
the Red Chinese indicate a desire to live at peace with the United States,
with other countries surrounding it, then quite obviously the United States
would reappraise its policies. We are not wedded to a policy of hostility to
Red China."[12]

With these ideas bubbling up from the bottom and similar public statements coming from the top, an end to the containment and isolation policy
seemed inevitable. Rusk, however, was perceived as the outlier, opposed
to any reevaluation of US policy on China. Thomson, by 1963 a special
assistant to the assistant secretary of state for Far Eastern affairs, described
Rusk as a "zealot" on maintaining the isolation of China; Rusk also reportedly told another staffer, "You know, there are some young men in this
government who think we're going to change our China policy, and I can
tell you they're dead wrong."[13]

In the fall of 1963, when Hilsman was asked to speak at the Commonwealth Club in San Francisco about US-Chinese relations, he felt the key
issue was accepting the permanence of the Communist regime. Believing
that the PRC was on shaky ground led directly to a policy of extended
pressure, and hopes that the regime would collapse on its own or through
ROC efforts. Assuming that Beijing's leaders were going to stay in power
for the long haul meant finding a way to open serious dialogue with them.[14]
Hilsman saw an opportunity to make that sentiment public.[15]

Within the State Department the speech was drafted by the staff at
the Far Eastern Bureau: Hilsman; Thomson; Desk Officer for Mainland
China Affairs Lindsey Grant; Director of the Office of Research Allen
Whiting; special assistant Joseph Neubert; Public Affairs Advisor Abram
Manell; and Deputy for Economic Affairs Robert Barnett. Hilsman and
Thomson felt that the initial drafts were weak. Thomson gave a draft to
NSC staffer for Far Eastern affairs Michael Forrestal, who also felt it
lacked the necessary boldness. Thomson made changes to the speech, and
his draft became the speech that Hilsman gave.[16] None of the descrip-

tions of the speech show participation by the Department of Defense, the CIA, any members of the NSC staff beyond Forrestal, or anyone outside the Far Eastern Bureau of State.

Hilsman describes the final draft as a "very careful speech" that would lay the groundwork for the second-term policy of the Kennedy administration. It would acknowledge the Beijing regime's hold on the mainland and make an appeal to China's leaders based on that reality: you can end your isolation by showing the world that you will no longer act aggressively. He described the notion as "out of that flows open door speech—'we will match you step by step.'"[17]

Following the Kennedy assassination, some in the Far Eastern Bureau wondered if Hilsman should cancel the speech. Thomson, Manell, and Neubert felt that the speech was important, but that Hilsman was taking a great "personal risk." Hilsman was seen as a Kennedy man, and an initiative on such a momentous foreign policy issue might be seen as undermining the authority of the new president.[18] It was unclear what Johnson's views on China were, and even a speech that echoed Kennedy's November statement on China could be too provocative or precedent setting for the transition period. Hilsman suggested that part of his reasoning for going ahead with the speech was to prod the new administration: "We might as well smoke out Johnson on this one."[19] Hilsman felt he could use the transition as a way to force the issue of ending China's isolation out of the depths of the Far Eastern Bureau and onto the front page of American newspapers.

To do this, however, Hilsman would need clearance from the upper levels of the State Department and the White House. Actual approval of the speech seemed to be sketchy at best. Hilsman's efforts to get approval began on December 9, only four days before he was scheduled to deliver it.[20] The draft was sent to Harriman's office for final clearance, but with Harriman out of town, the speech was cleared by his assistant William Sullivan. A copy of the speech was given to Rusk as he prepared to leave for a NATO conference in Europe. There are several versions of Rusk's reaction to the speech. Thomson claimed that after a quick glance at the speech and reassurance that it did not condone the pending French recognition of Communist China, Rusk approved. Thomson then cleared the speech with the White House by gaining approval from Michael Forrestal, Bundy's assistant on Asia. Bundy did not see the speech, nor did any of the all-purpose White House staffers of Kennedy (Theodore Sorensen or Arthur Schlesinger) or Johnson (Walter Jenkins, Bill Moyers). Hilsman gives a slightly different description of the Rusk approval: "I took the speech up to Rusk, told him what was in it, and said, 'Do you want to read it? There's going to be some flap about it.'" Rusk responded "'No, I'll let you do your own thing . . .'" In this version, Rusk never read the speech, but allowed Hilsman to use his own judgment on the substance of the speech and whether to give it. In either case, it is unlikely that Rusk was fooled; Hilsman had not gotten one past him. Rusk likely knew what Hilsman would say even if he did not review every word. He may have decided that Hilsman's views were not very different from those expressed by Kennedy in November, and continuity should carry the day during the transition.[21] Harriman and Ball did not see the speech until the morning of December 13 and were not thrilled about its content; they were even less pleased upon being told that Rusk, the White House, and Harriman's own office had already cleared the speech. Soon after, Forrestal called Thomson to explicitly tell him not to say that the White House had cleared the speech.[22] Given Rusk's approval of the speech, no one had the authority to unapprove it, but the upper levels of State and the NSC staff were backing away from the speech even before it was given.

Most of the speech given on December 13 showed continuity with Kennedy and Eisenhower policy on China. Though the speech is often seen as a break with the past, it was brutally critical of Chinese leaders, continuing with themes that echo back to Truman. Hilsman declared the Great Leap Forward a "failure" and was "astounded" at the "arrogance" of Chinese leaders who continued their collectivization of agriculture in defiance of all the evidence that these policies were always disastrous. He called Chinese leaders "parochial," "Marxist puritans," who showed a "stubborn addiction to theories which do not work in the modern world." He specifically ridiculed China's pretensions to global leadership: "The Chinese Communists have set themselves up as a model for the less-developed nations. But like the king in the fairy tale, they seem unaware that they have no clothes. . . . The tragedy of the closed and stagnant society on the mainland is dramatized by the robust survival of an alternative model for Chinese development: the record of the Government of the Republic of China . . . the results are extraordinarily impressive." The real meat of the speech comes in discussing Chinese aggression. Hilsman began by bluntly stating the basis of US policy: "Our prime objective concerning Communist China is that it not subvert or commit aggression against its free world neighbors. It must not be allowed to accomplish through force of arms that success which it has rarely achieved at the ballot box." He pointed out the paradox that the US continued to "maintain a policy of non-recognition and trade embargo of Communist China—at a time when we are willing to broaden contact with the Soviet Union." The reason for the paradox, he explained, was that China "remains wedded to a fundamentalist form of communism which emphasizes violent revolution." The last few paragraphs of the speech contain the seeds of the controversy that followed. Hilsman stated that

> we pursue today towards Communist China a policy of the open door: we are determined to keep the door open to the possibility of change, and not to slam it shut against any developments which might advance our national good, serve the free world, and benefit the people of China. . . . We hope that, confronted with firmness which will make foreign adventure unprofitable, and yet offered the prospect that the way back into the community of man is not closed to it, the Chinese Communist regime will eventually forsake its present venomous hatreds.[23]

The reaction to the speech was mixed. Hilsman states that newspaper editorials were supportive (15 of 21 written by January 1964 were supportive).[24] The reaction of the Committee of One Million was predictable. They accused the administration of being "soft on communism" and sent a letter of protest to every member of Congress.[25] Hilsman had actually sent a draft of the speech to committee president Marvin Liebman, but the gesture did not soften the committee's response as it accused Hilsman of accepting two Chinas and engaging in a "pursuit of policies based on illusions."[26] There was little congressional response.

Ultimately, the Hilsman speech made no real waves. The administration launched no major initiatives based on his ideas, nor did it condemn the speech in public. Hilsman did have lunch with Johnson aide Walter Jenkins and asked him for Johnson's opinion of the speech. Jenkins reported back to Hilsman and Hughes that Johnson felt the speech was "on the whole, very good."[27] Hilsman sums up the effort by labeling it "the beginning of the beginning."[28] Interestingly, Hilsman resigned from the administration in February 1964. No source connects the speech to the resignation. At the time, it was widely believed that Hilsman resigned over what he saw as an overmilitarization of US policy in Vietnam. Both the Johnson White House and Hilsman denied that the resignation had anything to do with differences over Vietnam.[29]

If Hilsman had tried to slip one past Rusk, he understood the risks. He felt compelled to send Rusk a memo explaining the speech and how it did not reflect a departure from previous policy.[30] In 1965, nearly two years later, the process was still being questioned. In response to a *Newsweek* article stating that Kennedy had personally approved the speech, McGeorge Bundy asked Thomson, by that point an NSC staffer, if that had been the case. Thomson informed him that Kennedy had not, in fact, cleared the speech.[31] Neither had Johnson. Any flap from the speech blew over quickly, and no significant change or serious interagency or upper-level thinking on China would occur until after Johnson was inaugurated for his own full term in 1965.

The Long Range Study 1965–1966

The first Kennedy/Johnson-era full interagency review of China policy began in the fall of 1965, four and a half years after Kennedy entered office. Incoming administrations typically take a six- to nine-month period to evaluate all major issues through their formal interagency committee process; the effort sets a baseline for administration policy. These reviews are particularly important if the new administration is of a different party. The new president has just run a multiyear campaign excoriating the "failed" policies of his political opponents, and the new course needs to be charted. Kennedy's informal processes meant that the president and his senior advisors never felt the need for such an effort. Johnson, however, initiated one in the first year after his election. Five aspects of the review are instructive. First, the change in president mattered; Johnson eventually gave a green light to a study that Kennedy had never considered important enough to launch. Second, interestingly, it was the Joint Chiefs of Staff and Secretary of Defense Robert McNamara who finally convinced Rusk and Bundy that a major study was necessary. Third, the interagency review was not initially connected to the upper-level thinking on whether to offer an olive branch to China in the summer of 1966; for that reason, they are examined here as two separate case studies. Fourth, the analysis was undertaken against the backdrop of the Vietnam War, yet it does not allow the war to define the study. The study considers China in the long term, out to 1976, in the context of its evolution and ambition, outside the prism of Vietnam and the possibility of US-Chinese conflict in Indochina. Fifth, while its disconnect from the upper level might be seen as a weakness, the strength of its analysis may be a direct result of that disconnect; it was not guided by the needs of the moment, nor were participants pressured to draw conclusions that supported current strategy.

The case confirms the evolution-balance model: the bureaucracies and the president's senior advisors successfully convinced the president to initiate a full formal interagency examination of a policy, essentially acknowledging a weakness in the administration's process and working to rectify it. By the time it had been completed, the formal SIG/IRG system had been established. The review was then vetted through the FE/IRG and a China Working Group that used the Long Term Study as its starting point.

Political Context

The years 1964 and 1965 were transitional years for US-Chinese relations. The most significant change, of course, was the occupant of the Oval Office. Johnson, like Kennedy before him, was a committed anti-Communist, perhaps even more acutely aware of the consequences for Democrats who appear soft on China. His escalation of the intervention in Vietnam is a testament to his belief in the domino theory and his fear that failure in Vietnam would cripple his presidency. Three sets of issues place the Long Term Study in its larger political context. First, the PRC's strategic position evolved significantly in a short time with victories (detonation of its first atomic bomb in October 1964) and defeats (the coup in Indonesia and Pakistan's failures in Kashmir). While its ability to deter the US and the USSR had taken a giant leap, regional defeats emphasized the limits of its influence. More importantly, China's own domestic politics entered a phase of turmoil during the Cultural Revolution (1966–76) that could cripple its potential to mount any serious threat to the US. Second, the ROC saw similar successes and failures during this period. While its standing at the UN eroded somewhat, US intervention in Vietnam gave Chiang Kai-shek hope that the US was warming up to the idea of military action to deal with the PRC. ROC lobbying for assistance gained renewed urgency. Third, and most significantly, the Johnson administration moved into Vietnam; Johnson's war began in 1964 and, for the administration, Vietnam was at root about the expansion of Chinese Communism. The US could not afford to allow another domino to fall, and Johnson could not allow his administration to be labeled by its domestic political opponents as the one "who lost Vietnam." The Long Term Study was undertaken with all these issues as its backdrop. In some ways, this was a poor time to begin assessing the future of US-China relations out to 1976 (the mandate of the study). East Asia was in such flux that predicting what might happen in one year was difficult; examining a decade-long window might have been impossible.

Johnson and China before the Presidency

That Johnson was a Cold War hawk should not be surprising. His instincts were exactly what could be expected from a southern conservative Democrat during the first few decades of the Cold War: Communism was a global threat, and the purpose of US foreign policy was to contain the spread of Communism and Soviet power wherever and whenever it threatened the US or its allies. Johnson was a New Dealer through and through, having served as director of the Texas office of the National Youth Administration from 1935 until he was elected to the House in 1937. He moved from the House to the Senate in 1948. Though absolutely loyal to FDR, Johnson was still a southern Democrat. He had always been more conservative than Kennedy; his selection on the ticket in 1960 was to reassure the southern conservative wing of the Democratic Party that a Northeastern liberal like Kennedy would not be allowed to push civil rights legislation too far or too fast.

On foreign policy, however, Johnson showed himself to be nearly a quintessential hawk after exhibiting some early idealistic support for the Baruch Plan (a proposal for giving all atomic weaponry to the UN) and opposition to the House Un-American Activities Committee (voting against its funding in 1946).[32] His campaign speeches illustrated an allegiance to the core of Truman's foreign policy and a belief in what would eventually be called the domino theory. In 1948 he said:

> The great Russian bear, a bear who walks like a man, is stalking across Europe; and to every citizen of that unhappy continent, a bear on the back doorstep is much more persuasive than an eagle across the ocean. . . . If Italy is lost, Greece will be cut off and Turkey isolated. The bell has tolled for Rumania, Yugoslavia, Czechoslovakia. It is tolling for Finland, Norway, Sweden. Each toll of the bell brings closer the day when it could toll for you and me.[33]

Johnson was one of Truman's most vocal supporters during the Korean War, seeing a weak stand in South Korea as akin to the appeasement of Hitler at the 1938 Munich Conference. Johnson explained that he "wasn't any Chamberlain umbrella man": accepting North Korean aggression "would mean a third world war, just as similar incidents had brought on the second world war." Truman's intervention in Korea was to guarantee "no more Munichs."[34] As soon as news reached Johnson that the North had invaded and Truman had pledged aid to the South, he had his aides begin drafting a letter praising Truman. He wanted it to be the first Truman would receive from a member of Congress, emphasizing to staffer Horace Busby that he wanted the letter "on Truman's desk when he gets there in the morning." Johnson expressed his "deep gratitude and admiration of your courageous response," adding that US support for South Korea gave a "new and noble meaning to freedom."[35] Johnson saw Vietnam through the same prism of lessons learned; it would be appeasement to ignore Communist aggression.[36]

Johnson's foreign policy beliefs and hawkish anti-Communism were not simply products of support for Democratic presidents. He had been a strong ally of Eisenhower while in the Senate. His bipartisanship did not always sit well with every Democrat in the Senate, but was crucial in Eisenhower's efforts to restrain the less internationalist wing of the Republican Party led by Senator Robert Taft of Ohio. Johnson had been a strong supporter of US ballistic missile programs and space programs, played a key role in the creation of NASA, and fought with Eisenhower against congressional limitations on presidential power in US foreign policy.[37] Johnson had developed his own ideas on "massive retaliation" two years before John Foster Dulles's famous speech declaring that the US might use nuclear weapons as a response to any Soviet provocation around the world. In 1952, a Johnson Senate newsletter stated: "We should announce, I believe, that any act of aggression, anywhere by any communist forces will be regarded as an act of aggression by the Soviet Union. . . . If anywhere in the world—by any means open or concealed—communism trespasses upon the soil of the free world, we should unleash all the power at our command upon the vitals of the Soviet Union."[38] Johnson supported Eisenhower's Formosa Resolution of 1955, granting the president congressional approval to use force to defend Taiwan and the Pescadores from Chinese aggression. During that Senate debate in January 1955, a possible amendment in the mix would have placed Quemoy and Matsu outside the area that Eisenhower would have permission to defend. From his hospital bed, Johnson voted against the amendment and for the defense of Quemoy and Matsu.[39]

Asia was a special case for Johnson. As he took office, Communism seemed to be on the march in the Pacific Rim at the same time as the post–Cuban Missile Crisis détente with the Soviet Union was being cultivated across the Atlantic. Kennedy had sent Johnson on a goodwill tour of Asia in May 1961. The trip may have been a way to reassure allies and give a sulking vice president something to do. Staffer Eric Goldman felt that for Johnson it was "the most satisfying episode in his whole three years as Vice-President." The visit took him to the Philippines, Thailand, South Vietnam, Taiwan, Pakistan, and India. In Taipei he met with Chiang Kai-shek and gave a speech in which he proclaimed: "I assure you on behalf of President Kennedy that we love our friends, and expect to stand behind them every day, today, tomorrow, and every day to come." He described his newspaper coverage as a "carnival when the New Frontier came to Taipei." For Johnson, the tour of US allies reaffirmed his belief that the US must be committed to stopping the spread of Communism in Asia. His trip report to Kennedy was clear in how he viewed the situation:

> The key to what is done by Asians in defense of Southeast Asian freedom is confidence in the United States. There is no alternative to United States leadership in Southeast Asia. . . . The battle against Communism must be joined in Southeast Asia with strength and determination to achieve success there—or the United States, inevitably must surrender the Pacific and take up our defenses on our own shores. . . . Without this inhibitory influence, the island outposts—Philippines, Japan, Taiwan—have no security and the Pacific becomes a Red Sea. . . . We must decide whether to help these countries to the best of our ability or to throw in the towel in the area and pull back our defenses to San Francisco and a "Fortress America" concept.[40]

Given that relations with the USSR were on the upswing, the root of the problem in Asia was China and its support for Communist movements, particularly in Laos, Indonesia, and Vietnam. US intervention in the Vietnam War, often called "Johnson's War," was simply an extension of the logic of containment.[41] Johnson's perceptions of China, its role in the Vietnam War, and the policies that grew out of these beliefs were the consensus beliefs at the time: the US must prevent the spread of Soviet-Chinese Communism in East Asia and do it by force if necessary; if Vietnam falls, the rest of Indochina would fall, then Japan, India, and on and on. Importantly, Rusk shared this domino theory view of the geopolitical challenge in East Asia.[42]

Of course, the domestic politics of the situation were also on Johnson's mind. Much of Johnson's views on policy toward China can be attributed to domestic political imperatives. In a transition period conversation with the US ambassador to South Vietnam, Henry Cabot Lodge, Johnson stated what would eventually become a mantra: "I am not going to be the President who saw Southeast Asia go the way China went."[43] Johnson feared the electoral and policy consequences of not succeeding in that task. He was absolutely certain that Republicans would use charges of being "soft" on Communism as a means to kill the Great Society social programs that he saw as the heart of his legacy.[44] Even if Johnson took suggestions from his less hawkish advisors on China, many of whom believed that the US isolation strategy was obsolete, the domestic imperative remained. A conversation with Senator Richard Russell in January 1964 about the impending French recognition of China summed up Johnson's domestic dilemma well; both men agreed that eventually the US would have to recognize China, but that was impossible in the short term. In Russell's words: "Politically, right now it's poison, of course."[45]

International Political Context

For China, the mid-1960s are difficult to classify. The year 1964 started off well. In January, France recognized the PRC as the legitimate China. The propaganda victory was invaluable; the former colonial power of Indochina now recognized the PRC. At the UN Security Council, the recognition score was now tied: two nations recognizing the PRC (France and the USSR) and two nations recognizing the ROC (the US and UK).[46] At home, however, the Great Leap Forward, Mao's policy of rapid agricultural collectivization begun in 1963, had already failed, destroying the agricultural system in China and generating a horrific famine. US intelligence estimates discounted the crisis in 1963, expecting China to recover quickly. The US assumed China would continue to make progress toward nuclear capability and remain the strongest land power in Asia.[47]

China ended 1964 on a high note as well, enhancing its strategic position with a successful detonation of an atomic bomb on October 16, 1964. Chinese pursuit of nuclear weapons had begun during the 1950s and accelerated after the Sino-Soviet split; out from under the Soviet umbrella, China emphasized self-reliance in its foreign policy and military developments, including nuclear weapons. For Chinese leaders crossing the nuclear threshold was an indication of its status, a message about its growing power, a way to defend national liberation movements by deterring their enemies, and a necessary measure that could prevent the PRC from being bullied again by the US over Quemoy, Matsu, and Taiwan.[48]

The successful test in October 1964 was no surprise to the US. A Special National Intelligence Estimate from July 1963, for example, speculated that given the "normal number of difficulties," the Chinese test might come in late 1964 or early 1965.[49] After the test, the PRC tried to use what it believed was newfound leverage to change US strategic doctrine. Premier Zhou Enlai pledged that the PRC would never use nuclear weapons first and offered direct US-PRC talks on a joint no-first use pledge. Zhou also suggested convening a conference of all the nuclear powers to draw up plans for the complete elimination of nuclear weapons. The US rejected each of the proposals.[50] The administration did assess the possibility of launching preemptive strikes to destroy the program, but decided that China's arsenal would lack any serious ability to strike the US or US allies for years; it had bragging rights, but little else.[51] Even a successful detonation of a thermonuclear device on June 17, 1967 made little difference. China's nuclear arsenal did not emerge as a serious political-military consideration for the US until the 1990s.[52] For Johnson, the PRC's conventional capabilities and its potential to nurture allies in the developing world were still the paramount threats.

Failures in Indonesia and Pakistan illustrated the limits of PRC power. In particular, the emergence of a strongly anti-Communist government in Indonesia tipped the balance of power in Southeast Asia toward the US. In the 1950s and 1960s, Indonesian leader Sukarno had been attempting to maintain a delicate balance between the Indonesian military and the Communist Party of Indonesia. The PRC had growing success in disrupting that balance, pulling Indonesia, the largest nation in Southeast Asia, leftward during the early 1960s. Indonesia was a key member of the Non-Aligned Movement in the 1950s, but moved steadily toward a more militant anti-Western, anti-imperialism stance, even using Chinese-style rhetoric of people's war and anti-imperialism as a rallying cry during its conflict with Malaysia from 1963 to 1965 (the "Konfrontasi").[53] China was certainly instrumental in Sukarno's pledge on September 25, 1965 that Indonesia was about to enter the "second stage of the Indonesian Revolution, namely implementation of socialism."[54] China's plans collapsed spectacularly in October 1965 when the Indonesian military overthrew Sukarno and crushed the Communist Party of Indonesia, while killing tens of thousands of left-leaning politicians and citizens, and thousands more who were suspected of harboring political thoughts that might challenge the new rulers in any way.[55] China's bid to lead Indonesia solidly into its revolutionary camp had failed. Instead, Indonesia's new military regime under General Suharto was firmly anti-Communist, anti-Chinese, and pro-Western. The role of the US in the coup is still debated, though it was obviously a significant shift in the regional balance of power welcomed by the administration.[56]

China also suffered a setback in South Asia when its ally Pakistan failed in its attempt to take territory in the disputed region of Jammu and Kashmir. Low-level conflict had begun in the summer of 1965 across the line of control that separated Indian and Pakistani-held areas of Jammu and Kashmir. Pakistan's August offensive was blunted by India and a cease fire was ultimately implemented on September 21/22, 1965. China had defeated

India in the 1962 war over disputed territory in the same region, but its ally in Pakistan could not repeat the feat.[57]

The Chinese representation issue was still the main diplomatic arena for the US and China. US policy of using the "important question" parliamentary tactic—raising the threshold for passage of a resolution on the China seat to a two-thirds vote at the UN General Assembly—had worked well. The 1961 vote tally was 61 votes for making the issue an important question, with 34 against and 9 abstentions. Even though the 1961 resolution calling for removal of the ROC and recognition of the PRC as the legitimate government of China favored Beijing, 48–37–19, it would remain a dead letter until the important question threshold was reached. The ROC's targeted foreign aid for developing nations, particularly in Africa, was successful in holding back the PRC's appeal to the developing world and switching African votes toward the ROC. The 1962 vote on replacing the ROC with the PRC flipped back in the ROC's direction: only 42 for making the switch, 56 against, and 12 abstentions. The year 1963 saw the same pattern. Over 50% of the General Assembly voted against replacement (41–57–12), and no important question vote was even held.[58]

The PRC responded to the new US strategy by downplaying the importance of the UN. In its propaganda, the important question resolution of 1961 was seen as one "which tramples upon the UN Charter."[59] On September 29, 1965 Foreign Minister Chen Yi stated a set of demands that would be prerequisites for China's entry into the UN, all nonstarters: the UN must adopt a revolutionary philosophy; reform its organization; withdraw its Korean War resolution identifying North Korea and China as aggressors and instead label the US as the aggressor; revise the UN charter; and expel "all imperialist puppets." Of course, removing the ROC from the UN was the core demand.[60]

In the zero-sum game across the Taiwan Strait, the ROC saw its fortunes rise. China's new atomic capability and the escalating war in Vietnam encouraged Chiang to forge a more aggressive policy toward China, particularly in 1964 and 1965 as the US moved into Vietnam, illustrating its willingness to use force in Asia. His lobbying for US assistance in retaking the mainland continued. He made his case to the Johnson administration forcefully from 1964 through 1966, reopening and expanding the arguments he had lost during the Kennedy administration. He renewed his calls for the US to help the ROC overthrow Mao's regime and argued that the US should give Taiwan nuclear weapons or use US nuclear weapons to preemptively destroy Chinese infrastructure before China launched a nuclear strike on Taiwan.[61] Chiang linked his fight with China to the

Vietnam struggle, offering to deploy ROC troops alongside US troops in Indochina, but the US worked hard to bury the idea.[62] Though Kennedy had agreed to the joint US-ROC Blue Lion Committee that studied plans for ROC attacks on the mainland, a committee that Chiang saw as the thin edge of the wedge, the Johnson administration spent years trying to blunt those hopes.[63]

Ultimately for the Johnson administration, China policy during this period could not be separated from the Vietnam War; Vietnam was a subset of the larger struggle against China and both nations' rivalry with the Soviet Union. The main arena of competition for the US and China was Indochina, and the main issue was China's ability to spread its revolution to Vietnam and beyond. The year 1965 was the key year for the US intervention in Vietnam. At the time of Kennedy's death, the US had roughly 16,000 troops in Vietnam, mostly advisors and Special Forces. Johnson added approximately another 7,000 through 1964. The Rolling Thunder bombing campaign began in March 1965, and large contingents of US ground forces began to deploy soon after, culminating in the July 1965 decision to add another 125,000 Americans to the war effort. By the end of 1965, the US had over 180,000 troops in the area and the US was committed to full combat operations.[64]

US intervention in Vietnam added complexity to a larger drama with three main players. China was not only combatting the West, but it was also competing with the Soviet Union to be the true leader of Communism in the world. A National Intelligence Estimate (NIE) from May 1965 stated it clearly: "We believe that the principal aims of Chinese Communist foreign policy over the next few years will be . . . to eject the West, especially the US, from Asia and to diminish US and Western influence throughout the world . . . and to supplant the influence of the USSR in the world at large."[65] Ray Cline, special assistant to the director of central intelligence and former CIA station chief, emphasized the domestic political aspects of China's policies in Southeast Asia. In a memo to Rostow in 1966, he argued that the factionalism within the Communist Party and the failure of the Great Leap Forward, which "succeeded in alienating" the Party leadership "from most of China's youth, intellectuals, and political cadres on whom the regime must depend to get its orders carried out," had increased the Communist Party's need for a foreign policy victory in Vietnam.[66]

One additional factor focused the administration's mind on the China threat. On September 3, 1965, *People's Daily*, the official Communist Party newspaper, published an essay by Chinese defense minister Lin Biao, entitled "Long Live the Victory of People's War."[67] The essay was written to commemorate the twentieth anniversary of the defeat of Japan in 1945, but it served as a loud proclamation to domestic and international audiences that China was rededicating itself to wars of national liberation. It was also a tutorial for the North Vietnamese in their expanding fight with the US. The essay was steeped in propaganda and the tortuous language required to maintain congruence with Communist doctrine, but its aggressive tone had administration officials comparing it to Hitler's *Mein Kampf.*[68] Most saw the speech as a call to arms for Communist movements all across the world and a clear warning to the US that it now faced a real challenge from China, even as, and perhaps because of, the possibilities of détente with the Soviet Union.[69]

In the context of Lin Biao's essay, the US could be forgiven for seeing China as unremittingly hostile. The essay, however, takes great pains to emphasize "self-reliance," even counseling the North Vietnamese to "rely on the strength of the masses in one's own country and prepare to carry on the fight independently." In short, China was signaling that it was not preparing to intervene directly as it had in Korea.[70] Tying the US down in a war fought by the North Vietnamese while focusing Communist Party energies on domestic priorities gave China the best of both worlds. China did send additional signs, however, that there were scenarios where it would intervene with its own forces.[71]

The administration made the case about the Chinese threat at every opportunity. Undersecretary of State George Ball told members of Congress the basic problem facing the US in 1965: "And what is really involved in the larger effort in South Vietnam is whether the Free World will be able to limit the expansionist drive of Communist China, not merely in the Southeast Asia peninsula but on down through those soft islands . . . Indonesia . . . the Philippines . . . and ultimately . . . Australia."[72] At his press conference of July 28, 1965, the day the administration announced an increase of 75,000 troops bound for Vietnam, Johnson answered a letter from a "woman in the Midwest" asking "why" the US was in Vietnam. He explained that the US was already at war:

> It is guided by North Viet-Nam and it is spurred by Communist China. Its goal is to conquer the South, to defeat American power, and to extend the Asiatic dominion of communism. There are great stakes in the balance. Most of the non-Communist nations of Asia cannot, by themselves and alone, resist the growing might and the grasping ambition of Asian communism.[73]

The administration was not deviating from the consensus and commitments the US had made during the Cold War. The logic of containment required US intervention in Vietnam. In his memoirs, even after the debate on Vietnam had become contentious and toxic, and US-Chinese relations had taken an abrupt turn toward normalization under Nixon, Johnson restated the themes that led him to escalate the war. He argued that China and its allies "were undoubtedly counting on South Vietnamese collapse and an ignominious US withdrawal. . . . Clearly the decisions we were making would determine not merely the fate of Vietnam but also the shape of Asia for many years to come."[74]

The US knew that China was assisting Vietnam, but the depth of China's commitment to Vietnam was uncertain. Would China intervene in Vietnam, the way it had in Korea, if the North Vietnamese regime were in danger of being overthrown? Both Johnson and Rusk felt that China almost assuredly would. Rusk considered the issue in his memoirs: "If anyone had asked me in 1963 whether we could put five hundred thousand American soldiers in South Vietnam and bomb almost every military target in North Vietnam up to the Chinese Border without bringing the Chinese in, I would have been hard pressed to say yes."[75] The US believed that the Soviet Union and China were competing for North Vietnam's allegiance, a situation that added pressure on China to come through for North Vietnam the way it had for North Korea a decade earlier.[76] That threat of Chinese intervention is essential to explaining the way the US fought in Vietnam. Johnson's limited war policies—counterinsurgency, gradual escalation, avoidance of major operations in Cambodia, and repeated bombing pauses in tandem with calls for negotiations—were restraints placed on the US military out of fear that these actions might lead to direct Chinese involvement. In short, China was always the main antagonist, and North Vietnam simply the proxy.

Domestic Political Context

Johnson feared that losing Vietnam would lead quickly to a replay of the "Who Lost China?" debate from the late 1940s and early 1950s. His political opponents would use a collapse in Vietnam as leverage to cripple his presidency and crush the Great Society programs he cherished. The administration felt this pressure from the beginning of its tenure. In a January 9, 1964, memo Bundy wrote to Johnson that "the political damage to Truman and Acheson from the fall of China arose because most Americans came to believe that we could and should have done more than we did to prevent it. This is exactly what would happen now if we should seem to be the first to quit on Saigon."[77] As he explained to one supporter over the phone, he had several options in Vietnam: "One is run and let the dominoes start falling over. And God almighty, what they said about us leaving China would just be warming up compared to what they'd say now."[78] In his memoirs, Johnson put that fear of a new round of recriminations in the context of the foreign policy consensus, rather than his own political fortunes:

> A divisive debate about "who lost Vietnam" would be, in my judgment, even more destructive to our national life than the argument over China had been. It would inevitably increase isolationist pressures from the right and left and cause a pulling back from our commitments in Europe and the Middle East as well as Asia.[79]

Whether the lessons of the "Who Lost China?" accusations against Truman made Johnson more worried about his political future or the future of the foreign policy consensus is unclear. In either case, it added to the core political context of Vietnam; internationally or domestically, the issue was China.

Narrative of Decision

NSC staffer Komer first suggested a bottom-up review to SANSA McGeorge Bundy in March 1961. He thought Bundy should ask the State Department to initiate it. In the margin of the memo, he wrote: "Do mention 5–10-year focus."[80] This would be the term of reference for the study once it began in 1965. Komer continued to press on the issue, writing in April that "having determined that very little thinking on China is going on in this town," he would try his hand at developing a statement of China policy. He made the case for why a large interagency review was absolutely essential.[81] His memos were read, but no action was taken. The Department of Defense (DoD) also had concerns about the lack of an interagency study. In June 1961 JCS chair Lyman Lemnitzer asked McNamara to consider a State-Defense-CIA interagency review on how Chinese acquisition of nuclear weapons might impact Chinese foreign policy in the long run. The JCS had examined the issue, but thought a major interagency review would be useful.[82] Chief of Naval Operations Arleigh Burke sent a similar memo to McNamara asking him to push State to begin a major evaluation of China strategy; the US needed a "comprehensive statement of policy toward communist China."[83] In 1961, memos from the Office of the Assistant Secretary of Defense for International Security Affairs were sent to senior members of the DoD asking whether an interagency review had been started. If none had been performed or were in the works, the memo to the DoD asked, is policy still based on a set of Eisenhower-era NSC documents? A similar memo was sent to the NSC staff.[84] The CIA also had its own NIEs on Chinese foreign policy, the Sino-Soviet split, and Chinese economic issues.[85] Of course, the State Department's Far Eastern Bureau had been working on the issue in great detail. All this activity occurred within each departmental or agency silo.

The idea for the Long Range Study seems to have come out of a shorter-range study initiated by the Joint Chiefs. In the winter of 1965, the JCS studied the possibilities of direct US-China war. This study was submitted to the Senior Policy Group, an ad hoc committee composed of the Deputy Secretary of Defense, Cyrus Vance; the chair of the Joint Chiefs of Staff, General Earle Wheeler; and the acting deputy under-secretary of state for political affairs, Llewelyn Thompson. The Senior Policy Group asked for further study of the issue, still focusing on the possibility that greater US action in Southeast Asia would lead to real US-Chinese confrontations. The new study would still be under the authority of the JCS, directed by Lt. General B. E. Spivey, director of the Joint Staff's J-5 Strategic Plans and Policy section. It would be an interagency study, however, including members of the State Department's Policy Planning Council and the CIA. The CIA seems to have been considered a junior member of the study group, never mentioned in memos as a participant, but showing up on attendance lists. All told, the study included 13 officers from the Joint Staff, two officials from the Department of Defense office of International Security Affairs, and one official each from State and the CIA. The study began on March 8, 1965 and was finished on April 30.[86]

Critically, on that same day, the Senior Policy Group agreed to establish a longer-range follow-on study that would begin in the fall of 1965.[87] That meant that the JCS-led study would be a preliminary warm-up to a larger interagency study co-led by State and Defense. The April 30 report specifically refers to itself as the "Communist China (Short Range Report)," and defines its study question as the potential for direct conflict between the US and China in Southeast Asia in the short term. The results of the report were narrowly focused on political-military considerations about the escalation of US operations in Vietnam, highlighting topics such as how to keep the war limited to Vietnam, the danger of US-PRC naval confrontations in the South China Sea (high), the likelihood that China might directly intervene in the war on the ground (low as long as the North

Vietnamese adhered to people's war strategies), and methods to intensify the Sino-Soviet split. The conclusion of the report was prescient given the unfolding of the war over the next few years. It predicted the long-term outcome of the Vietnam War: the prospects that the US could inflict enough harm on North Vietnam to convince it and China to give up their revolutionary goals were low. Since the US was also unlikely to find a way to end the flow of supplies to North Vietnam, it needed to come up with other options.[88] From that perspective, the story of the US in Vietnam is the failure to come up with those other options.

The senior leadership of the State Department met on July 6, 1965 to discuss the report. Attending the meeting were Rusk, Ball, Thompson, Assistant Secretary of State for Far Eastern Affairs William Bundy, as well as other officials from the Far Eastern Bureau, Policy Planning Council, and Bureau of Political-Military Affairs. Thompson briefed the members of the group on the study and each had his own view of the strengths and weaknesses of the report. Most importantly, the group suggested some of the terms of reference for the follow-on longer-range study. Rusk contributed two key parameters for the study. First, he felt that the long-range study should not make any assumptions about the direction of Chinese behavior. It should consider the potential for China to continue its current aggressive behavior as well as the possibility that the Sino-Soviet split, the potential of a turnabout in Indonesia, or difficulties in Vietnam might lead China "toward peaceful co-existence." Rusk also elevated participation in the discussions, asking for his staff to set up a meeting between himself, McNamara, and McGeorge Bundy.[89] Thompson quickly moved to set up the meeting but added other officials to the attendance list: all members of the Senior Policy Group (whom he called the "Board of Directors" for the study), as well as William Bundy of the Far Eastern Bureau and Assistant Secretary of Defense for International Security Affairs John McNaughton. A Thompson memo to Rusk a week later provided a set of guidelines for thinking about China, many of which formed the basis of the issues addressed in the Long Term Study.[90]

A meeting between Rusk, McNamara, and Bundy was held on August 27, 1965. It was preceded by a considerable amount of State Department and JCS memo traffic defining the parameters of the study. In addition to the key senior advisors, the meeting included five members of the State Department (Thompson and representatives from the Far Eastern and Politico-Military Bureaus, and the Policy Planning staff), and five members of the Department of Defense (Vance, McNaughton, Wheeler, Spivey, and an additional officer from the Joint Staff). The meeting produced little but the expectation that the Long Range Study should be high-quality. Both Bundy and McNamara stressed that what they wanted was not an "interdepartmental coordinated draft but a useful analysis." McNamara felt that "it is less important that this be a completed and fully coordinated job, than that it reflect the thoughtful work of a limited number of good minds."[91] The senior leadership did not want a lowest common denominator document filled with compromises and bureaucratic soft-pedaling, something they feared might happen if interagency consensus overshadowed rigorous analysis.

The Long Term Study began in fall 1965 and issued its report in June 1966. The Senior Policy Group gave "policy guidance" for the study. The committee was dubbed the "Special State-Defense Study Group." An interim report was submitted on December 1, 1965. The study directors were Joseph Yeager of the State Department Policy Planning Council and Brigadier General Stephen W. Henry of the Air Force and the Joint Staff. Its members included four officials from the State Department, one from the Office of the Secretary of Defense, one from the CIA, and six officers from the Joint Staff.[92] The membership leaned heavily toward the Joint Staff, suggesting that the report would be focused on the political-military dimensions of the US-Chinese relationship, rather than the diplomatic or economic aspects. The report, however, was as broad as possible, examining US-Chinese relations in all its political-military and economic dimensions.

The terms of reference for the report were concise, yet daunting: "The Study Group will examine the political-military position of the United States vis-à-vis Communist China and other potentially hostile or disruptive forces in the Far East through 1976."[93] The final report was over 300 pages long and contained an additional 3 appendices and 10 annexes. Instead of relying solely on government expertise, the Study Group "consulted" academic and think tank/foundation expertise. The report defined the basic problem facing the US: "The Chinese regime's objectives of regional hegemony and world revolution clash with our own fundamental interests in preventing domination of Asia by any single power and in developing a peaceful and open world society of free nations."[94] The Study Group based its recommendations on a set of moderate assumptions about the future of China; they excluded scenarios predicated on major changes in China or East Asia. Over the next decade they expected the Chinese economy to be poor; the leadership to be stable, but insecure; military modernization to be adequate, but without major breakthroughs; and its goals in Asia to remain the same as in 1966: attempts to spread revolution in Southeast Asia, to divide the US from its allies in Asia.[95] The report drew up three "broad national strategies" that the US could choose from: disengagement, containment, and showdown. The Study Group rejected outright the strategies of disengagement and showdown, choosing a containment policy that would attempt "concurrently to check the spread of Chinese Communist power and influence and to induce moderation of Peking's current expansionist policies."[96] The real meat of the report was an analysis of different types of containment strategy that ran over 100 pages. The study considered three options: "close-in containment and forward defense" with a continued US "presence on the mainland of Asia"; offshore balancing that focused on US forward presence and alliances with nations that form the island chain around mainland Asia; and "remote containment and mid-Pacific defense behind buffer zones." The Study Group rejected remote containment as not technologically feasible yet. A choice between the other two strategies, in effect, had already been made. Even if the offshore balancing strategy was optimal, it was not feasible until the Vietnam War came to some conclusion. US presence in Vietnam meant that the US was locked into close-in containment on the Asian mainland for the foreseeable future.

Interestingly, the report also considered policies aimed at moderating Chinese behavior including limited economic ties, reassurances that the US would not try to overthrow the Communist regime, ending "close-in Taiwan Straits patrols," confidence building measures to prevent military misunderstandings, humanitarian aid, and lifting travel restrictions. The report considered diplomatic recognition to be impossible due to China's demand that the US abandon Taiwan.[97] The report did, however, believe that changing China's behavior was possible.

> Our long term problem may well be how to ensure that, as containment succeeds, China will turn toward the free world rather than the Soviet Union. . . . On the one hand as Chinese policy moderates, we should try to draw China into activities on the broader world scene where, through exposure to outside reality and successful assumption of international responsibility, she might gain a degree of status and respect which could substitute in part for the unattainable goals of regional domination and super-power status. On the other hand, by gradually shifting as circumstances permit from a military policy of close-in containment to containment largely from offshore island positions, and by demonstrating in other ways that we are not committed to a policy of hostility or military "encirclement," we might ease the tension between China and ourselves, thereby facilitating

a decision that Chinese interests were better served by normalizing relations with us rather than risking another betrayal at the hands of the Russians.[98]

These ideas were essentially the basis for the détente policies of the Nixon administration. Squaring the Taiwan issue with the above paragraph was the major puzzle, something that the Johnson administration could not solve.

In terms of quality, the report was a thoughtful and comprehensive review of US options toward China. From the perspective of the inter-agency process, it was produced five years after it should have been written. The timing, however, fit with the development of decision making in the Johnson administration. The report was finished in June 1966, in time to be considered within the new SIG-IRG. The administration had finally established a set of almost formal interagency procedures.

The word "almost" is used deliberately. The Long Range Study initially existed in isolation from the informal reevaluation of China policy that led to Johnson's speech of July 12, 1966 and the subsequent strategy on Chinese representation. If the Long Range Study and the speeches are seen as two threads of decision making on China—one formal and one informal—the two threads did finally tie together in September 1966. Following the completion of the Long Range Study, the China issue was given to the Far Eastern IRG. The FE/IRG had been considering everything but China since it held its first meeting on March 21, 1966, issues such as economic development in Southeast Asia, Japanese security policy and the defense of the Ryukyus, financing South Korean and Filipino troops in South Vietnam, and food aid to Indonesia, for example.[99] Perhaps that was intentional; interagency deliberations could not get under way until the formal review of the Long Range Study was completed.

A July 26 memorandum from the Senior Policy Group suggested that the FE/IRG create a special subcommittee on China to explicitly consider the recommendations of the Long Range Study. It set a deadline of October 1 for completion. The FE/IRG then created the Interagency China Country Committee, or "China Working Group" as it was generally called. The CWG functioned as a subcommittee of the FE/IRG, submitting its recommendations to the FE/IRG and taking its direction from the FE/IRG chair, Assistant Secretary of State for Far Eastern Affairs William Bundy. The group was chaired by Harald Jacobson, director of the Asian Communist Affairs office of the Far Eastern Bureau of the State Department. Its membership included three additional officials from the State

Department (a second official from the Far Eastern Bureau and one each from the Bureau of Intelligence and Research, and USIA), one representative from the CIA, one from the DoD Office of International Security Affairs, and Alfred Jenkins, the China expert on the NSC staff.[100]

Analysis

The Long Range Study case confirms the evolution-balance model. Requests for a full formal interagency review of China policy had been bubbling up from the lower levels of the bureaucracy since 1961, but were ignored until Johnson's first postelection year in office. In this sense, both the Short Range and Long Range Studies emerged from the same frustration with the informal process that led to the creation of the SIG/IRG. There is no specific documentary evidence of when Johnson approved the study; however, given his micromanagement of policy and the fact that Rusk, McNamara, and Bundy were involved in the decision, Johnson must have given at least tacit support. It is hard to believe that Rusk and Bundy would initiate something of this nature without his knowledge.

If looked at chronologically, it would have made sense that the Long Range Study, completed in June 1966, might have been a significant influence on Johnson's July 1966 speech offering a tentative olive branch to China. The case study that follows this one, however, does not support that conclusion. The formal Long Range Study did not feed into the informal processes that led to the speech. The conclusions of the Long Range Study fed into the FE/IRG and CWG after the July speech had been given, at roughly the same time that these groups were asked to consider the implications of the speech. The two cases were independent of each other, but both ended up under the purview of the FE/IRG.

Johnson's July 1966 Speech and the Chinese Representation Issue

China scholars often see 1966 as a key year in the evolution of US policy toward China, the year that the Johnson administration took the first baby steps toward the rapprochement that would jump ahead in the Nixon years.[101] Johnson's speech of July 12, 1966, a very limited softening of the isolation, suggested the possibility of change. Very little came of it afterwards, however. In particular, US strategy at the UN remained consistent in its creative search for ways to keep the PRC out and the ROC in. The decision making that led to the July speech seemed completely isolated from the Long Range Study. Though the administration had created an interagency process to deal with China, decisions were still made at the top primarily through small group meetings between Johnson and whichever senior staff he chose to use for advice. This case, however, fits the evolution-balance model primarily because of two proposals for new interagency committees. A proposal for an assistant-secretary-level group that would focus on the possibility for a major shift in China policy was implemented. A second proposal, by US ambassador to the UN Arthur Goldberg, for a high-level interagency group was rejected. Both initiatives were attempts to add more formality to the informal style governing the process. In addition, following Johnson's speech, analysis of the key issues was delegated to the new formal structures of the CWG and FE/IRG.

The July 1966 speech was the result of an evolution in public and congressional opinion and the domestic political dynamics of US intervention in Vietnam, one that became evident in 1966. Important and well-publicized congressional hearings on China, Asia, and Vietnam were deeply influential in reshaping the debate on China outside and inside the administration. Johnson's decision to use the hearings as a window of opportunity flowed from two factors. First, Goldberg emerged as a key foreign policy advisor when he stepped down from his appointment as Supreme Court associate justice and became US ambassador to the UN; his views on engaging China influenced Johnson. Second, the working levels of the State Department seemed to have worn Rusk down, convincing him to at least consider an end to the isolation of China. Both these factors led to Johnson's speech and several other trial balloon speeches in the spring and summer of 1966. Rusk, however, ultimately could not escape a career of seeing Chinese Communism as the key postwar problem in Asia; he stopped any significant moves from going forward in the fall of 1966 when support for changes in US policy at the UN seemed the logical extension of the July speech. The US position—rejection of PRC membership and support for the ROC—remained unaffected by any of the discussions during 1966. Johnson's faith in Rusk was the key factor that led the administration, in effect, to pop its own trial balloons.

Political Context

Though this case study overlaps with the previous case study, there are some differences in the political context. The Long Range Study began in March 1965 and issued its report in June 1966. The Cultural Revolution in China began in 1966, and crucial trends on congressional and public opinion became evident in 1966. These issues helped reshape thinking on China at the top level of the administration, in ways that the Long Range Study could not.

International Political Context

The key event in China that might have had an impact on the administration's thinking was the Cultural Revolution. It began in full force in May 1966, and the administration watched events closely. Johnson received a constant flow of memos concerning China from NSC staff China expert Alfred Jenkins. These were memos Jenkins prepared for Rostow, and Rostow forwarded them to the president for his nighttime reading. Johnson, a voracious reader, continually asked Rostow for more. Jenkins's memos were Johnson's key source of analysis on the issue.[102] During the Cultural Revolution, Mao's mission could not have been more ambitious: consolidate his control over the party leadership and bureaucratic apparatus (party, government, and military); remove potential rivals for power (his successor Liu Shaoqi and his allies); bring a new revolution to the high school and college age Chinese born after 1949; and remake society, by destroying Chinese traditional culture in favor of a new Communist culture.[103] The ultimate result was political chaos in China that lasted until 1976, though the worst years were during the Red Guard phase of 1966–69, when students were mobilized to crush anything that hinted of Chinese traditions or was deemed not sufficiently revolutionary.

The failure of the Great Leap Forward and the crisis of legitimacy it created for the Communist Party in general and for Mao's grip on the Party cut in either direction when it came to foreign policy: toward a need for the tottering leadership of a weakening country to reduce threats from abroad and seek a better relationship with the US, or toward the use of a more nationalist and revolutionary foreign policy to firm up Mao's leadership and draw the people's attention away from domestic problems. The Sino-Soviet split cut several ways as well. Mao could decide that revolutionary fervor allowed China to capture global Communist leadership from the Soviets (as the Lin Biao speech of 1965 seems to imply), or Mao might seek to balance against the Soviets through a rapprochement with the US. The latter approach is essentially the one taken by Mao and Zhou Enlai during the Nixon administration.

The full importance of the Cultural Revolution, however, played little role in the thinking of the Johnson administration that led to the July speech. The issues that brought about the speech were the same as they had been since 1961: isolation did not seem to be working; it went against the grain of US policy toward the Soviet Union; and it was based on the anachronistically absurd notion that the Communist regime would fade quickly.

Domestic Political Context

The more relevant change in the political context came within the US. Domestic politics were obviously a key factor to a man as politically wired as Johnson. Public opinion on China and congressional opinions on China were changing. Much of this was due to shifts in the academic community: a consensus had grown that US policy toward China was obsolete and counterproductive. The public's perception of China was evolving or perhaps even contradictory. On the one hand, polling showed that, given a choice of China or Russia as the "number one" threat to the US, China had passed Russia in 1962 and continued to be seen as an increasingly greater threat through 1967. When asked in March 1966 by Gallup if they expected China to intervene directly in Vietnam, 46% of Americans thought China would intervene and 27% thought they would not. The same poll showed that 73% of Americans felt that if China intervened the US should stay and fight; only 8% saw Chinese intervention as a reason to withdraw from Vietnam. A June 1966 Harris survey found that 57% of Americans supported US recognition of China and 55% supported UN admission for China if this might ease a path toward an end to the war in Vietnam. A similar survey put the numbers as 2–1 in favor of Chinese admission into the UN if it would bring an end to the war. Moyers, increasingly important to Johnson at the time, reportedly encouraged Gallup and the Harris polling organization to take these polls regarding US relations with China. It was his way to get a sense of how much wiggle room the administration had to pursue contacts with China.[104] What these polls revealed was that public opinion on China was very closely tied to Chinese behavior. If the Chinese would help end the war in Vietnam, in other words, end its support for revolution, the US people were ready to extend a hand of friendship. If China wanted to escalate the war, the US people were ready to fight. These ideas echoed the rhetoric of every administration since the Communists came to power.

Two sets of congressional hearings in early 1966 were crucial institutional factors influencing the administration. The hearings before the House Foreign Affairs Committee's Subcommittee on the Far East and the Pacific, led by Chairman Clement Zablocki (D-WI) from January through March, and the Senate Foreign Relations Committee's hearings led by J. William Fulbright (D-AR) in March had a threefold impact. First, the hearings publicized the views of scholarly China experts, the vast majority of whom saw US policy as out of date and needlessly inflexible. During the Fulbright hearings 200 Asian area studies experts took out an ad in the *New York Times* calling for outright recognition of China.[105] Second, Fulbright likely used the hearings to send the administration a message: deeper US intervention in Vietnam could bring the Chinese into the war. Fulbright certainly felt that way on a personal level by 1966, but the hearings were his way to place it on the record as the sense of Congress.[106] Third, the hearings were clearly a congressional attempt to send a very public message to the administration on China; congressional views of China were changing. Zablocki himself had been a charter member of the Committee of One Million, but by the fall of 1966 was a leader of a movement to shift China policy. Later in 1966 Senators Abraham Ribicoff (D-CT), Jacob Javits (R-NY), and Paul Douglas (D-IL) all resigned from the Committee of One Million.[107]

The sense that the Committee of One Million was losing its power to define China policy was a crucial factor. Vietnam and the simple passage of time were having their impact on the domestic debate. The administration did not need to repeatedly impress the public with its hostility toward China. Certainly, Johnson still had to worry about losing Vietnam, but the shadow of the "Who Lost China" debate was significantly lighter. On the contrary, a better relationship with China might be the key to ending the Vietnam War, possibly a win-win where US-China reconciliation cleared the path for US withdrawal from Vietnam. These ideas were precisely the type of thinking that would eventually prevail in the Nixon White House.

Narrative of Decision

Administration policy on Chinese representation at the UN had remained essentially static since the 1961 important question innovation. Persistent efforts by various officials at the State Department who wanted to see a reexamination of the overall isolation strategy and the supporting tactic of keeping the PRC out of the UN had gone nowhere. At the senior levels of the administration there was little interest in reevaluating any aspect of China policy until 1966. Though Bundy and US Ambassador to the UN Adlai Stevenson had felt that the current approach had reached its limits as early as 1964, Johnson leaned toward Rusk's view. In a November 1964 meeting, Rusk reminded everyone that 15 years ago Rusk himself had "invented" the US tactics for keeping China out of the UN. He argued that accepting China into the UN would be tantamount to rewarding China for aggression. This was the ultimate ownership of a policy and gave it even more credibility in the eyes of Johnson. It had been Rusk's idea in the first place and Rusk was sticking to it. Johnson was holding the line and Rusk, the man he trusted most, gave him no reason to change.[108]

The continued crisis in Vietnam also mitigated against any wavering of US commitments. Isolating a nation that was supporting revolution seemed an obviously better choice than engaging it. In addition, the UN votes suggested that the policy was gaining strength, rather than weakening. Support for admitting the PRC was falling, while more nations backed the important question vote each year from 1965 through 1968.[109]

The working levels of the administration, however, never gave up trying, focusing their efforts on minor tweaks to travel restrictions. Of these early proposals, Thomson, a staffer at the Far Eastern Bureau and then the NSC staff, stated that "all of them died in the Secretary's in-box." Rusk rejected them or ignored them for an extended period of time and then sent them back to the lower levels for additional review. A minor shift in policy that allowed medical professionals to travel to China was only accomplished in 1965 after a six-month bureaucratic battle. It only succeeded through outside pressure from Representative Zablocki and Senator Fulbright; Dr. Paul Dudley White, Eisenhower's heart specialist; and letters from several medical organizations, including the American Public Health Association.[110]

The impetus for consideration of engagement came from Congress in 1966. Zablocki and Fulbright scheduled a series of congressional hearings on US-China relations for January through March 1966. Reevaluation of policy toward China was almost forced on Johnson by the need to respond to the hearings and the desire to stay ahead of Congress on these issues. Civil rights legislation had already created great fissures in the Democratic Party, and the Vietnam War was adding additional strains. Johnson could not afford to lose control of the public debate on Vietnam, and the hearings on Asia and China placed that control at risk.

The Zablocki hearings in the Subcommittee on the Far East and Pacific of the House Foreign Affairs Committee, *United States Policy toward Asia*, were held on January 25–27, February 1–3 and 15–16, and March 8–10.[111] They overlapped with Fulbright-led hearings on the Vietnam War in the Senate Foreign Relations Committee, the contentious "Vietnam Hearings," lasting from January 28 to February 18.[112] These hearings, often containing scathing attacks on Johnson's war strategy, added additional pressure on the administration. Rusk, Assistant Secretary of State for Far Eastern Affairs William Bundy, and Director of the Far Eastern Bureau's Office of Asian Communist Affairs Harald Jacobson testified before the Zablocki committee. The administration worked to steer the debate by having Bundy give a speech on February 12 at Pomona College, "The United States and Communist China." The speech was included in the hearings as part of Bundy's testimony. The hearings included 35 witnesses, all Asia and China experts. Among them was A. Doak Barnett, an Asia expert who had also consulted for the administration. Barnett called for the administration to "contain Communist China . . . but at the same time to strive . . . to search out possible areas of accommodation that do not require sacrifices of our vital interests or those of our friends."[113] Hans Morgenthau, one of the preeminent scholars of international relations who literally wrote the book on post–World War II realist theory, also testified, calling for the US to recognize China, bring it into the UN, and then challenge it to behave in ways befitting a member of the UN.[114] In his testimony, Hilsman, by then a professor at Columbia University, described the US and China as being on a "collision course" toward war. He reiterated the arguments from his December 1963 speech: the US must contain China, fight its aggression, but be clear that if China was willing to end its hostile policies, the US was willing to listen.[115] Other witnesses dismissed any potential for change in China's behavior, but all told, the hearings considered every possible option on China from direct war to withdrawal from Asia.

There is little documentary evidence of decisions being made on how to respond to the Zablocki hearings. The subcommittee scheduled the hearings; members of the State Department were called to testify and each prepared a statement that supported administration policies, basically off-the-shelf rearticulations of policy no different from the formula stated by President Kennedy on November 14 1963—the US is ready for dialogue when China shows us it is ready to behave. Rusk summed up the quid pro quo: "When Peiping abandons the aggressive use of force and shows that it is not irrevocably hostile to the United States, then expanded contacts and improved relations may become possible."[116] Bundy's speech of February 12 and his testimony in the hearings mirrored Rusk's formulation, emphasizing what he saw as China's deepening commitment to a "virulent revolutionary policy."[117]

Zablocki's management of the hearings reflected the dilemma for any Democrat. Just holding the hearings and placing the idea of UN admission and US recognition on the table would seem a risky play for an anti-Communist, supporter of the war in Vietnam, and former member of the Committee of One Million. Zablocki's subcommittee, however, had already called for more nonofficial contacts with China and recognition of Mongolia in May 1965.[118] Zablocki, however, was still clearly worried about the pressure from Republicans and the shadow of the China lobby. After asking Bundy about allowing China into the UN and perhaps opening up more contacts, he quickly backtracked to safe political ground, making it clear that he only asked about these issues "for the record" and his questions "are not in any way intended to indicate that I agree with the ideas or support the view covered by the questions."[119]

The Senate Committee on Foreign Relations hearings, *US Policy with Respect to Mainland China*, began in the latter days of the Zablocki hearings, stretching from March 8 through the 30th.[120] Led by Fulbright and on the heels of the Vietnam hearings, these proceedings had a clear intent. No members of the administration testified at this hearing, a fact that was deliberate and symbolic—administration policy on China was under attack. Fulbright used these hearings to make his case: isolation had failed; it was time to move on. Witness after witness delivered the message, often so strongly that Republican members of Congress complained that the hearing was imbalanced. Fulbright responded to pleas by Senate Republican leader Everett Dirksen by adding to the witness list some supporters of the continued hard line on China.[121] In spite of the token efforts to provide the other side of the argument, Fulbright sent his message loud and clear. Witness after witness hammered the administration for an obsolete and counterproductive policy. The first witness, Barnett, who had testified at the Zablocki hearings, set the tone for the entire slate of witnesses: "The time has come—even though the United States is now engaged in a bitter struggle in Vietnam—for our country to alter its posture toward Communist China and adopt a policy of containment, but not isolation."[122] The most crucial aspect of Barnett's argument and the testimony that followed was the fundamental challenge not just to administration strategy, but to administration goals. Containing China was necessary but not sufficient. Even successful containment left a revolutionary behemoth stewing on the Asian continent. The US needed to address the problem of China's existence and that required a new objective, taming or changing China. Isolation could never accomplish that. John King Fairbank, one of the most respected China experts in the US, concurred, arguing for a plan of action "to defuse or dampen Peking's militancy by getting China into greater contact with the outside world . . . American policy should work toward a gradual shift from trying to isolate Peking, which only worsens our problem."[123] Additional testimony emphasized how isolation simply exacerbated tensions and increased China's militancy (Alexander Eckstein), or failed to take advantage of the growing Sino-Soviet split by giving China the possibility of better relations with the US as a balance against the USSR (Donald Zagoria), or handed Peking the initiative (Robert Scalapino).[124]

Nearly all of Fulbright's witnesses supported Chinese entry into the UN in the form of a two-China policy, typically with the PRC taking the UNSC seat while the ROC remained only in the UNGA. Importantly, they also all endorsed containment of China and pressure on China to reduce its support for wars of liberation. Their views of the US effort in Vietnam were more varied.[125] An appendix to the hearings contained a memorandum from the Council for a Livable World, a nonprofit organization created by American physicists to address the nuclear arms race. The memorandum called for Chinese entrance into the UN, formal diplomatic recognition of China, an end to the trade embargo, and the establishment of negotiations on a range of political and cultural issues. The memorandum was signed by dozens of academics and a smaller number of business leaders representing 30 states.[126]

The hearings were the congressional version of a full court press, designed by Fulbright to take the ball out of the administration's hands. The administration, however, was not ready to relinquish control. Fulbright's message was heard within the administration and it gave hope to those officials who had been arguing for a change since the Kennedy administration. The hearings also gave Johnson some public reassurance that discussion of ending the policy of isolation might not be political suicide.

Supporters of a new approach to China moved quickly. White House assistant Jack Valenti asked James Thomson, the NSC staff China expert, for a memo that reviewed current policy. Valenti would have asked for such a memo only if Johnson had asked him to or if he felt that the president would eventually ask for such a memo. Thomson replied on March 1 with a detailed examination of why the US had been isolating China, a "residue of the bitterness and suspicion here at home over the 'loss of China' and the Korean War" to which the Democratic Party is "especially vulnerable." He argued that while the China lobby had weakened and polls showed less knee-jerk opposition to better relations, the administration had an opportunity. Even in 1963, Hilsman's speech had not produced tremendous protests from Congress. Thomson included a list of the types of changes the US could make to its policies, including lifting the travel ban, invitations to Chinese journalists, licensing of commercial sales in medicines and critical foods, adding China to multilateral disarmament talks, and moving toward a two-China solution at the UN. The memo also noted that the US should expect the Chinese leadership to reject everything and anything at first.[127]

Komer used his position as interim SANSA to gently float ideas that the Zablocki hearings had explored. On March 2, the week before the Fulbright hearings would publicize a new China policy, Komer sent Johnson a memo that foreshadowed the Fulbright argument. He prefaced his proposal with a nod to his status: "Though I am doing my best to be interim: unavailable, imperceptible, and invisible, I hope you will allow a few private thoughts on our Asian problem." Noting that Johnson had offered North Vietnam aid if it would negotiate an end to the war, Komer wondered if that same formula could work for China. If it ended its "expansion and pressures," the US might consider China's admission to the UN as well as trade and other contacts. His memo was entitled "Open Door for Red China?" Komer sent a copy to Moyers to make sure that Johnson would see it.[128]

Johnson watched the hearings closely; they were on the agenda for the Tuesday Lunch Group session of March 8 (the day the Fulbright hearings began), but there is no record of the conversation.[129] Thomson of the NSC staff sent summaries of each day's proceedings to Johnson through Moyers. Johnson reportedly liked the nature of the discussion in the hearings.[130]

On March 10, the administration tried to blunt the sting of the Fulbright hearings; the State Department announced that restrictions on travel to China for scholars would be lifted, subject to authorization and approval on an individual basis.[131] Supporters of ending China's isolation in the administration saw the hearings as a crucial factor in gaining Rusk's approval for the new travel policy; the hearings changed a lot of minds and to a certain extent isolated Rusk within the State Department.[132] Rusk saw the way the political winds were blowing and made a small concession.

Vice President Hubert Humphrey went on the record as a supporter of these new ideas right after the hearings began. In a speech on Vietnam at the National Press Club on March 11, Humphrey applauded the Fulbright hearings and may have been obliquely calling for a review of China policy by stating that the US needed to know much more about China.[133] More important were Humphrey's answers to a series of questions on China's role in Vietnam during *Meet the Press* on March 13. In response to a question on whether the US presence in Vietnam was truly about containing China, Humphrey presented US policy in the exact framework being used in the Fulbright hearings (at the time reaching their midpoint): "I do believe that containment of aggressive militancy of China is a worthy objective, but containment without necessarily isolation."[134]

Though the Humphrey *Meet the Press* statements were made on the vice president's own initiative, supporters of a new China approach used them as leverage, particularly since the press coverage was favorable. Komer sent

Johnson a memo on March 14 suggesting that Humphrey's approval of the Fulbright hearings could be used as a "trial balloon" for more flexibility toward China. They showed that the US was "prepared to reexamine coexisting peacefully" with China. If the Chinese leadership refused then it would be "isolating itself."[135] Thomson sent Moyers a memo on March 15 that essentially made the same argument. He noted that, because of Humphrey's appearance, many believed the administration had already officially shifted to the position of "containment—yes, isolation—no." The administration could use Humphrey's statements as official policy, essentially sliding in that direction and making the argument that this has always been, in effect, the US position; there has been no actual movement. The US should emphasize, he argued, that the door had always been open, but that China had continued to isolate itself.[136]

The debates and lobbying about how to respond to the hearings continued through the spring and into the summer. An interagency group began meeting in mid-April cochaired by the assistant secretaries of the State Department bureaus of Far Eastern Affairs and Economic, Energy, and Business Affairs, William Bundy and Anthony Solomon, respectively. The group consisted of officials from each bureau, the CIA, the White House, and NSC staff. The group met on April 12, June 13, and July 21. Its mandate was to consider what types of items might be included in a partial lifting of the trade embargo on China.[137] The documentary record, however, suggests that this group had little impact on overall policy, and there is little to indicate who instigated its formation.

The breakthrough may have come from an unexpected source. Arthur Goldberg had replaced Adlai Stevenson as US ambassador to the UN in July 1965 following Stevenson's death. Importantly, Goldberg was Johnson's first handpicked foreign policy advisor. Though he had been a member of Kennedy's cabinet (secretary of labor) and a Kennedy choice for the Supreme Court in 1962, Johnson convinced him to step down from the Court to take the UN ambassador's job.[138] Goldberg had sent Johnson a memo on April 8, 1966 suggesting that some thought be given to developing proposals on a joint US-Chinese foreign ministers meeting or a Big Five meeting of the foreign ministers of the US, China, Russia, the United Kingdom, and France. Johnson was "fascinated" with the idea and asked NSC staffer Komer to speak to Goldberg and sound out the idea. Komer summarized the issue in an April 19 memo to Johnson. Goldberg had explained to Komer that in his view US policy toward China at the UN was unsustainable. Switching to a two-China approach would place the burden on China as the "inflexible" party. Komer and Goldberg felt setting up a "small high level action group to work out across the board recommendations" would be the next best step. Goldberg had discussed the issue with Rusk, but the secretary was "noncommittal." Komer acknowledged to Johnson in writing the need for secrecy and the fact that the high-level group would operate outside regular decision making channels: "There's nothing to lose if we can only keep the matter from leaking. But it will take your proposing such a group to get it off the ground." Goldberg's group was composed of himself, Komer, and Ball, while Komer had suggested Goldberg, Rostow, Ball, and Edward Rice, the US Consul General in Hong Kong and Macau who was based in Washington during these deliberations. Both Goldberg and Komer must have seen Rusk as an obstacle to these ideas; both left Rusk off the membership of the high-level group. Johnson shut down the end run quickly. He made his sentiments clear about whom he trusted. His response on the memo was checking the recommendations for "I'll discuss with Rusk; Rostow see me."[139]

On April 23, Johnson met with Rostow and decided the next move. In a memo to Rusk, Rostow explained Johnson's thinking. The State Department was to look at the issue and seek "imaginative ways of handling the China problem," including asking the assistant secretaries at State to seek ideas from "the best brains that can be mobilized from outside the government." Johnson also wanted Goldberg and Rusk to speak directly about Goldberg's proposals.[140]

Through April and May, three channels of decision making were active: at State, in the NSC and White House staffs, and at the senior level. Within the State Department, the Bureau of International Organization Affairs, under Joseph Sisco, studied alternatives to current policy regarding Chinese representation at the UN. The Bureau of Far Eastern Affairs had the job of thinking about how to finesse potential changes with the ROC.[141] Since there was no full interagency process, much of this State Department work existed in isolation from the rest of the government. For example, information on Sisco's review was not shared with the NSC staff until Samuel Berger of State mentioned it to Alfred Jenkins after an early November FE/IRG meeting had ended.[142]

Within the NSC and White House staffs, lobbying for a new policy continued. Valenti spoke with Zagoria, a witness during the Fulbright hearings, who had been "enthusiastic" about ending China's isolation. Zagoria recommended a major speech by Johnson to spell out a new policy. He wrote a memo to Johnson on the idea, and Valenti forwarded it to Moyers.[143] Thomson also routed his own memos for Rostow to Moyers and Valenti to make sure that Johnson heard the ideas from more than one of his most trusted advisors. In an April 2 memo, Thomson mentioned that a cable from US analysts based in Hong Kong had argued that US flexibility on China makes "life more difficult for" the Chinese leadership. One of the cornerstones of Chinese foreign policy was the supposed threat of American imperialism: "We become a troubling phenomenon—and a potentially divisive factor in Chinese foreign policy—when we don't live up to the advertisement." Willingness to make peaceful overtures to China kept "Peking off balance."[144] Rostow was also searching for additional ideas. He asked Rice for suggestions on "what we might do or say now in the hope of reaching a better relationship with mainland China." Rice thought that offers to improve US-Chinese relations would not make a difference until Mao Zedong's death. Overtures today, however, could make a difference to the successor leadership. The US needed to persuade the Chinese leadership that the US was not an aggressor, in particular by convincing it that the US did not support ROC efforts to retake the mainland. Rice placed US isolation policy in the context of the history of US relations with Asia. He wondered why the US would have a trade embargo on China when the fundamental core of US strategy in Asia since the 19th century had been that no nation was allowed to "refuse to trade with the rest of the world."[145]

At the upper level, the informal discussions defined the policy. Goldberg sent a memo to Johnson (also Rusk and Sisco) on April 28 detailing his ideas: the US may lose the coming vote in the General Assembly; a new, more flexible option, perhaps "containment without isolation" that accepts two Chinas, would reverse the situation, placing China on the defensive.[146] Rostow met with Goldberg and sent Johnson a memo on April 30 detailing his thoughts on the meeting. Rostow urged caution. Three key political problems remained: the reaction of the ROC, which would likely be negative; past US promises to use the Security Council veto to prevent Chinese admission to the UN; and the possibility that Eisenhower might carry out his threat to publicly challenge the administration if it moved toward recognition of China at the UN.[147]

During this period, Rusk seemed to have had a change of heart, even if only temporarily. In May, he instructed the Far Eastern Bureau to compose a draft letter to China proposing a meeting of foreign ministers to "discuss means of lessening tensions in the Far East." Rusk expected China to reject the idea, but, as others had pointed out, this only strengthened the argument that Chinese policy was self-isolating. The letter would be sent secretly through the Warsaw channel; he recommended informing the governments of the ROC, Britain, Australia, and South Korea.[148] Goldberg and Rusk met on the issue around the same time in May. In a memo to

Johnson, Rusk wrote that after the meeting, he still felt that "there appears to be little prospect that our traditional position will be sustained by the forthcoming General Assembly." Both he and Goldberg agreed that the only realistic new option would be to support a two-China solution. They expected the PRC and ROC to reject the idea, but the US could work on convincing Taipei that a two-China representation formula was better than the alternative of seeing the ROC expelled. He noted a Gallup poll from April where 56% of the public would support UN membership for the PRC. He explicitly asked permission to begin discussions with the ROC about the new idea and to raise the idea with Canada, a candidate for introducing the resolution (already on the record as supporting two Chinas). Congress could be brought into the mix after the ROC's views were known.[149]

Rostow felt that Rusk's memo was "something of a landmark." Rusk's flexibility surprised him, but Rostow was still worried about Eisenhower's reaction and the reaction of Taipei. The memo gave Johnson two options to check: "Set up a meeting" or "Let it go." Johnson checked "Set up a meeting." Rostow then spoke with Johnson and Rusk, getting agreement from both men for a May 23 date. Rusk requested that Goldberg and William Bundy attend.[150]

The meeting was moved to May 24, but the most interesting aspect was that Johnson met with Goldberg alone for roughly an hour before sitting down with Goldberg, Rostow, Bundy, and Ball (sitting in for Rusk). No major decision was made. The only concrete result of the meeting may have been a request that State's instructions to the new US ambassador to Taipei, Walter McConaughy, include getting a sense of how the ROC would react to a change in US policy.[151] Johnson seemed to be leaving his options open and, in his eyes, the absence of Rusk may have made the meeting an inappropriate forum for a decision.

The process was essentially placed in stasis until after consultations with Taipei. As June turned to July, McConaughy, Bundy, and Rusk met with Chiang Kai-shek and several of his senior advisors. Rusk warned his counterparts that they needed to consider an option other than simply walking out if the UNGA voted to admit the PRC. Chiang actually tacked in the opposite direction. Rather than considering two Chinas, he appeared confident that the upheaval of the Cultural Revolution would produce an opportunity for the ROC to retake the mainland. Rusk, likely in an attempt to warn Chiang of the seriousness of any major attacks on the mainland, reminded him that if the US were drawn into any conflict with China, it would not remain a conventional war.[152]

Johnson decided he should wade into the debate in either late June or early July. Congressional hearings had been held; his administration had debated the issue; diplomats had sounded out the ROC. In addition, the Long Term Study had been submitted, though it is unclear if he had seen it. Only Johnson's voice remained absent. Rostow was given the job of organizing the drafting of a major speech on Asia. Unhappy with Rostow's draft, Johnson asked Moyers to rework it, but keep that fact a secret. The directive to Moyers represents not simply a request for a change in tone, but for a change in direction. Johnson had put his finger on the scale, finally, by elevating Moyers's role. From this point on, the fix was in. Moyers was a greater advocate for containment without isolation than either Rusk or Rostow; through Moyers, Johnson was able to push the policy in a very specific direction. Moyers gave the task of redrafting to Thomson, who was known to favor the Fulbright position and Humphrey statements. Thomson's guidance from Moyers, through Moyers's aide Hayes Redmon, was to pen a draft that fit what Thomson would say if he were president. Harriman, at the time US ambassador at large, may have influenced Moyers's thinking on the subject. He had been lobbying Moyers on the issue for some time. In a June 3 memo he argued for the "acceptance of 'containment, but not isolation' through adoption perhaps of a two-China policy." Referencing global public opinion that was turning against the US presence in Vietnam and turning against Johnson as a by-product, he felt that "the President could well gain in most parts of the world by a spectacular change in attitude towards Red China. It would then, I believe, be easier to gain better understanding of Vietnam."

Moyers touched up the draft and Johnson approved it. Only then did the draft go to Rusk for review. Importantly, Moyers told Rusk that Johnson had already approved the draft; this was not true, but it was bureaucratically significant. Given Rusk's absolute loyalty to Johnson and his conception of his role as secretary—to advance the president's policy and not make his own—it is not surprising that Rusk accepted the draft with minor changes. Thomson felt that the speech was the White House's way of "outflanking" Rusk and Rostow.[153]

Johnson had intended to deliver his speech to the American Alumni Council at the Greenbrier Hotel in White Sulphur Springs, West Virginia. His travel was canceled due to poor weather, and he instead spoke to a nationwide audience from the Oval Office. Given the Fulbright hearings and the Humphrey *Meet the Press* comments, the speech itself broke no new ground; however, the fact that Johnson himself was supporting these ideas and using a major televised address to reiterate these themes made the speech a potential breakthrough. Most of the speech reiterated traditional themes of US policy in Asia: containment, trade and alliances among the anti-Communist nations in Asia, and the strategic rationale for US intervention in Vietnam. Key passages, however, sounded a different note:

> There is a fourth essential for peace in Asia which may seem the most difficult of all: reconciliation between nations that now call themselves enemies. A peaceful mainland China is central to a peaceful Asia. . . . For lasting peace can never come to Asia as long as the 700 million people of mainland China are isolated by their rulers from the outside world . . . the greatest force for opening closed minds and closed societies is the free flow of ideas and people and goods. For many years, now, the United States has attempted in vain to persuade the Chinese Communists to agree to an exchange of newsmen as one of the first steps to increased understanding between our people. More recently, we have taken steps to permit American scholars, experts in medicine and public health, and other specialists to travel to Communist China. And only today we, here in the Government, cleared a passport for a leading American businessman to exchange knowledge with Chinese mainland leaders in Red China. All of these initiatives, except the action today, have been rejected by Communist China.[154]

Johnson did not specifically use the phrase "containment without isolation," but the speech mapped out that formula: the US was committed to fighting Communism in Asia for the long haul; however, it had and would continue to try to keep the door open to China. Chinese isolation was self-imposed; the US would try to end it, but Chinese aggression was the prime obstacle. Johnson reiterated these points on his Asia trip in October 1966. On October 18, at the East-West Center in Honolulu, Johnson even spoke specifically of an end to China's isolation:

> We shall keep alive the hope for a freer flow of ideas and people between mainland China and the United States, as I have said so recently on so many other occasions. For only through such exchange can isolation be ended and suspicion give way to trust. . . . We do not believe in eternal enmity. All hatred among nations must ultimately end in reconciliation. We hopefully look to the day when the policies of mainland China will offer and will permit such a reconciliation.[155]

If the Oval Office address is seen as a significant olive branch, rather than only a rhetorical flourish designed to allow Johnson to appear to offer a significant olive branch, China did not reciprocate. At the time, its leadership was fully engaged in the Cultural Revolution; no major foreign policy initiatives could have emerged from within such intense political turmoil.

Following the July speech, decision making in the administration operated on two tracks. The CWG examined long-range issues, including the possibility of an end to isolation, a link to the July 12 speech. Senior officials informally prepared for a possible change in US policy at the UN; importantly, there is no indication that the CWG or FE/IRG addressed the representation issue. It was immediate and important and left up to the senior decision makers. In this sense, the formal interagency process and the informal processes worked in separate but parallel grooves, with the reassessment of isolation as the only overlap.

On August 24, the FE/IRG officially tasked the CWG to review the Long Range Study with the intent of establishing guidelines for future policy. The CWG began its assessment of the Long Range Study at its third meeting on September 13, 1966; its first two meetings were largely organizational. It endorsed the Long Range Study, stating that the US should in the long term "move gradually to a strategy of containment primarily from the offshore island chain." The strategy would have three elements: "deterring or defeating communist aggression"; stabilizing and "strengthening" US Asian allies; and "inducing Asian Communist leaders to moderate, and eventually abandon their expansionist policies." The third element was influenced by the debate that led to Johnson's July speech. The guidelines were approved by the FE/IRG at its October 19 meeting.[156] The CWG continued to seek ways to take baby steps toward ending China's isolation. At its December 13 meeting it recommended lifting additional travel restrictions, some currency controls on dollar "transactions . . . outside the United States between third countries," and licensing restrictions on "foodstuffs, medical supplies and equipment and art objects." The CWG explicitly stated its goals: "The CWG believes these actions would contribute to the long term strategy of seeking peace and reconciliation with Communist China. The CWG also believes that a positive step on our part along these lines could encourage more pragmatic elements in Peking to question the wisdom of Peking's policy of hostility to the United States."[157] In this sense, the CWG was fully in line with the Long Range Study, the Fulbright hearings, and the consensus that emerged from the debate leading to the July speech. That connection can be viewed as the informal process guiding the formal process, or the working level finally having permission to pursue the policies it had preferred since 1961.

On the representation issue, informality still dominated decision making. The issue was not placed into the SIG/IRG system, and it was even unclear to various parts of the bureaucracy what other departments were doing. For example, Secretary of Defense McNamara had commissioned a study of the representation issue, feeling that DoD needed to have an iron in the fire. In his view, the US stance at the UN was isolating the US and hurting alliance cohesion in Asia, particularly with Japan. The existence of the study was unknown to anyone outside the DoD until Alfred Jenkins of the NSC staff had lunch with Morton Halperin of the DoD Office of International Security Affairs on September 1. Halperin mentioned it in passing, and Jenkins sent a memo to Rostow informing him later that day.[158]

In spite of all these developments during 1966, Rusk seemed to have let the things drift, perhaps a deliberate strategy to prevent any significant recasting of the policy. The issue finally came to a decision point when Rusk and Johnson discussed it at a TLG meeting on September 13. In preparation for the meeting, Jenkins advised Rostow that the US had two choices: find an ally to sponsor a two-China resolution, or reaffirm US opposition to the yearly Albanian-sponsored resolution that switched Chinese representation from the ROC to the PRC. He recommended sticking with strong opposition to the Albanian resolution. Though most analysts in the government believed that the UNGA vote was trending away from the ROC, it was possible that the Cultural Revolution might reverse that trend. Most critically, Jenkins explained his choice as being based on a lack of interagency staffing, explicitly saying that "since requisite groundwork for a clear change in policy or tactics has not been laid," the US could not adjust its UN tactics on the fly.[159] Here Jenkins was essentially pointing out a weakness in the process: informality left the administration unprepared.

Within the State Department, Rusk was also being prepared for the September TLG meeting. Assistant Secretary of State for International Organization Joseph Sisco reminded Rusk that at the meeting he would have to explain to Johnson why US policy at the UN had not been changed over the summer, even though a consensus on a two-China approach seemed to have been reached. With a nod to domestic political considerations, Sisco suggested that any China issues should wait until after the 1966 midterm elections. He also felt that Rusk should inform Johnson that Goldberg had been lobbying within the State Department for the US to announce its new policy at the opening of the new UNGA session.[160]

At the TLG meeting, Johnson, Rusk, McNamara, Rostow, and Moyers met for an unusually long time, from 2:15 to 3:45; Rusk and Johnson met alone from 3:45 to 4:01. Johnson's Daily Diary includes a note quoting Rostow as saying the meeting was "of unusual importance—as well as rather long."[161] There is no record of discussions at the meeting; however, Rusk must have been able to hold the line against a two-China option. Roughly five hours after the meeting, the State Department issued guidance to diplomatic posts that the US would not change its policy at the UNGA; it would oppose the Albanian resolution that would seat the PRC and remove the ROC, and it would continue to support a vote making the representation issue an important question requiring a two-thirds majority in the UNGA.[162]

The opening of the UNGA session in November added a bit of drama. Canada broke with the US on the issue, deciding to introduce a "one China—one Taiwan" resolution with the PRC gaining the UNSC seat. Rusk managed to delay Canada's decision, hoping to convince it to introduce a study commission resolution instead that would at least delay any vote for a year. Rusk and Johnson met on November 6, and Johnson approved the study commission tactic.[163] The US introduced its yearly resolution on making the China representation issue an important question on November 14; a November 15 TLG meeting reviewed the potential for success.[164] Ultimately, the votes on November 29 moved decisively in favor of the US. The issue of Chinese recognition remained an "important question" by a vote of 66 for, 48 against, and 7 abstaining. The Albanian-sponsored resolution was defeated (46 for, 57 against, 20 abstaining). In a surprise to the US, a Syrian-sponsored resolution making the study commission an important question, requiring a two-thirds vote, and adding another parliamentary hurdle to a direct vote on representation, passed (51–37–30). That led to the defeat of the study commission resolution itself. As David Popper, the deputy assistant secretary of state for international organization, put it, "Today's votes on Chinese representation were even better than we had anticipated."[165]

Any potential for real change in US policy toward China ended at this point. No matter what the working levels of the administration might have thought, Rusk retained what was effectively veto power through the rest of the administration's term in office. Johnson and his senior advisors were also unwilling to invest political capital in continued outreach to China as the Vietnam War became an ever more bitter experience.

Analysis

This case study confirms the evolution-balance model. In two instances, new formal interagency groups were proposed by members of the administration. A newly created assistant-secretary-level group met in April, June, and July to organize the administration's response to the congressional hearings. There is no record that the group's work had any input into Johnson's thinking. Goldberg's high-level group to assess China policy, however, was rejected. Johnson's informal and confidence structures—either the TLG or Rusk's advice—remained at the heart of decision making. Following the July 1966 speech, the China Working Group of FE/IRG, also a more formal structure, evaluated some of the issues, but there is no indication it had any impact on thinking at the upper levels of the administration. The debate of the spring and summer of 1966 could have led the administration to change its policy along the lines of the ideas expressed in the hearings: lifting of trade and travel restrictions, diplomatic recognition of China, and acceptance of two Chinas. Perhaps Johnson might have moved toward détente with China similar to the détente brewing with the USSR. Ultimately, Johnson trusted Rusk, and that allowed Rusk to define administration policy. He had the ability to choose which ideas would be implemented and which would wait for another day. The confidence structure was unchallenged. If lower level staffers were "dead wrong" about ending China's isolation, Rusk had the power to make them wrong.

Conclusions

Both the case studies in this chapter confirm the evolution-balance model; administration officials worked to add more formal structures to the informal structures that dominated decision making. The administration did initiate the formal interagency Long Range Study, establish an assistant-secretary-level group in the spring of 1966, and give the FE/IRG and CWG responsibility for assessing policy options after the July 1966 speech. Goldberg's high-level group, however, was not approved. Importantly, however, most of these formal structures seem to have been either irrelevant to the content of the July speech or only plugged into these senior-level decisions after the speech.

Several conclusions can be drawn from these case studies. First, the administration was still dominated by informality. The informal process had floated a trial balloon, then handed aspects of the policy off to the emerging formal structures to define what the new ideas might actually mean. A fully functioning formal interagency structure would have moved the analysis from the bottom up, and senior decision makers would have had the Long Range Study in their hands as they thought about initiatives like the July speech or Chinese representation at the UN; in all the memos moving back and forth between the senior officials regarding the Chinese representation issue, there is no mention of the Long Range Study. Second, China policy making illustrates the disconnect between the new SIG/IRG and actual decisions by the president. If the Long Range Study is the key interagency document on China, it plugged itself into the FE/IRG, but not into the TLG. If Johnson used the Long Range Study to inform his ideas about China, it was entirely informal, an aspect of his "night reading." There was no meeting scheduled for the NSC or TLG with an agenda entitled "Consideration of Long Term Study of China."

Third, no matter what lower level officials thought or what interagency reports concluded, the bottom line for Johnson's choices on China was the impact of domestic politics and his still rock-solid bond with Rusk. The July speech was prompted by congressional hearings; Johnson was following the shift in public opinion rather than initiating new policies that bubbled up from below. Even with the wiggle room that Congress had provided him, Johnson did little more than give a speech. Rusk's viewpoint was still definitive and after decades of thinking on China, Rusk would not or could not give serious ground on the policy of isolation. Johnson's reliance on Rusk illustrates the importance of the confidence structure.

Administration debates in 1967 and 1968 bear this out. A softening of Chinese rhetoric in the fall of 1967 and into 1968 and US intelligence reports indicated that less radical elements had regained control of China's foreign policy, moving it away from Mao's revolutionary rhetoric and back toward Marxist-tinged realism. The new information led to a reconsideration of isolation and engagement throughout the administration.[166] Most importantly, the developments renewed Johnson's interest in what might be done to open the door to China. Not only did he ask State and the NSC staff to think about the issue, but he met with a group of academic China experts to hear their views. The meeting, sponsored by the National Committee on United States-China Relations, was held on February 2, 1968. As the China lobby was losing its power, organizations such as this one were meeting with the president. Several witnesses from the Fulbright hearings attended (Scalapino, Barnett, and Eckstein), as well as Edwin Reischauer (former US Ambassador to Japan), and China experts Lucian Pye, George Taylor, Carl Stevens, and Executive Director of the Committee Cecil Thomas. Rostow and NSC staff China expert Alfred Jenkins sat in on the meeting. The experts concentrated on the need for a new China policy, while Johnson reminded them of the political difficulties he would encounter reaching a hand out to Communist China at the same time he was fighting North Vietnam. A consensus did emerge on the need for an official in the US government who would be a type of specialist and coordinator whose portfolio only focused on China. Johnson asked the experts to suggest some possible candidates. The group was asked to draft a memo on US options for China.[167]

Rusk, however, had not reconsidered his 1966 views. China had to make the first move by changing its aggressive policies. The message in public was not very different from the private counsel he gave to Johnson. In a January 1968 interview with *Maclean's*, Rusk presented the same formula as in 1966. Though China was not the primary aggressor in Vietnam, a victory for the North would "stimulate the expansionist ambitions of Communist China."[168] In private, Rusk sent a memo to Johnson on February 22, 1968 that echoed his public comments.[169] A few days later, February 24, Rostow gave Johnson another memo that summed up a series of communications from Rusk, William Bundy, Jenkins, and the academic experts. Rostow noted that Rusk, Bundy, and Jenkins agreed: due to the Cultural Revolution, "China is in a mess." He argued that its focus would be on domestic issues for the near future. While Mao still controlled the nation and pushed the Cultural Revolution line, there would be little chance of rapprochement. Selective trade liberalization and the relaxation of some travel restrictions might be the best that the US could accomplish. He also pointed out Rusk's position on the UN: "The Secretary is emphatic in his opposition to Peking entry."[170] On March 6, Bundy sent an "action memorandum" recommending that the US lift travel restrictions for Americans wishing to travel to China. These types of restrictions were in force for a handful of Communist nations (China, North Korea, Cuba, North Vietnam). Rusk rejected Bundy's memo on March 11.[171] The Johnson administration had gone as far as it could go, and Rusk defined that limit.

Johnson's historic March 31 speech fundamentally reshaped US policy in Vietnam and the legacy of the Johnson presidency itself. In a surprise to the nation and almost everyone within the administration, Johnson announced that he would end the Vietnam bombing, pursue peace talks with North Vietnam, and refuse the nomination of his party for the 1968 presidential election. The abrupt shift on Vietnam effectively ended serious thinking on China. No major initiatives concerning Asia would come from a wounded presidency committed to using its last months in office to extricate itself from the war.

SEVEN

∿ Richard M. Nixon

"If Men Were Angels . . ."

"If men were angels, no government would be necessary . . .
In framing a government which is to be administered by men
over men, the great difficulty lies in this: you must first enable
the government to control the governed; and in the next place
oblige it to control itself."

  —James Madison, *Federalist* 51[1]

In an interview during the 1968 presidential campaign, Richard Nixon explained his approach to decision making:

> I would disperse power, spread it among able people. . . . I would operate differently from President Johnson. Instead of taking all power to myself, I'd select cabinet members who could do their jobs, and each of them would have the stature and the power to function effectively. . . . when a President takes all power to himself, those around him become puppets. They shrivel up and become less creative. . . . And your most creative people can't develop in a monolithic, centralized power set-up.[2]

After his time in office, resignation, and a decade of reflection, Nixon amended those ideas in a 1983 interview:

> Cabinet government is a myth and can't work . . . no (President) in his right mind submits anything to his cabinet.[3]

Had Nixon learned something from his time in the White House? Perhaps this was the idealism of candidacy meeting the hard reality of governmental decision making. But Nixon was no novice in office. His years as Eisenhower's vice president certainly would have told him nearly everything he needed to know about the feasibility of cabinet government and the delegation of power. In that sense, these quotes reflect the words of a candidate differentiating himself from the previous occupant of the White House—however he did it, I'll do the opposite—compared to the unvarnished words of a man suffering political exile.

Another option is to see these quotes as simply a testament to the paradoxical impulses that warred within Nixon. Strategic brilliance and bureaucratic timidity coexisted in a unique way. That paradox was managed or mismanaged well enough that a decision process generally seen as horrid produced a coherent and often-admired grand strategy. Administration speechwriter William Safire explained the contradictions this way:

> He's like a layer cake and the top layer is patriot, and beneath that there's mild paranoia, and beneath that there's very good to people who work with him and thoughtful and not at all abusive, and underneath that the hard liner. So in terms of personal relationships and family relationships, and official family relationships, you had this different kind of guy. And in terms of willingness to go along with break-ins and things like that, somebody else. But the trouble is you cannot separate these things out. And I said, "If you want to say what was he really like?" You've got to take your fork and cut down, right down the seven or eight layers and then take a spoonful or whatever it is and you see the confluence of flavors.[4]

As a decision maker, Nixon exhibited many of these layers—searching for good advice and analysis throughout the government, wanting absolute presidential control of foreign policy, and delegating management and implementation to his national security advisor (ANSA), Henry Kissinger, while nurturing an intense jealousy of the attention and power that role granted Kissinger.

The best assessments of the Nixon process typically describe the administration as an example of a formalistic management style, elaborating on the numerous Kissinger-chaired interagency committees that supported the NSC.[5] Often Nixon's foreign policy is seen as a product of Nixon and Kissinger alone, a centralization so deep that only two men mattered. Nixon's relevance to his own foreign policy is often debated; Kissinger was and still is given credit for Nixon's success. Kissinger, not Nixon, won the 1973 Nobel Peace Prize for ending the Vietnam War. Today, as of this writing,

Kissinger continues to capture the world's imagination. His latest book, aptly titled *Kissinger on Kissinger*, was published in 2019. Seventeen books about Kissinger were listed on Amazon in 2020. In comparison, there are no books about William Rogers, three about Dean Rusk, and only one about Kissinger's successor, Carter's secretary of state Cyrus Vance. Of course, Watergate and Nixon's fate—the only president to resign from office—makes Nixon the object of even more fascination, often based in scorn, however, rather than approval; 27 biographies of Nixon are available.

The centralized decision making that is typically seen as the standard Nixon-Kissinger style—a series of Kissinger-chaired committees—actually did not exist at the outset of the administration. It began to be put in place after about six months when Nixon decided that he had been wrong about what type of decision making would work for him. Nixon redesigned the system to make it a better fit for his own personal style and to balance against his original formality. The reason for this shift supports elements of both the evolution and evolution-balance models.

As this chapter and the next illustrate, the picture of Nixon-Kissinger centralization is often exaggerated. The finding is especially true in the case of China policy. Kissinger worked diligently to keep the interagency process alive and of use to himself and the president. His elevation to the positions of both secretary of state and ANSA in the second term should be seen as an attempt to plug the State Department and the interagency process more directly into decision making, not as an effort to bypass the bureaucracies.

Nixon's initial decision making process was a formal structure that mirrored, yet deviated from, the Eisenhower formal system. First, like Eisenhower, Nixon hoped to build a strong National Security Council through the establishment of two NSC subcommittees, the Review Group (RG) and the Undersecretaries Committee (USC). Kissinger and the NSC staff would manage the NSC system, giving the White House control and demoting the State Department (which had secured the management role under Johnson within the SIG/IRG system). Second, Nixon's interagency process produced real and significant policy analysis on an ongoing basis through a very formal process. National Security Study Memorandums (NSSMs) reflected a thoroughness that Eisenhower would have been proud of. These studies and memos, however, were not always connected to the NSC. Third, Nixon did not want recommendations; instead, he sought well-staffed evaluations of a full range of options that he could use as a reference when he made his decisions. He hoped to avoid what he saw as the great flaw in the Eisenhower system: the bureaucracy would develop a consensus and present it to Eisenhower; the president then ratified that consensus, rather than decide the issue himself. In a sense, Nixon tried to slice decision making into discrete phases: analysis (performed by his bureaucracies through an interagency process led by the NSC staff); decision (made by Nixon alone or with one or two advisors); and implementation (in the hands of Nixon, Kissinger, or the relevant cabinet department, depending on the seriousness of the issue, Nixon's interest in the policy, and the secrecy necessary to carry through the idea). By many accounts, the hope to build a White House-managed cabinet was a sincere, but ultimately failed, effort.

The role of the president was simple: Nixon would be the center of strategy and decision, a sort of rational actor in the Oval Office, in control of both policy making and implementation, backstopped by an interagency process that produced detailed cost-benefit analyses of all available options. The fatal flaw in Nixon's plan was Nixon. His own character—the weaknesses in his personal management style—doomed his original design. He never found a way to deal psychologically with the rough and tumble and give and take of governmental decision making. His vicious political techniques, used in every election he contested, had its roots in a sense that he was under siege, his enemies always circling in for the kill.[6] He responded by using his campaign and White House staffs to attack his enemies in ever more elaborate ways, ultimately leading him to the Watergate scandal. That same impulse pushed Nixon toward eventually centralizing aspects of decision making in the White House to an even greater degree than Kennedy and Johnson. In an effort to insulate the presidency from the executive branch, Nixon tried to build an administrative fortress around himself, where Kissinger stood as a sentry, managing how information passed through its gates. This portrait of Nixon's decision process is an extreme version of the evolution model. Ironically, the expanding role of Kissinger and the NSC staff intensified the pathologies in the administration's organizational dynamics: Nixon's distrust of the cabinet departments; the feud between Kissinger and the NSC staff and Secretary of State William Rogers and the State bureaucracy; and Nixon's and Roger's very different conceptions of the reason Rogers was chosen by Nixon for the post.

The informal structure was warped by these pathologies. There was no analog for the Tuesday Lunch Group, no informal meetings of the national security advisor, the secretary of state, and the secretary of defense. This left the administration with no method of developing consensus among the senior decision makers. Kissinger did have weekly informal meetings with Undersecretary of State Elliot Richardson (and to a lesser extent his successor, Douglas Irwin), but these could hardly repair the day-by-day damage caused by the lack of a consensus-building process and the fact that Rogers and Kissinger had no real working relationship. This problem may have been baked in. Since Nixon insisted that he did not want his senior advisors to build a consensus and then present it to him as a fait accompli, he developed no mechanism for creating any rivalry-softening collegiality.

Kissinger was Nixon's most trusted advisor and became the heart of the confidence structure. The Nixon-Kissinger partnership rivals that of Truman-Acheson and Eisenhower-Dulles. Intellectually, Kissinger and Nixon were an excellent match—realists who had a similar view of the need to manage relations between the great powers. Their division of labor suited each man as well; Nixon hated the task of management, and Kissinger was willing to run the policy process on Nixon's behalf in exchange for the ability to advise the president on strategic matters and for playing the key role in implementation at the tactical level on many issues. Nixon trusted Kissinger's thinking on world affairs enough to delegate him immense authority, but their working "friendship" was marred by jealousy and anger. Perhaps it was as close to loyalty and trust as Nixon could come.

Three major changes in the administration's processes were established over time, two in the first six to 18 months, and the third in the first year of Nixon's second term. Each attempt at balancing and compensating grew out of Nixon and Kissinger's sense that the initial system had failed; its formality and absence of consensus building arrangements produced arguments, bitter rivalry, and leaks to the press, the exact results Nixon was hoping to avoid. Each was an adjustment to the formal process, and all three moved the administration toward a system that made the confidence structure—Kissinger—the hub of the formal structure; none of the adaptations created a real informal structure.

First, by February 1970, new interagency groups chaired by Kissinger that functioned, in theory, as subcommittees of the NSC were created for each of the administration's priority areas. Each excluded the secretaries of state or defense. The Washington Special Actions Group, the Verification Panel (arms control), Vietnam Special Studies Group, the Defense Program Review Committee, the Intelligence Committee, and the 40 Committee (covert operations) connected the president to the departments through Kissinger. The NSSM and National Security Decision Memorandums (NSDMs) process often flowed to and through these committees, rather than through the NSC. As the next chapter illustrates, China was an exception. These committees gave Nixon greater control, a way to avoid NSC meetings where the president was confronted with face-to-face debate, and a route around the secretaries of state and defense. Importantly, these were not methods of cutting out the departments and agencies, but ways for Nixon and Kissinger to shut out the senior officials of those departments while still using the expertise and manpower of each. In effect, the standard flow of interagency reports and analysis was now rerouted from the NSC and cabinet secretaries to Kissinger, allowing the confidence structure to capture the formal system.

Second, in September 1970, National Security Decision Memorandum 85, *The National Security Council Senior Review Group*, established a senior interagency group, the Senior Review Group (SRG), that would take over the day-to-day interagency process for the administration. It replaced the RG, a committee that had the same responsibilities but none of the clout that was given to the SRG. The RG had been chaired by Kissinger, but its membership merely specified "representatives" of each major department and agency for foreign policy, a lack of specificity that undermined its authority. The Kissinger-led SRG included the deputies of the major departments, the director of the CIA, and the chair of the Joint Chiefs. This elevated the group to the senior-most interagency group aside from the NSC. It met more frequently than the NSC and was a mandatory stopover before any policy made its way to the NSC. Again, with Kissinger as chair and the deputies of each cabinet department reporting to him, the formal system was routed through Kissinger's office, giving Kissinger the ability to interpret the product of the formal process for Nixon. Even with the proliferation of Kissinger-chaired committees, however, most committees met less and less over time.

Third, though the new committee system gave Nixon and Kissinger more control over the process, it also escalated the bureaucratic warfare between Rogers and Kissinger. Nixon could not resolve the problem until the first year of his second term when he fired Rogers and gave Kissinger both jobs: secretary of state and ANSA. At that point it was explicit: Nixon had formalized his confidence structure.

The Nixon case study confirms the evolution-balance model. Nixon's own weaknesses meant that the formal structure could never work the way he had hoped and prevented the informal structure from ever being formed. To compensate, Nixon relied on his confidence structure; Kissinger was given Nixon's proxy and a committee structure that allowed him to dominate the formal structure.

Table 9.3 uses the structured-focused comparison questions to compare the evolution of Nixon's overall decision making to the evolution of deci-

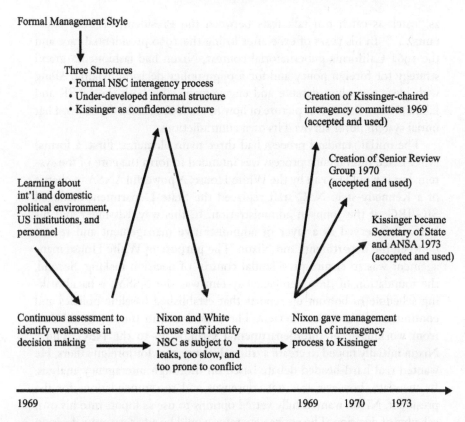

Formal Management Style

Three Structures
• Formal NSC interagency process
• Under-developed informal structure
• Kissinger as confidence structure

Creation of Kissinger-chaired
interagency committees 1969
(accepted and used)

Creation of Senior Review
Group 1970
(accepted and used)

Learning about
int'l and domestic
political environment,
US institutions, and
personnel

Kissinger became
Secretary of State
and ANSA 1973
(accepted and used)

Continuous assessment to
identify weaknesses in
decision making

Nixon and White
House staff identify
NSC as subject to
leaks, too slow, and
too prone to conflict

Nixon gave management
control of interagency
process to Kissinger

1969   1969   1970   1973

NSC – National Security Council
ANSA – Assistant tot eh President for National Security Affairs

Fig. 7.1. The Evolution of Nixon Administration Decision Making

sion making for China. Figure 7.1 traces the changes in the overall decision making process of the Nixon administration as illustrated in figure 2.2.

Initial Decision Making Process

Nixon entered office with the explicit intention of differentiating himself from his predecessor. As Vietnam consumed the Johnson presidency, it also discredited his foreign policy process. The changes in decision making as described in previous chapters were not publicly acknowledged, and Nixon could still describe the Johnson decision machinery during the campaign

as "catch-as-catch can talk fests between the President, his staff assistants . . ."[7] In his years of exile after losing the 1960 presidential race and
the 1962 California gubernatorial context, Nixon had fashioned a grand
strategy for foreign policy and for foreign policy decision making. Along
with ideas regarding détente and engagement with both the USSR and
China, Nixon had a clear picture of how he wanted to make decisions. That
initial system never survived its own contradictions.

The initial standard process had three main elements. First, a formal
NSC-based interagency process was intended to form the core of the system, but it would be run by the White House. A powerful ANSA in charge
of a Kennedy-style NSC staff replaced the State Department-managed
SIG/IRG of the Johnson administration. In this way, Kissinger and his
NSC staff served as a layer of administrative management and review
between the departments and Nixon. The purpose of White House management was to ensure presidential control of decision making. Second,
the foundation of the interagency system was the NSSM, a backbreak-
ing schedule of bottom-up reports that established baseline policies and
continuous departmental review. The paperwork, in theory, would flow
from working-level Interdepartmental Groups up to the NSC. Third,
Nixon initially hoped to create a true cabinet system for foreign affairs. He
wanted real hard-headed debate based on thorough interagency analysis.
Its mandate, however, was not consensus and recommendations for the
president. Nixon wanted fully vetted options to use as inputs into his own
calculus of decision. The entire apparatus would be advisory only; decision
making and implementation would be controlled by Nixon.

The original sin of the design becomes obvious: formal systems rooted
in a strong NSC-based interagency process are decentralized systems;
White House-managed decisions backed up by a powerful presidential
staff generally become centralized systems. Nixon tried to have it both
ways. The overall result was a series of terrible, now legendary, bureaucratic battles as the senior level of this nascent cabinet government crashed
and burned.

A Formal NSC Interagency Process under White House Control

After squeaking by Democratic candidate Hubert Humphrey in the 1968
election, the Nixon transition team began by commissioning memos on
different approaches to management. Surprisingly, Nixon chose Henry
Kissinger, a Harvard professor and chief foreign policy advisor to Nel-

son Rockefeller, his rival for the 1968 Republican presidential nomination, for the position of ANSA, the official who would organize the creation and then the execution of Nixon's foreign policy decision making. Given Nixon's difficulty with interpersonal communication and trust, choosing Kissinger, a man he hardly knew, to serve as his foreign policy alter ego is another of his many contradictions. While Nixon may not have known Kissinger on a personal level, he trusted Kissinger's intellect and political judgment. Nixon admired Kissinger's scholarly writing as well as his bed-rock beliefs on the nature of international relations. Both men were real-ists, believing that world politics was fundamentally a competition between nation-states whose power capabilities made them rivals. War, however, was not inevitable; stability, even extended periods of peace, could be achieved through a well-managed balance of power. Though Kissinger had turned down an offer to work on the Nixon campaigns in 1960 and 1968, once elected, Nixon courted Kissinger anew. The two met on November 25 at the Pierre Hotel in New York where they discussed global affairs.[8] As a result of some transition disorganization, Nixon did not explicitly offer Kissinger the ANSA post. Two days later when Nixon campaign chair and transition advisor John Mitchell asked Kissinger if he was ready to take the position of ANSA, Kissinger replied, "I did not know that I had been offered it." Mitchell responded, "Oh, Jesus Christ," and quickly arranged for Nixon to formally offer Kissinger the post.[9] As a foreshadowing of things to come, Kissinger's new role was announced on November 29, but the cabinet selections, including secretary of state and secretary of defense, were not announced until December 11. In spite of Nixon's rhetoric or musings about an NSC-led decision process, his White House staff came first.[10]

Kissinger's priority was designing a decision making system that fit Nixon's preferences. Nixon was very clear about what he wanted: NSC-based interagency procedures that would advise him, but not make deci-sions; Nixon would control foreign policy from the White House. In a campaign radio address in 1968, Nixon tied decision style to decision qual-ity, blaming failures of Kennedy and Johnson's national security strategy on informality and poor use of the NSC:

> Since 1960 this Council has virtually disappeared as an operating function. . . . I attribute most of our serious reverses abroad since 1960 to the inability or disinclination of President Eisenhower's successors to make effective use of this important Council.[11]

Nixon stated publicly that he would "restore the National Security Council to its preeminent role in national security planning." It would not be a replication of the Eisenhower system, but Nixon explicitly told Kissinger in their pre-inauguration meetings that he wanted a "more formal decision making process."[12] As Kennedy had designed his informal spokes of the wheel to be the antithesis of Eisenhower's formality, Nixon saw a return to the Eisenhower architecture as an antidote to what he saw as Johnson's adhocracy. Like Nixon, Kissinger had been a critic of Johnson, arguing in a Rockefeller campaign press release from June 21, 1968 that

> there exists no staff procedures for arriving at decisions; instead ad hoc groups are formed as the need arises. . . . Without a central administrative focus, foreign policy turns into a series of unrelated decisions—crisis-oriented, ad hoc and after the fact in nature. We become prisoners of events.[13]

Kissinger's task was to translate Nixon's vision into an actual formal system.

General Andrew Goodpaster, a veteran of the Eisenhower NSC staff then serving in Vietnam, was brought back to Washington to help Nixon and Kissinger during the transition. Kissinger had hired Morton Halperin to draft a memo detailing a new national security interagency process based, in part, on Goodpaster's analysis of the Eisenhower system. Halperin had been deputy assistant secretary of defense for international security affairs in the Johnson administration and had lamented how the Tuesday Lunch Group left the middle layers of the bureaucracy in the dark about decisions made at the cabinet level. Lawrence Eagleburger, who had worked on the Johnson NSC staff and in Rusk's State Department, also reviewed Halperin's memo. The group met in New York and Cambridge, Massachusetts as they considered a concept for a new NSC process.[14]

Two memos illustrate the debate during this period: the notes of a dinner meeting on December 9, 1968 between Kissinger and members of his advising team in Cambridge, and a draft of the memorandum that Kissinger would give to Nixon laying out the parameters of a new NSC. The notes of the meeting do not indicate who attended, but they do contain Kissinger's handwritten comments. The NSC system would have four levels. First, the NSC would meet monthly or for a "special call" and include statutory members and advisors and anyone else the president chose to add. Second, an Executive Group of the NSC, which included the president, secretaries of state and defense, and Kissinger, would meet on a weekly basis.

This group was essentially Nixon's version of the Tuesday Lunch Group. Because criticism of the TLG was a key part of Nixon's attacks on Johnson and the Democrats, the memo was careful to specifically say that the group would meet "but not at lunch." The notes called for the Executive Group to be "formally established," and for its deliberations to be "publicized" as a way of showing the press that the NSC was "continuously at work." Records of the meetings would be taken by a member of the NSC staff, "a Non-person"—meaning someone who would not participate, but only observe. These "confidential notes" would not be "formal minutes." Importantly, Kissinger rejected the formal creation of the group, writing on the draft the comment "do not establish formally; if done membership will grow." He also rejected publicity concerning the group's meetings. This is crucial. Kissinger understood that this group would do the real work of advising the president on foreign policy, and it could only do so if it were small and informal, and if it were insulated from larger bureaucratic debates and organizational rivalries; only then could Nixon use the Executive Group the way Johnson used the TLG, as his senior-level brain trust where full and open debate flourished.

Third, a Review Committee of the NSC, consisting of Kissinger, the assistant secretary of defense for international security affairs, and the equivalent official at State, would manage the interagency system, bringing issues to the Executive Group, assigning tasks to assistant-secretary-level regional groups, recommending national security directives, and creating "study assignments" inside and outside the government. The Review Committee essentially managed the NSC similar to the way the Planning Board had managed Eisenhower's NSC. Fourth, the Interdepartmental Regional Groups of the Johnson administration would be decommissioned and then "reconstituted" to perform the exact same jobs they had done since NSAM 341 had created them. Each would be an assistant-secretary-level committee focusing on a specific region, with membership from all the relevant departments and agencies. The very important difference between these new committees and the Johnson IRGs was that these would be chaired by members of the NSC staff, not by the State Department.

The latter two points illustrate the shift of power in foreign affairs from State to the NSC staff. Along with the NSC staff-run non-IRG interdepartmental groups, the Senior Interdepartmental Group (SIG), chaired by the undersecretary of state, was eliminated, thereby ending State's leadership role in the interagency process. The memo also called for merging the ANSA position with the director of the NSC staff and the executive secretary of the NSC. These changes would give Kissinger authority over the policy process, personnel, and communications between the bureaucracies and the president. The entire NSC staff apparatus would also be formally created as part of the Executive Office of the President, tying it to Nixon more directly, rather than as an adjunct to the NSC.[15]

The undated draft memorandum for Nixon, written by Kissinger, reinforced the main points of the dinner meeting notes, but with several important differences.[16] First, it did not mention the Executive Group of the NSC; the inclusion of a regularized informal meeting of the senior advisors to the president was not suggested to Nixon, even as it was being discussed by those designing the system. Second, the memo retained the Johnson IRGs with State Department leadership. Third, it proposed an Undersecretaries Committee, led by the undersecretary of state, and including the deputy secretary of defense, ANSA, and other officials at the subcabinet level. Its job was to deal with issues unresolved by the IRGs, or those that did not rise to cabinet-level importance. It also named the new presidential directive series that would replace the National Security Action Memorandums of the Kennedy/Johnson era: National Security Study Memorandums would initiate reviews of key topics; and National Security Decision Memorandums would officially transmit presidential decisions to the executive branch. The memo, however, did not specify the process for these documents.

The contrast between the two documents suggests that there was still debate about whether State or the NSC staff would lead the system. The undated memo gave greater power to the State Department than the notes of the dinner meeting (maintaining the IRGs and establishing the Undersecretaries Committee.). It even implied that the NSC staff would not be a significant producer of policy analysis, stating that "only in exceptional circumstances would the NSC staff prepare its own papers."[17]

During this period Kissinger and Goodpaster visited Eisenhower, then seriously ill and resting in Walter Reed National Military Medical Center (he would pass away on March 28, 1969). Eisenhower was adamant; the SIG/IRG had to be dismantled. Coordination of the interagency system must come from the White House. In particular, he saw a State-led system as mistakenly elevating the State Department over the Defense Department on national security issues. Kissinger felt that the SIG could still be useful and argued for retaining it, but Nixon was unyielding on the subject, arguing forcefully that the "influence of the State Department must be reduced."[18]

Kissinger gave Nixon his final draft on December 27, 1968.[19] Many sections of this memo are repeated verbatim in the official directive that established Nixon's NSC system, NSDM 2, *Reorganization of the National Security Council System*, signed by Nixon on January 20, 1969.[20] This final proposal and NSDM 2 resolved most, but not all, of the key debates in favor of the NSC staff. Some flexibility, however, was built into it, allowing Nixon to use the NSC, but not be tied to it as the sole advisory body.

First, Kissinger's draft described the NSC as the "the principal forum for issues requiring interagency coordination," while NSDM 2 referred to the NSC as "a principal forum." This slight change of the article, representing a wariness of forcing all presidential decisions into the NSC, replaced a paragraph in Kissinger's December memo explicitly stating that the "the NSC should not be considered the sole forum for presidential discussion in the National Security field. The President will reserve the option of constituting subcommittees." Second, the NSC Review Group (no longer the Review Committee) under Kissinger's direction was created to "examine papers" on their way to the NSC and to decide which issues should be placed before the NSC, given to the Undersecretaries Committee, or assigned to NSC Interdepartmental Groups (which replaced the IRGs) or Ad Hoc Groups. Importantly, while NSDM 2 gave Kissinger the chairmanship of the RG, additional members of the committee were listed only as "a representative" of the secretaries of State and Defense, the Chairman of the Joint Chiefs of Staff (CJCS), and the Director of Central Intelligence (DCI). Third, the USC was renamed the "NSC Ad Hoc Under Secretaries Committee." The committee's existence was a victory for the State Department, but the "Ad Hoc" designation seems to have been a slap in the face, implying that it was a temporary structure. The "Ad Hoc" disappeared quickly, and the committee was simply called the USC. Its membership was not changed from early drafts—chaired by the undersecretary of state (State's second-ranked official at the time) and consisting of the deputy secretary of defense, CJCS, and DCI. NSDM 2 placed it as subordinate to the RG: "It would deal with matters referred to it by the NSC Review Group." The arrangement was awkward and ultimately unworkable since the unspecified membership on the RG meant that members of the USC could be asked to take direction from their departmental subordinates.

Fourth, both Kissinger's draft and NSDM 2 elevated the role of the ANSA and NSC staff at the direct expense of the State Department. The ANSA was given the job of "determining the agenda" for the NSC and "ensuring that the necessary papers are prepared." This power was not absolute, however. The ANSA would perform these tasks under presidential "direction" and "in consultation with the Secretaries of State and Defense." The State-chaired IRGs were "reconstituted as part of the

National Security Council structure" and renamed NSC Interdepartmental Groups (IGs). This implied that NSC staffers would chair the IGs, and that the NSC staff rather than assistant secretaries of state now managed the preparation of IG policy papers and crisis contingency papers. That, however, did not turn out to be the case. Regional issue IGs were ultimately still chaired by the relevant State assistant secretary.

Importantly, NSDM 2 omitted the Executive Group from the final document; no small senior-level committee was established. It also explicitly rescinded NSAM 341, Johnson's directive that had institutionalized the SIG/IRG system, eliminating the SIG and all the IRGs.

NSDM 1, *Establishment of NSC Decision and Study Memoranda Series*, signed by Nixon on January 20, 1969, officially created the NSSM and NSDM system, but did not specify the process through which these documents would be produced.[21] Its wording reflected Kissinger's memo of December 27, which was equally unclear about the production of these documents.

Approval of Kissinger's December draft was somewhat rocky, foreshadowing the bureaucratic battles to come. The State Department and to a lesser extent the Department of Defense fought back against the concentration of power in the White House. At a meeting in Key Biscayne, Florida on December 28, Nixon met with Kissinger, Secretary of State-designate William Rogers, Secretary of Defense-designate Melvin Laird, Vice President Spiro Agnew, and Goodpaster. Unknown to Rogers and Laird, Nixon had already approved Kissinger's NSC system proposal. At the meeting Nixon sought their consent, which they granted that same night.[22]

Between this meeting and the signing of the first NSDMs following the inauguration on January 20, 1969, both Laird and Rogers began lobbying to modify the system they had already approved. Laird felt that a representative of the intelligence community needed to be a member of the RG. Kissinger's early draft of the December 27 memo had included the DCI in the RG, but Nixon had circled "Central Intelligence" and scrawled "no" on the draft. Kissinger lobbied Nixon and had the DCI put back into the membership of the RG in the final draft of NSDM 2.[23]

The objections from the State Department were more fundamental. U. Alexis Johnson, newly appointed as the undersecretary of state for political affairs, had been one of the architects of the SIG/IRG system as deputy undersecretary for political affairs in Lyndon Johnson's State Department. He clearly saw that the new system was emasculating State in favor of White House dominance. Even before the Key Biscayne meeting, he had tried to convince Kissinger to give the Secretary of State power to review all papers before they would go to the RG, and lobbied Rogers to object to the new design. Both Kissinger and Rogers rebuffed him.[24] Following the Key Biscayne approval, Johnson continued to argue against the dismantling of the SIG/IRG. On January 6 Johnson met with Rogers and Kissinger again but made little headway. Johnson also met with Rogers and Elliot Richardson, the new undersecretary of state, to convince them to make a forceful protest. Johnson hoped that they would "mount the ramparts . . . against the Kissinger/NSC takeover of State's international functions."[25] In early January, Richardson sent a memo to Kissinger with revisions to the December 27 document.[26] Richardson's draft eliminated the RG completely. Instead, Richardson's draft emphasized that the "Secretary of State should be the principal advisor to the President in the conduct of foreign policy. The Department of State has principal responsibility for the overall direction, coordination, and supervision of interdepartmental activities of the US Government overseas," language taken directly from NSAM 341 that had established the SIG/IRG. The agenda of the NSC would be set by consultations between the ANSA and the secretary of state. In theory, if the ANSA and secretary set the agenda and the RG did not even exist, any vacuum that existed would be filled by the department with the "principal responsibility" in foreign affairs—the State Department.

Kissinger sent a three-page memo to Nixon on January 7 that detailed State's objections, and gave a thorough assessment the pros and cons of Richardson's revisions. Two aspects of the memo stand out. First, Kissinger did not shrug off State's objections; he described them faithfully in the memo, even including excerpts from NSAM 341. Here, Kissinger was being an honest broker of the process, bringing to the president points of view that he believed the president needed to hear, even if Kissinger disagreed with them. Second, Kissinger also allowed himself to be an advocate, making it clear that he did disagree with Richardson:

> The only way the President can ensure that all options are examined, and all the arguments fairly presented, is to have his own people— responsive to him, accustomed to his style, and with a Presidential rather than departmental perspective—oversee preparation of the papers. If the President wants to control policy, he must control the policy process.[27]

Kissinger described Nixon's response to the memo this way: "Suddenly, Nixon was unavailable for days on end." Nixon's inability to handle confrontation led him to avoid the dispute. When the two finally spoke on the matter, Nixon told Kissinger that the issue would take care of itself. Kissinger still needed to engineer a consensus, however. He met with Goodpaster, Eagleburger, Rogers, and Richardson at the State Department to hash it out, but resolved little. Ultimately H. R. Haldeman, Nixon's chief of staff, called Kissinger to tell him that the president would stick with the language of the December 27 memo agreed upon at Key Biscayne. In Kissinger's words, Haldeman told him "that anyone opposing it should submit his resignation."[28] In this case, Haldeman played a role that would become familiar. When Nixon could not bear the awkwardness of confronting his advisors and overruling them in person, Haldeman stepped in as the blunt enforcer of the president's wishes.

In hindsight, Goodpaster argued that the purpose of the White House-managed system went beyond "Presidential control." He felt Nixon "was going to do foreign policy. And he was going to direct it: he was going to engage in it."[29] In short, Nixon desired to be his own secretary of state. Nixon stated it plainly in his memoirs: "From the outset of my administration, however, I planned to direct foreign policy from the White House."[30]

State did get a concession, however. NSDM 3, *The Direction, Coordination, and Supervision of Interdepartmental Activities Overseas*, of January 20 and NSDM 7, *Direction, Coordination, and Supervision of Interdepartmental Activities Overseas—Interdepartmental Groups*, dated February 7, used language from NSAM 341 and Richardson's memo to emphasize the secretary of state's role as Nixon's "principal foreign policy advisor" and State's authority to manage both the process and implementation of foreign policy.[31] Both these NSDMs would, in theory, be fulfilled through the Undersecretaries Committee.

Implementation of the System

In practice, the heart of the system was intended to be a series of interagency studies that analyzed options for the president and NSC principals—NSSMs. Each NSSM tasked a specific IG to write a report that answered a detailed set of questions that could run for multiple pages (NSSM 1 on Vietnam used seven pages to outline the key questions the report must consider).[32] The language used in the NSSM and the reports is sometimes confusing about whether the request for the study or the actual study is the NSSM. Importantly, the study questions were drafted by the NSC staff, sent to the IGs by Kissinger with his signature authorizing the NSSM.

The Nixon administration issued 206 NSSMs from January 21, 1969 to July 29, 1974, each a request for a large interagency review; that averaged roughly three per month. In Nixon's first year of office alone, Kissinger tasked the bureaucracy with 85 NSSMs, a pace of seven major interagency studies initiated per month.[33] Each study was assigned to a specific IG or ad hoc group, and given a due date for submission to the appropriate senior-level, Kissinger-chaired committee (initially the RG, but eventually the SRG or one of the six other committees established through 1969 and 1970). From there, in theory, the policy analysis would make its way to the NSC unless the president chose to make a decision outside the NSC. The entire process was managed by the NSC staff.[34] A quick look at NSSMs shows how explicitly formal the system was intended to be. NSSM 2, *Middle East Policy*, directed the NSC Interdepartmental Group for the Near East to write two papers. The first was to consider three potential negotiation avenues for resolving the Arab-Israeli conflict; the second was to analyze US interests. The memorandum specified that "the first paper should be forwarded to the NSC Review Group by January 25, 1969. The second paper should be forwarded to the NSC Review Group by February 24, 1969."[35] NSSM 3, *US Military Posture and the Balance of Power*, of January 21, 1969 created an ad hoc interagency group to examine US defense strategy and force deployment. It explicitly specified the group's membership and gave an exact due date and oversight body for the report: "The report of the group shall be forwarded to the NSC Review Group by July 1, 1969."[36]

While this looks like an inclusive, rigorous interagency process, it spawned a debate from the moment it was first publicized: Is it a replication of the Eisenhower NSC tweaked to avoid a consensus that traps the president, or is it busywork given to the departments and agencies that allowed Nixon, Kissinger, and the NSC staff to operate without interference? In other words, was the system designed to prevent the departments and agencies from giving meaningful input by drowning them in policy papers?[37] As described in the next chapter, in the case of China the NSSM/NSDM process was absolutely essential to most but not all of Nixon's decisions.

Kissinger explained it this way:

> The interdepartmental machinery was applied to real problems; it was designed to elicit the best thinking within the government and to define the range of choices available to the President. The final decision was often made alone by Nixon or in consultation with me; but though the bureaucracy did not participate in the decision, it played—paradoxically—a major role in the process of reach-

ing it. For the options produced by it were the raw material of our deliberation.[38]

Kissinger's description answers an additional question: How did NSSMs and NSDMs connect to the NSC and the president? Early NSSMs created a system where the product of established IGs or ad hoc interagency groups was given to the RG. There was no explicit paper flow beyond this. If the NSSMs were simply busywork, the RG was a great black hole; Kissinger could file the reports (where researchers like the author might be the first people ever to read them), and then he and Nixon would make policy however they wanted. If Nixon honored the Eisenhower model, the RG would refine papers or ask the interagency groups to revise papers until they were ready for NSC review or presidential decision. Kissinger's quote made it clear that he and Nixon used the interagency process as the foundation of their decisions, but did not allow the interagency groups to make the decisions for the president. As Herbert Levin, NSC staffer and State Department official for Japan and East Asia, explained, the work of the interagency system "was the mortar and the bricks of what happened when the policy designs actually took form."[39] Again, this is an Eisenhower-like system that went to great lengths to correct Nixon's sense of the older version's flaws—it sought to make sure that the president could never be trapped by departmental consensus or limited by the interagency process.

The Undersecretaries Committee focused on implementation of decisions; it was the Nixon administration's version of the Eisenhower-era Operations Coordination Board that oversaw the implementation of policy. Chaired by the undersecretary of state, the department's number-two official, and including the deputy secretary of defense, the ANSA, the DCI, and the CJCS, it carried the weight of NSDMs 3 and 7 giving the secretary of state responsibility for "the overall direction, coordination and supervision of interdepartmental activities of the United States Government overseas."[40] NSDM 2 spelled out the USC role, but the verbiage is not necessarily helpful in identifying what that actually encompassed.[41] An examination of USC declassified documents makes its job much clearer. In cases where NSSMs and NSDMs explicitly tasked the USC with creating implementation plans for presidential decisions, the USC actually designed those plans for presidential approval, generally after consultations between the USC chair and Kissinger. The USC was originally scheduled to meet every Thursday at 4:00 p.m., with an acknowledgment that such a regularized schedule might not be necessary. It also had its own memorandum series—

Undersecretaries Committee Decision Study Memorandum (NSC-U/SM) and Undersecretaries Committee Decision Memoranda (NSC-U/DM). The USC produced 150 study memoranda (with multiple iterations of each based on interagency negotiation) and 126 decision memorandums (again with numerous versions hashed out through interagency bargaining).[42] The USC also inherited the staff that had supported the Johnson-era SIG.[43] From the documentary record, USC activity appears essential to the administration. Once Nixon began to consider a specific policy goal, he asked the USC the question: What are the ways I might accomplish this? The USC then staffed out a range of possibilities—here are the ways and here are their potential impacts.

USC activities reveal a rigorous interagency process; however, it was not explicitly plugged into the NSC. The committee did include the ANSA, which was ultimately its true connection to Nixon, through Kissinger. Its records indicate the initial centrality of the Kissinger-Richardson relationship. What is missing is any indication of a role for the secretary of state. Rogers's influence should have come from the fact that the undersecretary of State was his number two. As discussed in the next chapter, on China decision making the USC took on the central task of exploring implementation options for policies decided at the NSC or by Nixon or Kissinger, or both.

Once up and operating, the system filled in the gaps that had not been adequately specified by NSDM 1 and 2. The bottom line, though, was clear: Nixon would make decisions based on full interagency evaluation of available options. On paper, Kissinger and the NSC staff were given immense power to manage foreign policy by setting the NSC's agenda, the assignment of policy reviews, and the management of those reviews. Kissinger, however, did work to make sure that every issue had full interagency participation. The NSSM and USC processes illustrate the way the system actually provided Nixon with the information and analysis he desired before he was ready to make a decision.

An Advisory Cabinet, But a Presidential Decision

As Eisenhower's vice president for eight years, Nixon had the opportunity to observe the president typically seen as the father of presidential management. He chose to replicate the Eisenhower formal interagency process, but tried to establish two related distinctions; he wanted wide open debate of all options at the NSC, but no specific recommendations. The NSC was advisory, not a place to iron out a consensus decision that he would accept or reject. Versions of the draft minutes of the first NSC meeting on January 21, 1969 stressed both ideas.

> The President emphasized that he wanted deliberations of the group to be open and free and to assure each member that they should feel completely free to speak their piece. . . . The President emphasizes that he will insist upon a free give and take discussion at NSC meetings. He does not want recommendation; he wishes to hear all points of view, and as a matter of practice, he will, after careful consideration, make his decisions after the NSC meetings. . . . the President stated that the NSC was not a decision-making body, that he would not call for votes on a particular issue and that he did not want them to feel obliged to hammer out a consensus . . . The President interjected that he felt strongly about this point and if minority views existed that he wanted to see them clearly stated.[44]

To Nixon, the Achilles heel of Eisenhower's interagency system was not its lack of speed or its proliferation of paperwork, as the Jackson subcommittee had argued, but the way it produced a ready-made consensus for Eisenhower to ratify, a consensus that represented a bureaucratically achievable compromise rather than a policy that actually solved a problem. Its goal was not innovation or creativity, but making sure each department and agency could walk away somewhat satisfied. Nixon felt that Eisenhower had been boxed in, giving him no real choice once the interagency process had made up its mind. Nixon reportedly told Kissinger that he wanted the "Eisenhower system . . . without the concurrences."[45] The last thing he wanted, in the words of Helmut Sonnenfeldt, a Nixon NSC staffer, was "precooked decisions that were bargained out in the bureaucracies and among cabinet officers and then presented to him in such a way that he could only accept or reject them."[46] Nixon's Foreign Policy Report to Congress of February 18, 1970 had unusual candor for a public document. Nixon wrote: "I refuse to be confronted with a bureaucratic consensus that leaves me no options but acceptance or rejection and that gives me no way of knowing what alternatives exist."[47]

In this sense, Nixon was trying to separate decision making into components. The advisory process would be cabinet-style—undertaken by the departments and agencies. Its analysis would reach Nixon through a hierarchical interagency process. Nixon would then make the decision by himself or with individuals of his own choosing. Implementation would be either delegated to the departments and agencies or handled by Nixon himself. White House staffer William Safire quoted Chief of Staff H. R. Haldeman explaining the initial concept at a staff meeting: "Our job is not to do the work of the government, but to get the work out where it belongs—out to the departments."[48]

To ensure that the NSC would be a forum for open discussion, Nixon hoped to keep NSC membership restrictive. The first NSC meeting reflected Nixon's desire for a small NSC reserved for principals; the only officials invited were Nixon, Vice President Spiro Agnew, Secretary of State Rogers, Secretary of Defense Laird, Secretary of the Treasury David Kennedy, DCI Richard Helms, Chairman of the Joint Chiefs General Earle Wheeler, Goodpaster, director of the Office of Emergency Preparedness George Lincoln, and Kissinger. NSDM 123 of July 27, 1971 added the secretary of the treasury and the attorney general to the NSC on a permanent basis.[49]

Though Nixon did not want recommendations from his NSC, the documentary record shows that he did, in fact, receive written recommendations to accept or reject. These came from Kissinger, however, not the NSC. All the interagency staff work could produce mountains of paper that no president could or should try to scale. The administration developed a two-phase process where the NSC staff managed Kissinger's time and effort (first phase) in the same way Kissinger and the NSC staff managed Nixon's time and effort (second phase). First, Kissinger's NSC staff had the job of filtering the product of the interagency process into a manageable form—departmental or interagency reports/memos reached Kissinger under an NSC staff-written covering memo that included specific recommendations for Kissinger to approve or disapprove. Kissinger would also receive memos from his staff in preparation for meetings with the president or other senior cabinet officials, outlining the topics he should raise. For each type of memo, Kissinger would check a box, "Approve or Disapprove" or "I have discussed this with the President . . . Yes_____ . . . No_____."[50] The style allowed Kissinger to use his staff as a brain trust to make sure he could set priorities and stick to the big picture while his staff made sure that nothing would fall through the cracks.

Second, as heads of the RG and USC, Kissinger and Richardson (and his replacement Douglas Irwin) used the same memo format to formally organize Nixon's decisions—a covering memo with recommendations that were followed by "Approved_____" and "Disapprove_____." Nixon would initial in one space or the other, indicating his decision, or sometimes initial neither and write in further instructions.[51] This paperwork procedure gave both Kissinger and Richardson real influence on the president's thinking through the covering memo by translating the work of the bureaucracy. Kissinger had far greater power than anyone else, however. Every memo relating to foreign policy was subject to a Kissinger covering memo. Nixon had delegated the task of making recommendations to Kissinger and to a lesser extent to the chair of the USC, the same task he adamantly refused to grant to the NSC. This delegation was a measure of Nixon's trust in Kissinger, his belief that Kissinger understood what Nixon wanted—someone who would present all the options (honest broker), but also provide proposals that flowed from Nixon's concept of US national interests (advocate). This dual role for Kissinger is evident in the fact that Nixon did not simply approve every recommendation, and Kissinger often counseled Nixon to reject recommendations that came from the RG or USC.

Table 7.1 shows that during the first six months of the administration's tenure in office, Nixon's NSC system functioned in reality much like its design (if we assume that the quantity of meetings is a reflection of effort and intent). From January to June 1969, the administration held 23 NSC meetings in roughly 23 weeks. During this period, the RG met 26 times. The USC met 9 times.[52] A schedule like this indicates that no deep centralization had yet taken root during the first six months of Nixon's time in office.[53] The evolution model suggests that the standard interagency process operates as intended for roughly six months. As discussed below, this six-month estimate appears accurate for the Nixon administration.

Role of the President

In many ways, Nixon was trying to build what amounted to a rational actor system of decision making. In foreign policy analysis, the classic rational actor model views the government as a unified actor making decisions through unemotional cost-benefit analysis.[54] Nixon was essentially putting the idea into practice with the president as that rational actor, a single brain performing cost-benefit analysis based on the foundational work of the executive branch and the NSC staff. The real decisions were made by Nixon when he was alone. Kissinger's memos must have been useful to him or he would have discontinued them, but in no way was this designed to be a system where Nixon simply ratified Kissinger's recommendations. Kissinger explained it to reporters as a process through which Nixon listened to all the arguments then "stews about it and decides by himself." H. R. Haldeman, Nixon's chief of staff, also used the word "stew" to describe Nixon's deliberations.[55] Harold Saunders, an NSC staffer, described Nixon

TABLE 7.1. Major Committees and NSSMs of the Nixon Administration

Date (by Quarter)	National Security Council (NSC)	NSC Review Group (RG)[a]	NSC Senior Review Group (SRG)[b]	NSC Undersecretaries Committee	NSSMs
Jan.–March 1969	11	11	—	3	35
April–June 1969	12	15	—	6	26
July–Sept. 1969	6	5	—	6	15
October–Dec. 1969	6	8	—	5	9
Jan.–March 1970	9	10	—	6	6
April–June 1970	6	10	2	6	4
July–Sept. 1970	6	—	8	4	8
October–Dec. 1970	3	—	18	3	8
Jan.–March 1971	5	—	11	6	9
April–June 1971	3 (all June)	—	15	1	12
July–Sept. 1971	3	—	12	0	5
October–Dec. 1971	3	—	8	1	6
Jan.–March 1972	2	—	8	4	9
April–June 1972	1 (May)	—	4	1	3
July–Sept. 1972	0	—	5	1	6
October–Dec. 1972	1 (Nov)	—	4	1	5
Jan.–March 1973	1 (March)	—	3	0	12
April–June 1973	1 (April)	—	4	0	7
July–Sept. 1973	0	—	5	1	0
October–Dec. 1973	0	—	0	0	3
Jan.–March 1974	2	—	1 (February)	1	9
April–June 1974	1	—	0	1	4
July–August 8, 1974	0	—	0	0	3

Sources: NSC, RG, and SRG meetings: National Security Council Institutional Files, Finding Aid, 43–73, RNPL, https://www.nixonlibrary.gov/sites/default/files/forresearchers/find/textual/institutional/finding_aid.pdf. NSSMs: NSSMs, Nixon Administration, 1969–1974. Federation of American Scientists, https://fas.org/irp/offdocs/nssm-nixon/index.html. Undersecretaries Committee: NSC Institutional ("H") Files, Under Secretaries Committee Memorandum Files (1969–1974), Boxes H-249-H-281, RNPL.

a Operated from 1/20/69 through 9/14/70. Replaced by SRG by NSDM 85, September 14, 1970.

b Created by NSDM 85. Operated under Nixon from 9/14/70 to 8/9/74.

as "lonely in his study, with his long yellow pad, making up his pro and con columns."[56] Though Nixon wanted options and assessments and the views, no matter how disparate, of all departments and agencies, he reserved the making of decisions to himself. At the first NSC meeting he stated it simply: "I will make the decisions. To do this, I will need all points of view. I will then deliberate in private and make the decisions. In this process, I might talk to individuals prior to finalizing my decision."[57] Nixon's aides touted his brilliance and felt that he attacked problems, devouring every bit of information and always reaching out for more. That thirst for more was similar to Johnson's. Nixon's staff had standing orders to send interesting articles to Nixon for weekly reading.[58] He was often described as a president who wanted to make the best decision that he could, even if, as NSC staffer and second-term Chief of Staff Alexander Haig felt, he "took anguishing time to do it." Haldeman believed that "Nixon was about as conversant with the range of national security affairs on an hour by hour, minute by minute basis, as Kissinger was."[59] Kissinger summed up Nixon's style this way: "No modern President was more solitary, more studious, or spent so much of his time alone, reading or outlining options on his ubiquitous yellow legal pads."[60]

Interestingly, Nixon's perception of Eisenhower himself allowing his NSC system to trap him into decisions is disputed by Eisenhower and much of the research on his administration. Eisenhower too wanted full debate of all the options in the NSC but made decisions with small groups of select advisors following those meetings. When asked if Nixon ever made decisions at an NSC meeting, Undersecretary of State Elliot Richardson answered sharply: "Never. Neither did Eisenhower."[61]

Organizational Dynamics

The conventional wisdom about organizational dynamics in the Nixon administration is accurate in its assessment of the depth of the bureaucratic infighting. Moving foreign policy into the White House was never going to please the cabinet departments. Laird and the Department of Defense fought Kissinger's control of the interagency process, complaining about being excluded, and eventually used an NSC staff-assigned member of the Joint Staff to report back to the JCS on what was happening in Kissinger's shop, essentially spying on the NSC staff.[62] The Rogers vs. Kissinger and State vs. NSC staff hostilities, however, were the most significant and most revealing about the Nixon foreign policy machinery. Their rivalry became a vicious war over power and turf where each antagonist fought the other, leaked to the press, and endlessly lobbied Haldeman and Nixon. Over time, as Kissinger mastered the art of bureaucratic combat, Rogers was excluded from more and more key aspects of decision making. Any examination of Nixon decision making will elaborate on how Kissinger cut Rogers and the State Department bureaucracy out of policy making on Cambodia, the Soviet Union, and China (chapter 8 reevaluates this conclusion) or used back channels to seize control of negotiations where State believed it had authority—the Paris Peace Talks, the Strategic Arms Limitation Talks, and years' worth of Middle East negotiations.[63] The Rogers-Kissinger feud is now legend. The crucial question is why the Rogers-Kissinger relationship deteriorated so profoundly.

Three elements of the initial organizational dynamics explain how Nixon's administration became the quintessential example of bureaucratic and organizational politics gone bad: Nixon's distrust of the bureaucracies and State in particular; State's sense that the NSC staff had seized its rightful sovereignty over foreign policy; and the differing conceptions that Nixon and Rogers had about Rogers's role, particularly when it came to implementation. A fourth element cuts both ways, toward participation and exclusion. Kissinger attempted to make sure that a full interagency process continued to backstop Nixon's decisions. As the disputes between Rogers and Kissinger evolved into open hostilities, the interagency process still functioned; only Rogers's relevance to it was in question.

First, Nixon's desire to run foreign policy from the White House was based partly on his need for control and partly on his deep distrust of the executive branch bureaucracies, the CIA, and particularly the State Department.[64] At their first meeting at the Pierre Hotel, Nixon told Kissinger how badly he had been treated by the Foreign Service when he was vice president; he distrusted its members and felt that the State Department was filled with Democrats who would never be sufficiently loyal to Nixon.[65] He also saw State as lacking in creativity, hidebound, and unable to move beyond its own standard operating procedures. John Holdridge, a Foreign Service officer who became an NSC staffer under Kissinger, quotes Nixon as saying: "If the Department of State has had a new idea in the last 25 years, it is not known to me."[66] Another NSC staffer, William Watts, felt that Nixon had "contempt for the State Department, just total," and quotes him as demanding to "keep those bastards out of it, the White House will just do it."[67] Nixon spent a worrisome amount of time trying to hunt down State officials who were not sufficiently loyal. This included using a career Foreign Service officer, Turner Shelton, as Nixon's man in the Foreign Service, tasked with feeding the White House "information" on State and making a list of those Foreign Service officers who were not loyal to Nixon.[68]

Second, senior and midlevel officials at State were aware of Nixon's resentment. As noted above, after the Key Biscayne meeting of December 26, the senior officials at State argued that Kissinger had stolen their authority and responsibility. William Bundy, a holdover from the Johnson administration as assistant secretary of state for East Asian and Pacific affairs until May 1969, called it a "palace coup."[69] From then on, State fought back to regain some of its lost power. To retain relevance, State would need either a strong secretary who could persuade Nixon of State's usefulness or a way to reestablish a solid role in the interagency process. Rogers never achieved the former, but Kissinger actually worked to guarantee the latter as illustrated below.

Third, Nixon and Rogers had very different conceptions of Rogers's mission as secretary. According to Kissinger, Nixon saw Rogers as his chief negotiator, rather than a decision maker, "a role he reserved for himself" and Kissinger. Rogers's lack of experience in foreign affairs was an "asset because it guaranteed that policy direction would remain in the White House." Kissinger remarked that "few Secretaries of State have been selected because of their President's confidence in their ignorance in foreign policy."[70] Haldeman echoed the concept: Nixon "saw Rogers as being a negotiator . . . but the foreign policy would be established at the White House by the President. The President would be in effect his own Secretary of State with Bill Rogers as his chief negotiator." Haldeman also stated that, in his view, Rogers never understood Nixon's view of Rogers's role.[71] Nixon had been open about this concept in a 1967 interview: "All you need is a competent Cabinet to run the country at home. You need a President for foreign policy; no Secretary of State is really important; the President makes foreign policy."[72] What Rogers did give Nixon was loyalty. They had been personal friends for decades and served together in Eisenhower's administration, Nixon, of course, as vice president and Rogers as deputy attorney general (1953–57), then attorney general (1957 to 1961). Rogers also showed strong loyalty to Nixon during the slush fund/Checkers controversy of 1952 (where Nixon was accused of diverting campaign money into a secret fund), providing Nixon with personal and legal counsel, and lobbying with Republican leaders to keep Nixon on the 1952 ticket.[73] In Nixon's mind, therefore, Rogers's job was to faithfully execute Nixon's designs, including, in Nixon's words, the "formidable task of managing the recalcitrant bureaucracy of the State Department."[74]

Ironically, Rogers was eventually excluded from all the key negotiations undertaken by the administration—the Paris Peace Talks, SALT, the Middle East, and the secret communications with China. Kissinger became Nixon's chief negotiator. This change in role was part of the balancing and compensating process, discussed below, but it stems in part from Nixon's distrust of the State Department and his growing sense that Kissinger was more faithful to Nixon's goals than Rogers was. For Nixon, Rogers had been captured by State, becoming its representative to Nixon, rather than Nixon's man taming the monster at State.

Rogers's view of his role as secretary of state can only be inferred from his actions. He declined to write memoirs and rarely granted interviews or answered questions relating to his relationship with Kissinger, even though he remained a public figure, notably chairing the Reagan administration's Presidential Commission on the Space Shuttle Challenger Accident in 1986. Even before the inauguration in 1969, both he and Richardson began to fight back against White House primacy. Complaints about Kissinger's direct diplomacy with US allies started immediately.[75] Rogers made sure he met with Nixon several times per week, and Richardson eventually required all assistant secretaries to route Interdepartmental Group work through his office before it would go to Kissinger.[76] Rogers's battle to regain State's influence was prominent enough that, in reading Haldeman's diaries, you might get the impression that Rogers was the aggressor and Kissinger the victim. Haldeman's published diaries contain multiple entries from 1969 and 1970 where Kissinger complained and threatened to resign because he felt that Rogers was trying to undermine him and take the lead on key issues. Passages read more like the court transcripts from a very bad divorce (K = Kissinger; P = Nixon):

> K very agonized, finally late today told P that State and Rogers were engaged in all out systematic effort to destroy NSC apparatus (1/23/70). . . . Biggest problems of the day came via phone call from P after I got home. K had apparently hit him again on the Rogers problem, said Rogers is out to get him (3/17/70). . . . Rogers clearly maneuvers to clobber Henry (4/1/70). . . . K still feels this is all part of a plan to do him in, and to take over foreign policy by State from the White House (7/15/70).[77]

At the Nixon Presidential Library there is at least one archive box filled with folder after folder of memos regarding the State Department's counterattack against the White House. One typical memo from Haig to Kissinger, sent on October 27, 1969, points to State's suggestion for a SALT negotiation structure that would give State "almost autonomous control" of arms control policy. The same memo laments that even after the president sent a directive to all the major bureaucracies ordering them to clear all public communications with the White House, State issued a directive in response that ordered State officials to "limit coordination and collaboration with members of the NSC staff."[78]

If Rogers saw himself as John Foster Dulles to Nixon's Eisenhower, Nixon did not. While Kissinger and Rogers fought against each other using all the tricks of bureaucratic warfare, Nixon refused to shield either man from the other. Kissinger was, in effect, used by Nixon to restrain Rogers. The toll it took on both men was brutal. Kissinger brought his never-ending litany of grievances to Haldeman over what he perceived as a stream of outrages from Rogers.[79] Rogers's bitterness over the experience again can only be inferred by his silence after he left the administration in September 1973. Joseph Sisco, assistant secretary of state for Near Eastern affairs, put it succinctly: "The humiliations—and there were numerous—heaped upon (Rogers) have scarred him indelibly."[80] Kissinger won the war against Rogers because Nixon wanted him to win. If foreign policy was to be run out of the White House, Kissinger's victory was necessary and inevitable.

The fourth point here is crucial. In spite of all this day-to-day contentiousness, Kissinger worked hard to keep an inclusive interagency process functioning, but firmly under his control. State had lost the management role it had gained under Johnson, and Rogers would be a much less powerful secretary of state than Rusk and light years less important than Dulles or Dean Acheson, Truman's secretary of state, but the State bureaus would be full and important participants in the interagency process through NSSMs; NSSMs assigned reviews to IG committees that had full interagency participation. For example, an early draft of NSSM 106 on China policy, assigned in the fall of 1970, placed the review in the hands of a new China Policy Group chaired by the undersecretary of state. Kissinger rewrote the NSSM placing the study back into the regular channel of the East Asian and Pacific Affairs IG. Similarly, at roughly the same time Kissinger was handed a draft of NSSM 107 that called for an analysis of the China representation issue at the UN to be led by a member of the NSC staff; Kissinger had the draft redone, handing chair duties to the assistant secretary of state for international organization affairs.[81] In both cases, Kissinger was reinforcing the standard interagency process and defending State's role in it.

Kissinger's efforts to include the career levels of the State Department while at the same time exclude Rogers may have been a loyal effort to remain faithful to Nixon's original design—White House management of policy. If Rogers continued to try to move the coordination role back to State, Kissinger's job became one of defending NSC staff authority while making sure the expertise of State contributed to the advisory process. For example, in August 1969, Richardson suggested forming a SALT back-stopping group, chaired by Rogers with membership that nearly mirrored NSC membership. Rogers and Richardson had cleared the idea with Laird at Defense, Wheeler at the JCS, and Gerard Smith, the director of the

Arms Control and Disarmament Agency, before sending it to Nixon. In a memo to the president, Kissinger argued that the proposal was another attempt by State to sabotage the White House:

> This is essentially the same proposal made earlier by State with respect to Vietnam. Its practical consequence is to circumvent the NSC and nullify its procedures. The sole difference between the proposed committee and the NSC is your participation. It is a bad idea to put you into the position of having to make the decision . . . in a forum in which you might have to overrule the Secretary of State. . . . RECOMMENDATION: That the operational monitoring of SALT be vested in the Under Secretaries Committee which is chaired by Elliott Richardson. Policy issues should remain with the NSC.[82]

In short, Kissinger was not trying to cut the State Department out of decision making completely. He was reinforcing presidential control of the policy process through the established NSC system. State had a role and Kissinger valued that, but he would not allow State to reconstitute the SIG/IRG on an ad hoc basis and would not allow Rogers to transform himself into a powerful secretary. Chester Crocker, an NSC staffer, saw it as a way to keep important issues out of Rogers's hands, by essentially intercepting them in the USC and RG and directing them into the NSC staff.[83]

Development and Use of the Three Structures

Nixon's personal quirks and the rivalry between Rogers and Kissinger stunted the growth of any informal processes, leaving meetings between Kissinger and Richardson as the only informal element. In contrast, the confidence structure solidified within six months; Kissinger eclipsed all other advisors in the area of foreign policy, anchoring his unchallenged role. The Nixon-Kissinger relationship was as integral to foreign policy as that of Eisenhower-Dulles or Truman-Acheson. Nixon's confidence structure dominated at times, and was typically used to manage the formal structure.

Informal Structure

The informal decision making structure of the Nixon administration remained underdeveloped throughout Nixon's tenure in office. As discussed below, this had the effect of enhancing the role of the confidence structure. The evolution model suggests that the informal structure should be established after roughly six months. While a key aspect of informal decision making did form in May of 1969 (regular lunches between Kissinger and Richardson), a fully functioning informal decision structure working in parallel to the formal NSC structure, like the Tuesday Lunch Group of the Johnson administration, never existed, for two reasons. First, since Nixon explicitly told his senior advisors that he wanted options and would not accept a system that presented him with a fait accompli, a bureaucratic consensus that limited his options, he never created a consensus-building apparatus. The last thing he wanted was his cabinet officials meeting in a small group to prepare a prebaked compromise for presentation to him at an NSC meeting. The warning against negotiating any interagency unanimity before Nixon could hear the full range of ideas from every department and agency was almost an invitation for advisors to compete with each other for Nixon's favor. Second, the Rogers-Kissinger feud ruled out any regularized informal process that might include both men. Rogers, as secretary of state, could be forgiven for thinking that his views would be at least as influential if not more influential than anyone else's. Kissinger also understood that his power in the administration was surpassed only by that of Haldeman; he had no incentive ever to back down from a Rogers challenge or make any compromise with him. He could even repeatedly threaten to resign knowing full well that the result in the Oval Office would be anger aimed more at Rogers than Kissinger.

Richardson and Kissinger, however, did create an informal process based on the chairmanships of the RG and the USC. Beginning on May 29, 1969 and continuing until June 12, 1970, shortly before Richardson became Secretary of Health, Education, and Welfare, Kissinger and Richardson met for lunch on a Tuesday 30 times, an average of just under one meeting every two weeks. These meetings had agendas, and Kissinger's staff set a list of items for Kissinger to raise with Richardson.[84] The two men also phoned each other frequently.[85] The origins of the meetings seem to have come out of Richardson's initial fear that State was being pushed out of the policy process. He had been trying to regain a prominent role for State since the December 1968 Key Biscayne decisions creating the White House-centered system. One of his deputies, Jonathan Moore, had been a colleague of Kissinger, and, through Moore, Richardson set up the weekly meetings. Both Nixon and Kissinger felt that Richardson was the only senior official in the State Department worth including in serious decision making, and both Haldeman and Nixon felt that Richardson was perhaps the only official who could go head-to-head with Kissinger.[86] The meetings were designed to coordinate the work of both State and the NSC staff as well as the RG and USC. In particular, the meetings also decided the NSSM agenda and 10–15 possible questions that an NSSM might address. Richardson saw the lunches as State's "principal point of contact" with the NSC system and Kissinger. Richardson also used the meetings to try to repair the Rogers-Kissinger relationship and Nixon's mistrust of State.[87]

Kissinger met with Douglas Irwin, Richardson's replacement, on a similar basis. They intended to meet every other Thursday for breakfast, but the record is spotty; documentation exists for only nine meetings between October 1970 and February of 1972. The routinization of these less frequent meetings seemed to fade in early 1972, and no regularly scheduled meetings between them were held from June to October 1972.[88] Kissinger did meet with Laird once or twice a month at the Pentagon.[89] There is no record of any such meeting with Rogers.

Confidence Structure

It is tempting to simply write "Kissinger" and then move on to the next section, but the Nixon-Kissinger relationship needs some elaboration. In part, the relationship deepened over time due to the Rogers-Kissinger feud that crippled both the formal and informal process. The key question, however, is why Nixon and Kissinger formed their unique partnership from the beginning of the administration's term. Nixon-Kissinger rivals Truman-Acheson and Eisenhower-Dulles as a partnership that defined US foreign policy during its era. Their relationship is unique, however. Where Acheson and Dulles had been major players in US foreign affairs and were well known to their respective presidents before they were appointed secretary of state (Acheson as a State Department official since 1941; and Dulles as consultant to Truman, a negotiator of the US Japanese Peace Treaty of 1952, and a prominent foreign policy wise man of the Republican Party), Kissinger was a Harvard professor, a scholar, a part-time consultant to the Johnson administration, and an advisor to the Rockefeller campaign in 1968. Nixon and Kissinger's primary knowledge of each other was through their published works. The two men first met face to face at a 1967 Christmas party thrown by Claire Boothe Luce in New York; their encounter lasted a reported five minutes. Their next meeting was at the Pierre Hotel in November when Nixon intended to ask Kissinger to assume the national security advisor post.[90] In spite of an absence of history between the two men, Nixon and Kissinger worked so closely that often it seemed difficult to tell which man was running the show. Kissinger managed the NSC system, wrote cover memos for Nixon that summarized the analysis of the rest of the executive branch, gave Nixon weekly or biweekly reports on foreign policy activities of the US government, had nearly unfettered access to the Oval Office, and spoke to the president by phone or in person daily.[91] In Nixon's first 100 days, Nixon met with Kissinger 198 times one-on-one or in small groups, compared to Rogers and Laird who met with Nixon only 30 times.[92] How did Kissinger, a man Nixon had spoken to for five minutes, instantly merit so much more contact and trust from Nixon than Rogers, a friend for decades, and Laird, a Republican member of the House of Representatives (since 1952) while Nixon was vice president and a key leader of the Republican Party?

Three aspects of this tight partnership between near strangers are relevant: the similarity in their thinking on foreign affairs; the division of labor they created; and the trade-offs inherent in the relationship that made them partners and rivals at the same time. First, Nixon and Kissinger's thinking on foreign affairs was nearly perfectly in sync. Haldeman explains it this way: "I attended countless meetings between Kissinger and Nixon and, from the first, realized that they, although as different as any two people could be, were in almost perfect communion on foreign policy philosophy and strategy."[93] Both men were realists, believing that international relations was always fundamentally defined by the rivalries between the great powers and that international stability was only achieved through management of the balance of power.[94] Both men also mistrusted and resented the foreign affairs bureaucracies. Kissinger felt the same to a lesser extent when he entered the administration, but grew to share that contempt for much of the executive branch apparatus for foreign affairs.[95] To staffers observing their behavior, both men shared an administrative style best described as "conspiratorial," "malignant," and defined by "secrecy and paranoia."[96]

Second, memoirs from administration veterans, even Kissinger's, identify a clear division of labor: the strategic design belonged to Nixon; the management of tactical diplomacy and intra-administration warfare rested in Kissinger's hands.[97] The decision making system made Kissinger function as Nixon's alter ego, permitting Kissinger to try to be both honest broker of administration debates and an advocate for specific policies, while giving him unequaled access to the Oval Office and Nixon's own perspectives on foreign policy.[98] Nixon simply did not want to manage the decision making process. His inability to handle conflict meant that he needed someone else to take that role. He had managed his 1960 presidential campaign and lost, then delegated management of his 1968 presidential campaign and won. The lesson he thought he had learned was that he should be the grand strategic thinker and allow someone else to work the day-to-day operations. Haldeman explained it this way:

> He had no interest in managing. . . . there are people who think great thoughts and have great abilities, but don't have either the inclination or the discipline . . . to manage them—to manage the process. And they need someone to manage things for them.[99]

The two men quickly understood how interdependent they were. Kissinger's power was derived wholly from Nixon, and Nixon understood that he needed Kissinger to do the dirty work on his behalf or else the bureaucracies would suffocate his foreign policy.[100]

Third, the White House atmosphere of distrust fueled by Nixon's characteristic paranoia led to a strange relationship in which Nixon and Kissinger relied on each other yet saw each other as rivals, manipulated each other, and mocked each other when meeting with other close advisors.[101] Neither man ever trusted the other. Early on Nixon had warned Richardson: "I don't trust Henry, but I can use him. . . . Watch Henry! Check on him."[102] Nixon fumed about how much credit Kissinger received for Nixon's achievements, particularly the opening to China.[103] In March 1969, worried about the media impression that Kissinger was the real architect of the administration's foreign policy, Nixon instructed Haldeman to order Kissinger to stay off television.[104] Kissinger was also worried about that same public perception even as he courted the press and encouraged his growing celebrity. In March 1971 Senator Stuart Symington (D-MO) suggested that since Kissinger was the driving force behind US foreign policy, he should have to testify before Congress. In response, and perhaps out of a guilty conscience, Kissinger wrote a five-page memo to Nixon defending his role in the process; it included a point-by-point refutation of Symington's argument.[105] Nixon convened a committee called the "Henry-Handling Committee" in the summer of 1969 and again in January 1971. Kissinger's complaining about Rogers had so unnerved the president that he asked Haldeman, White House assistant John Ehrlichman, and Attorney General John Mitchell to reassure Kissinger and convince him to end his tirades against Rogers; the committee failed.[106]

In the context of the evolution model, the Nixon administration had a formal standard interagency process plagued with feuding, but no significant informal structure. That led him to give the confidence structure a more prominent role than he had originally intended.

Balancing and Compensating

Haldeman's diary entry from June 4, 1969 records an unofficial Nixon decision: "Decided no more NSC meetings. Result of leak. Can't trust to papers. Will make decisions privately with K."[107] The evolution-balance model explains how the disconnect between what Nixon thought he wanted (open cabinet government) and what he really wanted (unchallenged control, secrecy, and centralization) led to changes in the administration's decision making. In effect, Nixon had learned about his own weaknesses.

To revise this system, Nixon took three steps. First, during the latter half of 1969, the administration created of a new series of issue-based interagency committees chaired by Kissinger—the Washington Special Actions Group, Vietnam Special Studies Group, Defense Program Review Committee, Verification Panel, Intelligence Committee, and 40 Committee. Each excluded Rogers and nearly all of the cabinet-level members of every important foreign policy department or agency. Second, the Review Group was reestablished as the Senior Review Group with a standard membership, again chaired by Kissinger and again excluding Rogers and the cabinet-level representatives of major departments. In both these cases, Kissinger's committees allowed the confidence structure to essentially act as the interpreter of the formal structure for Nixon. Third, Nixon finally replaced Rogers with Kissinger for his second term, giving Kissinger the positions of both secretary of state and ANSA. The move was a complete and explicit takeover of the system by Kissinger, and a merging of the formal and confidence structures.

The centralization and domination by Kissinger and the NSC staff that is the hallmark of most analyses of Nixon's decision making really begins here, after six months in office, as the new interagency committees were inaugurated in 1969–70. Kissinger chaired every major committee and sat on the NSC. Only the undersecretary of state could rival that level of inclusion. The undersecretary, however, did not have immediate and nearly unlimited access to Nixon. Kissinger's central role in the process made him more powerful than any cabinet officer, and excluded Rogers and Laird from the bulk of the important interagency meetings on key policies. Laird had an advantage over Rogers; most of these committees had two representatives from the Defense Department—the deputy secretary and a member of the JCS. Given that the new SRG had an explicit mandate allowing it to bypass the NSC, it was possible for Kissinger to use the new array of committees to completely push Rogers and Laird out of the loop on most issues unless the State and Defense representatives were willing to gum up the works and force the debate into the NSC, something that everyone understood would displease Nixon.

Kissinger's second-term role as both secretary of state and ANSA made him arguably the most dominant foreign policy advisor to a president since the post–World War II national security establishment had been created. In effect, Nixon had done what Eisenhower decided not to do: he created a first secretary of the government and placed Kissinger in that post.

Nixon may have reached the conclusion that his cabinet-style decision making was not working as early as April 1969.[108] Crocker, an NSC official, also states that after about six months the NSC system stopped functioning and Kissinger's power grew.[109] Safire commented that though cabinet government was the goal, it "was not the view that prevailed, but it was not a matter of being two-faced—Nixon and Haldeman honestly thought in the beginning that was the way it could and should be done."[110] The frequency of NSC meetings dropped significantly after about six months, illustrating how Nixon put his dissatisfaction into action. Table 7.1 charts the frequency of NSC meetings. From January to June 1969, the NSC met 23 times, nearly once per week. During the next six months, the NSC met only 12 times. The once-every-two-weeks schedule was maintained through 1970, but the NSC seems all but forgotten by 1971, meeting only 14 times. In 1972, it was convened only four times.[111] A similar disenchant-ment with cabinet-level decision making outside the area of national secu-rity and foreign policy occurred at the same time. Nixon asked Haldeman to restrict access to the president in the summer of 1969. Only Haldeman, Ehrlichman, and Kissinger were to have day-to-day access; everyone else, even cabinet officers, had to request an audience with the president, then wait for permission to be granted, learning to their dismay that the answer might be "no." The impression at the time was that Haldeman, Ehrli-chman, and Kissinger were acting as a "palace guard" or "Berlin Wall," but Nixon himself asked for the new procedures.[112] Beyond Nixon's suspicions, demands for loyalty, and fear of leaks was the reality that every president faces: each cabinet member is a lobbyist for their department or pet idea, and unless the president controls his own schedule he could end up spend-ing 24 hours a day meeting with people who absolutely, positively, urgently have to see the him immediately. By all accounts, Nixon, not Kissinger, was the impetus for the changes. Nixon had always wanted White House domi-nance. When the initial process disappointed him, he moved to reshape it, hoping to achieve his original goals. The mission was to tighten presiden-tial control; the chosen instrument was Kissinger.

Four problems made a cabinet-based design that encouraged open debate among advisors increasingly uncomfortable for Nixon: he could not deal with direct interpersonal confrontation; he harbored a deep suspicion and paranoia about the motives of everyone around him; he was obsessed about leaks to the press that might spring from the formal NSC; and he, Kissinger, and the NSC staff felt that the system had become overloaded to such a degree that it no longer functioned efficiently.

First, Nixon's reputation as a vicious politician, a pioneer of the ad hominem attack who would do anything to secure election, is well deserved. From slush funds and service at Senator Joseph McCarthy's side in the 1950s to Watergate in the 1970s, Nixon was the archetypal political streetfighter and dirty trickster. Ironically, this malicious side coexisted with a timidity and awkwardness when it came to interpersonal bargaining and conflict, a crippling weakness for a president who hoped to control foreign policy. Nixon could not manage his administration himself, nor could he step in from time to time as an enforcer. His reliance on others for these roles meant that he either dispersed power to other officials (Kissinger, Haldeman, and Ehrlichman) or he let bureaucratic pathologies and feuds fester for far too long. He had created a system that required strong presidential management and yet he detested confrontation and was simply unable to handle intra-administration bureaucratic politics.[113] Haig described it as an "almost pathological distaste for confrontation."[114] He tried to avoid dealing with direct conflict as much as possible, working to insulate, even isolate, himself from the growing feud between Kissinger and Rogers, at one point avoiding meetings with his own secretary of state. Haldeman was handed the job of pouring water on each particular fire on a daily basis.[115]

Second, Nixon's paranoia and suspicion are legendary and led directly to the Watergate scandal. There is little need to recount it here.[116] Nixon's sense that he was the kid who was brought up on the wrong side of the tracks, but who succeeded anyway, mixed deep resentment with even deeper insecurity, baking into his personality a need for revenge against the wealthy and powerful establishment. "They" were his enemies and sought to destroy him, whether they were members of the press, the Democratic Party, Congress, career members of the bureaucracy, or even his own cabinet. His paranoia led him to see conspiracies around every corner; disagreement was disloyalty, and no one could be trusted. Only a small group was considered truly loyal. These men, led by Haldeman, were so dedicated to Nixon that many of them committed crimes to protect him or damage his enemies. Ultimately, more than a handful served time in jail as a result of the Watergate investigations.[117]

The third piece of the puzzle that destroyed Nixon's original design for his role in decision making was his obsession with leaks. He was convinced that leaks to the press would kill his ability to accomplish anything in foreign policy, particularly the type of secret diplomacy he saw as essential for the success of negotiations to end the Vietnam War, to limit the nuclear arsenals of the US and USSR, to move toward Middle East peace, and to open communications with China.[118] Minutes of the first NSC meeting highlighted specific warning against leaks and indicated that attendance at NSC meetings would be limited in an effort to prevent staff from being able to recount meeting discussions to the press.[119] Added to his paranoia and resentment, the fear of leaks led to a sense that his administration was under siege. The Nixon White House became the encyclopedic definition of a self-fulfilling prophecy. The secret dirty tricks unit, named the "Plumbers," was initially created by Nixon aides to plug leaks about the covert bombing of Cambodia in 1969. It eventually was used for the failed break-in at the Watergate hotel in June 1972. That burglary led investigators to Nixon and eventually forced him from office. As Kissinger remarked: "The Nixon team drew the wagons around itself from the beginning; it was besieged in mind long before it was besieged in fact."[120]

Finally, the pace of the NSSMs, the heavy load carried by the NSC staff, and the wide open agendas encouraged by Nixon's emphasis on hearing all sides, overloaded the system and made it difficult for the administration to set priorities. Like Bundy and Rostow before him, Kissinger routinely asked his staff for assessments of NSC procedures. As early as February 1969, Haig began writing memos suggesting ways of dealing with the lack of organization in the NSC staff, and, in particular, the need for a deputy ANSA.[121] Memos sent to Kissinger during 1969 in response to a general call for ideas on how to improve NSC staff procedures came back to him with similar themes. Haig and others argued that the departments were being "overloaded with NSC requirements."[122] Halperin, who wrote the original memo that outlined the Nixon NSC, felt that the Nixon NSC was becoming too much like the "Eisenhower system of using the NSC for low priority issues and dealing with important issues in other ways. Unless a line is drawn and these issues are moved back in the system there will be increasing pressure to deal with other major issues on an ad hoc basis."[123] Most importantly, Nixon made the same complaints to Kissinger, Haldeman, and Ehrlichman: the administration needed to learn to prioritize if it was to be successful. Nixon wanted to focus on the "big battles." Everything else should be "delegated to the Departments and within the White House staff." In foreign policy, Nixon specified a short set of topics he wanted to address: East-West Relations, the Soviet Union, China, Eastern Europe (if related to the USSR), Western Europe (Britain, Germany, France, Spain, Italy, and Greece), the Middle East, and Vietnam. He was blunt: "I do not want matters submitted to me unless they require Presidential decision and can only be handled at the Presidential level."[124]

Kissinger-Chaired Interagency Groups

Typically, the Nixon-Kissinger decision making system of seven Kissinger-chaired committees—the RG and six issue-based committees—is described as if it was designed this way from day one. Only the RG, however, was part of the original Nixon NSC system. The first to be added was the Washington Special Actions Group (WSAG). The WSAG was a formalized version of an ad hoc crisis management committee created in April 1969 to manage the US response to North Korea shooting down an EC-121 reconnaissance place over international waters, killing 31 American servicemen. Though the plane was attacked on April 14, Kissinger did not create a special crisis group until April 17, when he and Nixon decided that crisis-style decision making was overloading routine decision mechanisms. The new Interdepartmental Coordinating Committee on Korea was chaired by Kissinger and included the undersecretary of state for political affairs, the deputy secretary of defense, the deputy director of the CIA, and the vice chairman of the Joint Chiefs.[125] Nixon saw the utility of the crisis committee and directed on May 16, 1969 that it be institutionalized as a permanent committee and renamed the WSAG; it remained under Kissinger's leadership. The committee and its membership were formalized by NSDM 19 of July 3, 1969.[126] The original crisis management structure of the administration as established in NSDM 8 (March 21, 1969) gave the IGs the responsibility for drafting contingency plans that would be reviewed by both the RG and USC. The IG chairs would manage crises in their respective areas under the guidance of the USC.[127] Though NSDM 19 suggested that the WSAG was merely charged with assessing the contingency plans created by the IGs, in practice the WSAG became the crisis management body for the administration. Authority for crisis decision making that had been given to the IG chairs and USC, committees led by the State Department, had been handed over to the WSAG. The frequency of its meetings illustrates its new role. The WSAG generally met more than any other interagency group, and the dates of its meetings track with crises and important decision points. It might meet once or twice per month when there was no crisis, but several times per week during a crisis. For example, from July

TABLE 7.2. Kissinger-Chaired Committees

Date (by Quarter)	Washington Special Actions Group (WSAG)[a]	Vietnam Special Studies Group (VSSG)[b]	Defense Program Review Comm. (DPRC)[c]	Verification Panel[d]
Jan.–March 1969	—	—	—	—
April–June 1969	—	—	—	—
July–Sept. 1969	7	—	—	4
October–Dec. 1969	4	3	4	2
Jan.–March 1970	9	2	4	4
April–June 1970	32	2	1	3
July–Sept. 1970	19	2	2	3
October–Dec. 1970	7	0	3	3
Jan.–March 1971	26	0	4	4
April–June 1971	2	0	6	8
July–Sept. 1971	3	0	3	4
October–Dec. 1971	16	0	2	3
Jan.–March 1972	5	0	2	5
April–June 1972	43	0	5	3
July–Sept. 1972	8	0	2	3
October–Dec. 1972	6	0	1	3
Jan.–March 1973	8	0	0	6
April–June 1973	6	0	0	3
July–Sept. 1973	8	0	2	6
October–Dec. 1973	17	0	0	4
Jan.–March 1974	1	0	0	5
April–June 1974	1	0	0	3
July–August 1974	10	0	0	1

Source: National Security Council Institutional Files Finding Aids, 43–73, RNPL, www.nixonlibrary.gov/sites/default/files/forresearchers/find/textual/institutional/finding_aid.pdf

Note: Dates for meetings of the Intelligence Committee (November 1971) and the 40 Committee (February 1970) remain unavailable.

a WSAG created July 3, 1969 by NSDM 19

b VSSG created by September 16, 1969 by NSDM 23.

c DPRC created October 11, 1969 by NSDM 26.

d Verification Panel created in June 1969.

1969 to March 1970 it met 20 times; from April to September 1970, it convened 51 times (crises on Laos and Cambodia); from October to December 1970, it met 7 times; from January to March 1971, it met 26 times (all on Vietnam-related issues); from April to June 1972, it met 43 times.[128] See table 7.2 for all data on these committees.

The Vietnam Special Studies Group (VSSG) was the second Kissinger-chaired interagency committee. In a September 5, 1969 memo Kissinger explained that he had "become convinced of the need for systematic analysis of US policies and programs in Vietnam" and suggested that Nixon create a new committee chaired by Kissinger to undertake that task. Nixon agreed, and NSDM 23 creating the VSSG was signed on September 16, 1969. Membership included the undersecretary of state, deputy secretary of defense, DCI, and CJCS.[129] Before the VSSG, decision making for Vietnam had been by-the-book cabinet decision making. Nixon issued NSSM 1 asking for a full review of US policy toward Vietnam on his first full day in office, January 21, 1969. Departments were instructed to respond by February 10, and an NSC meeting on March 28 gave Nixon the opportunity to hear his senior advisors' views. On April 1 he signed NSDM 9, which spelled out his decisions on Vietnam.[130] Over the next six months, Kissinger saw the need for further review, but these follow-up decisions were not placed back into the NSC system. Instead, Kissinger assumed the lead through the VSSG. The VSSG, however, had a short-lived influence. It met nine times from October 1969 to July 1970, then never met again. Why it was cast aside is unclear. It is possible that the Special Review Group for Southeast Asia created by NSDM 79 of August 13, 1970, which had the same membership as the VSSG, had replaced it, and it is also possible that Nixon and Kissinger eventually moved to limit participation in Vietnam decisions even further, nullifying the real impact of either committee. The most likely explanation, however, is that the WSAG simply took over the key role on Vietnam. From January 1970 to July 1974, 152 of 227 meetings (67%) of the WSAG concerned the Vietnam War.[131]

The Verification Panel was created to backstop the SALT negotiations in June 1969 at the suggestion of Gerard Smith, head of the Arms Control and Disarmament Agency and the US representative at SALT. The Verification Panel met at least once a month until August 1974. Membership on the Verification Panel was nearly identical to the VSSG, adding only the attorney general and the ACDA head. The Defense Program Review Committee was created by NSDM 26 (October 11, 1969) to handle defense budget and force deployment issues. The membership of the Defense Program Review Committee was exactly the same as that of the VSSG. It met about once per month through fall 1971 and then generally met once every six weeks, until the fall of 1972. Thereafter it met only three times from October 1972 to August 1974.[132] Two additional panels, the Intelligence Committee (oversight of the intelligence community) and the 40 Committee (review of covert operations), were also created. Most details concerning the frequency of meetings of these committees is still unavailable. The Intelligence Committee was created on November 5, 1971 through a memorandum rather than an NSDM. Its membership included Kissinger (chair), the secretaries of defense and treasury (replaced by the undersecretary of the treasury in April 1974), the attorney general, the deputy secretary of state (the new number-two position at State as of July 13, 1972), the DCI, and the CJCS.[133] The 40 Committee had existed as the 303 Committee, the name given to it by the Johnson administration in June 1964. It was renamed by NSDM 40 of February 1970; its members were Kissinger (chair), the undersecretary of state for political affairs, the deputy secretary of defense, the attorney general, and the DCI.[134]

Four aspects of these committees are important. First, Kissinger chaired them all. Through these committees, he could steer policy in the direction desired by Nixon or at least manage key policies to prevent interagency conflict from clogging the gears of decision. Second, membership on the committees had such significant overlap that it might have been difficult to remember which committee was meeting once everyone arrived. The number two or three official at State served on all of them; the deputy secretary of defense, DCI, and CJCS had membership in five of the six committees. In effect, these officials were meeting as a mini-NSC, metaphorically using different letterhead for different issues, but still essentially one set of advisors managing the decision process, gaining more authority as the number of NSC meetings declined in the second half of 1969. Third, Rogers was not a member of any of the committees. In effect, he was nearly neutralized. Laird sat only on the Intelligence Committee. Fourth, the ability of Kissinger to work with all them on a regular basis in an environment that always excluded Rogers and usually excluded Laird institutionalized Kissinger's power as essentially the only de facto cabinet-level official in the room for every committee save the Intelligence Committee. It also gave him access to senior department officials on a regular basis outside the supervision of Rogers and Laird. In particular, Kissinger had routine meetings with the DCI and CJCS; Rogers and Laird met as a group with these individuals only in NSC meetings where the president was in attendance, making those meetings a very different environment. The message was clear: nothing significant happened unless Kissinger was in the room and in command.

The Senior Review Group (NSDM 85)

In the original NSDM 2 design of the Nixon NSC system, the RG played a role similar to Eisenhower's Planning Board. The RG handled paper flow from the IGs to the NSC, deciding if and when issues should be passed up to the NSC or given to the USC or settled at the IGs; it also could set the agenda of policies addressed in the IGs and other ad hoc groups. In short, it directed traffic, set agendas, and tried to prevent the NSC from being overloaded. Kissinger was chair of the RG, but the rest of its membership was not specified beyond "representative" of the departments of State and Defense, the CIA, and the JCS.[135]

The RG as originally established lasted into the summer of 1970, when a consensus was reached among all the participating agencies that the RG needed to be reconstituted into something more powerful. As part of his ongoing assessment of the NSC process, Kissinger asked NSC staffers Richard Kennedy and William Watts to consider flaws in the system. Their April 3, 1970 report identified several problems: members of the RG were uncertain about the paper flow to and from the RG; the RG was staffed with assistant-secretary-level officials who did not have the authority to speak for their respective departments; often several assistant secretaries from a department attended meetings and could not agree on what their own department's preferences were; and RG ineffectiveness led to ad hoc committees taking over its role. As a result, the RG had failed in its job of protecting the NSC from being overloaded with less important topics.[136]

Laird had begun meeting with the JCS to discuss their assessments of the NSC since September 1969. At the third meeting on March 9, 1970 Laird commissioned the JCS to write a report on NSC weaknesses. Their May 27 paper echoed many of the Kennedy/Watts views—complaints about the proliferation of ad hoc groups and the growing need for the RG to take a more decisive role in the NSSM process. Haig received a copy of the JSC report and gave it to Kissinger in June.[137] Sometime in August, Kissinger and Laird spoke on the subject, and Kissinger promptly brought the issue to Nixon. Kissinger's assessment was captured in an August 14 internal JCS memo for new chair of the JCS, Admiral Thomas Moorer: "It has become increasingly clear that Dr. Kissinger is disenchanted with the Review Group. He considers it a useless strata of middle-management people who waste his time as well as their own. This is probably true."[138]

On August 25, 1970, in a memo to Nixon, Kissinger reiterated the common complaints about the RG. He suggested restructuring the RG into an undersecretary-level committee that would have the authority to resolve interagency and intra-agency disagreements (a particular problem with State, he noted). His memo included a draft NSDM 83 that Nixon signed on September 4. Kissinger did not immediately disseminate the NSDM, however. NSC staffer Winston Lord had sent a note to Kissinger arguing for a delay in establishing the group; Kissinger then shelved the NSDM temporarily.[139] On September 8, Kennedy sent Kissinger a memo giving him a heads-up about a State Department study of the NSC. A report by Deputy Undersecretary of State for Management William Macomber recommended giving the USC a larger role in managing the NSC system, essentially handing it the RG's job. Kennedy felt it would "preempt" the role of the new SRG. He also noted that if Rogers suggested boosting the USC's responsibilities, Kissinger's proposal for a more powerful SRG would be seen as a ploy to weaken State and the USC. Any reservations Kissinger or other members of the NSC staff may have had about a new committee dissipated as soon as they saw State angling to empower the USC to fill the void left by the dysfunctional RG. Upon receiving the memo, Kissinger wrote on the top of the memo "OK—establish Senior Group."[140] Kennedy wrote at least two drafts of the NSDM over the next few days, sending each to Haig.[141]

On September 14, Nixon signed a renumbered NSDM 85, *NSC Senior Review Group*. It remedied the basic problem by making the SRG a senior-level committee, with a familiar list of members: Kissinger as chair, the undersecretary of state, the deputy secretary of defense, director of central intelligence, and chairman of the Joint Chiefs of Staff, nearly identical in membership to all the other new interagency committees set up in 1969. The role of the SRG as written in the directive remained mostly unchanged from the RG's mandate: it managed the flow of policy review from the IGs to the USC and NSC, focusing on both quality control and readiness for decision. One important section is notable:

> The Senior Review Group shall recommend whether a paper, after review by it, should be referred for consideration by the National Security Council, forwarded directly to me for decision or returned to the originating body for revision before further consideration by the Senior Review Group.[142]

The SRG was given the option of bypassing the NSC and sending recommendations directly to the president. The frequency of meetings reflects the new center of action. During its first year (October 1970 to September 1971), the SRG held 56 meetings; the NSC met 14 times.[143]

Rogers and State understood very quickly that they had been hoodwinked again, just as they had at the December 1968 Key Biscayne meeting. On October 27, 1970, Kissinger and Irwin had their regularly scheduled meeting. While it is unclear what the two men discussed, Irwin had been given a memo by William Cargo, director of planning and coordination at State, explaining that the new SRG had made a bad system worse, at least for State and Defense. Given that issues could go straight from the SRG and any of the other Kissinger-chaired committees to the president,

Rogers and Laird were effectively frozen out of many decisions.[144] For Nixon and Kissinger, that was part of the plan. If each cabinet department is illustrated by a pyramid with layers representing each level or hierarchy, Nixon had effectively lopped off the top cabinet layer and replaced it with Kissinger.

Kissinger as Secretary of State and ANSA

The ultimate method of centralization for Nixon and Kissinger was unprecedented. If Kissinger had eclipsed Rogers and the two men simply could not work together, the solution was obvious: fire Rogers. Kissinger's elevation, however, had occurred along with an institutional evolution of the NSC staff into a power center that rivaled State and Defense, a trend begun under Kennedy. Given that Nixon wanted to be his own secretary of state and hoped Kissinger and the NSC staff would manage the foreign policy process and corral the rest of the bureaucracies, Nixon reached what seemed like a logical conclusion: the secretary of state and ANSA roles should be merged. Nixon could then control the interagency process, end any State freelancing, and turn implementation over to Kissinger, someone he believed would be absolutely faithful to his foreign goals, even if not entirely loyal.

The problem was how to deal with Rogers.

Even with all the structural machinations of 1969–1970, Rogers fought on. His statutory and institutional power meant that he could not truly be ignored, no matter how much Nixon and Kissinger tried to shove him aside. Irwin joined the battle as well, bringing multiple staffers to the significant interagency meetings as a way to drown out the voices of other agencies. Rogers and Irwin hoped to bypass the new SRG by directing IG and USC papers to Rogers, where they were "approved" and then designated as official US policy before being sent to the Kissinger.[145] Haldeman's diaries contain numerous post-SRG descriptions of the battlefront:

> I had a three hour lunch with Rogers . . . his principal concern was to try to work out the Henry K. problem. Basically he is sincerely trying to do what he thinks is best for the P. and of course so is Henry, but the two of them just stay on a collision course. . . . Henry caught me later and made it clear that his dissatisfaction is again reaching a peak. . . . (2/22/71) . . . (Kissinger) also thinks that Rogers has declared total war on him (11/11/71). . . . (Rogers) also stated that he's got to have a direct line of communication with the P. so

that when he does something, he can do it directly to the P without going through Henry. (1/11/72).[146]

Nixon fought back against Rogers by giving more and more responsibility for diplomacy to Kissinger. Of course, Kissinger's usurpation of Rogers's role at the Paris Peace Talks, SALT, the Middle East negotiations, and China initiative is well known. Less well known were Nixon's attempts to force State, Defense, and the CIA to clear all significant diplomatic meetings, correspondence, and foreign policy press releases with the White House. A September 1, 1969 letter to Rogers, Laird, and Helms stated that anything of "known or potential presidential interests" had to be cleared. In January 1972, Nixon was still trying to push State to seek White House clearance on all contacts with foreign officials.[147] Rogers simply would not comply, and Kissinger's complaints to Haldeman about being cut out of the loop continued at the Paris Peace Talks, during Middle East negotiations, and even over China.[148]

After his 49-state victory over McGovern in November 1972, Nixon made his move. Cabinet changes after reelection are not unusual, but Nixon went beyond the norm by asking his entire cabinet and White House staff to submit their resignations the day after the election.[149] In part, the exercise was a formality based in tradition; everyone served at the pleasure of the president and would continue that service only if the president asked. Nixon, however, in 1972 and 1973 replaced the leadership at seven of 12 cabinet departments. Most of the new cabinet secretaries were in place by February 1973, including Richardson, who succeeded Laird at Defense. Amazingly, Rogers remained in place.

As was the case with other cabinet members Nixon intended to fire, Haldeman or Ehrlichman were tasked with meeting the soon-to-be-gone official shortly after the election. Nixon's deep aversion to confrontation meant that he was nearly incapable of directly firing anyone. With the formal resignations already requested, those who would actually be leaving were summoned for the bad news. Haldeman met with Rogers on November 16 at Camp David. When told that he was to be replaced, Rogers adamantly made it clear that he did not want to leave until the summer of 1973; he refused to be part of the general second-term house cleaning and insisted on talking to the president. Haldeman brought Rogers to Nixon, and Rogers successfully persuaded Nixon to keep him on until the summer of 1973; face to face, Nixon was unable to fire Rogers. Rogers had made it personal, a matter of his professional dignity, in a way he hoped Nixon would understand; he explained to Nixon that leaving immediately would be seen as a "victory for Kissinger" (Haldeman's words). Kissinger reacted badly to the news that Rogers was staying on. Haldeman quotes Kissinger's tirade: "You promised me, Haldeman. You gave me your word! And now he's hanging on just like I said he would. . . . He will be with me forever—because he has this President wrapped around his little finger."[150]

Nixon had actually decided in November 1972 to replace Rogers with Kenneth Rush, the deputy secretary of defense. As the number two at Defense, Rush had worked with Kissinger on nearly all of the Kissinger-chaired interagency committees, and Nixon felt confident that Rush was loyal enough to help him tame the State Department. A few days earlier, before his meeting with Rogers, Nixon had told Kissinger and Haldeman that his "one legacy is to ruin the foreign service. I mean ruin it—the old foreign service—and to build a new one. I'm going to do it." Of Rush, he said, "I am going to take the responsibility for cleaning up that State Department and I want him to be my man."[151] Once Nixon allowed Rogers to stay, however, Rush was appointed deputy secretary of state as of February 1973, in effect, an interim post preparing him to take over the department.[152] Over the first six months of 1973, Nixon and Kissinger changed their minds; both came to believe that Kissinger should replace Rogers. Watergate had become a growing threat to Nixon, and Kissinger was rapidly accruing a reputation for diplomatic miracles following the Paris Peace Accords that ended the Vietnam War (January 27, 1973); he received the Nobel Peace Prize for the accomplishment in December 1973. Nixon's popularity was collapsing, while Kissinger's soared. Nixon's reputation had become so tarnished that the US press began to give Kissinger full credit for all of the administration's successes.[153] The result was that Nixon now needed Kissinger to help him shore up his political support. As Nixon explained: "With the Watergate problem, I didn't have any choices."[154] Both Haldeman and Ehrlichman resigned on April 30, 1973 as their participation in the scandal was revealed, and Haig, Kissinger's deputy, became the new chief of staff, technically Kissinger's new boss. The new arrangement led to a rivalry between Kissinger and Haig. Given his growing legend and the prospect of a new rivalry, Kissinger issued an ultimatum: make him secretary of state or he would resign.[155]

When it came time to leave in June 1973, Rogers decided he wished to continue in the position. When asked by Haig to leave on August 8, 1973, Rogers reportedly shouted: "Tell the president to go f— himself." Rogers threw Haig out of his office, arguing that if Nixon wanted him to leave, Nixon would have to ask in person. Finally, on August 16, Nixon did just that.[156] Amazingly, after deciding to fire his secretary of state, one of the most vicious American politicians of the 20th century took a full nine months to muster up the courage to ask him to leave face to face.

Rogers officially resigned on September 3 and Kissinger assumed his duties on September 21 after Senate confirmation (Rush served as interim secretary). Kissinger retained his ANSA role, ending any rivalries over who controlled foreign policy in the administration, except the one between Nixon and Kissinger. As president, of course, Nixon still held the reins, but Kissinger had gained unequaled authority over the management of the NSC interagency system, implementation, and advice and access to Nixon. His former deputy ANSA was chief of staff; the new deputy ANSA, General Brent Scowcroft, was absolutely faithful to the interagency design. Kissinger even inaugurated a new informal process where he, Scowcroft, and Haig would have lunch together on a regular basis when all three were in Washington.[157]

Conclusion

The evolution-balance model is confirmed by this case study of Nixon foreign policy decision making. Though Nixon had initiated a cabinet-based formal structure that he thought would allow him to evaluate all the potential options through open and freewheeling debates, it clashed with Nixon's own nature. His inability to handle conflict, his suspicion and paranoia, his obsession with leaks, and the sense that the NSC had become overloaded led Nixon to seek a process that fit his style better. The original formal design had become untenable, and Nixon moved to change it.

Several aspects of this analysis are important. First, in this case, Nixon himself is the one who decided his own system had failed him. He was not pressured by other officials to adapt his style to the needs of the bureaucracies. Instead, he concluded that the nature of the bureaucracies meant that he needed a better way to manage them. He did not, however, have any interest in hands-on management. Kissinger was given that challenge. Second, the creation throughout 1969 and 1970 of the six ANSA-chaired committees and ultimately the SRG were Nixon's way of limiting the debate he had originally sought and placing power into the hands of Kissinger, the one person in the foreign policy area he had faith in administratively and strategically. In the context of the evolution model, it was a merging of the formal structure with the confidence structure. Third, initially, Nixon hoped to establish a decision making system based on the formal Eisenhower machinery, but with one key change: the interagency process would assess options, but not provide recommendations. In this sense,

Kissinger's original role is analogous to the role of Robert Cutler in Eisenhower's Planning Board, and the USC played the same part as Eisenhower's Operations Coordination Board. Nixon's dissatisfaction with what he thought would work for him led him to elevate Kissinger, but it also meant that Nixon often received recommendations rather than options to choose from, actual boxes to check "yes" or "no," exactly what he had originally hoped to avoid. In this case, however, rather than being produced through a consensus-driven interagency process, the vast majority of recommendations came from Kissinger, while some came from Richardson and Irwin at the USC. That reality gave Kissinger significant power to shape policy. As seen in the following chapter, however, Kissinger was faithful to Nixon's grand design; while he may have freelanced on details, Nixon's goals and strategies to achieve those goals always served as the foundation of the administration's foreign policy.

Fourth, one of the key reasons to make changes was the need to end the Kissinger-Rogers feud. Nixon's choice of Rogers was, in hindsight, a poor one; the administration never really recovered from it. The innovations of 1969 and 1970 could be seen as Nixon's way of compensating for his inability to work with Rogers. A counterargument would be that Nixon never found a way to deal with any cabinet members. The secrecy and the paranoia meant that he never trusted anyone in his administration whose stature and legitimacy were not based on their proximity and loyalty to Nixon. In other words, anyone with an independent power base in a bureaucracy or political stature was suspect. Nixon's sense of being under siege led him to give his loyalists in the White House staff the authority to run the system. The notion of assistants to the president who would manage, even rule over, the bureaucracies has been called a "counter-bureaucracy" or the "administrative presidency." Nixon had followed up the creation of the six Kissinger-chaired committees and the SRG in 1969 and 1970 with a similar design under Ehrlichman for domestic politics.[158]

A fifth and related point is that Kissinger, in effect, became the "First Secretary of Government" that Eisenhower had considered creating late in his second term.[159] Nixon had toyed with the idea of creating "super-secretaries," cabinet officials who would run their own departments and also serve as Nixon's chief advisors on a range of issues that might span more than one cabinet department's area of responsibility; in effect, these super-secretaries would form another administrative layer between the cabinet secretaries and Nixon, a layer where interagency disagreements could be resolved without presidential intervention. The super-secretary, as a single individual, would have the authority to make a decision, preventing interagency disagreements from being simply bumped up to the Oval Office.[160] Nixon's super-secretaries idea focused on the domestic side and was never implemented. For foreign policy, however, Kissinger seems to have assumed that role implicitly; as secretary of state and ANSA, he was a cabinet secretary who managed the full range of national security affairs on behalf of the president. Interestingly, Nixon was opposed to the first secretary idea when Eisenhower had brought it to the cabinet in 1959. In a telephone conversation with John Foster Dulles, then-Vice President Nixon had argued that Eisenhower's proposal would be a political disaster, signaling that Eisenhower was taking it easy as president for the rest of his term. Nixon called it the "most revolutionary change in 150 years" to the structure of the US government. He argued against it every chance he had.[161] After four years in office, however, Nixon implemented a version of that idea. Staff managers simply did not have the legitimacy to run the bureaucracies; they needed legitimacy and a power base of their own. As Kissinger argued, by August 1973 the administrative presidency had clearly failed: "in short, Nixon's style of government by means of Presidential assistants had become unworkable."[162] The Kissinger move to State while retaining the ANSA post was designed to solve that problem. Kissinger would have control of the interagency machinery and the statutory authority over foreign policy that comes with a cabinet position, a deeper and more permanent merger of the formal and confidence structures. Most importantly, it was a system that fit Nixon's style.

EIGHT

~ Nixon and China

> "There's an old Vulcan proverb, 'Only Nixon could go to China.'"
>
> —Mr. Spock, *Star Trek VI*[1]

In hindsight, the 1968 campaign slogan "Nixon's the One" seems unfortunate. In the context of China, however, it is accurate and flattering: Nixon was the president who finally allowed US-Chinese relations to catch up with geopolitical reality. Nixon took advantage of the political timing of his election and of his unique place in American politics to engage China in ways that both Kennedy and Johnson had felt were absolutely necessary but completely impossible. Coming to power in 1969 gave Nixon an advantageous position; he could blame Kennedy and Johnson for the failures in Vietnam, while spinning those failures as a new freedom to reevaluate US containment policy. Trading intervention for détente and a Triangular Diplomacy that improved US relations with both the USSR and China, Nixon became the peacemaker. He also had one thing the other two lacked: he was Nixon. Unmatched in the ferocity of his anti-Communism, and heir to Eisenhower, he was nearly immune to criticism from his right flank. He could never be labeled soft on Communism; he nearly invented the charge. "Only Nixon could go to China" has become an axiom of world politics, a historical legacy of US foreign policy and a case study for research on policy innovation.[2] In part, it was true because Nixon did not have to worry about Nixon attacking him.

Freed from almost all domestic political restraints on China, Nixon not only allowed the foreign policy bureaucracies to seek rapid advances in US policy toward China, he actually outpaced them. Nixon came into office committed to engagement in China, and he was very public about his hopes. In an interview with *Time* magazine in October 1970, he revealed an item on his bucket list: "If there is anything I want to do before I die, it is to go to China."[3] The only questions were how and when.

This chapter looks at three case studies: National Security Study Memorandum (NSSM) 14 in 1969; the Chinese representation issue in 1971 as defined in NSSM 107 (1970–71); and the decision on withdrawing US troops from Taiwan in 1973–74 made as part of NSSM 171 (1973) and codified by National Security Decision Memorandum (NSDM) 248 (1974). Nixon administration decision making on China does not strongly support the evolution-balance model; only the third case study provides partial support. In each case study, decisions are dominated by the formal interagency process. Eisenhower would have been proud; Senator Jackson must have been appalled.

NSSM 14 was a quintessential example of the Nixon formal process. Neither the evolution or evolution-balance model adds understanding to an analysis of decision making in this case; it was by-the-book formal interagency decision making. The China Working Group of the East Asian Interdepartmental Group (EAIG) drafted the study; sent it to the Review Group, which refined it; and then passed it on to the NSC for a scheduled meeting on August 14, 1969. At the level of the China Working Group and the EAIG, the State department dominated the process, precisely as defined in NSDMs 1 and 2. It assessed US options, but gave Nixon no specific recommendations. Kissinger, however, did inform Nixon that of the three options presented in the review—current policy, intensified deterrence and isolation, or reduction of points of conflict—the departments all agreed with Nixon's view; it was time to end China's isolation.

In decisions on Chinese representation, NSSM 107 of November 1970 moved through the interagency process from a State-led ad hoc interdepartmental group to the Senior Review Group, and on to the NSC in March 1971. Nixon ultimately made his decisions in July and August at two rare informal meetings with Rogers and Kissinger. Rogers announced the new US position in a speech on August 2, 1971—the US would switch to a two China policy, acceptance of both China and Taiwan in the UN. Though this second case study does not support the evolution-balance model, it does confirm the evolution model. In the end the process was narrowed to meet a deadline for implementation—the upcoming meeting of the UN General Assembly and its yearly debate on Chinese representation.

The final case study in this chapter examines NSSM 171, the post-Vietnam review of US policy in Asia that began in February 1973. That review led to decisions on the withdrawal of US troops from Taiwan, made official in NSDM 248 (March 1974). It illustrates Nixon and Kissinger's continued reliance on the interagency process even as the two men changed policies in fundamental ways, such as the opening to China, the end of the

Vietnam War, and the departure of Rogers. The interagency process continued to function as it always had, perhaps with fewer perturbations echoing down from the upper levels. Without Rogers and Kissinger battling over policy at the top, the rest of the bureaucracy knew that their efforts were guided by one unified institutional and geopolitical architecture. This third case study partially confirms the evolution-balance model in one sense. The final 1974 decision on how swiftly to remove US troops from Taiwan contained in NSDM 248 ratified an informal agreement between ANSA Kissinger and then Secretary of Defense Elliot Richardson from February 1973. Nearly a year later, even when Richardson was no longer secretary of defense, Kissinger's enhanced power as ANSA and secretary of state allowed him to guide the interagency process toward upholding that 1973 compromise. The merger of the formal and confidence structures that gave Kissinger such influence, however, was a result of overall changes in decision making, not anything related to Taiwan. For that reason, this case should not be considered a full confirmation of the evolution-balance model.

Nixon's China decisions and overall decision making are compared in table 9.3. Figure 8.1 diagrams Nixon's China policy using the framework of figure 2.2.

It is hard to square this faithfulness to the interagency process with the exclusion of Rogers and the State Department from participation and even knowledge of the Kissinger–Zhou Enlai diplomacy of 1970–71 and Kissinger's trip to China in July 1971. This chapter illustrates some weaknesses in aspects of our scholarly approach to decision making, weaknesses that ignore the impact of implementation. Once implementation of a policy begins, particularly if it requires secrecy as a prerequisite to success, decision making is fundamentally changed. Those implementing the policy can become the sole decision makers. The difference between strategy and tactics becomes useful here. Overall strategy—how should the Nixon administration deal with China—was developed through the interagency process. Diplomatic overtures to China—some public and some secret—began early in the administration's tenure and were fully vetted through the interagency process. Once China responded, far more quickly than anyone anticipated, Nixon, Kissinger, and the NSC staff dominated the secret tactical maneuvering. The interagency process continued to assess potential avenues for convincing China to end its isolation without ever being given explicit knowledge that some of their ideas were feeding into actual conversations with China, rather than remaining hypothetical scenarios for several years down the road. Kissinger states it this way: "One

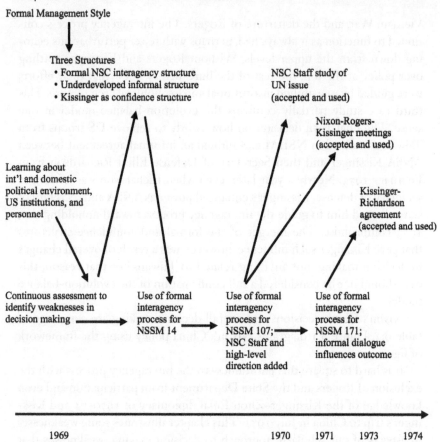

Fig. 8.1. The Evolution of Nixon Administration Decision Making on China

of the advantages of the NSC system for secret diplomacy in which we were now involved is that it enabled the President and me to obtain agency views and ideas without revealing our tactical plan."[4] At the level of secret diplomacy, decision making and implementation necessarily merge. It was there that Rogers and the rest of the administration were cut out of the loop. In that sense, the secret diplomacy and Kissinger's trip to China are similar to the backchannel negotiations at the Paris Peace Talks, Kissinger's Middle East negotiations that excluded Rogers, and even the bombing of Cambodia in 1969. The interagency system evaluated options and even received copies of NSDMs deciding policy, but it did not necessarily know when or how policy would be implemented, nor would it always have a key role in the real execution of that policy. The Nixon administration provides an excellent case study for examining how decision making power shifts to those who carry out policy once implementation begins.

NSSM 14 and the Opening to China

National Security Study Memorandum 14, issued February 5, 1969, called for a full bottom-up interagency review of China policy. The study was conducted in a by-the-book interagency process exactly as envisioned in NSDMs 1 and 2, a style that mirrored the formality of the Eisenhower administration. Drafting began in the China Working Group subcommittee of the East Asia Interdepartmental Group, then moved through the EAIG, the NSC Review Group (RG), and finally to the NSC, where it was considered by the president and his principal advisors on August 14. NSSM 14, *U.S. China Policy*, presented the president with options rather than recommendations, exactly what Nixon wanted out of the interagency process. Of the three options considered—current policy, intensified deterrence and isolation, and reduction of points of conflict—all agencies supported the latter. That fact was not indicated in the study, but it was made clear in NSC discussions and informal conversations throughout the bureaucracy. Stories of China decisions being forged in an almost closed circle comprised of Nixon, Kissinger, and a few others are only accurate for aspects of the implementation of the new policy. For example, Nixon's decision to sign NSDM 17 on June 26, 1969, asking for policies to implement a lifting of restrictions on travel and trade with China, was an early product of the same interagency committees preparing for the NSC meeting and backstopping the informal consultations between Nixon, Kissinger, and Undersecretary of State Elliot Richardson. The implementation plans for the new policies were developed in the interagency Undersecretaries Committee, again a full interagency process. During this period, both Nixon and Rogers began sending diplomatic signals to China through back channels (Pakistan, France, and Romania). These were necessarily secret, Nixon and Kissinger operating outside regular administration channels, but they reflected the consensus in the interagency process and public statements by Nixon, Rogers, and Kissinger.

Political Context

Politically, 1969 seems light years from 1968. The international and domestic political situations shifted rapidly, but the biggest change was the occupant of the White House. Nixon's pre-presidential record as a committed anti-Communist and foe of China was unmatched. By the mid-1960s, however, he had rethought this stance, coming to the same conclusion as the lower levels of the Johnson administration and academic experts: engagement with China would serve US interests better than isolation. Nixon also understood the politics of a potential breakthrough; he had more political leeway on China than any Democrat could ever have, and he intended to use it for both strategic and political reasons. In China, the excesses of the Cultural Revolution had led Mao Zedong to backtrack, restraining his Red Guards and attempting to bring order to the chaos he had unleashed. Below Mao, rivalries within the Chinese leadership between Zhou Enlai, Lin Biao, and Jiang Qing prevented any clear direction in foreign policy. Possible withdrawal of US forces from Vietnam and the collapse of relations with the USSR, however, suggested a way forward: the Soviet threat was increasing just as the US threat declined. Old fashioned balancing might be the remedy. After Mao commissioned a special People's Liberation Army study of Chinese foreign policy by a group of respected marshals, Zhou's proposal for reaching out to the US as a counterweight to the Soviets ultimately won the argument. The increasing possibility of large-scale war with the USSR was the final impetus for Mao's own acceptance of rapprochement with the US; by 1969 the USSR was perceived as a greater threat to China than the US. Across the Taiwan Strait, the ROC could read the handwriting on the wall and was reforming its economy to prepare for the possibility of losing the support of Washington and its place in the UN. Domestically, Nixon's ascendance to the White House gave the US a chance to essentially reboot its policy in Asia. Belief in the domino theory and hard containment of China had led the US into Vietnam. As the nation turned against the war and its architects, Nixon had the opportunity Johnson never have had: he had the political space to engage with China. The mistakes of Vietnam could be blamed on Johnson and the Democrats; the China lobby had lost much of its power; and Nixon hoped to use the window of opportunity he had been given.

Nixon and China before the Presidency

With the exception of perhaps Senator Joseph McCarthy, no mainstream American politician of the early Cold War era had used his antiCommunist fervor to greater political effect than Nixon. His ultimate campaign weapon, used again and again, was not only to question his opponents' commitment to fighting Communism, but to eventually accuse them of harboring Communist sympathies. Running in the 12th Congressional District in California against incumbent Jerry Voorhis in 1946, Nixon accused Voorhis of being a "registered socialist," backed by communists. He argued that his election was essential to stopping a strategy "calculated to gradually give the American people a Communist form of government."[5] Nixon was front and center during the McCarthy era as a member of the House Un-American Activities Committee (HUAC) from the moment he began serving in the House in 1947 (following his defeat of Voorhis). Nixon made his name and fame in Congress at HUAC's 1948 Hiss-Chambers hearings. Whittaker Chambers, a *Time* magazine editor, accused Alger Hiss, a former senior State Department diplomat, of being a Communist spy for the USSR. Nixon was one of the lead questioners of both Chambers and Hiss during the famous hearings that led to perjury charges against Hiss.[6] Following Mao's victory in October 1949, Nixon rallied Republicans, blaming Truman and Democrats for losing China; he decried what he saw as the abandonment of Chiang Kai-shek and a surrender to Mao's forces.[7] Having become a rising star, Nixon turned his eyes toward the Senate. He denounced his 1952 opponent for a Senate seat in California, Helen Gahagan Douglas, as supportive of Communist China's entry into the UN, even stating a few days after China's intervention into the Korean War (October 19, 1950) that Douglas "was committed to the State Department policy of appeasing Communism in Asia, which finally resulted in the Korean War." He summed up his view of Douglas by arguing that she "follows the Communist Party line."[8] Nixon opposed Truman's limited war strategy in Korea, publicly calling for taking the war to China by bombing its territory and linking up with ROC forces for a counteroffensive into the mainland. He saw a negotiated path to ending the Korean War and acceptance of North Korea's continued existence as a "laying the foundation for eventual communist domination of all of Asia."[9]

Nixon's blanket indictments of nearly all Democrats as communist sympathizers and the notoriety they brought him were the reasons Eisenhower chose him as vice president on the 1952 ticket. As an attack dog second-in-command, Nixon was a perfect complement to Eisenhower's genial image. Nixon escalated his attacks on Truman Secretary of State Dean Acheson during the 1952 campaign: "China wouldn't have gone Communist—if the Truman administration had had backbone."[10] Truman and Acheson had "invited the Communists to begin the Korean War." He linked the 1952 democratic nominee to the policies he had been opposing for years, labeling Adlai Stevenson a "graduate of Acheson's 'Cowardly College of Communist Containment.'"[11] Nixon, of course, followed Eisenhower's policies for eight years: the US would defend Taiwan from Communist China, refuse to recognize the PRC as a legitimate government, and fight the inclusion of the PRC in the UN at the expense of ROC representation.[12] In 1953, Nixon was the conduit for a strong message to Chiang—the US was committed to the ROC, but would not use its own military power to assist it with any mainland invasion. Nixon's credibility on China and the fact that he considered Chiang a "friend" made the warning a potent one.[13] During the 1954–55 Quemoy and Matsu crisis, Nixon threatened the use of tactical nuclear weapons as a response to Chinese aggression.[14] Though he was never formally considered a member of the China lobby, in private administration deliberations Nixon gave the same unyielding support to the ROC. Before leaving the country for his trip to Latin America in April 1958, he wrote a memo to Eisenhower's special assistant for national security affairs, Robert Cutler, stating that if the issue of Chinese representation at the UN should come up at any NSC meeting, Nixon wanted his "view put on the record as follows: I am unequivocally opposed at this time to recognition of Red China, admission of Red China to the United Nations and to any concept of 'Two Chinas.'"[15]

During the 1960s, Nixon's views evolved significantly. As the Republican nominee for president in 1960, he began the decade competing with the Democratic nominee, Senator John Kennedy, for which man could be toughest on China. In the second presidential debate on October 7, 1960, Kennedy argued that while the defense of Taiwan was crucial, defending Quemoy and Matsu was unnecessary and perhaps futile. Nixon responded forcefully, viewing the defense of Quemoy and Matsu in the context of the domino theory. Refusal to defend the islands would only embolden the Communists: "In my opinion this is the same kind of woolly thinking that led to disaster for America in Korea. I am against it. I would never tolerate it as president of the United States."[16] On the campaign trail he pledged that if elected he would veto any resolution at the United Nations that gave the ROC seat to the PRC.[17] Nixon's loss in the 1960 election and subsequent defeat in the 1962 California gubernatorial race left him out of politics, but only temporarily. These years out of the "arena," as he called it, had allowed him time to reflect. The US experience in Vietnam and the widening Sino-Soviet split had altered his views of how to deal with China. Nixon believed it was time to make overtures. In a March 12, 1966 meeting with Johnson, Nixon recounts how he "urged a diplomatic communication as soon as possible. 'Mr. President,' I said 'time is on their side. Now is the time to confront them on the diplomatic front'"[18]

Nixon unveiled his new views on China in a 1967 *Foreign Affairs* article, "Asia after Vietnam."[19] Nixon argued that the US had missed the great progress in East Asia while it was fighting in Vietnam. US ability to thwart Communist expansion in Vietnam had bought time for the other nations in Asia to stabilize themselves politically and economically. Most notably, Indonesia—the "greatest prize in Southeast Asia"—had defeated its Communist threat.[20] The nations in the region no longer saw the West in the context of anticolonial nationalism; instead, they saw China as the growing problem and the US as a "protector."[21] That did not mean, however, a future of persistent hostility toward China. He argued that it was up to the US to end China's isolation, to make attempts to bring it peacefully into the community of nations, and to reform the excesses of Maoism.

> Any American policy toward Asia must come urgently to grips with the reality of China. This does not mean, as many would simplistically have it, rushing to grant recognition to Peking, to admit it to the United Nations and to ply it with offers of trade. . . . It does mean recognizing the present and potential danger from Communist China, and taking measures designed to meet that danger. . . . Taking the long view, we simply cannot afford to leave China forever outside the family of nations, there to nurture its fantasies, cherish its hates and threaten its neighbors. There is no place on this small planet for a billion of its potentially most able people to live in angry isolation. But we could go disastrously wrong if, in pursuing this long-range goal, we failed in the short range to read the lessons of history. The world cannot be safe until China changes. Thus our aim, to the extent that we can influence events, should be to induce change. The way to do this is to persuade China that it must change: that it cannot satisfy its imperial ambitions, and that its own national interest requires a turning away from foreign adventuring and a turning inward toward the solution of its own domestic problems.[22]

He summed up the idea by suggesting "Containment without isolation" as a defining "concept" that might "keep the peace" and "help draw off the poison of the Thoughts of Mao."[23] Nixon's ideas as fleshed out in the article mirrored the thinking of the working-level Kennedy/Johnson interagency groups as well as the China experts who testified in the spring 1966 congressional hearings. Nixon reiterated this theme during the 1968 elections, essentially quoting from his *Foreign Affairs* piece during foreign policy addresses.[24] Nelson Rockefeller, Nixon's rival for the Republican nomination, and Democratic nominee Hubert Humphrey had made similar statements about changing US policies toward

China.[25] Humphrey carried through the arguments he had begun to make in 1966 about ending China's isolation. Rockefeller's views on repairing US-PRC relations were, in part, the product of Kissinger's evolving views of China.[26]

The evolution of Nixon's thinking reflected the same evolution within academia and government, among major political figures in the US, and around the world. Perhaps any president elected in 1968 would have made overtures to China. Given Nixon's history, his opening to China was both more shocking and more durable.

International Political Context

In a short time during the late 1960s and early 1970s, Chinese foreign policy experienced a fundamental evolution. If Nixon's opening to China and détente with the USSR is seen as epic change, shifts in China's view of the world during this period are equally stunning. When Nixon and Kissinger reached out to China to test the possibilities for engagement, it found a willing partner.

As described in the previous chapter, the Cultural Revolution was Mao's largest and boldest campaign. The goal was no less than a transformation of Chinese society, to be achieved through a mass mobilization of urban high school and university students—the Red Guards. One scholar describes it as a "mass insurgency from below" aimed at identifying and removing anyone in society and the Communist Party who did not fully support Mao's ideas.[27] It was also a factional battle at the top levels of the Communist Party, designed to crush those individuals and cliques judged ideologically impure ("Capitalist Roaders") or infatuated with the wrong kind of Communist ideas (leaning toward "Khrushchevite Revisionism"). Equally important for Mao was an effort to root out the largest threats—those who were not absolutely loyal to Mao. The course of the Cultural Revolution and its impact on Chinese foreign policy was also shaped by the rivalries between the key Communist Party factions: more hardline elements led by Defense Minister Lin Biao (Mao's designated successor as of 1966, leading a military faction); a radical faction led by Jiang Qing, Mao's wife and a vice chair of the Central Cultural Revolution Group; and a relatively moderate wing led by Premier Zhou Enlai. These were rivalries about ideology, policy, and personal power.[28]

Lin Biao saw the US as China's main enemy; he supported a foreign policy that might repair the damage in PRC-USSR relations. Jiang's faction viewed both the US and USSR as imperialist aggressors; China needed to be prepared to go it alone. Zhou focused on the growing Soviet threat and sought to balance against it with better ties to the US. His views can be seen as a realism colored by a mix of ideology and pragmatism. He rejected any attempts for any nation, even China, to establish hegemony in Asia; both the US and Soviet Union were dangers to China and East Asia, but the US was the lesser danger.[29]

Ironically, as the Johnson administration debated whether to end its policy of isolation toward China during 1967 and 1968, the Cultural Revolution was leading China toward isolating itself. Most high ranking officials in Chinese embassies and consulates and an estimated 50% to 67% of all embassy staff had been forced to return to China by mid-1967. Outside the Communist bloc, stable diplomatic relations had dwindled to a handful of states: mainly Afghanistan, Pakistan, Zambia, Tanzania, and Nepal. Communist Party leaders who had a history of dealing with other nations through regular diplomatic channels had their revolutionary credentials challenged from both left and right. Both Foreign Minister Marshal Chen Yi and the Chinese representative at the Warsaw talks, Wang Bingnan, then considered members of the Zhou's moderate faction, became targets of the radical-faction-inspired Red Guards. Ultimately, in the summer of 1967, the Foreign Ministry itself was seized by Red Guards who then began to dictate policy to embassies that still functioned.[30] The Red Guards had launched a reign of terror against perceived enemies of Mao's ideas, but then divided into factions and turned on each other in 1968, battling on campuses around the nation. Mao's solution was to first place the Red Guards under the direction of the People's Liberation Army in August 1968, using the army to regain control over them (a factional victory for Lin Biao). Next, he reassigned the Red Guards to work in the countryside to teach them how to be proper members of the Communist peasantry, essentially an ideological cover for internal exile.[31] The excesses of the Red Guards reflected poorly on the radical faction, elevating the military and moderate groups.

Events in 1968 and 1969 gave the moderates the power to redirect Chinese foreign policy, allowing Zhou Enlai to make his case that the Soviet Union was the real threat and better relations with the US were part of the solution. The Sino-Soviet rift widened throughout the 1960s. Instead of global Communist solidarity, China and the Soviet Union were competing for the allegiance of developing world Communist regimes and movements.[32] China had been the primary supporter of Vietnam in its struggle with the US, but the post-Khrushchev Soviet leadership had begun to compete with China for Hanoi's favor. When President Johnson announced a decision to halt US bombing of Vietnam in exchange for peace negotiations in March 1968, China counseled Hanoi to continue the war rather than negotiate. North Vietnamese leaders chose to take Soviet advice instead, agreeing to negotiations.[33] At that point, the Chinese leadership could see the handwriting on the wall. Post–Vietnam War East Asia might become a struggle against the Soviet Union. It foreshadowed the late 1970s wars between Vietnam and Cambodia and China and Vietnam.

The seriousness of the Soviet threat escalated on August 20, 1968, as Soviet and Warsaw Pact troops entered Czechoslovakia to crush a reform movement led by Alexander Dubcek. The Soviets saw the "Prague Spring" as a direct challenge to its ideological and political hegemony in Eastern Europe. Soviet propagandists and Soviet Communist Party general secretary Leonid Brezhnev justified the invasion by arguing that the Soviets had a duty within the communist world to place nations back on the true path to communism if they began to stray; other Communist states only retained "limited sovereignty" within the international Communist movement. The new policy was dubbed the Brezhnev Doctrine.[34] The implications for China were significant: Had the Soviets just warned China that it could be the target of Soviet military intervention if their ideological differences widened? The Chinese response was swift. The Soviets were accused of "imperialism," and the Soviet vision of a Moscow-led and managed Communist bloc was compared to Japan's East Asian Co-Prosperity Sphere and Hitler's European order.[35] At the 12th Plenum of the Eighth Central Committee, October 13–31, 1968, Mao began tilting toward the moderates. Reportedly, he referred to the Soviet Union as a "greater threat to China than the weary paper tigers of American imperialism." Zhou was even given permission to restart the Warsaw talks with the US.[36]

In 1969, while the new Nixon administration studied the possibility of engagement with China, Sino-Soviet antagonism nearly erupted into a major war. The Ussuri River Crisis of spring and fall pushed China even further toward engagement with the US. Chinese-Russian clashes over their border date back long before the PRC, USSR, or even Marx was born. Serious disagreements were muted by Communist solidarity during the early Cold War years; the Sino-Soviet split allowed them to resurface.[37] A long-standing dispute over the Chenpao/Damasky Island in the Ussuri River flared up into actual fighting on March 2, 1969. China launched an attack in response to what it claimed had been multiple Soviet violations of the border since January 1967.[38] Clashes continued through the spring and summer of 1969 as both nations mobilized their militaries and their propaganda forces. The order of battle is estimated to have been 380,000 to 480,000 Chinese troops and 250,000 to 300,000 Soviet troops aligned on the border.[39] Both nations also mobilized thousands of citizens to protest at each other's embassies in their respective capitals.[40] After continued lower-level clashes through the summer and fall, diplomacy finally led to negotiations in Peking beginning in October 1969. Diplomacy reduced immediate tensions, but did little to move the two nations toward each other in any substantive way.[41]

Mao had already begun to think about a new direction for Chinese foreign policy even before the Ussuri River crisis. The possibility of US withdrawal from Vietnam, the Brezhnev Doctrine, and a new administration in Washington required much study. A possible US attempt to begin a dialogue with China had already become a significant factor in China's calculations. Mao had read Nixon's *Foreign Affairs* article and given it to Zhou.[42] In making his case for rebalancing China's strategic calculations, Zhou was able to capture Mao's curiosity. On February 19, 1969, Mao began his own review of Chinese foreign policy: "The Four Marshal Symposium." The review was headed by Marshal Chen Yi. The fact that Chen, who had been under attack by the Red Guards in 1967, could regain his authority and lead this study was significant. Some aspects of bureaucratic politics are the same everywhere: choosing the leader of an important study group is a political act that, in itself, shapes the outcome. The other three marshals who led the study—Xu Xiangqian, Nie Rongzhen, and Ye Jianying—had all been demoted during the Cultural Revolution, reassigned to factories in Beijing.[43] Their elevation and Chen's leadership role were victories for Zhou.

The marshals gave four reports to Mao. Given that the studies began before the Ussuri River Crisis and the important 9th Party Congress of April 1969, and that the final report was finished in September 1969, the marshals' ideas evolved over time. How much their conclusions were influenced by Mao, Zhao, or Lin is unclear. Mao, however, is quoted telling the Cultural Revolution Leading Group on March 15, 1969, shortly after the first battles on the Ussuri River, that "we are now isolated."[44] Lin Biao's power was elevated at the 9th Party Congress as the looming threat of larger scale war with the Soviets emphasized the military's importance; half of the new members of the central committee were military officers.[45] The 9th Party Congress's decision to allow ambassadors to return to the embassies, a reopening to the world, was a victory for Zhou.[46] In short, the reports could have gone in several directions as Mao continued to balance the factions. Neither of the first two reports (completed before the end of March) mentioned possible rapprochement with the US. After the party congress, Zhou counseled the marshals to continue their review and explicitly encouraged them not to fear contradicting any of the decisions made at the congress. The party congress had reiterated the traditional attacks on US "imperialists" and escalated attacks on Soviet "revisionists." The third and fourth reports (June and September 1969) moved toward a strategic shift in China's foreign policy. The marshals felt that war with the Soviet Union was a serious possibility; "US imperialism" was less of a threat than "Soviet revisionism." China should "play the card of the United States" and balance against the increasingly aggressive Soviet threat. Privately, Chen Yi was reported to have recommended to Zhou that he open a negotiation with the US "so that basic and related problems in Sino-American relations can be solved." The marshals were counseling Zhou and Mao to engage in the traditional balancing behavior of realists—side with the lesser threat against the greater threat—recalling strategic balancing behavior by various factions during the Warring States era (475–221 BC). They even argued that one of the reasons the Soviet Union had not attacked China in 1969 was the possibility that a Soviet attack on China might push the US and China into an "alliance." The marshals worried about their "unconventional thoughts," but again Zhou assured them that Mao wanted open and honest views.[47] The balancing logic found a receptive home in Mao's political realism. Mao was reported to have explained relations with the US by employing a historical analogy: "Didn't our ancestors counsel negotiating with faraway countries while fighting with those that are near?"[48] As this new thinking suggests, China did respond rapidly to Nixon's diplomatic feelers.

In Taipei, ROC leaders might have had too much confidence in the US alliance to fully appreciate how the situation had been transformed. The US had already cut economic aid to Taiwan in 1965, and drastically cut military aid by over 75% from 1968 to 1969.[49] Certainly, the use of Taiwan as essentially a forward base of operations during the Vietnam War had continued to cement the alliance (a home for 20,000 US troops).[50] Any drawdown of US aid could be interpreted as the natural outcome of US plans for withdrawal from the war. Though Taipei saw an evolution in US policy, rather than an abrupt break, the ROC would have to prepare to be more self-reliant. Taiwan was buying more weapons from the US to build up its own capability, and its rapid economic development was partly geared toward creating an economy that could sustain large defense expenditures in the long term. Perhaps most importantly, Chiang Kai-shek was relieved when Nixon, his old friend and ardent enemy of China, entered the White House.[51] In 1969, the US reassured Chiang that any US overtures to China were simply a part of the Nixon administration's willingness for open dialogue with anyone. The ROC leadership, however, had a clandestine intelligence channel to Zhou Enlai through Hong Kong. It likely knew that secret US-Chinese talks were proceeding more rapidly than the US let on. The channel may have been Zhou's way of convincing Chiang that the US was ready to abandon it or an attempt to develop a joint ROC/PRC stance against the acceptance of two Chinas.[52]

Domestic Political Context

Two key aspects of the US domestic political situation influenced Nixon's foreign policy decisions overall and on China: US movement out of Vietnam; and the weakening of the China lobby. First, a growing number of Americans were concluding that intervention to prevent the spread of Communism in East Asia was no longer worth the effort. How would that impact China policy? At the time of the Tet Offensive in January 1968, public opposition to the Vietnam War surpassed support for the first time. By the time of Nixon's inauguration, disapproval of the war was about 50% and growing; support for the war had fallen to 30% and would fall further. The US public's thinking on the war was actually more complex than these numbers seem at first glance. As late as October 1968, by a tally of 44–42% (within the margin of error), Americans identified themselves as "hawks" more than "doves," meaning that they wanted to "step up US military effort in Vietnam." By November of 1969, only 31% described themselves as hawks, while 55% identified as doves.[53] China was still seen as the greatest threat to the US in 1967, by 70% to 20% over Russia.[54] The decline in support for the Vietnam War was not an indication that Americans no longer saw Chinese aggression in Vietnam as a problem; it was instead a sign of the dissatisfaction over how the Johnson administration had fought the war.

Johnson had already moved to deescalate. On March 31, 1968, after winning the New Hampshire primary by a much smaller margin than anticipated, 48–42% over antiwar candidate senator Eugene McCarthy, Johnson announced he intended to halt the bombing of Vietnam in exchange for peace talks and would not seek reelection. Once elected, Nixon still had the choice to escalate or deescalate the war in Vietnam; some might argue he did both. Leaving Vietnam, however, even if gradually, would open the path to relations with China. As seen below, both Nixon and Kissinger firmly believed that a withdrawal from Vietnam was a prerequisite to engagement with China.

Second, the administration had to account for the China lobby. By

June 1968, the Committee of One Million still counted 96 members in the House (42 Democrats and 54 Republicans), but had lost so much support in the Senate that it no longer kept track of its numbers there. The committee felt certain that Nixon would maintain a hard line against China and its admission into the UN.[55] That perhaps explains why the administration never felt as much pressure from conservatives as Nixon and Kissinger expected.[56] The committee had sponsored a number of polls, but ended the practice in June 1971 after the opening to China was under way; the polls showed increasing support for Nixon's engagement with China. It had also published a newsletter starting in April 1969, "China Report," lobbying against Nixon's policies toward China. The newsletter was discontinued in October 1971 after the UN General Assembly vote that gave the Chinese seat in the UN to the PRC.[57] Nixon could not be outflanked on the right; when he moved to engage China and allow the admission of the PRC to the UN along with the expulsion of the ROC, he effectively neutered the China lobby.

Narrative of Decision

During Nixon's first postelection meeting with Kissinger at the Pierre Hotel, on November 25, 1968, Nixon told Kissinger that he believed the time was right for a new approach to China. He recommended his *Foreign Affairs* article as an indication of his thinking.[58] Though Kissinger often gets the credit as the strategic thinker of the administration, Nixon was the driver of the new China policy from the outset; Kissinger saw China in the context of US-USSR relations—a way to balance against Soviet power.[59] During the 1968 campaign, he had advised Rockefeller that China would need to change before the rest of the world approached it. He expected it to do so in the future, ending its hostility toward the West out of pure national interest.[60] To him, any reformulation of China policy was a medium- to long-term issue. Nixon felt that a shift could occur much more quickly as the US withdrew from Vietnam. He saw it as part of his legacy, ending the isolation of one of the great powers and permanently restructuring the post–World War II international order. General Alexander Haig, Kissinger's NSC military assistant, even recounts a story from early in Nixon's term when Kissinger returned from a meeting with Nixon somewhat incredulous. He told Haig, "Al, this madman wants to normalize our relations with China," and then laughed. In an understatement, Haig described Kissinger as "very skeptical."[61]

Secretary of State William Rogers echoed Nixon's *Foreign Affairs* article

in his nomination testimony before the Senate Foreign Relations Committee on January 15, 1969. He felt that the Sino-Soviet split was "probably one of the most important things that has happened in international
relations since the takeover of mainland China" and suggested opening up
"channels of communication with Red China, if it is possible and as soon
as it is possible." His argument was the same as Nixon's: "I think in the
long run you can't have a billion people outside the world community."[62]
Nixon's inaugural speech contained two sentences designed as messages
to both the Soviet Union and China that his administration was open to
serious discussions: "Let all nations know that during this administration
our lines of communication will be open. We seek an open world—open
to ideas, open to the exchange of goods and people—a world in which no
people, great or small, will live in angry isolation."[63] In particular, the last
line was aimed directly at Beijing. Given that the career officials of the
State Department had supported attempting a dialogue with China, only
to feel that they had been thwarted by Rusk, both Nixon's and Roger's
attitude must have been a huge boost to morale. Importantly, Nixon and
Rogers agreed on the overall parameters of US policy toward China. Dean
Rusk might smile in approval; there was no "blue sky" between the president and his secretary of state.

In spite of his doubts, Kissinger quickly moved to give Nixon what he
wanted: a review of US policy toward China. What would become NSSM
14 was initiated on January 27, 1969, one week after the inauguration. NSC
staff secretary Richard Moose sent a memo to NSC East Asia staffer Richard Sneider directing him to begin "an NSSM on China policy in general,
but focusing specifically on the problem of what we will say at the Warsaw
meeting on February 20." Moose's memo stated explicitly that Kissinger had
asked for the NSSM.[64] Presumably Nixon had asked Kissinger for an NSSM,
but no record of when that conversation was held is available. In a February
1 memo Sneider gave his short summary of key China issues to Kissinger.[65]

NSSM 14 ultimately became a bottom-up review, even though Sneider's memo providing guidance for the NSSM mentions the resumption of
the Warsaw talks as its highest priority. The shift in focus may have been
partly due to delays in restarting the talks. The last Johnson-era Warsaw
meeting had been held in January 1968. Discussions on setting a date for
resumption lasted until after the November 1968 elections. Johnson then
acted as a go-between for President-elect Nixon and China in setting up
a date for the next round of talks, eventually scheduled for February 20,
1969.[66] These were cancelled due to the defection of the Chinese charge
d'affaires at The Hague in January.

There were essentially two views on how to approach China in late 1968 and early 1969. One view supported a tentative outreach that waited for China to indicate it was willing to change before the US would commit itself to any concrete action. Outgoing ANSA Walt Rostow had written to incoming ANSA Kissinger in December defining what he felt should be the objectives of the Nixon administration over the next 12–18 months. The third point on the list was "beginnings of normalizing our relations with Communist China." He referenced the upcoming February 20 talks as a time for "finding out if mainland China is about ready to come to terms for a while with the rest of Asia and the US."[67] State concurred with this approach. It produced its first study of China relations in preparation for the February 1969 Warsaw meeting. It was given to Nixon sometime in late January or early February in the form of a 12-page memo from Rogers, with eight annexes. Deputy Assistant Secretary of State for East Asian and Pacific Affairs (EAP) Affairs Winthrop Brown, his predecessor Robert Barnett, and Thomas Shoesmith (ROC country director for the EAP Bureau) had reviewed and approved the memo. The memo began with a top-to-bottom summary of available options that included "two Chinas" or "one China, one Taiwan," the possibilities of normalization, the withdrawal of US troops from Taiwan, and an analysis of later-term Johnson policy. Rogers recommended that Nixon hold discussion of normalization "in reserve for further consideration" until the US could get a sense of China's willingness to reduce its hostilities and engage with the US on "outstanding issues" between the two nations.[68]

Nixon was an advocate of a bolder approach where the US took the initiative. In a February 1 memo, Nixon wrote: "I think we should give every encouragement to the attitude that this administration is exploring possibilities of rapprochement with the Chinese. This, of course, should be done privately and should under no circumstances get into the public print from this direction."[69]

If Nixon wanted this to be private, he did a poor job of maintaining that privacy. The rhetoric coming out of the administration nearly shouted across the Pacific that the US was ready for a new relationship with China. Rogers publicly called for greater US-Chinese cultural and educational contacts on February 18; Kissinger told members of the press on February 21 that when it came to China, "the President has always indicated that he favors a policy of maximum contact." While in France as part of a trip to Europe, Nixon met with President Charles de Gaulle on March 1 and asked him to send a message to the Chinese leadership that the US wished to open a dialogue.[70] The public pronouncements at this point echoed Nixon's 1967 *Foreign Affairs* article. The diplomatic messages were essentially feelers; the administration was testing to see if China had any inclination to go beyond the Warsaw channel. NSSM 14 framed the policy within the overall strategic context: If China is willing to talk, what are US interests?

On February 5, 1969, NSSM 14 was signed by Kissinger, its contents likely based on Sneider's memo of February 1. It called for a comprehensive review of China policy: "The President has directed that a study be prepared on U.S. Policy Towards China, on U.S. objectives and interests involved and the broad lines of appropriate U.S. policies." NSSM-14 identified four areas of focus: "current" policy; the "nature of the Chinese threat and intentions in Asia"; the "interactions between U.S. policy" and the policies of other powers in the region; and, most importantly, "alternative U.S approaches on China and their costs and risks." The study was assigned to the East Asia Interdepartmental Group and given a deadline of March 10 for submission to the Review Group.[71]

The process at this point was faithful to the design of NSDMs 1 and 2—formal, interagency, and inclusive.

The EAIG created a China Working Group under the leadership of Brown of EAP; this new group produced the study under the supervision of the EAIG, chaired by the assistant secretary of state for East Asian and Pacific affairs, William Bundy until May 1969 and thereafter Marshall Green.[72] The memo traffic (as described below) indicates that membership in the Working Group and the EAIG included representatives from at least the departments of State and Defense, JCS, and the CIA, though no formal membership list has been found in the documentary record. The NSC staff's Sneider had given the Working Group very clear instructions to avoid anything that was similar to the Johnson administration's Long Range China Study of 1965; he directed it to keep the paper to roughly 20 single-spaced pages. Though the original NSSM called for a paper to be sent to the RG on March 10, the schedule slid repeatedly. Inclusivity within the interagency process necessarily meant delays as multiple agencies reviewed drafts and gave their comments, and the Working Group attempted to meld those comments into a coherent whole. For example, merely within the State Department, each draft of NSSM 14 was reviewed by several offices in the East Asian and Pacific Bureau, but also by officials in the Bureaus of Intelligence and Research, Educational and Cultural Affairs, and Legal Affairs, and the US Embassy in Taiwan. The Working Group produced a first draft that was sent to all participating bureaucracies sometime in mid-March. Based on the comments of the agencies involved, the Working Group reviewed its draft and produced a second draft, dated

March 29 (though it continued tinkering with that second draft until April 1). Both the March 29 and April 1 drafts were sent to participating agencies and the embassy for a second look. The third draft was dated April 24 in some memos and April 29 in others. Though the EAIG was scheduled to review the draft on April 10 and 15 for submission to the RG on April 18, that slipped to April 29.[73] It is unclear what dates the EAIG actually did meet; however, it was formally submitted by Brown to the RG with a covering memo dated April 30, 1969.[74]

As the interagency drafting of NSSM 14 proceeded, other channels related to China were active. Undersecretary of State Elliot Richardson, chair of the Undersecretaries Committee (USC), sent Nixon a memo sometime in March or April with his thoughts on how the US could change policy. Nixon marked up the memo and returned it to Richardson with suggestions on what the US might do.[75] On instructions from Kissinger, Sneider organized and convened a group of outside consultants to advise the administration on China. The consultants were given a sanitized version of the NSSM 14 draft to read in preparation for a meeting on April 24. The outside consultants—academic China scholars A. Doak Barnett, Lucian Pye, Edwin Reischauer, George Taylor, and Henry Rosovsky—met with Kissinger, Sneider, and additional NSC staffers Morton Halperin, Dean Moar, and Lindsey Grant. Following that meeting they met with Nixon. Sneider's schedule for the meeting also listed a set of questions for the consultants. The tenor of the questions mirrored Nixon's thinking: "What kind of deterrence is necessary to prevent expansion of Chinese power . . . what sort of evolution in China is possible in direction favorable to our interests, and how can US actions contribute to bringing it about. . . . How does Taiwan relate to our China problem? What do we do about Taiwan?"[76]

The administration also issued NSSM 35, *US Trade Toward Communist Countries*, on March 28. It asked for an assessment of trade restrictions on Eastern Europe, Asian Communist nations, and Cuba, whether they should be modified, and, if so, in what ways. The review was assigned to an ad hoc committee chaired by the assistant secretary of state for economic affairs, and included representatives from the departments of Defense, Commerce, Agriculture, and Treasury, the CIA, the Export-Import Bank, the Office of the Special Representative for Trade Negotiations, and the NSC staff. The study was assigned a due date for submission to the RG on May 9.[77]

By the date of that report's submission, the EAIG had already discussed the drafts of NSSM 14 in preparation for submitting its final version to the RG. A consensus within the group had formed around a policy that reflected Nixon's hopes, an option entitled at that stage "Reduction of Points of Conflict and International Isolation," in short—engagement. EAIG members were in agreement on efforts to lift some trade and travel restrictions during 1969 (though some in the committee hoped for an immediate end to all trade restrictions). The group also agreed that US policy on the Offshore Islands need not be changed. There was less unity on the UN representation issue and whether the US should draw down some of its forces from Taiwan commensurate with US troop withdrawals from Vietnam.[78]

On May 15, the RG met to discuss the EAIG's draft of NSSM 14. The meeting was chaired by Kissinger and included three officials from State (including Brown and Arthur Hartman, the staff secretary for the USC), and one each from the departments of Defense and Treasury, the CIA, the JCS, USIA, and the Office of Emergency Preparedness. Four NSC staffers attended as well. The minutes open with a statement that the NSSM report would not be ready for the May 21 NSC meeting. Importantly, State was given the responsibility of redrafting the NSSM based on comments by the other participating agencies. The key revisions mentioned were the need for a clear delineation in the options section between "early decision issues . . . (trade and travel)"; those "dependent on other issues," such as "use of Taiwan as a base"; and "those of longer term nature (US policy toward Taiwan, Offshore Islands, the UN, and perhaps diplomatic relations)." Kissinger noted that the paper presented two alternatives to current policy: "intensify containment" and "reduction in tensions." He questioned whether these were "phony" options. He asked the group, "Does anybody favor intensifying our pressures on China? The President has made it clear that he does not wish to be presented with artificial options." Kissinger also wanted the paper to consider fundamental questions: "Why is bringing China into the world community inevitably in our interest?" and why do we assume that "an isolated China, so long as it caused no major problems, is necessarily against our interests?" He wanted the NSSM to place all the key aspects in the context of large strategic issues. A consensus was reached among the State Department and NSC staff representatives that the relaxation of tensions approach was the best; the minutes noted State assurances that Rogers supported this option as well. The group also agreed that the threat from China was greater in the longer term than in the short term; therefore, the NSSM did not need to be addressed at an NSC meeting until debates over the language in the study had been resolved; there was no rush. Kissinger noted in his memoirs that he was initially unhappy with the draft's focus on narrow topics such as UN representation, Taiwan, and the Sino-Soviet split "as if they existed in a vacuum," rather than as pieces of a larger strategic puzzle the US needed to solve to move relations in a positive direction. Kissinger also felt that the paper overemphasized the character of Chinese leadership; it identified the goal of US policy as one of "changing the minds of the Chinese leadership . . . from militancy to conciliation." He felt that to understand the China challenge for the US, the paper needed to consider "which of our problems with China are caused by its size and situation and which of them are caused by leadership." As a realist scholar, Kissinger felt the study underplayed the basic dilemma: a powerful state "surrounded by weaker states was a geopolitical problem no matter who governed it." In other words, NSSM 14 at that point saw a solution in convincing a revolutionary state to be less revolutionary, whereas Kissinger saw shifts in the East Asian balance of power between the US, China, the USSR, and Japan as the key.[79]

The Asian Communist Affairs office of the East Asian and Pacific Bureau of State organized the revision process after the May 15 RG meeting. It sent a revised draft, dated June 14, to RG members on June 17; they were asked to return comments by June 20 in anticipation of the June 25 NSC meeting. The covering memo summarized the paper. This revised version explicitly defined one of the US "interests and objectives" as "to achieve relax of tensions between the US and PRC, including participation of PRC in discussions on measures for arms control and disarmament, and normalization of US pol and econ relations with PRC." It still considered two very different alternatives to current US policy: "Intensified Deterrence and Isolation" and "Reduc(tion) of PRC Isolation and Points of US-PRC Conflict." The latter alternative, however, was given more attention in the memo, specifically outlining the short- and long-term advantages and disadvantages of the approach.[80]

In late June, the Asian and Communist Affairs office received comments back from the Office of International Security Affairs of the DoD, the CIA, Treasury, the JCS, the Vice President's Office, the Bureau of the Budget, and the Political-Military Bureau at State.[81] Neither the VP's office nor the Budget Bureau had representation on the RG, but in the interest of an inclusive process, they were able to view and comment on the NSSM draft.

At roughly the same time, Kissinger and Richardson informally discussed actions the US could take immediately to send signals to China about the possibility of rapprochement and preparations for ending policies that diplomatically and economically isolated China. Nixon had specifically asked Kissinger and Richardson to brainstorm on these issues during their luncheons. On June 21, Richardson sent Kissinger a detailed memo on possible initiatives that he felt would "do more to promote US foreign policy and econ interests than it would benefit China." He organized them into four sets: controls on foreign subsidiaries; bunkering restrictions; liberalization of US tourist purchases; and selective reduction of controlled items. These included very technical regulatory restrictions, the kinds of minutiae that would make trade with China easier but not provide significant economic assistance to China, such as lifting restrictions on the purchase of oil from US companies by Chinese Communist Party–owned ships or even non-Chinese ships bound for China, or allowing licensing for sales of food grains, agricultural equipment, pharmaceuticals, or chemical fertilizers. Kissinger summarized Richardson's ideas in a covering memo for Nixon on June 23 under the title "Actions to Indicate a Possible Opening Toward China"; Richardson's memo was added in an attachment. Kissinger recommended that Nixon approve Richardson's proposals. Nixon accepted softening "prohibitions on transactions with China" by "foreign corporations owned by US interests" and allowing American tourists to buy "limited" amounts of Chinese manufactured goods. He rejected the lifting of the oil sales restrictions, and made no comment on the licensing idea.[82]

The result of these memos was NSDM 17, *Relaxation for Economic Controls Against China*, of June 26, 1969. The memorandum asked the USC to draw up implementation plans for three of the four Richardson/Kissinger ideas; though Nixon did not agree to the licensing proposal initially, he did give Kissinger the green light to include it in the NSDM along with the tourism and foreign subsidiaries restrictions. The USC was directed to write new regulations regarding these areas, and to prepare a "press and diplomatic" strategy for announcing the changes and an approach to Congress. Richardson's memo to the USC, dated June 28, set up an interagency working group to staff out possible regulatory modifications and set a meeting date for July 3 as well as a July 7 deadline for submitting proposals to the president. The memo was addressed to the standard USC roster: deputy secretary of defense, director of central intelligence, chairman of the Joint Chiefs, undersecretary of commerce, undersecretary of the treasury, and Kissinger.[83]

On May 24, 1969, Rogers visited Pakistan and spoke with President Yahya Khan about Nixon's hopes to open a secret diplomatic channel to China. The message was a simple one—the US was serious about beginning a dialogue.[84] Though Kissinger became known as the master of the back channel, secret communications to China through Pakistan began with Rogers. More importantly, the policy was being implemented before the review was completed. Nixon, Rogers, and Kissinger, however, knew

what the consensus was at the interagency level; there was no real substantive disagreement at any level of the bureaucracy. There was a strong
agreement that the US should move forward to end its policy of isolation
and initiate a new engagement.

Nixon traveled to Asia and Europe from July 26 to August 3. While
in Pakistan, August 1–2, he met with President Yahya Khan and reiterated Rogers' message: the US would like to help end China's isolation.
Nixon traveled on to Romania, August 2–3, and sent a similar message
through Romanian president Nicolae Ceausescu. The US goal was to end
China's isolation and to have solid relations with both China and the Soviet
Union.[85] The messages carried short- and long-term implications. In the
short run, in the midst of the Sino-Soviet clashes, the US would not ally
itself with the Soviet Union in an attempt to weaken China. In the long
run, the US hoped to establish a normal relationship with China.

On August 8, 1969, the official completion date of NSSM 14 and the
day that China broke off talks with the USSR over the border, Rogers
gave a speech in Canberra, Australia during an Australia, New Zealand, US
(ANZUS) Council meeting.

> We recognize, of course that the Republic of China on Taiwan and
> Communist China on the mainland are facts of life. We know, too,
> that mainland China will eventually play an important role in Asian
> and Pacific affairs—but certainly not as long as its leaders continue
> to have such an introspective view of the world. . . . This is the rea-
> son we have been seeking to open up channels of communication.[86]

It was a clear distillation of the administration's hopes for China, and an
argument that could have been made by any of Kennedy's or Johnson's
Asia experts. At the highest levels of the administration, both publicly and
privately, the US had made its new policy clear. Internally, the interagency
process produced a document that backstopped the change of direction.

NSSM 14, as transmitted to NSC members on August 8 in anticipation
of a scheduled NSC meeting on August 14, included a four-page outline,
a 10-page executive summary, a 22-page report (the core of the paper),
and eight annexes. The annexes covered "Premises and Factors" of the
geopolitical context; "Modes of Military Deterrence"; US policy toward
Taiwan; Taiwan as a US military base; the Offshore Islands; the diplomatic
approach to China; UN issues; and trade policy.[87] The paper summarized
its own purpose as an analysis of "(1) US interests and objectives and the
nature and degree of threats that Peking may present to the US or to other

countries in Asia, and (2) present US strategy and alternatives thereto." It defined present US policy as having "two elements: (1) deterrence of any possible direct Chinese threat across its borders or to the US, and (2) limited efforts to suggest to the Chinese the desirability of changing their policies in the direction of a more tolerant view of other states and of the present world political system."[88]

Two alternatives to current policy were examined: "Intensified Deterrence and Isolation" or "Reduction of PRC's Isolation and Points of US-PRC Conflict." These were the same two alternatives addressed in the May 15 RG meeting, even though Kissinger wondered if the intensified deterrence alternative was a realistic option: the president did not support it; did anyone? In spite of this question, the two options presented essentially took the carrot and stick menu of the old policy and emphasized one aspect over the other. Should the US increase the size of the stick with intensified deterrence, or make the carrot more appetizing through a serious effort at fundamentally reshaping the US-China relationship? As the report stated:

> There is also a basic agreement that our policy must be a combination of deterrence, aimed at making clear to the Chinese that nuclear or conventional military actions will be unprofitable, and of limited steps to suggest the possibility of improved relations with the U.S. The disagreement (discussed below in considering alternatives to our current posture) centers around the "mix" of these elements.[89]

The study clearly fell on the side of engagement, supporting implicitly and explicitly the "reduction of isolation" alternative. Though it began with the premise that in the short term the US and China would continue to be at odds and that even in the long term the two nations were unlikely to find common ground on most issues, the authors were optimistic. They felt that "over the next five to ten years, depending in part on when Mao dies, certain changes are possible." While there was the possibility that China might "move toward a policy of more aggressive action," they argued that "we believe, however, that it is more likely that China's policy ultimately will moderate, given an international climate conducive to moderation." Elements of a new strategy could include "improved relations with the US and/or Japan, in part as a counter-balance to Soviet pressures," reduced Chinese "support for revolutionary movements," "seeking increased contact with the nations of Asia and membership in international organizations," and an "interest" in arms control.[90] The study argued that "there is little reason to believe . . . that this present level of conflict and antagonism will endure indefinitely." US policy can be "set in more flexible terms and in the direction of the achievement of an improved and more relaxed relationship with the PRC."[91]

The section on intensified deterrence was three and a half pages long and considered both the advantages and disadvantages of its political, military, and economic aspects. The policy might include "explicit endorsement" of the ROC "claim to be the only legitimate government of China," opposition to PRC membership in international organizations unless it made significant changes in its foreign policies, refusal to increase communications with China, continued military deployments throughout East Asia (including South Vietnam, even after the war had ended), treaty commitments with Malaysia and Singapore, tightening of the economic embargo of China, and greater deployment of tactical nuclear weapons in the region.[92] Obviously, some of these ideas were nonstarters. The US had already begun to reach out to China and loosen trade restrictions.

The section on reduction of isolation was seven and a half pages long. It also considered the advantages and disadvantages of the political, military, and economic aspects of that option, but each advantage and disadvantage was broken down into short- and long-term perspectives. The authors argued that short-term steps were necessary "to initiate changes now, when China poses only a limited threat, in an effort to set in motion as improvement over the longer term, when China's power could make her a greater potential danger." The types of policy options listed included ending travel restrictions, greater attempts at dialogue, ending opposition to PRC admission to the UN (but still supporting ROC membership), recognition of the PRC as the legitimate government of the mainland ("while insisting that settlement of the Taiwan question . . . must be by peaceful means"), reduction or withdrawal of US forces on Taiwan, and loosening of economic restrictions on China.[93]

The NSC staff prepared talking points for Kissinger in anticipation of the August 14 NSC meeting. Kissinger added comments in the margins in a few places, generally stressing geopolitical considerations. The talking points followed the structure of the NSSM, basically serving as another executive summary of the paper, with some additional commentary. Importantly, the last item in the section on "Intensified Deterrence and Isolation" was "No agency supports this strategy," Kissinger's summary of the bureaucratic landscape on the option. Description of the "Reduction of Points of Conflict" alternative was no different from NSSM 14.[94] The talking points for Kissinger were written from the perspective of an honest broker; it was a fair and clear restatement of NSSM 14.

Kissinger used these staff talking points to prepare NSC meeting talking points for Nixon and an additional memo for Nixon where Kissinger took on the ANSA's other role: advocate and enforcer of Nixon's choices. The set of memos tried to resolve some of the issues addressed in NSSM 14, emphasizing that the US had begun to move in the direction of reduction of tensions, and suggesting that Nixon should remind attendees that the US had already instituted policies to "show our willingness to have a more constructive relationship with Communist China while maintaining our commitment to the GRC" (Government of the Republic of China). They also pointed out that the NSC would meet in the fall regarding the Sino-Soviet split, but that Nixon had already "made clear to Asian leaders during my trip that we do not intend to join the Soviets in any plan to 'gang up' on China." Importantly, the memo noted that Nixon had yet to make a final decision to implement the recommendations made in NSDM 17. The memo also included the NSC staff's talking points for Kissinger and a copy of the "Outline and Key Issues" section of NSSM 14.[95]

Before the NSC meeting, Kissinger briefed Nixon on the debate as he saw it. He felt there were three different views of China policy within the bureaucracy. First, a "Slavophile" position, held by Soviet specialists, worried that given the state of USSR-PRC relations any tilt by the US toward China might jeopardize US-USSR détente. Second, a "Realpolitik" group emphasized the benefits of a growing relationship with China on US policy toward the Soviets; Moscow would likely become more cooperative if it worried about US-Chinese rapprochement. Third, "Sinophiles" delinked the Soviet-Chinese relationship from US-Chinese relations; the US should move toward engagement with China because it was right for the current situation in Asia. Stepping away from his honest broker role, Kissinger made it clear that he fell into the Realpolitik camp.[96] That balancing act became known as Triangular Diplomacy: the ability for the US to play the Chinese and Soviet against one another, each worried about the other's friendship with the US.

The NSC meeting on August 14 considered the NSSM 14 study and Korean peninsula questions. Attendees included Nixon, Kissinger, Rogers, Laird, Attorney General John Mitchell, Richardson, JCS Chair General Earle Wheeler, DCI Richard Helms, Office of Emergency Preparedness director George Lincoln, and Assistant Secretary of State for East Asian and Pacific Affairs Marshall Green. Nixon outlined his views, and again set the tone for how the US would think about China and US-Soviet-Chinese relations. He felt that "we have always assumed that the Chinese are hard liners and that the Soviets are the more reasonable. But I think this is open to question. . . . China can't stay permanently isolated. To me, China uses the dispute with Russia for internal use. But to me the Soviets are the more aggressive." He speculated that, given Soviet actions in Czechoslovakia and along the Sino-Soviet border, the Soviets could have a "'knock them off now' policy developing with respect to China." Both Nixon and Rogers felt that it was not in the US interest to see the USSR win a conflict with China. Rogers added that the State Department feels "that the Chinese threat is greatly overemphasized." Green felt that Asian nations' fear of China was large enough that they "might accept the Soviets as an alternative." Nixon disagreed, arguing that Asian nations "don't want the Soviets in."[97]

No formal decision came out of the meeting, but the consensus, even if never put on paper, was clear: no official, department, or agency supported an intensified hard line toward China. Kissinger believed that a US president openly espousing an end to Chinese isolation at an NSC meeting was "a major event in American foreign policy."[98]

The Ussuri River crisis that began in March 1969 added some immediacy to these mid-year deliberations. What had begun as a bottom-up review for a new administration became more critical as the possibility of a larger war between China and the USSR emerged. Nixon emphasized his view: a clash that left the PRC weakened was not in the US interest. Kissinger described it this way: the US "had a strategic interest in the survival of a major Communist country, long an enemy, and with which we had no contact." He felt that increasingly that "need for contact was becoming urgent."[99] The implicit direction for US policy was to send signals through every possible channel and to let the Chinese dictate the pace of the dialogue.

Analysis

NSSM 14 was conducted through a by-the-book interagency process. From the China Working Group of the EAIG to the full EAIG to the RG to the NSC, it appears to have been an inclusive bottom-up review of alternatives to current policy, exactly the type of comprehensive assessment that is undertaken when a new administration enters after eight years of the opposition political party occupying the Oval Office. Two aspects of it, however, are instructive. First, even though Nixon wanted an interagency process to assess only his options, not make recommendations, Nixon knew that the administration's consensus was to end isolation and move toward engagement. The only question was what type of engagement and how quickly to proceed. The interagency process was tasked to consider the former, while, as shown below, China determined the pace. Second, Nixon remained firmly in charge. From the February tasking for NSSM 14 to the August NSC meeting, Nixon received updates on the study through Kissinger. In mid-June, when he felt that he had enough information to institute a first step toward engagement—relaxation of some trade controls—he directed the Undersecretaries Committee to design specific policies to implement those plans in NSDM 17 of June 26, 1969. As laid out in NSDMs 1 and 2, the formal interagency process produced options for overall strategy and policy implementation, while Nixon directed the nature of the inquiry (through NSSM 14) and the policies to be implemented at every stage (though NSDM 17).

Though the NSSM 14 and NSDM 17 decisions were both interagency, the first was formal and the second added some informality. Briefly, the Nixon system had the best of both worlds. Given the prominence of the Rogers-Kissinger feud in the scholarship on the Nixon administration, it is telling that there is no evidence of its impact during decisions on NSSM 14. The lack of rivalry, however, was not due to any informal structures that reduced conflicts. No record of a Nixon, Rogers, Kissinger meeting on NSSM 14 exists; Kissinger claims that he never discussed overall strategic issues related to China with Nixon and Rogers in a small informal setting.[100] Though no analog for Johnson's Tuesday Lunch Group existed, the documentary record captures frequent communication between Nixon and Kissinger and between Kissinger and Richardson. Rogers did meet with Nixon multiple times each week and was granted as much access as any cabinet member; they also talked by phone frequently.[101] While this did not match Kissinger's access to Nixon, Rogers was certainly not a bystander in the China decision process, even if his name does not come up frequently in the narrative of NSSM 14. The review was firmly under control of the State Department—the China Working Group and EAIG were chaired by State officials—and therefore under Rogers's authority and direction. Perhaps at this point, at least on China policy, Rogers felt no threat from Kissinger, and Kissinger's relationship with Nixon gave him confidence in his own status.

Chinese Representation at the UN, 1971

On October 25, 1971 the United Nations General Assembly (UNGA) voted to give the China seat at the UN to the PRC; the ROC, knowing the outcome of the pending vote, had withdrawn from the UN earlier in the day. The PRC had accomplished its goal of replacing the ROC at the UN almost exactly 22 years after taking power in Beijing. The US policy designed by Truman, continued by Eisenhower, modified by Kennedy, and defended by Johnson had finally failed. The Nixon team, realizing that the votes in the UNGA to keep China out and Taiwan in were likely to disappear by 1971, moved to a dual representation formula: the US would support the PRC's claim to both the UNGA and UN Security Council (UNSC) seat, but also hoped to allow Taiwan to retain a seat in the UNGA. Rogers announced the policy on August 2, 1971. No one in the administration truly thought it would prevent the ROC from being tossed out of the UN, but most hoped it would at least give the appearance of a good faith effort by the US.

The decision to develop the new policy began in November 1970 with NSSM 107 and was once again a by-the-book formal interagency process: an ad hoc interagency group chaired by Assistant Secretary of State for International Organization Affairs Samuel De Palma developed the response to NSSM 107 and delivered it to the SRG, which prepared it for an NSC meeting on March 25, 1971. From there State took charge of the policy, and key decisions were made in two private meetings between Nixon, Rogers, and Kissinger. Nixon was firmly in control; State had been delegated the implementation of the policy; and Kissinger and Nixon worked to make sure the representation issue did not interfere with the outreach to the PRC that had been the core policy of the administration since it entered office. This case study does not confirm the evolution-balance model. The informal meetings of Nixon, Rogers, and Kissinger, however, do give support to the original evolution model. In the end, as a deadline approached, Nixon needed to speed up the process. He used these informal sessions of principals to go the last mile.

Of course, between November 1970 and August 1971, Kissinger made his secret trip to China (July 1971), and Nixon's intention to visit China in 1972 was announced. The backdrop to analysis of the UN policy was the secret diplomacy between the US and China that bypassed the interagency system, excluded the State Department, and explicitly kept Secretary of State Rogers out of the loop until July 8, the day before Kissinger left for Asia and a side trip from Pakistan to Beijing. Reconciling the seeming faithfulness to the interagency process and the secret decision making of the diplomacy to China is difficult. The case studies here suggest that, in spite of Nixon's resentments and disappointments with the State Department and Kissinger's rivalry with Rogers, during 1971 and 1972, the State Department and Rogers were integral to the formulation of policy except in cases where secrecy was necessary.

Political Context

Internationally, the key backdrop during this decision was the secret diplomacy that led to Kissinger's trip to Beijing in 1971. China responded positively to the administration's overtures, and the two nations moved more rapidly toward direct talks than even Nixon envisioned. Through 1969 and 1971, Zhou Enlai had solidified the policy of engagement within the Chinese leadership. Crucially, the death of Lin Biao, the party's number-two who leaned toward the Soviets, left Zhou without serious challengers. Only the Taiwan issue could have derailed the momentum toward rapprochement. China's view of the UN had evolved in the late 1960s and early 1970s from outright hostility and rejection of membership back to its earlier policy of lobbying for the Chinese seat at the UNGA and UNSC. It wanted in and wanted the ROC out. In contrast, the ROC never wavered; Chiang refused to accept two Chinas in the UN and hoped that the US would continue to support Taiwan's seat. The administration, however, believed that within only a few years, the UNGA would vote to remove the ROC and replace it with the PRC. As it reconsidered its policy in 1970, the Nixon administration understood that it was out of options. Kennedy's important question strategy was about to fail. The domestic political context, however, moved in Nixon's favor. Public approval for Nixon's Vietnam policy was accompanied by a shift to support for engagement with China, a peaceful alternative to fighting China's perceived expansion into Southeast Asia. Though Nixon's Cambodia invasion of April 1970 derailed the diplomatic momentum, it was back on track by late 1970. Kissinger's trip in July 1971 and the promise of a Nixon visit to China in 1972 were a moment in history that reshaped how people viewed the future of East Asia and US-Chinese relations. These successes gave Nixon enough public support to walk away from two decades of Taiwan policy with few political consequences at home.

International Political Context

The tale of the administration's diplomacy toward China is beyond the scope of this study and well told in memoirs, journalism, and historical analyses. The importance of the public and back-channel diplomacy rests in its role as context for the decisions that had yet to be made. US communication with China occurred through two channels: secret communications through Pakistan and to a lesser extent France and Romania that were used to send messages intended for the Communist Party leadership alone; and the continuation of the Warsaw dialogue, employed for more traditional diplomacy that required less stringent operational secrecy.[102] The former channel was controlled by Nixon and Kissinger, and few outside the White House and the NSC staff knew of its existence. Rogers did not know the extent of the communications through 1970. This point is crucial. In effect, much of State's public diplomacy called for the initiation of a policy that was already being implemented. Its lack of knowledge added a complicating factor. Public statements by State, particularly regarding Taiwan or the Chinese seat at the UN, might undermine or contradict the private diplomacy.[103]

In the fall of 1969, US ambassador to Poland Walter Stoessel had been working to make contact with representatives of the Chinese Embassy in Warsaw. He finally succeeded in December, and soon the US and China agreed to resumption of the talks on January 20, 1970. The US invasion of Cambodia on May 1, 1970, however, ended them. Under the leadership of Prince Norodom Sihanouk, Cambodia had attempted to remain neutral during the Vietnam War. North Vietnam had repeatedly violated that neutrality. A coup by US allied General Lon Nol on March 18, 1970 overthrew Sihanouk, and the new government made it clear that North Vietnamese actions would no longer be tolerated. The joint US and South Vietnamese invasion in May hoped to drive out any North Vietnamese presence and to find the North Vietnamese headquarters in Cambodia, the Central Office for South Vietnam, though many still doubt that it ever existed. The Chinese had been counting on US withdrawal from Vietnam, and suddenly the US was escalating the war and complicit in the overthrow of Sihanouk. With the North Vietnamese moving closer to Moscow and the US gaining an ally in Lon Nol's government, China needed some local champion. That became Sihanouk.[104] The invasion was seen as an escalation within the Chinese leadership, one that it had to respond to forcefully and publicly, even as it hoped to continue the path toward engagement. Suspending the Warsaw talks was an easy and low-cost way of showing the world China's displeasure while not jeopardizing the secret channels.

Even through third-party intermediaries, China made it clear that Taiwan was the priority. No matter how large the Soviet threat loomed and how logical it was to use the US as a counterweight, the main goal for Beijing was driving a wedge between the US and Taiwan. China wanted eventual recognition of the PRC and de-recognition of the ROC, withdrawal of US forces from Taiwan, and a cancellation of the US-Taiwan Mutual Defense Treaty of 1954.[105] Taiwan issues were deal breakers, policies on which no Chinese leader could give significant ground. China did not expect a quick resolution of the Taiwan problem, and was willing to address other topics first: an end to its isolation, a US withdrawal from Vietnam but not Asia, and US help in balancing against the Soviet threat.[106]

Factionalism at the top levels of the Communist Party of China were (and still are) an inevitable feature of a system built on personal loyalties, political intrigue, and limited institutional restraints on leadership. By 1969, the disastrous path of the Cultural Revolution had led to a weakening of the radical faction under Jiang Qing; the core contest over foreign policy narrowed to a battle between Lin Biao and Zhou Enlai. At the 2nd Plenum of the 9th Central Committee in August and September 1969 in Lushan, Lin's faction overplayed its hand, calling for a revision of the government constitution and the creation of a state chairman position that would presumably be Lin. Mao himself argued against the idea and thereafter saw Lin's ambition as a direct personal threat. Over the next year, Mao moved to reduce Lin's stature.[107] Lin and his family died on September 13, 1971 while trying to flee the country; their plane ran out of fuel. Whether he had been plotting to assassinate Mao or whether he feared Mao was about to purge him is still a matter of debate. Most sources claim that Mao had been encouraged to shoot the plane down but refused to give the order.[108] With Lin's death and subsequent discrediting of both his allies and arguments, Zhou had gained nearly complete freedom to pursue his policy of rapprochement as long as Mao still supported Zhou's key argument: the Soviet threat was increasing and the US threat was receding. Better relations with the US were the key to rebalancing power in the region.

The August-September meeting of the Central Committee also reshaped China's policy toward the UN. The anger that had been the hallmark of China's policy in the mid-1960s switched back toward a lobbying effort at gaining support for China's entry into the UN. China's own hope to end its isolation meant reaching out to both international organizations and nations that had yet to extend recognition to the PRC. Isolating Taiwan diplomatically and stealing votes at the UNGA was the ultimate goal. The new policy met with measurable success; 20 nations, including NATO members Canada, Italy, and Turkey, recognized the PRC from 1969 to 1971.[109]

Voting patterns at the UNGA had turned against Taiwan and the US since Nixon entered office, but only slightly. In 1969, the vote on keeping the China issue an important question (requiring a two-thirds vote to pass the UNGA) carried by 71 for, 48 against, and 7 abstentions. That support fell in 1970 to 66 for, 52 against, and 7 abstentions. Support for the Albanian resolution that would give the Chinese seat at the UN to the PRC and remove the ROC from the UN entirely failed in 1969 by a vote of 48 for, 56 against, and 22 abstentions. In 1970, the resolution gained a simple majority: 51 for, 49 against, and 27 abstentions. The vote was short of the two-thirds necessary (only 41%), but still illustrated how precarious the US and Taiwanese position had become.[110]

Chiang Kai-shek, however, remained steadfast; he was not about to make changes in US policy easy for the Nixon administration. During the 1960s, the ROC had moved toward a focus on its economy, pioneering government-business partnership and export-led growth policies.[111] In part, this was a hedging strategy—building up Taiwanese wealth in case the US continued to withdraw its support; economic and military aid had already been cut during the Johnson years. When the administration ended permanent patrols of the Taiwan Strait in October 1969 and Nixon announced in November that US Cold War policy in the developing world would no longer include intervention but instead be based on aid and arms sales to anti-Communist allies who would do the fighting (the Nixon Doctrine), Chiang gave the administration a shopping list of weapons it wished to purchase.[112] The ROC did not expect the US to proceed so quickly toward rapprochement with China, nor did it believe China was capable of such a rapid turnaround in its foreign policy toward the US and USSR. Chiang's overconfidence in Nixon reinforced his defiance at the UN: the China seat belonged to the ROC; he would never accept a two-China solution.[113]

Domestic Political Context

In an attempt to avoid the fate of Johnson, Nixon portrayed himself as the peacemaker in a new "era of negotiation."[114] Ending the war in Vietnam was the key issue that would shape Nixon's domestic political wiggle room on China. Vietnamization, the administration's policy for withdrawing US troops and replacing them with troops from South Vietnam, was fully under way by 1970. Troop levels fell from 535,454 in September 1969 to 223,025 in September 1971.[115] Support for Nixon's policies in Vietnam tracked with those numbers, rising from about 45% in March 1969 to over 60% in January 1970 (with some drops in support in September 1969). It thereafter fluctuated due to events (the Cambodian invasion of April 1970, and the South Vietnamese incursion into Laos—Lam Son 719—of February 1971), but ultimately recovered in mid-1972 when approval moved upwards to over 60% and even 70% as US troops had nearly completed their withdrawal.[116]

Polls indicated that even as the American public still saw China as a threat, opinion on China's entry into the UN changed significantly. In 1971, 55% of Americans saw China as a greater threat than Russia. Only 23% had a favorable view of China (compared to 53% holding a favorable view of Taiwan). At the same time, however, 55% of Americans supported establishing normal diplomatic ties with China. Support for China's entry into the UN was divided by age cohorts, revealing a clear difference between older Americans who still saw China in the context of the 1949 Revolution and the Korean War. In 1969, Americans ages 21–30 supported/opposed China's entry into the UN 45/46. In 1970, that grew to 55/35, but dropped to 48/34 in May 1971. Older Americans polled were strongly opposed to China's entry into the UN in 1969 and 1970: 33/56 and 33/51 for 31–50 year olds and 27/56 and 28/54 for those 51+ in age. By May 1971, before Kissinger's trip, however, these opinions had shifted: 31–50 year olds supported China's entry 45/41, and the 51+ age group supported China's entry by 42/36.[117] With the China lobby weakened, public opinion fluctuating, and Nixon's credentials as an anti-Communist inoculating him from critics to his right, the domestic political obstacles to rapprochement were disappearing. The administration was attentive to these issues. It tracked newspaper editorials that had been written about Chinese representation at the UN, finding in March 1970 that over 80% of them supported PRC admission.[118]

Narrative of Decision

Even as the Nixon administration opened secret channels to Beijing and used speeches to explicitly state its willingness to mend relations with the PRC, three debates continued. First, how quickly should the US move in its efforts to engage China? Though the State Department counseled for a slow approach that would be less unsettling to other diplomatic ties than rapid progress might (USSR or Japan), this question was settled by Nixon, who wanted to move as quickly as possible. Second, if the US reached out to China, what were US priorities: the East Asian balance of power, global balancing against the USSR, or moderating Chinese behavior? No clear battle lines existed within the administration on this subject. Third, if the US and China did normalize relations, how should the US finesse the Taiwan issue? The question was fundamental for the US and existential for Taiwan. Would rapprochement with the PRC require abandoning the ROC? Did the US have any options for continuing aspects of its relationship with Taiwan? The highest-profile dilemma and the one requiring immediate attention was US support for the ROC at the UN. Here again, the State Department and the president were at odds. State worried about the way allies might begin to question US commitments if the US abandoned Taiwan at roughly the same moment it withdrew from Vietnam. Nixon and Kissinger's understanding of the situation reflected their realist philosophy. The great power relationships between the US, China, and Russia outweighed the importance of Taiwan and the US-Taiwan relationship.

Given that the UN representation issue was by its nature the responsibility of the State Department, Rogers had been sending memos framing the complexities of the problem from the early days of the administration. In a memo to Nixon of January or February 1969, Rogers outlined State's position: "Our current policy on the Chinese representation question would be seriously undermined if Peking were to respond favorably to an offer to normalize relations or if its rejection of such an offer became common knowledge."[119] Another memo from Rogers to Nixon on June 19, 1970, prepared by Undersecretary of State John Irwin and De Palma, reiterated the same view as in 1969. Operating from the premise that the UNGA would vote to add the PRC and oust the ROC by 1971, State explored seven different options for US policy, most of them based on some variant of a "two China" approach.[120]

Responding to Rogers's June memo, Kissinger wrote to Nixon on July 11. He agreed with the pessimistic analysis on the longevity of current US policy, but argued for continuing current US policy for the fall 1970 UNGA session—reliance on the important question tactic—and hoped to "avoid" any talk of two Chinas unless it looked like the US would lose the important question vote. The US should emphasize its commitment to ROC membership in the UNGA, not a policy of "excluding the Chinese Communists." Nixon approved Kissinger's recommendation and US policy on the issue for 1970 was settled.[121] On November 19, the UNGA sustained the important question resolution by a vote of 66 to 52 to 7. The Albanian resolution to expel the ROC and seat the PRC passed for the first time: 51–49–25, but it was not even close to a two-thirds majority.[122]

That same day Kissinger signed NSSM 107, *Study of Entire UN Membership Question: U.S.-China Policy*. State and NSC staff support for a full interagency study of the issue had begun earlier in the fall. In October Dick Smyser, NSC staffer for Asia, had suggested to Winston Lord, also an expert on China and Asia, but serving as a general NSC staff assistant to Kissinger, that the US move to a two-China policy, where both the PRC and the ROC would be members of the UN, but the PRC would inherit the UN Security Council seat. In an October 27, 1970 memo Lord suggested that Kissinger launch an NSSM on Chinese representation, but keep the idea quiet until after the UNGA vote. Kissinger accepted both recommendations. Kissinger and Lord also began a parallel NSC staff study on the same subject, led by Marshall Wright, John Holdridge, and Helmut Sonnenfeldt.[123]

The secret diplomacy was accelerating during this period, having recovered from the interruption of Cambodia. It was, however, not truly that secret. For example, on October 26, 1970, Nixon met with Romanian leader Nicolae Ceausescu at the White House, remarking during his dinner toast that Ceausescu was "one of the few world leaders" with ties to the US, USSR, and PRC. He noted how "extremely valuable" it was for the US and Romanian presidents to speak to one another. The implication was clear; Ceausescu was in a unique position to be a conduit from Nixon to both nations. Nixon's toast was the first time a US president had publicly referred to China as the "People's Republic of China," another olive branch across the Pacific.[124] In this sense, the existence of diplomatic activity between the US and China could be inferred by anyone with a half-decent imagination who had been paying attention. The rapid success of these communications was the real secret.

State initiated a large study on the issue just as the UNGA prepared to vote. On November 17, 1970, Deputy Assistant Secretary of State Winthrop Brown sent a memo to Rogers calling for an internal State review of the Chinese representation question. Rogers approved the idea, informing the likely participants—the East Asian, International Organization, and Politico-Military Bureaus and the Policy Planning Staff. He also told the president on November 18.[125]

The next day, Kissinger signed NSSM 107, establishing the large interagency study suggested by Lord in October. Current policy was likely to fail in 1971; Nixon needed options. The study called for an examination of new approaches and their implications for US diplomacy around the world. Universality, a concept that might allow for UN membership by both Taiwan and China, North and South Korea, and East and West Germany, was of particular interest. The study was due to the SRG by January 15, 1971.[126] The NSSM preempted the internal State study; whether it was a way to prevent State from controlling the issue through its own intradepartmental work, or simply Kissinger waiting until after the UN vote to begin the study, is not clear. Participation included State, the CIA, and NSC staff; leadership of the study, however, was given to State's De Palma, an assignment that should be seen as faithful to the by-the-book interagency process. As head of State's International Organization Affairs

Bureau, he would be the official to directly manage implementation of the policy. De Palma's group was a new ad hoc IG, but that was not a deviation from the standard interagency procedures of NSDM 2. It reflected the complexities of a cross-cutting issue that had implications for a number of UN-related topics—Soviet actions at the UN, as well as membership for North and South Korea and East and West Germany. The NSC IGs were regionally based with one exception, the Political Military IG, and Chinese representation did not fit there. The solution was a new IG led by the State official with the most direct responsibility.

On the same day, Kissinger signed NSSM 106, *China Policy*. Essentially an updating of NSSM 14, it was assigned to the EAIG, chaired by State, and scheduled for submission to the SRG on February 15, 1971. NSSM 106 called for an examination of China policy from the ground up: long-range (5–10 years) and short-range goals, policy toward Taiwan, coordination with allies, and the impact of China policy on US-Soviet relations and US "interests in Southeast Asia."[127]

A few days later, on November 22, Nixon sent Kissinger a memo asking for an NSC staff analysis of Chinese representation "on a very confidential basis . . . without any notice to people who might leak." Kissinger wrote back on November 27 that he had already begun the study (based on Lord's recommendation). Lord had tasked Wright, Holdridge, Sonnenfeldt, and Richard Kennedy on November 10.[128]

At this point, the standard formal interagency process operated as envisioned by NSDMs 1 and 2. A parallel channel controlled by the NSC staff and White House gave Nixon an alternate source of advice, and, of course, the secret diplomacy gave him explicit direction over its implementation.

One crucial point is important to note. Though Nixon sought a measure of centralized management, Kissinger tried to be faithful to the formal interagency process. An early draft of NSSM 106, not numbered and referred to as an NSDM, was entitled *Establishment of China Policy Group*. The new committee was to be chaired by the undersecretary of state and have full interagency participation. The original idea came in an October 8 letter from Richard Moorsteen, a former member of Nixon's NSC staff who had moved on to the RAND Corporation; Moorsteen's letter suggested that Kissinger chair the new group. Kissinger initially liked the idea and directed Lord to ask Holdridge and Kennedy to write an NSDM creating the group; Lord spelled out the parameters of the NSDM in memos of October 30 and November 10.[129] Though the draft NSDM still had a State Department official as chair, it pulled the Chinese representation issue out of the hands of the EAIG. Kissinger, however, had a change of heart. In his own handwriting, Kissinger redrafted the NSDM into NSSM 106, giving responsibility for the study back to the EAIG, and eliminating the China Policy Group.[130] Here Kissinger was faithful to the original interagency design. The EAIG had undertaken NSSM 14; it should maintain that leadership in the follow-on study.

While the gears of the interagency machinery turned around these issues, a diplomatic breakthrough occurred through the Pakistan channel. On December 9, 1970, Pakistani ambassador to the US Agha Hilaly came to the White House to read Kissinger a handwritten note from Zhou Enlai. In the note Zhou called for US-Chinese talks on US "vacation of Chinese territories called Taiwan," and invited "a special envoy of President Nixon's" to China.[131] To a certain extent, it changed the context and stakes associated with the NSSMs, though few of the interagency participants knew it. The existence of the letter from Zhou and the drafting of the US response were kept secret. Only Nixon, Kissinger, and at least Haig and Lord of the NSC staff knew about them.[132] Kissinger drafted a response based on conversations with Nixon, and a letter for Zhou was given to Hilaly on December 16. In accepting the invitation, the letter made it clear that the US wished to discuss ways to "improve relations and reduce tensions." Importantly, the letter also stated clearly that "with respect to the US military presence on Taiwan . . . the policy of the United States Government is to reduce its military presence in the region of East Asia and the Pacific as tensions in this region diminish."[133]

Initial drafts of NSSM 107 were completed on January 25, 1971 and submitted to SRG members for review along with a draft of a State-written issues paper on the subject. The documentary record of the NSSM 107 drafting is spotty; it is unclear exactly which officials participated in the drafting process and when meetings were held. Records indicate that the ad hoc IG included the full range of participation of any IG: State, Defense, the JCS, the CIA, and NSC staff. The draft response to NSSM 107 was sent to SRG members, including Undersecretary of State Irwin, Deputy Secretary of Defense David Packard, JCS chair Admiral Thomas Moorer, DCI Richard Helms, and the deputy secretaries of both Treasury and Commerce. The director of the Office of Emergency Preparedness, the Department of Justice, and the Vice President's office received revised versions dated in mid-March.[134] The State issues paper, which was still being revised into the first week of February, was a joint product of several bureaus—International Organization, East Asia and Pacific (including its sections on the ROC, Asian Communist Affairs, and Regional Affairs), and

European Affairs—as well as the office of the counselor of the department and the Planning and Coordination staff.[135]

The NSSM 107 paper was finally submitted to Kissinger on February 6 and sent to the rest of the SRG members on February 9. An SRG meeting to discuss the NSSM was tentatively scheduled for February 26.[136]

The study response to NSSM 107 fit the standard pattern: it examined options but did not provide recommendations. In that sense, it served as a bottom-up review on the issue of Chinese representation that framed the administration's thinking, and provided Nixon with the necessary information and analysis he could use to make a decision. It was 41 pages long and contained seven annexes on topics ranging from dual representation at the UN, legal considerations, and related UN-membership problems such as Germany and Korea, to the ROC's opposition to dual representation. The advantages and disadvantages of four options were considered. First, the then-current policy of relying on the important issue threshold of a two-thirds vote at the UN might be continued. Of course, the premise of the study was that it would fail in 1971. Second, the US could support some type of universality-based option. Universality had been a foundational concept for US policy makers at the inception of the UN. Any nation-state that was recognized by other nation-states should be admitted as a member of the UN, regardless of international political dynamics. With a universality-based policy, both China and Taiwan qualified for admission to the UN. The proposal, however, would likely be rejected by both Beijing and Taipei. Third, the US could turn to a number of dual representation strategies, variations on "Two Chinas," "One China—One Taiwan," "One China—Two States," "One China—Two Delegations," and "Two Delegations." Again, all the potential benefits were outweighed by the probability that both the PRC and ROC would reject them out of hand. A fourth strategy—a mixture of the dual representation and universality approaches—was mentioned but not fully examined.[137]

Annex G, "ROC Opposition to Dual Representation," highlighted the core of the US dilemma:

> The ROC has given no sign of flexibility or willingness to consider seriously new approaches. . . . President Chiang ruled out any compromise of the ROC's basic policy of insisting that it is the only legitimate representative of China in the UN. . . . it is the estimate of our China experts that it will be virtually impossible to persuade Chiang to remain in the UN if a dual representation is passed.[138]

The overall conclusion was not optimistic: current policy was going to fail, and any change in policy would lead to the ROC either being expelled from the UN or withdrawing in protest. None of the options examined in the NSSM 107 paper resolved that fundamental quandary.

Perhaps the most important section of the NSSM 107 response was a brief section on US interests toward the PRC and ROC. While these objectives included more traditional policy goals of deterrence and conflict avoidance, the first objective was "normalize US political and economic relations with the PRC and achieve a relaxation of tensions."[139]

These ideas fit with the NSSM 106 study of *US China Policy*, dated February 16, 1971. The two studies were obviously related—tasked on the same day, written by IGs with significant overlap, due at roughly the same time, and to be delivered to the same committee, the SRG.[140] As a follow-up to NSSM 14, NSSM 106—56 pages with a single nine-page annex—illustrated how far the administration had come since August 1969. The options generated and analyzed were not about whether the US should engage China, as was the case in NSSM 14. The issue here was how to move forward with the new policy:

> The question arises as to how in the seventies we can best cope with the PRC's new-found dynamism in the international arena. Return to a strategy of attempted isolation does not seem to be appropriate, or perhaps even feasible. . . . Accordingly, it is not treated as a policy alternative in this paper. It is assumed that the US strategy of the past few years toward a reduction of the PRC's isolation and points of conflict will be followed and refined.[141]

In 1969, the notion of ending isolation and reducing points of conflict was one of the alternative strategies; in 1971, it was the baseline policy.

At roughly the same time, the USC completed its study of expanding trade and travel with the PRC, an extension of Richardson's work with the USC from NSDM 17 in June 1969. Irwin's USC, augmented with officials from the departments of Agriculture, Commerce, Justice, and Treasury, delivered its report to Nixon on February 23, in time to be part of the discussion at the next meeting of the SRG. The seven-page list of recommendations for Nixon, with spaces for Nixon to check "Approve" or "Disapprove," was accompanied by the USC's own study U/SM 91, "Travel and Trade with Communist China," a 35-page (with a two-page annex) analysis of all the travel and trade restrictions on China that the US might tinker with to bring the two nations closer.[142]

An SRG meeting on Chinese representation was scheduled for March 9, 1971, postponed from February 26. Six days before the meeting, on March 3, NSC staffer Marshall Wright submitted a seven-page memo to Kissinger on Chinese representation. It is unclear if this was the product of the NSC staff's in-house study; however, no other NSC staff document on the issue during this time period is available in the archival record. Since Wright had been one of the staffers assigned to the in-house study, it is safe to assume that the memo reflected the thinking of the staff at the time. Wright's memo outlined the basic dilemma: the inevitable failure of current policy and ROC rejection of any new policy. Wright supported a dual representation formula that would include universality; he wrote talking points for Kissinger's attendance at the upcoming SRG meeting based on that analysis.[143]

The SRG met on March 9 to discuss Chinese representation in preparation for a possible NSC meeting. The meeting, chaired by Kissinger, included six participants from State (including Irwin, Undersecretary U. Alexis Johnson, Green, and a participant from the Arms Control and Disarmament Agency), three from Defense, three from the JCS, two from the CIA (including Helms), four from the NSC staff (including Wright and Holdridge), and one each from USIA and Treasury. By the numbers, State and Defense both had six officials in attendance. SRG members reached no specific conclusion on policy, but Kissinger gently nudged the conversation in a desired direction. Most debates on the topic began with the expected demise of current policy. Kissinger added a second premise: every policy change led to membership for the PRC. He also hinted at a bottom line: "My judgment is that the President would react very badly if the end result of this exercise is the passage of the Albanian Resolution, the seating of Communist China, and the expulsion of Taiwan." In other words, the SRG needed to come up with a plausible blueprint for keeping the ROC in the UN, whether this was universality or dual representation or some combination of the two. The consensus of the meeting placed the issue into the hands of State. The SRG recommended that Nixon "should be asked to authorize the Department of State to consult with allied and friendly countries on alternatives to the Important Question-Albanian Resolution formula." State was specifically asked to study dual representation or a mix of dual representation and universality.

In an unusual twist for the administration, the SRG minutes specified that the SRG should make recommendations to the president. Typically, Nixon wanted options; here the SRG was stating its intention to give the president its consensus on where to go. In addition, Rogers was given the authority to decide if an NSC meeting on the subject should be held. Kissinger even said at the meeting: "My view is that whenever a cabinet member wants an NSC meeting, we arrange one if the President's schedule permits."[144] In effect, the SRG was delegating much of the advisory process to the State Department. Given the speed of the secret diplomacy with China, Kissinger knew that a decision was even more time-urgent than generally understood.

The SRG met again on March 12, this time regarding NSSM 106; Kissinger began the meeting by announcing that Rogers had requested an NSC meeting on NSSM 107 and that Kissinger had scheduled it for March 25.[145] Between the SRG and NSC meetings, Kissinger wrote Nixon a seven and a half-page, single-spaced memo on the issue. Moving toward his role as advocate, Kissinger gave Nixon his views. The 1971 UNGA vote would likely lead to Taiwan's expulsion and significant loss of "prestige" for the US abroad. The administration's domestic reputation for deft leadership would also suffer. The goal should be a strategy that led to both the ROC and PRC having UN membership. A dual representation policy that delinked "conflicting claims of sovereignty by Taipei and Peking" might work. In short, they could both be UN members even as they wrestled with their existential disagreements and their definitions of sovereignty. Kissinger suggested a new strategy for the fall: making the expulsion of the ROC an important question, but allowing the admission of the PRC under a dual representation formula as simply a regular question. This approach granted the PRC membership in the UN and at least delayed the day when the ROC lost its UN seat. Kissinger passed on State's request for permission to consult allies, but he hoped that this request would be delayed until the administration worked out a very specific guidance for those consultations, something that State felt was not necessary. He worried that State's priority was to use the representation issue to improve US-PRC relations, while he hoped to design a policy to soften the blow to the ROC.[146]

Nixon opened the March 25 NSC meeting on NSSM 107 with his sense that the US should have the votes to keep current policy on track until 1972. He turned the meeting over to Kissinger, who quickly summarized the problem: if the US chose to introduce a dual representation resolution, it had to give up on the important question resolution; a dual representation resolution would be passed by simple majority. It could fail, however, and leave the Albanian resolution (PRC in; ROC out) as the alternative, a resolution that had won a majority in 1970. He introduced his idea: the US would "modify the Important Question by making it only apply to the expulsion of Taiwan." He also highlighted the dilemma the administration faced over US military commitments to Taiwan. If the US accepted PRC membership in the UN as part of rapprochement, the ROC would ask for reassurances about those military commitments as compensation. US-PRC relations, however, might become contingent on reductions in those very same commitments to Taiwan. Rogers explained his sense that if the US bypassed the important question resolution, a dual representation resolution would pass, and the PRC would likely reject it. It could be another two or three years before China might reconsider, accepting dual representation or convincing enough UNGA members to try the Albanian resolution again. Nixon made the case for a strong military package for Taiwan as compensation for any reformulation of US policy. Laird, however, warned that Chiang "may prefer to be expelled rather than to accept a change." The US needed to be ready for that scenario. Nixon reminded the group that polls showed Americans opposing China's membership in the UN by a 3–2 margin. He worried about the public fallout, but was certain that China would not accept a UN resolution that hinted at dual representation. That left the issue centered on how to keep Taiwan in, rather than how to keep China out. Both Agnew and Connally held a completely different perspective from the rest of the group. They argued that the US could stick to its guns on Taiwan, stay with the important question, and if Taiwan were expelled from the UN and China were admitted, the US should be happy to accept the outcome. The administration would have shown its commitment to its Asian allies; those nations who voted for the changes would be seen as unreliable; the US public would admire the administration's grit and principled stand; and as long as the US stood behind Taiwan with a firm military commitment, why did Chiang need the UN? Nixon closed the meeting by saying: "We need to talk about this some more. I will look it over again over the weekend." Minutes of the NSC meeting reveal nothing about Kissinger's own preferences.[147]

Following the meeting, Nixon told Kissinger that he was inclined to agree with Agnew and Connally. Nixon's sense at the time was that the best policy was to delay a decision on the issue until the diplomacy through the Pakistani channel took on a more distinct direction. Kissinger felt that making a principled stand, sticking with current policy, even if it were defeated, would benefit the US in the long run. They both felt that for the time being, they were, in Kissinger's words, "reluctant to go to the mat with Rogers on this issue."[148] Rogers and State would be given the lead on the UN issue in the interagency process, while Nixon and Kissinger controlled the back channels that led to rapprochement with China.

On April 9, Kissinger sent a memo to Nixon that recommended specific courses of action on the Chinese representation issue. The memo was based on a draft written by Wright on April 1. In contrast to his behavior at the NSC meeting, Kissinger gave his frank views to Nixon in the memo. He felt a change was "worth considering if—but only if—it has a real chance of preventing Taiwan's expulsion for the foreseeable future—not just for a year or two." He suggested a strategy of universality linked to dual representation, and a modified important question that only covered the expulsion of Taiwan. China could be admitted by a simple majority, but Taiwan could only be expelled by a two-thirds vote. Convincing Chiang to remain in the UN after such a shift in US policy was be a diplomatic challenge, the key to which would be emphasizing the alternative—PRC entry and ROC expulsion. The final page of the memo had four recommendations and spaces for Nixon to sign his approval or disapproval. First, Kissinger recommended that former diplomat Robert Murphy be appointed Nixon's "personal representative" on the issue. Second, Murphy's goal should be to convince Chiang of the merits of the approach. Third, Nixon should defer his final decision on the issue until after the consultations with Chiang. Fourth, while the decision was on hold, State should be "instructed to avoid any indication of a new US position on the Chirep issue." Nixon approved them all.[149]

The April 9 memo illustrated Nixon's method for maintaining control. He always planned on making decisions himself, based on an assessment of options generated through the interagency process. He never intended to delegate to the State Department. To that extent, Rogers actually had more autonomy than could be expected, given Nixon's distaste for State. Once again, as the advisor Nixon trusted most, Kissinger's role in the confidence structure gave him unchallenged prominence and ability to influence Nixon's thinking. This was only true because Nixon wanted it that way.

Putting the decision on hold pending talks with Chiang paid off for Nixon and Kissinger in April. The US table tennis team, playing at the time in Japan, had been asking its Chinese counterparts about a possible visit to China. On April 6, Mao decided to invite the team to Beijing for an exhibition. Once conveyed to team members, then to the US Embassy in Japan, Rogers took the news to Nixon, who immediately agreed. The 15 members of the team's delegation visited China from April 10 through 17 and even met with Zhou Enlai on April 14.[150] The signal foreshadowed China's next, even more important, move. The administration quickly reciprocated. The USC had delivered its list of recommendations for lifting trade and travel restrictions, along with U/SM 91, "Travel and Trade with Communist China," on February 23. Nixon approved them on April 12, and Kissinger issued NSDM 105, *Steps Towards Augmentation of Travel and Trade Between the People's Republic of China and the United States*, on April 13. The NSDM accepted the USC's recommendations for ending a host of restrictions on interactions with China, including relaxation of currency controls, permission to for US ships to "carry Chinese cargoes between non-Chinese ports, and for US-owned foreign flag vessels to call at Chinese ports," and easing restrictions on direct trade for specific items pending further USC study.[151]

Just a few weeks later, the back-channel diplomacy reached a breakthrough. On January 5, 1971, the Chinese received the US message of December 16. The Chinese sent their reply on April 23 and Ambassador Hilaly of Pakistan delivered it to Kissinger on April 27. The message from Zhou stated:

> If the relations between China and the USA are to be restored fundamentally, the US must withdraw all its Armed forces from China's Taiwan and Taiwan Straits area. A solution to this crucial question can be found only through direct discussions between high level responsible persons of the two countries. Therefore, the Chinese Government reaffirms its willingness to receive publicly in Peking a special envoy of the President of the U.S. (for instance, Mr. Kissinger) or the U.S. Secretary of State or even the President of the U.S. himself for direct meeting and discussions.[152]

The communication included good news (an invitation) and bad news (the prominence of the Taiwan issue), but these contradictions were likely the product of factional battles within the Chinese leadership. Lin Biao's military faction still held some influence and likely demanded a strong statement regarding US military forces in Taiwan as a concession for the invitation of an American envoy. In light of the Chinese representation decision, one key fact was crucial: none of Zhou's messages mentioned the UN. The US could infer that it was not a priority and not an obstacle to direct talks. The representation issue and the secret diplomacy remained on separate tracks, just as long as US policy on the former did not derail the latter. To maintain that secrecy, the deliberations and even knowledge of the existence of US-China direct diplomacy were limited to Nixon, Kissinger, and select members of the NSC staff.

After Hilaly left the White House, Kissinger met with Nixon to give him the news. Nixon called Kissinger roughly an hour later to discuss who might be sent to China as the special envoy. The two considered the pros and cons of several candidates: David Bruce, then serving as the US chief delegate to the Paris Peace Talks; Nelson Rockefeller (as long as he was accompanied by chaperones, possibly Haig and Green from State); or Richardson (a possibility dismissed quickly because of the "Rogers problem"). Rogers himself, the secretary of state, was never considered as an envoy during the phone call. Kissinger explained in his memoirs that this was impossible "given Nixon's determination that he, not the State Department, should be seen—justly—as the originator of China policy."[153]

The next morning Nixon met with Kissinger and Haldeman in the Oval Office. While discussing who should go to China, Nixon ruled out himself, Rogers, and Kissinger, the latter "because that would break all the china with State." Again, the choice revolved around Bruce or Rockefeller. Nixon wrote in his memoirs that he considered Henry Cabot Lodge and even suggested Rogers:

> "What about Bill then," I asked. "If we send the Secretary of State, they'll sure as hell know we're serious." Kissinger rolled his eyes upward. I knew he would have opposed Rogers on personal grounds, but in this case he had good policy reasons. The Secretary of State had too high a profile for those first talks. Besides there was almost no way he could go to China secretly.[154]

According to Haldeman, the three met again later in the day, during which Kissinger made the case for himself as the envoy. Nixon agreed with his argument, deciding that, in Kissinger's words, "Nixon's overriding motive was undoubtedly that I understood our policy best, and that being familiar with my complicated chief I would be able to arrange the sort of Peking visit for him with which Nixon would be most comfortable."[155] Kissinger met with Hilaly hours later on April 28, instructing him to tell Chinese officials that the US would give China a formal reply in early May. On May 9, the US sent a message to Zhou through Pakistan that accepted the invitation for Nixon to visit China and proposed a secret trip by Kissinger to prepare for the Nixon visit, sometime after June 15. Both Haig and NSC staff China expert Winston Lord helped draft the reply. China received the message on May 17, and Hilaly brought Kissinger Zhou's reply on June 2; Zhou approved of the preparatory trip and called for an envoy to visit China between June 15 and 20. Kissinger and Lord responded on June 4, suggesting bumping the travel date to mid-July. Zhou agreed in a message received by the US on June 11.[156] Kissinger's secret trip was given the green light. The only question was whether routine decision making in Washington and noise from the US government might derail the plans, a problem Nixon and Kissinger had already faced.

Complications arose almost immediately after Zhou's April 27 message inviting an envoy or Nixon to China. Having no knowledge of the secret diplomacy, while at a London meeting of the Southeast Asia Treaty Organization on April 29, Rogers discussed journalist and Mao-confidant Edgar Snow's assertion in the April 20 issue of *Life* magazine that Mao would welcome a visit to China by Nixon, saying "he did not see it as serious invitation." Rogers also criticized China as "expansionist," a nation whose policies had a "disruptive role" in Southeast Asia, and remarked that US-PRC rapprochement could only happen after China began to follow the "rules of international law." Nixon and Kissinger worried that China might see Rogers's comments as the US response to Zhou's letter.[157] During a press conference on the same day, Nixon reiterated his goals for China policy:

> The long-range goal of this Administration is a normalization of our relationships with Mainland China, the People's Republic of China. . . . But now when we move from the field of travel and trade to the field of recognition of the Government, to its admission to the United Nations, I am not going to discuss those matters, because it is premature to speculate about that. . . . When I have an announcement to make, when a decision is made—and I have not made it yet—I will make it. . . . I would finally suggest that—I know this question may come up if I don't answer it now—I hope, and, as a matter of fact, I expect to visit Mainland China sometime in some capacity—I don't know what capacity.[158]

Nixon and Kissinger hoped that a personal statement from the president compensated for any damage done by Rogers.

This delicate diplomacy was complicated further by Ambassador Murphy's meeting with Chiang Kai-shek in Taipei on April 27. Chiang preferred sticking with the important question for as long as possible, but in the event that a new strategy was absolutely essential, he insisted that the ROC must retain its UNSC seat. If changes in US policy led to the PRC gaining both the UNGA and UNSC, the ROC would likely leave the UN, and "the world would know that she has been forced out not by the Communists, but by the United States."[159] NSC staff members Richard Kennedy and Melvin Levine drafted a memo for Kissinger to give to Nixon on May 19 that spelled out the dilemma and the results of the Murphy-Chiang meeting. Kissinger approved the memo and sent it to Nixon on May 26. Both the NSC staff and State believed there was little chance that the ROC could keep the UNSC seat if dual representation were passed in the UNGA; the PRC would almost assuredly be handed the UNSC seat. US ambassador to the UN George H. W. Bush had assured Kissinger that this was a "basic fact" in a memo of April 17. Fighting the hopeless fight seemed to be the only policy that might satisfy Chiang. Importantly, sticking with the old policy did not seem to create problems for US rapprochement with Beijing. Chinese leaders expected the US to stand by the ROC and were willing to continue their outreach to the US. Kissinger recommended that Nixon approve another Murphy mission to Taipei. This time, Murphy was to tell Chiang that "there is no way we can guarantee his Security Council seat." If he insisted on the UNSC seat as a bottom line that, if crossed, would lead him to withdraw from the UN, the US was prepared to stay with current policy and accept defeat.[160]

Nixon did not accept Kissinger's May 26 memo as the last word. He used that memo as background for a May 27 meeting between Nixon, Rogers, and Kissinger. The meeting was likely originally scheduled in preparation for Rogers' trip to Europe to discuss the Mutual and Balanced Forced Reductions negotiations on conventional weapons deployments, but the Chinese representation issue was added to the agenda. Kissinger was still the dominant voice whispering in the president's ear; he wrote Nixon's talking points for a meeting in which he participated, but Nixon still wanted Rogers' input. State would be implementing the policy, and that fact kept Rogers in the room at the crucial moment. Kissinger's talking points summarized his earlier memo, but gave a bit more detail on US options. The talking points recommended that Nixon get Rogers's views before he made any decision.[161]

A transcript of the May 27 meeting is fascinating in what it reveals about each participant's view. Nixon worried about the domestic political implications of any leaks, suggesting the administration was considering a two-China policy such as dual representation. He hoped to consult with "the China lobby, which is still a considerable group," to soften their criticism of any change: "I don't want them to descend on me like a pack of little jackals." Nixon was fatalistic about the policy itself, willing to accept the loss at the UNGA, a tactical maneuver that would show support for the ROC, and remove it as an obstacle to US-PRC rapprochement in one roll of the dice: "The two-China thing. It's probably what we're going to end up with. . . . I am greatly tempted to stand on principle and get rolled and get them out. I am concerned about one thing: we've got to think very selfishly." Rogers worried about the delay in coming up with a position. The world was waiting for the US to decide how to deal with the probability that the important question vote would fail in 1971. Further hesitation raised the pressure on other nations to make their own policies without knowing where the US was headed. Rogers questioned the wisdom of waiting another six weeks to two months for a decision. He also felt that sticking with current policy and losing might be just as bad for Nixon: "I think your conservative friends will think that it's a terrible defeat and you followed a policy that's doomed to failure." Kissinger barely participated until Rogers left the meeting after roughly 90 minutes. He then raised the issue of tweaking the important question tactic by allowing the PRC admission to pass on majority vote, but keeping the Taiwan expulsion as an important question requiring a two-thirds vote. He and Nixon also discussed another key reason for allowing a delay: waiting to see how the Chinese would respond to the latest secret communication about a presidential visit. Kissinger did state that the tactical issues here were not "worth overruling the Secretary of State."[162] Rogers was eventually going to be given permission to float a dual representation formula.

Though the transcript does not indicate any specific decision, immediately after the meeting State began consulting with the ROC and other US allies about their views of Chinese representation and whether current US policy had a chance to succeed beyond the 1971 UNGA session. Essentially, the administration was gathering intelligence and sounding out the allies. At a June 1 news conference, Nixon made the process public:

> We are now analyzing that situation in consultations with the Republic of China on Taiwan and with third countries. After we have completed our analysis, which I would imagine would take approximately 6 weeks, we will then decide what position we, the Government of the United States, should take at the next session of the United Nations this fall.[163]

Nixon held faithful to this estimate. He did not meet with Rogers and Kissinger on the subject again until July 22.

During June, the Senate Foreign Relations Committee had the first session of its hearings on *US Relations with the People's Republic of China*. The hearing considered four resolutions that called for seating the PRC at the UN, introduced by Senators Jacob Javits (R-NY), George McGovern (D-SD), Edward Kennedy (D-MA), and Mike Gravel (D-AK). Two of the four called for dual representation, while the other two made no mention of the ROC's status at the UN. All called for better relations with the PRC, one even for normalization.[164] As an indication of public support for PRC entry into the UN, the hearings might have been helpful; as a congressional attempt to dictate policy, Nixon saw them as most unwelcome.

Of course, part of the delay in the UN decision was due to the fact that Kissinger would be traveling to Beijing in mid-July, information that was deliberately being kept secret from nearly everyone involved in thinking about strategy for the UN session. In this sense, the formal decision process continued to operate without knowledge of the most important aspect of US policy toward China and Taiwan. Again, this is not an example of Nixon ignoring the interagency system, but instead a reflection of the need to keep leaks from spoiling a diplomatic initiative; Nixon and Kissinger believed that public knowledge of the trip gave potential opponents, such as the Soviet Union or allies of the ROC in the US, the opportunity to sabotage it. It was also an attempt to make sure that one of the most important postwar geopolitical events was firmly credited to Nixon and not to Rogers or State. The latter had been kept out of the loop on the secret diplomacy from the beginning.

The dates for Kissinger's July trip were set by June 11, but Rogers was not told by Nixon that Kissinger was traveling to China until July 8, one day before Kissinger would take a detour from a visit to Pakistan and head to Beijing.[165] Kissinger had been scheduled for a well-publicized visit to Asia lasting from July 1 through 13, visiting Saigon, Bangkok, New Delhi, and Islamabad. Once in Pakistan, he used the excuse of stomach troubles to hide for a few days, supposedly at the Pakistani president's guest house in the mountains. In reality, he embarked from Islamabad for Beijing on July 9 for roughly 48 hours, returning to Pakistan on July 11, then heading back to the US. Only a small number of people accompanied Kissinger: NSC staffers Lord, Holdridge, and W. Richard Smyser, and two Secret Service agents, Jack Ready and Gary McCleod. Another set of people knew about the trip but did not go: NSC staffers Haig, Hal Saunders, and David Halperin; DCI Helms; CIA Deputy Director for Plans and Operations Thomas Karamessines; NSC staff administrative assistants Diane Matthews and Florence Gwyer; and three other Secret Service agents.[166] The number of people in the administration who knew about Kissinger's trip can be estimated at 19, but that is likely an inaccurate number. Some of this information, of course, still remains classified, but it would be a safe assumption that members of the intelligence community, military officers who were responsible for logistics, and White House staffers who worked directly for Nixon or Haldeman also knew. What is instructive here was that only one official from the State Department had knowledge of the secret diplomacy for the trip—US ambassador to Pakistan Joseph Farland. He had been brought into the discussion on May 3, even before a concrete date had been set. It would be his job to make arrangements with the Pakistani government.[167]

Following Kissinger's return to the US, Nixon gave a prime-time speech on July 15 from the NBC affiliate in Burbank, California revealing Kissinger's secret trip and announcing that he himself would visit China in 1972. The entire framework of US relations with Asian nations and the USSR had been changed. Of lesser global but more immediate importance, the issue of Chinese representation was thrown into a new context. While in China, Zhou told Kissinger that China absolutely rejected dual representation, but Kissinger got the sense that the UN seat was a much lesser priority than US-China rapprochement. US policy at the UN would not jeopardize Nixon's trip. If the US proposed dual representation and the Chinese rejected it, the US might appear to the world as the reasonable nation and China the belligerent who refused to compromise. China seemed willing to stand on principle at the UN but still seek out a new relationship with the US. Kissinger was also informed by the NSC staff on July 12 that the ROC would approve of a dual representation resolution that reserved the UNSC seat for the ROC in tandem with another resolution keeping expulsion of the ROC as an important question.[168]

At a July 22 meeting, Nixon, Rogers, and Kissinger met alone on the issue for the second time that year and for the first time since the announcement. Rogers and Kissinger worried that if the US continued to oppose China's entry in the UN, it made "us look like a bunch of hypocrites," in Rogers's words, or "tricky" in Kissinger's words. Both argued for supporting PRC admission but finding a way to defend ROC membership as well, in short, a dual representation resolution. Nixon agreed with their joint assessment. Nixon and Kissinger hoped to convince both the ROC and the PRC that the US was on their side. Nixon stated that "what we really need here, Bill, is to have George [Bush] or whatever, not to make a great big damn legal case for it, just say the nation shouldn't be expelled, and we're going to fight for them." Kissinger argued that "I'd like to be in a position where we have made a genuine fight, but at the same time, Peking could figure that anytime they could get two-thirds, they could get rid of Taiwan and that seems to be something they could look forward to in two or three years, maybe even one year."[169] In short, the US would fight the good fight and likely lose in a way that reassured Taipei the US was not abandoning it, while reassuring Beijing that even if the US won in the short term, it always intended on losing in the long term.

Though the record of the meeting does not indicate a specific decision, State began to lay the groundwork for the new dual representation policy: support for PRC admission to the UN, and use of the important question to prevent expulsion of the ROC.[170] It also tried to convince the ROC to accept UNGA membership even if it lost the UNSC seat, a notion the ROC rejected immediately.[171]

On August 2, Rogers met with the press to explain the new policy. He began his statement with the same premise that Nixon had used in his 1967 *Foreign Affairs* article: the world had changed significantly since the end of World War II. The US had been "adapting" to these new realities since Nixon entered office. In the case of China, accepting the reality of a new era meant that "the United States accordingly will support action at the General Assembly this fall calling for seating the People's Republic of China. At the same time the United States will oppose any action to expel the Republic of China or otherwise deprive it of representation in the United Nations." The US hoped to make the expulsion of the ROC an important question. Rogers pointed out that possession of the UNSC seat was up to the UNSC, and the US would accept whatever decision was made there. Though the implication was that the US would not use its veto to prevent the PRC from gaining the UNSC seat, Rogers refused to elaborate on specifics, declining to discuss what he called "tactics."[172]

In response to criticisms by Walter Judd, former House member and then chairman of the Committee of One Million, Nixon went even further than Rogers on the UNSC question. At a press conference on September 16, Nixon stated that the US would not oppose a UN decision to remove Taiwan from the UNSC, replacing it with mainland China. Nixon argued that this was not an issue for the UNSC, but for the UNGA; once the PRC was "admitted to the United Nations, the seat in the Security Council would go to the People's Republic and that, of course, meant the removal of the Republic of China from the Security Council seat."[173]

The logic of this argument might be challenged, but the fact that Nixon was making it illustrated how far the US had come. All the senior decision makers had come to see rapprochement with China as a much greater priority for the US than its traditional commitments to Taiwan. China policy was rooted in fundamental great power relations: from the use of China to balance against Russia, to easing US withdrawal from Vietnam, to the simple realist sense that isolating a powerful nation was geopolitical malpractice. The administration perceived Taipei as an obstacle to major issues, an irritant that the US would manage in the best way that it could. As the Nixon-Rogers-Kissinger meetings suggest, Nixon's primary worry was domestic politics. Since US public opinion had moved toward acceptance of the PRC in the UN and applauded Nixon's trip to China, the decision to risk Taiwan's expulsion was much easier.

The diplomacy at the UN from August through October is beyond the scope of this study. In short, US ambassador to the UN George H.W. Bush tried nearly every trick in the parliamentary handbook to secure a dual representation formula with Beijing controlling the UNSC seat. The UNGA agenda for the fall had a vote on the Albanian resolution coming before a vote on dual representation. If the Albanian proposal passed—expelling the ROC and seating the PRC—the dual representation resolution would be rendered irrelevant. During September, Bush tried to combine the two resolutions into one but lost the vote in the UNGA General Committee (the subcommittee of the UNGA that dealt with agenda items). On October 25, Bush then tried to make the Albanian resolution an important question, arguing that the expulsion of a UN member must be considered important; this idea never came to a vote since the resolution had already been placed on the agenda. The ROC opposed Bush's actions, strongly contending that there could only be one China; the UNGA had to choose one or the other. Later in the October 25 session, the important question resolution failed: 55 for, 59 against, 15 abstentions. Bush tried one more tactic, calling for dividing the Albanian resolution into two votes: one to add the PRC and one to expel the ROC. It failed 51–61–19. Before the UNGA voted on the Albanian resolution, the ROC formally withdrew from the UN, in hope of preserving its dignity by rejecting the UN before the UN could reject it. Later that evening, the Albanian resolution passed 76–35–17.[174]

Nixon did face heavy criticism from the right for not defending Taiwan at the UN. Kissinger described the congressional response as "bitter and surprisingly widespread."[175] Nixon worried most that columnist William Buckley and California governor Ronald Reagan, the intellectual and political standard bearers for the more conservative wing of the Republican Party, might stir up immense protests against the replacement of Taipei with Beijing, blaming Nixon for the loss at the UN. Given the weakness of the China lobby at the time, Buckley and Reagan were the biggest potential headaches. The administration reached out to both men to keep them behind Nixon or at least to mute their arguments for the sake of party unity.[176] In spite of the brief fury from the right, nothing seemed able to derail administration planning for Nixon's trip, or the trajectory of the policy that would take Nixon to Beijing in February 1972. The political ground had shifted, and Nixon was the beneficiary. Gallup polls in March 1972 showed that 68% of Americans thought that Nixon's visit would assist in "improving world peace" (18% very effective; 50% fairly effective). Nixon's public approval jumped from 49% in January to 56% following the February trip. In the coming months, Nixon added the Moscow Summit where the SALT agreements were signed, and neared completion of the withdrawal of US troops from Vietnam. His approval spiked to over 60%.[177] Of course, he won 49 states in November of 1972, securing himself a landslide with 96.7% of the Electoral College, at that time the second largest margin of victory in the 20th century (FDR won in 1936 with 98.5%; in 1984, Reagan passed Nixon, winning with 97.6% of the electoral vote).

Analysis

The case study of Chinese representation reinforces the argument that Nixon did want full interagency participation in decision making unless secrecy was necessary to prevent leaks that might undermine the policy. This case does not confirm the evolution-balance model. The NSSM 107 decision does not deviate from the standard interagency process, and suggestions for changes such as the senior-level China Working Group were considered as part of NSSM 106, not NSSM 107. The Chinese representation issue remained within the standard interagency committees. At key points, however, Nixon met alone with Rogers and Kissinger, in an informal setting (May 27 and July 22). These meetings support the original evolution model; when Nixon felt the need to move the decision along, he met with only a small group.

Interestingly, the Rogers-Kissinger feud was not relevant to China at this point. The system may have worked well because Rogers and Kissinger agreed on a direction—toward engagement with China. State managed the interagency studies, defining the analysis of US strategy, and Richardson's USC had control over the concrete recommendations on how policy could be changed in the short run. More importantly, Nixon and Kissinger could give Rogers power in the standard interagency process because the real action—negotiations with China over an envoy—were secret, and firmly in the hands of Nixon and Kissinger. If Rogers knew about the dialogue with Zhou Enlai through Pakistan, decisions on China might have exhibited the same type of bitterness that developed over the Middle East or the Paris Peace Talks. That kind of intense bureaucratic battle did erupt over the Shanghai Communique, the official joint US-China statement released at the conclusion of the Nixon-Mao Summit in February 1972. After Kissinger's July trip, while the administration publicly basked in its triumphs, Rogers and State were still being excluded from key decisions. Again, secrecy was the reason. The communique had been in the works since Kissinger left for China in July, but serious efforts began on September 1, and included plans for Kissinger-Zhou consultations in Beijing set for October. Importantly, that job was done by the NSC staff alone.[178] Rogers was not even told that Kissinger would go to China in late October until a few days before it was announced to the nation; he tried to stop Kissinger from going, forcing Nixon to spend some time playing referee.[179] During Nixon's trip in February, numerous State Department officials and NSC staffers traveled with Nixon to China. Of course, that included both Rogers and Kissinger. While Rogers was busy with official diplomatic nice-ties, Kissinger negotiated with Qiao Guanhua (Ch'iao Kuan-hua), the dep-uty foreign minister. Over 20 hours of talks, Kissinger and Qiao hammered out the language of the communique; Nixon received what he thought was the final text at 2:00 a.m. on February 25.[180] On February 26, the text of the communique was given to the State Department for approval. This was the first time any State officials saw the draft, a draft already approved by Nixon and submitted to Chinese negotiators. Shortly after receiving the text, the US delegation was informed that the Communist Party Politburo had approved the draft.[181] Both Rogers and Assistant Secretary of State Marshall Green rejected the text and insisted that Kissinger renegotiate aspects of it. Diplomatically, returning to the Chinese after language had been agreed upon was a potential disaster. It was also embarrassing for the nation and for Kissinger personally. Nixon, however, told Kissinger to reopen negotiations, if possible. He worried that State would sabotage the summit by leaking their objections, complaining about their unhappiness with the communique to the press and to the right wing of the Repub-lican Party. He felt he had little choice. State could possibly reenergize the China lobby if it were unhappy. Kissinger returned to Qiao and with some persuading, renegotiated the text to satisfy the State Department; the revised draft was completed on February 27.[182] Nixon met with Rogers on the 27th, a meeting that began with Rogers still complaining about the text but ended after Nixon, in Haldeman's words, "clearly hit Bill hard and said he expected him to instruct his bureaucracy to stay behind us 100 percent and support it fully."[183]

Again, when secrecy was necessary, State was shut out. Nixon had no regrets about it. Only his fear that State might spoil his greatest diplo-matic masterstroke allowed Rogers to have any role in the drafting of the communique.

Troop Levels in Taiwan: NSSM 171 and NSDM 248

One of the implicit agreements between the US and China during the early stages of engagement and the negotiations over the Shanghai Communique was the shared understanding that full normalization would not occur until the US withdrew its military forces from Taiwan. What forces to withdraw and when to remove them was partly decided through NSSM 171, *US Strategy for Asia*, of February 13, 1973, and NSDM 248, *Changes in US Force Levels on Taiwan*, of March 14, 1974. Given Nixon and Kissinger's willingness to use the interagency machinery as the crucible for assessing options, it is no surprise that the process relied on standard interagency channels. A close look at the withdrawal plan, however, reveals that the NSDM 248 troop withdrawals are nearly exactly the same as those settled on in February 1973: ironed out by Kissinger and Richardson, approved by Nixon and then communicated by Kissinger to Zhou Enlai on February 16. In that sense, this case study partially confirms the evolution-balance model. As Kissinger's power increased through 1973, culminating in his dual role, his ability to guide the interagency process grew even more. In addition, the informal Kissinger-Richardson relationship, which existed while Richardson was undersecretary of state (January 1969–June 1970), was renewed when Richardson was appointed secretary of defense in January 1973. It was a factor only in the early parts of this decision, however; Richardson accepted a new appointment as Attorney General in May 1973. Nixon's merger of the formal and confidence structures had successfully smoothed over the rivalries of the first term. The full interagency process was still used to assess options, but after adding the secretary of state position to his responsibilities in September 1973, Kissinger had the bureaucratic muscle to put his thumb on the scale even more than before. This case study is considered only a partial confirmation of the evolution-balance model, however, because Kissinger's new power, though important to the outcome, was not initiated by anything specifically related to the decision on troop levels in Taiwan. The merger of the confidence and formal structures was due to the overall changes in Nixon's decision making as detailed in chapter 7.

Political Context

The political context of this decision was self-made. Nixon's perceived triumphs had reshaped world politics; the early success of détente, no matter its future viability, had changed the nature of the challenges Nixon faced. At home, these achievements and his reelection by historic margins left him seemingly invincible. Of course, Watergate unraveled Nixon's standing in the US. His foreign policy, however, with Kissinger firmly at the helm, proved durable, lasting into the Ford and Carter presidencies.

International Political Context

From 1972 to 1974 the list of administration triumphs is impressive: a summit in Beijing promising a new relationship between the US and the PRC; a summit in Moscow and the signing of the SALT agreements limiting US and Soviet ballistic missile deployments and banning nationwide antiballistic missile systems; an overall shift in the global balance of power through a Triangular Diplomacy that improved the US geopolitical position in fundamental ways; and withdrawal of US forces from Vietnam accompanied by the Paris Peace Accords. Détente had the potential to remake the postwar world, managing great power relations in a way that reduced the risk of serious conflict between the two superpowers. The Sino-Soviet relationship was still tense enough for the US to play one against the other, but it was clearly on more stable ground than in 1969.[184] Overall, the world seemed to be a safer place because of the relationships between Nixon and Brezhnev and Nixon and Mao.

In China, though Zhou had fought off the challenge from the right, the radical faction renewed its attacks on his rapprochement policies. In 1972 and 1973, and escalating after the 10th Party Congress of August 1973, the left moved against Zhou, often using articles in party journals to criticize his policies or to vilify Confucian ideas, which served as a surrogate for attacks on Zhou. The left pushed back against growing US-China ties, but it was not strong enough to force Mao and Zhou away from their own strategy of engagement.[185]

The ROC government could be forgiven if it felt like an endangered species. It had lost its seat at the UN and watched Nixon travel to Beijing. It understood that Nixon or his successors would need to withdraw US troops from Taiwan and end the Mutual Defense Treaty (both realized by Carter in 1978). In 1973, the US began treating Taiwan as less than a nation, even though it still recognized the ROC as the legitimate China. Taiwanese government delegations and diplomats were no longer allowed to meet with their US counterparts when in Washington; their new avenue for communications was the Taiwan desk in the State Department—a bureau within EAP—meaning that even the ROC ambassador would only have a direct line to the US through an official whose boss was an assistant secretary of state. Access to Kissinger also ended.[186] The US compensated with accelerated arms sales to Taiwan in hopes of helping it help itself through the transition in US policy.[187] The sales were also a sign that the China lobby, though weakened, still had some strength. Chiang Kai-shek had suffered a severe heart attack in July 1972 and fell into a coma.

He awakened in January of 1973 and remained somewhat active until he passed away on April 5, 1975. Chiang's son, Chiang Ching-quo, premier since May 1972, had consolidated the succession process during his father's illness.[188] Both men prepared Taiwan for the inevitable by building up Taiwan's economy, an attempt to prepare itself for going it alone if necessary, to build up enough wealth to purchase the armaments it needed to defend itself from China, and to tie itself economically to East Asia, the US, and Europe in hopes that economic ties might prevent abandonment.[189] The remaining question for Taipei and Washington was how quickly the US would withdraw its forces from Taiwan.

Domestic Political Context

The great heights of Nixon's tremendous electoral victory in 1972 were followed by the Watergate scandal. The fall was immense: from a 49-state landslide to resignation in disgrace over roughly 20 months. During much of 1973 and all of 1974, the administration's decision making was severely warped by the increasing legal and political pressures. In an ironic twist, Kissinger's stature in the nation seemed to grow along with the scandal. Haldeman and Ehrlichman resigned on April 30, 1973 when it became clear that both were implicated in Watergate. As a result, Kissinger remained the lone survivor of the inner administrative team around Nixon. When Kissinger officially became secretary of state on September 23, 1973, he stood as a pillar of stability in contrast to most of the rest of Nixon's senior advisors and to a president facing escalating accusations so damning that he felt the need to defend himself by publicly declaring "I am not a crook" (on November 17, 1973, at Disney World no less).

Public support for Nixon's China policy, both the opening and the possible distancing from Taiwan, illustrates mixed success for Nixon's efforts to use the bully pulpit to rally Americans.[190] Nixon's trip to China was tremendous news; in a Gallup poll of March 1972, 98% of those polled had heard about the trip, the highest "awareness score" for any event ever subject to a Gallup poll. The image of China as a rival, however, was tough to erase. A June 1972 poll gave China a 23% favorable rating (71% unfavorable) compared to 40% favorability for the Soviet Union and 53% for Taiwan. By 1973, however, the favorability of China increased to 49% with 43% unfavorable, but reversed again to 20% favorable and 73% unfavorable by 1976. Taiwan's numbers remained roughly the same as in 1972: 55% favorable.[191] An August 1974 Gallup poll suggested that most Americans had not yet accepted the notion of recognizing China and derecognizing Taiwan. Support for such a trade-off was only 11%; opposition was at 72%, with 17% uncertainty. The Mutual Defense Treaty had support from 48% of Americans, opposition from 35%, and again 17% uncertain.[192]

Narrative of Decision

The Shanghai Communique can be seen as the initial baseline for the renewal of US-Chinese relations. Three aspects of the February 27 document are notable. First, engagement was so important for both nations that they agreed to sign a document that outlined agreements and disagreements, rather than allow a lack of consensus on key issues to stop the momentum for rapprochement. This style of communique had been Zhou's idea; Kissinger called the idea "unprecedented," and Lord felt it was "brilliant."[193] Second, the communique took clear aim at the Soviets, stating that "neither should seek hegemony in the Asia–Pacific region and each is opposed to efforts by any other country or group of countries to establish such hegemony." Third, the two nations agreed to disagree on Taiwan, each spelling out its view. For the Chinese, Taiwan was a province, and its "liberation" was "China's internal affair in which no other country has the right to interfere; and all U.S. forces and military installations must be withdrawn from Taiwan." While the US accepted the notion "that all Chinese on either side of the Taiwan Strait maintain there is but one China and that Taiwan is a part of China," it hoped for "a peaceful settlement of the Taiwan question by the Chinese themselves." The US also agreed to what was once considered unthinkable: "the ultimate objective of the withdrawal of all U.S. forces and military installations from Taiwan."[194]

Richard Nixon's second inauguration was on January 20, 1973. One week later, January 27, the Paris Peace Accords were signed, charting a path to end the Vietnam War, and most importantly for the US, a completion of the withdrawal of US combat troops. Implementation of the Accords still required much diplomacy. Leaving for Asia on February 7, Kissinger planned to travel to Bangkok, Vientiane, and Hanoi, finally arriving in Beijing on February 15. In preparation for the trip, Kissinger spoke with Nixon on February 1. They discussed the fact that Kissinger had given Zhou Enlai assurances that the US would remove its troops from Taiwan. Nixon brought up the issue in a way that made it clear there had been little thinking on how to accomplish that withdrawal: "Another point we have to have in mind is what the hell we do on Taiwan? Now, as you know, I think they might call in our chip on that. You think they will?"

Kissinger explained the sequence; forces related to Vietnam would be withdrawn "immediately. And the other ones would be reduced gradually." Kissinger told Nixon he planned to give Zhou a schedule of withdrawal for the Vietnam forces and hoped that Zhou would not press him on the remaining forces. Nixon replied, "So do it." Kissinger explained to Nixon that in his view, "for the time being, what they really want from us is protection against Russia. Taiwan is subsidiary."[195]

Kissinger and Secretary of Defense designate Elliot Richardson had already been working on a timetable for withdrawal of US forces. On February 6, Richardson offered suggestions that Kissinger used in his discussions with Zhou while in China.[196] This Richardson-Kissinger timetable defined the administration's baseline for troop withdrawals from that moment on, a rare prominence for informal decision making, rooted in the Richardson-Kissinger relationship from the first year and half of Nixon's first term.

Nixon and Kissinger decided to fold the issue into the larger strategic picture of how the withdrawal from Vietnam would impact US interests in Asia. NSSM 171, *US Strategy in Asia*, was signed on February 13, 1973. The study memorandum created an ad hoc IG group chaired by a Department of Defense representative and including membership from State, the CIA, and the NSC staff. Its report was due to the Defense Program Review Committee (DPRC) by March 30, 1973. The NSSM asked the IG to focus on the political-military aspects of US policy: "security assistance programs," "conventional force requirements," nuclear weapons issues, and military basing requirements. As always, the study asked for an analysis of options.[197] It specifically directed that the study be a continuation of the work for NSSM 69, *US Nuclear Policy in Asia*, of July 14, 1969 that had reached the SRG on March 12, 1971.[198]

During his trip to China, Kissinger met with Zhou several times from February 15 to 19. On the 16th, Kissinger gave Zhou a specific timeline: withdrawal of five squadrons of F-4s in 1973—roughly half of the 9,000 US troops in Taiwan—and at least two additional F-4 squadrons in 1974, numbers based on Richardson's memo.[199] In a meeting on February 19, Kissinger and Zhou discussed what information each side would make public concerning the dialogue between the two nations. Kissinger stated that "if I am asked about Taiwan, about the forces on Taiwan, I will say we will study this problem in terms of the tensions in the area and when we have anything to do we will say it. We have no immediate decision."[200] In effect, Kissinger honestly stated that the US was involved in an interagency study and had not made up its mind yet. In contrast to the honesty with

Zhou, Kissinger misled James Shen, Taiwan's ambassador to the US, in a meeting on February 21, telling Shen any news reports that the US might reduce its forces on Taiwan were "ridiculous."[201]

Though NSSM 171 directed the IG to have its report ready by March 30, 1973, the DPRC did not meet until July 26, 1973 (the second-to-last DPRC meeting). In his capacity as chair of the committee, Kissinger relayed the interim DPRC decisions in a memo of August 28, 1973. The Defense Department was directed to study "alternative withdrawal objectives and schedules" for troops deployed in Taiwan. The report was due back to the DPRC on September 10.[202] The DPRC, however, held its final meeting on August 17. DPRC members received the report when it was done, but never again met formally.

While the study was being conducted, political dynamics in Washington shifted. Kissinger's prestige grew in expected and unexpected ways. Rogers finally left the administration and Kissinger became both secretary of state and ANSA on September 23. On Tuesday, October 16, Kissinger, not Nixon, was awarded a Nobel Peace Prize for ending the Vietnam War. A few days later, the Watergate scandal intensified and Nixon was under siege politically until he resigned on August 8, 1974. Nixon had tried to fire the Watergate special prosecutor, Archibald Cox, on Saturday, October 20, only to see the top two officials of the Justice Department—Richardson (who had left Defense to become attorney general on May 25, 1973) and William Ruckelshaus—resign rather than carry out the president's directive. The number three official, Solicitor General Robert Bork, finally fired Cox that same night. On Monday, October 22, in response to the "Saturday Night Massacre," the House of Representatives began impeachment proceedings against Nixon. Not only did Kissinger steal Nixon's credit for ending Vietnam, but he now towered above the rest of the administration as the completely innocent one.[203]

Without formal DPRC meetings, the bureaucracies negotiated a decision on a withdrawal schedule in an ad hoc manner. Importantly, State, rather than the NSC staff, took the lead. Arthur Hummel, acting assistant secretary of state for EAP, explained it in a memo to Alfred Jenkins, formerly the NSC staffer for China during the Johnson administration, now a senior official in the US Liaison Office in Beijing: "the center of gravity in US-PRC relations seems to have followed Henry into the State Department." Lord, Kissinger's chief China advisor at the NSC staff, moved with Kissinger to State, becoming director of the Planning and Coordination Staff (soon to be renamed the Policy Panning Office). Hummel felt that as Kissinger's plate was more than full, he and Lord were the point men for China policy. He wrote that Kissinger had mapped out a "scenario for future military withdrawals from Taiwan, which we are slowly and painfully working out with different agencies in Washington."[204]

Deputy Secretary of Defense William Clements, the Defense representative on the DPRC, issued his report to DPRC members in early November, though the exact date is unclear. It analyzed several options for a three-phased withdrawal and made a recommendation on which option it preferred.[205] Hummel replied to the November Clements memo on December 15, 1973, and Clements gave his response to Kissinger on February 20, 1974. On March 11, 1974, Kissinger sent a memo to Nixon detailing the interagency recommendations on Taiwan troop withdrawals. The memo noted that these suggestions were based on work by both State and Defense. The Kissinger memo was drafted by Kennedy, Smyser, and Solomon on March 7. It included a draft NSDM 248, *Changes in US Force Levels on Taiwan*, which specifically referenced the NSSM 171 study as the basis for the NSDM. The US was already nearly finished withdrawing its forces associated with the Vietnam War, cutting US force levels roughly in half as Kissinger had promised Zhou, and leaving a deployment of 4,619 troops on Taiwan as of September 30, 1974. The bulk of the troops, 3,496, accounted for the Air Force deployment.[206] Importantly, the interagency process produced a decision that nearly mirrored what Richardson had suggested and Kissinger had promised Zhou in February 1973. Initially, two additional squadrons of F-4s would have been withdrawn by the end of 1974. State and Defense, however, felt that withdrawal of both squadrons would "create serious problems for . . . Chiang Ching-quo . . . and this could be interpreted in Taipei as forcing on them an agreement made in Peking." State, Defense, and Kissinger found a compromise—delaying the withdrawal of one squadron until the end of May 1975. Nixon initialed in the approval space, and NSDM 248 was signed by Kissinger on March 14. One F-4 squadron was withdrawn by July 31, 1974, while the second squadron left by May 30, 1975. As compensation, the US sold F-5A fighters to Taiwan. Further studies of US staffing levels, communications infrastructure, and intelligence capabilities on Taiwan by Defense and the CIA were directed by the NSDM. Due dates were set for April 15, 1974.[207]

Analysis

The decision regarding withdrawal of US troops from Taiwan illustrates the administration's continued reliance on the interagency system, yet it also shows Kissinger's unchallenged power to move the policy in a desired direction. Through an informal process, he and Richardson set the direction of the debate in February 1973, and Kissinger was able to direct the bureaucratic and international compromises on the issue in March and April 1974. The fact that the DPRC stopped meeting in the summer of 1973 should be seen as a reflection of Kissinger's formal consolidation of authority. The DPRC was originally created to grant Nixon greater clout over defense policy through Kissinger. Making the DPRC, rather than the NSC, the key venue for defense decisions pushed the secretary of defense out of the room and gave Kissinger regularized access to deputy-level defense officials. As secretary of state and ANSA, Kissinger did not need the DPRC to dominate decision making. His stature allowed him unrivaled power, primarily because it was clear Nixon wanted it that way. His status was enhanced as the administration crumbled; Kissinger was perceived as the rock-solid foundation of US foreign policy.

The evolution-balance model helps explain the dynamics of this case study. Kissinger's ability to dominate, even while making sure to keep the interagency machinery functioning, reflects the culmination of Nixon's hopes to restyle his decision structure. Kissinger was given the dual role of ANSA and secretary of state to end the rivalries and leaks caused by formal cabinet decision making and Nixon's unwillingness or inability to resolve bureaucratic conflicts. Kissinger became exactly what Nixon had hoped Kissinger could be: he managed the interagency process, consulted with cabinet officers, and made sure the policy outcomes were those Nixon preferred. The evidence for this is deductive: the outcome of the interagency deliberation in NSDM 248 was nearly the same as the initial ideas decided during the Nixon/Kissinger conversation of February 1, 1973, the Kissinger/Richardson dialogue of February 6, 1973, and as explained to Zhou on February 16, 1973 in Beijing. In this sense, the decision on troop withdrawals from Taiwan is best described as a product of the merging of the formal and confidence structures. As Nixon sank into the quagmire of Watergate, his confidence structure—Kissinger—gained more and more authority, perhaps even actually earning the title "Kissinger's foreign policy."

Conclusions

The case studies of China decision making suggest that Nixon and Kissinger worked hard to keep the formal interagency system running smoothly. Though the NSC itself and most of the new committees faded in use over time, the interagency process continued to function well. The ultimate destination for NSSM 14 was the NSC. NSSM 107, however, moved from the standard interagency hierarchical committees into small informal meetings of Nixon, Rogers, and Kissinger. The existence of an informal structure was a rarity for the administration, which reflected State's important role in diplomacy at the UN. The decision on Taiwan troop withdrawals was made through an interagency process guided in its latter stages by Kissinger's new authority as ANSA and secretary of state.

Several points flow from this analysis. First, the original evolution model is a useful explanatory model for the Chinese representation case. In the end, small group meetings between the principals framed the decision. In the absence of any informal structures, Nixon met with Rogers and Kissinger in a rare moment of civility and common purpose to iron out a compromise as a deadline approached. Second, Rogers's role in China policy is still one that can be debated. His prominence in the Chinese representation decision might be due to the fact that it was the State Department that had implementation responsibility. A more cynical argument is that Rogers and the State Department were given the lead here specifically to make them the fall guys for a policy that was collapsing. Who would take the blame for the US inability to keep Taiwan in and China out? Kissinger traveled to China for a second time on October 20–26, 1971, and the UNGA decision on Chinese representation occurred on October 25. The timing was brutal for the ROC, but also for Rogers. While Kissinger received the glory of another successful diplomatic achievement, State felt the sting of a debacle at the UN.

Third, the final case study illustrates both Kissinger's bureaucratic supremacy and his faithfulness to the interagency system, a mixing of the formal and confidence structures, as was the case with the overall evolution of Nixon's foreign policy decision making. Though his discussions with Richardson gave him a definite idea of how he wanted troop withdrawals to proceed, he still did not make a choice on his own. He pushed the policy into the interagency process, even if this meant a delay. If he wanted to or was able to simply dictate the schedule of withdrawal, why did it take until April of 1974 to draft an NSDM? Clearly, Kissinger still saw the value of the formal interagency mechanisms.

Fourth, an alternative perspective could be that changes to the decision making on China were unnecessary because the overall changes had already solved the decision making problems. NSSM 14 is standard interagency process, and NSSM 107 and NSSM 171 fed into the SRG and DPRC, respectively, the new committees created by the overall evolution. In that sense, the latter two decisions were products of the new system; they benefited from the adjustments already made. These two cases might then confirm the evolution-balance model. To be rigorous methodologically, however, confirmation of the evolution-balance model for these case studies requires identifying changes that are caused by dissatisfaction with the specific decision making processes for China. For that reason, the Chinese representation case is explained better by the original evolution model, and the Taiwan troop withdrawal case could be explained by either model depending on the perspective taken. In the latter case, perhaps it is best to judge it as a partial confirmation of the evolution-balance model.

Fifth, the important role of the interagency system in the China decisions discussed in this chapter seems to run counter to the infamous exclusion of Rogers in the diplomatic maneuvering that led to the breakthroughs in 1971. Again, the difference between analyzing policy options and implementing policy is crucial here. Both Nixon and Kissinger saw the interagency process as the bedrock on which to base their planning. Implementation, however, directly communicating with China, was still a case where secrecy was an absolute necessity. The standard formal system may have actually been doubly important while the two men led a secret diplomatic initiative. Knowing that the bureaucracy was behind the policy, even if only hypothetically, provided them with some psychological bolstering. Making sure that every aspect had been thoroughly examined by all the experts also helped to guarantee that the few officials involved in the secret diplomacy were not missing any important pieces of the puzzle. For implementation, however, the need for secrecy and the importance of preventing leaks meant that in a need-to-know situation, very few people needed to know. Rogers was excluded because Nixon simply did not trust him to execute Nixon's plans faithfully. He also worried that Rogers would steal the credit for the opening, something Kissinger eventually did. Again, this suggests a difference between decision making for general strategic assessments of policy and on-the-fly decision making for tactical implementation. Rogers and the full interagency process were central to the former, but excluded from the latter.

NINE

∽ Conclusions

If Shakespeare had been alive during the latter half of the 20th century, his epic tragedies chronicling the rise and fall of Kings John, Lyndon, and Richard would have brought thrills, tears, and a warning to millions. Camelot's promise ended with an assassin's bullet. The Great Society perished in jungles 10,000 miles away. The champion of the silent majority with a historic electoral victory left office in disgrace, betrayed by his own inner demons. As Nixon speechwriter William Safire said, Nixon "may be the only genuine tragic hero in our history, his ruination caused by the flaws in his own character."[1] One can imagine the final play in the series ending with a lonely and uncertain Gerald Ford sitting in the Oval Office hesitantly rearranging the office supplies on the Wilson Desk.

In terms of drama, these three presidents are amazing case studies for historians, or political scientists, and even fiction writers. The question of whether they mattered as individuals, however, is still one of the central debates in presidential scholarship. Do individuals matter? Or are institutional pressures the defining characteristics in administrative dynamics?

The preceding chapters illustrate how the evolution-balance model can be used to explain the changes made to overall foreign policy decision making during the Kennedy, Johnson, and Nixon administrations, changes designed to compensate for weaknesses in the president's preferred management style. Kennedy and Johnson added or considered adding formality to their informal decision making processes. Nixon added a new layer of committees, rooted in his confidence structure, to manage the unintended consequences of his formal interagency system.

For China decision making, the model has greater explanatory power the longer an administration has been in office; in the timeline of each administration the evolution-balance model is more useful in explaining the later case studies than the earlier ones. This finding makes sense. If we are studying the way decision making evolves over time, the length of time is an important variable. Results that find a relationship between the length of time in office and the probability of changes in decision making structure are instructive: the longer an administration has been in office, the greater the likelihood of modifications to decision making.

The difference between the overall evolution of decision making (where all three presidents considered or actually did move to balance out the weaknesses in their decision processes) and the China case studies seems to be the increased requirement for expertise when it came to making decisions on specific issues. That need for advice from specialists on China led to a greater reliance on the interagency machinery (Johnson and Nixon) or delegation to departmental leadership (Kennedy). Tables 9.1 to 9.3 summarize the findings of the case studies for each presidency; table 9.4 uses these tables to generate a comparison of the overall decision making for each president.

Perhaps most important is the question of why presidents choose to accept or reject new structures suggested by staff (Kennedy, Johnson), or come to believe on their own that new methods of decision making are needed (Nixon). This study supports two explanations. First, proposals that ask a president to change his style will be rejected (Kennedy). Those proposals that enhance his ability to be himself may be accepted (Johnson, Nixon). Second, proposals for change that come from the individual or individuals in the confidence structure and that reinforce the relationships in the confidence structure are the likeliest to be accepted. Anything that complicates or inhibits the confidence structure is headed for rejection. The quote at the beginning of this book is testament to a president's need for someone he can trust. As FDR said, "You'll discover the need for somebody like Harry Hopkins who asks for nothing except to serve you."[2] Presidents come into office as fully finished products; they are unlikely, unwilling, or unable to remodel themselves. They may, instead, search for someone who understands how they operate. If they do find such a person or persons, they want a system that places that individual or individuals in a preeminent position as alter ego, confidant, manager, or all three. That need may be the greatest ordering principle in any administration. Changes in decision making must enhance that relationship and give the president more freedom to be himself; if that freedom creates problems for everyone else, it is the job of the advisor in the confidence structure to deal with it.

This study views the key idiosyncratic variable—presidential management style—as a constant. When faced with institutional pressures that clearly point to presidential style as a problem, the remedies are twofold: changes in the institutional structures of decision making, or greater reliance on the idiosyncratic relationships between the key decision makers. The above conclusion suggests, though, that institutional adaptations may only be undertaken if they satisfy the idiosyncratic preferences of the president. The lessons of decision making in the Trump administration point to a third possibility—breakdown. Trump refused to be tamed by any process, and advisor after advisor concluded that the president's management style was the source of the trouble. The result was more overall personnel turnover than in any previous administration and a high body count of senior level resignations and firings (one secretary of state, two secretaries of defense, and two national security advisors in four years).[3] President Joe Biden, one of the most experienced men in history to enter the Oval Office, seems to have made a clear and explicit choice at the outset of his term. For his secretary of state, he chose Antony Blinken, an official with vast experience, service in the Clinton NSC staff, and a deputy national security advisor and deputy secretary of state in the Obama administration. More importantly, perhaps, was his service as staff director for the senate Committee on Foreign Affairs while Biden served as chairman and as Vice President Biden's national security advisor during the Obama-Biden first term. This record means that from 2002 to the end of 2012, Blinken was Biden's foreign policy brain trust; no one knows Biden's sense of foreign policy or foreign policy process more than Blinken. In the context of the evolution-balance model, Biden has built his confidence structure into his formal interagency process. Future research on the Biden administration should seek to understand whether Biden's choice is a reflection of learning from the experience of being vice president or a lesson from Trump's chaotic management, or both.

Possibly it is all a lesson in learning. Incoming presidents believe they have learned things from the previous presidents' experiences. After making decisions of their own, they believe they have learned again. The dilemma is when that learning suggests the president must change his ways.

This chapter looks at the big-picture comparisons and what they tell us about overall presidential decision making on foreign policy and issue-specific decisions regarding China. The structured-focused comparison framework is used to organize the chapter. The goal is to identify patterns in the changes or lack of changes in decision making. Five comparisons can be made: overall decision making between presidencies; China decision making within each presidency; overall decision making to China decision making within presidencies; China decision making between presidencies;

TABLE 9.1. Summary of Kennedy Decision Making

Decision Case	Overall Administration Decision Making	UN Decision 1961	Return to the Mainland 1962
Domestic Political Context	N/A	Pressure from the China lobby Public opinion against entrance of the PRC into the UN	Pressure from China lobby minimized Residual issue of how much support to give to ROC
International Political Context	N/A	Moratorium strategy failing ROC and PRC both reject "two Chinas"	Worry that ROC action will spur a regional war
Initial Standard Decision Making	Informal Downgrading of NSC Initial plan for State Department primacy NSC staff becomes president's own foreign policy staff	Informal Leading role for the secretary of state and State Department NSC staff in a supporting role	Informal Leading role for the State Department assistant secretary Inclusion of all relevant departments Policy considered at one NSC meeting
Role of the President	Spokes-of-the-wheel President as his own secretary of state	Spokes-of-the-wheel Information, analysis sent to Kennedy Kennedy made all key decisions	Spokes-of-the-wheel Information, analysis sent to Kennedy Kennedy made all key decisions
Organizational Dynamics	NSC staff grows in absence of adequate State Department leadership No major bureaucratic rivalries Collegial decision making	Initial dominance of State Department Greater participation of special assistants and NSC Staff over time Debate on all issues allowed long after presidential decision	State and CIA shared diplomatic role State, CIA, and NSC staff advised No organizational rivalry
Informal Structure	Dominated the process Small group meetings with key advisors Use of special assistants in White House	Dominated the process Small group meetings with key advisors Use of special assistants in White House	Dominated the process Informal meetings with State Department and CIA officials
Confidence Structure	Bundy and sometimes Sorensen	During final days of decision Bundy, Sorensen, and Schlesinger roles increased	Bundy
Balancing and Compensating	Greater use of special assistants 1961: Accepted/Used Planning Group 1961: Accepted/Ignored Standing Group I 1962: Accepted/Ignored ExComm 1962: Accepted/Used almost exclusively for Cuba Standing Group II 1963: Accepted/Ignored	None	Full formal cabinet-level interagency meeting in June 1962 Discussed at NSC meeting June 1962 Offshore Islands Working Group Summer 1962: Accepted then ignored

TABLE 9.1—*Continued*

Decision Case	Overall Administration Decision Making	UN Decision 1961	Return to the Mainland 1962
Institutional Variables	Pressures from NSC staff to create more formal structures for interagency decision making	No significant pressure to change the informal process since the State Department always had dominant role	Pressure from departments and NSC staff for a more formal interagency process to examine the issue
Idiosyncratic Variables	Kennedy insistence on using informal processes for all decisions that involved him	Kennedy's preferences prevailed	Kennedy's preferences made the new interagency group merely an adjunct to the informal structure
Analysis	Evolution-balance model confirmed	Evolution-balance model not confirmed Evolution model confirmed	Evolution-balance model confirmed

and overall decision making to China decision making between presidencies. Table 9.5 summarizes these comparisons. Discussion of each will be within the context of the structured-focused comparison categories below. Each section will generate lessons that can be learned about the way decision making changes over time. A following section considers the evolution of US policy on China and the importance of domestic politics in foreign policy. The final pages consider some lessons learned and thoughts on further research.

Testing the Evolution-Balance Model; Comparing Presidencies

The following section compares the Kennedy, Johnson, and Nixon administrations using the structured-focused comparison categories. The four elements of the evolution-balance model are built into category five, "Balancing and Compensating." That category serves as the test of the model: How well did it predict and explain changes in each administration's decision making?

Initial Decision Making Process

Two perspectives help explain each president's initial decision making system. First, the Kennedy and Johnson informality can be seen as a reaction to the perception that Eisenhower's system was too formal. Nixon's per-

TABLE 9.2. Summary of Johnson Decision Making

Decision Case	Overall Administration Decision Making	Long Range Study 1965–66	Speech of July 1966 and Chinese Representation
Domestic Political Context	N/A	Pressure to remain tough on Asian Communism in Vietnam and toward China Fear that loss of Vietnam would destroy domestic priorities	Pressure from Congress to reconsider China policy (Zablocki and Fulbright hearings) Pressure from Congress over Vietnam intervention (Fulbright hearings)
International Political Context	N/A	Major Chinese successes and failures Escalation of US intervention in Vietnam Vietnam War linked to Chinese expansionism Surprising ROC success at the UN; PRC attacks on the UN Escalation of Chinese threats: Lin Biao speech	Chaos unleashed by the Cultural Revolution creating uncertainty over Chinese foreign policy Chinese rhetoric becoming more radical Deepening US commitments in Vietnam
Initial Standard Decision Making	Reliance on cabinet officers in informal settings Minimal use of NSC No standard interagency process Priority on consensus Delegation to the State Department	Formal interagency process Senior Policy Group Defense and State led process Process approved in meeting of secretaries of state, defense, and SANSA	No formal interagency process at the senior level Reliance on cabinet officers Lobbying by working-level officials hoping to change senior decision makers' opinions Working-level interagency group on trade issues (April to July)
Role of the President	Top heavy spokes-of-the-wheel Domination by presidential action	None	Monitoring of the debates in the administration through Komer, Moyers, and Rostow
Organizational Dynamics	No major bureaucratic rivalries Cabinet officers with full access to the president	State and DoD led CIA and NSC staff participation No organizational rivalry	No organizational rivalry Humphrey freelancing State Department still in lead
Informal Structure	Tuesday Lunch Group (TLG) dominated the process	Direction by Rusk, McNamara, and Bundy Senior Policy Group	Goldberg enhanced role Rostow keeping Johnson appraised of new ideas Informal meetings of cabinet officers with Johnson TLG meeting Sept. 13

TABLE 9.2—*Continued*

Decision Case	Overall Administration Decision Making	Long Range Study 1965–66	Speech of July 1966 and Chinese Representation
Confidence Structure	Rusk Sometimes Moyers After 1966 Rostow added	Not relevant	Rusk following Johnson's interest in exploring new policies, but retained ability to veto all changes Moyers acting as Johnson alter ego (speech drafting)
Balancing and Compensating	SIG/IRG: Accepted/ Used, but not as a core structure for major decisions New TLG 1966–68: Accepted/Used as the key forum for decision making	Creation of China Working Group (CWG) as subcommittee of the FE/IRG	Issues related to July 1966 speech considered in CWG and FE/IRG Assistant-secretary-level interagency group created Goldberg suggests high-level group (rejected)
Analysis	Evolution-balance model confirmed	Evolution-balance model confirmed	Evolution-balance model confirmed

ception that Kennedy and Johnson were disorganized brought the presidency full circle, back to the formal Eisenhower style. A second way of viewing it might be through a partisan lens. Republicans lean toward more formal hierarchies in their administrative structures, while Democrats tend to view formal systems as an impediment to multiple perspectives and creativity. In part, for these reasons, Kennedy and Johnson downgraded the NSC, while Nixon proposed to make it the center of decision making.

If there are lessons to be learned from the initial choices of each president, the key issue might be their expectations. Both Kennedy and Nixon expected to be underwhelmed by the State Department, and desired to be their own secretaries of state. While Kennedy relished the diplomatic stage, Nixon actively resented the State Department. Playing the role of secretary of state was a way to control it, punish it, and keep it from getting in the way of his diplomacy. Johnson delegated to State because he trusted Rusk. All three men received what they expected from State: Kennedy was disappointed, Johnson was satisfied, and Nixon was at war. Whether these outcomes were self-fulfilling prophecies is a solid question for further research.

In all three administrations, initial decision making on China reflected the initial overall process. Kennedy delegated to State, but often made key decisions in informal settings. Johnson made no serious decisions on China

TABLE 9.3. Summary of Nixon Decision Making

Category Decision	Overall Decision Making	1969: NSSM 14	1970/71: Chinese Representation	1973–74: US Troops in Taiwan
Domestic Political Context	N/A	Public opinion turning against LBJ Vietnam policy Weakness of China lobby Nixon's impeccable anti-Communist credentials Nixon's belief in the potential for US-PRC engagement	Public support for withdrawal of US forces in Vietnam Public support for engagement with PRC and UN membership growing Support for Nixon's breakthrough to China in 1971	Nixon electoral landslide in 1972 Watergate
International Political Context	N/A	Worsening Sino-Soviet split Chaos of Cultural Revolution weakens hard line and pro-Soviet CPC factions Zhou wins argument over US-PRC relations	Belief that UNGA would replace ROC with PRC Success of secret diplomacy Death of Lin; Zhou policy wins PRC warms to UN ROC and PRC rejection of two-Chinas	Success of détente with PRC and USSR Paris Peace Accords Leftist pressure on Zhou US distancing of ROC
Initial Standard Decision Making	Formal NSC-based system controlled by White House through ANSA management Formal review process Goal of producing options for presidential decision	Formal NSC-based system EAIG-based review RG meeting on May 15, 1969 NSC meeting on August 14, 1969 Assessed options for Nixon	Formal NSC-based system (NSSM 107) NSC staff-based study Assessed options for Nixon USC recommendations for policy implementations	Formal NSC-based system (NSSM 171)
Role of the President	Sole decision maker As rational actor judge of policy options	Defining policy goals and implementing them	Defining policy goals Reserving final decisions for himself Controlling policy	Making final decision

TABLE 9.3—*Continued*

Category Decision	Overall Decision Making	1969: NSSM 14	1970/71: Chinese Representation	1973–74: US Troops in Taiwan
Organizational Dynamics	NSC staff vs. State Department Kissinger vs. Rogers Nixon distrust of bureaucracies Nixon vs. Rogers on Rogers's role	No major disagreements that impacted the policy process	State given the lead on policy Reasonable debate on how to implement policy	Rogers eclipsed then replaced by Kissinger Kissinger at State and ANSA
Informal Structure	Underdeveloped; no system for consensus-building Kissinger and Richardson meetings Rogers not involved	Kissinger/Richardson meetings	Nixon-Rogers-Kissinger meetings on May 27 and July 22	Kissinger and Richardson dialogue early 1972
Confidence Structure	Kissinger	Kissinger	Kissinger: honest broker in interagency meetings; privately giving Nixon his views	Kissinger
Consideration of Additional Changes	Kissinger-chaired interagency committees 1969: Accepted/ Used SRG 1970: Accepted/Used Kissinger as secretary of state and ANSA 1973: Accepted/Used	None	Creation of new IG for NSSM 107, chaired by State	Merger of secretary of state and ANSA jobs
Analysis	Evolution-Balance Model Confirmed	Evolution-balance model not confirmed	Evolution-balance model not confirmed Partial confirmation of evolution model	Evolution-balance model partially confirmed

TABLE 9.4. Comparison of Overall Decision Making in Three Administrations

Decision Case	Kennedy	Johnson	Nixon
Initial Standard Decision Making	• Informal • Downgrading of NSC • Initial plan for State Department primacy • Creation of the president's own foreign policy staff in NSC staff	• Reliance on cabinet officers in informal settings • Minimal use of NSC • No standard inter-agency process • Priority on consensus • Delegation to the State Department	• Formal NSC-based system controlled by White House through ANSA management • Formal review process • Goal of producing options for presidential decision
Role of the President	• Spokes-of-the-wheel • President as his own secretary of state	• Top-heavy spokes-of-the-wheel • Domination by presidential action	• Sole decision maker • As rational actor judge of policy options
Organizational Dynamics	• NSC staff role grows in absence of adequate State Department leadership • No major bureaucratic rivalries • Collegial decision making	• No major bureaucratic rivalries • Cabinet officers with full access to the president	• NSC staff vs. State • Kissinger vs. Rogers • Nixon distrust of bureaucracies • Nixon and Rogers differ on Rogers's role
Informal Structure	• Dominated the process • Small group meetings with key advisors • Use of White House special assistants	• Tuesday Lunch Group (TLG) dominated the process	• Underdeveloped; no system for consensus-building • Kissinger and Richardson meetings • Rogers not in informal system
Confidence Structure	• Bundy and sometimes Sorensen	• Rusk • Sometimes Moyers • After 1966 Rostow added	• Kissinger
Balancing and Compensating	• Greater use of special assistants 1961: Accepted/Used • Planning Group 1961: Accepted/Ignored • Standing Group I 1962: Accepted/Ignored • ExComm 1962: Accepted/Used for Cuba • Standing Group II 1963: Accepted/Ignored	• SIG/IRG: Accepted/Used, but not as a core structure for major decisions • New TLG 1966–68: Accepted/Used as the key forum for decision making	• Kissinger-chaired interagency committees 1969: Accepted/Used • SRG 1970: Accepted/Used • Kissinger as secretary of state and ANSA 1973: Accepted/Used
Analysis	• Evolution-balance model confirmed	• Evolution-balance model confirmed	• Evolution-balance model confirmed

until 1965, also delegating policy to State. Nixon played it by the book; NSSM 14 was a formal interagency review that faithfully followed the Eisenhower model as tweaked by Nixon.

Role of the President

Saying that each president desires to be the last word on every subject seems too obvious. This observation does not mean that the president truly believes he knows more than anyone else on every issue (even though that argument is precisely the one often made by President Donald Trump).[4] For each president, the point is this: the responsibility is mine, therefore the authority must also be mine. This need to keep their hands on the wheel might be an acceptance of the great burden that comes with the job or a fear that someone else somewhere in the government will do something foolish. It is probably a little bit of both. In any case, presidents are ambitious people, generally overflowing with confidence. How many individuals can honestly say that they believe they deserve to be the most powerful person in the world? Each man studied here drove himself to the White House for similar and unique reasons: Kennedy's ambition and confidence in his right to leadership; Johnson's ambition and need to control the levers of power for the purpose of creating a legacy; and Nixon's ambition coupled with a resentment pushing him to best his rivals and detractors.

Each man saw himself sitting behind a desk in the Oval Office in total command of the executive branch and its choices. They would neither ratify consensus nor be boxed in by past decisions (though each man could not avoid that fate on many issues). Kennedy's and Johnson's spokes-of-the-wheel structures placed them at the heart of the process, while Nixon used an elaborate interagency machine to essentially check his work and toss him ideas to use when he sat alone calculating his next moves. Kennedy and Nixon operated as their own secretaries of state. Johnson wanted Rusk running State; it is more accurate to say that Johnson was his own chief of staff.

The lessons learned here reinforce the existing scholarly literature. Alexander George's seminal studies of presidential decision making in foreign policy saw presidential management as the function of three characteristics: the individual's cognitive style; his sense of his decision making strengths and weaknesses; and his orientation toward conflict.[5] That analysis has only grown stronger over time. Kennedy liked to weigh all sides of a problem before making a decision, seeing his strengths in his own analytical ability; structured systems might reduce his effectiveness,

TABLE 9.5. Summary of Comparisons

Comparison	Case Study Results
Comparison of Overall Decision Making between Presidencies	Evolution-Balance Model Confirmed for Each Presidency • JFK: New formal structures created, but not used (Standing Groups). • LBJ: New formal structures created and used to varying degrees (SIG/IRG functioned, but not connected to LBJ; new TLG becomes epicenter of decision making). • RMN: New Kissinger-chaired committees used in favor of NSC-based cabinet decision making; Kissinger connects interagency process to Nixon; Kissinger eventually becomes secretary of state and ANSA.
Comparison of China Decision Making within Each Presidency	JFK: • UN Decision 1961: Evolution Model confirmed. • Return to Mainland 1962: Evolution-Balance Model confirmed. LBJ: • Long Range Study 1965–66: Evolution-Balance Model confirmed. • July 1966 Speech and Chinese Representation: Evolution-Balance Model confirmed. RMN: • NSSM 14 1969: Evolution-Balance Model not confirmed. • Chinese Representation 1970–71: Partial confirmation of Evolution Model; Evolution-Balance Model not confirmed. • US Troops in Taiwan 1973–74: Evolution-Balance Model partially confirmed.
Comparison of Overall Decision Making to China Decision Making within Each Presidency	JFK: • Overall decision making shows attempts to add formality to an informal process; China decision making does not add formality in 1961; does add formality in 1962; China decision making is less informal than overall decision making. LBJ: • Overall decision making does add formality to an informal process; both China case studies also add formality; China decision making follows the pattern of overall decision making. RMN: • Overall decision making merges formal and confidence structures (Kissinger-chaired committees) to compensate Nixon unhappiness with formal cabinet decision making; China decisions use formal interagency process in 1969, adds some informality by 1971, with growing Kissinger power in 1973–74. China decision making follows the pattern of overall decision making.
Comparison of China Decision Making between Presidencies	Over time each administration made changes to balance for weaknesses in presidential style. • JFK: the fewest changes in China decision making, adding some formal aspects to an informal process. • LBJ: the largest changes in China decision making, plugging it into new formal processes. • RMN: few changes to formal process until 1973–74 when Kissinger's role as secretary of state and ANSA gave him power to direct the formal process that had been merged with the confidence structure.

TABLE 9.5—*Continued*

Comparison	Case Study Results
Comparison of Overall Decision Making to China Decision Making between Presidencies	Over time LBJ and RMN used the new administration processes for China decision making; JFK did not change his processes significantly • JFK: Some formal processes added to Return to Mainland decision, but overall process remained informal. • LBJ: New formal processes for overall decision making used for China decisions by 1966. • RMN: Interagency process continued to be used for China decisions, ultimately placed into Kissinger-dominated processes.

and reliance on the "experts" was sure to lead him astray; he thrived on the give and take, the competition and conflict. Johnson was more of a political than analytical man; he searched for the possible, rather than the optimal; his strengths were in turning policy solutions into reality; conflict was appropriate only if it was necessary to get people to see things his way, and challenges were not welcome. Nixon thought of himself as a scholar, analytically inclined to hash out the greatest geopolitical conundrums and find the best solution; anyone who could not see how political trends factored into the calculus of decision was missing the crucial variables; he also understood his greatest weaknesses—inability to psychologically tolerate and administratively manage conflict among his subordinates.

Initially, the role of each president in China decision making matched their overall roles. Kennedy sat down with his key advisors in informal settings and hashed out decisions on Chinese representation in 1961. Johnson left China up to Rusk and other cabinet officers initially, keeping informed of all the issues, but allowing delegation. Nixon allowed the interagency process to take care of the overall review of China. When NSSMs were ready they made their way to Nixon, through the NSC or Kissinger. Nixon considered each interagency product, and used that analysis to back up his thoughts on each step toward engagement with China.

Organizational Dynamics

Here is where the contrasts get interesting and instructive. The Kennedy and Johnson administrations are examples of teamwork and relative harmony; the Nixon administration was a nightmare of brutal rivalry and dysfunction. The key to explaining the difference is a twofold question. First, is there a gap between how the secretary of state viewed his role and how the president viewed the secretary's role? Second, how do the secretary of state and the ANSA view their relationship? The easiest way to answer why the Kennedy and Johnson administrations did not develop the furious battles seen under Nixon, Ford, Carter, Reagan, G. W. Bush, and Trump might be simply to say "Dean Rusk." Rusk lived by his belief that there should be "no blue sky between" the president and his secretary of state.[6] Rusk's task was to represent the president's foreign policy, not create his own, nor tutor the president in foreign affairs, nor undermine the president by challenging his judgment in public or in meetings. If Rusk disagreed with the president, as Johnson contends he did, that disagreement was a private matter between Rusk and the president, and once it was stated in private, the president would decide and the disagreement would end; the private blue sky would never be heard from again. The NSC staff's emergence as a potential rival to State's primacy in foreign affairs did not lead to bureaucratic battles because Rusk saw Bundy and Rostow as extensions of the president. If Kennedy wanted Bundy to play an important role in policy making, even performing duties that might have been the secretary of state's in earlier administrations (for example, managing some diplomatic exchanges between Taiwan and the US), then Rusk had to accept it, or resign. Johnson had Rusk's loyalty from the moment he took the oath of office, but they developed a closeness that Kennedy and Rusk never shared. The Rusk-Bundy relationship remained solid because both Kennedy and Johnson wanted it that way, and both men understood their job as serving the president. The Rusk-Rostow relationship was even closer; Rostow had worked for Rusk at State as director of policy planning from November 1961 to the end of March 1966. Their relationship, with Rostow subordinate to Rusk, had been solidified before Rostow became ANSA. Rusk had an old-fashioned notion of public service. His highest ambition was to serve his president; if the president was successful, he had done his job.

As chapter 7 illustrates, Nixon and Rogers had different conceptions of Rogers's role. Worse, Rogers saw Kissinger as a rival, not an extension of Nixon. Kissinger's initial role was as Nixon's right hand, and Kissinger accepted that understanding. Rogers, however, could not countenance Kissinger's access to Nixon and what he must have seen as Kissinger's independent action. As the case studies here show, Kissinger was not an independent actor on China; he implemented Nixon's policy designs. That faithfulness on China and other areas was the key to Kissinger's ascension to the secretary of state position. At its core, the roots of the Rogers-Kissinger feud lay in Nixon's hope to use State as a resource for his own hands-on diplomacy, not as the true representative of the US in important matters. Rogers's view will remain a mystery; since he left no record of how he felt about his time as secretary of state, his judgments on Nixon's decision making style and Kissinger's role in the process can only be inferred. Rogers and Nixon were both veterans of the Eisenhower administration. If that was the model for the incoming Nixon team, Rogers may have believed he was chosen to become Nixon's John Foster Dulles, a towering figure with significant tactical independence, and the public face of American diplomacy, while the president managed overall strategy carefully and quietly behind the scenes. Instead, Nixon usurped the secretary of state's responsibility and authority, grew furious over Rogers's bouts of independent action, and used Kissinger as the mechanism of Oval Office dominance. Nixon was not going to change his view of the State Department as a disloyal and overly liberal bureaucracy, and Rogers would not back down from his hope to elevate the secretary's role. To resolve the growing feud, Nixon had two options: find a Republican Dean Rusk who made loyalty his priority, or make Kissinger secretary of state.

A more succinct way of putting it is this: if a president wants to be his own secretary of state, he needs a secretary of state who will accept the backseat. In that sense, Rusk was a better choice as secretary of state than Kennedy believed; a more outspoken secretary, eager to take the initiative, might have undermined Kennedy's own desire for leadership in foreign affairs. Johnson inherited Rusk but found the right man, absolutely loyal to Johnson and Johnson's policy preferences. Nixon's choice of Rogers was disastrous for both men. The fact that William Rogers lasted so long, into Nixon's second term, is a stunning illustration of Nixon's inability to handle direct conflict, or his sense of loyalty to Rogers given their history together, or both.

The lessons from this look at organizational dynamics are a reinforcement of ideas contained in the study of the original evolution model.[7] The George H. W. Bush foreign policy process was a well-functioning system free of feuds and public acrimony. After the successive controversies of Nixon, Ford (firing of Secretary of Defense James Schlesinger in November 1975), Carter (resignation of Secretary of State Cyrus Vance in April 1980), and Reagan (resignation/firing of Secretary of State Alexander Haig in June 1982, and a record six people serving as ANSA), the Bush administration was a welcome turn toward boredom and competence. Solid professional and personal relationships and a clear understanding of the roles each senior official was to play prevented rivalries. All of Bush's top advisors had a Rusk-like conception that their job was to serve the president, and all of them trusted that their counterparts shared that priority.[8] Useful comparisons can also be made between the relative peace of the Clinton and Obama administrations and the factional infighting during the George W. Bush years or the near-collapse of decision making under Trump.[9]

If there is a lesson for presidents, it is that they must choose their foreign policy advisors more carefully. Presidents should pick a set of advisors who have worked together before (likely at lower levels in a previous administration), who are experienced enough to know that overt feuds will undermine the administration's foreign policy no matter how well designed it might be, and who understand that while debate and disagreement within the councils of the administration are important, public disagreements, particularly with the president, will be and should be the fastest way to a seat on a corporate board or a publishing contract for your memoirs. A clear understanding of roles and responsibilities, even with the knowledge that those roles and responsibilities will evolve over time, is absolutely necessary. Kennedy is reported to have lamented the problem: "I must make the appointments now; a year hence I will know who I really want to appoint."[10] Can a president know who he trusts the most and who he can rely upon on day one of his tenure in office? Perhaps this is possible if the president and his advisors have long experience in Washington and with each other—the lesson of the George H. W. Bush administration. Replicating that, however, is unlikely if the US continues to elect presidents with little experience in Washington or in making foreign policy decisions. Newness and novelty seem to be a plus for candidates, but decision making suffers from that level of inexperience. If nothing else, the Trump administration is an excellent lesson in how a lack of governmental experience can create administrative chaos. The Biden administration may be a test case for the value of experience. The majority of the key advisors served together in the Obama administration. From day one, they have known the job and each other.

Development and Use of the Three Structures

The original evolution model is something of a starting point for this analysis. An initial formal process is created at the inception of an administration, and the informal and confidence structures develop over the first six months to a year of its time in office. The main role of the informal structure—a small committee of principals without the president's attendance—is to iron out disagreements and develop senior-level consensus and teamwork. The confidence structure represents the president's ultimate sounding board, the one or two officials the president relies on for advice, support, and camaraderie. Figures 9.1, 9.2, and 9.3 provide illustrations of the three structures in the Kennedy, Johnson, and Nixon administrations.

When using the three structures idea as an analytical tool, again, Kennedy and Johnson are similar in their decision making style, and Nixon is the outlier. Both Kennedy and Johnson downplayed their formal structures, deliberately diminishing the use of the NSC. Their informal structures were used as the routine backbone of the foreign policy process. Kennedy's spokes of the wheel system placed him at the center of informal lines of communication that reached throughout the departments. Johnson focused on his senior advisors and used the Tuesday Lunch Group to manage a consensus he built himself. Kennedy's confidence structure was rooted in the Kennedy-Bundy relationship. To a lesser extent, White House assistant Theodore Sorensen and Attorney General Robert Kennedy were elements of the confidence structure. Johnson relied on Rusk as his core confidant, and on White House assistant Bill Moyers to a lesser extent. The contrast here fits the overall nature of the two administrations. Kennedy's relationship with Rusk was often strained and Kennedy was skeptical about State's usefulness. His elevation of the NSC staff was partly based on his confidence in Bundy. Johnson, more attuned to who had responsibility and authority for specific issues, relied on Rusk. He and Rusk also bonded over their outsider status and southern roots.

Nixon's three structures are nearly the opposite of those of Kennedy and Johnson. Instead of a system rooted in informal processes, Nixon created an elaborate formal process that was ultimately directed by the confidence structure. No important informal structures developed, and that absence of any mechanism to iron out a consensus or even quietly identify areas of disagreement made a bad situation intolerable. It appears that this lack of an informal system was deliberate. Nixon wanted to prevent Rogers, Laird, and Kissinger from bargaining out a consensus and coming to him with a precooked recommendation, essentially a Nixon administration decision made without Nixon. Here is a lesson about being careful what you wish for. Instead of consensus, Nixon got a four-year-long war between his senior advisors. The outcome was never in doubt. Kissinger would win the war because Nixon wanted him to win. The confidence structure was always based in the Nixon-Kissinger relationship. In hindsight, Nixon might believe that his biggest decision making mistake was not removing Rogers after six months, roughly about the time the new Kissinger-chaired interagency committees were created. Again, Nixon needed a Republican Rusk to make his system work.

China policy in each administration initially followed the overall deci-

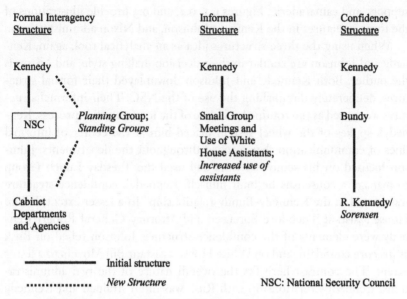

Fig. 9.1. Three Structures of Decision Making: Kennedy

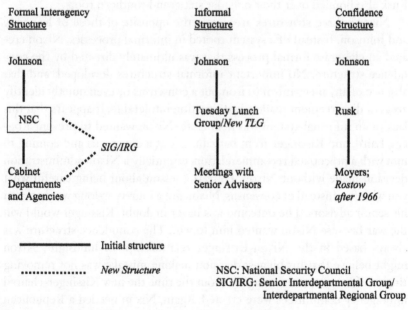

Fig. 9.2. Three Structures of Decision Making: Johnson

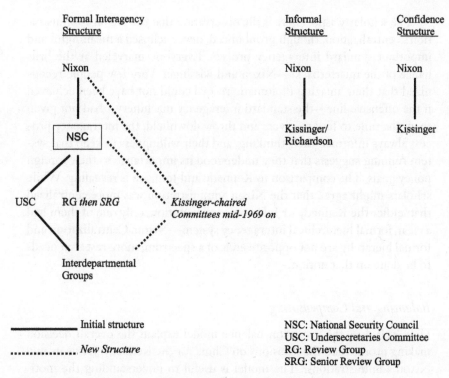

Formal Interagency Structure	Informal Structure	Confidence Structure

Nixon | Nixon | Nixon

NSC

Kissinger/ Richardson | Kissinger

USC | RG *then SRG* | Kissinger-chaired Committees mid-1969 on

Interdepartmental Groups

―――――――― Initial structure

·············· *New Structure*

NSC: National Security Council
USC: Undersecretaries Committee
RG: Review Group
SRG: Senior Review Group

Fig. 9.3. Three Structures of Decision Making: Nixon

sion making structures. Kennedy and Johnson initially made China decisions informally. China was just another issue running through the spokes of the wheel. Nixon's China policy was backed up by the rigor of State-led formal interagency NSSMs. Behind the scenes, however, Nixon and Kissinger pushed engagement forward on their own; it was implementation by confidence structure.

Lessons learned here might be twofold, one for policy making and one scholarly. The key lesson of the Carter, Reagan, and Bush study was the importance of the informal structure as the glue that keeps the formal structure from shattering into rivalry and prevents the confidence structure from narrowing the range of advice in counterproductive ways (a president hears only one voice, and that voice may not be giving the president all that he needs to make the best decision). The Kennedy, Johnson, and Nixon cases reiterate that. With well-functioning informal structures under Kennedy and Johnson, there were no serious rivalries. Nixon's mix of formal and confidence structures, in the absence of informal systems, led to a bureaucratic meltdown.

The scholarly aspect here is the observation that the Nixon administration's centralization, though pronounced, never eclipsed a meaningful and important standard interagency process. Everyone marveled at the brilliance of the quarterbacks—Nixon and Kissinger. Very few people recognized that their amazing diplomatic record could not have been achieved if the offensive line—the standard interagency machinery—had not given them the time to find receivers and throw downfield; the interagency process always informed their thinking, and their willingness to keep that system running suggests that they understood its importance to their foreign policy goals. The comparison to Kennedy and Johnson is revealing. While scholars might agree that the Nixon administration was more centralized than either the Kennedy or Johnson administration, only one of them had a clear, formal hierarchical interagency system—Nixon. Centralization and formal hierarchy are not opposite ends of a spectrum; more research needs to be done on that notion.

Balancing and Compensating

How well does the evolution-balance model explain the overall decision making process and the decisions on China for the Kennedy, Johnson, and Nixon administrations? The model is useful to understanding the motivations for change and the actual changes that shaped the overall decision making in each administration. The model's explanatory power on China decision making varies over time. Early case studies show fewer of the dynamics predicted by the evolution-balance model. Only over time do China decisions reflect each administration's desire to compensate for the management problems caused by the president's initial administrative choices.

Presidential Management Style

The evolution-balance model treats presidential style as a constant, and the case studies bear this out. None of the presidents studied here became a different man or fundamentally altered the way he thought about decision making. Kennedy accepted the creation of formal committees recommended by advisors (the Planning and Standing Groups), then ignored them because they encroached on his freedom. Both Johnson and Nixon created new structures designed to better adapt the system to their styles. As Johnson's chief of staff approach overloaded him, he added formal structures to take care of the balls he might drop while juggling. The SIG/IRG took hold of secondary issues that Johnson simply could not add to his inbox. His new TLG, however, gave his informal structure a connection to the formal side of the administration. Nixon desired greater insulation from the departments and agencies than his formal process could give him; he simply could not face the daily disagreements that resulted from open cabinet government, even if it was what he initially thought would work best for him. The new Kissinger-chaired committees and Kissinger's eventual dual secretary of state/ANSA role gave Nixon that much-needed buffer, allowing him to concentrate on overall strategy and the politics of implementation. If Nixon were a king, Kissinger was asked to construct a moat around the castle and manage all traffic across the drawbridge.

Continuous Assessment to Identify Weaknesses

The case studies support the notion that every administration reassesses its decision making on a routine basis. That "deciding how to decide" occurred for overall decision making and for China decisions in all three administrations.[11] Advisors and the president all seemed to understand that the initial design of the administration was a first cut, a theory about what the best way to make decisions might be. After repeatedly making decisions, the weaknesses of the system became apparent. In the cases of Kennedy and Johnson, the weaknesses were identified by ANSAs Bundy and Rostow, and the problems were caused by the informality of the process—detachment from the departments, confusion about what the president's preferred policies were, and even uncertainty among many in the departments and agencies about if, when, and what decisions had been made. Nixon, ever the outlier, returned the NSC to prominence, then found himself plagued with leaks, feuds, and a plodding pace. Along with Kissinger, he evaluated his own system and found it wanting. In China decision making, continuous assessment of the process was also the norm, and proposals for change came from the same sources as it had for overall decision making: State and the NSC staff. Under Johnson and Nixon, proposals for new committees also came from other sources: UN ambassador Arthur Goldberg and outside consultant Richard Moorsteen, respectively. These two cases reflect the openness of each administration to ideas about decision making from nearly anywhere. The new arrangements may not have been accepted, but they were taken seriously, an indication that the search for better processes is fundamental and ongoing.

As the case studies show, in all three administrations there was an extensive dialogue about the process and how the president's management style impacts the functioning of foreign policy decision making. The surprising aspect of this is how frank the president's advisors could be with the president, explicitly giving him some unflattering advice: the way you do your job is the way you do your job, but here is the long list of problems it creates. During my research in the presidential archives of Eisenhower to Clinton, I have never found a memo from the president expressing outrage that anyone would suggest his decision making needed improvement.

Proposals for Change to Compensate and Find Better Balance

Once weaknesses had been identified, each administration developed proposals for change. All were significant modifications that had the potential to restructure decision making in fundamental ways. In the language of the evolution-balance model, the proposals sought to create a better balance between the formal, informal, and confidence structures. For both Kennedy and Johnson, the goal was to add formality to an informal process in an effort to build a better balance into the system, a remedy accepted then ignored by Kennedy and accepted and used by Johnson. In the Kennedy administration, Bundy and the NSC staff suggested the Planning Group and Standing Groups, more formal committees to provide some formal structures that connected the informal structures to the departments and agencies. Under Johnson, both the State Department and special advisor Maxwell Taylor, with the help of State's U. Alexis Johnson, created proposals for a new interagency system, the SIG/IRG, led by State. The SIG/IRG was in effect a reconstruction of an Eisenhower-like system to manage the interagency process through a set of committees with formal roles, responsibilities, and relationships. At the senior level, ANSA Rostow refined the TLG into an actual functioning NSC analog, a more formal TLG with routinized connections to the departments and agencies.

Nixon began with a formal system and could have added more informality. Work on the original evolution model illustrates how the Carter, Reagan, and George H. W. Bush administrations evolved in precisely that manner. Nixon's management style precluded that type of evolution. Face-to-face frank dialogue and efforts to build consensus were simply impossible for him. His solution was to give Kissinger, the source of his confidence structure, the ability to directly manage and guide the formal process. Nixon could not be a hands-on manager, but Kissinger could. Nixon believed that he had Kissinger's unwavering loyalty and that, more importantly, the two men shared the same outlook on international affairs and the US national interest. The new Kissinger-chaired committees of the first term and the dual secretary of state/ANSA role for Kissinger in the second term meant that Nixon had found what he wanted—an assistant he could trust who would manage the formal system and insulate Nixon from it at the same time.

Of the seven China case studies examined here, four follow the dynamics predicted by the evolution-balance model and reflect the patterns of
overall decision making: Kennedy's 1962 Return to the Mainland, both
Johnson case studies, and Nixon's 1973/74 decision on US Troops in Taiwan (partial confirmation). In these cases, the pattern of change matches
the overall evolution of decision making. Kennedy and Johnson added formality to their informality—interagency committees dedicated specifically
to China issues. Nixon's second-term informal processes worked briefly as
he had hoped, with Kissinger and Richardson negotiating a consensus in
February 1973. Ultimately, Kissinger's dual role allowed him to manage
the formal process from Foggy Bottom and the White House, a merger of
the confidence and formal structures that matched the overall pattern of
decision making.

In two cases China decisions do not match the overall evolution of the
administration. The original evolution model explains decision making
better than the evolution-balance model for Kennedy's 1961 and Nixon's
1970/71 cases on Chinese representation. In both cases, the president's
decision was made ultimately in small group meetings. Kennedy began
with informal processes that also delegated issues to the State Department
(in a bit of formality), but his thinking was sharpened by Bundy and special
assistants Theodore Sorensen and Arthur Schlesinger. No suggestions to
use a more formal process for China decisions had surfaced yet; however,
the debates on how to modify the process following the Bay of Pigs were
already under way. Kennedy's use of special assistants in small, private settings illustrates that he already believed he had learned something—before
making his final determination he needed to sound out the ideas with
trusted advisors; he needed a moment to lean on the confidence structure.
Similarly, Nixon's 1970–71 decision on Chinese representation shows a
by-the-book interagency system that fed into two ad hoc, informal meetings between Nixon, Rogers, and Kissinger. While the overall evolution-
balance model illustrates Nixon's use of new structures to grant Kissinger
his managerial proxy, in this case, Nixon did something rare; he sat down
with Rogers and Kissinger for frank and open discussions of China policy
strategy and tactics in an informal setting.

Only in one case did decision making show virtually no significant
departure from the initial design. NSSM 14 of 1969 followed the standard
interagency process without deviation, traveling its way from the Far Eastern Interdepartmental Group to the Review Group to the NSC, exactly as
NSDM 2, Nixon's memorandum on NSC procedures, had outlined.

Since time is a key factor in the model, it is not surprising that the
evolution-balance model predicts decision making dynamics better the

longer an administration has been in office. The one case study that shows no change in style, NSSM 14, is from the first eight months of Nixon's term in office. The original evolution model is better at explaining Kennedy's and Nixon's Chinese representation decisions, made during Kennedy's first year in office and Nixon's first two years in office. The evolution-balance model works best to explain later decisions. Johnson's 1965–66 Long Term Study and his speech of July 1966 leading to reconsideration of Chinese representation in the fall may have been undertaken in Johnson's first and second year in office, but they were also decisions made in the fourth and fifth year of Rusk's, Bundy's, and Rostow's tenures in the Kennedy/Johnson administration. Nixon's 1973–74 decisions on Taiwan troops were in the fifth and sixth year of his term. Time matters, and the case studies bear that out. Over time, administrations search for greater balance and, believing that they have learned something valuable, attempt to compensate for weaknesses in the process.

Presidential Choice

When confronted with decisions about decision making, presidential choice seems guided by how changes might impact the confidence structure. For Kennedy, the new interagency Standing Groups went against the grain of what he thought he had known before becoming president and what he believed he had learned during the Bay of Pigs. Formal processes channel information and advice to the president based on who the organizational chart determines are the most useful individuals; it traps the president with predetermined sources of counsel. That rigid structure led Kennedy to the Bay of Pigs disaster and he would simply not allow any additional formalities to box him in. Johnson's confidence structure was enhanced by the formal additions. The SIG/IRG system gave more control to Rusk, the core member of Johnson's confidence structure, and did not interfere with Johnson's mastery over the issues that mattered to him. Once Rostow had moved into Johnson's confidence structure, he accepted Rostow's suggestions for the new TLG. As always, the TLG allowed Johnson the informal meetings he preferred, and Johnson trusted Rostow enough to allow him to plug that informal process into the rest of the departmental and agency bureaucracy in a more formal way.

Nixon was unlikely to build any type of informal process that could create a consensus. His initial decision making structure was predicated on preventing a consensus among his advisors that might limit his freedom of decision. Even if he had sought agreement among his advisors, it was likely impossible. The two key individuals who would form that consensus were at each other's throats. Instead, Nixon built a committee hierarchy that used the confidence structure to manage the formal process. Nixon approved the new system because it enhanced Kissinger's power in ways that benefited Nixon. Two aspects of this analysis are particularly interesting. First, Nixon came to office adamant that he would not accept precooked recommendations. Yet Kissinger had the explicit task of doing just that, making recommendations for Nixon on memos with boxes for Nixon to check: "Approve" or "Disapprove." The difference seems to be that Nixon rejected recommendations that might be derived from bureaucratic consensus, assuming that these were lowest-common-denominator compromises, rather than policies that advanced a strategic goal. He accepted Kissinger's recommendations because he knew that Kissinger understood Nixon's goals and his way of thinking. Nixon had found an alter ego whose judgment he trusted and who was ready to dive head first into the dirty work of bureaucratic bargaining and management, allowing Nixon to be above the fray in the rare air of pure strategic thought. Second, the only real informal processes during Nixon's first term were based in the Kissinger-Richardson meetings, similar to meetings between the heads of the Planning Board and Operations Coordination Board under Eisenhower. There, the two managers of the important committees could have steered the entire system in the direction Nixon desired. Richardson's appointment as secretary of defense for Nixon's second term at the time that Kissinger was to be appointed secretary of state was likely an effort to create an informal structure that might oversee the process on a more comprehensive level. Kissinger, of course, did not move to State until September 1973, and Richardson left Defense for the attorney general position in May 1973, an effort by Nixon to place another official he trusted at the head of the Department of Justice as Watergate became a growing concern. The delay in Kissinger's appointment and Richardson's jump to Justice preempted the emergence of a real informal structure.

From Isolation to Engagement: The Political Context of China Decision Making

In 1948, as he threw support behind Democratic president Harry Truman's nascent containment policies, Senator Arthur Vandenberg, Republican chairman of the Senate Foreign Relations Committee, said that the US should end "partisan politics at the water's edge."[12] For a brief moment,

Republicans and Democrats set aside partisanship, allowing strategic calculation of US national interests to guide foreign policy. Perhaps the threat of the Soviet Union during the early days of the Cold War was so great that it outweighed partisan politics. In contrast, partisanship was one of the defining factors in China decisions during the Kennedy, Johnson, and Nixon years. The Republican Party used China as a weapon against Democrats, convincing them that they must defend a policy of isolation that most no longer supported, and, in effect, delaying opportunities for engagement from 1961 to 1969. Once Nixon entered office, he implemented the engagement that the Democrats could not. With some grumbling, his party fell in line. Nixon basked in the glory of an achievement he himself had been partly responsible for postponing.

Decisions on whether to engage China diplomatically, or to devise a formula for recognition of China at the UN, or how much support to give to Taiwan, are political questions decided by international and domestic politics. As this research has shown, from the moment Kennedy entered office, the Asia and China experts at the working levels of the departments and agencies were ready to move away from the Truman-Eisenhower isolation policy toward what they saw as a more realistic and productive engagement strategy. It was not a belief that Communism was no longer a threat, or that China had watered down its revolutionary ideology. Isolation only made sense if it led to the fall of Mao's regime. Once it was clear that the PRC was not a temporary phenomenon, dialogue rather than silence seemed the logical path to stability in Asia.

Certainly, Kennedy and Johnson were cold warriors; both men's policies on Vietnam should testify to that. They brought the US into a war to stop the spread of Asian Communism, risking their entire presidencies on military intervention across the Pacific, even ignoring the all-important post–Korean War warning: never get into a ground war in Asia. From a strategic perspective, both men shared a belief in China's culpability in supporting, even instigating, North Vietnamese operations against South Vietnam. Chinese-sponsored aggression could be the logical answer to why détente with the USSR was acceptable and a similar policy toward China was not. If the Vietnam War was an overt manifestation of Chinese hostility, then engagement with China had to wait until it ended that aggression. US statements on China during the Kennedy and Johnson administrations all support this strategic formulation.

Private discussions portray a different perspective. Kennedy was quoted as believing that isolating China was "irrational," arguing that "it really doesn't make any sense—the idea that Taiwan represents China."[13] A Johnson conversation with Richard Russell in 1964 echoed the dilemma. While Johnson thought that the US would eventually recognize China, he agreed with Russell's assessment that domestically, such recognition was "poison."[14] The internal debates of both administrations suggest that officials held a complex view of the dynamics in East Asia: the US believed that China's efforts to spread communism in Southeast Asia had to be contained, and it also believed that communications with China might realign the balance of power in the region. In this sense, the US could approach China with both the carrot and the stick and let China's response dictate which one the US chose to use. Isolation combined with intervention, however, was counterproductive, leaving no avenues for dialogue. Even Nixon's 1967 *Foreign Affairs* article implies that isolation made China more dangerous: "We simply cannot afford to leave China forever outside the family of nations, there to nurture its fantasies, cherish its hates and threaten its neighbors."[15] The question of whether isolating a nation deters it, coerces it, or antagonizes it is at the heart of debates on détente during the Cold War or on Iran and North Korea today.

Kennedy and Johnson were unable to make significant moves toward China because they were prisoners of a narrative about the Democratic Party that had persisted since Truman, a narrative pushed to great effectiveness by the Republican Party and one of its rising leaders—Richard Nixon. Neither Kennedy nor Johnson could suffer another "Who Lost China?" or "Who Lost Vietnam?" charge. As Democrats, neither man could make a move toward engagement without bringing the wrath of the China lobby and Republican Party down on them, risking every policy their administration believed in and the success of their entire presidencies. Engagement, no matter how logical from a strategic point of view, was simply out of the question for Democrats in the 1960s. The narrative of Democratic weakness in fighting Asian Communism was baked into Cold War partisan politics, and Vandenberg's hopes aside, partisanship was not afraid of the water; it extended across the Pacific and Atlantic.

The Kennedy-Johnson experience benefits from the use of the poliheuristic model, which sees policy making as a two-stage process.[16] First, policies that are politically impossible are ruled out, and then decision makers choose the best of the remaining options. Engagement with China was ruled out for domestic political reasons, leaving both administrations trying to find ways to extend the life of an isolation strategy each viewed as approaching a certain death. Both Kennedy and Johnson fought to come up with new strategies for keeping China out of the UN, never seriously considered removing US troops from Taiwan, and seemed resigned to their political inability to take advantage of the Sino-Soviet split. They fought to maintain the status quo and hoped that time might lead to reform from within China.

The analysis comes back around to the notion that only Nixon could go to China, primarily because Nixon would not be hounded by Nixon if he supported engagement. With the ability to neutralize his right flank, Nixon became the great hope for a new China policy. Ironically, it was Nixon who changed Eisenhower's policy, one he supported for eight years as vice president. Equally ironic is the fact that Nixon was the man who finally gave the green light to the ideas of the liberal Democrats in the State Department whom he detested.

Neorealist scholars of international relations, who argue that system-level factors are the independent variable for any change in state behavior, might argue that the beginnings of US-China engagement must be seen as Washington's and Beijing's reactions to the changing strategic environment. The independent variables are the shifts in the power balance among the three major nations in the system. The USSR and China moved away from each other just as the US was attempting to withdraw from Vietnam; as the Soviet threat to China grew, rapprochement with the US was the obvious balancing strategy for Beijing. Similarly, for the US a decline in its power due to the failures in Vietnam led to a similar strategy of balancing against the stronger Communist power (the USSR) by engaging the weaker (China). At the same time, US-USSR détente used engagement as a method to restrain Soviet actions, again a calculation based on the failure of intervention. In this sense, Triangular Diplomacy was the logical step for both the US and China.

Neoclassical realist scholars, who see a mix of system- and state-level factors as the independent variables, might argue that shifts in the global balance of power created an impetus for new policies. Those shifts might not actually lead to new policies, nor will they automatically lead to any predictable policy outcome. Great power dynamics had changed, but why did that lead to US-China engagement, and why did it lead to US-China engagement when it did, from 1969 to 1972? The domestic political variables add explanatory value. In China, the failures of the Cultural Revolution were a gain for relative moderates like Zhou Enlai; gains against the military and radical factions led to a reassessment of foreign policy goals. Instead of treating the 1969 hostilities with the USSR as a reason to back off and find common ground with Moscow (the hope of Lin Biao's military faction) or going it alone with even greater hostility toward both Washington and Moscow (the radical faction choice), Zhou was able to remind Mao of what Western scholars would think of as his more realist roots: use of the US to balance against the Soviets. Again, Nixon's strong anti-Communist credentials gave him more leeway to deal with China than any other US politician. Though those farther to the right, such as California governor Ronald Reagan, criticized him, Republican Party solidarity muted their protests. If Nixon's return to power is seen as a result of the Democratic Party's failures in Vietnam, then system-level factors are still the independent variable. At another level of analysis, Nixon's victory in 1968 was due to the passage of civil rights legislation, which pushed the traditionally solid Democratic South toward Alabama governor George Wallace in 1968, toward Nixon in 1972, and firmly into the Republican camp by the 1990s. In this sense, rapprochement with China is a side effect of electoral realignment in the US. Both system-level and domestic-level factors can explain the end of isolation and the emergence of engagement.

Further Research

Scholarly debates are never really settled. At best, solid research points us toward better questions. Three areas of further research can follow from this study. First, the relationship between implementation and decision needs much greater attention. Planning and bottom-up reviews seem to be the purview of a formal interagency structure. When implementation of policy begins, however, those with the responsibility for implementation seem to gain control over the decision. Rather than thinking about large strategic issues, decision making becomes about tactics, on-the-fly adjustments to events and negotiating proposals—the type of topics that cannot be sent back to the full interagency machinery because of potential leaks to the press and because of time urgency. Scholars should be able to learn a great deal about decision making by explicitly focusing on the transition from big-picture strategic analysis to tactical cost-benefit analysis of implementation options. A narrower lens on that transition to implementation helps square the contradiction of the Nixon administration. Nixon's decision making is typically seen as highly centralized, almost Nixon-and-Kissinger-alone-on-an-island. That version centers on areas where Nixon and Kissinger were directly implementing the policy. As the Nixon case studies illustrate, the interagency process served a crucial role in backstopping Nixon and Kissinger, even as the departments and agencies were unaware that the policies they had been considering were already being implemented.

Second, scholars who hope to understand the president's influence on the policy process have two case studies that can be compared to great effect, though the research design is somewhat morbid. Following Kennedy's assassination, Johnson was the only difference in the administration. Similarly, when Nixon stepped down on August 9, 1974, the only administrative change was Gerald Ford's move to the White House. A deep examination of those transitions using archival material is sure to yield great insights. What is the impact when everything stays the same except the president? The transition from Kennedy to Johnson was tragically abrupt, while the transition from Nixon to Ford followed more than a year of administrative turmoil and was in some ways expected once impeachment proceedings began. In that sense, the cases are not equivalent in their research design. Research on the cases would nonetheless provide interesting results.

A third area of study is more of a normative suggestion. The importance of a president's management style is a given. Scholars and journalists are still writing articles and books explaining the decision processes that led to the Johnson administration's intervention in Vietnam or the George W. Bush administration's invasion of Iraq. Trump's style of management or mismanagement during the COVID-19 pandemic has already been the subject of many journalistic accounts and will no doubt become the subject of bestsellers and scholarly publications to come. If decision making style and management skill are that important to policy outcomes, why is it rarely, if ever, even mentioned when the US considers a candidate for president? Understanding how a candidate managed their decision making process as governor or senator or business executive could tell us volumes. Since this work and most others suggest that the president's style is nearly a constant, then the way a candidate makes decisions at their current administrative level is a preview of how they would operate in the Oval Office. During a presidential election all candidates should be asked to explain their administrative philosophy or to sketch out an organization chart or explain a time when they had learned something about making decisions and adjusted their management style to incorporate their new understanding. We might even go as far as taking a lesson from parliamentary systems by requiring candidates to identify possible cabinet officers before the election. Identifying the "shadow" secretary of state or "shadow" national security advisor can give a voter a much better idea of the type of administration that would be taking office. Explicit to this research, all candidates could be asked how they would react to advisors who propose modifications in the policy process. The answers should be revealing.

A predictive value of the evolution-balance model is its acceptance of dynamism in presidential decision making. Too often any restructuring or reorganization of decision making is seen as presidential weakness and administrative chaos. The evolution-balance model argues that the opposite may be true; innovations in an administration's decision making structure may be indications of learning. When changes are made, perhaps it is a moment where the public can learn about the president and his management ideas, an immediate case study of managerial and presidential leadership. We should avoid the knee-jerk "administration in disarray" conclusion, and ask the president how his new arrangements benefit him.

Interestingly, each of the presidents studied here did talk about their style of decision making during their run for president. The NSC as a subject for discussion, however, has seemed to disappear. Of course, my dream would be to see the following question asked during a presidential debate: "How will you manage your NSC interagency system?" I'll keep dreaming.

～ Notes

ONE

1. Kathryn Dunn Tenpas, *Crippling the Capacity of the National Security Council*, Brookings, January 21, 2020, https://www.brookings.edu/blog/fixgov/2020/01/21 /crippling-the-capacity-of-the-national-security-council/. Pottinger may be the sixth sequentially, but he is the seventh overall. During 2017, the NSC staff had two deputies.

2. See Peter Bergen, *Trump and His Generals* (New York: Penguin Press, 2019); and Daniel Drezner, *The Toddler in Chief* (Chicago: University of Chicago Press, 2020).

3. I. M. Destler, "Jonestown." *Foreign Affairs*. April 30, 2009, https:// www.foreignaffairs.com/articles/united-states/2009-04-30/jonestown; Karen DeYoung, "Despite Stature, James L. Jones Was Awkward Fit in Obama White House as National Security Advisor," *Washington Post*, October 8, 2010; and David Rothkopf, "More on the Jones-Donilon Transition," *Foreign Policy*, October 11, 2010, https://foreignpolicy.com/2010/10/11/more-on-the-jones-donilon-transition/

4. Jeffrey Bader, *Obama and China's Rise* (Washington, DC: Brookings, 2012), 115.

5. "Minutes of Committee Meeting with the President," June 18, 1957, Flemming, Arthur S. Papers, 1939–1975, Box 162, folder "PACGO: Foreign Affairs Organization—1955–1957 (2)," Dwight Eisenhower Presidential Library (DDEL).

6. PACGO [President's Advisory Committee on Government Organization] to Eisenhower, January 13, 1959, White House Office, Office of the Staff Secretary: Records, 1952–1961, Subject Series, White House Subseries, Box 5, folder "Rockefeller—Committee on Reorganization of the Government (5)," 8, DDEL.

7. J. F. Dulles telephone call to Vice President Richard Nixon, January 24, 1959, Papers of John Foster Dulles, Telephone Calls Series, Box 9, folder "Memoranda of Tel. Conv—Gen Jan. 4, 1959—May 8, 1959 (3)," DDEL.

8. Alfred Sander, *Eisenhower's Executive Office* (New York: Praeger, 1999), 174–91; William W. Newmann, "Searching for the Right Balance: Managing Foreign Policy Decisions under Eisenhower and Kennedy," *Congress and the Presidency* 42, no. 2 (May–August 2015): 119–46.

9. William W. Newmann, *Managing National Security Policy: The President and the Process* (Pittsburgh: University of Pittsburgh Press, 2003).

10. Newmann, *Managing National Security Policy*, 199–203.

11. Richard Neustadt, *Presidential Power and the Modern Presidents* (New York: Free Press, 1990).

12. Terry Moe, "The Politics of Bureaucratic Structure," in *Can the Government Govern*, ed. John Chubb and Paul Peterson (Washington, DC: Brookings Institution, 1989), 285–323; and Terry Moe, "The Revolution in Presidential Studies," *Presidential Studies Quarterly* 39, no. 4 (December 2009): 701–24.

13. John Burke, *The Institutional Presidency* (Baltimore: Johns Hopkins University Press, 1992); and John Hart, *The Presidential Branch* (Chatham, NJ: Chatham House, 1995, 2nd ed.).

14. See US Department of State, *Foreign Relations of the United States, 1981–1988, Reagan Administration*. https://history.state.gov/historicaldocuments/reagan

TWO

1. William Newmann, *Managing National Security Policy* (Pittsburgh: University of Pittsburgh Press, 2003).

2. Chester Barnard, *The Functions of the Executive* (Cambridge: Harvard University Press, 1968 [1938]); Philip Selznick, *Leadership in Administration* (Evanston, IL: Row, Peterson, and Co., 1957); James MacGregor Burns, *Leadership* (New York: Harper and Row, 1978); Bert Rockman, *The Leadership Question* (New York: Praeger, 1984); Robert Jervis, "Do Leaders Matter and How Would We Know?," *Security Studies* 22 (2013): 153–79. For a focused examination of the tragic and abrupt transition from Kennedy to Johnson and its impact on the policy process, see William W. Newmann, "Kennedy, Johnson, and Policy toward China: Testing the Importance of the President in Foreign Policy Decision Making," *Presidential Studies Quarterly* 44, no. 4 (December 2014): 640–72.

3. Alexander George, "The Operational Code," *International Studies Quarterly* 13, no. 2 (1969): 190–222; Alexander George, "Assessing Presidential Character," *World Politics* 26, no.2 (1974): 234–82; James David Barber, *The Presidential Character*, 4th ed. (Englewood Cliffs, NJ: Prentice-Hall, 1992); Stanley Renshon and Deborah Welch Larson, eds., *Good Judgment in Foreign Policy* (Lanham, MD: Rowman and Littlefield, 2003); Mark Schafer and Scott Crichlow, *Groupthink vs. High Quality Decision Making in International Relations* (New York: Columbia University Press, 2010); Alex Mintz and Karl DeRouen Jr., *Understanding Foreign Policy Decision Making* (Cambridge: Cambridge University Press, 2010); and Steve Yetiv, *National Security through a Cockeyed Lens* (Baltimore: Johns Hopkins University Press, 2013).

4. Patrick Anderson, *The President's Men* (Garden City, NY: Doubleday, 1968); Stephen Hess, *Organizing the Presidency* (Washington, DC: Brookings Institution Press, 1988); and Fred Greenstein, ed., *Leadership in the Modern Presidency* (Cambridge: Harvard University Press, 1988).

5. First (individual), second (state), and third (system) images are the classic formulation of how to define the independent variable in international relations. See Kenneth Waltz, *Man, the State, and War* (New York: Columbia University

Press, 1954). Explicitly first image analyses include Jonathan Keller and Dennis Foster, "Don't Tread on Me," *Presidential Studies Quarterly* 46, no. 4 (December 2016): 808–27; and Maryann Gallagher and Susan Allen, "Presidential Personality," *Foreign Policy Analysis* 10 (2014): 1–21.

6. Danile Krcmaric, Stephen Nelson, and Andrew Roberts, "Studying Leaders and Elites," *Annual Review of Political Science* 23 (2020): 133–51.

7. Vincent Boucher, Charles-Philippe David, and Karine Premont, *National Security Entrepreneurs and the Making of American Foreign Policy* (Montreal: McGill-Queen's University Press, 2020).

8. Lloyd Etheredge, "Personality Effects on American Foreign Policy, 1898–1968," *American Political Science Review* 72, no. 2 (June 1978): 434–51; Miriam Steiner, "The Search for Order in a Disorderly World," *International Organization* 37, no. 3 (1983): 373–414; Bruce Buchanan, "Constrained Diversity," in *The Managerial Presidency*, ed. James P. Pfiffner (Pacific Grove, CA: Brooks/Cole Publishing, 1991), 78–104; Margaret Hermann and Thomas Preston, "Presidents, Advisors, and Foreign Policy," *Political Psychology* 15, no. 1 (1994): 75–96; Daniel Bynam and Kenneth Pollack, "Let Us Now Praise Great Men," *International Security* 25, no. 4 (Spring 2001): 107–46; and Stephen Dyson, "Personality and Foreign Policy," *Foreign Policy Analysis* 2 (2006): 289–306.

9. Richard Neustadt, *Presidential Power and the Modern Presidents* (New York: Free Press, 1990). On the impact of this work, see James Pfiffner, "Presidential Decision Making," *Presidential Studies Quarterly* 35, no. 2 (June 2005): 217–28; and, Matthew Dickinson, "We All Want a Revolution," *Presidential Studies Quarterly* 39, no. 4 (December 2009): 736–70.

10. On this debate, see the classic work by Graham Allison, *Essence of Decision* (Boston: Little, Brown, 1971). For cognitive analysis-based modifications of the rational actor model that focus on the limits to rational analysis, see Herbert Simon, *Administrative Behavior* (New York: Free Press, 1965 [1945]); and James March and Herbert Simon, *Organizations* (New York: John Wiley and Sons, 1958).

11. Samuel Huntington, *The Common Defense* (New York: Columbia University Press, 1961); Warner Schilling, Paul Y. Hammond, and Glenn Snyder, *Strategy, Politics, and Defense Budgets* (New York: Columbia University Press, 1962); Morton Halperin and David Halperin, "The Key West Key," *Foreign Policy* 52 (1983–84): 114–28, and Graham Allison and Philip Zelikow, *Essence of Decision*, rev. ed. (New York: Addison-Wesley, 1999), 143–96.

12. Graham Allison and Morton Halperin, "Bureaucratic Politics," *World Politics* 24 (supplement 1972): 40–79; Morton Halperin and Arnold Kanter, "The Bureaucratic Perspective," in *Readings in American Foreign Policy*, ed. Morton Halperin and Arnold Kanter (Boston: Little, Brown, 1974), 1–42; and Allison and Zelikow, *Essence of Decision*, 255–324.

13. Richard. T. Johnson, *Managing the White House* (New York: Harper and Row, 1974); Alexander George, *Presidential Decision Making in Foreign Policy* (Boulder: Westview Press, 1980); Philip Henderson, *Managing the Presidency* (Boulder: Westview Press, 1988); and Alexander George and Juliette George, *Presidential Personality and Performance* (Boulder: Westview Press, 1998).

14. Johnson, *Managing the White House*, 1–8 and 230–41; George, *Presidential Decision Making*, 145–68; George and George, *Presidential Personality*, 199–280;

and Colin Campbell, *Managing the Presidency* (Pittsburgh: University of Pittsburgh Press, 1986).

15. I. M. Destler, *Presidents, Bureaucrats, and Foreign Policy* (Princeton: Princeton University Press, 1974), 90.

16. Bundy to Kennedy, January 31, 1961, National Security Files (NSF), Departments and Agencies Series, Box 283A, folder "National Security Council Organization and Administration 1/30/61–1/31/61," John F. Kennedy Presidential Library (JFKL).

17. Walt Rostow, *The Diffusion of Power* (New York: Macmillan, 1972), 160.

18. Henry Kissinger, *White House Years* (Boston: Little, Brown, 1979), 31.

19. H. R. Haldeman, "The Nixon White House and the Presidency," in *The Nixon Presidency*, ed. Kenneth W. Thompson (Lanham, MD: University Press of America, 1987), 74 and 85.

20. Terry Moe, "The Revolution in Presidential Studies," *Presidential Studies Quarterly* 39, no. 4 (December 2009): 701–24.

21. Thomas Weko, *The Politicizing Presidency* (Lawrence: University Press of Kansas, 1995), 11.

22. Quoting Edward Corwin, *The President: Office and Powers*, 4th ed. (New York: New York University Press, 1957), 171. See also Cecil V. Crabb and Pat M. Holt, *Invitation to Struggle*, 3rd ed. (Washington DC: Congressional Quarterly, 1989).

23. James March and Johan Olsen, "The New Institutionalism," *American Political Science Review* 78, no. 3 (September 1984): 743.

24. Terry Moe, "The Politicized Presidency," in *The New Direction in American Politics*, ed. John Chubb and Paul Peterson (Washington, DC: Brookings Institution, 1985), 235–72.

25. David Lewis, *The Politics of Presidential Appointments* (Princeton: Princeton University Press, 2008), 6–10 and 141–71; and David Lewis, *Presidents and the Politics of Agency Design* (Stanford: Stanford University Press, 2003).

26. Graham Allison and Peter Szanton, *Remaking Foreign Policy* (New York: Harper and Row, 1975), 21.

27. Duncan Clarke, *The Politics of Arms Control* (New York: Free Press, 1979); and David Forsythe, *Human Rights and US Foreign Policy* (Gainesville: University Press of Florida, 1988).

28. M. K. Bolton, *U.S. National Security and Foreign Policymaking after 9/11* (Lanham, MD: Rowman and Littlefield, 2007).

29. I. M. Destler, "National Security Advice to U.S. Presidents," *World Politics* 29, no. 2 (1977): 143–76; I. M. Destler, "A Job That Doesn't Work," *Foreign Policy* 38 (Spring 1980): 80–88; Peter Szanton, "Two Jobs, Not One," *Foreign Policy* 38 (Spring 1980): 89–91; and Bert Rockman, "America's Departments of State," *American Political Science Review* 75, no. 4 (December 1981): 911–27.

30. The Supreme Court ruling, *US v. Curtiss-Wright Export Co.*, established the modern conception of presidential dominance in foreign affairs, arguing that what have been called "plenary" or "inherent" powers in foreign affairs are powers of the presidency. See "*United States v. Curtiss-Wright Export Corporation*," Oyez, https://www.oyez.org/cases/1900-1940/299us304. See also Roy E. Brownell, "The Coexistence of *United States v. Curtiss-Wright* and *Youngstown Sheet & (and) Tube v. Sawyer* in National Security Jurisprudence," *Journal of Law & Politics* 16, no. 1 (Winter 2000): 1–112.

31. Arthur Schlesinger Jr. *The Imperial Presidency* (Boston: Houghton-Mifflin, 1973).

32. Eric Posner and Adrian Vermeule, *The Executive Unbound* (New York: Oxford University Press, 2010), 31.

33. Andrew Rudalevige, *The New Imperial Presidency* (Ann Arbor: University of Michigan Press, 2005).

34. Benjamin Kleinerman, *The Discretionary President* (Lawrence: University Press of Kansas, 2009); James Pfiffner, "The Contemporary Presidency: Constraining Executive Power," *Presidential Studies Quarterly* 38, no. 1 (March 2008): 123–43; and Rudalevige, *New Imperial Presidency*.

35. Kenneth Mayer, *With the Stroke of a Pen* (Princeton: Princeton University Press, 2001); Phillip Cooper, *By Order of the President* (Lawrence: University Press of Kansas, 2002); Steven Calabresi and Christopher Yoo, *The Unitary Executive* (New Haven: Yale University Press, 2008); Jeffrey Crouch, Mark J. Rozell, and Mitchel A. Sollenberger, "The Unitary Executive Theory and President Donald J. Trump," *Presidential Studies Quarterly* 47, no. 3 (September 2017): 561–73; and Graham Dodds, *The Unitary Presidency* (New York: Routledge, 2020).

36. Richard Nathan, *The Plot That Failed* (New York: Wiley, 1975); Bert Rockman. "Does the Revolution in Presidential Studies Mean 'Off with the President's Head?,'" *Presidential Studies Quarterly* 39, no. 4 (December 2009): 786–94; Joel Aberbach and Bert Rockman. "The Appointments Process and the Administrative Presidency," *Presidential Studies Quarterly* 39, no. 1 (March 2009): 38–59; David Lewis, "Revisiting the Administrative Presidency," *Presidential Studies Quarterly* 39, no. 1 (March 2009): 60–73.

37. Charlie Savage, "Trump Lawyer's Impeachment Argument Stokes Fears of Unfettered Power," *New York Times*, January 3, 2020, https://www.nytimes.com/2020/01/30/us/politics/dershowitz-trump-impeachment.html; Michael Brice-Saddler, "While Bemoaning Mueller Probe, Trump Falsely Says the Constitution Gives Him 'the Right to Do Whatever I Want'," *Washington Post*, July 23, 2019, https://www.washingtonpost.com/politics/2019/07/23/trump-falsely-tells-auditorium-full-teens-constitution-gives-him-right-do-whatever-i-want/

38. Rockman. "Does the Revolution in Presidential Studies Mean 'Off with the President's Head?,'" 793.

39. Ivano Cardinale, "Beyond Constraining and Enabling: Toward New Microfoundations for Institutional Theory," *Academy of Management Review* 43, no. 1 (2018): 132–55.

40. Newmann, *Managing National Security Policy*.

41. Luther Gulick, "Notes on the Theory of Organization," in *Papers on the Science of Administration*, ed. Luther Gulick and L. Urwick (New York: Taylor and Francis, 2003), 1–49; and William Y. Elliott, *US Foreign Policy* (New York: Columbia University Press, 1952), 66.

42. The EOP grew exponentially during World War II, topping out at over 194,000 in 1943. Following World War II, the size decreased to 1,100–1,400 under Truman. Eisenhower doubled its size and Nixon brought the staff to over 5,000, before Ford reduced its size. The Obama White House reported its Executive Office of the President size at 1,800. See "Size of the Executive Office of the President (E.O.P)," The American Presidency Project; http://www.presidency.ucsb.edu/data

/eop.php; and Obama Administration, "The Executive Branch," http://www.white house.gov/our-government/executive-branch

43. John Burke, *The Institutional Presidency* (Baltimore: Johns Hopkins University Press, 1992); and John Hart, *The Presidential Branch*, 2nd ed. (Chatham, NJ: Chatham House, 1995).

44. Destler, "National Security Advice"; Destler, "A Job That Doesn't Work"; Szanton, "Two Jobs, Not One"; Zbigniew Brzezinski, "The NSC's Midlife Crisis," *Foreign Policy* 69 (Winter 1987–88): 81–95; Amy Zegart, *Flawed by Design* (Stanford: Stanford University Press, 1999).

45. I. M. Destler and Ivo Daalder, *A New NSC for a New Administration*, Brookings Institution, November 15, 2000, https://www.brookings.edu/research/a-new -nsc-for-a-new-administration/; and Alexander Bobroske, *Reforming the National Security Council*, American Action Forum, December 21, 2016, https://www.americ anactionforum.org/research/reforming-national-security-council/

46. Public Law 114–328, *National Defense Authorization Act for Fiscal Year 2017*, December 23, 2016, Section 1085. https://www.congress.gov/114/plaws/publ328 /PLAW-114publ328.pdf

47. Moe, "The Politicized Presidency"; Hess, *Organizing the Presidency*, 221; and Andrew Rudalevige, *Managing the President's Program* (Princeton: Princeton University Press, 2002).

48. Alex Mintz and Carly Wayne, *The Polythink Syndrome* (Stanford: Stanford University Press, 2016); and Irving Janis, *Groupthink* (Boston: Houghton Mifflin., 1982).

49. Charles Hermann, ed., *International Crises* (New York: Free Press, 1972); and Ole Holsti, "Theories of Crisis Decision Making," in *Diplomacy*, ed. Paul Lauren (New York: Free Press, 1979), 99–136.

50. Alex Mintz, "The Decision to Attack Iraq: A Noncompensatory Theory of Decision Making," *Journal of Conflict Resolution* 37, no. 4 (December 1993): 595–618; and Alex Mintz, "How Do Leaders Make Decisions? A Poliheuristic Perspective," *Journal of Conflict Resolution* 48, no. 1 (2004): 3–13.

51. Newmann, *Managing National Security Policy*, 39–40.

52. Newmann, *Managing National Security Policy*.

53. Johnson, *Managing the White House*; and George and George, *Presidential Personality*.

54. Newmann, *Managing National Security*.

55. Newmann, *Managing National Security*, 38–42.

56. Stephen Hess, *Organizing the Presidency*.

57. Neustadt, *Presidential Power*, 169; and Paul Light, *The President's Agenda* (Baltimore: Johns Hopkins University Press), 40–45.

58. James Best, "Presidential Learning," *Congress and the Presidency* 15, no. 1 (Spring 1988): 25–26; and Harold Seidman, *Politics, Position, and Power* (New York: Oxford University Press, 1986), 83.

59. George and George, *Presidential Personality*, 201–3.

60. Paul Anderson, "Deciding How to Decide in Foreign Affairs," in *The Presidency and Policy Making*, ed. George Edwards, Steven Shull, and Norman Thomas (Pittsburgh: University of Pittsburgh Press, 1985), 152.

61. Hugh Heclo, "The Changing Presidential Office," in *The Managerial Presidency*, ed. James Pfiffner (Pacific Grove, CA: Brooks/Cole Publishing, 1991), 40.

62. George Reedy, *Twilight of the Presidency* (New York: Mentor Books, 1979), 17–28.

63. Alexander George, "Case Studies and Theory Development: The Method of Structured, Focused Comparison," in *Diplomacy: New Approaches in History, Theory, and Policy*, ed. Paul Lauren (New York: Free Press, 1979), 43–68: Alexander George and Timothy J. McKeown, "Case Studies and Theories of Organizational Decision Making," in *Advances in Information Processing in Organizations*, vol. 2, ed. Robert Coulam and Richard Smith (Greenwich, CT: JAI Press, 1985): 29–41; Alexander George and Andrew Bennett, *Case Studies and Theory Development in the Social Sciences* (Cambridge: MIT Press, 2004); and Andrew Bennett and Jeffrey T. Checkel, eds., *Process Tracing: From Metaphor to Analytical Tool* (Cambridge: Cambridge University Press, 2015).

64. George, *Presidential Decision Making*; Charles Walcott and Karen Hult, *Governing the White House* (Lawrence: University Press of Kansas, 1995); Newmann, *Managing National Security Policy*; and David Mitchell, "Does Context Matter?," *Presidential Studies Quarterly* 40, no. 4 (December 2010): 631–59.

65. George and Bennett, *Case Studies and Theory Development in the Social Sciences*, 205–32; and Bennett and Checkel, *Process Tracing*.

66. David Waldner, "Process Tracing and Qualitative Causal Inference," *Security Studies* 24 (2015): 239–50; and Nina Tannenwald, "Process Tracing and Security Studies," *Security Studies* 24 (2015): 219–27.

67. James Mahoney, "Process Tracing and Historical Explanation," *Security Studies* 24 (2015): 200–218.

68. Respectively, Alex Mintz, Nehemia Geva, Steven Redd, and Amy Carnes, "The Effect of Dynamic and Static Choice Sets on Political Decision Making," *American Political Science Review* 91, no. 3 (September 1997): 553–66; Jeffrey Friedman and Richard Zeckhauser, "Analytical Confidence and Political Decision-Making," *Political Psychology* 39, no. 5 (2018): 1069–87; Janet Weiss, "Coping with Complexity," *Journal of Public Policy Analysis and Management* 2, no. 1 (Autumn 1982): 66–87; and Rod Albuyeh and Mark Paridis, "Thawing Rivalries and Fading Friendships," *Political Psychology* 39, no. 4 (2018): 811–27.

THREE

1. *The Federalist Papers*, Number 76, Avalon Project, https://avalon.law.yale.edu/18th_century/fed76.asp

2. Bundy to Kennedy, November 16, 1962, National Security Files (NSF) Departments and Agencies, Box 283A, "National Security Council (NSC) Organization and Administration 12/27/61–11/22/63," 2, John F. Kennedy Presidential Library (JFKL).

3. Quoted in Arthur Schlesinger Jr., "A Biographer's Perspective," in *The Kennedy Presidency*, ed. Kenneth Thompson (Lanham, MD: University Press of America, 1985), 22–23.

4. George Ball, *The Past Has Another Pattern* (New York: W. W. Norton, 1982), 167–68.

5. Quoted in Theodore Sorensen, *Kennedy* (New York: Bantam, 1965), 316.

6. President John F. Kennedy, Inaugural Address, January 20, 1961, Kennedy Presidential Library, https://www.jfklibrary.org/learn/about-jfk/historic-speeches/inaugural-address

7. Richard T. Johnson, *Managing the White House* (New York: Harper and Row, 1974), 120–58.

8. Graham Allison, "Conceptual Models and the Cuban Missile Crisis," *American Political Science Review* 63, no. 3 (1969): 689–718; and Graham Allison, *Essence of Decision* (Boston: Little, Brown, 1971).

9. On the Eisenhower process, see Robert Cutler, "The Development of the National Security Council," *Foreign Affairs* 34, no. 3 (April 1956): 441–58; Stanley Falk, "The National Security Council under Truman, Eisenhower, and Kennedy," *Political Science Quarterly* 79, no. 3 (September 1964): 403–34; Philip Henderson, *Managing the Presidency* (Boulder: Westview Press, 1988); and Fred Greenstein and Richard Immerman, "Effective National Security Advising: Recovering the Eisenhower Legacy," *Political Science Quarterly* 115, no. 3 (2000): 335–45.

10. John F. Kennedy, "A Democrat Looks at Foreign Policy," *Foreign Affairs* 36, no. 1 (October 1957): 56.

11. The subcommittee changed its name to the Subcommittee on National Security Staffing and Operations from 1962 to 1965 and then operated as the Subcommittee on National Security and International Operations thereafter. See Henry Jackson, ed., *The National Security Council* (New York: Praeger, 1965), 30–54.

12. Jackson, *The National Security Council*, xii; and John Burke, *Honest Broker* (College Station: Texas A&M University Press, 2009), 57.

13. Bromley Smith, *Organizational History of the National Security Council during the Kennedy and Johnson Administrations* (Washington, DC: National Security Council, 1988), 6.

14. Richard Neustadt, "Memorandum on Staffing the President-Elect," in *The Managerial Presidency*, ed. James Pfiffner (College Station: Texas A&M University Press, 1999), 56, 65, and 67.

15. Clark Clifford, *Counsel to the President* (New York: Anchor Books, 1991), 328–29; and James Pfiffner, *The Strategic Presidency*, 2nd ed. (Lawrence: University Press of Kansas, 1988), 40.

16. Bundy to Kennedy, 11/16, 1962, NSF Departments and Agencies, Box 283A, "NSC Organization and Administration, 12/27/61–11/22/63," 1, JFKL.

17. Dean Rusk, *As I Saw It* (New York: Penguin, 1990), 518.

18. John Prados, *Keeper of the Keys* (New York: William Morrow, 1991), 101–2.

19. *Foreign Relations of the United States* (FRUS), *1961–1963*, Volume XXV, Document 4.

20. Bundy to Kennedy, January 31, 1961, NSF, Departments and Agencies, Box 283A, "NSC Organization and Administration 1/30/61–1/31/61," 1–2, JFKL.

21. Sorensen, *Kennedy*, 319.

22. Bundy to Kennedy, January 24, 1961, 13.

23. Prados, *Keepers of the Keys*, 106.

24. Bundy to Kennedy, January 24, 1961, 13–14. The Office of Civil Defense and

Mobilization was renamed the Office of Emergency Planning in September 1961. The attendees at the first meeting were the statutory members: Kennedy, Vice President Lyndon Johnson, Secretary of State Rusk, Secretary of Defense McNamara, Director-designate of the Office of Civil Defense and Mobilization Frank Ellis; statutory advisors: Chairman of the Joint Chiefs of Staff Lyman Lemnitzer, Director of Central Intelligence Allen Dulles; and invitees: Secretary of the Treasury C. Douglas Dillon, Budget Director David Bell, Undersecretary of State Chester Bowles, Counselor-designate of the State Department George McGhee, Assistant Secretary of Defense Paul Nitze, Deputy Director of Central Intelligence Robert Amory, Special Assistant to the President for Science and Technology Jerome Wiesner, Bundy, and Military Aide to the President General Chester Clifton. See "Record of Actions by the NSC at its 475th held on February 1, 1961," NSF, Meetings and Memoranda, Box 313, "NSC Meetings 1961, No. 475, 2/1/61," 1, JFKL; and Smith. *Organizational History*, 31.

25. "Record of Actions by the NSC at its 475th Meeting held on February 1, 1961," 5.

26. Keith Clark and Laurence Legere, *The President and the Management of National Security* (New York: Praeger, 1969), 71.

27. Administrative History, Department of State, Volume 1, Chapters 1–3, Box 1, "Chapter 2 (Leadership and Structure of the Department): Sections A, B," 7, Lyndon Johnson Presidential Library (hereafter LBJL).

28. Prados, *Keepers of the Keys*, 106; and "Record of Actions by the NSC at the 475th Meeting held on October 13, 1961," NSF Meetings and Memoranda, Box 313, "NSC Meetings, 1961," 1. Data compiled from Clinton Administration. National Security Council Archives, https://clintonwhitehouse4.archives.gov/media/pdf/Kennedy_Admin.pdf

29. Sorensen, *Kennedy*, 319.

30. I. M. Destler, *Presidents, Bureaucrats, and Foreign Policy* (Princeton: Princeton University Press, 1974), 100.

31. Roger Hilsman, *To Move a Nation* (Garden City, NY: Doubleday and Co., 1967), 23; Arthur Schlesinger, *A Thousand Days* (New York: Fawcett, 1965), 377–81; and Patrick Anderson, *The President's Men* (Garden City, NY: Doubleday and Co, 1968), 264.

32. McGeorge Bundy, "The National Security Council of the 1960's," in Jackson, *National Security Council*, 278.

33. Bundy to Senator Jackson, September 4, 1961, NSF. Departments and Agencies, Box 283, "NSC General 5/61–12/61," 3–4.

34. Schlesinger, *Thousand Days*, 377.

35. Sorensen, *Kennedy*, 302.

36. *FRUS, 1961–1963*, Volume XXV, Document 6; Anderson, *President's Men*, 264; and Clark and Legere, *The President*, 77; Destler, *Presidents*, 98; and Smith, *Organizational History*, 11, 14, 21–22.

37. *FRUS, 1964–1968*, Volume XXXIII, Document 155; Anderson, *President's Men*, 264; Prados, *Keeper of the Keys*, 102; and Clarke and Legere, *The President*, 78–79.

38. Memorandum for the President, June 22, 1961, NSF Departments and Agencies, Box 283A, "NSC Organization and Administration 5/5/61–7/25/61," 1–2, JFKL.

39. Bundy to Kennedy, January 31, 1961, 1.

40. Memorandum for the President, June 22, 1961, 1–2.

41. Schlesinger, *Thousand Days*, 198.

42. Anderson, *President's Men*, 202, 261, and 265.

43. Prados, *Keeper of the Keys*, 110.

44. Smith, *Organizational History*, 17.

45. Anderson, *President's Men*, 196–97 and 270.

46. Alexander George, "The Case for Multiple Advocacy in Making Foreign Policy," *American Political Science Review* 66, no. 3 (September 1972): 751–85; David Hall, "The 'Custodian-Manager' of the Policy-Making Process," *Commission on the Organization of the Government for the Conduct of Foreign Policy (Murphy Commission)*, vol. 2, appendix D, chapter 12, June 1975, 100–118; and John Burke, *Honest Broker*, 1–14.

47. Sorensen, *Kennedy*, 317.

48. Burke, *Honest Broker*, 56–104. Quote from Walt W. Rostow, *The Diffusion of Power* (New York: Macmillan, 1972), 169. Scholars have debated whether an official can be both honest broker and advocate. On this debate, see I. M. Destler, "A Job That Doesn't Work," *Foreign Policy* 38 (Spring 1980): 80–88; Peter Szanton. "Two Jobs, Not One," *Foreign Policy* 38 (Spring 1980): 89–91; and Burke, *Honest Broker*.

49. Smith, *Organizational History*, 23; and Andrew Preston, "The Little State Department," *Presidential Studies Quarterly* 31, no. 4 (2001): 644.

50. Stephen Hess, *Organizing the Presidency* (Washington, DC: Brookings, 1988), 74–75; James David Barber, *Presidential Character*, 4th ed. (Englewood Cliffs, NJ: Prentice-Hall, 1992), 341–85; Arthur Schlesinger, "Effective National Security Advising," *Political Science Quarterly* 115, no. 33 (2000): 347–51; Thomas Preston, *The President and His Inner Circle* (Baltimore: Johns Hopkins University Press, 2001), 97–113; Robert Dallek, *Camelot's Court* (New York: Harper Collins, 2013), 35 and 67–76.

51. Schlesinger, *Thousand Days*, 625.

52. Sorensen, *Kennedy*, 436.

53. Schlesinger, *Thousand Days*, 121, 393, and 466; Rostow, *Diffusion of Power*, 128 and 162; Johnson, *Managing the White House*, 124; Dallek, *Camelot's Court*, 99; Sorensen, *Kennedy*, 419; Anderson, *President's Men*, 265; and Robert Dallek, *An Unfinished Life* (New York: Back Bay Books, 2003), 307. Quote from Johnson, *Managing the White House*, 130.

54. Schlesinger, *Thousand Days*, 631; Anderson, *President's Men*, 196; Johnson, *Managing the White House*, 126–29; Schlesinger, "A Biographer's Perspective," 20–24. Quoted from Johnson, *Managing the White House*, 133.

55. Anderson, *President's Men*, 195; and Memorandum for the President, June 22, 1961, 1–2, JFKL.

56. Schlesinger, *Thousand Days*, 120.

57. Johnson, *Managing the White House*, 126–29.

58. Bundy to Kennedy, January 31, 1961, 1, JFKL.

59. Hilsman, *To Move a Nation*, 35; Rusk, *As I Saw It*, 294; Barry Rubin, *Secrets of State* (Oxford: Oxford University Press, 1987), 99 and 110–111; *Arthur Schlesinger Jr., Robert Kennedy and His Times* (New York: Ballantine, 1978), 465–70; Rostow, *Diffusion of Power*, 163; Sorensen, *Kennedy*, 322; Clark and Legere, *The President*,

74–75; Anderson, *President's Men*, 264–267; Paul Hammond, *LBJ and the Management of Foreign Relations* (Austin: University of Texas Press, 1992), 5–6; and Kai Bird, *The Color of Truth* (New York: Simon and Shuster, 1998), 188–89.

60. Schlesinger, *Thousand Days*, 377

61. Nicholas deB. Katzenbach, *Some of It Was Fun: Working with RFK and LBJ* (New York: W. W. Norton, 2009), 221.

62. Schlesinger, *Thousand Days*, 406–14; and U. Alexis Johnson, *The Right Hand of Power* (Englewood Cliffs, NJ: Prentice-Hall, 1984), 221.

63. Smith, *Organizational History*, 49–50. The memo is a response to criticisms of the Kennedy NSC process by Eisenhower. Director of Central Intelligence John McCone had been regularly briefing former president Eisenhower on national security issues. Eisenhower had taken the opportunity at one of the briefings to advise McCone on the defects of the new administration's NSC system: it needed weekly meetings and some established committees to perform the functions of his OCB and PB committees. McCone had given Kennedy a memo summarizing Eisenhower's views, which Kennedy passed on to Bundy.

64. Dallek, *Unfinished Life*, 300 and 306.

65. Johnson, *Managing the Presidency*, 6–8, 120–58, and 238.

66. Memorandum for the President, June 22, 1961, 1–2.

67. Schlesinger, *Thousand Days*, 389–90; and Thomas Schoenbaum, *Waging Peace and War* (New York: Simon and Shuster, 1988), 283–85.

68. Bundy to Senator Jackson. September 4, 1961, 4.

69. Bundy to Senator Jackson. September 4, 1961, 2; Schlesinger, *Thousand Days*, 389–90; Clark and Legere, *The President*, 78; and Schoenbaum, *Waging Peace and War*, 283–85.

70. Rusk, *As I Saw It*, 518.

71. Rusk, *As I Saw It*, 293.

72. Schlesinger, *Thousand Days*, 144–45; and Schoenbaum, *Waging Peace and War*, 284.

73. Dean Rusk, "The President," *Foreign Affairs* 38, no. 3 (April 1960): 355.

74. Hilsman, *To Move a Nation*, 59; Ball, *Past Has Another Pattern*, 169; Rubin, *Secrets of State*, 98; and Schoenbaum, *Waging Peace and War*, 12–14. Quote from Hilsman.

75. Rusk, *As I Saw It*, 516–17.

76. Ball, *The Past Has Another Pattern*, 169.

77. Sorensen, *Kennedy*, 319–20; Rostow, *Diffusion of Power*, 162–63; and Rusk, *As I Saw It*, 516.

78. Rusk, *As I Saw It*, 336–37.

79. Sorensen, *Kennedy*, 319; Schlesinger, *Thousand Days*, 632; Clark and Legere, *The President*, 79; and Smith, *Organizational History*, 17.

80. Dean Rusk Oral History Interview I, July 28, 1969, 18, LBJL, http://www.lbjlibrary.net/assets/documents/archives/oral_histories/rusk/rusk01.pdf

81. Theodore Sorensen, *Decision Making in the White House* (New York: Columbia University Press, 1963), 63.

82. Memorandum for the President, June 22, 1961, NSF Departments and Agencies, Box 283A, "NSC Organization and Administration 5/5/61–7/25/61," 1–2, JFKL.

83. Anderson, *President's Men*, 264–67; Rostow, *Diffusion of Power*, 168–69; Bird, *Color of Truth*, 189; Sorensen, *Kennedy*, 317; Hilsman, *To Move a Nation*, 56; and Ball, *Past Has Another Pattern*, 172–73.

84. Theodore Sorensen. *Counselor* (New York: Harper Perennial, 2008), 233–37.

85. Robert Kennedy *Thirteen Days* (New York: Signet, 1969). Robert Kennedy first sat in on an NSC meeting on April 22, 1961, immediately following the Bay of Pigs disaster, a clear sign that the president wanted another set of trusted eyes and ears. See Smith, *Organizational History*, 33.

86. Bundy to Kennedy, November 16, 1962, JFKL, 2.

87. Maxwell D. Taylor, *Swords and Ploughshares* (New York: W. W. Norton, 1972), 184–94.

88. Schlesinger, *Thousand Days*, 277–78; Johnson, *Managing the White House*, 138; Rusk, *As I Saw It*, 213; Prados, *Keeper of the Keys*, 104; Irving Janis, *Groupthink* (Boston: Houghton Mifflin, 1982); 14–47; Lloyd Etheredge, *Can Governments Learn?* (New York: Pergamon Press, 1985).

89. Schlesinger, *Thousand Days*, 391–92.

90. Memorandum for the President, June 22, 1961, 1.

91. Johnson, *Managing the White House*, 138; and Prados, *Keeper of the Keys*, 104.

92. Fowler to Dillon, May 5, 1961, NSF Departments and Agencies, Box 283, "NSC General 5/61–12/61," 1–3, JFKL.

93. Komer to Bundy, November 5, 1963, NSF Robert W. Komer, Box 410, "China (CPR) Nuclear Explosion 1961–1963 (2 of 2)," JFKL. See also Prados, *Keeper of the Keys*, 104.

94. Komer to Rostow, "Thoughts on Staff Organization," May 1, 1961, Papers of Robert W. Komer, Box 1, "RWK Chron File January-June 1961 (2 of 3)," 1, LBJL.

95. Smith to Bundy, June 22, 1961, NSF Departments and Agencies Box 283A, "NSC Organization and Administration 5/5/61–7/25/61," 1–3, JFKL.

96. Bundy to Kennedy, May 16, 1961, NSF Departments and Agencies, Box 290, "White House General 1961–1962," 1–2, JFKL; and Bundy to Kennedy, (no date), NSF Departments and Agencies Box 283A, "NSC Organization and Administration 9/10/61–12/26/61," 1, JFKL.

97. On the NSC staff functions under Truman and Eisenhower, see Falk, "National Security Council," and Anna Kasten Nelson, "President Truman and the Evolution of the National Security Council," *Journal of American History* 72, no. 2 (1985): 360–78.

98. NSC Record of Action, January 10, 1962, NSF Meetings and Memoranda Box 314, "NSC Standing Group Meetings 1/62," JFKL; and *FRUS, 1961–1963*, Volume XXV, Document 16.

99. "NSC Meetings—Kennedy Administration (1961–1963)." Clinton Administration, National Security Council Archives, https://clintonwhitehouse4.archives .gov/media/pdf/Kennedy_Admin.pdf

100. See NSF Meetings and Memoranda Box 314, "NSC Standing Group Meetings 1/62" through "NSC Standing Group Meetings to 5/18/62–8/3/62," JFKL.

101. Smith, *Organizational History*, 51.

102. Graham Allison and Philip Zelikow, *Essence of Decision* (New York: Addison-Wesley Longman, 1999).

103. Burke, *Honest Broker*, 65; "NSC Meetings—Kennedy Administration (1961–1963)," National Archives, Record of Clinton White House. http://clinton4.nara.gov/media/pdf/Kennedy_Admin.pdf; and David Coleman, NSC ExComm Meetings, 1962–1963, http://historyinpieces.com/research/meetings-excomm-executive-committee-national-security-council

104. Bundy to Kennedy, November 16, 1962, NSF Departments and Agencies, Box 283A, "NSC Organization and Administration 12/27/61–11/22/63," JFKL.

105. Bundy to Kennedy, April 2, 1963, NSF, Departments and Agencies, Box 283A, "NSC Organization and Administration 12/27/61–11/22/63," JFKL. See also Burke, *Honest Broker*, 66.

106. Bundy to Kennedy, April 12, 1963, NSF Meetings and Memoranda Box 315, "Standing Group Meetings General, 4/63–5/63. JFKL."

107. "National Security Action Memorandum No.—, Establishment of Standing Committee of the NSC." NSF Meetings and Memoranda, Box 315, "Standing Group Meetings General, 4/63–5/63," JFKL.

108. NSC Standing Group Record of Actions, April 16, 1963, NSF Files Meetings and Memoranda, Box 315, "Standing Group Meeting, General Meeting 1, 4/16/63," JFKL. Each Standing Group meeting has its own folder in the Kennedy Presidential Library. Copies of the documentation used for each meeting are contained there. See NSF Meetings and Memoranda, Box 315.

109. NSF, Meetings and Memoranda, Box 315, JFKL.

FOUR

1. Quoted in Arthur Schlesinger, *A Thousand Days* (New York: Fawcett, 1965), 446.

2. See Chen Jian, *Mao's China and the Cold War* (Chapel Hill: University of North Carolina Press, 2001), 25–32; and Tang Tsou, *America's Failure in China, 1941–1950*, vol. 2 (Chicago: University of Chicago Press, 1967). The Truman administration's defense of its policy is contained in United States Department of State, *United States Relations with China*, August 1949, published by the Internet Archive https://archive.org/stream/VanSlykeLymanTheChinaWhitePaper1949/Van+Slyke%2C+Lyman+-+The+China+White+Paper+1949_djvu.txt

3. See Ross Koen, *The China Lobby in American Politics* (New York: Harper and Row, 1974); and Stanley Bachrack, *The Committee of One Million* (New York: Columbia University Press, 1973). The China lobby was powerful enough to coerce the original publisher of Koen's book to stop its first printing and to "destroy" over 4,000 copies. Fewer than 800 were circulated and a concerted effort by the China lobby had them removed from libraries or locked away. Koen, *China Lobby*, ix.

4. William Bueler, *US China Policy and the Problem of Taiwan* (Boulder: Colorado Associated University Press, 1971), 50.

5. Walter LaFeber, *The Clash* (New York: W. W. Norton, 1997), 284–95.

6. Well into the 1960s, US officials used the older name "Formosa" to refer to Taiwan. For the text of the resolution see *Inside the Cold War*, available at http://insidethecoldwar.org/sites/default/files/documents/Formosa%20Resolution%20January%2029,%201955.pdf. The resolution was passed by the House 409-3 on January 25, 1955, and by the Senate 85-3 on January 28, 1955.

7. Bueler, *US China Policy*, 22; A. Doak Barnett, *A New US Policy toward China* (Washington, DC: Brookings Institution, 1971), 82–83; and Robert Accinelli, *A Thorn in the Side of Peace* (Cambridge: Harvard East Asia Monographs, 2001), 125.

8. David Allen Meyers, *Cracking the Monolith* (Baton Rouge: Louisiana State University Press, 1986), 127–50; John Lewis Gaddis, "The American Wedge Strategy," in *Sino-American Relations*, ed. Harry Harding and Yuan Ming (Wilmington, DE: Scholarly Resources, 1989), 157–83; and Nancy Tucker, *The China Threat* (New York: Columbia University Press, 2012), 92–96.

9. Donald Zagoria, *The Sino-Soviet Split* (Princeton: Princeton University Press, 1962); Gordon Chang, *Friends and Enemies* (Stanford: Stanford University Press, 1990); and Chen, *Mao's China*, 49–84.

10. Kenneth Young, *Negotiating with the Chinese Communists* (New York: McGraw-Hill, 1968), 3–12.

11. James Fetzer, "Clinging to Containment; China Policy," in *Kennedy's Quest for Victory*, ed. Thomas Paterson (Oxford: Oxford University Press, 1989), 179–80.

12. John Shaw, *JFK in the Senate* (New York: Palgrave, 2013), 25.

13. Ball, *The Past Has Another Pattern* (New York: W. W. Norton, 1983), 166–67; Foster Rhea Dulles, *American Policy toward Communist China* (New York: Crowell, 1972), 189.

14. Shaw, *JFK*, 33; and Ira Stoll, *JFK, Conservative* (Boston: Houghton Mifflin, 2013), 3, 36, 38, and 45.

15. John F. Kennedy, "A Democrat Looks at Foreign Policy," *Foreign Affairs* 36, no. 1 (October 1957): 50.

16. Remarks of Senator John F. Kennedy in the Senate, Washington, DC, June 14, 1960. JFKL. https://www.Kennedylibrary.org/Research/Research-Aids/Kenne dy-Speeches/United-States-Senate-U-2-Incident_19600614.aspx

17. *1960 Democratic Party Platform*, July 11, 1960. American Presidency Project, http://www.presidency.ucsb.edu/ws/?pid=29602

18. UN General Assembly, Official Records of the 332nd Plenary Meeting, 747–49, http://repository.un.org/bitstream/handle/11176/298929/A_PV.332-EN .pdf?sequence=1&isAllowed=y; and John Kuo-Chang Wang, "United Nations Voting on Chinese Representation, 1951–1971," PhD diss., University of Oklahoma, 1977, https://shareok.org/bitstream/handle/11244/4401/7815387.PDF?sequen ce=1

19. On the overall state of the ROC and PRC relationship and each government's relationship with the rest of the world, see Chang, *Friends and Enemies*, 217–52; and Evelyn Goh, *Constructing the U.S. Rapprochement with China, 1961–1974* (Cambridge: Cambridge University Press, 2005), 17–45.

20. Wang, *United Nations Voting*.

21. General studies of Taiwan's foreign policy and its relations with the US in the 1950s and early 1960s include Sheldon Appleton, *The Eternal Triangle* (East Lansing: Michigan State University Press, 1961); Nancy Tucker, *Patterns in the Dust* (New York: Columbia University Press, 1983); Robert Accinelli, *Crisis and Commitment* (Chapel Hill: University of North Carolina Press, 1996); Richard Bush, *At Cross Purposes* (New York: Taylor and Francis, 2004); and John Garver, *The Sino-American Alliance* (Armonk, NY: M. E. Sharpe, 1999).

22. Garver, *Sino-American Alliance*, 93–111; Victor Kaufman, "Trouble in the

Golden Triangle," *China Quarterly* 166 (June 2001): 440–56; and Jay Taylor, *The Generalissimo* (Cambridge: Harvard University Press, 2009), 510–11.

23. Translation of letter from Chiang Chung-cheng, April 1, 1961, President's Office Files, Countries, Box 113A. "China, Security, 1961," 4, JFKL. Chiang Kai-shek was also referred to as Chiang Chung-cheng.

24. Taylor, *Generalissimo*, 507 and 519.

25. Excellent general works on Chinese foreign policy in this era include A. Doak Barnett, *Communist China and Asia* (New York: Vintage, 1961) and Chen, *Mao's China*.

26. Barnett, *Communist China and Asia*, 65–67.

27. On this point, see Michael Hunt, *The Genesis of Chinese Communist Foreign Policy* (New York: Columbia University Press, 1996), 17–25 and 212–25; and Zhang Weng, *Never Forget National Humiliation* (New York: Columbia University Press, 2012). Chen Jian refers to it as "victim mentality"; see *Mao's China*, 12.

28. A. M. Halperin, "Communist China's Foreign Policy," *China Quarterly* 11 (July–September 1962), 95–96; and Joseph Camilleri, *Chinese Foreign Policy* (Seattle: University of Washington Press, 1980), 78–106.

29. See Alice Langley Hsieh, *Communist China's Strategy in the Nuclear Era* (Santa Monica, CA: RAND Corporation, 1962), 76 and 121–30; Qiang Zhai, *China and the Vietnam Wars, 1950–1975* (Chapel Hill: University of North Carolina Press, 2000), 114–23; Jung Chung and Jon Halliday, *Mao* (London: Vintage Books, 2006), 444–72, and John Garver, *China's Quest* (Oxford: Oxford University Press, 2016), 130–42 and 171–77. The Five Principles of Peaceful Coexistence, the foreign policy campaign of Zhou in the mid-1950s, consisted of mutual respect for territorial integrity and sovereignty, nonaggression, noninterference in the internal affairs of other nations, equality and mutual benefit, and peaceful coexistence. See Ronald Keith, *The Diplomacy of Zhou Enlai* (New York: St. Martin's, 1989), 150–53.

30. See Byron Weng, *Peking's UN Policy* (New York: Praeger, 1972), 73–82; Michael Lindsay, "A New China Policy," *China Quarterly* 10 (April–June 1962), 56; and Rosemary Foot, *The Practice of Power* (Oxford University Press, 1995), 24–27.

31. Young, *Negotiating*, 236–37.

32. Clark Clifford, *Counsel to the President* (New York: Anchor Books, 1992), 344–45; and Noam Kochavi, *A Conflict Perpetuated* (New York: Praeger, 2002), 56.

33. Leonard Kusnitz, *Public Opinion and Foreign Policy* (Westport, CT: Greenwood Press, 1984), 101–11.

34. Bachrack, *The Committee*, 154 and 183–84. On the Committee's legislative ties and work during the 1950s, see 3–67 and 179–96.

35. *Nomination of Dean Rusk, Secretary of State-designate*, Hearing before the Committee on Foreign Relations, United States Senate, 87th Congress, 1st Session, January 12, 1961, 7, Hathi Trust, https://babel.hathitrust.org/cgi/pt?id=uc1.$b643311&view=1up&seq=5

36. *Foreign Relations of the United States* (FRUS), *1961–1963*, Volume XXII, Document 20.

37. Harland Cleveland to Abram Chayes, "Chinese Representation in the United Nations," March 24, 1961, Papers of James C. Thomson, Jr. Communist China, Box 1, "General 1/61–6/61," JFKL

38. Foot, *Practice of Power*, 264–66; Kochavi, *Conflict Perpetuated*, 62; and

Schlesinger, *Thousand Days*, 443. Rusk contends that Stevenson even considered recognition of the PRC, though he believed that it would come to nothing; China would reject it. See Dean Rusk, *As I Saw It* (New York: Penguin, 1990), 284.

39. Rusk, *As I Saw It*, 99–191.

40. June Grasso, *Truman's Two-China Policy, 1948–1950* (Armonk, NY: M. E. Sharpe, 1987), 127.

41. Rusk, *As I Saw It*, 282–83.

42. McGhee, "US Policy Toward China," April 3, 1961, Papers of James C. Thomson, Jr., Communist China, Box 1, "General 1/61–6/61," JFKL.

43. Kochavi, *A Conflict Perpetuated*, 63; and Cleveland to Chayes, Papers of James C. Thomson, Jr., Communist China, Box 1, "General 1/61–6/61," JFKL

44. *FRUS, 1961–1963*, Volume XXII, Document 13.

45. *FRUS, 1961–1963*, Volume XXII, Document 9. Kennedy brought up his domestic dilemmas in detail. He specifically mentioned Eisenhower's strong objection to US recognition and the pressures he faced from the Committee of One Million.

46. *FRUS, 1961–1963*, Volume XXII, Document 18.

47. See multiple memos in NSF Meetings and memoranda, Box 321, "Staff Memoranda Robert W. Komer 1/1/61–3/14/61," JFKL.

48. *FRUS, 1961–1963*, Volume XXII, Document 8.

49. *FRUS, 1961–1963*, Volume XXII, Document 23.

50. Thomas Schoenbaum, *Waging Peace and War* (New York: Simon and Shuster, 1988), 387–88; Rusk, *As I Saw It*, 282–84; and Schlesinger, *Thousand Days*, 443.

51. Rusk, *As I Saw It*, 283–84.

52. Memorandum of Conversation, May 24, 1961, NSF, Countries Files, Box 22, "China General 5/1/61–6/12/61," JFKL; and *FRUS, 1961–1963*, Volume XXII, Document 27.

53. *FRUS, 1961–1963*, Volume XXII, Document 28.

54. Komer to Bundy and Rostow, June 15, 1961, NSF Countries, Box 22, "China, General 6/13/61–6/27/61," JFKL. CPR was an abbreviation for Communist People's Republic.

55. *FRUS, 1961–1963*, Volume XXII, Document 34.

56. Vice President Johnson hand delivered one of these letters to President Chiang on May 14. See *FRUS, 1961–1963*, Volume XXII, Northeast Asia Documents 21, 26, and 42, 51–52, 58–62, and 95–97; and Komer to Bundy and Rostow, June 28, 1961, Papers of Arthur Schlesinger Jr., White House Files, Classified Subject File, Box WH29, "China 6/61–6/62," JFKL.

57. Lucius Battle to Bundy, June/July 1961, President's Office Files, Countries Series, Box 113A, "China, Security, 1961," JFKL.

58. *FRUS, 1961–1963*, Volume XXII, Document 20; and Papers of James C. Thomson, Jr., Box 14, "General 1/61–6/61," JFKL; and Gilpatric to Chairman of the Joint Chiefs of Staff, "US Policy Toward Communist China," July 3, 1961, NSF, Robert W. Komer Series, Box 410, "China (CPR) 1961–1963 [2 of 3]," JFKL.

59. On the March meeting, see Papers of Robert W. Komer, Box 1, "RWK Chron File, January–June 1961 (3 of 3)," Lyndon B. Johnson Presidential Library (hereafter LBJL).

60. Komer to Bundy and Rostow, June 28, 1961, Papers of Arthur Schlesinger

Jr., White House Files, Classified Subject File, Box WH29, "China 6/61–6/62," JFKL; and Rostow to Assistant Secretary of State for Far Eastern Affairs, July 12, 1961, President's Office Files, Countries, Box 113A, "China, General, 5/61–12/61," JFKL.

61. *FRUS, 1961–1963*, Volume XXII, Document 39. Here Bundy referred to past secretaries of state George Marshall (1947–49) and Dean Acheson (1949–53).

62. *FRUS, 1961–1963*, Volume XXII, Document 45; Kusnitz, *Public Opinion and US Foreign Policy*, 98–99; and Foot, *Practice of Power*, 38–39.

63. *FRUS, 1961–1963*, Volume XXII, Document 44.

64. Rusk to Kennedy, July 31, 1961, President's Office Files, Countries, Box 113A, "China, Security, 1961," JFKL.

65. *FRUS, 1961–1963*, Volume XXII, Documents 46, 71, 72, and 74; and Foot, *Practice of Power*, 39.

66. Schlesinger, *Thousand Days*, 442–44; and FRUS, 1961–1963, Volume XXII, Document 48.

67. *FRUS, 1961–1963*, Volume XXII, Document 58.

68. Schlesinger, *Thousand Days*, 446.

69. Rusk to Stevenson, September 13, 1961, NSF Countries, Box 22, "China, General 9/61," JFKL.

70. *FRUS, 1961–1963*, Volume XXII, Documents 69 and 75.

71. Komer to Bundy, October 19, 1961, Papers of Robert W. Komer. Box 1, "RWK Chron File June–December 1961 (2 of 4)," LBJL. During roughly the same time in October, Komer sent Bundy a memo suggesting that the administration should consider the use of blackmail against leaders of the China lobby and their allies in the ROC, here referred to as the Government of the Republic of China (GRC), to relieve some of the political pressures on the administration. He wrote: "There might be some useful payoffs if we could get Robert Kennedy interested in a very discreet investigation of the so-called 'China Lobby.' Who knows what a tracing of funds might indicate? If nothing there would be no loss so long as the fact of investigation did not become public. If some interesting tie-ins were developed, they might be excellent leverage in the many further encounters with our GRC ally, whose bargaining skill is a lesson for us all." The memo may have been in jest or it may have been a sign of potential serious illegality. Either way, there is no documentary evidence that Bundy considered the idea or even responded to it. See Komer to Bundy, October 16, 1961, NSF Robert W. Komer, Box 411, "China (Taiwan and the Offshore Islands) 1961–1963 (1 of 3)," JFKL.

72. *FRUS, 1961–1963*, Volume XXII, Document 75. For the text of the resolution, see UN Resolutions Adopted by the General Assembly, 16th Session, http://www.un.org/en/ga/search/view_doc.asp?symbol=A/RES/1668(XVI)

73. Foot, *Practice of Power*, 40.

74. Weng, *Peking's UN Policy*, 127–41.

75. Roger Hilsman, *To Move a Nation* (Garden City, NY: Doubleday, 1967), 302–3, 310, and 315; and Garver, *Sino-American Alliance*, 88.

76. *FRUS, 1961–1963*, Volume XXII, Document 90.

77. *FRUS, 1961–1963*, Volume XXII, Document 84.

78. *FRUS, 1961–1963*, Volume XXII, Document 86.

79. *FRUS, 1961–1963*, Volume XXII, Document 88.

80. Memorandum for the Record, March 19, 1962, Roger Hilsman Papers, Box 1, "China Planning on Mainland Operations, 3/62," JFKL.

81. *FRUS, 1961–1963*, Volume XXII, Document 89.

82. *FRUS, 1961–1963*, Volume XXII, Document 90.

83. *FRUS, 1961–1963*, Volume XXII, Documents 91 and 92.

84. Memorandum for the Record, March 31, 1962, Roger Hilsman Papers, Box 1, "China Planning on Mainland Operations, 3/62," JFKL; and *FRUS, 1961–1963*, Volume XXII, Part 1, Document 94, 199–200. Hilsman states that this was the "only time I ever saw Rusk speak with feeling in a meeting." Hilsman, *To Move a Nation*, 314–15.

85. *FRUS, 1961–1963*, Volume XXII, Document 98.

86. *FRUS, 1961–1963*, Volume XXII, Document 105.

87. *FRUS, 1961–1963*, Volume XXII, Document 110.

88. *FRUS, 1961–1963*, Volume XXII, Document 115. Hilsman's memo restated the basic conclusions of the State Department: the ROC feels that the mainland is ready for counterrevolution, but does not believe it can achieve this goal without some level of direct US help. State's Intelligence and Research Bureau argued that any counterrevolutionaries are unlikely to be loyal to the ROC even if they hate the Communist regime, and any real success would lead to Soviet intervention. See *FRUS, 1961–1963*, Volume XXII, Document 113.

89. Hilsman, *To Move a Nation*, 318.

90. Kennedy noted that columnist Joseph Alsop had reported on the PRC military buildup and wanted to know how that information had leaked. *FRUS, 1961–1963*, Volume XXII, Documents 116 and 118.

91. "President's Intelligence Checklist," June 19, 1962, President's Office Files, Countries, Box 113A, "China, Security, 1962–1963," JFKL.

92. *FRUS, 1961–1963*, Volume XXII, Document 120.

93. "President's Intelligence Checklist," June 20, 1962, President's Office Files, Countries, Box 113A, "China, Security, 1962–1963," JFKL.

94. Hilsman Meeting Notes, June 20, 1962, Roger Hilsman Papers, Box 1, "China–Offshore Islands Crisis 6/62," JFKL; and Hilsman, *To Move a Nation*, 318–19. Hilsman's version of the meeting is the only one on record, but the pattern of discussion fits with debates being held during this period. Hilsman's notes are also reprinted *FRUS, 1961–1963*, Volume XXII, Document 122. A full list of participants included 18 people: seven from State, five from Defense, one each from the CIA and the NSC staff, one from the US Information Agency, and three from the Executive Office of the Presidency, including Komer. See NSF, Robert W. Komer, Box 411, "China (Taiwan and Offshore Islands) 1961–1963 (3 of 3)," JFKL.

95. *FRUS, 1961–1963*, Volume XXII, Document 123.

96. *FRUS, 1961–1963*, Volume XXII, Document 128.

97. Young, *Negotiating*, 250–51.

98. *FRUS, 1961–1963*, Volume XXII, Document 131.

99. Papers of John F. Kennedy, Presidential Papers, NSF, Meetings and Memoranda, National Security Council Meetings, 1962: No. 500, 26 June 1962, JFKL Digital Collection.

100. President John F. Kennedy, News Conference, June 27, 1962. JFKL, https://

www.Kennedylibrary.org/Research/Research-Aids/Ready-Reference/Press-Confe
rences/News-Conference-37.aspx

101. *FRUS, 1961–1963*, Volume XXII, Documents 161, 165, 166, and 184.

102. See Hilsman, *To Move a Nation*, 311; *FRUS, 1961–1963*, Volume XXII, Documents 91 and 153.

FIVE

1. *The Federalist Papers*, Number 70, Avalon Project, https://avalon.law.yale.edu
/18th_century/fed70.asp

2. Quoted in Mark Updegrove, *Indomitable Will* (New York: Crown, 2012), 10–11.

3. Clark Clifford, *Counsel to the President* (New York: Anchor Press, 1991), 381.

4. Bill Moyers, "Epilogue: Second Thoughts," in *Lyndon Baines Johnson and the Uses of Power*, ed. Bernard J. Firestone and Robert Vogt (New York: Greenwood Press, 1988), 349.

5. Quoted in Doris Kearns Goodwin, *Lyndon Johnson and the American Dream* (New York: Signet, 1976), 253.

6. George Reedy, *Lyndon B. Johnson* (New York: Andrews and McMeel, 1982), ix.

7. Dean Rusk, *As I Saw It* (New York: Penguin, 1990), 33.

8. David Fromkin, "Lyndon Johnson and Foreign Policy," *Foreign Affairs* 74, no. 1 (January–February 1995): 161–70; Robert Dallek, "Lyndon Johnson as a World Leader," in *The Foreign Policies of Lyndon Johnson*, ed. H. W. Brands (College Station: Texas A & M Press, 1999), 6–18; Matthew Jones, "Groping toward Coexistence," *Diplomacy and Statecraft* 12, no. 3 (September 2001): 175. While in graduate school the author worked for Paul Hammond while he was writing a book on the foreign policy of the Johnson administration. The initial goal of the book was to study Johnson's decision making, but not include Vietnam. That was to be the unique aspect of the study. Professor Hammond ultimately came to the conclusion that such an endeavor was not feasible. The Vietnam War extended its tentacles into every corner of Johnson's policy. The published book contains a chapter on Vietnam policy. See Paul Hammond, *LBJ and the Presidential Management of Foreign Relations* (Austin: University of Texas Press, 1992).

9. Rowland Evans and Robert Novak, *Lyndon Johnson* (New York: Signet, 1966), 358–62; and Goodwin, *Lyndon Johnson*, 162.

10. Dean Rusk Oral History Interview I, 7/28/69, LBJ Library (hereafter LBJL), 9–10; and Robert Caro, *The Passage to Power* (New York: Knopf, 2012), 320.

11. Bundy to Johnson, November 23, 1963, National Security Files (NSF), Files of McGeorge Bundy, Chron File, November 1963, Box 1, "November 23–30, 1963 (2 of 2)," LBJL.

12. Evans and Novak, *Lyndon Johnson*, 365–68. The text of the speech can be found at the American Presidency Project, http://www.presidency.ucsb.edu/ws/?pi
d=25988

13. Eric Goldman, *The Tragedy of Lyndon Johnson* (New York: Dell, 1968), 120.

Sorensen announced his resignation on January 15, 1964, effective February 29. Schlesinger resigned on January 28, effective March 1.

14. Komer to Bundy, December 18, 1963, Papers of Robert W. Komer, Box 3, "RWK Chron File July-December 1963 (1 of 3)," LBJL.

15. Smith to the President, January 31, 1964, NSF, Memos to the President, Box 1, "Vol. 1 11/63–2/64 (1 of 2)," LBJL.

16. Richard T. Johnson, *Managing the White House* (New York: Harper and Row, 1974), 159–98; and Thomas Preston, *The President and His Inner Circle* (New York: Columbia University Press, 2001), 137–89.

17. Bundy to Rusk, November 30, 1965, NSF, Memos to the President McGeorge Bundy, Vol. 15–17, Box 5, "McGeorge Bundy Vol. 17, Nov. 20-Dec. 31, 1965 (2 of 3)," LBJL.

18. Bundy to the President, December 5, 1963, NSF, Memos to the President, Box 1, "Vol. 1, 11/63–2/64 (2 of 2)," LBJL.

19. Bromley Smith, "National Security Affairs during the Johnson Administration," in *The Johnson Presidency*, ed. Kenneth Thompson (Lanham, MD: University Press of America, 1986), 201–2.

20. Smith, "National Security Affairs," 200–201.

21. Rusk Oral History Interview I, LBJL, 18–19.

22. Bundy to Valenti, March 4, 1964, NSF Memos to the President, Box 1, "McGeorge Bundy, Vol. 2, 3/1–31, 64 (1 of 2)," LBJL.

23. Lyndon B. Johnson. *The Vantage Point* (New York: Holt, Rinehart, and Winston, 1971), 65.

24. Goodwin, *Lyndon Johnson*, 335. On Johnson's constant worry about leaks, see Nicholas deB. Katzenbach Oral History Interview II, 11/23/68, LBJL, 17; Robert S. McNamara Oral History Interview I, 1/8/75, LBJL, 17; Rusk Oral History Interview I, 3, and 17–19, LBJL; Walt W. Rostow Oral History Interview I, 3/21/69, 9, 14, 16–17, 21, and 36, LBJL; and W. Marvin Watson and Sherwin Markman, *Chief of Staff* (New York: Thomas Dunne Books, 2004), 104–10.

25. The vice presidency remained vacant for slightly over a year under Johnson. Previous administrations operated without vice presidents for far longer. The vice presidency remained vacant under Truman from April 1945 to January 1949. President John Tyler, who assumed the presidency after William Henry Harrison's death, had no vice president for one month shy of a full four-year term.

26. Smith, "National Security Affairs during the Johnson Administration." 200–201.

27. *Foreign Relations of the United States* (hereafter FRUS), *1964–1968*, Volume XXXIII, Document 144.

28. McGeorge Bundy Oral History Interview I, 1/30/69, 38, LBJL.

29. *FRUS, 1964–1968*, Volume XXXIII, Document 170.

30. David Humphrey, "NSC Meetings during the Johnson Presidency," *Diplomatic History* 18, no. 1 (January 1994): 35.

31. Data on NSC meetings is from Clinton Administration. National Security Council Archives, https://clintonwhitehouse4.archives.gov/media/pdf/Johnson_Admin.pdf

32. Humphrey, "NSC Meetings," 31–32.

33. Keith Clark and Laurence Legere, *The President and the Management of*

National Security (New York: Praeger, 1969), 88; John Prados, *Keeper of the Keys* (New York: Morrow, 1991), 149; and Hammond, *LBJ*, 7. The best analysis of Johnson's use of the NSC is Humphrey, "NSC Meetings," 29–45.

34. Richard Goodwin, *Remembering America* (Boston: Little, Brown, 1988), 382.

35. Rusk Oral History Interview I, 4, LBJL; Bundy Oral History Interview I, 21, LBJL; and Preston, *The President*, 162.

36. Irving Janis, *Groupthink* (Boston: Houghton Mifflin, 1982), 97–130.

37. Rusk Oral History Interview I, 26–27, LBJL; Preston, *The President*, 155; and David DiLeo, *George Ball, Vietnam, and the Rethinking of Containment* (Chapel Hill: University of North Carolina Press, 1991).

38. Johnson, *Managing the White House*, 180; Goodwin, *Lyndon Johnson*, 251; Warren Cohen, *Dean Rusk* (Totowa, NJ: Cooper Scientific, 1980), 221.

39. *FRUS, 1964–1968*, Volume XXXIII, Document 180.

40. Bundy, Oral History Interview I, LBJL, 25.

41. Rusk, *As I Saw It*, 335–336. Jack Valenti, one of Johnson's White House staffers, echoed this assessment. Johnson made decisions with his cabinet officers, not with staff. Jack Valenti, "Managing the White House; Leading the Country," in Thompson, *Johnson Presidency*, 29.

42. Thomas Schoenbaum, *Waging Peace and War* (New York: Simon and Shuster, 1988), 413–14; Hammond, *LBJ*, 1–2.

43. Tom Wicker, *JFK and LBJ* (Baltimore: Penguin, 1968), 1.

44. James C. Thomson Oral History Interview I, 7/22/1971, 23, LBJL.

45. Patrick Anderson, *The President's Men* (Garden City, NY: Doubleday and Co., 1968), 301.

46. Prados, *Keeper of the Keys*, 138.

47. Benjamin H. Read Oral History Interview I, 1/13/69, LBJL, 4.

48. NSAM 280, February 14, 1964, LBJL, https://www.discoverlbj.org/item/nsf-nsam280

49. NSAM 281, February 11, 1964, LBJL, https://www.discoverlbj.org/item/nsf-nsam281; and *FRUS, 1964–1968*, Volume XXXIII, Document 6.

50. See, for example, Goldman, *Tragedy*; George Christian, *The President Steps Down* (New York: Macmillan, 1970); Harry McPherson, *A Political Education* (Austin: University of Texas Press, 1972); Reedy, *Lyndon Johnson*; Goodwin, *Remembering America*; Joseph Califano, *The Triumph and Tragedy of Lyndon Johnson* (New York: Simon and Shuster, 1991); and Watson and Markman, *Chief of Staff*.

51. Bundy Oral History Interview I, LBJL, 23–24; and Goodwin, *Lyndon Johnson*, 251.

52. Bundy Oral History Interview I, LBJL, 23.

53. Humphrey, "NSC Meetings," 33.

54. Anderson, *President's Men*, 339; Bundy Oral History Interview I, LBJL, 42; and Prados, *Keeper of the Keys*, 154.

55. The complete list was Johnson, Vice President Hubert Humphrey, Bundy, NSC executive secretary Bromley Smith, Rusk, McNamara, Deputy Secretary of Defense Cyrus Vance, Assistant Secretary of Defense for International Security Affairs John McNaughton, Chairman of the Joint Chiefs General Earle Wheeler, Director of the Defense Intelligence Agency General Joseph Carroll, and Moyers. Memorandum for Bromley Smith. September 16, 1965, Remote Archives Cap-

ture Project File, Box 3, "Documents from the National Security File, Intelligence Briefings File, Boxes, 1–10," LBJL.

56. *FRUS, 1964–1968*, Volume XXXIII, Documents 161 and 164, respectively. Francis Bator of the NSC staff actually drafted a memo on March 31, 1966 stating that until Johnson chose a successor to Bundy, Moyers would serve as ANSA. The memo was never disseminated; Johnson named Rostow as ANSA later than day.

57. Helms to Moyers, September 23, 1966, NSF, Agency File, Box 10, "CIA Helms Memoranda," LBJL.

58. Robert Komer Oral History Interview, November 15, 1971, "AC-94-3," 22, LBJL.

59. Humphrey, "NSC Meetings," 30–31; Johnson, *Managing the White House*, 176–77; and Goldman, *Tragedy*, 119–20.

60. John Macy, "Personnel and Presidential Advisors," in Thompson, *Johnson Presidency*, 135.

61. Clark and Legere, *The President*, 82–83; H. W. Brands. "Introduction," in *The Foreign Policies of Lyndon Johnson*, ed. H. W. Brands (College Station: Texas A&M Press, 1999), 4.

62. Robert Dallek, *Flawed Giant* (New York: Oxford University Press, 1998), 89–90.

63. On these debates, see Goldman, *Tragedy*, 447–48; Prados, *Keeper of the Keys*, 148. Bundy quoted in Bundy Oral History Interview I, LBJL, 1.

64. Rusk Oral History Interview I, LBJL, 3; and Rostow Oral History, LBJL, 7.

65. Quoted in, respectively, Walt Rostow, *The Diffusion of Power* (New York: Macmillan, 1972), 363; and Goldman, *Tragedy*, 121. See also Rusk, *As I Saw It*, 333; and Smith, "National Security Affairs during the Johnson Administration," 206.

66. Christian, *President Steps Down*, 7.

67. See NSF, Memos to the President McGeorge Bundy and Robert Komer, Box 6 (1 of 2), "McGeorge Bundy Vol. 18, January 1–18, 1966 (1 of 2)," LBJL; and Rostow, *Diffusion of Power*, 360–61.

68. Robert Komer Oral History Interview, 1/30/70, "AC 94-1," LBJL.

69. Rusk Oral History Interview I, 29, LBJL; and George Ball, *The Past Has Another Pattern* (New York: W. W. Norton, 1982), 339.

70. Rusk Oral History Interview I, 28, LBJL.

71. Vaughan Davis Barnett, *The Presidency of Lyndon Johnson* (Lawrence: University Press of Kansas, 1983), 15–17; Goodwin, *Remembering America*, 260; and Larry Berman, "Paths Chosen and Opportunities Lost," in *Leadership in the Modern Presidency*, ed. Fred Greenstein (Cambridge, MA: Harvard University Press, 1988), 140–43.

72. See Goodwin, *Lyndon Johnson*, 185; and Rusk Oral History Interview I, 1, LBJL. Quote in Rusk, *As I Saw It*, 332.

73. Califano, *Triumph and Tragedy*, 28–29; Goodwin. *Remembering America*, 258–59.

74. Bundy Oral History Interview I, 34–35, LBJL; and McGeorge Bundy Oral History Interview II, 2/17/69, 8–9, LBJL

75. Goodwin, *Lyndon Johnson*, 248–49; Goldman, *Tragedy*, 120. One tale of the "treatment" tells the story of Eisenhower asking his attorney general, William Rog-

ers, to stay in between the president and Senator Johnson to keep Johnson from grabbing Eisenhower's suit lapels. Larry Berman, "Paths Chosen," 139.

76. Anderson, *President's Men*. 303.

77. When Johnson thought Jack Valenti, a White House staffer, was getting too much publicity, Johnson temporarily ended Valenti's unrestricted access to the Oval Office and forced him to make an appointment to see Johnson. Johnson, *Managing the White House*, 178. White House staffers generally knew when Johnson was displeased with them; he would deliberately mispronounce their names. McGeorge Bundy Oral History Special Interview I, 3/30/93, 8, LBJL.

78. Goldman, *Tragedy*, 121.

79. Janis, *Groupthink*; and Kevin Mulcahy, "Rethinking Groupthink," *Presidential Studies Quarterly* 25, no. 2 (Spring 1995): 237–50.

80. McNamara Oral History Interview I, 1/8/75, 10, LBJL.

81. Quoted in Rusk Oral History Interview I, 22, 5, 21, and 19, respectively, LBJL.

82. Bundy Oral History Interview I, 15–18, LBJL.

83. Watson, *Chief of Staff*, 110.

84. Rusk, *As I Saw It*, 296 and 336–37.

85. On the Robert Kennedy–Johnson rivalry, see Jeff Shesol, *Mutual Contempt* (New York: W. W. Norton, 1997).

86. See President Lyndon B. Johnson's Daily Diary Collection, February 4, 1964, LBJL, http://www.lbjlibrary.net/collections/daily-diary.html

87. Rusk Oral History Interview I, 16, LBJL; Komer, Oral History Interview, "AC 94–2," 38–40, LBJL; and Henry Graff, *The Tuesday Cabinet* (Englewood Cliffs, NJ: Prentice Hall, 1970). The meetings themselves were not secret. The press even gave the group a nickname—the "awesome foursome." Graff, *Tuesday Cabinet*, 3–4.

88. Graff, *Tuesday Cabinet*; Prados, *Keeper of the Keys*, 149: Hammond, *LBJ*, 9–10; David Humphrey, "Tuesday Lunch at the Johnson White House," *Diplomatic History* 8, no. 1 (Winter 1984): 83 and 90.

89. Bundy Oral History Interview I, 38–39, LBJL.

90. Rusk Oral History Interview I, 16–17, LBJL.

91. McNamara Oral History Interview I, 16–17, LBJL.

92. Quoted in Humphrey, "Tuesday Lunch," 92.

93. See Robert Caro, *Master of the Senate* (New York: Knopf, 2016), 507–10; and Humphrey, "Tuesday Lunch," 83.

94. Humphrey, "Tuesday Lunch," 82 and 89–90; Hammond, *LBJ*, 9; "Lunch Meeting with the President, Tuesday, January 24, 1967," NSF, Files of Walt W. Rostow, Box 1, "Meetings with the President January thru June 1967," LBJL; and Tom Johnson's Notes of Meetings, Boxes 1–4, LBJL.

95. These numbers differ slightly from those calculated by David Humphrey. The difference may be a judgment for what counts as a TLG meeting (there often was no official designation of these meetings until 1966) and a greater availability of data as of this writing in 2020 compared to Humphrey's accounting in 1984. See Humphrey, "Tuesday Lunch," 84–86.

96. See Dwight D. Eisenhower, *Mandate for Change* (Garden City, NY: Doubleday and Co, 1963), 115; and Robert Cutler, *No Time for Rest* (Boston: Little, Brown, 1965), 306.

97. Prados, *Keeper of the Keys*, 149; Humphrey, "Tuesday Lunch," 84; and "Lunch with the President, Wednesday, February 23, 1967, Agenda," NSF, Files of Walt W. Rostow, Box 1, "Meetings with the President January thru June 1967," LBJL.

98. Humphrey, "Tuesday Lunch," 87

99. Data on the number of meetings, their dates, and their attendance is calculated from President Lyndon B. Johnson's Daily Diary Collection, LBJL, http://www.lbjlibrary.net/collections/daily-diary.html; Humphrey, "Tuesday Lunch at the Johnson White House," 82–88; and NSF, Files of Walt W. Rostow, Box 1, "Meetings with the President April-December 1966"; "Meetings with the President January thru June 1967"; "Meetings with the President July thru December 1967"; "Meetings with the President January-April 1968 (1)"; "Meetings with the President May-June 1968 (1 of 5)"; "Meetings with President July-December 1968 (4 of 5);" and "Meetings with the President January 1969 (1 of 5)."

100. I. M. Destler, *Presidents, Bureaucrats, and Foreign Policy* (Princeton: Princeton University Press, 1972), 108; Preston, *The President*, 141; John Burke, *Honest Broker* (College Station: Texas A&M University Press, 2009), 89; Rostow, *Diffusion of Power*, 360.

101. Rusk, *As I Saw It*, 519–20.

102. On these criticisms, see Goodwin, *Lyndon Johnson*, 337; Prados, *Keeper of the Keys*, 150–51; Destler, *Presidents*, 109–10; Clark and Legere, *The President*, 89–90; William Bundy, "The National Security Process: Plus Ca Change . . . ?," *International Security* 7, no. 3 (Winter 1982–83): 101.

103. Smith, "National Security Affairs during the Johnson Administration," 203.

104. Rostow Oral History Interview I, 34, LBJL; and Read Oral History Interview I, 5–6, LBJL.

105. See NSF, Files of Walt W. Rostow, Boxes 1–3, LBJL.

106. Howard Wriggins to Rostow, July 26, 1966, NSF, Files of Walt W. Rostow, Box 1, "Meetings with the President April–December 1966," LBJL.

107. Johnson, *Vantage Point*, 20.

108. Quoted in Berman, "Paths Chosen and Opportunities Lost," 146.

109. U. Alexis Johnson, *The Right Hand of Power* (Englewood Cliffs, NJ: Prentice-Hall, 1984), 395; and Rusk, *As I Saw It*, 337.

110. Destler, *Presidents*, 90.

111. Wicker, *JFK and LBJ*, 197–98.

112. Rusk Oral History Interview I, 3 and 9, LBJL.

113. Rusk, *As I Saw It*, 337.

114. Bundy, Oral History Special Interview I, 6, LBJL

115. Cohen, *Dean Rusk*, 219.

116. Maxwell Taylor, *Swords and Ploughshares* (New York: W. W. Norton, 1972), 191–92.

117. See NSAM 124, *Establishment of the Special Group (Counter-Insurgency)*, January 18, 1962, Federation of American Scientists (FAS), https://fas.org/irp/offdocs/nsam-jfk/nsam124.htm; and Jeffrey Michaels, "Managing Global Counterinsurgency," *Journal of Strategic Studies* 35, no. 1 (February 2012): 33–61.

118. *FRUS, 1964–1968*, Volume XXXIII, Document 149.

119. *FRUS, 1964–1968*, Volume XXXIII, Document 16.

120. *FRUS, 1964–1968*, Volume XXXIII, Document 17.

121. NSAM 280, February 14, 1964, FAS, https://fas.org/irp/offdocs/nsam-lbj/ns am-280.htm; and NSAM 310, July 8, 1964, LBJL, https://www.discoverlbj.org/it em/nsf-nsam310

122. *FRUS, 1964–1968*, Volume XXXIII, Document 42.

123. Taylor officially became a special consultant to the president on September 17, 1965. See note 5 in *FRUS, 1964–1968*, Volume XXXIII, Document 50.

124. Taylor to the President, May 17, 1967, NSF, NSAMs, Box 7, "NSAMs, NSAM 341, The Direction, Coordination, and Supervision of Interdepartmental Activities Overseas," (2 of 2), LBJL; Administrative History, Department of State, Volume 1, Chapters 1–3, Box 1, "Chapter 2 (Leadership and Structure of the Department): Sections A, B," LBJL; Taylor, *Swords and Ploughshares*, 359–61; and Johnson, *Right Hand of Power*, 398–99.

125. On the July 1965 decisions, see Larry Berman, *Planning a Tragedy* (New York: W. W. Norton, 1983).

126. *FRUS, 1964–1968*, Volume III, Document 93; and President Johnson's Press Conference, July 28, 1965, *American Presidency Project*, http://www.presidency.ucsb .edu/ws/?pid=27116

127. See Humphrey, "NSC Meetings," 38.

128. *FRUS, 1964–1968*, Volume XXXIII, Document 48.

129. See Johnson, *Right Hand of Power*, 398–401.

130. See note 1 in *FRUS, 1964–1968*, Volume XXXIII, Document 48. Early versions of the IRGs had been created on an experimental basis in either 1965 or 1966. The assistant secretaries of state for Latin America and Africa had agreed to run interagency committees for their region. See Rostow Oral History Interview I, 27, LBJL, and *FRUS, 1964–1968*, Volume XXXIII, Document 51.

131. The report is reprinted in *FRUS, 1964–1968*, Volume XXXIII, Document 50.

132. Taylor to the President, May 17, 1967, NSF, NSAMs, Box 7, "NSAMs, NSAM 341, The Direction, Coordination, and Supervision of Interdepartmental Activities Overseas," (2 of 2), LBJL; and Taylor, *Swords and Ploughshares*, 359–61.

133. Taylor, *Swords and Ploughshares*, 361.

134. *FRUS, 1964–1968*, Volume XXXIII, Documents 51, 52, and 53.

135. *FRUS, 1964–1968*, Volume XXXIII, Document 55.

136. *FRUS, 1964–1968*, Volume XXXIII, Document 56. The SIG/IRG system was created in tandem with a new system within the regional bureaus of State: the country director system in which one State Department official would be the central coordinator for all interbureau issues related to that country. See William Bacchus, *Foreign Policy and the Bureaucratic Process* (Princeton: Princeton University Press, 1974).

137. Comments on NSAM 341 Prepared for President Johnson for use at the Cabinet Meeting, March 4, NSF, "Memos to the President McGeorge Bundy and Robert Komer 3/1–31/66, vol. 21 (3 of 3)"; Fact Sheet on NSAM 341, NSF, Memos to the President McGeorge Bundy and Robert Komer 3/1–31/66, vol. 21 (3 of 3); and Background Briefing—SIG by Taylor and U.A. Johnson, March 4, 1966, NSF, NSAMs Box 7, "NSAM 341 The Direction, Coordination and Supervision of Interdepartmental Activities Overseas, (2 of 2)," LBJL.

138. *FRUS, 1964–1968*, Volume XXXIII, Document 153.

139. Destler, *Presidents*, 104–5 and 117; Clark and Legere, *The President*, 92; and Hammond, *LBJ*, 31–32.

140. See "The Secretary of State and the Problem of Coordination: New Duties and Procedures, March 4, 1966," prepared by the Senate Subcommittee on National Security and International Operations, Senate Committee on Government Operations, 89th Congress, 2nd Session, May 9, 1966. See also *FRUS, 1964–1968*, Volume XXXIII, Document 58.

141. Authority given to the State Department and the SIG/IRG by NSAM 341 explicitly excludes "military forces operating in the field."

142. On these analyses of the SIG and the view of Johnson and his senior advisors, see Johnson, *Right Hand of Power*, 400–401; Smith, "National Security Affairs during the Johnson Administration," 203; Bundy Oral History Interview I, 39, LBJL; Nicholas deB. Katzenbach Oral History Interview III, 12/11/68, 6, LBJL; and Nicholas deB. Katzenbach, *Some of It Was Fun* (New York: W. W. Norton, 2008), 203.

143. NSAM 341, "The Direction, Coordination and Supervision of Interdepartmental Activities Overseas," 3/2/1966, LBJL, https://www.discoverlbj.org/item/nsf-nsam341

144. Clark and Legere, *The President*, 148.

145. For details on SIG meetings, see NSF, Agency File, Department of State Senior Interdepartmental Group, Box 56, LBJL.

146. Komer wrote: "As a minor example of the kind of cutthroat piddling that goes on in an interregnum . . . it reminds me of grammar school." Komer to Moyers, March 8, 1966. NSF, Files of Robert W. Komer (1966–1967), Box 1, "Chrono: March 1–20, 1966 (2 of 2)," LBJL.

147. SIG Assignments to Other Agencies and Departments. NSF, Agency File, Box 62, "State Department, Special Group (CI)," LBJL.

148. Taylor to the President, March 29, 1966. NSF, Memos to the President McGeorge Bundy and Robert Komer Box 6 (2 of 2), "Memos to the President Robert Komer 3/1–3/31/66, Volume 21 (1 of 3)," LBJL; and Memo from Rostow to the President, 10/13/66, NSF, Files of Walt W. Rostow, Box 15, "Files of Walt Rostow Non-Vietnam, March-June 1967 (1 of 2)," LBJL.

149. Taylor, *Swords and Ploughshares*, 361.

150. Administrative History, Department of State, Volume 1, Chapters 1–3, Box 1, "Chapter 2 (Leadership and Structure of the Department): Sections A, B," 35, LBJL

151. Clark and Legere, *The President*, 126; and Rostow, *Diffusion of Power*, 362.

152. Rostow to the President, March 30, 1967, NSF, Files of Walt W. Rostow, Box 15, "Files of Walt Rostow Non-Vietnam, March-June 1967 (1 of 2)," LBJL.

153. Draft memo from the President, June 27, 1967, NSF, NSAMs Box 7, "NSAM 341 The Direction, Coordination and Supervision of Interdepartmental Activities Overseas (2 of 2)," LBJL.

154. Clark and Legere, *The President*, 126; and Rostow, *Diffusion of Power*, 126.

155. *FRUS, 1964–1968*, Volume XXXIII, Document 153.

156. David Halberstam, *The Best and the Brightest* (New York: Fawcett, 1973), 758–50; and David Milne, *America's Rasputin* (New York: Hill and Wang, 2008), 153–54. Bundy discounts Vietnam as his reason for leaving. He described it as

essentially fatigue, feeling that "in a wider and a deeper sense toward the end of 1965, it became clear to me that I was really running out of steam. This was not just this complicated question of relations with the President. It was a much more deep-seated thing. I had been doing this job for going on five years . . . but it was just not workable from my point of view that I should still be doing that, let's say, for another two years." Bundy Oral History Interview I, 13, LBJL.

157. *FRUS, 1964–1968*, Volume XXXIII, Documents 153 and 161.

158. Bundy to Rusk, November 30, 1965. NSF Memos to the President, McGeorge Bundy Vol. 15–17, Box 5, "McGeorge Bundy vol. 17 Nov. 20-Dec. 31, 1965 (2 of 3)," LBJL; and Bundy to the President, February 19, 1966. NSF Memos to the President McGeorge Bundy and Robert Komer Box 6 (1 of 2), "McGeorge Bundy vol. 20 February 5–28, 1966 (1 of 2)," LBJL; and *FRUS, 1964–1968*, Volume XXXIII, Document 163.

159. *FRUS, 1964–1968*, Volume XXXIII, Document 164.

160. P. M. Kamath, *Executive Privilege versus Democratic Accountability* (Atlantic Highlands, NJ: Humanities Press, 1982), 170.

161. President Lyndon B. Johnson's New Conference, March 31, 1966, American Presidency Project, http://www.presidency.ucsb.edu/ws/index.php?pid=27524. See also Kevin Mulcahy, "Walt Rostow as National Security Advisor," *Presidential Studies Quarterly* 25, no. 2 (Spring 1995): 229. In private, he illustrated the point in quintessential Johnson style: "I'm getting Walt Rostow as my intellectual. He's not your intellectual. He's not Bundy's intellectual. He's not Galbraith's intellectual. He's not Schlesinger's intellectual. He's going to be my Goddam intellectual and I'm going to have him by the short hairs." Quoted in Halberstam, *Best and the Brightest*, 762.

162. Arthur Schlesinger, *A Thousand Days* (New York: Fawcett, 1965), 412.

163. *FRUS, 1964–1968*, Volume XXXIII, Document 170.

164. See Humphrey, "NSC Meetings," 41. Clinton Administration. National Security Council Archives, https://clintonwhitehouse4.archives.gov/media/pdf/Johnson_Admin.pdf

165. President Lyndon B. Johnson's Daily Diary Collection, LBJL, http://www.lbjlibrary.net/collections/daily-diary.html; NSF, Files of Walt W. Rostow, Box 1, Lyndon B. Johnson Presidential Library; and Humphrey, "Tuesday Lunch," 82–88.

166. Read Oral History Interview I, 7, LBJL.

167. Read Oral History Interview I, 5–6, LBJL.

168. Rostow Oral History Interview I, 34, LBJL.

169. See, for example, Howard Wriggins to Rostow, July 26, 1966, NSF, Files of Walt W. Rostow, Box 1, "Meetings with the President April-December 1966," LBJL.

170. Oral History Interview with Robert Komer, August 18, 1970, "AC-94-2," LBJL; and Graff, *Tuesday Cabinet*.

171. NSF, Files of Walt W. Rostow, Box 1, "Meetings with the President April-December 1966," LBJL.

172. Read Oral History Interview I, 6; LBJL.

173. NSF, Files of Walt W. Rostow, Box 1, "Meetings with the President April-December 1966," LBJL; and Tom Johnson's Notes of Meetings, Boxes 1–4, LBJL.

174. In some quarters Rostow has been criticized for becoming almost a second

secretary of state, due to proximity to the president, rather by intention. None of the principals, however, have made this charge. He has also been accused of using his control of the paper flow to limit the president's exposure to alternate opinions. Scholars of groupthink have labeled Rostow a "mindguard"—the person whose job it is to "suppress" alternate points of view. Given Johnson's need for information, his mastery of the process and personnel, and his boundless energy, it is hard to imagine anyone could have successfully prevented Johnson from seeking out ideas or analysis that he wanted. On the former argument, see Katzenbach Oral History Interview II, 7 and 16, LBJL. On the latter, see Janis, *Groupthink*, 40–41 and 119.

175. Rostow Oral History Interview I, 3/21/69, 16, LBJL.

SIX

1. James Thomson, Oral History Interview, July 22, 1971, 40–41, Lyndon Johnson Presidential Library (hereafter LBJL).

2. This chapter does not include a case study that examines decision making concerning China's acquisition of an atomic bomb. The advisory process on China's nuclear capability was placed into a special committee chaired by former deputy secretary of defense Roswell Gilpatric in 1964. In that sense, it is not standard decision making and is therefore less relevant to the research questions here. Ultimately, the administration accepted China's new capability and moved on to assess its impact. As McGeorge Bundy stated of China's first nuclear bomb: "It was the dog that did not bark." McGeorge Bundy Oral History Interview II, 2/17/69, 39, LBJL. On the decision, see William Burr and Jeffrey Richelson, "Whether to 'Strangle the Baby in the Cradle,'" *International Security* 25, no. 3 (2001): 54–99; and Hal Brands, "Rethinking Nonproliferation," *Journal of Cold War Studies* 8, no. 2 (Spring 2006): 83–113.

3. Komer to M. Bundy and Walt Rostow, March 6, 1961, NSF, Meetings and Memoranda Series, Box 321, "Staff Memoranda Robert W. Komer, 1/1/61–3/14/61," JFKL; Komer to M. Bundy, "Check List on China Policy," July 7, 1961, NSF, Robert W. Komer Series, Box 410, "China (CPR) 1961–1963 [2 of 3]," JFKL; Komer to Bundy and Rostow, "First Thoughts on China," April 7, 1961, NSF, Robert W. Komer Series, Box 410, "China (CPR) 1961–1963 [3 of 3]," JFKL; and Thomson, Oral History Interview, 48, LBJL. See also James Thomson, "On the Making of US China Policy," *China Quarterly* 50 (April–June 1972): 223–25; and Gordon Chang, *Friends and Enemies* (Stanford: Stanford University Press, 1990), 271. Bowles had called for a de facto acceptance of two Chinas, while containing Chinese expansionism, and upholding the US alliance with the Republic of China. See Chester Bowles, "The 'China Problem' Reconsidered," *Foreign Affairs* 38, no. 3 (April 1960): 476–86.

4. Papers of James C. Thomson, Box 14, "Proposed Presidential Speech on a Two China's Policy, November 1961," JFKL.

5. Thomson, "On the Making," 226.

6. China scholars consider the Kennedy administration to be the first that acknowledged permanent Communist sovereignty over the mainland. See William Bueler, *US China Policy and the Problem of Taiwan* (Boulder: Colorado Associated

University Press, 1971), 42; and A. Doak Barnett, *A New US Policy toward China* (Washington, DC: Brookings Institution, 1971), 15.

7. Roger Hilsman. *To Move a Nation* (Garden City, NY: Doubleday, 1967), 344–45; Thomson, "On the Making," 227.

8. See, for example, Rostow to Members of the Tuesday Planning Group, 7/23/63; and Komer to Bundy, November 5, 1963, NSF, Robert W. Komer Series, Box 410, "China (CPR) Nuclear Explosion 1961–1963 [2 of 2]," JFKL.

9. Hilsman, *To Move a Nation*, 346–47.

10. Hilsman, *To Move a Nation*, 353.

11. John F. Kennedy, Commencement Address at American University, June 10, 1963, John F. Kennedy Presidential Library (JFKL), https://www.jfklibrary.org/Asset-Viewer/BWC7I4C9QUmLG9J6I8oy8w.aspx

12. John F. Kennedy, "News Conference 64," November 14, 1963, JFKL, https://www.jfklibrary.org/Research/Research-Aids/Ready-Reference/Press-Conferences/News-Conference-64.aspx

13. Thomson, Oral History Interview, 40–41, LBJL.

14. Roger Hilsman, Oral History Interview. Association for Diplomatic Studies and Training Foreign Affairs Oral History Project, May 15, 1969, 21; https://www.adst.org/OH%20TOCs/Hilsman,%20Roger.toc.pdf

15. Hilsman, *To Move a Nation*, 351.

16. Hilsman, *To Move a Nation*, 351–53; Thomson, Oral History Interview, 37–39, LBJL; and Thomson, "On the Making," 229–31.

17. Hilsman, Oral History Interview, 21. For the text of Dulles speech, see *FRUS, 1955–1957*, Volume III, Document 268.

18. Hilsman, *To Move a Nation*, 351.

19. Hilsman, Oral History Interview, 21.

20. Kevin Quigley, "A Lost Opportunity," *Diplomacy and Statecraft* 13, no. 3 (2002): 186.

21. For additional analysis on this question, see Quigley, "A Lost Opportunity," 186, and Warren Cohen, *Dean Rusk* (Totowa, NJ: Cooper Scientific, 1980), 172–73.

22. Hilsman, *To Move a Nation*, 355; Thomson, Oral History Interview, 39, LBJL; and Thomson, "On the Making," 231.

23. Roger Hilsman, "Communist China: The United States Policy," *Vital Speeches of the Day* 30, no. 7 (1963): 203–7.

24. Thomson, "On the Making," 230.

25. Hilsman, *To Move a Nation*, 356; Rosemary Foot, "Redefinitions: The Domestic Context of America's China Policy in the 1960s," *in Reexamining the Cold War*, ed. Robert Ross and Changbin Jiang (Cambridge, MA: Harvard University Press, 2001), 278.

26. Stanley Bachrack, *The Committee of One Million* (New York: Columbia University Press, 1976), 209–10; and Stanley Hornbeck, "United States Policy regarding China: What Did Mr. Hilsman Disclose at San Francisco?," *World Affairs* 126, no. 4 (1963–64): 238–43.

27. Hilsman, Oral History Interview, 22.

28. Hilsman, *To Move a Nation*, 357.

29. See David Halberstam, *The Best and the Brightest* (New York: Fawcett, 1973), 455–57; and "Hilsman Resigns Key Policy Post," *New York Times*, February 26,

1964, https://www.nytimes.com/1964/02/26/archives/hilsman-resigns-key-policy-post-us-adviser-on-far-east-plans.html

30. Hilsman to Adlai Stevenson, no date, Roger Hilsman Papers, Countries Series, Box 1, "China—Policy Speech, 12/13/63," JFKL.

31. Thomson to M. Bundy, November 29, 1965, NSF, Country Files: Asia and the Pacific, China, Box 239, "China Vol. V Memos 10/65–1/66 [1 of 2]," LBJL.

32. Robert Dallek, *Lone Star Rising* (Oxford: Oxford University Press, 1991), 275.

33. Doris Kearns Goodwin, *Lyndon Johnson and the American Dream* (New York: Signet, 1976), 102.

34. Eric Goldman, *The Tragedy of Lyndon Johnson* (New York: Dell, 1968), 450–51.

35. See Thomas Gaskin, "Lyndon B. Johnson, the Eisenhower Administration and US Foreign Policy, 1957–1960," *Presidential Studies Quarterly* 24, no. 2 (Spring 1994): 341–61; and Robert Caro, *Master of the Senate* (New York: Knopf, 2016), 307.

36. Goodwin, *Lyndon Johnson*, 269.

37. Caro, *Master of the Senate*, 525–41.

38. Ronnie Dugger, *The Politician* (New York: Morrow, 1982), 371.

39. Kennedy, also in the hospital at the time, voted for the limiting amendment. See Dwight Eisenhower, *Mandate for Change* (Garden City, NY: Doubleday and Co, 1963), 468–69.

40. Quoted in Goldman, *Tragedy*, 459–63.

41. On Vietnam as an extension of previous policies, see Leslie Gelb, *The Irony of Vietnam* (Washington, DC: Brookings, 1979).

42. Foster Rhea Dulles, *American Foreign Policy toward Communist China, 1949–1969* (New York: Crowell, 1972), 212–18.

43. Halberstam, *Best and the Brightest*, 364.

44. An excellent overview of these issues is Francis Bator, "No Good Choices," *Diplomatic History* 32, no. 3 (June 2008): 309–40.

45. *FRUS, 1964–1968*, Volume XXX, Document 2.

46. The UK had actually tied to recognize the PRC in 1950, but that recognition was rejected.

47. NIE, Number 13–63, "Problems and Prospects in Communist China." May 1, 1963, 1–2, NSF, NIEs, Box 4, "13–61 to 13–65, Communist China, (2 of 2)," LBJL. On US assessments of the impact of the Great Leap Forward, see SNIE [Special National Intelligence Estimate] Number 13–61, "The Economic Situation in China," April 4, 1961; and NIE Number 13-4-62, "Prospects for Communist China." May 2, 1962, NSF, NIEs, Box 4, "13–61 to 13–65, Communist China (1 of 2)," LBJL.

48. John Lewis and Xue Litai, *China Builds the Bomb* (Stanford: Stanford University Press, 1988), 11–72.

49. SNIE [Special National Intelligence Estimate] Number 13-2-63, "Communist China's Advanced Weapons Program," July 24, 1963, 2. NSF, National Security Estimates, Box 4, "13–61 to 13–65, Communist China (2 of 2)," LBJL.

50. Dulles, *American Foreign Policy*, 223.

51. Burr and Richelson, "Whether to 'Strangle the Baby in the Cradle.'"

52. M. Taylor Fravel and Evan S. Medeiros, "China's Search for Assured Retaliation," *International Security* 35, no. 2 (Fall 2010): 53–55.

53. John Sutter, "Two Faces of Konfrontasi," *Asian Survey* 6, no. 10 (October 1966): 523–46. On the relationship between Indonesia and China during this period, see Sheldon Simon, *The Broken Triangle* (Baltimore: Johns Hopkins University Press, 1969).

54. Sutter, "Two Faces of Konfrontasi," 538.

55. On the coup and its aftermath, see Daniel Lev, "Indonesia 1965," *Asian Survey* 6, no. 2 (February 1966): 103–10; and Robert Cribb, "Unresolved Problems in the Indonesian Killings of 1965–1966," *Asian Survey* 42, no. 4 (July–August 2002): 550–63.

56. H. W. Brands, "The Limits of Manipulation," *Journal of American History* 76, no. 3 (December 1989): 785–808; and Matthew Jones, "U.S. Relations with Indonesia, the Kennedy-Johnson Transition, and the Vietnam Connection, 1963–1965," *Diplomatic History* 26, no. 2 (April 2002): 249–81.

57. Klaus H. Pringsheim, "China's Role in the Indo-Pakistani Conflict," *China Quarterly* 24 (October–December 1965): 170–75.

58. John Kuo-Chang Wang, "United Nations Voting on Chinese Representation: An Analysis of General Assembly Roll Calls, 1951–1971," PhD diss., University of Oklahoma, 1977, 95–122. https://shareok.org/bitstream/handle/11244/4401/7815387.PDF?sequence=1

59. Byron S. J. Weng, *Peking's UN Policy* (New York: Praeger, 1972), 124.

60. Weng, *Peking's UN Policy*, 138–41.

61. Memorandum of Conversation, October 24, 1964. NSF, Agency File, Box 8, "Central Intelligence Agency, Volume 1 (2 of 2)," LBJL.

62. *FRUS, 1964–1968*, Volume XXX, Documents 16 and 20.

63. On the Blue Lion committee, see *FRUS, 1964–1968*, Volume XXX, Documents 20, 44, 45, 119, 120, 165, and 166.

64. Larry Berman, *Planning a Tragedy* (New York: W. W. Norton, 1983).

65. NIE Number 13-9-65, "Communist China's Foreign Policy." May 5, 1965, 1, NSF, NIEs, Box 4, "13–61 to 13–65, Communist China (2 of 2)," LBJL.

66. Cline to Rostow, April 13, 1966, 2. NSF, Agency File, Box 9, "Central Intelligence Agency, Volume 2 (1 of 2)," LBJL.

67. The text of the essay can be found in Lin Biao, *Long Live the Victory of People's War!*, as posted by Marxists Internet Archive, https://www.marxists.org/reference/archive/lin-biao/1965/09/peoples_war/index.htm. See also an excellent analysis of the essay, D. P. Mozingo and T. W. Robinson, *Lin Piao on "People's War"* (Santa Monica, CA: RAND Corporation, 1965).

68. Dulles, *American Policy toward Communist China*, 224; and Nancy Tucker, "Threats, Opportunities, and Frustration in East Asia," in *Lyndon Johnson Confronts the World*, ed. Warren Cohen and Nancy Tucker (Cambridge: Cambridge University Press, 1994), 103.

69. Lyndon B. Johnson, *The Vantage Point* (New York: Holt, Rinehart, and Winston, 1971), 134; and George Ball, *The Past Has Another Pattern* (New York: W. W. Norton, 1982), 179.

70. On this point, see Mozingo and Robinson, *Lin Piao on "People's War"*, 18–20.

71. James Hershberg and Chen Jian, "Reading and Warning the Likely Enemy," *International History Review* 27, no. 1 (March 2005): 47–84. On China's overall policy during the Vietnam War, see Chen Jian, *Mao's China and the Cold War* (Chapel Hill: University of North Carolina Press, 2001), 205–37. China did angrily deny February 1967 press reports that it had given the US reassurance at the Warsaw talks that it would not intervene directly in Vietnam unless it was attacked. See Kenneth Young, *Negotiating with the Chinese Communists* (New York: McGraw-Hill, 1968), 274.

72. Randall Woods, *LBJ* (New York: Free Press, 2006), 618.

73. President's News Conference, July 28, 1965. American Presidency Project, http://www.presidency.ucsb.edu/ws/index.php?pid=27116

74. Johnson, *Vantage Point*, 136.

75. Rusk, *As I Saw It*, 456.

76. See John Garver, "The Chinese Threat in the Vietnam War," *Parameters* 22, no. 1 (Spring 1982): 73–85.

77. Bundy to Johnson, January 9, 1964. NSF, Memos to the President, Box 1, "Volume 1 11/63–2/64 (2 of 2)," LBJL.

78. Robert Caro, *The Passage of Power* New York: Knopf, 2012), 534.

79. Johnson, *Vantage Point*, 152.

80. *FRUS, 1961–1963*, Volume XXII, Document 8.

81. Komer to Bundy and Rostow, "First Thoughts on China," April 7, 1961, NSF, Robert W. Komer, Box 410, "China (CPR) 1961–1963 (2 of 3)," JFKL. The memo provides an excellent overview of the strengths and weaknesses of the US and its allies in East Asia and provides three long-term options for the US: "active hostility," "middle road" containment through alliances along the periphery of China, and "accommodation" by accepting a level of neutrality of the lesser powers in East Asia and exploiting the Sino-Soviet split as a way to weaken China.

82. *FRUS, 1961–1963*, Volume XXII, Document 36.

83. Burke to McNamara, June 16, 1961, NSF, Robert W. Komer, Box 410, "China (CPR) 1961–1963 (2 of 3)," JFKL.

84. Office of International Security Affairs, Department of Defense, "US Policy Toward Communist China," NSF, Robert W. Komer Series, Box 410, "China (CPR) 1961–1963 [2 of 3]," JFKL. The internal DoD memo lists three specific documents, NSC 5906/1, NSC 5913/1, and NSC 5723.

85. For example, see National Intelligence Council, *Tracking the Dragon*, October 2004, 313–63.

86. "Communist China (Short Range Report)," prepared by the Special State-Defense Study Group, April 30, 1965; and Memorandum from Chester Cooper to McGeorge Bundy, July 12, 1965, NSF, Agency File, Box 61, "State, Department of, Special State-Defense Study Group re China," LBJL.

87. "Communist China—Long Range Study," June 1966, NSF, Country File, Asia and the Pacific, China, Box 245, "China—Communist China Long Range Study by the Special State-Defense Study Group (vol. 1)," LBJL.

88. See "Communist China (Short Range Report)"; and Memorandum from Chester Cooper to McGeorge Bundy, July 12, 1965, NSF, Agency File, Box 61, "State, Department of, Special State-Defense Study Group re China," LBJL. The

authors of the study concluded that US options were "punitive rather than inter-dictory and even when militarily successful may not achieve the desired political goal. . . . However, these operations are predicated on persuading our adversaries that they will undergo unacceptable damage if they do not desist. With determined and fanatical enemies, like those in control in Peiping and perhaps Hanoi, there is serious danger that they will refuse to so long as they are physically able to carry on, thus facing the US with difficult problems of what to do next."

89. *FRUS, 1961–1963*, Volume XXII, Document 92.

90. *FRUS, 1961–1963*, Volume XXII, Document 94.

91. Memo from R. C. Bowman to Bundy, August 26, 1965; and State Department Memorandum of Conversation, August 27, 1965 in NSF, Agency File, Box 61, "State, Department of, Special State-Defense Study Group re China," LBJL.

92. "Communist China—Long Range Study," v.

93. "Communist China—Long Range Study," vi.

94. "Communist China—Long Range Study," 1 and 222–24.

95. "Communist China—Long Range Study," 2–13.

96. "Communist China—Long Range Study," 1–2.

97. "Communist China—Long Range Study," 214–22 and Annex IV.

98. "Communist China—Long Range Study," 23.

99. See NSF, Agency File, Box 63, "State, Department of, Interdepartmental Regional Group (IRG) (2 of 2)," LBJL.

100. Memorandum for the Deputy Secretary of Defense, the Chairman Joint Chiefs of Staff, and the Deputy Undersecretary of State for Political Affairs, July 26, 1966; and Alfred Jenkins to Rostow, September 14, 1966; and Minutes of the Inter-Agency China Committee, October 31, 1967, in NSF, Files of Alfred Jenkins, Box 1, "Chicom—China Working Group—1966–1967," LBJL.

101. Michael Lumbers, *Piercing the Bamboo Curtain* (Manchester: University of Manchester Press, 2008); and Katherine Klinefelter, "The China Hearings," *Congress & the Presidency* 38 (2011): 60–76.

102. Walt Rostow, *The Diffusion of Power* (New York: Macmillan, 1972), 360–36; and NSF, Files of Alfred Jenkins, Boxes 1–3, LBJL.

103. Roderick MacFarquhar and Michael Schoenhals, *Mao's Last Revolution* (Cambridge, MA: Harvard University Press, 2008); and Andrew Walder, *China under Mao* (Cambridge, MA: Harvard University Press, 2015), 180 315.

104. Leonard Kusnitz, *Public Opinion and Foreign Policy* (Westport, CT: Greenwood Press, 1984), 111–19; and Lumbers, *Piercing the Bamboo Curtain*, 154–55.

105. Chang, *Friends and Enemies*, 274.

106. Klinefelter, "China Hearings." 62.

107. Bachrack, *The Committee of One Million*, 231 and 245.

108. *FRUS, 1964–1968*, Volume XXX, Document 66.

109. Wang, *United Nations Voting*, 95–122; and Weng, *Peking's UN Policy*, 231.

110. See Thomson, "On the Making," 233–38; Thomson, Oral History Interview, 41–2, LBJL; Bundy to Johnson, December 2, 1965, NSF, Memos to the President, "McGeorge Bundy, Vol. 17, Nov. 20, 1965-Dec. 31, 1965 (2 of 3)," LBJL; and Lumbers, *Piercing the Bamboo Curtain*, 76.

111. *United States Policy toward Asia*, Subcommittee on the Far East and the Pacific,

Committee on Foreign Affairs, US House of Representatives, 89th Congress, 2nd Session, January–February 1966. Hathi Trust, https://catalog.hathitrust.org /Record/007608252

112. *Supplemental Foreign Assistance, Fiscal Year, 1966*: Vietnam, Hearings before the Committee on Foreign Relations, United States Senate, 89th Congress, 2nd Session, on S. 2793, to amend further the Foreign Assistance Act of 1961, as amended: January 28, February 4, 8, 10, 17 and 18, 1966. Hathi Trust, https://catal og.hathitrust.org/Record/010309694

113. Testimony of A. Doak Barnett, *United States Policy*, 63–64.

114. Testimony of Hans Morgenthau, *United States Policy*, 125. See Hans Morgenthau, *Politics Among Nations*, 5th ed., Revised (New York: Alfred A. Knopf, 1978).

115. Testimony of Roger Hilsman, *United States Policy*, 136–40.

116. Testimony of Dean Rusk, *United States Policy*, 525–32.

117. Testimony of William Bundy, *United States Policy*, 536–48. Bundy's speech is reprinted in William Bundy, "The United States and Communist China," February 28, 1966, *Department of State Bulletin* 54 (1392): 310–18.

118. Matthew Jones, "Groping toward Coexistence," *Diplomacy and Statecraft* 12, no. 3 (September 2001): 185.

119. *United States Policy toward Asia*, 547–48.

120. *US Policy with Respect to Mainland China*, US Congress, Hearings before the Committee on Foreign Relations, United States Senate, 89th Congress, 2nd Session, March 8, 10, 16, 18, 21, 30, 1966, https://babel.hathitrust.org/cgi/pt?id=umn .31951d01984992t&view=1up&seq=2

121. Klinefelter, "China Hearings," 63–64.

122. Testimony of A. Doak Barnett, *US Policy*, 4.

123. Testimony of John K. Fairbank, *US Policy*, 106.

124. Testimony of Alexander Eckstein, Donald Zagoria, Robert Scalapino, *US Policy*, respectively, 335, 368–75, and 570.

125. On the UN issue, see *US Policy*, 4, 106, 212, 215, 247–48, 288, and 571.

126. Memorandum from the Council for a Livable World, March 25, 1966, *US Policy with Respect to Mainland China*, 615–30.

127. Thomson to Valenti, March 1, 1966, NSF, Country File: Asia and the Pacific, Box 239, "China Vol. VI, Memos 3/66–9/66 (1 of 2)," LBJL.

128. NSF, Files of Robert W. Komer (1966–67), Box 1, "Chrono: March 1–20, 1966 (2 of 2)," LBJL.

129. "Tuesday Lunch Agenda," March 8, 1966, NSF, Memos to the President McGeorge Bundy and Robert Komer Files, Box 6 (2 of 2), "Robert Komer 3/1–31/66, vol. 21 (3 of 3)," LBJL.

130. Thomson Oral History Interview, 42–43, LBJL.

131. *FRUS, 1964–1968*, Volume XXX, Document 133. See note 2.

132. Thomson Oral History Interview, 42–43, LBJ.

133. Hubert Humphrey, "United States Tasks and Responsibilities in Asia," March 11, 1966. *Department of State Bulletin* 54 (1397): 523–29.

134. *Meet the Press*, vol. 10, no. 11, March 13, 1966, 10–11 and 15. Minnesota Historical Society, http://www2.mnhs.org/library/findaids/00442/pdfa/00442-018 19.pdf

135. Komer to Johnson, March 14, 1966, NSF Memos to the President,

McGeorge Bundy and Robert Komer, Box 6 (2 of 2), "Robert Komer 3/1–31/66, Vol. 21 (2 of 3)," LBJL.

136. *FRUS, 1964–1968*, Volume XXX, Document 136.

137. NSF, Country File: Asia and the Pacific, Box 240, "China Vol. VII Memos 9/66–11/66 (3 of 3)," LBJL.

138. Goldberg, a hero to liberals, may have been picked by Johnson to deflect criticism of his foreign policy from within the Democratic Party. It also opened a slot on the Court for Johnson's friend Abe Fortas. David Stebenne, *Arthur J. Goldberg* (Oxford: Oxford University Press, 1966), 346–48.

139. *FRUS, 1964–1968*, Volume XXX, Document 141.

140. *FRUS, 1964–1968*, Volume XXX, Document 145.

141. *FRUS, 1964–1968*, Volume XXX, Document 143 and 148.

142. *FRUS, 1964–1968*, Volume XXX, Documents 195 and 199.

143. Valenti to Moyers, April 5, 166, NSF, Country File: Asia and the Pacific, Box 240, "China Vol. VI, Memos (continued) 3/66–9/66 (2 of 3)," LBJL.

144. Thomson to Rostow, Moyers, and Valenti, April 2, 1966, White House Confidential Files, Box 7 (2 of 2), "CO 50 China," LBJL

145. Rice to Rostow, April 15, 1966, NSF, Country File: Asia and the Pacific, Box 240, "China Vol. VI, Memos (continued) 3/66–9/66 (2 of 3)," LBJL.

146. *FRUS, 1964–1968*, Volume XXX, Document 144.

147. *FRUS, 1964–1968*, Volume XXX, Document 145.

148. *FRUS, 1964–1968*, Volume XXX, Document 148.

149. *FRUS, 1964–1968*, Volume XXX, Document 149.

150. *FRUS, 1964–1968*, Volume XXX Document 150; and Rostow to Marvin Watson, May 18, 1966, NSF, Country File: Asia and the Pacific, Box 240, "China Vol. VI, Memos (continued) 3/66–9/66 (1 of 3)," LBJL.

151. *FRUS, 1964–1968*, Volume XXX, Document 154.

152. The summary of these meetings is contained in four telegrams from the embassy in the Republic of China to the Department of State. See *FRUS, 1964–1968*, Volume XXX, Documents 162 through 165.

153. Thomson Oral History Interview, 42–45, LBJL; and *FRUS, 1964–1968*, Volume XXX, Document 156.

154. "Remarks to the American Alumni Council: United States Asian Policy," American Presidency Project. http://www.presidency.ucsb.edu/ws/?pid=27710

155. "Remarks at the East-West Center in Honolulu," October 18, 1966, American Presidency Project. http://www.presidency.ucsb.edu/ws/index.php?pid=27941. See also "Remarks Upon Arrival at Bangkok, Thailand," October 28, 1966, American Presidency Project. http://www.presidency.ucsb.edu/ws/index.php?pid=27964

156. Jenkins to Rostow, September 14, 1966, "General Endorsement of the Policy Recommendation in the Long-Range Communist China Study," no date; and Minutes of the Inter-Agency China Committee, October 31, 1967, in NSF, Files of Alfred Jenkins, Box 1, "Chicom—China Working Group—1966–1967," LBJL.

157. Jacobson to W. Bundy, no date, NSF, Files of Alfred Jenkins, Box 1, "Chicom—China Working Group—1966–1967," LBJL.

158. *FRUS, 1964–1968*, Volume XXX, Document 178.

159. *FRUS, 1964–1968*, Volume XXX, Document 179.

160. *FRUS, 1964–1968*, Volume XXX, Document 182.

161. *FRUS, 1964–1968*, Volume XXX, Document 182; and President's Daily Diary, September 13, 1966, LBJL, http://www.lbjlibrary.net/collections/daily-diary.html

162. *FRUS, 1964–1968*, Volume XXX, Document 185.

163. *FRUS, 1964–1968*, Volume XXX, Documents 194 and 200.

164. *FRUS, 1964–1968*, Volume XXX, Document 206.

165. *FRUS, 1964–1968*, Volume XXX, Document 220.

166. Lumbers, *Piercing the Bamboo Curtain*, 216–18.

167. Memorandum for the Record, February 4, 1968, NSF, Meeting Notes Files, Box 2, "February 2, 1968, Meeting with China Experts," LBJL.

168. "Secretary Rusk Discusses Vietnam in Canadian Magazine Interview," *Department of State Bulletin* (February 12, 1968), 208–9.

169. *FRUS, 1964–1968*, Volume XXX, Document 302.

170. Rostow to Johnson, February 24, 1968, NSF, Country File, Asia and the Pacific, Box 244, "China, CODEWORD, Vol. 1, 2/65–4/67," LBJL. For Jenkins's memo, see Alfred Jenkins, "Thoughts on China," February 22, 1968, NSF, Alfred Jenkins File, Box 3, "CHICOM—Cultural Revolution, January–June 1968," LBJL. Jenkins's memo was a brilliant analysis of Chinese history, politics, and its impact on foreign policy. It placed the Cultural Revolution, China's "madness" (1), in the context of the colonial era, the birth of Republicanism, and the ongoing attempts by Mao's regime to "destroy its Confucian past and to come into the modern world" (1). He suggested that Mao would not change; his political fortunes had risen and fallen in the last decade based on the successes and failures of his policies. The Cultural Revolution reflected, in part, Mao's sense that his power rested with his ability to stoke continued revolutionary radicalism at home and abroad. His successors might have a more traditional outlook, holding a foreign policy goal of "carving out in some fashion what it considers to be its legitimate sphere of influence in Asia" (7). The year 1968 would not be the time for new initiatives. The radicalism of the Cultural Revolution required a rejection of any softening toward the US. Even a successor regime might feel compelled to refuse US overtures as a defense against Mao loyalists and to retain its legitimacy. Jenkins concluded that an opening might have been possible prior to the Cultural Revolution (8). He recommended maintaining the current policy of deterring and defending against Chinese aggression, while reminding China that when it is ready to end its aggression, the US was ready to talk.

171. *FRUS, 1964–1968*, Volume XXX, Document 306.

SEVEN

1. *The Federalist Papers*, Number 51, Avalon Project, https://avalon.law.yale.edu/18th_century/fed51.asp

2. Earl Mazo and Stephen Hess, *Nixon* (New York: Harper and Row, 1968), 314–15.

3. Joan Hoff Wilson, "Richard M. Nixon: The Corporate Presidency," in *Leadership in the Modern Presidency*, ed. Fred Greenstein (Cambridge, MA: Harvard University Press, 1988), 170.

4. William Safire Oral History Interview, March 28, 2008, 11. Richard M. Nixon Presidential Library (hereafter RMNL), https://www.nixonlibrary.gov/sites/default/files/forresearchers/find/histories/safire-2008-03-27.pdf

5. Richard Johnson, *Managing the White House* (New York: Harper and Row, 1974), 199–229; and Alexander George, *Presidential Decision Making in Foreign Policy* (Boulder: Westview Press, 1980), 145–68.

6. See Fawn Brodie, *Richard Nixon* (New York: Norton, 1981); and Tom Wicker, *One of Us* (New York: Random House, 1991).

7. Nixon from a *New York Times* interview of October 25, 1968, quoted in I. M. Destler, *Presidents, Bureaucrats, and Foreign Policy* (Princeton: Princeton University Press, 1974), 18.

8. Richard Nixon, *The Memoirs of Richard Nixon*, vol. 1 (New York: Warner Books, 1978), 421–22; Rowland Evans and Robert Novak, *Nixon in the White House* (New York: Vintage, 1972), 19–21; Marvin Kalb and Bernard Kalb, *Kissinger* (New York: Dell, 1975), 24–41; and Winston Lord, *Kissinger on Kissinger* (New York: All Points Books, 2019), 14.

9. Henry Kissinger, *White House Years* (Boston: Little, Brown, 1979), 10–16.

10. Nixon had chosen his White House staff—H. R. Haldeman and John Ehrlichman—two weeks before the Kissinger selection. See Stephen Hess, "First Impressions: A Look Back at Five Presidential Transitions," Brookings Institution, March 1, 2001 https://www.brookings.edu/articles/first-impressions-a-look-back-at-five-presidential-transitions/

11. A, James Reichley, *Conservatives in an Age of Change* (Washington, DC: Brookings, 1981), 67.

12. Kissinger, *White House Years*, 38 and 11.

13. Kissinger, *White House Years*, 38–39.

14. NSDM 1, *Establishment of NSC Decision and Memoranda Series*, NSC H Files Records of the Staff Secretary (1969–1974), National Security Decision Memorandum Working Files, Box H-284, "NSDM-1," Richard M. Nixon Presidential Library; Roger Morris, *Uncertain Greatness* (New York: Harper and Row, 1977), 78–80; Seymour Hersh, *The Price of Power* (New York: Simon and Shuster, 1983), 29–30; "The Nixon Administration National Security Council," Brookings Institution National Security Council Project, Oral History Roundtable, 1998, 2–3, https://www.brookings.edu/wp-content/uploads/2016/07/19981208.pdf; and Peter Rodman, *Presidential Command* (New York: Knopf, 2009), 38–39. Goodpaster's memos are compiled in NSC Files, HAK Office Files, HAK Administrative and Staff Files—Transition, Box 1, RMNL.

15. "Notes of Dinner Meeting, December 9, 1968," NSC H Files, Records of the Staff Secretary (1969–1974), NSDM Working Files, Box H-284, "NSDM-1," RMNL.

16. Kissinger to Nixon, undated, NSC H Files POLICY PAPERS (1969–1974), NSDMs, NSDM 1 to NSDM 12, Box H-209, "NSDM 1," RMNL.

17. Kissinger to Nixon, "Proposal for a New National Security Council System," undated, NSC H Files POLICY PAPERS (1969–1974), NSDMs, NSDM 1 to NSDM 12, Box H-209, "NSDM 1," 7, RMNL.

18. Kissinger, *White House Years*, 42–43; and Rodman, *Presidential Command*, 38.

19. *Foreign Relations of the United States* (hereafter *FRUS*), *1969–1976*, Volume II, Document 1.

20. *FRUS, 1969–1976*, Volume II, Document 11.

21. *FRUS, 1969–1976*, Volume II, Document 10.

22. Kissinger to Nixon, "Memorandum on a New National Security Council System," undated, NSC H Files POLICY PAPERS (1969–1974), NSDMs, NSDM 1 to NSDM 12, Box H-209, "NSDM 1," RMNL; Kissinger, *White House Years*, 44–45; Morris, *Uncertain Greatness*, 90.

23. Kissinger to Nixon, "Memorandum on a New National Security Council System"; and Kissinger, *White House Years*, 44–45.

24. Morris, *Uncertain Greatness*, 89–90.

25. U. Alexis Johnson, *The Right Hand of Power* (Englewood Cliffs, NJ: Prentice-Hall, 1984), 513–16.

26. *FRUS, 1969–1976*, Volume II, Document 4.

27. Kissinger to Nixon, January 7, 1969, NSC H Files POLICY PAPERS (1969–1974), NSDMs, NSDM 1 to NSDM 12, Box H-209, "NSDM 1," RMNL.

28. Kissinger, *White House Years*, 45–46.

29. *Nixon Administration National Security Council*, 3–4.

30. Nixon, *Memoirs*, Volume I, 421.

31. See *FRUS, 1969–1976*, Volume II, Document 12; and "NSDM 7," NSDMs, Nixon Administration. Federation of American Scientists (FAS), https://fas.org/irp/offdocs/nsdm-nixon/nsdm-7.pdf

32. NSSM 1, *The Situation in Vietnam*, January 1, 1969, FAS, https://fas.org/irp/offdocs/nssm-nixon/nssm_001.pdf

33. National Security Study Memorandums of the Nixon Administration, FAS, https://fas.org/irp/offdocs/nssm-nixon/index.html

34. Memo from Kissinger, January 23, 1969, NSC H Files, Minutes of Meeting (1969–1974), Box H-120, "NSC Meeting, NSC Meeting—January 21, 1969," 13–15, RMNL; Chester Crocker, "The Nixon-Kissinger National Security Council System, 1969–1972," Commission on the Organization of Government for the Conduct of Foreign Policy, Volume 6, Appendix o, June 1975, 86–87.

35. NSSM 2, FAS, https://fas.org/irp/offdocs/nssm-nixon/nssm_002.pdf

36. NSSM 3, FAS, https://fas.org/irp/offdocs/nssm-nixon/nssm_003.pdf

37. Official descriptions of policy, such as Nixon's 1970 Report to Congress, maintain that the interagency process was the backbone of policy making. See "Nixon's Report on Foreign Policy," *New York Times*, February 19, 1970, https://www.nytimes.com/1970/02/19/archives/nixons-report-to-congress-on-foreign-policy-introduction-genuine.html. For arguments highlighting the important role of the interagency system, see Johnson. *Managing the White House*, 224–25; Alexander Haig, Oral History Interview, November 30, 2007, RMNL, https://www.nixonlibrary.gov/sites/default/files/virtuallibrary/documents/histories/haig-2006-11-30.pdf. Those who saw the system as busywork included NSC staffers Richard Allen and Helmut Sonnenfeldt; See "The Role of the National Security Advisor," Brookings Institution National Security Project Oral History Roundtables, 1990, 3, https://www.brookings.edu/wp-content/uploads/2016/07/19991025.pdf; and *Nixon Administration National Security Council*, 14. Goodpaster, as well as NSC staffer Winston Lord, say that the NSSM system was designed with both motivations in mind. See *Nixon Administration National Security Council*, 7; and Winston Lord Oral History Interview, April 28, 1998, 74–75, Association for Diplomatic

Studies and Training Foreign Affairs Oral History Project (ADST), https://www.ad st.org/OH%20TOCs/Lord,%20Winston.pdf

38. Kissinger, *White House Years*, 414.

39. *China Policy and the National Security Council*, Brookings Institution National Security Council Project, Oral History Roundtable, 1999, 4, http://cissmdev.devcl oud.acquia-sites.com/sites/default/files/papers/china.pdf

40. NSDM 3, https://fas.org/irp/offdocs/nsdm-nixon/nsdm-3.pdf

41. NSDM 2, https://fas.org/irp/offdocs/nsdm-nixon/nsdm-2.pdf

42. Richardson to USC Members, "NSC U/DM-1," February 7, 1969, NSC H Files, Under Secretaries Committee Memorandum Files (1969–1974), "U/DM-1," Box H-270, RMNL. On the Study Memorandums and Decision Memorandums, respectively, see NSC H-Files, Under Secretaries Committee Memorandum Files (1969–1974), Under Secretaries Study Memorandums, Boxes H-249-H-269, RMNL, and NSC H-Files, Under Secretaries Decision Memorandums (1969–1974), Under Secretaries Decision Memorandums, Boxes H-270-H-281, RMNL.

43. *FRUS, 1969–1976*, Volume II, Document 301.

44. Memo from Kissinger, January 23, 1969. NSC H Files, Meeting Files (1969–1974), Box H-019, "NSC Meeting, NSC Procedures and Meeting Schedule," 1, RMNL; and "Minutes of the First Meeting of the National Security Council, January 21, 1969." NSC H Files, Minutes of Meetings (1969–1974), Box H-120, "NSC Meeting—January 21, 1969," 4, RMNL.

45. See Morris, *Uncertain Greatness*, 63; quote from Destler, *Presidents*, 118.

46. Helmut Sonnenfeldt, "Reconstructing the Nixon Foreign Policy," in *The Nixon Presidency*, ed. Kenneth Thompson (Lanham, MD: University Press of America, 1987), 320.

47. Nixon's Report on Foreign Policy.

48. William Safire, *Before the Fall* (New York: Tower Publications, 1975), 116.

49. "List of Invitees, NSC Meeting," January 21, 1969, NSC H Files, Meeting Files (1969–1974), Box H-019, "NSC Meeting, NSC Procedures and Meeting Schedule," RMNL. The Office of Emergency Preparedness was abolished by Nixon's Reorganization Plan No. 2 of 1973. As of July 1973, the office and its seat on the NSC were eliminated. Richardson claims he attended all NSC meetings, but he was not on the original list of invitees for the first meeting. See Elliot Richardson Oral History Interview, May 30, 1996, ADST, 4, https://www.adst.org/OH%20TO Cs/Richardson,%20Elliot.toc.pdf. See NSDM 123, July 27, 1971, FAS, https://fas .org/irp/offdocs/nsdm-nixon/nsdm-123.pdf

50. There are dozens of examples of these memos in the Nixon Presidential Library. For an example, see Haig to Kissinger, February 25, 1970, NSC Files, Subject Files, Box 334, "Items to Discuss with the President 1/5/70–30 Apr 70, (2 of 3)," RMNL.

51. For example, see Kissinger to Nixon, June 3, 1971, NSC Files, HAK Office Files, Country Files-Far East, Box 86, "US China Policy 1969–1972 Secret (1 of 2)," RMNL; and Douglas Irwin to Nixon, February 23, 1971, NSC H Files, Study Memorandums (1969–1974), NSSMs, Box H-176, "NSSM-106 (1 of 3)," RMNL.

52. NSC H Files, Records of the Staff Secretary (1969–1974), History, Box H-297, "Admin Files," RMNL.

53. Policy related to the war in Vietnam, however, is often seen to have taken

on many of the classic characteristics of the centralized Nixon-Kissinger style very early on. See William Shawcross, *Sideshow* (New York: Cooper Square Press, 2002); and Kissinger, *White House Years*, 239–54 and 277–82.

54. Graham Allison and Philip Zelikow, *Essence of Decision*, 2nd ed. (New York: Addison Wesley Longman, 1999), 13–75.

55. Kissinger quoted in Kalb and Kalb, *Kissinger*, 104; Haldeman quoted from H. R. Haldeman, Oral History, August 13, 1987, 13, RMNL, https://www.nixonlibr ary.gov/sites/default/files/forresearchers/find/histories/haldeman-1987-08-13.pdf

56. Quoted in David Rothkopf, *Running the World* (New York: Public Affairs, 2005), 114.

57. "Minutes of the First Meeting of the National Security Council, January 21, 1969," 4, RMNL.

58. Richard Moose to NSC staff, May 7, 1969, US National Security Council Institutional Files 1974–1977, Box 79, "Administrative Files—NSC Staff Instructions," Gerald R. Ford Presidential Library.

59. Quote from Alexander Haig Oral History, November 30, 2007, 29. See also H. R. Haldeman Oral History Interview, August 13, 1987, 58–60, RMNL, https://www.nixonlibrary.gov/sites/default/files/forresearchers/find/histories/haldeman -1987-08-13.pdf; quotes from H. R. Haldeman Oral History Interview April 11, 1988, 104–5, RMNL, https://www.nixonlibrary.gov/sites/default/files/forresearch ers/find/histories/haldeman-1988-04-11.pdf

60. Henry Kissinger, *Years of Renewal* (New York: Simon and Shuster, 1999), 30.

61. Elliot Richardson. Oral History Interview, May 31, 1988, 10, RMNL, https://www.nixonlibrary.gov/sites/default/files/forresearchers/find/histories/ric hardson-1988-05-31.pdf. On Eisenhower's decisions, see Robert Cutler, *No Time for Rest* (New York: Little, Brown, 1965), 306; Dwight Eisenhower, *Mandate for Change* (Garden City, NY: Doubleday and Co., 1963), 115; Douglas Kinnard, *Eisenhower and Strategy Management* (Lexington: University Press of Kentucky, 1977), 16, 133; and Stephen Ambrose, *Eisenhower: The President*, vol. 2 (New York: Simon and Shuster, 1984), 443–46.

62. Kenneth Rush, "An Ambassador's Perspective," in *Nixon Presidency*, ed. Thompson, 340; and *Nixon Administration National Security Council*, 7–8 and 10.

63. For example, see Raymond Garthoff, *Détente and Confrontation* (Washington, DC: Brookings, 1985); William Bundy, *A Tangled Web* (New York: Hill and Wang, 1998); and Robert Dallek, *Nixon and Kissinger* (New York: Harper and Row, 2007).

64. On Nixon's dislike for the CIA as well, see Richard Helms, *A Look over My Shoulder* (New York: Ballantine, 2003), 377.

65. Kissinger, *White House Years*, 11 and 26; John Holdridge, *Crossing the Divide* (Lanham, MD: Rowman and Littlefield, 1997), 33; and Evans and Novak, *Nixon in the White House*, 12.

66. Rodman, *Presidential Command*, 42–43; quote from "China Policy and the National Security Council," 10.

67. William Watts, Oral History Interview, ADST Oral History Project, August 17, 1995, 42, https://adst.org/oral-history/oral-history-interviews/#gsc.tab=0

68. Shelton had gained favor with the administration by sending a letter lamenting the disloyalty he saw in the State Department. Kissinger, Haldeman, Ehrli-

chman, and Nixon discussed the issue from April through June 1970. Turner was rewarded for what was essentially a willingness to spy for the White House with the position of US ambassador to Nicaragua in November 1970. See Kissinger to Nixon, April 10, 1970, NSC Subject Files, Box 339, "HAK/Richardson Meetings April-May 1970 (2 of 2)," RMNL; Haldeman to Kissinger, May 14, 1970, NSC Files, Subject Files, Box 339, "HAK/Richardson Meetings April-May 1970 (1 of 1)," RMNL; and Ehrlichman to Kissinger, June 1, 1970, NSC Subject Files, Box 339, "HAK/Richardson Meetings, June 1970 (1 of 2)," RMNL.

69. Bundy, *Tangled Web*, 55.

70. Kissinger, *White House Years*, 26.

71. Haldeman Oral History Interview, April 11, 1988, 153, RMNL.

72. Evans and Novak, *Nixon in the White House*, 11.

73. Richard Nixon, *Six Crises* (Garden City, NY: Doubleday, 1962), 77–138; Nixon, *Memoirs*, 420; Herbert Klein, *Making It Perfectly Clear* (Garden City, NY: Doubleday, 1980), 138; Brodie, *Richard Nixon*, 218–219 and 277; and Haldeman Oral History Interview, April 11, 1988, 153–54, RMNL.

74. Nixon. *Memoirs*, 420.

75. *FRUS, 1969–1976*, Volume II, Document 19.

76. Destler, *Presidents, Bureaucrats, and Foreign Policy*, 130–32; Richard Reeves, *President Nixon* (New York: Simon and Shuster, 2001), 82–83.

77. See H. R. Haldeman, *The Haldeman Diaries* (New York: Berkley, 1995), 48, 101, 116, 118, 120, 122–24, 152–53, 169, 211, 218, 224, 231, 234, and 235–36; quotes from 147, 166–67, 174, 219.

78. See Haig to Kissinger, October 27, 1969, NSC Files, Henry Kissinger Office Files, US Domestic Agency Files, Box 148, "State/WH Relationship Vol. 1 (2 of 3)," RMNL.

79. Entries discussing Kissinger's threats to resign are numerous. See Haldeman, *Haldeman Diaries*, 260–61, 277–78, 281, 308, and 462.

80. Wicker, *One of Us*, 424.

81. See NSSM Drafts contained in NSC H Files Study Memorandums (1969–1974), NSSMs, Box H-177, "NSSM 106 (2 of 3)," RMNL. On Kissinger's use of the bureaus, see Helmut Sonnenfeldt's comments in *Nixon Administration National Security Council*, 15–16.

82. Kissinger to Nixon, August 27, 1969, and Richardson to Nixon, August 13, 1969, NSC Files, Subject Files, Box 334, "Items to Discuss with the President 2/5–7/14, 1969 (1 of 1)," RMNL.

83. Crocker, "Nixon-Kissinger National Security Council System, 1969–1972," 85.

84. The number of meetings may be 29. The records of these meetings are sparse and there may be one meeting that was scheduled then postponed for the next week given that the agenda items are the same. See NSC Files Subject Files, HAK/Richardson Meetings, Boxes 337–339, RMNL.

85. Elliot Richardson, "The Paradox," in *Nixon Presidency*, ed. Thompson, 62.

86. See Kalb and Kalb, *Kissinger*, 107; Morris, *Uncertain Greatness*, 134; and Haldeman, *Haldeman Diaries*, 657. Nixon's confidence in Richardson is clear. Richardson served as secretary of health, education, and welfare, secretary of defense, and attorney general.

87. See Richardson Oral History Interview, ADST, 4; John Leacacos, "Kissinger's Apparat," *Foreign Policy* 5 (Winter 1971–72): 18.

88. Leacacos, "Kissinger's Apparat," 18; and NSC Files, Subject Files, HAK/Irwin Meetings Oct 70, Box 340, RMNL.

89. Kalb and Kalb, *Kissinger*, 109.

90. Dallek, *Nixon and Kissinger*, 78–79.

91. On the reports, see NSC Files, Subject Files, President/Kissinger Memos, Box 341, RMNL. See also Morris, *Uncertain Greatness*, 144.

92. Calculated by Dallek, *Nixon and Kissinger*, 100.

93. H. R. Haldeman, *Ends of Power* (New York: Times Books, 1978), 123.

94. Nixon, *Memoirs*, vol. 1, 422; Robert Schulzinger, *Henry Kissinger* (New York: Columbia University Press, 1989), 19–20; Kalb and Kalb, *Kissinger*, 16; and Garthoff, *Détente and Confrontation*, 25–26.

95. Morris, *Uncertain Greatness*, 63; Joseph Sisco; "Nixon's Foreign Policy," in *Nixon Presidency*, ed. Kenneth Thompson (Lanham, MD: University Press of America, 1987), 395; Robert Litwak, *Détente and the Nixon Doctrine* (Cambridge University Press, 1984), 65.

96. NSC staffers Lawrence Eagleburger and Peter Rodman quoted, respectively, in Walter Isaacson, *Kissinger* (New York: Simon and Shuster, 1992), 140, and Peter Rodman Oral History Interview, May 24, 1994, ADST, https://www.adst.org/OH%20TOCs/Rodman,%20Peter%20W.toc.pdf?_ga=2.21510331.1254488540.1567791004-424886806.1566917469. See also quotes from Roger Morris, *Haig* (New York: Playboy Press, 1982), 107; and Watts Oral History Interview, ADST, 40.

97. Haldeman, *Ends of Power*, 122–23; Kissinger, *White House Years*, 162; Alexander Haig, *Inner Circles* (New York: Warner Books, 1992), 204; Lord Oral History Interview, ADST, 78; Watts Oral History Interview, ADST, 45; and Richardson Oral History Interview, 2, RMNL.

98. Whether a single person can be both advocate and honest broker has been debated by scholars. See John Burke, *Honest Broker* (College Station: Texas A&M Press, 2009). Burke argues that Kissinger's advocacy role overshadowed his brokerage role, see 106–50.

99. Haldeman Oral History Interview, August 13, 1987, 60–62, RMNL.

100. On this point, see Safire, *Before the Fall*, 160–64.

101. Dallek, *Nixon and Kissinger*, 614–16.

102. Isaacson, *Kissinger*, 142.

103. Kissinger, *White House Years*, 734; Haldeman, *Haldeman Diaries*, 444 and 655.

104. Haldeman to Herbert Klein, March 24, 1969, NSC Files, Subject Files, President/Kissinger Memos, Box 341, "President /Kissinger Memos," RMNL.

105. Kissinger to Nixon, n.d., NSC Files, HAK Office Files, US Domestic Agency Files, Box 148, "State/WH Relationship Vol. 5 Feb 1, 1971-March 1972 (3 of 3)," RMNL.

106. Isaacson, *Kissinger*, 209–11.

107. Haldeman, *Haldeman Diaries*, 78.

108. Haldeman Oral History Interview, April 11, 1988, 152–53, RMNL.

109. Crocker, "Nixon-Kissinger National Security Council System," 91.

110. Safire, *Before the Fall*, 116.

111. NSC H Files, Records of the Staff Secretary (1969–1974), History, Box H-297, "Admin Files," RMNL.

112. Safire, *Before the Fall*, 281–82; Haldeman Oral History Interview, April 11, 1988, 49–59 and 153–54, RMNL. See also Dan Rather and Gary Paul Gates, *The Palace Guard* (New York: Warner Books, 1975).

113. Alexander George and Juliette George, *Presidential Personality and Performance* (Boulder: Westview Press, 1998), 212–13; Johnson, *Managing the White House*, 213; Evans and Novak, *Nixon in the White House*, 5; Kissinger, *White House Years*, 28–29; and Kissinger, *Years of Renewal*, 44 and 68.

114. Haig, *Inner Circles*, 194–95.

115. Haldeman, *Haldeman Diaries*.

116. For excellent scholarly examinations of Nixon's character, see Brodie, *Richard Nixon*; James David Barber, *Presidential Character*, 4th ed. (New York: Pearson, 2008); and David Greenberg, *Nixon's Shadow* (New York: W. W. Norton, 2003), 232–69.

117. On these issues, see, for example, Klein, *Making It Perfectly Clear*, 132–52; Haldeman Oral History, August 13, 1987, 58–61; Richardson, "The Paradox," 51–54; Wicker, *One of Us*, 403. On Watergate and loyalty, see Bob Woodward and Carl Bernstein, *All the President's Men* (New York: Warner Books, 1976); and Stanley Kutler, *The Wars of Watergate* (New York: W. W, Norton, 1982).

118. Nixon, *Memoirs*, 443, 478–82; Alexander Haig, *Inner Circles*, 210–11; Burke, *Honest Broker*, 128–30.

119. "Minutes of the First Meeting of the National Security Council, January 21, 1969," 3, RMNL.

120. Kissinger, *White House Years*, 19–20.

121. Haig to Kissinger, February 7, 1969, Kissinger-Scowcroft West Wing Office Files, 1969–1977: Administrative File, Box 45, "National Security Council Organization—(2), 2/7/69–2/11/69," Gerald R. Ford Presidential Library.

122. Haig to Kissinger, May 2, 1969, NSC Files, Subject Files, Box 334, "Items to Discuss with the President (8/8/69–9/5/69)," RMNL.

123. NSC Files, Name Files, Box 817, "Halperin, Morton H. Staff Memos (1969)," RMNL.

124. Nixon to Haldeman, Ehrlichman, and Kissinger, March 2, 1970, NSC Files, Subject Files, Box 341, "President/Kissinger Memos April 69-July 70 (4 of 4)," RMNL.

125. Kissinger, *White House Years*, 313–19; and Asif Siniver, "The Nixon Administration and the Cienfuegos Crisis of 1970," *Review of International Studies* 34 (2008): 77–78.

126. Kissinger to Rogers, Laird, and William Colby (CIA), May 16, 1969, NSC H Files, Meeting Files (1969–1974), Washington Special Actions Group Meetings, Box H-070, "Washington Special Actions Group May 1969–1971 (5 of 5)," RMNL; and NSDM 19, July 3, 1969, FAS, https://fas.org/irp/offdocs/nsdm-nixon/nsdm-19.pdf

127. *FRUS, 1969–1976*, Volume 11, Document 31.

128. NSC H Files, Records of the Staff Secretary (1969–1974), History, Box H-297, "Admin Files," RMNL; National Security Council Institutional Files Finding Aids, RMNL, www.nixonlibrary.gov/sites/default/files/forresearchers/find/textual/institutional/finding_aid.pdf

129. Kissinger to Nixon, September 5, 1969, *FRUS, 1969–1976*, Volume VI, Document 115; and NSDM 23, September 16, 1969, *FRUS, 1969–1976*, Volume II, Document 73.

130. *FRUS, 1969–1976*, Volume VI, Document 1; NSDM 9, April 1, 1969, FAS, https://fas.org/irp/offdocs/nsdm-nixon/nsdm-9.pdf

131. National Security Council Institutional Files Finding Aids, RMNL, www.nixonlibrary.gov/sites/default/files/forresearchers/find/textual/institutional/finding_aid.pdf

132. For the origins of the Verification Panel, see Gerard Smith, *Doubletalk* (Lanham, MD: University Press of America, 1985), 108–9. On the frequency of meetings, see National Security Council Institutional Files Finding Aids, RMNL, www.nixonlibrary.gov/sites/default/files/forresearchers/find/textual/institutional/finding_aid.pdf. On membership of the DPRC, see *FRUS, 1969–1976*, Volume II, Document 79; and Smith, *Doubletalk*, 108–9.

133. NSDM 253, April 24, 1974, FAS, https://fas.org/irp/offdocs/nsdm-nixon/nsdm_253.pdf

134. NSDM 40, February 17, 1970, FAS, https://fas.org/irp/offdocs/nsdm-nixon/nsdm-40.pdf; and "Chronology of the 40 Committee," CIA Reading Room, https://www.cia.gov/library/readingroom/docs/LOC-HAK-301-1-9-6.pdf

135. *FRUS, 1969–1976*, Volume II, Document 11.

136. Kennedy and Watts to Kissinger, April 3, 1970, NSC H-Files Misc., Box H-299, "New NSC System," RMNL. See also Crocker, "Nixon-Kissinger National Security Council System," 93.

137. JCS to Laird, May 28, 1970, and Haig to Kissinger, June 10, 1970, NSC H-Files Misc., Box H-299, "New NSC System," RMNL; Laird to Assistant Secretary of Defense for International Security Affairs, May 9, 1970, and "Report to the Joint Chiefs of Staff on the NSC System, May 27, 1970," NSC H-Files Misc., Box H-300, "Institutional Files General 1969–1974 (3 of 3)," RMNL.

138. Memorandum for Admiral Moorer, August 14, 1970, NSC H-Files Misc., NSC System, "NSC Organization (1 of 3)," RMNL.

139. *FRUS, 1969–1976*, Volume II, Document 118.

140. Kennedy to Kissinger, September 8, 1970. NSC H Files Policy Papers (1969–1974), NSDMs, Box H-219, "NSDM-85," RMNL.

141. Kennedy to Haig, September 11, 1970, and Kennedy to Haig, September 14, 1970, NSC H-Files Misc., Box H-299, "New NSC System," RMNL.

142. *FRUS, 1969–1976*, Volume II, Document 121.

143. Records of these meetings begin recording SRG meetings as of June 27, 1970, even though the RG was not officially renamed until September. This is likely an artifact of post-hoc record keeping. See NSC Files, Institutional Files, Finding Aid, 55, RMNL, https://www.nixonlibrary.gov/sites/default/files/forresearchers/find/textual/institutional/finding_aid.pdf

144. *FRUS, 1969–1976*, Volume II, Document 126.

145. Jeanne Davis to Kissinger, October 14, 1970; and Haig to Kissinger, October 28, 1970, NSC Files, Subject Files, Box 340, "HAK/Irwin Meetings, October 1920 (1 of 1)," RMNL. Quote from Davis memo.

146. Haldeman, *Haldeman Diaries*, 301, 453, and 479.

147. This battle over clearance began in 1969 and never ended. See Nixon to

Rogers, Laird, and Helms, September 1, 1969, *FRUS, 1969–1976*, Volume II, Document 70; Nixon to Rogers and Kissinger, January 19, 1972, NSC Files, HAK Office Files, US Domestic Agency Files, Box 148, "State/WH Relationship Vol. 5 Feb 1, 1971-March 1972 (2 of 3)," RMNL. See also Rodman, *Presidential Command*, 46–48.

148. Kissinger to Haldeman, February 1, 1972, NSC Files, HAK Office Files, US Domestic Agency Files, Box 148, "State/WH Relationship Vol. 5, Feb. 1, 1971-March 1972, (2 of 3)," RMNL.

149. Haldeman, *Ends of Power*, 224.

150. Haldeman, *Ends of Power*, 237–38.

151. *FRUS, 1969–1976*, Volume II, Document 347.

152. Rush, "Ambassador's Perspective," 340–41.

153. C. L. Sulzberger, *The World and Richard Nixon* (New York: Prentice-Hall, 1987), 173–74.

154. Isaacson, *Kissinger*, 503.

155. Isaacson, *Kissinger*, 492–94.

156. Kissinger, *Years of Upheaval*, 422; and Isaacson, *Kissinger*, 503. Quote from Isaacson. One quirk of this delay was the satisfaction that Rogers must have felt when Nixon asked him to inform Haldeman that he should resign from the chief of staff position or be fired. See Raymond Price, *With Nixon* (New York: Viking, 1977), 99. Haldeman was deeply implicated in the Watergate scandal, eventually serving 18 months in prison for conspiracy to obstruct justice, obstruction of justice, and lying under oath.

157. Robert McFarlane, *Special Trust* (New York: Cadell and Davies, 1994), 156.

158. Richard Nathan, *The Plot That Failed* (New York: Wiley and Sons, 1975).

159. Alfred Sander, *Eisenhower's Executive Office* (New York: Praeger, 1999), 174–91; William W. Newmann, "Searching for the Right Balance: Managing Foreign Policy Decisions under Eisenhower and Kennedy," *Congress and the Presidency* 42, no. 2 (May–August 2015): 119–46.

160. Mordecai Lee, *Nixon's Super-Secretaries* (College Station: Texas A&M Press, 2010).

161. Dulles to Nixon telephone call, January 24, 1959. Papers of John Foster Dulles, Telephone Calls Series, Box 9, folder "Memoranda of Tel. Conv—Gen Jan. 4, 1959—May 8, 1959 (3)," Dwight David Eisenhower Presidential Library; and Sander, *Eisenhower's Executive Office*, 187.

162. Kissinger, *Years of Upheaval*, 418.

EIGHT

1. YouTube, https://www.youtube.com/watch?v=X_gwnFSFzv0

2. Tyler Cowen and Daniel Sutter, "Why Only Nixon Could Go to China," *Public Choice* 97, no. 4 (1998): 606–15; and Alex Cukierman and Mariano Tommasi, "When Does It Take a Nixon to Go to China?," *American Economic Review* 88, no. 1 (March 1998): 180–97. An overview of the evolution in Nixon's beliefs on China can be found in Fu-mei Chiu Wu, *Richard M. Nixon, Communism, and China* (Washington, DC: University Press of America, 1978).

3. William Safire, *Before the Fall* (New York: Tower Publications, 1975), 371.

4. Henry Kissinger, *White House Years* (Boston: Little, Brown, 1979), 705.

5. Stephen Ambrose, *Nixon* (New York: Simon and Shuster, 1987), 128–38.

6. Chambers, a former Communist himself, produced documents suggesting Hiss had passed information to the Soviets in the 1930s. The statute of limitations for charges of espionage had run out by the late 1940s, but Hiss was convicted of perjury (for lying about his Communist Party membership) and served nearly four years in prison. See Ambrose, *Nixon*, 166–96; Irwin Gellman, *The Contender* (New York: Free Press, 1999), 196–244; and Allen Weinstein, *Perjury* (New York: Random House, 1997).

7. Tom Wicker, *One of Us* (New York: Random House, 1991), 120–22. For an examination of the evolution of Nixon's rhetoric on China, see Denise Bostdorff, "The Evolution of Surprise," *Rhetoric and Public Affairs* 5, no. 1 (Spring 2002): 31–56.

8. Fawn Brodie, *Richard Nixon* (New York: Norton, 1981), 239–40.

9. Ambrose, *Nixon*, 251.

10. Marvin Kalb and Bernard Kalb, *Kissinger* (New York: Dell, 1974), 249.

11. Nixon expressed "regret" for the "intensity of those attacks" against Acheson in his *Memoirs*, but admitted that Acheson's "clipped moustache, his British tweeds, and his haughty manner made him the perfect foil for my attacks on the snobbish foreign service personality and mentality that had been taken in hook, line, and sinker by the Communists." Acheson actually advised Nixon during his presidency; Nixon called him "one of my most valued and trusted unofficial advisors." Nixon, *The Memoirs of Richard Nixon*, vol. 1 (New York: Warner Books, 1978), 136.

12. Bostdorff, "Evolution of Diplomatic Surprise," 33–35.

13. Nixon, *Memoirs*, 154.

14. Richard Johnston, "Nixon Gives Reds Warning on Atom," *New York Times*, March 18, 1955, 16, https://timesmachine.nytimes.com/timesmachine/1955/03/18/issue.html

15. Ambrose, *Nixon*, 460.

16. The Second Kennedy-Nixon Presidential Debate, October 7, 1960, Commission on Presidential Debates, https://www.debates.org/voter-education/debate-transcripts/october-7-1960-debate-transcript/

17. Nancy Tucker, *Strait Talk* (Cambridge, MA: Harvard University Press, 2009), 35.

18. Nixon, *Memoirs*, 336–37.

19. Richard Nixon, "Asia after Vietnam," *Foreign Affairs* 46, no. 1 (October 1967): 111–25.

20. Nixon, "Asia after Vietnam," 111.

21. Nixon, "Asia after Vietnam," 113.

22. Nixon, "Asia after Vietnam," 121.

23. Nixon, "Asia after Vietnam," 123.

24. See, for example, Richard Nixon, "To Keep the Peace," remarks on the CBS Radio Network, October 19, 1968. American Presidency Project, https://www.presidency.ucsb.edu/documents/remarks-the-cbs-radio-network-keep-the-peace

25. Xia Yafeng, *Negotiating with the Enemy* (Bloomington: Indiana University Press, 2006), 136.

26. Chris Tudda, *A Cold War Turning Point* (Baton Rouge: Louisiana State University Press, 2012), 3; and Jeremy Suri, *Henry Kissinger and the American Century* (Cambridge: Harvard University Press, 2007), 182.

27. Andrew Walder, *China under Mao* (Cambridge, MA: Harvard University Press, 2015), 201.

28. This three faction assessment is based on Thomas Gottlieb, *Chinese Foreign Policy and the Origins of the Strategic Triangle* (Santa Monica: RAND Corporation, 1977); and John Garver, *China's Decision for Rapprochement with the United States, 1968–1971* (Boulder: Westview Press, 1982), 108–48.

29. Ronald Keith, *The Diplomacy of Zhou Enlai* (New York: St. Martin's Press, 1989), 183–84.

30. Robert Sutter, *Chinese Foreign Relations after the Cultural Revolution, 1966–1977* (Boulder: Westview Press, 1978), 6–7; Joseph Camilleri, *Chinese Foreign Policy* (Seattle: University of Washington Press, 1980), 109–11; and Barbara Barnouin and Yu Changgan, *Chinese Foreign Policy during the Cultural Revolution* (London: Kegan Paul International, 1998), 1–22; and Chen Jian, *Mao's China and the Cold War* (Chapel Hill: University of North Carolina, Press), 244.

31. Walder. *China under Mao*, 200–271.

32. On Sino-Soviet relations during this period, see A. Doak Barnett, *China and the Major Powers in East Asia* (Washington, DC: Brookings, 1977), 45–48.

33. Chen, *Mao's China*, 230–37.

34. Matthew Ouimet, *The Rise and Fall of the Brezhnev Doctrine* (Chapel Hill: University of North Carolina Press, 2003), 66–69.

35. Kenneth W. Rea, "Peking and the Brezhnev Doctrine," *Asian Affairs* 3, no. 1 (September–October 1975): 22–26.

36. John Garver, *China's Decision*, 125; and Gottlieb, *China's Foreign Policy*, 94–95.

37. See George Ginsburgs and Carl Pinkele, *The Sino-Soviet Territorial Dispute* (New York: Praeger, 1978).

38. Thomas Robinson, "The Sino-Soviet Border Dispute," *American Political Science Review* 66, no. 4 (December 1972): 1182.

39. Robinson, "Sino-Soviet Border Dispute," 1184–85.

40. Kissinger, *White House Years*, 172.

41. Harold Hinton, "Conflict on the Ussuri: A Clash of Nationalisms," *Problems of Communism* 20, nos. 1–2 (January–April 1971): 45–61.

42. Chen, *Mao's China*, 245.

43. Chen, *Mao's China*, 245; and Li Jie, "Changes in China's Domestic Situation in the 1960s and Sino-US Relations," in *Reexamining the Cold War*, ed. Robert Ross and Jiang Changbin (Cambridge, MA: Harvard University Press, 2001), 313.

44. Li "Changes in China's Domestic Situation," 311.

45. Byung-Joon Ahn, *Chinese Politics and the Cultural Revolution* (Seattle: University of Washington Press, 1976), 242–43.

46. Rosemary Foot, *The Practice of Power* (Oxford: Oxford University Press, 1995), 218.

47. On the marshal's reports, see Li, "Changes in China's Domestic Situation," 313–14; Chen, *Mao's China and the Cold War*, 246–49; Gong Li, "Chinese Decision Making and the Thawing of US-China Relations," in *Reexamining the Cold War*, ed. Ross and Jiang, 333–35; and Barnouin and Yu, *Chinese Foreign Policy*, 142–44.

48. Li Zhisui, *The Private Life of Chairman Mao* (New York: Random House, 1994), 514.

49. Nancy Tucker, *Taiwan, Hong Kong, and the United States, 1945–1992* (New York: Twayne, 1994), 61–62; and Steven Goldstein, *The United States and the Republic of China, 1949–1978* (Stanford: Asia/Pacific Research Center, Institute for International Studies, Stanford University, 2000), 30.

50. Tucker, *Strait Talk*, 34.

51. Jay Taylor, *The Generalissimo* (Cambridge: Harvard University Press, 2011), 538–45.

52. Taylor, *Generalissimo*, 548–49.

53. John Mueller, *War, Presidents, and Public Opinion* (New York: Wiley, 1973), 56 and 106. See also Leslie Gelb, *The Irony of Vietnam* (Washington, DC: Brookings, 1979), 172.

54. Leonard Kusnitz, *Public Opinion and Foreign Policy* (Westport, CT: Greenwood Press, 1984), 111.

55. Stanley Bachrack, *The Committee of One Million* (New York: Columbia University Press, 1976), 258.

56. Winston Lord, Association for Diplomatic Studies and Training Foreign Affairs (ADST) Oral History Project, April 28, 1998, 187; https://www.adst.org/OH%20TOCs/Lord,%20Winston.pdf

57. Bachrack, *Committee of One Million*, 261–62.

58. Nixon, *Memoirs*, 422.

59. Kalb and Kalb, *Kissinger*, 253; Herbert Klein, *Making It Perfectly Clear* (Garden City, NY: Doubleday and Co, 1980), 371; *China Policy and the National Security Council*, Brookings National Security Council Oral History Roundtables, November 4, 1999, 6, https://www.brookings.edu/wp-content/uploads/2016/07/19991104.pdf; and Winston Lord, *Kissinger on Kissinger* (New York: All Points Books, 2019), 26.

60. Suri, *Henry Kissinger*, 182.

61. Alexander Haig Oral History, November 30, 2007, 16, RMNL, https://www.nixonlibrary.gov/sites/default/files/virtuallibrary/documents/histories/haig-2006-11-30.pdf

62. *Foreign Relation of the United States, 1969–1972* (hereafter *FRUS*), Volume I, Document 8.

63. Klein, *Making It Perfectly Clear*, 5; and Richard Nixon, Inaugural Address, January 20, 1969, American Presidency Project, https://www.presidency.ucsb.edu/documents/inaugural-address-1

64. Moose to Sneider, January 27, 1969, NSC H Files, Study Memorandums (1969–1974), NSSMs, Box H-134, "NSSM-14 (2 of 2)," RMNL.

65. Moose to Kissinger, February 1, 1969, NSC H Files, Study Memorandums (1969–1974), NSSMs, Box H-134, "NSSM-14 (2 of 2)," RMNL.

66. Li, "Changes in China's Domestic Situation," 313; Camilleri, *Chinese Foreign Policy*, 118; and Xia, *Negotiating with the Enemy*, 140.

67. Rostow to Kissinger, December 23, 1968, NSC Files, HAK Office Files, HAK Administrative and Staff Files Transition, Box 4, "World Situation," RMNL.

68. Rogers to Nixon, n.d. 1969, 11, RG General Records of the Department of State, Central Policy Files, 1967–1969, Political and Defense, Box 1973, "POL 2 Chicom US," National Archives and Records Administration (NARA).

69. Kalb and Kalb, *Kissinger*, 252.

70. Kalb and Kalb, *Kissinger*, 254.

71. NSSM 14, *US China Policy*, February 5, 1919, Federation of American Scientists (FAS), https://fas.org/irp/offdocs/nssm-nixon/nssm_014.pdf

72. John Holdridge, *Crossing the Divide* (Lanham, MD: Rowman and Littlefield, 1997), 31.

73. See memos between Thomas Shoesmith, country director, Republic of China Affairs, Bureau of East Asian and Pacific Affairs, Department of State, and Oscar Armstrong, deputy chief of mission, US Embassy, Taipei, Taiwan, dated March 21, April 3, April 4, and April 25 in RG 0059 Department of State, Bureau of East Asian and Pacific Affairs/Office of the Country Director for Entry# A1 5412: Subject Files; 1951–1978, Container # 8, "NSSM 14 U.S. China Policy, 1969," NARA; "NSDM 17, Draft Chronology," RMNL; Jeanne Davis to RG Members, April 30, 1969, NSC H Files, Records of the Staff Secretary (1969–1974), National Security Decision Memorandum Working Files, Box H-284, "NSDM 17," RMNL; and Holdridge, *Crossing the Divide*, 27.

74. Brown to Kissinger, April 30, 1969, NSC H Files, Meeting Files (1969–1974), Senior Review Group Meetings, Box H-037, "China NPG (part 2)," May 15, 69, RMNL. Brown was acting assistant secretary for East Asian and Pacific affairs during the transition from Bundy to Green though Bundy would not officially leave until May.

75. Elliot Richardson, "The Paradox," in *The Nixon Presidency*, ed. Kenneth Thompson (Lanham, MD: University Press of America, 1987), 54.

76. Sneider to Kissinger, April 22, 1969, NSC H Files, Miscellaneous Institutional Files of the Nixon Administration, NSC System, Box H-299, "NSC Vol II 4/1/69–5/30/69 (2 of 2)," RMNL.

77. NSSM 35, *U. S. Trade Policy Toward Communist Countries*, March 28, 1969, FAS, https://fas.org/irp/offdocs/nssm-nixon/nssm_035.pdf

78. Shoesmith to David Dean, political counselor, US Embassy, Taipei, Taiwan, May 9, 1969, RG 0059 Department of State, Bureau of East Asian and Pacific Affairs/Office of the Country Director for Entry# A1 5412: Subject Files; 1951–1978, Container # 8, "NSSM 14 U.S. China Policy, 1969," NARA.

79. Winston Lord to Kissinger, May 19, 1969, "NSC Review Group Meeting," NSC H Files, Minutes of Meetings (1969–1974), Senior Review Group, Box H-111, "SRG Minutes Originals 1969 (3 of 3)," RMNL; and Kissinger, *White House Years*, 178.

80. Davis to RG Members plus USIA, June 17, 1969, RG Meeting Minutes, May 15, 1969, Summary, NSC H Files, Records of the Staff Secretary (1969–1974), National Security Decision Memorandum Working Files, Box H-284, "NSDM 17," RMNL.

81. Harry Thayer to Brown, June 24, 1969, in RG 0059 Department of State, Bureau of East Asian and Pacific Affairs/Office of the Country Director for Entry# A1 5412: Subject Files, 1951–1978, Container # 8, "NSSM 14 U.S. China Policy, 1969," NARA; Kaakon Lindjord (Office of Emergency Preparedness) to Davis, June 19, 1969; G. Warren Nutter (ISA DoD) to Kissinger, June 23, 1969; "Memo for File" NSC, June 26, 1969; and "Additional Distribution—NSSM 14." NSC H Files, Study Memorandums (1969–1974), NSSMs, Box H-134, "NSSM-14 (2 of 2)," RMNL.

82. Richardson to Kissinger, June 21, 1969, and Kissinger to Nixon, June 23, 1969, NSC H Files, Records of the Staff Secretary (1969–1974), National Security Decision Memorandum Working Files, Box H-284, "NSDM 17," RMNL.

83. NSDM 17, *Relaxation of Economic Controls Against China*, June 26, 1969, https://fas.org/irp/offdocs/nsdm-nixon/nsdm-17.pdf; and Richardson to USC, June 28, 1969, NSC H Files, Policy Papers (1969–1974), NSDMs, Box H-210, "NSDM 17 (1 of 2)," RMNL.

84. Tad Szulc, *The Illusion of Peace* (New York: Viking Press, 1978), 115–16.

85. Kissinger, *White House Years*, 180.

86. Kissinger, *White House Years*, 181–82.

87. NSSM 14 US China Policy, August 8, 1969, NSC Institutional "(H)" Files, Meeting Files (1969–1974), National Security Council Meetings, Box H-023, "NSC Meeting (San Clemente) 8/14/69 Briefings: Korea; China (2 of 3)," RMNL.

88. NSSM 14, Outline and Key Issues, 1.

89. NSSM 14, Executive Summary, 3–4.

90. NSSM 14, 3–4.

91. NSSM 14, 7.

92. NSSM 14, 12–15.

93. NSSM 14, 15–22.

94. "HAK Talking Points: U.S. China Policy," n.d., NSC Institutional "(H)" Files, Meeting Files (1969–1974), National Security Council Meetings, Box H-023, "NSC Meeting (San Clemente) 8/14/69 Briefings: Korea; China (2 of 3), 10," RMNL.

95. NSC H Files, Study Memorandums (1969–1974), NSSMs, Box H-134, "NSSM-14 (1 of 2)," RMNL.

96. Kissinger, *White House Years*, 182. On the Soviet specialists' concerns over the impact of any changes in US China policy, see Llewellyn Thomson to Rogers, February 7, 1969, RG 59 General Records of the Department of State, Central Foreign Policy Files 1967–1969, Political and Defense, Box 1973, "Political Aff. and Rel. Chicom-US, 3/1/69," NARA. Ambassador to the USSR Thompson had retired in January 1969, but still consulted with State, Kissinger, and Nixon. See Jenny Thompson and Sherry Thompson, *The Kremlinologist* (Baltimore: Johns Hopkins University Press, 2018), 466.

97. Draft Minutes of NSC Meeting, August 14, 1969, NSC H Files, Minutes of Meetings (1969–1974), NSC Draft Minutes, Box H-121, "NSC Meeting—August 14, 1969," RMNL. DCI Helms briefing on China, submitted in writing to NSC members on August 12, provides an overview of what US intelligence knew about China at the time—the impact of the Cultural Revolution, the economy, the Sino-Soviet split, and internal politics. From a historical perspective, it is an amazing document. See "DCI Briefing for 8/14 NSC Meeting," NSC H Files, NSC Meetings, Box H-023, "NSC Meeting (San Clemente), 8/14/69, Briefings: Korea; China (2 of 3)," RMNL.

98. Kissinger, *White House Years*, 182.

99. Kissinger, *White House Years*, 182.

100. Kissinger, *White House Years*, 733–34.

101. I. M. Destler, *Presidents, Bureaucrats, and Foreign Policy* (Princeton: Princeton University Press, 1974), 130; and Richard Reeves, *President Nixon* (New York: Simon and Shuster, 2001), 82–83.

102. Kissinger, *White House Years*, 163–94, 684–732; Robert Ross, *Negotiating Cooperation* (Stanford: Stanford University Press, 1995), 17–36; Xia, *Negotiating with the Enemy*, 135–61; Tudda, *Cold War Turning Point*, 33–78.

103. Kissinger, *White House Years*, 684 and 720.

104. See Ben Kiernan, *How Pol Pot Came to Power* (London: Verso, 1985), 300–322.

105. Robert Sutter, *The China Quandary* (Boulder: Westview Press, 1983), 24; and Ross, *Negotiating Cooperation*, 1–3.

106. Garver, *China's Decision*, 84–107; Foot, *Practice of Power*, 218; and William Bundy, *A Tangled Web* (New York: Hill and Wang, 1998), 235.

107. Garver, *China's Decision*, 134–37.

108. See Harrison Salisbury, *The New Emperors* (New York: Avon, 1992), 284–306; and Jung Chang and Jon Halliday, *Mao* (London: Vintage, 2006), 574–84.

109. Byron Weng, *Peking's UN Policy* (New York: Praeger, 1972), 167–70 and 271; and Camilleri, *Chinese Foreign Policy*, 125.

110. John Kuo-Chang Wang, "United Nations Voting on Chinese Representation: An Analysis of General Assembly Roll Calls, 1951–1971," PhD diss., University of Oklahoma, 1977, 122.

111. See Robert Wade, *Governing the Market* (Princeton: Princeton University Press, 1991); and Ezra Vogel, *The Four Little Dragons* (Cambridge: Harvard University Press, 1991).

112. Kissinger, *White House Years*, 187; and Taylor, *Generalissimo*, 545.

113. Tucker, *Strait Talk*, 32–48.

114. Zbigniew Brzezinski, "Half Past Nixon," *Foreign Policy* 3 (Summer 1971): 3–21, quoted on 6.

115. See Worldwide Manpower Distribution by Geographical Area (M05), Historical Reports—Military Only—1950, 1953–1999. Defense Manpower Data Center, Department of Defense, https://www.dmdc.osd.mil/appj/dwp/dwp_reports.jsp

116. Andrew Z. Katz, "Public Opinion and Foreign Policy," *Presidential Studies Quarterly* 27, no. 3 (Summer 1997): 498.

117. Kusnitz, *Public Opinion*, 111–19; and Michael Y. M. Kau, Pierre M. Perrolle, Susan H. Marsh, and Jeffrey Berman, "Public Opinion and Our China Policy," *Asian Affairs* 5, no. 3 (January–February 1978): 136.

118. Marshall Wright to Kissinger, March 3, 1971, 3, NSC Files, HAK Office Files, Country Files—Far East, Box 86, "Chirep," RMNL.

119. Rogers to Nixon (n.d.), 11, and Annex D, 1, RG 59 General Records of the Department of State, Central Foreign Policy Files 1967–1969, Political and Defense, Box 1973, "Pol 2 Chicom US," NARA.

120. *FRUS, 1969–1976*, Volume XVII, Document 290.

121. *FRUS, 1969–1976*, Volume XVII, Document 290.

122. Resolution 2642, 25th General Assembly, UN General Assembly, Quick Links, 25th Session, http://research.un.org/en/docs/ga/quick/regular/25

123. *FRUS, 1969–1976*, Volume V, Document 302.

124. Kalb and Kalb, *Kissinger*, 267; and Tad Szulc, "Ceausescu Visits Nixon at the White House for Talks on World Issues," *New York Times*, October 27, 1970, https://www.nytimes.com/1970/10/27/archives/ceausescu-visits-nixon-at-the-white-house-for-talks-on-world-issues.html

125. Rogers to Nixon, November 18, 1970. *FRUS, 1969–1976*, Volume XVII, Document 311.

126. *FRUS, 1969–1976*, Volume XVII, Document 312.

127. NSSM 106 *China Policy*, November 19, 1970, FAS, https://fas.org/irp/off docs/nssm-nixon/nssm_106.pdf. William Gleysteen, who served in UN and East Asia–related positions in State's International Organization Affairs and Intelligence and Research Bureaus under Nixon, felt that NSSM 106 and 107 "were rewrites of the transition team papers prepared for the 1968 elections." See *China Policy and the National Security Council*, 5.

128. Nixon, *Memoirs*, 9–10; *FRUS, 1969–1976*, Volume XVII, Document 312; and Lord to Wright, Holdridge, Sonnenfeldt, and Kennedy, November 10, 1970, NSC H Files, Study Memorandums (1969–1974) NSSMs, Box H-177, "NSSM 106 (3 of 3)," RMNL.

129. Moorsteen to Kissinger, October 8, 1970; Lord to Kennedy and Holdridge, October 30, 1970; and Lord to Holdridge and Kennedy, November 10, 1970. NSC H Files, Study Memorandums (1969–1974) NSSMs, Box H-177, "NSSM 106 (3 of 3)," RMNL.

130. Draft NSDM, "Establishment of China Policy Group," November 18, 1970, NSC H Files, Study Memorandums (1969–1974) NSSMs, Box H-177, "NSSM 107 (1 of 2)," RMNL.

131. Kissinger, *White House Years*, 700–701.

132. Kissinger, *White House Years*, 718.

133. Kissinger, *White House Years*, 702.

134. Distribution List for "UN Membership Question: US-China Policy (NSSM 107)," January 27, 1971, NSC H Files, Study Memorandums (1969–1974), NSSMs, Box H-177, "NSSM 107 (2 of 2)," RMNL.

135. Marshall Green to Thomas Shoesmith, February 5, 1971, RG 0059, Bureau of East Asian and Pacific Affairs/Office of the Country Director for Entry# A1 5142: Subject Files; 1951–1978, Container #8, "NSSM 107," NARA. The State Department issues paper was similar to NSSM 107, but with a greater focus on the political and diplomatic implications of representation options. *Issues Paper—NSSM 107*, NSC H Files, Meeting Files (1969–1974), NSC Meetings, Box H-031, "NSC Meeting UN Representation and China (part 1), 3/25/71," RMNL; and Wright to Kissinger, March 3, 1971, 7, NSC Files, HAK Office Files, Country Files—East Asia, Box 86, "Chirep," RMNL.

136. DePalma to Kissinger, February 6, 1971; and NSC staff Secretary Jeanne Davis to SRG Members, February 9, 1971. NSC H Files, Study Memorandums (1969–1974), NSSMs, Box H-177, "NSSM 107 (1 of 2)," RMNL.

137. *Study of the Entire UN Membership Question: US/China Policy*, January 25, 1971, NSC H Files, Study Memorandums (1969–1974), NSSMs, Box H-177, "NSSM 107 (2 of 2)," RMNL.

138. *Study of the Entire UN Membership Question*, Annex G, 1–2.

139. *Study of the Entire UN Membership Question*, 19.

140. NSSM 106, *United States China Policy*, February 16, 1971, NSC H Files, Meeting Files (1969–1974), National Security Council Meetings, Box H-031, "NSC Meeting UN Representation and China (part 2), 3/25/71," RMNL.

141. NSSM 106, 22.

142. Irwin to Nixon, February 23, 1971; and NSC U/SM 91 Travel and Trade with Communist China, February 22, 1971, NSC H Files, Study Memorandums (1969–1974), NSSMs, Box H-176, "NSSM-106," RMNL

143. Wright to Kissinger, March 3, 1971, NSC Files, HAK Office Files, Country Files—East Asia, Box 86, "Chirep," RMNL.

144. *FRUS, 1969–1976*, Volume V, Document 335.

145. *FRUS, 1969–1976*, Volume XVII, Document 108.

146. Kissinger to Nixon, (n.d.), NSC Files, HAK Office Files, Country Files—Far East, Box 86, folder "Chirep," RMNL.

147. *FRUS, 1969–1976*, Volume V, Document 342. Attendees at the March 25 NSC meeting included Nixon, Vice President Spiro Agnew, Rogers, Laird, Secretary of the Treasury John Connally, Attorney General John Mitchell, Director of the Office of Emergency Preparedness George Lincoln, US ambassador to the UN George H. W. Bush, JCS chair Admiral Thomas Moorer, Deputy DCI General Robert Cushman, Acting ACDA director Philip Farley, U. A. Johnson, DePalma, Green, Kissinger, Holdridge, Wright, and Kennedy. The totals include five members of State and four from the NSC staff.

148. Kissinger, *White House Years*, 773. Within a week of the meeting, Connally had a change of heart on the policy, and favored a dual representation with universality. Wright to Kissinger, April 1, 1971, NSC H Files, Study Memorandums (1969–1974), NSSMs, Box H-177, "NSSM 197 (1 of 2)," RMNL.

149. Kissinger to Nixon, April 9, 1971, NSC H Files, Study Memorandums, NSSMs, Box H-177, "NSSM-107 (1 of 2)," RMNL.

150. Zhaohui Hong and Yi Sun, "The Butterfly Effect and the Making of 'Ping-Pong Diplomacy,'" *Journal of Contemporary China* 9, no. 25 (2000): 429–48.

151. NSDM 105, *Steps towards Augmentation of Travel and Trade between the People's Republic of China and the United States*, April 13, 1971, FAS, https://fas.org/irp/offd ocs/nsdm-nixon/nsdm-105.pdf. See also Kissinger, *White House Years*, 711–12. On the USC's reports, see Kennedy to Kissinger, July 16, 1971, NSC H-Files, Miscellaneous Institutional Files of the Nixon Administration, NSC System, Box 300, "Institutional Files General 1969–1974 (3 of 3)," RMNL.

152. Kissinger, *White House Years*, 713–14; and *FRUS, 1969–1976*, Volume XVII, Document 118.

153. See Nixon-Kissinger phone conversation, April 27, 1971, 8:16–8:36 p.m., in nixontapes.org, http://nixontapes.org/hak/1971-04-27_Nixon_002-052.mp3; and Kissinger, *White House Years*, 715–16.

154. Nixon, *Memoirs*, vol. 2, 14–15.

155. H. R. Haldeman. *The Haldeman Diaries* (New York: Berkley, 1995), 340–41; and Kissinger, *White House Years*, 717.

156. Kissinger, *White House Years*, 718 and 724–28; Nixon, *Memoirs*, vol. 1, 16. The US eventually discovered that the Chinese were worried about the secrecy, fearing that the US was leaving itself the option to cancel the trip. Kissinger, *White House Years*, 724.

157. Kissinger, *White House Years*, 719–20; Holdridge, *Crossing the Divide*, 47; and Terence Smith, "Rogers Bids China Be 'Constructive' in Southeast Asia," *New York Times*, April 28, 1971, https://www.nytimes.com/1971/04/28/archives/rogers-bids -china-be-constructive-in-southeast-asia-he-says-us.html

158. President Nixon's News Conference, April 29, 1971, American Presidency Project, https://www.presidency.ucsb.edu/documents/the-presidents-news-confer ence-133

159. *FRUS, 1969–1976*, Volume V, Document 349.

160. Kennedy and Melvin Levine to Kissinger, May 19, 1971, NSC H-Files, Study Memorandums (1969–1974), NSSMs, Box H-177, "NSSM 107," RMNL; and *FRUS, 1969–1976*, Volume V, Document 346.

161. Kissinger to Nixon, May 27, 1971, NSC H-Files, Study Memorandums (1969–1974), NSSMs, Box H-177, "NSSM 107 (1 of 2)," RMNL.

162. *FRUS, 1969–1976*, Volume V, Document 358.

163. Nixon News Conference of June 1, 1971, American Presidency Project, https://www.presidency.ucsb.edu/documents/the-presidents-news-conference-135

164. *United States Relations with the People's Republic of China*, Hearings before the Committee on Foreign Relations, United States Senate, 92–1, June 24, 25, 28, and 29, and July 20, 1971, books.gooogle.com.

165. Kissinger, *White House Years*, 739.

166. Lord Interview, ADST, 123–125; Jussi Hanhimaki, *The Flawed Architect* (Oxford: Oxford University Press, 2004), 135; and *FRUS 1969–1976*, Volume XVII, Documents 135 and 137.

167. Kissinger, *White House Years*, 721–23.

168. Kissinger, *White House Years*, 759–760 and 773; and *FRUS, 1969–1976*, Volume V, Document 371.

169. *FRUS, 1969–1976*, Volume V, Document 377.

170. *FRUS, 1969–1976*, Volume V, Document 384.

171. *FRUS, 1969–1976*, Volume V, Document 379 and 380.

172. "Secretary Rogers Announces U.S. Policy on Chinese Representation in the U.N," *Department of State Bulletin* 65, no. 1678 (August 23, 1971): 193–96.

173. President's News Conference, September 16, 1971, American Presidency Project, https://www.presidency.ucsb.edu/documents/the-presidents-news-confer ence-139

174. John Garver, *The Sino-American Alliance* (Armonk, NY: M. E. Sharpe, 1997), 253–63; and Wang, *United Nations Voting on Chinese Representation*, 170–82.

175. Kissinger, *White House Years*, 785.

176. Haldeman, *The Haldeman Diaries*, 448–49.

177. Lydia Saad, *Gallup Vault: Nixon's China Visit Was a Game Changer*, February 17, 2017, Gallup, https://news.gallup.com/vault/204065/gallup-vault-nixon-china -visit-game-changer.aspx; and *Presidential Approval Ratings—Gallup Historical Sta-tistics and Trends*, Gallup, https://news.gallup.com/poll/116677/presidential-appro val-ratings-gallup-historical-statistics-trends.aspx

178. *FRUS 1969–1976*, Volume XVII, Document 137; and Holdridge, *Crossing the Line*, 68.

179. *FRUS 1969–1976*, Volume XVII, Document 158; Kissinger, *White House Years*, 775; and Haldeman, *Haldeman Diaries*, 440.

180. Kissinger, *White House Years*, 1074–80.

181. Lord Interview, ADST, 165–67; and Haldeman, *Haldeman Diaries*, 509.

182. Lord Interview, ADST, 167–68; and Kissinger, *White House Years*, 1082–84.

183. Haldeman, *Haldeman Diaries*, 513–14.

184. Robert Horn, "Sino-Soviet Relations in an Era of Détente," *Asian Affairs* 3, no. 5 (May–June 1976): 290.

185. See Thomas Robinson, "China in 1973," *Asian Survey* 14, no. 1 (January 1974): 1–21; Henry Bradsher, "China: The Radical Offensive," *Asian Survey* 13, no. 11 (November 1973): 989–1009; Peter Moody Jr., "The New Anti-Confucian Campaign in China," *Asian Survey* 14, no. 4 (April 1974): 307–24; and Parris Chang, "The Anti–Lin Piao and Confucius Campaign," *Asian Survey* 14, no. 10 (October 1974): 871–86.

186. Tucker, *Strait Talk*, 65.

187. Leslie Gelb, "Arms Sales," *Foreign Policy* 25 (Winter 1976–77): 13.

188. Taylor, *Generalissimo*, 581–82; and J. Bruce Jacobs, "Taiwan 1972," *Asian Survey* 13, no. 1 (January 1973): 105.

189. On this point, see Douglas Mendel Jr., "Taiwan Adjusts to Isolation," *Asian Affairs* 3, no. 1 (September–October 1975): 63–66.

190. On Nixon's efforts, see Jean Garrison, "Framing the National Interests in US-China Relations," *Asian Perspective* 24, no. 3 (2000): 103–34. Polling data on 115.

191. Garrison, "Framing the National Interests," 115; and Kusnitz, *Public Opinion and Foreign Policy*, 140.

192. Mendel, "Taiwan Adjusts," 65.

193. Lord Interview, ADST, 145–46; and Kissinger, *White House Years*, 1075.

194. *FRUS, 1969–1976*, Volume XVII, Document 203.

195. *FRUS, 1969–1976*, Volume XVIII, Document 5.

196. *FRUS, 1969–1976*, Volume XVIII, Document 18.

197. NSSM 171, *US Strategy for Asia*, February 12, 1973, FAS, https://fas.org/irp/offdocs/nssm-nixon/nssm_171.pdf

198. NSSM 69, *US Nuclear Policy in Asia*, July 14, 1969. FAS, https://fas.org/irp/offdocs/nssm-nixon/nssm_069.pdf; and National Security Institutional Files, Finding Aid, RMNL, https://www.nixonlibrary.gov/sites/default/files/forresearchers/find/textual/institutional/finding_aid.pdf

199. *FRUS, 1969–1976*, Volume XVIII, Documents 9 and 18.

200. *FRUS, 1969–1976*, Volume XVIII, Document 14.

201. *FRUS, 1969–1976*, Volume XVIII, Document 16.

202. Kissinger to DPRC members, August 28, 1973, NSC H Files, Study Memorandums (1969–1974), NSSMs, Box II-196, "NSSM 171 (1 of 2)," RMNL.

203. The impression that Kissinger had no role in the activities that encompassed Watergate was inaccurate. Kissinger had been involved in asking for wiretaps on NSC staffers and reporters. See Stanley Kutler, *The Wars of Watergate* (New York: W. W. Norton, 1992), 119–20.

204. *FRUS, 1969–1976*, Volume XVIII, China, Document 71.

205. Clements to [Defense Program Review Committee] members (n.d.), NSC H Files, Study Memorandums (1969–1974), NSSMs, Box H-196, "NSSM 171 (1 of 2)," RMNL.

206. See Worldwide Manpower Distribution by Geographical Area (M05), Historical Reports—Military Only—1950, 1953–1999.

207. *FRUS, 1969–1976*, Volume XVIII, China, Document 73; and NSDM 248, *Changes in US Force Levels on Taiwan*, March 14, 1974, FAS, https://fas.org/irp/offdocs/nsdm-nixon/nsdm_248.pdf

414 ~ Notes to Pages 327–53

1. William Safire, *Before the Fall* (New York: Belmont Tower Books, 1975), 8.

2. FDR to Wendell Wilkie, January 1941, quoted in Robert Sherwood, *Roosevelt and Hopkins* (New York: Harper and Brothers, 1948), 3.

3. The list references only those advisors who left the administration over differences with the president concerning policy or decision making: Secretary of State Rex Tillerson, Secretaries of Defense James Mattis and Mark Esper, and National Security Advisors H. R. McMaster and John Bolton. Trump's first national security advisor, Michael Flynn, is excluded from this list; he was fired after lying to the FBI about contacts with Russian government officials.

4. Haley Britzky, "Everything Trump Says He Knows 'More about Than Anybody,'" *Axios*, January 5, 2019, https://www.axios.com/everything-trump-says-he-knows-more-about-than-anybody-b278b592-cff0-47dc-a75f-5767f42bcf1e.html?te=1&nl=frank-bruni&emc=edit_fb_20200311

5. Alexander George and Juliette George, *Presidential Personality and Performance* (Boulder: Westview Press, 1998), 201–3.

6. Dean Rusk, *As I Saw It* (New York: Penguin, 1990), 516–17.

7. William Newmann, *Managing National Security Policy* (Pittsburgh: University of Pittsburgh Press, 2003).

8. Newmann, *Managing National Security Policy*, 138–70.

9. Solid introductions to decision making in each administration are the following. For Clinton, see David Halberstam, *War in a Time of Peace* (New York: Scribner, 2001). For George W. Bush, see Ivo Daalder and James Lindsay, *America Unbound* (Washington, DC: Brookings Institution, 2003), and James Mann, *The Great Rift* (New York: Henry Holt, 2020). For Obama, see Mark Landler, *Alter Egos* (New York: Random House, 2016). For Trump, see John Burke, "The Trump Transition, Early Presidency, and National Security Organization," *Presidential Studies Quarterly* 47, no. 3 (September 2017): 574–96, and John Burke, "Struggling with Standard Order: Challenges and Performance of the Trump National Security Council System," *Presidential Studies Quarterly* 48, no. 4 (December 2018): 640–66.

10. As quoted in John Kenneth Galbraith, *Ambassador's Journal* (Boston: Houghton Mifflin, 1969), 7.

11. The phrase comes from Paul Anderson, "Deciding How to Decide in Foreign Affairs," in *The Presidency and Policy Making*, ed. George Edwards, Steven Shull, and Norman Thomas (Pittsburgh: University of Pittsburgh Press, 1985), 151–72.

12. Arthur Vandenberg, "Bipartisan Foreign Policy," *Vital Speeches of the Day* 15, no. 1 (October 15, 1948), 13.

13. Arthur Schlesinger, *A Thousand Days* (New York: Fawcett, 1965), 442–46.

14. *Foreign Relations of the United States, 1964–1968*, Volume XXX, Document 2.

15. Richard Nixon, "Asia after Vietnam," *Foreign Affairs* 46, no. 1 (October 1967): 121.

16. Alex Mintz, "The Decision to Attack Iraq: A Noncompensatory Theory of Decision Making," *Journal of Conflict Resolution* 37, no. 4 (December 1993): 595–618; and Alex Mintz, "How Do Leaders Make Decisions? A Poliheuristic Perspective," *Journal of Conflict Resolution* 48, no. 1 (2004): 3–13.

∼ Bibliography

ARCHIVES AND GOVERNMENT HISTORICAL SERIES

The following sources were used throughout this research; they are cited in the endnotes, but do not have individual bibliographic entries.

Central Intelligence Agency Reading Room, https://www.cia.gov/library/reading room/home
Dwight David Eisenhower Presidential Library, Abilene, KS
Federation of American Scientists, Presidential Directives and Executive Orders, https://fas.org/irp/offdocs/direct.htm
Gerald R. Ford Presidential Library, Ann Arbor, MI
John F. Kennedy Presidential Library, Boston, MA
Lyndon B. Johnson Presidential Library, Austin, TX
Richard M. Nixon Presidential Library, Yorba Linda, CA
University of California at Santa Barbara, American Presidency Project, https://www.presidency.ucsb.edu/
US State Department, Foreign Relations of the United States, https://history.state.gov/historicaldocuments

WORKS ON THE PRESIDENCY, MULTIPLE PRESIDENCIES, FOREIGN POLICY, PUBLIC POLICY, AND METHODOLOGY

Aberbach, Joel, and Bert Rockman. "The Appointments Process and the Administrative Presidency." *Presidential Studies Quarterly* 39, no. 1 (March 2009): 38–59.
Albuyeh, Rod, and Mark Paridis. "Thawing Rivalries and Fading Friendships." *Political Psychology* 39, no. 4 (2018): 811–27.
Allison, Graham. *Essence of Decision*. Boston; Little, Brown, 1971.
Allison, Graham, and Morton Halperin. "Bureaucratic Politics." *World Politics* 24 (supplement 1972): 40–79.
Allison, Graham, and Peter Szanton. *Remaking Foreign Policy*. New York: Harper and Row, 1975.

Allison, Graham, and Philip Zelikow. *Essence of Decision*. Rev. ed. New York: Addison-Wesley, 1999.

Ambrose, Stephen. *Eisenhower: The President*. Vol. 2. New York: Simon and Shuster, 1984.

Anderson, Patrick. *The President's Men*. Garden City, NY: Doubleday and Co., 1968.

Anderson, Paul. "Deciding How to Decide in Foreign Affairs: Decision Strategies as Solutions to Presidential Problems." In *The Presidency and Policy Making*, edited by George Edwards, Steven Shull, and Norman Thomas, 151–72. Pittsburgh: University of Pittsburgh Press, 1985.

Bacchus, William. *Foreign Policy and the Bureaucratic Process: The State Department's Country Director System*. Princeton: Princeton University Press, 1974.

Bader, Jeffrey. *Obama and China's Rise*. Washington, DC: Brookings, 2012.

Barber, James David. *The Presidential Character*. 4th ed. Englewood Cliffs, NJ: Prentice-Hall, 1992.

Barnard, Chester. *The Functions of the Executive*. Cambridge: Harvard University Press, 1968.

Bennett, Andrew, and Jeffrey Checkel, eds. *Process Tracing: From Metaphor to Analytical Tool*. Cambridge: Cambridge University Press, 2015.

Bergen, Peter. *Trump and His Generals*. New York: Penguin Press, 2019.

Best, James J. "Presidential Learning: A Comparative Study of the Interactions of Carter and Reagan." *Congress and the Presidency* 15, no. 1 (Spring 1988): 25–48.

Bobroske, Alexander. *Reforming the National Security Council*. American Action Forum. December 21, 2016, https://www.americanactionforum.org/research/refo rming-national-security-council/

Bolton, M. K. *U.S. National Security and Foreign Policymaking after 9/11*. Lanham, MD: Rowman and Littlefield, 2007.

Boucher, Vincent, Charles-Philippe David, and Karine Premont. *National Security Entrepreneurs and the Making of American Foreign Policy*. Montreal: McGill-Queen's University Press, 2020.

Brice-Saddler, Michael. "While Bemoaning Mueller Probe, Trump Falsely Says the Constitution Gives Him 'the Right to Do Whatever I Want'." *Washington Post*, July 23, 2019, https://www.washingtonpost.com/politics/2019/07/23/tru mp-falsely-tells-auditorium-full-teens-constitution-gives-him-right-do-whate ver-i-want/

Britzky, Haley. "Everything Trump Says He Knows 'More about Than Anybody.'" *Axios*, January 5, 2019, https://www.axios.com/everything-trump-says-he-kno ws-more-about-than-anybody-b278b592-cff0-47dc-a75f-5767f42bcf1e.html ?te=1&nl=frank-bruni&emc=edit_fb_20200311

Brownell, Roy. "The Coexistence of *United States v. Curtiss-Wright* and *Youngstown Sheet & Tube v. Sawyer* in National Security Jurisprudence." *Journal of Law & Politics* 16, no. 1 (Winter 2000): 1–112.

Brzezinski, Zbigniew. "The NSC's Midlife Crisis." *Foreign Policy* 69 (Winter 1987–88): 81–95.

Buchanan, Bruce, "Constrained Diversity: The Organizational Demands of the Presidency." In *The Managerial Presidency*, edited by James P. Pfiffner, 78–104. Pacific Grove, CA: Brooks/Cole Publishing, 1991.

Bundy, William. "The National Security Process: Plus Ça Change . . . ?" *International Security* 7, no. 3 (Winter 1982–83): 94–109.

Burke, John. *Honest Broker*. College Station: Texas A&M University Press, 2009.

Burke, John. *The Institutional Presidency*. Baltimore: Johns Hopkins University Press, 1992.

Burke, John. "Struggling with Standard Order: Challenges and Performance of the Trump National Security Council System." *Presidential Studies Quarterly* 48, no. 4 (December 2018): 640–66.

Burke, John. "The Trump Transition, Early Presidency, and National Security Organization." *Presidential Studies Quarterly* 47, no. 3 (September 2017): 574–96.

Burns, James MacGregor. *Leadership*. New York: Harper and Row, 1978.

Byman, Daniel, and Kenneth Pollack. "Let Us Now Praise Great Men." *International Security* 25, no. 4 (Spring 2001): 107–46.

Calabresi, Steven, and Christopher Yoo. *The Unitary Executive*. New Haven: Yale University Press, 2008.

Campbell, Colin. *Managing the Presidency*. Pittsburgh: University of Pittsburgh Press, 1986.

Cardinale, Ivano. "Beyond Constraining and Enabling: Toward New Microfoundations for Institutional Theory." *Academy of Management Review* 43, no. 1 (2018): 132–55.

Clark, Keith, and Laurence Legere. *The President and the Management of National Security*. New York: Praeger, 1969.

Clarke, Duncan. *The Politics of Arms Control*. New York: Free Press, 1979.

Cooper, Phillip. *By Order of the President*. Lawrence: University Press of Kansas, 2002.

Corwin, Edward. *The President: Office and Powers*. 4th ed. New York: New York University Press, 1957.

Crabb, Cecil V., and Pat M. Holt. *Invitation to Struggle*. 3rd ed. Washington, DC: Congressional Quarterly, 1989.

Crouch, Jeffrey, Mark Rozell, and Mitchel Sollenberger. "The Unitary Executive Theory and President Donald J. Trump." *Presidential Studies Quarterly* 47, no. 3 (September 2017): 561–73.

Cutler, Robert. "The Development of the National Security Council." *Foreign Affairs* 34, no. 3 (April 1956): 441–58.

Cutler, Robert. *No Time for Rest*. New York: Little, Brown, 1965.

Daalder, Ivo, and James Lindsay. *America Unbound*. Washington, DC: Brookings Institution, 2003.

Destler, I. M. "A Job That Doesn't Work." *Foreign Policy* 38 (Spring 1980): 80–88.

Destler, I. M. "Jonestown." *Foreign Affairs*, April 30, 2009, https://www.foreignaffairs.com/articles/united-states/2009-04-30/jonestown

Destler, I. M. "National Security Advice to U.S. Presidents." *World Politics* 29, no. 2 (1977): 143–76.

Destler, I. M. *Presidents, Bureaucrats, and Foreign Policy*. Princeton: Princeton University Press, 1974.

Destler, I. M., and Ivo Daalder. "A New NSC for a New Administration." Brookings Institution. November 15, 2000, https://www.brookings.edu/research/a-new-nsc-for-a-new-administration/

DeYoung, Karen. "Despite Stature, James L. Jones Was Awkward Fit in Obama White House as National Security Adviser." *Washington Post*, October 8, 2010.

Dickinson, Matthew J. "We All Want a Revolution: Neustadt, New Institutionalism, and the Future of Presidency Research." *Presidential Studies Quarterly* 39, no. 4 (December 2009): 736–70.

Dodds, Graham. *The Unitary Presidency*. New York: Routledge, 2020.

Drezner, Daniel. *The Toddler in Chief*. Chicago: University of Chicago Press, 2020.

Dyson, Stephen. "Personality and Foreign Policy: Tony Blair's Iraq Decisions." *Foreign Policy Analysis* 2, no. 3 (2006): 289–306.

Eisenhower, Dwight D. *Mandate for Change*. Garden City, NY: Doubleday and Co., 1963.

Elliott, William Y. *US Foreign Policy*. New York: Columbia University Press, 1952.

Etheredge, Lloyd. *Can the Government Learn?* New York: Pergamon Press, 1985.

Etheredge, Lloyd. "Personality Effects on American Foreign Policy, 1898–1968." *American Political Science Review* 72, no. 2 (June 1978): 434–51.

Falk, Stanley. "The National Security Council under Truman, Eisenhower, and Kennedy." *Political Science Quarterly* 79, no. 3 (September 1964): 403–34.

The Federalist Papers. Avalon Project, https://avalon.law.yale.edu/subject_menus/fed.asp

Forsythe, David. *Human Rights and US Foreign Policy*. Gainesville: University Press of Florida, 1988.

Friedman, Jeffrey, and Richard Zeckhauser. "Analytical Confidence and Political Decision-Making." *Political Psychology* 39, no. 5 (2018): 1069–87.

Galbraith, John K. *Ambassador's Report*. Boston: Houghton-Mifflin, 1969.

Gallagher, Maryann, and Susan Allen. "Presidential Personality." *Foreign Policy Analysis* 10 (2014): 1–21.

George, Alexander. "Assessing Presidential Character." *World Politics* 26, no. 2 (1974): 234–82.

George, Alexander. "The Case for Multiple Advocacy in Making Foreign Policy." *American Political Science Review* 66, no. 3 (September 1972): 751–85.

George, Alexander. "Case Studies and Theory Development: The Method of Structured, Focused Comparison." In *Diplomacy: New Approaches in History, Theory, and Policy*, edited by Paul Lauren, 43–68. New York: Free Press, 1979.

George, Alexander. "The Operational Code: A Neglected Approach to the Study of Political Leaders and Decision Making." *International Studies Quarterly* 13, no. 2 (1969): 190–222.

George, Alexander. *Presidential Decision Making on Foreign Policy*. Boulder: Westview Press, 1980.

George, Alexander, and Andrew Bennett. *Case Studies and Theory Development in the Social Sciences*. Cambridge: MIT Press, 2004.

George, Alexander, and Juliette George. *Presidential Personality and Performance*. Boulder: Westview Press, 1998.

George, Alexander, and Timothy J. McKeown. "Case Studies and Theories of Organizational Decision Making." In *Advances in Information Processing in Organizations*, vol. 2, edited by Robert Coulam and Richard Smith, 29–41. Greenwich, CT: JAI Press, 1985.

Greenstein, Fred, ed. *Leadership in the Modern Presidency*. Cambridge: Harvard University, 1988.

Greenstein, Fred, and Richard Immerman. "Effective National Security Advising: Recovering the Eisenhower Legacy." *Political Science Quarterly* 115, no. 3 (2000): 335–45.

Gulick, Luther. "Notes on the Theory of Organization." In *Papers on the Science of Administration*, edited by Luther Gulick and L. Urwick, 1–49. New York: Taylor and Francis, 2003.

Halberstam, David. *War in a Time of Peace*. New York: Scribner, 2001.

Hall, David K. "The 'Custodian-Manager' of the Policy-Making Process." *Commission on the Organization of the Government for the Conduct of Foreign Policy (Murphy Commission)*, vol. 2, appendix D, chapter 12, June 1975, 100–118.

Halperin, Morton, and David Halperin. "The Key West Key." *Foreign Policy* 52 (1983–84): 114–28.

Halperin, Morton, and Arnold Kanter. "The Bureaucratic Perspective." In *Readings in American Foreign Policy*, edited by Morton Halperin and Arnold Kanter, 1–41. Boston: Little, Brown, 1974.

Hart, John. *The Presidential Branch*. 2nd ed. Chatham, NJ: Chatham House, 1995.

Heclo, Hugh. "The Changing Presidential Office." In *The Managerial Presidency*, edited by James Pfiffner, 33–42. Pacific Grove, CA: Brooks/Cole Publishing, 1991.

Henderson, Philip. *Managing the Presidency: The Eisenhower Legacy from Kennedy to Reagan*. Boulder: Westview Press, 1988.

Hermann, Charles. "Changing Course: When Governments Choose to Redirect Foreign Policy." *International Studies Quarterly* 34, no. 1 (March 1990): 3–21.

Hermann, Charles, ed. *International Crises*. New York: Free Press, 1972.

Hermann, Margaret, and Thomas Preston. "Presidents, Advisers, and Foreign Policy." *Political Psychology* 15, no. 1 (1994): 75–96.

Hess, Stephen. *Organizing the Presidency*. Washington, DC: Brookings Institution Press, 1988.

Holsti, Ole. "Theories of Crisis Decision Making." In *Diplomacy: New Approaches in History, Theory, and Policy*, edited by Paul Lauren, 99–136. New York: Free Press, 1979.

Huntington, Samuel. *The Common Defense*. New York: Columbia University Press, 1961.

Jackson, Henry, ed. *The National Security Council*. New York: Praeger, 1965.

Janis, Irving. *Groupthink*. Boston: Houghton Mifflin, 1982.

Jervis, Robert. "Do Leaders Matter and How Would We Know?" *Security Studies* 22, no. 2 (2013): 153–79.

Johnson, Richard T. *Managing the White House*. New York: Harper and Row, 1974.

Johnson, U. Alexis. *The Right Hand of Power*. Englewood Cliffs, NJ: Prentice-Hall, 1984.

Kamath, P. M. *Executive Privilege versus Democratic Accountability*. Atlantic Highlands, NJ: Humanities Press, 1982.

Keller, Jonathan, and Dennis Foster. "Don't Tread on Me." *Presidential Studies Quarterly* 46, no. 4 (December 2016): 808–27.

Kinnard, Douglas. *Eisenhower and Strategy Management.* Lexington: University Press of Kentucky, 1977.

Kleinerman, Benjamin. *The Discretionary President.* Lawrence: University Press of Kansas, 2009.

Krcmaric, Danile, Stephen Nelson, and Andrew Roberts. "Studying Leaders and Elites." *Annual Review of Political Science* 23 (2020): 133–51.

Landler, Mark. *Alter Egos.* New York: Random House, 2016.

Lewis, David. *The Politics of Presidential Appointments.* Princeton: Princeton University Press, 2008.

Lewis, David. *Presidents and the Politics of Agency Design.* Stanford: Stanford University Press, 2003.

Lewis, David. "Revisiting the Administrative Presidency." *Presidential Studies Quarterly* 39, no. 1 (March 2009): 60–73.

Light, Paul Charles. *The President's Agenda.* Baltimore: Johns Hopkins University Press, 1982.

Mahoney, James. "Process Tracing and Historical Explanation." *Security Studies* 24 (2015): 200–218.

Mann, James. *The Great Rift.* New York: Henry Holt, 2020.

March, James, and Johan Olsen. "The New Institutionalism." *American Political Science Review* 78, no. 3 (1984): 734–49.

March, James, and Herbert Simon. *Organizations.* New York: John Wiley and Sons, 1958.

Mayer, Kenneth. *With the Stroke of a Pen.* Princeton: Princeton University Press, 2001.

Mintz, Alex. "The Decision to Attack Iraq: A Noncompensatory Theory of Decision Making." *Journal of Conflict Resolution* 37, no. 4 (December 1993): 595–618.

Mintz, Alex. "How Do Leaders Make Decisions? A Poliheuristic Perspective." *Journal of Conflict Resolution* 48, no. 1 (2004): 3–13.

Mintz, Alex, and Karl DeRouen Jr. *Understanding Foreign Policy Decision Making.* Cambridge: Cambridge University Press, 2010.

Mintz, Alex, Nehemia Geva, Steven Redd, and Amy Carnes. "The Effect of Dynamic and Static Choice Sets on Political Decision Making." *American Political Science Review* 91, no. 3 (September 1997): 553–66.

Mintz, Alex, and Carly Wayne. *The Polythink Syndrome.* Stanford: Stanford University Press, 2016.

Mitchell, David. "Does Context Matter?" *Presidential Studies Quarterly* 40, no. 4 (December 2010): 631–59.

Moe, Terry. "The Politicized Presidency." In *The New Direction in American Politics,* edited by John Chubb and Paul Peterson, 235–72. Washington, DC: Brookings Institution, 1985.

Moe, Terry. "The Politics of Bureaucratic Structure." In *Can the Government Govern?,* edited by John Chubb and Paul Peterson, 285–323. Washington, DC: Brookings Institution, 1989.

Moe, Terry. "The Revolution in Presidential Studies." *Presidential Studies Quarterly* 39, no. 4 (December 2009): 701–24.

Morgenthau, Hans. *Politics Among Nations,* 5th ed., Revised. New York: Alfred A. Knopf, 1978.

Mueller, John. *War, Presidents, and Public Opinion*. New York: Wiley, 1973.

Mulcahy, Kevin. "Rethinking Groupthink." *Presidential Studies Quarterly* 25, no. 2 (Spring 1995): 237–50.

Nelson, Anna Kasten. "President Truman and the Evolution of the National Security Council." *Journal of American History* 72, no. 2 (1985): 360–78.

Neustadt, Richard. *Presidential Power and the Modern Presidents*. New York: Free Press, 1990.

Newmann, William W. *Managing National Security Policy: The President and the Process*. Pittsburgh: University of Pittsburgh Press, 2003.

Newmann, William. "Searching for the Right Balance: Managing Foreign Policy Decisions under Eisenhower and Kennedy." *Congress and the Presidency* 42, no. 2 (May–August 2015): 119–46.

Obama Administration. "The Executive Branch." http://www.whitehouse.gov/our -government/executive-branch

Pfiffner, James. "The Contemporary Presidency: Constraining Executive Power." *Presidential Studies Quarterly* 38, no. 1 (March 2008): 123–43.

Pfiffner, James. "Presidential Decision Making: Rationality, Advisory Systems, and Personality." *Presidential Studies Quarterly* 35, no. 2 (June 2005): 217–28.

Pfiffner, James P. *The Strategic Presidency*. 2nd ed. Lawrence: University Press of Kansas, 1988.

Posner, Eric A., and Adrian Vermeule. *The Executive Unbound*. New York: Oxford University Press, 2010.

Prados, John. *Keeper of the Keys*. New York: William Morrow, 1991.

Preston, Thomas. *The President and His Inner Circle*. New York: Columbia University Press, 2001.

Public Law 114–328. *National Defense Authorization Act for Fiscal Year 2017*. December 23, 2016. Section 1085. https://www.congress.gov/114/plaws/publ328/PL AW-114publ328.pdf

Renshon, Stanley, and Deborah Welch Larson, eds. *Good Judgment in Foreign Policy*. Lanham, MD: Rowman and Littlefield, 2003.

Rockman, Bert. "America's Departments of State: Irregular and Regular Syndromes of Policy Making." *American Political Science Review* 75, no. 4 (1981): 911–27.

Rockman, Bert. "Does the Revolution in Presidential Studies Mean 'Off with the President's Head?'" *Presidential Studies Quarterly* 39, no. 4 (December 2009): 786–94.

Rockman, Bert. *The Leadership Question*. New York: Praeger, 1984.

The Role of the National Security Adviser. Brookings Institution National Security Project Oral History Roundtables, 1990, https://www.brookings.edu/wp-cont ent/uploads/2016/07/19991025.pdf

Rothkopf, David. "More on the Jones-Donilon Transition." *Foreign Policy*, October 11, 2010, https://foreignpolicy.com/2010/10/11/more-on-the-jones-donilon -transition/

Rothkopf, David. *Running the World*. New York: Public Affairs, 2005.

Rubin, Barry. *Secrets of State*. Oxford University Press, 1987.

Rudalevige, Andrew. *Managing the President's Program*. Princeton: Princeton University Press, 2002.

Rudalevige, Andrew. *The New Imperial Presidency*. Ann Arbor: University of Michigan Press, 2005.

Sander, Alfred. *Eisenhower's Executive Office*. Westport, CT: Greenwood Press, 1999.

Savage, Charlie. "Trump Lawyer's Impeachment Argument Stokes Fears of Unfettered Power." *New York Times*, January 3, 2020, https://www.nytimes.com/2020/01/30/us/politics/dershowitz-trump-impeachment.html

Schafer, Mark, and Scott Crichlow. *Groupthink vs. High Quality Decision Making in International Relations*. New York: Columbia University Press, 2010.

Schilling, Warner, Paul Y. Hammond, and Glenn Snyder. *Strategy, Politics, and Defense Budgets*. New York: Columbia University Press, 1962.

Schlesinger, Arthur. "Effective National Security Advising." *Political Science Quarterly* 115, no. 3 (2000): 347–51.

Schlesinger, Arthur, Jr. *The Imperial Presidency*. Boston: Houghton Mifflin, 1973.

Seidman, Harold. *Politics, Position, and Power*. New York: Oxford University Press, 1986.

Selznick, Philip. *Leadership in Administration*. Evanston, IL: Row, Peterson, and Co., 1957.

Sherwood, Robert. *Roosevelt and Hopkins*. New York: Harper and Brothers, 1948.

Simon, Herbert. *Administrative Behavior*. New York: Free Press, 1965.

Steiner, Miriam. "The Search for Order in a Disorderly World." *International Organization* 37, no. 3 (1983): 373–414.

Szanton, Peter. "Two Jobs, Not One." *Foreign Policy* 38 (Spring 1980): 89–91.

Tannenwald, Nina. "Process Tracing and Security Studies." *Security Studies* 24 (2015): 219–27.

"United States v. Curtiss-Wright Export Corporation." *Oyez*, https://www.oyez.org/cases/1900-1940/299us304

Vandenberg, Arthur. "Bipartisan Foreign Policy." *Vital Speeches of the Day* 15, no. 1 (October 15, 1948): 11–14.

Walcott, Charles, and Karen Hult. *Governing the White House*. Lawrence: University Press of Kansas, 1995.

Waldner, David. "Process Tracing and Qualitative Causal Inference." *Security Studies* 24 (2015): 239–50.

Waltz, Kenneth. *Man, the State, and War*. New York: Columbia University Press, 1954.

Weiss, Janet. "Coping with Complexity." *Journal of Public Policy Analysis and Management* 2, no. 1 (Autumn 1982): 66–87.

Weko, Thomas. *The Politicizing Presidency*. Lawrence: University Press of Kansas, 1995.

Yetiv, Steve. *National Security through a Cockeyed Lens*. Baltimore: Johns Hopkins University Press, 2013.

Zegart, Amy. *Flawed by Design*. Stanford: Stanford University Press, 1999.

THE KENNEDY AND JOHNSON PRESIDENCIES

Allison, Graham. "Conceptual Models and the Cuban Missile Crisis." *American Political Science Review* 63, no. 3 (1969): 689–718.

Ball, George. *The Past Has Another Pattern*. New York: W. W. Norton, 1982.

Barnett, Vaughan Davis. *The Presidency of Lyndon Johnson*. Lawrence: University Press of Kansas, 1983.

Bator, Francis. "No Good Choices: LBJ and the Vietnam/Great Society Connection." *Diplomatic History* 32, no. 3 (June 2008): 309–40.

Berman, Larry. "Paths Chosen and Opportunities Lost." In *Leadership in the Modern Presidency*, edited by Fred Greenstein, 134–63. Cambridge, MA: Harvard University Press, 1988.

Berman, Larry. *Planning a Tragedy*. New York: Norton, 1983.

Bird, Kai. *The Color of Truth*. New York: Simon and Shuster, 1998.

Brands, H. W. "Introduction." In *The Foreign Policies of Lyndon Johnson*, edited by H. W. Brands. College Station: Texas A&M Press, 1999.

Bundy, McGeorge. "The National Security Council of the 1960's." In *The National Security Council*, edited by Henry Jackson. New York: Praeger, 1965.

Califano, Joseph. *The Triumph and Tragedy of Lyndon Johnson*. New York: Simon and Shuster, 1991.

Caro, Robert. *Master of the Senate*. New York: Knopf, 2016.

Caro, Robert. *The Passage to Power*. New York: Knopf, 2012.

Christian, George. *The President Steps Down*. New York: Macmillan, 1970.

Clifford, Clark. *Counsel to the President*. New York: Anchor Books, 1991.

Clinton Administration. "NSC Meetings—Kennedy Administration (1961–1963)." National Security Council Archives, https://clintonwhitehouse4.archives.gov/media/pdf/Kennedy_Admin.pdf

Cohen, Warren. *Dean Rusk*. Totowa, NJ: Cooper Scientific, 1980.

Coleman, David. NSC ExComm Meetings, 1962–1963, http://historyinpieces.com/research/meetings-excomm-executive-committee-national-security-council

Dallek, Robert. *Camelot's Court*. New York: Harper Collins, 2013.

Dallek, Robert. *Flawed Giant*. New York: Oxford University Press, 1998.

Dallek, Robert. *Lone Star Rising*. Oxford University Press, 1991.

Dallek, Robert. "Lyndon Johnson as a World Leader." In *The Foreign Policies of Lyndon Johnson*, edited by H. W. Brands, 6–18. College Station: Texas A & M Press, 1999.

Dallek, Robert. *An Unfinished Life*. New York: Back Bay Books, 2003.

DiLeo, David. *George Ball, Vietnam, and the Rethinking of Containment*. Chapel Hill: University of North Carolina Press, 1991.

Dugger, Ronnie. *The Politician*. New York: Morrow, 1982.

Evans, Rowland, and Robert Novak. *Lyndon Johnson: The Exercise of Power*. New York: Signet, 1966.

Fromkin, David. "Lyndon Johnson and Foreign Policy." *Foreign Affairs* 74, no. 1 (January–February 1995): 161–70.

Gaskin, Thomas. "Lyndon B. Johnson, the Eisenhower Administration, and US Foreign Policy, 1957–1960." *Presidential Studies Quarterly* 24, no. 2 (Spring 1994): 341–61.

Goldman, Eric. *The Tragedy of Lyndon Johnson*. New York: Dell, 1968.

Goodwin, Doris Kearns. *Lyndon Johnson and the American Dream*. New York: Signet, 1976.

Goodwin, Richard. *Remembering America*. Boston: Little, Brown, 1988.

Graff, Henry. *The Tuesday Cabinet*. Englewood Cliffs, NJ: Prentice Hall, 1970.

Halberstam, David. *The Best and the Brightest*. New York: Fawcett, 1973.

Hammond, Paul. *LBJ and the Presidential Management of Foreign Relations*. Austin: University of Texas Press, 1992.

Hilsman, Roger. Oral History Interview. Association for Diplomatic Studies and Training Foreign Affairs Oral History Project (ADST), May 15, 1969, 21; https://www.adst.org/OH%20TOCs/Hilsman,%20Roger.toc.pdf

"Hilsman Resigns Key Policy Post," *New York Times*, February 26, 1964, https://www.nytimes.com/1964/02/26/archives/hilsman-resigns-key-policy-post-us-adviser-on-far-east-plans.html

Hilsman, Roger. *To Move a Nation*. Garden City, NY: Doubleday and Co., 1967.

Humphrey, David. "NSC Meetings during the Johnson Presidency." *Diplomatic History* 18, no. 1 (January 1994): 29–45.

Humphrey, David. "Tuesday Lunch at the Johnson White House." *Diplomatic History* 8, no. 1 (Winter 1984): 81–101.

Johnson, Lyndon B. *The Vantage Point*. New York: Holt, Rinehart, and Winston, 1971.

Katzenbach, Nicholas deB. *Some of It Was Fun*. New York: W. W. Norton, 2008.

Kennedy, John F. "A Democrat Looks at Foreign Policy." *Foreign Affairs* 36, no. 1 (October 1957): 44–59.

Kennedy, Robert. *Thirteen Days*. New York: Norton, 1969.

Macy, John. "Personnel and Presidential Advisors." In *The Johnson Presidency*, edited by Kenneth Thompson, 127–36. Lanham, MD: University Press of America, 1986.

McPherson, Harry. *A Political Education*. Austin: University of Texas Press, 1972.

Meet the Press. Vol. 10, no. 11, March 13, 1966, 10–11 and 15. Minnesota Historical Society, http://www2.mnhs.org/library/findaids/00442/pdfa/00442-01819.pdf

Michaels, Jeffrey. "Managing Global Counterinsurgency: The Special Group (CI) 1962–1966." *Journal of Strategic Studies* 35, no. 1 (February 2012): 33–61.

Milne, David. *America's Rasputin: Walt Rostow and the Vietnam War*. New York: Hill and Wang, 2008.

Moyers, Bill. "Epilogue: Second Thoughts." In *Lyndon Baines Johnson and the Uses of Power*, edited by Bernard J. Firestone and Robert Vogt, 349–62. New York: Greenwood Press, 1988.

Mulcahy, Kevin. "Walt Rostow as National Security Advisor." *Presidential Studies Quarterly* 25, no. 2 (Spring 1995): 223–36.

Neustadt, Richard. "Memorandum on Staffing the President-Elect." In *The Managerial Presidency*, 2nd ed., edited by James Pfiffner, 54–68. College Station: Texas A&M University Press, 1999.

Newmann, William W. "Kennedy, Johnson, and Policy toward China: Testing the Importance of the President in Foreign Policy Decision Making." *Presidential Studies Quarterly* 44, no. 4 (December 2014): 640–72.

Nomination of Dean Rusk, Secretary of State-Designate. Hearing before the Committee on Foreign Relations, United States Senate, 87th Congress, 1st Session, January 12, 1961. Hathi Trust, https://babel.hathitrust.org/cgi/pt?id=ucl.$b64 3311&view=1up&seq=5

Preston, Andrew. "The Little State Department: McGeorge Bundy and the National Security Council Staff, 1961–65." *Presidential Studies Quarterly* 31, no. 4 (December 2001): 635–59.

Reedy, George. *Lyndon B. Johnson*. New York: Andrews and McMeel, 1982.

Reedy, George. *Twilight of the Presidency*. New York: Mentor Books, 1979.

Rostow, Walt W. *The Diffusion of Power*. New York: Macmillan, 1972.

Rusk, Dean. *As I Saw It*. New York: Penguin, 1990.

Rusk, Dean. "The President." *Foreign Affairs* 38, no. 3 (April 1960): 353–69.

Schlesinger, Arthur, Jr. "A Biographer's Perspective." In *The Kennedy Presidency*, edited by Kenneth Thompson, 19–40. Lanham, MD: University Press of America, 1985.

Schlesinger, Arthur, Jr. *Robert Kennedy and His Times*. New York: Ballantine, 1978.

Schlesinger, Arthur. *A Thousand Days*. New York; Fawcett, 1965.

Schoenbaum, Thomas. *Waging Peace and War*. New York: Simon and Shuster, 1988.

"The Secretary of State and the Problem of Coordination: New Duties and Procedures, March 4, 1966." Prepared by the Senate Subcommitee on National Security and International Operations, Senate Committee on Government Operations, 89th Congress, 2nd Session, May 9, 1966, books.google.com.

Shaw, John T. *JFK in the Senate*. New York: Palgrave, 2013.

Shesol, Jeff. *Mutual Contempt*. New York: W. W. Norton, 1997.

Smith, Bromley. "National Security Affairs during the Johnson Administration." In *The Johnson Presidency*, edited by Kenneth W. Thompson, 199–208. Lanham, MD: University Press of America, 1986.

Smith, Bromley. *Organizational History of the National Security Council during the Kennedy and Johnson Administrations*. Washington, DC: National Security Council, 1988.

Sorensen, Theodore. *Counselor*. New York: Harper Perennial, 2008.

Sorensen, Theodore. *Decision Making in the White House*. New York: Columbia University Press, 1963.

Sorensen, Theodore. *Kennedy*. New York: Bantam, 1965.

Stebenne, David. *Arthur J. Goldberg: New Deal Liberal*. Oxford: Oxford University Press, 1966.

Stoll, Ira. *JFK, Conservative*. Boston: Houghton Mifflin Harcourt, 2013.

Taylor, Maxwell D. *Swords and Ploughshares*. New York: W. W. Norton, 1972.

Tenpas, Kathryn Dunn. *Crippling the Capacity of the National Security Council*. Brookings Institution, January 21, 2020, https://www.brookings.edu/blog/fixgov/20 20/01/21/crippling-the-capacity-of-the-national-security-council/

Updegrove, Mark. *Indomitable Will*. New York: Crown, 2012.

Valenti, Jack. "Managing the White House; Leading the Country." In *The Johnson Presidency*, edited by Kenneth W. Thompson, 21–39. Lanham, MD: University Press of America, 1986.

Watson, W. Marvin, and Sherwin Markman. *Chief of Staff*. New York: Thomas Dunne Books, 2004.

White, William. *The Professional*. Boston: Houghton Mifflin and Co., 1964.

Wicker, Tom. *JFK and LBJ*. Baltimore: Penguin, 1968.

Woods, Randall B. *LBJ: Architect of American Ambition*. New York: Free Press, 2006.

THE NIXON PRESIDENCY

Ambrose, Stephen. *Nixon: the Education of a Politician*. New York: Simon and Shuster, 1987.

Brodie, Fawn. *Richard Nixon*. New York: Norton, 1981.

Brzezinski, Zbigniew. "Half Past Nixon." *Foreign Policy* 3 (Summer 1971): 3–21.

Bundy, William. *A Tangled Web*. New York: Hill and Wang, 1998.

Crocker, Chester. "The Nixon-Kissinger National Security Council System." *Commission on the Organization of Government for Foreign Policy*, vol. 6, appendix O, June 1975, 79–99.

Dallek, Robert. *Nixon and Kissinger*. New York: Harper and Row, 2007.

Evans, Rowland, and Robert Novak. *Nixon in the White House*. New York: Vintage, 1972.

Garthoff, Raymond. *Détente and Confrontation*. Washington, DC: Brookings, 1985.

Gellman, Irwin. *The Contender*. New York: Free Press, 1999.

Greenberg, David. *Nixon's Shadow*. New York: W. W. Norton, 2003.

Haig, Alexander. *Inner Circles*. New York: Grand Central Publications, 1992.

Haldeman, H. R. *Ends of Power*. New York: Times Books, 1978.

Haldeman, H. R. *The Haldeman Diaries*. New York: Berkley, 1995.

Haldeman, H. R. "The Nixon White House and the Presidency." In *The Nixon Presidency*, edited by Kenneth W. Thompson, 73–98. Lanham, MD: University Press of America, 1987.

Hanhimaki, Jussi. *The Flawed Architect*. Oxford: Oxford University Press, 2004.

Helms, Richard. *A Look over My Shoulder*. New York: Ballantine, 2003.

Hersh, Seymour. *The Price of Power*. New York: Simon and Shuster, 1983.

Hess, Stephen. "First Impressions: A Look Back at Five Presidential Transitions." Brookings Institution, March 1, 2001, https://www.brookings.edu/articles/first-impressions-a-look-back-at-five-presidential-transitions/

Isaacson, Walter. *Kissinger*. New York: Simon and Shuster, 1992.

Johnston, Richard. "Nixon Gives Reds Warning on Action." *New York Times*, March 18, 1955, 16, https://timesmachine.nytimes.com/timesmachine/1955/03/18/issue.html

Kalb, Marvin, and Bernard Kalb. *Kissinger*. New York: Dell, 1975.

Kissinger, Henry. *White House Years*. Boston: Little, Brown, 1979.

Kissinger, Henry. *Years of Renewal*. New York: Simon and Shuster, 1999.

Klein, Herbert. *Making It Perfectly Clear*. Garden City, NY: Doubleday, 1980.

Kutler, Stanley. *The Wars of Watergate*. New York: W. W. Norton, 1982.

Leacocos, John. "Kissinger's Apparat." *Foreign Policy* 5 (Winter 1971–72): 3–27.

Lee, Mordecai. *Nixon's Super-Secretaries*. College Station: Texas A&M Press, 2010.

Litwak, Robert. *Détente and the Nixon Doctrine*. Cambridge: Cambridge University Press, 1984.

Lord, Winston. *Kissinger on Kissinger*. New York: All Points Books, 2019.

Lord, Winston. Oral History Interview, April 28, 1998. Association for Diplomatic Studies and Training Foreign Affairs Oral History Project, https://www.adst.org/OH%20TOCs/Lord,%20Winston.pdf

Mazo, Earl, and Stephen Hess. *Nixon*. New York: Harper and Row, 1968.

McFarlane, Robert. *Special Trust*. New York: Cadell and Davies, 1994.

Morris, Roger. *Haig*. New York: Playboy Press, 1982.

Morris, Roger. *Uncertain Greatness*. New York: Harper and Row, 1977.

Nathan, Richard. *The Plot That Failed*. New York: Wiley and Sons, 1975.

Nixon, Richard. *The Memoirs of Richard Nixon*, Vol. 1. New York: Warner Books, 1978.

Nixon, Richard. *Six Crises*. Garden City, NY: Doubleday, 1962.

The Nixon Administration National Security Council. Brookings Institution National Security Project Oral History Roundtables, 1998, https://www.brookings.edu /wp-content/uploads/2016/07/19981208.pdf

"Nixon's Report on Foreign Policy." *New York Times*, February 19, 1970, https:// www.nytimes.com/1970/02/19/archives/nixons-report-to-congress-on-foreign -policy-introduction-genuine.html

Price, Raymond. *With Nixon*. New York: Viking, 1977.

Rather, Dan, and Gary Paul Gates. *The Palace Guard*. New York: Warner Books, 1975.

Reeves, Richard. *President Nixon*. New York: Simon and Shuster, 2001.

Reichley, A. James. *Conservatives in an Age of Change*. Washington: DC: Brookings, 1981.

Richardson, Elliot. Oral History Interview, May 30, 1996. Association for Diplomatic Studies and Training Foreign Affairs Oral History Project, https://www .adst.org/OH%20TOCs/Richardson,%20Elliot.toc.pdf

Richardson, Elliot. "The Paradox." In *The Nixon Presidency*, edited by Kenneth Thompson, 51–70. Lanham, MD: University Press of America, 1987.

Rodman, Peter. Oral History Interview, May 24, 1994. Association for Diplomatic Studies and Training Foreign Affairs Oral History Project, https://www.adst .org/OH%20TOCs/Rodman,%20Peter%20W.toc.pdf?_ga=2.21510331.1254 488540.1567791004-424886806.1566917469

Rodman, Peter. *Presidential Command*. New York: Knopf, 2009.

Rush, Kenneth. "An Ambassador's Perspective." In *The Nixon Presidency*, edited by Kenneth Thompson. 335–55. Lanham, MD: University Press of America, 1987.

Safire. William. *Before the Fall*. New York: Tower Publications, 1975.

Schulzinger, Robert. *Henry Kissinger*. New York: Columbia University Press, 1989.

The Second Kennedy-Nixon Presidential Debate, October 7, 1960. Commission on Presidential Debates, https://www.debates.org/voter-education/debate-tran scripts/october-7-1960-debate-transcript/

Shawcross, William. *Sideshow*. New York; Cooper Square Press, 2002.

Siniver, Asif. "The Nixon Administration and the Cienfuegos Crisis of 1970." *Review of International Studies* 34 (2008): 69–88.

Sisco, Joseph. "Nixon Foreign Policy." In *The Nixon Presidency*, edited by Kenneth Thompson, 391–416. Lanham, MD: University Press of America, 1987.

Smith, Gerard. *Doubletalk*. Lanham, MD: University Press of America, 1985.

Sonnenfeldt, Helmut. "Reconstructing the Nixon Foreign Policy." In *The Nixon Presidency*, edited by Kenneth Thompson, 315–34. Lanham, MD: University Press of America, 1987.

Sulzberger, C. L. *The World and Richard Nixon*. New York: Prentice-Hall, 1987.

Suri, Jeremi. *Henry Kissinger and the American Century*. Cambridge: Harvard University Press, 2007.

Szulc, Tad. *The Illusion of Peace*. New York: Viking Press, 1978.

Thompson, Jenny, and Sherry Thompson. *The Kremlinologist*. Baltimore: Johns Hopkins University Press, 2018.

Thompson, Kenneth, ed. *The Nixon Presidency*. Lanham, MD: University Press of America, 1987.

Watts, William. Oral History Interview, August 7, 1995. Association for Diplomatic Studies and Training Foreign Affairs Oral History Project, https://adst.org/oral-history/oral-history-interviews/#gsc.tab=0

Weinstein, Allen. *Perjury*. New York: Random House, 1997.

Wicker, Tom. *One of Us*. New York: Random House, 1991.

Wilson, Joan Hoff. "Richard M. Nixon: The Corporate Presidency." In *Leadership in the Modern Presidency*, edited by Fred Greenstein, 164–98. Cambridge, MA: Harvard University Press, 1988.

Woodward, Bob, and Carl Bernstein. *All the President's Men*. New York: Warner Books, 1976.

YouTube. "There's an Old Vulcan Proverb . . . 'Only Nixon Could Go to China.'" https://www.youtube.com/watch?v=X_gwnFSFzv0

WORKS ON CHINA AND ASIA

Accinelli, Robert. *Crisis and Commitment: United States Policy toward Taiwan, 1950–1955*. Chapel Hill: University of North Carolina Press, 1996.

Accinelli, Robert. *A Thorn in the Side of Peace*. Cambridge, MA: Harvard East Asia Monographs, 2001.

Ahn, Byung-Joon. *Chinese Politics and the Cultural Revolution*. Seattle: University of Washington Press, 1976.

Appleton, Sheldon. *The Eternal Triangle: Communist China, the United States, and the United Nations*. East Lansing: Michigan State University Press, 1961.

Bachrack, Stanley. *The Committee of One Million*. New York: Columbia University Press, 1976.

Barnett, A. Doak. *China and the Major Powers in East Asia*. Washington, DC: Brookings, 1977.

Barnett, A. Doak. *Communist China and Asia*. New York: Vintage, 1961.

Barnett, A. Doak. *A New US Policy toward China*. Washington, DC: Brookings Institution, 1971.

Barnouin, Barbara, and Yu Changgan. *Chinese Foreign Policy during the Cultural Revolution*. London: Kegan Paul International, 1998.

Bostdorff, Denise. "The Evolution of Surprise: Richard's Nixon's Rhetoric on China, 1952-July 15, 1971." *Rhetoric and Public Affairs* 5, no. 1 (Spring 2002): 31–56.

Bowles, Chester. "The 'China Problem' Reconsidered." *Foreign Affairs* 38, no. 3 (April 1960): 476–86.

Bradsher, Henry. "China: The Radical Offensive." *Asian Survey* 13, no. 11 (November 1973): 989–1009.

Brands, H. W. "The Limits of Manipulation: How the United States Didn't Topple Sukarno." *Journal of American History* 76, no. 3 (December 1989): 785–808.

Brands, Hal. "Rethinking Nonproliferation: LBJ, the Gilpatric Committee, and U.S. National Security Policy." *Journal of Cold War Studies* 8, no. 2 (Spring 2006): 83–113.

Bueler, William. *US China Policy and the Problem of Taiwan*. Boulder: Colorado Associated University Press, 1971.

Bundy, William. "The United States and Communist China." *Department of State Bulletin* 54, no. 1392 (February 28, 1966): 310–18.

Burr, William, and Jeffrey Richelson. "Whether to 'Strangle the Baby in the Cradle': The United States and the Chinese Nuclear Program, 1960–64." *International Security* 25, no. 3 (Winter 2001): 54–99.

Bush, Richard. *At Cross Purposes*. New York: Taylor and Francis, 2004.

Camilleri, Joseph. *Chinese Foreign Policy*. Seattle: University of Washington Press, 1980.

Chang, Gordon. *Friends and Enemies*. Stanford University Press, 1990.

Chang Jung, and Jon Halliday. *Mao*. London: Vintage, 2006.

Chang, Parris. "The Anti-Lin Piao and Confucius Campaign." *Asian Survey* 14, no. 10 (October 1974): 871–86.

Chen Jian. *Mao's China and the Cold War*. Chapel Hill: University of North Carolina Press, 2001.

China Policy and the National Security Council. Brookings National Security Council Oral History Roundtables, November 4, 1999, https://www.brookings.edu/wp-content/uploads/2016/07/19991104.pdf

Cowen, Tyler, and Daniel Sutter. "Why Only Nixon Could Go to China." *Public Choice* 97, no. 4 (1998): 606–15.

Cribb, Robert. "Unresolved Problems in the Indonesian Killings of 1965–1966." *Asian Survey* 42, no. 4 (July–August 2002): 550–63.

Cukierman, Alex, and Mariano Tommasi. "When Does It Take a Nixon to Go to China?" *American Economic Review* 88, no. 1 (March 1998): 180–97.

Dulles, Foster Rhea. *American Policy toward Communist China*. New York: Crowell, 1972.

Fetzer, James. "Clinging to Containment; China Policy." In *Kennedy's Quest for Victory*, edited by Thomas Patterson, 178–97. Oxford: Oxford University Pres, 1989.

Foot, Rosemary. *The Practice of Power*. Oxford: Oxford University Press, 1995.

Foot, Rosemary. "Redefinitions: The Domestic Context of America's China Policy in the 1960s." In *Reexamining the Cold War*, edited by Robert Ross and Changbin Jiang, 262–87. Cambridge, MA: Harvard University Press, 2001.

Fravel, M. Taylor, and Evan S. Medeiros. "China's Search for Assured Retaliation: The Evolution of Chinese Nuclear Strategy and Force Structure." *International Security* 35, no. 2 (Fall 2010): 48–87.

Gaddis, John Lewis. "The American Wedge Strategy." In *Sino-American Relations*, edited by Harry Harding and Yuan Ming, 157–83. Wilmington, DE: Scholarly Resources, 1989.

Garrison, Jean. "Framing the National Interests in US-China Relations." *Asian Perspective* 24, no. 3 (2000): 103–34.

Garver, John. *China's Decision for Rapprochement with the United States, 1968–1971*. Boulder: Westview Press, 1982.

Garver, John. *China's Quest*. Oxford: Oxford University Press, 2016.

Garver, John. "The Chinese Threat in the Vietnam War." *Parameters* 22, no. 1 (Spring 1982): 73–85.

Garver, John. *The Sino-American Alliance*. Armonk, NY: M. E. Sharpe, 1997.

Gelb, Leslie. "Arms Sales." *Foreign Policy* 25 (Winter 1976–77): 3–23.

Gelb, Leslie. *The Irony of Vietnam*. Washington, DC: Brookings, 1979.

Ginsburgs, George, and Carl Pinkele. *The Sino-Soviet Territorial Dispute*. New York: Praeger, 1978.

Goh, Evelyn. *Constructing the U.S. Rapprochement with China, 1961–1974*. Cambridge: Cambridge University Press, 2005.

Goldstein, Steven. *The United States and the Republic of China, 1949–1978*. Stanford: Asia/Pacific Research Center, Institute for International Studies, Stanford University, 2000.

Gottlieb, Thomas. *Chinese Foreign Policy and the Origins of the Strategic Triangle*. Santa Monica, CA: RAND Corporation, 1977.

Gong Li. "Chinese Decision Making and the Thawing of US-China Relations." In *Reexamining the Cold War*, edited by Robert Ross and Jiang Changbin, 321–60. Cambridge, MA: Harvard University Press, 2001.

Grasso, June. *Truman's Two-China Policy, 1948–1950*. Armonk, NY: M. E. Sharpe, 1987.

Halperin, A. M. "Communist China's Foreign Policy." *China Quarterly* 11 (July–September 1962): 89–104.

Hershberg, James, and Chen Jian. "Reading and Warning the Likely Enemy: China's Signals to the United States about Vietnam in 1965." *International History Review* 27, no. 1 (March 2005): 47–84.

Hilsman, Roger. "Communist China: The United States Policy." *Vital Speeches of the Day* 30, no. 7 (1963): 203–7.

Hinton, Harold. "Conflict on the Ussuri: A Clash of Nationalisms." *Problems of Communism* 20, nos. 1–2 (January–April 1971): 45–61.

Holdridge, John. *Crossing the Divide*. Lanham, MD: Rowman and Littlefield, 1997.

Hong Zhaohui, and Yi Sun. "The Butterfly Effect and the Making of 'Ping-Pong Diplomacy.'" *Journal of Contemporary China* 9, no. 25 (2000): 429–48.

Horn, Robert. "Sino-Soviet Relations in an Era of Détente." *Asian Affairs* 3, no. 5 (May–June 1976): 287–304.

Hornbeck, Stanley. "United States Policy Regarding China: What Did Mr. Hilsman Disclose at San Francisco?" *World Affairs* 126, no. 4 (1963–64): 238–43.

Hsieh, Alice Langley. *Communist China's Strategy in the Nuclear Era*. Santa Monica, CA: RAND Corporation, 1962.

Humphrey, Hubert. "United States Tasks and Responsibilities in Asia." *Department of State Bulletin* 54, no. 1397 (March 11, 1966): 523–29.

Hunt, Michael. *The Genesis of Chinese Communist Foreign Policy*. New York: Columbia University Press, 1996.

Jacobs, J. Bruce. "Taiwan 1972." *Asian Survey* 13, no. 1 (January 1973): 102–12.

Johnston, Richard. "Nixon Gives Reds Warning on Atom." *New York Times*, March 18, 1955, 16, https://timesmachine.nytimes.com/timesmachine/1955/03/18/issue.html

Jones, Matthew. "Groping toward Coexistence: US China Policy during the Johnson Years." *Diplomacy and Statecraft* 12, no. 3 (September 2001): 175–90.

Jones, Matthew. "U.S. Relations with Indonesia, the Kennedy-Johnson Transition, and the Vietnam Connection, 1963–1965." *Diplomatic History* 26, no. 2 (April 2002): 249–81.

Jung Chang and Jon Halliday. *Mao: The Untold Story*. London: Vintage Books, 2006.

Katz, Andrew. "Public Opinion and Foreign Policy: The Nixon Administration and the Pursuit of Peace with Honor in Vietnam." *Presidential Studies Quarterly* 27, no. 3 (Summer 1997): 496–513.

Kau, Michael Y. M., Pierre M. Perrolle, Susan H. Marsh, and Jeffrey Berman. "Public Opinion and Our China Policy." *Asian Affairs* 5, no. 3 (January–February 1978): 133–47.

Kaufman, Victor. "Trouble in the Golden Triangle." *China Quarterly* 166 (June 2001): 440–56.

Keith, Ronald. *The Diplomacy of Zhou Enlai*. New York: St. Martin's Press, 1989.

Kiernan, Ben. *How Pol Pot Came to Power*. London: Verso, 1985.

Klinefelter, Katherine. "The China Hearings." *Congress & the Presidency* 38, no. 1 (2011): 60–76.

Kochavi, Noam. *A Conflict Perpetuated*. Westport, CT: Praeger, 2002.

Koen, Ross. *The China Lobby in American Politics*. New York: Harper and Row, 1974.

Kusnitz, Leonard. *Public Opinion and Foreign Policy*. Westport, CT: Greenwood Press, 1984.

LaFeber, Walter. *The Clash*. New York: W. W. Norton, 1997.

Lev, Daniel. "Indonesia 1965: The Year of the Coup." *Asian Survey* 6, no. 2 (February 1966): 103–10.

Lewis, John, and Xue Litai. *China Builds the Bomb*. Stanford: Stanford University Press, 1988.

Li Jie. "Changes in China's Domestic Situation in the 1960s and Sino-US Relations," In *Reexamining the Cold War*, edited by Robert Ross and Jiang Changbin, 288–320. Cambridge, MA: Harvard University Press, 2001.

Lin Biao. *Long Live the Victory of People's War!* Marxists Internet Archive, https://www.marxists.org/reference/archive/lin-biao/1965/09/peoples_war/index.htm

Lindsay, Michael. "A New China Policy: Difficulties and Possibilities." *China Quarterly* 10 (1962): 56–63.

Li Zhisui. *The Private Life of Chairman Mao*. New York: Random House, 1994.

Lumbers, Michael. *Piercing the Bamboo Curtain*. Manchester: University of Manchester Press, 2008.

MacFarquhar, Roderick, and Michael Schoenhals. *Mao's Last Revolution*. Cambridge, MA: Harvard University Press, 2008.

Mendel, Douglas, Jr. "Taiwan Adjusts to Isolation." *Asian Affairs* 3, no. 1 (September–October 1975): 63–66.

Meyers, David. *Cracking the Monolith: US Policy against the Sion-Soviet Alliance, 1949–1955*. Baton Rouge: Louisiana State University Press, 1986.

Moody, Peter, Jr. "The New Anti-Confucian Campaign in China." *Asian Survey* 14, no. 4 (April 1974): 307–24.

Mozingo, D. P., and T. W. Robinson. *Lin Piao on "People's War": A Second Look at Vietnam*. November. Santa Monica, CA: RAND Corporation, 1965.

National Intelligence Council. *Tracking the Dragon*. October 2004.

Nixon, Richard. "Asia after Vietnam." *Foreign Affairs* 46, no. 1 (October 1967): 111–25.

Ouimet, Matthew. *The Rise and Fall of the Brezhnev Doctrine*. Chapel Hill: University of North Carolina Press, 2003.

Presidential Approval Ratings—Gallup Historical Statistics and Trends. Gallup, https://news.gallup.com/poll/116677/presidential-approval-ratings-gallup-historical-statistics-trends.aspx

Pringsheim, Klaus H. "China's Role in the Indo-Pakistani Conflict." *China Quarterly* 24 (October–December 1965): 170–75.

Qiang Zhai. *China and the Vietnam Wars, 1950–1975*. Chapel Hill: University of North Carolina Press, 2000.

Quigley, Kevin. "A Lost Opportunity: A Reappraisal of the Kennedy Administration's China Policy in 1963." *Diplomacy and Statecraft* 13, no. 3 (September 2002): 175–98.

Rea, Kenneth. "Peking and the Brezhnev Doctrine." *Asian Affairs* 3, no. 1 (September–October 1975): 22–30.

Resolution 2642, 25th General Assembly, UN General Assembly. Quick Links, 25th Session, http://research.un.org/en/docs/ga/quick/regular/25; and FRUS, 1969–1976, vol. 17, Document 167.

Robinson, Thomas. "China in 1973: Renewed Leftism Threatens the 'New Course.'" *Asian Survey* 14, no. 1 (January 1974): 1–21.

Robinson, Thomas. "The Sino-Soviet Border Dispute." *American Political Science Review* 66, no. 4 (December 1972): 1175–1202.

Ross, Robert. *Negotiating Cooperation*. Stanford: Stanford University Press, 1995.

Saad, Lydia. "Gallup Vault: Nixon's China Visit Was a Game Changer." February 17, 2017. Gallup, https://news.gallup.com/vault/204065/gallup-vault-nixon-china-visit-game-changer.aspx

Salisbury, Harrison. *The New Emperors*. New York: Avon, 1992.

"Secretary Rogers Announces U.S. Policy on Chinese Representation in the U.N." *Department of State Bulletin* 65, no. 1678 (August 23, 1971): 193–96.

Simon, Sheldon. *The Broken Triangle: Peking, Djakarta, and the PKI*. Baltimore: Johns Hopkins University Press, 1969.

Smith, Terence. "Rogers Bids China Be 'Constructive' in Southeast Asia." *New York Times*, April 28, 1971. https://www.nytimes.com/1971/04/28/archives/rogers-bids-china-be-constructive-in-southeast-asia-he-says-us.html

Supplemental Foreign Assistance, Fiscal Year, 1966: Vietnam. Hearings before the Committee on Foreign Relations, United States Senate, 89th Congress, 2nd Session, on S. 2793, to amend further the Foreign Assistance Act of 1961, as amended: January 28, February 4, 8, 10, 17 and 18, 1966. Hathi Trust, https://catalog.hathitrust.org/Record/010309694

Sutter, John. "Two Faces of Konfrontasi: 'Crush Malaysia' and the Gestapu." *Asian Survey* 6, no. 10 (October 1966): 523–46.

Sutter, Robert. *The China Quandary*. Boulder: Westview Press, 1983.

Sutter, Robert. *Chinese Foreign Relations after the Cultural Revolution, 1966–1977*. Boulder: Westview Press, 1978.

Szulc, Tad. "Ceausescu Visits Nixon at the White House for Talks on World Issues." *New York Times*, October 27, 1970. https://www.nytimes.com/1970/10/27/arch ives/ceausescu-visits-nixon-at-the-white-house-for-talks-on-world-issues.html

Tang Tsou. *America's Failure in China, 1941–1950*. Vol. 2. Chicago: University of Chicago Press, 1967.

Taylor, Jay. *The Generalissimo*. Cambridge: Harvard University Press, 2011.

Thomson, James. "On the Making of US China Policy." *China Quarterly* 50 (April–June 1972): 220–43.

Tucker, Nancy. *The China Threat*. New York: Columbia University Press, 2012.

Tucker, Nancy. *Patterns in the Dust*. New York: Columbia University Press, 1983.

Tucker, Nancy. *Strait Talk*. Cambridge, MA: Harvard University Press, 2009.

Tucker, Nancy. *Taiwan, Hong Kong, and the United States, 1945–1992*. New York: Twayne, 1994.

Tucker, Nancy. "Threats, Opportunities, and Frustration in East Asia." In *Lyndon Johnson Confronts the World*, edited by Warren Cohen and Nancy Bernkopf Tucker, 99–134. Cambridge: Cambridge University Press, 1994.

Tudda, Chris. *A Cold War Turning Point*. Baton Rouge: Louisiana State University Press, 2012.

United Nations General Assembly, Official Records of the 332nd Plenary Meeting, 747–49, http://repository.un.org/bitstream/handle/11176/298929/A_PV.332 -EN.pdf?sequence=1&isAllowed=y

United Nations Resolutions Adopted by the General Assembly, 16th Session, http://www.un.org/en/ga/search/view_doc.asp?symbol=A/RES/1668(XVI)

United States Policy toward Asia. U. S. Congress, Subcommittee on the Far East and the Pacific, Committee on Foreign Affairs, US House of Representatives, 89th Congress, 2nd Session, January–February 1966. Hathi Trust, https://catalog.ha thitrust.org/Record/007608252

United States Relations with China, August 1949, Internet Archive, https://archive .org/stream/VanSlykeLymanTheChinaWhitePaper1949/Van+Slyke%2C+Ly man+-+The+China+White+Paper+1949_djvu.txt

United States Relations with the People's Republic of China. Hearings before the Committee on Foreign Relations, United States Senate, 92–1, June 24, 25, 28, and 29, and July 20, 1971. books.google.com.

US Policy with Respect to Mainland China. Hearings before the Committee on Foreign Relations, US Senate, 89th Congress, 2nd Session. Hathi Trust, https://ba bel.hathitrust.org/cgi/pt?id=umn.31951d01984992t&view=1up&seq=2

Vogel, Ezra. *The Four Little Dragons*. Cambridge: Harvard University Press, 1991.

Wade, Robert. *Governing the Market*. Princeton: Princeton University Press, 1991.

Walder, Andrew. *China under Mao*. Cambridge, MA: Harvard University Press, 2015.

Wang, John Kuo-Chang. "United Nations Voting on Chinese Representation: An Analysis of General Assembly Roll Calls, 1951–1971." PhD diss., University of Oklahoma, 1977.

Weng, Byron. *Peking's UN Policy*. New York: Prager, 1972.

Worldwide Manpower Distribution by Geographical Area (M05), Historical Reports—Military Only—1950, 1953–1999. Defense Manpower Data Center, Department of Defense, https://www.dmdc.osd.mil/appj/dwp/dwp_reports.jsp

Wu, Fu-mei Chiu. *Richard M. Nixon, Communism, and China*. Washington, DC: University Press of America, 1978.

Xia Yafeng. *Negotiating with the Enemy*. Bloomington: Indiana University Press, 2006.

Young, Kenneth T. *Negotiating with the Chinese Communists:* The United States Experience, 1953–1967. New York: McGraw-Hill, 1968.

Zagoria, Donald. *The Sino-Soviet Split*. Princeton: Princeton University Press, 1962.

Zhang Weng. *Never Forget National Humiliation*. New York: Columbia University Press, 2012.

Index

Note: Page numbers in *italics* indicate figures and tables. JFK refers to John F. Kennedy; LBJ refers to Lyndon B. Johnson; RMN refers to Richard M. Nixon.